THE ENCYCLOPEDIA
OF TV SCIENCE FICTION

ROGER FULTON

Boxtree

First published in 1990 by Boxtree Limited
in association with Independent Television Books Ltd
Text copyright © 1990 Roger Fulton

Illustrations
The publishers and author wish to thank the
following for providing illustrations:
The TVTimes Picture Library and especially
Tracey Whitton for all her patience and
efficiency; Associated Television; Delphi
Assoc.; ABC Television; Scottish Television
and the BBC.

Edited by John Gilbert and Christopher Walker
Designed by Penny Mills
Typeset by Cambrian Typesetters, Frimley, Surrey
Printed and bound in the UK by Richard Clay PLC,
Bungay, Suffolk

Jacket Illustration
Captain Kirk (William Shatner) has a ruck
with an android (Ted Cassidy) in the *Star
Trek* episode 'What are Little Girls made
of?'. © Columbia Pictures

CONTENTS

Single dramas/One-off productions

ACKNOWLEDGEMENTS

To the following, who gave freely and gladly of their time, knowledge and advice, I am deeply grateful:

Andrew Pixley, Neil Alsop and Tony McKay – the Time Screen Bandits whose knowledge of telefantasy knows no final frontier and who answered my numerous questions and helped fill in the gaps. Gary Russell, of the BBC Press Office, for his help on BBC shows in general, but most especially, for putting flesh on the bones of the last eight years of *Doctor Who*. Phil Bevan, for his encouragement in the beginning, his help along the way and the loan of his magazine collection. Tony Mechele, of the British Film Institute, for getting me one step nearer. Bill Parker, of Euston Films, for letting me plunder his archives. Maria Smith at TVS, Di Hall at Channel 4, Meg Armsby at LWT, Janice Jaggers at Thames Television, Fran Mannion and Graham King at Granada Television, Naomi Phillipson at Central, Don Mead and Don Harrington at ITC, and Peter Harley and Michael Thomas at the Filmcentre, London, for looking . . . and sometimes finding. John Braybon for his memories of *The Master*; Johnny Goodman for his hopes on *Outpost*. Warren Bennett and Keith Gilman of the *TV Times* library for the heavy stuff. The staff of the British Newspaper Library, Colindale, London. Elizabeth Wilcox for the *Avengers* and *Champions* scripts (it's not every mother-in-law who worked on so many classic shows). My publishers for their patience; my friends and colleagues for listening.

Last, but definitely not least, I want to thank my wife Ros and children Shelley and Sean. A book like this doesn't just happen – it takes many, many hours of work to research, process and write up all the material involved. And if you've already got a full-time job, that means eating into evenings and weekends – precious time spent in selfish pursuit when it might have been spent with them. So, to Ros, for poring through a good many copies of *TV* and *Radio Times* herself, and to all my family, for putting up with my absences and solitude, I couldn't have done it without you and it's good to be back!

SOURCES

Putting this book together meant leafing through more than 70 combined years of BBC and ITV schedules. Nearly all that information came from *TV Times* (1955–89, including many regional editions) and *Radio Times* (1952–89). Both magazines, with their devotion to casts and credits, were like a route map through nearly four decades of television.

Aside from information gleaned from the individuals named above, I also accumulated original publicity and billing material, where available – much of it, fortunately, still logged in the *TV Times* library. Other invaluable sources were: *Time Screen* (the Magazine of British Telefantasy), *Doctor Who Monthly*, and the collected wit and sometimes wisdom of Fleet Street. I tried to avoid *too* many other books on the subject (it can get disheartening in the small hours), but volumes I did find useful were: *Fantastic Television* by Gary Gerani, *The ITV Encyclopedia of Adventure* and the *Avengers* books by Dave Rogers (also published by Boxtree), the *Starlog* guides, *The Best of Science Fiction TV* by John Javna, *Blake's 7 Programme Guide* by Tony Attwood and *The Doctor Who Programme Guide* by Jean-Marc Lofficier.

If you want some additional reading, look no further than *Time Screen*. Address is 574 Manchester Road, Stockbridge, Sheffield S30 5DI.

PREFACE

The story of this book really began in 1953, when Professor Bernard Quatermass first saved the world from a rubber glove, covered in strips of leather and vegetation, that was threatening to destroy a cardboard cut-out of Westminster Abbey.

My mother recalls how she recoiled in fear and excitement, fingers covering her eyes but determined not to miss a second. The nation had seen nothing like it – and television had found its newest form of popular drama.

I wasn't even born when *The Quatermass Experiment* went horribly wrong. And I was too young to catch the second or third series, or even to watch ITV take its first faltering steps into the unknown with *The Strange World of Planet X* or *The Trollenberg Terror*. Neither could I stay up to watch the first disappearance of *The Invisible Man*, and the Andromeda serials were the stuff 'five more minutes' bedtime appeals were made of.

But once I learnt to control the horizontal and the vertical on the flickering black and white box in the corner, I was hooked. When Jimmy Wedgwood took off for the moon in *Target Luna* he opened a window on the imagination for thousands of kids like me. Suddenly it was possible to go anywhere, do anything.

Soon, you could fly round the world in *Supercar*, reach for the stars with *Fireball XL5* and *Space Patrol*, travel in time with *Doctor Who*, and voyage to the bottom of the ocean in *Seaview* and *Stingray*. I fought the Daleks (and won), thwarted the designs of THRUSH, did the Tracy airwalk, pinned Emma Peel's picture on my wall (next to Fulham FC and the Stones), and later queued for Tara King's autograph when *The Avengers* came to film at my school.

Programmes such as *UNCLE*, *Adam Adamant Lives!*, *The Avengers* and *Doctor Who* helped satisfy my thirst for TV adventure. Soon, too, series such as *Out of the Unknown* were unravelling my imagination, while *The Prisoner* was stretching it.

Throughout the 1960s, 1970s and, indeed, through most of the past decade, science fiction and its cousins have provided some of my most memorable TV moments. TV, on the other hand, has not always seemed totally committed to the cause.

Star Trek has hardly missed a year since its debut on BBC1 in 1969 as the summer season Saturday teatime filler between *Doctor Who*'s second and third incarnations, but we're *still* waiting for Auntie to show those three missing episodes. (How about it, BBC?)

On ITV, *U.F.O.* and *Space 1999* struggled to find a home, one disappearing into the night and the other jostling for room with the Saturday morning crowds. *The Secret Service* remained a secret to most of the country and ITV's regionalisation has meant that series after series has never been seen at the same time, on the same day, all across the country. The BBC started down *The Time Tunnel*, but never reached the end; and it dropped completely one episode each of *Counterstrike* and *Doomwatch*. Lately, *The Tripods* were cut off in mid-stride and Channel 4's *Max Headroom*, a brilliant British invention, had to go west to be developed into a series.

Doctor Who fell foul of the nervous watchdogs over its violence, yet it produced some of its best stories when at its most controversial. It escaped the axe once, but has seen its screen presence diminish from an initial ten months a year to just 14 weeks.

There's undoubtedly been a lot of juvenile science fiction – from both sides of the Atlantic – and not all of it intended purely for kids (remember *Man from Atlantis* or *Logan's Run*?). But TVSF has also been one of the medium's most potent messengers for conveying morality of thought, word and deed, from *Star Trek*'s righteous humanity and optimism to the eloquent parables of *The Twilight Zone*; from the ecological sermons of *Doomwatch* to the grim bell-tolling of *Survivors*; from the rebel-rousing of *Blake's 7* to the anti-fascist fervour of '*V*'. Even the young have not been neglected. Through the eyes of alien oddballs such as Uncle Martin, Mork and ALF, human aspirations and failings have been seen in sharper focus.

Nowadays, it seems, science fiction is regarded with great suspicion by the programme executives and – *Star Trek: the Next Generation* aside – it is difficult to see where the next big TVSF show is coming from. The last couple of years have already been lean. Gerry Anderson's *Space Police* pilot remains unscreened, while the revived *Twilight Zone* and its confederates have been banished to the graveyard slot of ITV's 24-hour schedules, some of them even having to go under assumed names to get a look in.

As the purse strings tighten even further all round, and the ITV companies look to the franchise struggle in 1992, the corporate conservatism will inevitably reassert itself through entrenchment in the family formula of soaps, variety, quiz shows, cop shows and sitcoms. HTV's *Outpost* may make it, otherwise it seems there's only the Doctor to carry the flag of British TVSF into the 1990s.

Meanwhile, inside this book you'll find details – background, storylines, casts and production credits – on every major science fiction series and play, British *and* American (sometimes even Australasian) to have inspired or insulted the imagination of this country's box watchers since 1951. There's also a sprint through some of the hundreds of hours of animated fantasy, plus a chronological stroll past the landmarks of science fiction television.

And that's about it. I look forward eagerly to *Star Trek: the Next Generation* but I hope the next generation has something more to look forward to, as well. With such a glorious past to wallow in, this volume is a celebration of the TVSF story so far. I hope it won't turn out to be its obituary.

Roger Fulton
December 1989

ENTRY FORMAT

With so many diverse productions to include, there are bound to be exceptions, but this is the general rule . . .

Each entry covers one programme in its entirety and consists, more or less, of the following:

Series name, e.g. BLAKE'S 7
and background, followed by regular cast, e.g.
Roj Blake Gareth Thomas   *Avon* Paul Darrow

Production credits, e.g. *Creator:* Terry Nation
Production company, e.g. *A BBC Production*
Number and duration of episodes and whether colour or black and white, e.g.

52 colour 50-minute episodes
(ITV times are based on traditional slots, including commercials)

followed by season breakdown (where appropriate) and UK premiere dates, e.g.

Season One:
2 January–27 March 1978
(ITV dates are networked, unless stated)

This is followed, where relevant, or possible, by a guide to every episode transmitted (and in some cases ones that weren't), in chronological order of transmission, reading downwards through left- and then right-hand entries. (In the case of most American series, this is the original US running order.)

Episodes are treated as follows:
Title and author, e.g.

Redemption

---

w Terry Nation

followed by synopsis and appropriate supporting cast, plus director and, in some instances, designer credits, e.g.

Alta One Sheila Ruskin
Director: Vere Lorrimer
Designer: Sally Hulke

(Some entries include episode titles only, others consist solely of numbers of episodes.)

Single plays include either full or main cast (as stated), relevant production credits and transmission dates.

The animated section is restricted (loosely) to production house, number of episodes shown in UK, whether colour or black and white, and UK premiere date.

SERIES

A FOR ANDROMEDA/THE ANDROMEDA BREAKTHROUGH

A for Andromeda and its sequel, *The Andromeda Breakthrough*, screened in 1961–2, were television's first attempts to create adult science fiction since the Quatermass sagas of the Fifties.

Scripted by BBC producer John Elliot, from an original storyline by renowned astronomer and novelist Fred Hoyle, they dealt with the impact of an alien intelligence upon life on Earth and with the ruthless pursuit by rival factions of the scientific secrets that could prove the breakthrough of the century. The machinations of governments and big business were Elliot's territory (he went on to produce the power games of *Mogul* and *The Troubleshooters*) but the astronomical and scientific concepts were Hoyle's. In his novels such as *The Black Cloud*, Hoyle, professor of astronomy and philosophy at Cambridge, contended that man's first contact with an alien civilisation would come through radio-astronomy and this idea forms the basis for the series, which begin with signals from space being received by a new radio telescope.

In the first series the signals are found to contain the 'assembly and operating' instructions for a highly advanced computer which then enables the research team literally to create life, first a misshapen blob, then a human embryo which grows rapidly into a beautiful young woman – Andromeda. *The Andromeda Breakthrough* dramatically upped the tempo of the power politics, set the intrigue against a worldwide environmental disaster, and revealed the purpose behind the original message – that of steering mankind down a less destructive path than the one it has taken. John Elliot's influence was greater in the second series – as well as scripting it he also produced and directed.

The hero of both series is Dr John Fleming, an outspoken, idealistic young scientist. It is he who first decodes the signals from outer space – 'It's a do-it-yourself kit, and it isn't human!' – and it is he who first recognises the dangers of extending the frontiers of human knowledge too far, too fast.

No one-dimensional cipher this one, Fleming is a scientist with a conscience, in the grand Quatermass tradition, who ends up saving the world from a chain of events he himself set in motion. (The character of Fleming has been seen as being based on the maverick qualities of Hoyle himself.)

Throughout, Fleming finds himself in conflict with most people around him, including his own and foreign governments; a shady, Swiss-based business cartel called Intel (headed by the villainous Kaufman); and an amoral biologist, Dr Madeleine Dawnay, who sees the Andromeda project as one great research opportunity.

A for Andromeda also marked the TV debut of a glamorous young actress called Julie Christie (plucked from a drama school by producer Michael Hayes), initially as the lab assistant, Christine, whose death provides the 'blueprint' for Dawnay's embryo, and then as Andromeda herself, whose ambivalent relationship with Fleming blossoms in the sequel. In this, the part was taken over by another relative newcomer, Susan Hampshire. Frank Windsor, stalwart of *Z-Cars* and *Softly, Softly*, appeared in the first series as Fleming's self-seeking colleague Dennis Bridger.

Both *A for Andromeda* and *The Andromeda Breakthrough* are now hailed as early classics of British science fiction.

(Author's note: Although there is some overlapping of cast and production details, for ease of reference the story guides to each series are treated separately, beginning with the main cast, followed by synopsis, supporting cast and production details.)

A FOR ANDROMEDA

w Fred Hoyle and John Elliot *(A 7-part serial)*

MAIN CAST:

THE SCIENTISTS:
John Fleming Peter Halliday   *Prof. Reinhart* Esmond Knight
Madeleine Dawnay Mary Morris   *Dr Geers* Geoffrey Lewis
Christine (Eps 2–4)/*Andromeda* (Eps 5–7) Julie Christie
Dennis Bridger Frank Windsor   *Harvey* John Murray-Scott
Dr Hunter Peter Ducrow

SECURITY:
Judy Adamson Patricia Kneale   *Maj. Quadring* Jack May
Harries John Nettleton

WHITEHALL:
J.M. Osborne Noel Johnson   *Gen. Vandenberg* Donald Stewart
Minister of Science Ernest Hare   *Prime Minister* Maurice Hedley
Defence Minister David King

INTEL:
Kaufman John Hollis   *Egon* Peter Henchie

The year is 1970. While conducting routine checks at a new radio-telescope high in the Yorkshire Dales, Prof. Reinhart's staff pick up unexpected signals from the direction of the constellation Andromeda. These are taped and decoded by brilliant scientist John Fleming who reveals them to be a series of arithmetical instructions for building a highly advanced computer.

Once the implications sink in, Whitehall gives the go-ahead for the machine to be built at Thorness, a remote island rocket base off the Scottish coast. 'Project Andromeda' is classified top secret but scientists, military and the shady cartel, Intel, all begin to compete for the information and Fleming's friend Bridger is found to be selling secrets to Kaufman. While trying to evade arrest he falls to his death.

Meanwhile, the completed computer

has begun to show its power and Fleming, increasingly wary, finds himself at loggerheads with biologist Madeleine Dawnay when the machine provides information that enables her to manufacture a living organism.

Later, the computer, in an attempt to extend its knowledge of humanity, compels lab assistant Christine to seize two exposed terminals – electrocuting her. Despite the incident, Dawnay continues her experiments. The result is a human embryo which matures rapidly, showing a startling resemblance to the dead Christine. Christened Andromeda, the girl learns at a phenomenal rate and also establishes a mental link with the computer, getting it to design a new missile system for the government which has grown worried at the deteriorating political situation.

More than ever, Fleming sees the liaison as a menace and tries to sabotage the computer which retaliates by 'creating' a toxic enzyme that leaves Dawnay fighting for her life (though the full significance of the substance only becomes clear in the series' sequel). When Andromeda tries to kill him, Fleming convinces her that if the computer were destroyed she would be free of its control. After wrecking the machine and burning the plans, they escape into the night . . .

Whelan **Bernard Kilby**
Osborne's secretary **Brenda Peters**
Interviewer **Kenneth Kendall**
Jenkins **Terry Lodge**
Oldroyd **John Barrett**
Capt Lovell **Frederick Treves**
Mrs Tate-Allen **Margaret Denyer**
Air Cmdre Watling **Jack Gwillim**
Corporal **Anthony Valentine**
Lieut. de Felice **Hugh Lund**

Producers: **Michael Hayes, Norman Jones**
Designer: **Norman James**
Film cameraman: **Peter Sargent**
Film editor: **Agnes Evan**

A BBC Production
Seven 45-minute episodes, black and white
The Message
The Machine
The Miracle
The Monster
The Murderer
The Face of the Tiger
The Last Mystery (50 mins)

3 October–14 November 1961

THE ANDROMEDA BREAKTHROUGH

w Fred Hoyle and John Elliot *(A 6-part story)*

MAIN CAST

THE SCIENTISTS:
John Fleming **Peter Halliday**   *Andromeda* **Susan Hampshire**
Madeleine Dawnay **Mary Morris**   *Prof. Neilson* **Walter Gotell**
Dr Geers **Geoffrey Lewis**

AZARAN
Col. Salim **Barry Linehan**   *Dr Abu Zeki* **David Saire**
Abu Zeki's assistant **Assad Obeid**   *President* **Arnold Yarrow**
Nurse **Heather Emmanuel**   *Lemka (Abu Zeki's wife)* **Jean Robinson**
Lemka's mother **Miki Iveria**

INTEL
Kaufman **John Hollis**   *Mlle Gamboule* **Claude Farell**

WHITEHALL
J.M. Osborne **Noel Johnson**   *Burdett (defence minister)* **David King**
Prime Minister **Maurice Hedley**   *Osborne's PA* **Philip Latham**

Having destroyed the Thorness super-computer, Fleming is picked up by the security forces but manages to escape and, reunited with Andromeda, takes refuge on a small island. A recovered Dawnay is lured to the Middle East country of Azaran where Intel is developing a new computer from information supplied by Bridger (Series One). Fleming and Andromeda are recaptured by the British government but are then kidnapped by Intel, joining Dawnay in Azaran.

Already there are signs that something strange is happening to the world's weather – as a result of the toxic enzyme (Series One) finding its way into the sea where it has multiplied and spread, absorbing nitrogen and lowering the air pressure. The outcome: tidal waves, hurricanes and tornadoes, as well as a drop in the atmosphere's oxygen level. In short, the world is slowly suffocating.

Fleming and Dawnay work to develop an antidote, although for Fleming the most pressing problem is the failing health of Andromeda who, though dying, is determined to work out the purpose of the message from space.

In Azaran, Col. Salim launches a military coup, backed by Intel. In turn, Gamboule, obsessed by ideas of world domination, seizes power by killing Salim. She, in *her* turn, is killed when a hurricane devastates Azaran, and Kaufman assumes (temporary) control before the President is ulti-mately reinstated. Andromeda is too weak to help as Fleming and Dawnay attempt to smuggle the antidote formula to Britain through a Canadian, Prof. Nielson, but she does convince Fleming that the 'message' was meant for him all along and that he should try to realise his dream of helping mankind.

Preen **Geoffrey Dunn**
RAF officer **Frederick Treves**
Gunman **James Urquhart**
Jan Neilson **Roy Wilson**
Burdett's PA **Jeffrey Gardiner**
Ratcliffe **Norman Space**
Intel agent **Michael Jacques**
Yusel (Abu Zeki's brother) **Earl Cameron**
Sharpling **David Chivers**

Producer: **John Elliot**
Directors: **John Elliot (Eps 1,3,5)**
John Knight (Eps 2,4,6)
Designer: **Norman James**
Film cameraman: **Ken Westbury**
Film editor: **James Colina**

A BBC Production
Six 45-minute episodes, black and white
Cold Front
Gale Warning
Azaran Forecast
Storm Centres
Hurricane
The Roman Peace (50 mins)

28 June–2 August 1962

ACE OF WANDS

This highly successful ITV children's adventure series of the early 1970s conjured up one of television's most dashing fantasy heroes – Tarot. A master magician, illusionist, escapologist and telepathic super-sleuth, Tarot was hailed at the start as 'a 20th-century Robin Hood, with a pinch of Merlin and a dash of Houdini'.

With his companions, Tarot tackled and despatched a collection of outrageous villains who wouldn't have felt out of place in *Batman* – adversaries such as Madame Midnight, the evil magician Mr Stabs, art thief Tun-Ju, mad chessmaster Ceribraun and the malevolent Mama Doc.

Created by Trevor Preston, the series wove magic, the supernatural and science fiction into a set of fantasy adventures that weren't afraid to send out a shiver or two. Several tales had especially sinister storylines; in *The Beautiful People*, domestic machines turned on their owners; the unnerving *Mama Doc* turned people into dolls that 'bled' when they broke; and *Nightmare Gas* induced horrific dreams that could literally scare victims to death.

Sharing Tarot's adventures were, in the first two seasons, his stage assistant Lulli, who had a telepathic link with Tarot, his enterprising ex-convict stage manager Sam, and the eccentric Mr Sweet, an antiquarian bookseller with a computer-like mind.

By Season Three, Mr Sweet was still around, but Lulli and Sam had given way to Mikki, a young journalist, and her photographer brother Chas. Mikki, too, had a telepathic link with Tarot. Completing the regulars was an inscrutable owl, Ozymandias.

REGULAR CAST

Tarot **Michael Mackenzie**   *Sam* **Tony Selby** *(Seasons One and Two)*
Lulli **Judy Loe** *(Seasons One and Two)*   *Mr Sweet* **Donald Layne-Smith**
Mikki **Petra Markham** *(Season Three*   *Chas* **Roy Holder** *(Season Three)*
Ozymandias **Fred the Owl**

Created by: **Trevor Preston**
Producer: **Pamela Lonsdale (Seasons One and Two), John Russell** *(Season Three*
Music: **Andrew Brown**
Magical adviser: **Ali Bongo**

A Thames Television Production
46 colour 30-minute episodes
Season One: 13 episodes
29 July–21 October 1970
Season Two: 13 episodes
21 July–13 October 1971
Season Three: 20 episodes
19 July–29 November 1972

Season One

One and One and One are Four

w **Trevor Preston** *(A 3-part story)*
Tracking down a professor's stolen brain-child leads Tarot and his friends to arch-criminal Madame Midnight and her wicked henchman Teddy Talk, whose lair is guarded by a battery of scientific traps.
Madame Midnight **Hildegard Neil**
Teddy Talk **Michael Standing**
Professor Ekdorf **Frederick Peisley**
Kal **Dave Prowse**
Six **Tony Caunter**
Eight **Chris Webb**
Ma Epps **Daphne Heard**
Dr Calder **Kenneth Watson**
Mr America **Bruce Boa**
Mr Russia **Jan Conrad**
Reporter **Carla Challoner**
Boutique girl **Nita Lorraine**

Director: **John Russell**
Designer: **Tony Borer**

The Mind Robbers

w **William Emms** *(A 4-part story)*
Tarot investigates the mysterious disappearance of two government ministers and clashes with an old adversary Señor Zandar and his cohort Fat Boy. Lured into a trap when Zandar hypnotises Lulli, Tarot must face a poisonous snake that hates people . . .
Señor Zandar **Vernon Dobtcheff**
Fat Boy **Michael Wynne**
Sir William Rowlands **Geoffrey Lumsden**
Miss Jellicoe **Sheelah Wilcocks**
Mr Hardy **John Golightly**
John Copney **Roger Kemp**
General Craig **Gerald Case**
Castor **Terry Walsh**
Pollux **Alan Chuntz**
Guard **Matthew Robertson**

Director: **Michael Currer-Briggs**
Designer: **Bernard Spencer**

Now You See It, Now You Don't

w Don Houghton *(A two-part story)*
A daring bank robbery leads Tarot, Lulli and Sam to an encounter with Falk, a power-mad Nazi-style villain whose base is a houseboat packed with computers.
Falk Christopher Benjamin
Macreedy Ray Barron
Gaston Alan Tucker
Cashier Tim Curry
Guard Billy Cornelius
Bank manager Kevin Stoney

Director: John Russell
Designer: Colin Andrews

The Smile

w Trevor Preston *(A 4-part story)*
Tun-Ju, 'The Emperor of the Art Thieves', and his accomplice Mrs Kite plot to steal the Mona Lisa. Sam loses his memory, and Tarot's head-on clash with the villain results in a deadly double-cross.
Tun-Ju Willoughby Goddard
Mrs Kite Dorothy Reynolds
Bartlett Bonnington John Barron
Digger farmer Reg Lye
Japanese bodyguard Tom Gan
Sir Patrick Landau Patrick McAlinney
Lady Landau Diana King

Director: Michael Currer-Briggs
Designer: Frank Gillman

Season Two

Seven Serpents, Sulphur and Salt

w Trevor Preston *(A 3-part story)*
Tarot and company face the formidable Mr Stabs, an evil magician who, aided by the beautiful Polandi and his wicked servant Luko, will stop at nothing to retrieve from Tarot the key to the secret of the Seven Serpents – not even murder.
Mr Stabs Russell Hunter
Polandi Harriet Harper
Luko Ian Trigger
Charlie Postle Jack Woolgar
Mr Christopher Llewellyn Rees
Mr Thwaites Jonathan Cecil

Director: Pamela Lonsdale
Designer: Tony Borer

Joker

w P.J. Hammond *(A 3-part story)*
Why should well-behaved children suddenly go beserk and wreck their classrooms? Tarot shuffles a pack of surprises dealt by Uncle Harry and his troupe of travelling entertainers 'Spells on Wheels' and rescues Lulli from the hands of the joker.
Uncle Harry Dermot Tuohy
The Jack Roy Holder
The Queen Carmen Munroe
The King Walter Sparrow
Miss Pascoe Lorna Heilbron
Headmaster George Waring
Headmistress Sheila Raynor

Director: John Russell
Designer: Bernard Spencer

Nightmare Gas

w Don Houghton *(A 3-part story)*
The beautiful but deadly Thalia and her monosyllabic brother Dalbiac steal a top-secret new gas, H23, which induces deep sleep and nightmares so vivid that the victim dies from shock.
Thalia Isobel Black
Dalbiac Jonathan Newth
Dr Richard Winthrop Laurence Carter
Sergeant Lewis Wilson
Trooper Alan Chuntz

Director: Ronald Marriott
Designer: Harry Clark

The Eye of Ra

w Michael Winder *(A 4-part story)*
Ceribraun, an eccentric, wheelchair-bound chessmaster, plots to steal the Eye of Ra, a priceless diamond said to have the power to turn people into chalk statues. Tarot finds himself the prisoner of Ceribraun's talking computer and is menaced by giant chesspieces.
Ceribraun Oscar Quitak
Sir John Packham Howard Goorney
Fredericks Nicholas Smith
Mr Quince Edward Jewesbury
Computer Charles Morgan
Sir Henry Carstairs Peter Williams

Director: John Russell
Designer: Bernard Spencer

Season Three

The Meddlers

w P.J. Hammond *(A 3-part story)*
Tarot acquires his new companions Chas
and Mikki and investigates a supposed
curse hanging over the London street
market where they live.
Spoon Michael Standing
Mockers Barry Linehan
Mr Dove Paul Dawkins
Drum Stefan Kalipha
Madge Honora Burke
Accordion player Neil Linden
Chauffeuse Norma West

Director: John Russell
Designer: Bill Palmer

The Power of Atep

w Victor Pemberton *(A 4-part story)*
A strange dream about Egypt, shared by
Tarot and Mikki, and a powerful voice at
a seance, lead Tarot and friends to the
tomb of Atep in Egypt's Valley of the
Kings. There Tarot confronts his former
stage partner and double, Quabal.
John Pentacle Sebastian
   Graham-Jones
High Priest Michael Mulcaster
Tramp Michael Rose
Fergus Wilson Joe Dunlop
Arab boy Lynval May

Director: Nicholas Ferguson
Designer: Harry Clark

Peacock Pie

w P.J. Hammond *(A 3-part story)*
Tarot and his friends clash with the bizarre
Mr Peacock whose astonishing power of
suggestion causes a bank robbery with no
robber, traps Chas in a room without a
door and strands Tarot at the top of a high
building with no way down.
Mr Peacock Brian Wilde
Mrs Macfadyean Dorothy Frere
Young Mrs Macfadyean Jean
   McCracken
Manageress Valerie Ost

Director: John Russell
Designer: Gordon Toms

Mama Doc

w Maggie Allen *(A 3-part story)*
One of Mr Sweet's university colleagues
disappears and the trail leads Tarot and
his friends to a doll's hospital run by the
eccentric Mama Doc, who, with her ac-
complice Bobby, turns people into dolls.
Mama Doc Pat Nye
Posy Peagram Wendy Hamilton
Bobby Michael Mundell
Prof. Darian Robert Grange
Dr Macdonald Ivor Roberts
Children Bobby Collins
   Claire McLellan
Mrs Darian Angela Rooks
Lorry driver David Parsons

Director: Nicholas Ferguson
Designer: Philip Blowers

Sisters Deadly

w Victor Pemberton *(A 3-part story)*
Chas returns from a photo assignment at
an old lady's 100th birthday party unable
to recall what happened, including that
while under hypnosis, he robbed a village
post office. Tarot uncovers a bizarre plot
by 'old ladies' to kidnap the Commander
in Chief of the British Land Forces.
Letty Edginton Sylvia Coleridge
Mathilda Edginton Henrietta Rudkin
Postmaster Bartlett Mullins
The Major James Bree
General Frank Duncan
Old ladies Lucy Griffiths, Mysie Montie,
   Kathleen St John, May Warden
General's driver Ronald Tye

Director: Darrol Blake
Designer: Andrew Drummond

The Beautiful People

w P.J. Hammond *(A 4-part story)*
Mikki is suspicious when she is barred
from a village fete by two strange but
beautiful girls and a handsome young
man. Tarot discovers that very valuable
prizes are on offer but are part of a bizarre
alien plot.

Jay **Edward Hammond**
Emm **Vivien Heilbron**
Dee **Susan Glanville**
Old woman **Kathleen Sainsbury**
Old man **Harry Hutchinson**

Old lady **Hilda Barry**
Vicar **Alex McDonald**

Director: **Vic Hughes**
Designer: **Eric Shedden**

ADAM ADAMANT LIVES!

Adam Llewellyn De Vere Adamant was a man out of his time, an Edwardian adventurer frozen in 1902 and revived 64 years later to bring his towering intellect, deadly fighting skills and implacable integrity to a world whose values are no longer those he had defended.

Adamant's references – as detailed in *Radio Times* at the start of this BBC series in 1966 – were impeccable. He was the ideal gentleman – elegant, courteous, honourable, charming and chivalrous, a friend of kings and statesmen. An *athlete*, boxer and swordsman, he moved like lightning and could handle any weapon with a deadly skill. A brilliant *scholar*, he was learned in every field of human knowledge. An *adventurer*, he was dedicated to fighting evil and undertook delicate and dangerous missions on behalf of his sovereign and country, in defence of the weak – especially women.

In 1902, Adam is lured by the beautiful Louise to a house where his arch-enemy The Face – a megalomaniac hiding his identity behind a leather mask – injects him with an eternal life drug and freezes him in a block of ice.

In 1966, workmen on a building site discover the ice block and the stage is set for Adam Adamant's return – but in the strange new world of the Swinging Sixties, shown as a bewildering collage of sights and sounds.

As Adam finds his feet he discovers two companions. The first, Georgina Jones, is a fan, whose grandfather regaled her with tales of Adamant's heroic exploits. And in episode two, Adam meets former music hall artist and jack-of-all-trades William E. Simms, who becomes his loyal factotum.

For two seasons the trio foiled a succession of oddball villains and bizarre plots in an enjoyable series whose resemblance to ITV's *The Avengers* was hardly surprising – its script editor Tony Williamson had written several Avengers episodes and both series shared some of the same writers – including Brian Clemens!

The second series also added spice to Adam Adamant's role as caped crusader by regularly pitting him against his old nemesis The Face – alive, well and plotting in the present as he had been in the past.

Suave actor Gerald Harper was cast as Adam, who despite his

many talents was given to smugness and a naive trust of women. Harper built on the cultured, elegant image in successive roles, including ITV's country squire *Hadleigh*.

REGULAR CAST

Adam Adamant **Gerald Harper** *Georgina Jones* **Juliet Harmer**
William E. Simms **Jack May** *The Face* **Peter Ducrow**

Creators: **Don Cotton, Richard Harris**
Script editor: **Tony Williamson**
Producer: **Verity Lambert**

A BBC Production
29 50-minute episodes, black and white
Season One:
23 June–13 October 1966
Season Two:
31 December 1966–25 March 1967
(BBC1)

Season One
16 episodes

A Vintage Year for Scoundrels

w **Tony Williamson**, *additional material by* **Donald Cotton, Richard Harris**
In 1902, gentleman adventurer Adam Adamant is lured into a trap where his arch-enemy, The Face, condemns him to 'die forever', entombed in a block of ice . . . In 1966, workmen discover Adam, still perfectly preserved. Reviving in hospital, he is plunged into modern London – an alien world of mini-skirts, cars, strip clubs, neon signs, blaring music and escalators. He is 'rescued' by Georgina Jones who helps him to come to terms with his new situation. In turn, Adam helps her against villainess Margot Kane and her henchmen Hicks and Hoggett.
Sir James **Kenneth Benda**
The Face **Peter Ducrow**
Gramps **Bartlett Mullins**
Hoggett **Ivor Slater**
Hicks **Frank Jarvis**
Detective **Joby Blanshard**
Margot Kane **Freda Jackson**

Director: **David Proudfoot**
Designer: **Darrol Blake**

Death Has a Thousand Faces

w **Tony Williamson**
A man is stabbed to death, a stick of Blackpool rock is the only clue, and a £50

million crime is in the making as Adam and Georgina face the 'perils' of Blackpool's Golden Mile.
Parky **Geoffrey Hinsliff**
Jeffreys **Michael Robbins**
Susie **Sheila Fearn**
Danny **Patrick O'Connell**
William E. Simms **Jack May (intro)**
Madame Delvario **Stephanie Bidmead**
Kelvin **John Rolfe**

Director: **Philip Dudley**
Designer: **Evan Hercules**

More Deadly Than the Sword

w **Terence Frisby**
Adam helps a government minister who is being blackmailed into handing over defence secrets at a Japanese geisha house.
Sir Ernest Hampton **Maurice Hedley**
McLennon **Barry Linehan**
Suzu **Lucille Soong**
Hitomi **Mona Chong**
Madame Nagata **Mary Webster**
Ikezawa **Andy Ho**
Kodama **Yuri Borienko**
Hiram **Geoffrey Alexander**

Director: **Leonard Lewis**
Designer: **Gwen Evans**

The Sweet Smell of Success

w **Robert Banks Stewart**
A blue carnation, the emblem of success

for a high-pressure sales campaign, is also the symbol for something far more sinister.

Badenoch John Gatrell
Kinthly Charles Tingwell
Sales manager Bryan Kendrick
Advertising manager David Lander
Shani Mathieson Adrienne Corri
McLintock William Hurndell
Spalding Jack Howlett

Director: Philip Dudley
Designer: Gwen Evans

Allah Is Not Always With You

w Tony Williamson
A dying girl's last words lead Adam into the world of nightclubs, gambling . . . and murder.
Vargos Kevin Brennan
Lukas Nosher Powell
Ahmed David Spenser
Helen Jennifer Jayne
Fluffy Valerie Stanton
Calvert John Hollis
Sheik John Woodnutt

Director: Paul Ciappessoni
Designer: Evan Hercules

The Terribly Happy Embalmers

w Brian Clemens
The mystery of financiers who always seem to die twice, leads Adam into a world of embalmers – and an appointment with death.
Sir George Marston John Scott
Wilson Jeremy Young
Mr Percy Arthur Brough
Grantham Deryck Guyler
Velmer John Le Mesurier
George Hamilton Dyce
Susan Ilona Rodgers

Director: Paul Ciappessoni
Designer Darrol Blake

To Set a Deadly Fashion

w Tony Williamson
The frantic world of high fashion and eccentric designers is a confusing one for

Adam – until he finds it is also the setting for espionage and murder.

Oretta Dorvetti Nancy Nevinson
Maj. Fitzgibbon Bryan Coleman
Leo Dorvetti Alan Foss
Janine Gwendolyn Watts
Roger Clair Colin Jeavons
Mrs Smythe Audrey Noble
Howarth Alister Williamson

Director: Leonard Lewis
Designer: Evan Hercules

The Last Sacrifice

w Richard Harris
A pleasant weekend party becomes a nightmare for a man who finds himself involved in black magic and human sacrifice.
Huge man Kenneth Ives
Esta Canfield Jennifer Daniel
Statton Glyn Dearman
Lord Rufus Pearmain William Dexter
James Denton Hugh Dickson
Minister John Dawson
Barber Ian Fairbairn

Director: Philip Dudley
Designer: Darrol Blake

Sing a Song of Murder

w John Pennington
Georgina is arrested for attempting to rob a bank, she and Adam find themselves in the world of pop music – and a sinister plot unfolds.
Kinkhead Michael Standing
Sgt Denis Cleary
Inspector Michael Beint
Melville Jerome Willis
Chauffeur James Blake
Carson Alex Scott
Felina Anne Kristen

Director: Moira Armstrong
Designer: Austin Ruddy

The Doomsday Plan

w Richard Harris
An outbreak of mysterious crimes, including the kidnapping of a BBC newsreader,

leads Adam into the fanatical realm of Dr Mort – prophet of doom!

BBC newsreader Kenneth Kendall
Dr Mort Peter Vaughan
Streek Roy Hanlon
Maddox Andrew Robertson
Hinchcombe Geoffrey Lumsden
Man with parcel Talfryn Thomas
Samantha Isobel Black

Director: Paul Ciappessoni
Designer: Mary Rea

Death by Appointment Only

w Tony Williamson
Big business and high-priced escorts involve Adam in a wave of murders which shake the financial capitals of the world.

Sandra Webb Patricia Haines
Phillippe Jervais Colin Vancao
Sir Nigel Dee David Garth
Daniels John Walker
Pamela Wentworth-Howe Christine Finn
Charles Fellows James Cairncross
Von Reison Edward Palmer

Director: Moira Armstrong
Designer: Ray London

Beauty Is an Ugly Word

w Vince Powell *and* Harry Driver
The world of beauty contestants and physical culture experts is the strange setting for a plot to destroy the human race.

Ryan Esmond Webb
Petherbridge John Baddeley
Paula Carter Annette André
Max Eddie Stacey
Sinoda Peter Jeffrey
Victor Barry Jackson
PC Mullins John McKelvey

Director: Philip Dudley
Designer: Ken Jones

The League of Uncharitable Ladies

w John Pennington
The murder of a man in St James' Park leads Adam to a strange womens' club in Pall Mall, and a committee of three old ladies called Faith, Hope and Charity, who are not what their names imply.

Prudence Geraldine Moffatt
Abstinence Eve Gross
Jarrot Gerald Sim
Charity Amelia Baynton
Hope Sheila Grant
Faith Lucy Griffiths
Randolph John Carson

Director: Ridley Scott
Designer: Mary Rea

Ticket to Terror

w Dick Sharples
Four hundred commuters – including Simms – disappear without trace on an underground line, in one of the most sinister conspiracies in British criminal history.

Miss Caldwell Ann Lynn
Dr Klein Max Adrian
Susan Denby Jan Quy
Harold Reg Lye
Engineer Jack Bligh
George Tommy Eytle
Armitage Michael Barrington

Director: Tina Wakerell
Designer: Evan Hercules

The Village of Evil

w Vince Powell *and* Harry Driver
A dead mouse, a young boy and a lonely mill lead Adam into a sinister web of evil that interrupts a quiet finishing holiday.

Joe Christopher Coll
Dr Craigshaw John Bailey
Mr Burke Trevor Baxter
Myra Bamford Colette O'Neil
Daniel Dinny Powell
Jerry Fletcher Len Jones
Mr Corbett John Law

Director: Anthea Browne-Wilkinson
Designer: Sally Hulke

D for Destruction

w Tony Williamson
A series of deadly accidents in Adamant's old regiment draws him back into uniform

and an encounter with the fanatical Col. Mannering who is infuriated by plans to phase out the Territorial Army.
Sgt Major Jeffers **Michael Ripper**
Corp. Grey **Walter Sparrow**
Bailey **Bryan Mosley**
General Mongerson **Parick Troughton**
Corp. Jenkins **Anthony Blackshaw**
Col. Mannering **Iain Cuthbertson**
Major **Michael Sheard**

Director: **Moira Armstrong**
Designer: **Ken Jones**

Season Two
13 episodes

A Slight Case of Reincarnation

w **Tony Williamson**, from a story by **Brian Clemens**
Adam Adamant is asked to protect an African leader from assassination – and recalls an old enemy.
Hinkaya **Horace James**
Hammond **Patrick Kavanagh**
Charlesworth **Norman Pitt**
Simpson **John Cazabon**
Logan **William Hurndell**
Dr Sanderson **Peter Madden**
Dr Heindrick **Martin Miller**
Sir Charles Thetford **John Frawley**
Lady Thetford **Peggy Ann Wood**
Louise **Mary Yeomans**

Director: **Roger Jenkins**
Designer: **Ken Jones**

Black Echo

w **Donald** and **Derek Ford**
An oil tanker delivers its load to a country house and the driver gets a shock that turns his hair white. And Adam Adamant again faces The Face.
Oil delivery man **Kenneth Ives**
Sir Henry **Donald Eccles**
Sir George **Peter Bathurst**
Beardsley **Trevor Baxter**
Sergei **Brian Gilmar**
Ireyna **Judy Parfitt**
Grand Duchess Vorokhov **Gladys Cooper**

Director: **Moira Armstrong**
Designer: **Peter Kindred**

Conspiracy of Death

w **Vince Powell** and **Harry Driver**
Jankers Johnson, an old wartime buddy of Simms, is mysteriously murdered at their former RAF aerodrome – but manages to get a message to Adam before he dies.
Johnson **John Scott Martin**
Davison **Harold Goodwin**
Onslow **Derek Farr**
Penrose **George Woodbridge**
Monique **Annette Carell**
Connelly **David Blake Kelly**
Dolly **Fanny Carby**

Director: **Roger Jenkins**
Designer: **Michael Young**

The Basardi Affair

w **Ian Stuart Black**
Adam gets involved in the world of international exploitation after the ruler of an oil-rich country is the victim of fierce intimidation.
Eileen Smith **Suzanne Mockler**
Sonia Fawzi **Kate O'Mara**
Chauffeur **Joe Cornelius**
Sheikh Abdul **Zia Mohyeddin**
Guard **Roy Stewart**
Prince Mahmud **Salmaan Peer**
Sir Robert **William Kendall**

Director: **Henri Safran**
Designer: **Peter Kindred**

The Survivors

w **Vince Powell** and **Harry Driver**
When inventions start appearing on the market after the death of their inventors, Adam is drawn into a sinister plot.
Minister **Anthony Dawes**
Singleton **Edwin Richfield**
Mrs Granger **Elizabeth Benson**
Critchley **Erik Chitty**
Marty **Roy Evans**
Mrs Clasp **Hilda Fenemore**
Blundell **Edward Evans**

Director: **Moira Armstrong**
Designer: **Michael Young**

Face in a Mirror

w John Pennington
The Face devises a plan to rid the world of
Adamant by first discrediting and then
destroying him. The scheme is so cunning
it may just succeed.
Farnley Gerald Harper
Gladwin Edward Brayshaw
Lady Lydia Jean Marsh
Livingstone Fred McNaughton
Hudson Billy John
Roach Bob Godfrey
Baker Basil Dignam

Director: Henri Safran
Designer: Michael Young

Another Little Drink

w Ian Stuart Black
Georgina goes to a party organised by the
manufacturer of a new soft drink, but
finds it is not as innocuous as it appears.
Supervisor Norman Wynne
Carol Shelley Sally Bazely
Dr Loton Meredith Edwards
Yorke Fredric Abbott
Addison Robert McBain
D.K. Davies Peter Bowles
Guard Michael Golden

Director: Laurence Bourne
Designer: Malcolm Middleton

Death Begins at Seventy

w Dick Sharples
When Simms gets a message from an old
theatre friend, he and Adam find them-
selves mixed up in strange goings-on at an
old folks' home
Timothy Henshaw George Benson
Charlie Pearson Windsor Davies
Matron Sheila Burrell
Mary Smith Cyd Hayman
Dr Henry Heason Kenneth J. Warren
Harry Newley John Glyn-Jones
Young man Bill Maclean

Director: Ridley Scott
Designer: Peter Kindred

Tunnel of Death

w Richard Waring
When Georgina is nearly arrested, Adam
becomes involved in uncovering the latest
plot by The Face who is busy organising
his biggest coup yet.
Sewerman Tex Fuller
Commissioner Hobson Geoffrey Chater
Scarlatti Arnold Diamond
Bruno Kenneth Ives
Constance Geraldine Newman
Brooke Walter Sparrow
Barker Jerold Wells

Director: Moira Armstrong
Designer: Michael Young

The Deadly Bullet

w Vince Powell and Harry Driver
After illusionist The Great Manton is
killed while performing the bullet-catching
trick, Adam uses his deductive skills to
help a reluctant policeman find his
murderer.
George Manton Henry Gilbert
Wanda Manton Sheila Brennan
Juanita Jill Curzon
Carlos Graham Corry
Oliver Meadows Nigel Stock
Insp. Foster Bill Kerr
Pop Williams Harold Bennett

Director: Henri Safran
Designer: Peter Kindred

The Resurrectionists

w Derek and Donald Ford
When a scientist destroys his invention for
calming wild animals and then vanishes,
Adam is drawn into a sinister encounter
with agents of The Face.
Dr Morris Vaine Bernard Kay
Sara Linden Wendy Gifford
Mr Byers-Thompson Frank Williams
The Minister Peter Stephens
Miss Coburn Sheila Grant
Susan Tracey Crisp
Mrs Withenshaw Cicely Paget-Bowman

Director: Ridley Scott
Designer: Malcolm Middleton

Wish You Were Here

w James MacTaggart

Simms's mother is charged with disturbing the peace, and when Simms goes to her aid he stumbles on a sordid plot.

Saville Peter Birrel
Mrs Simms Hilda Barry
Sonia Marion Mathie
Lord Hawksmoor Michael Gwynn
Old lady Kitty Attwood
Hercules Skip Martin
Matron Terry Richards

Director: Moira Armstrong
Designer: Peter Kindred

A Sinister Sort of Service

w Tony Williamson

A number of carefully planned robberies take place throughout the country, and it's clear that only one man can be behind them – The Face.

Sir Nigel Dee David Garth
Jason Lang T.P. McKenna
Thomas Mark Moss
Miklo Josef Zaranoff
Sandra Verrel Frances Cuka
SS girl Clare Jenkins
Furrier David Kelly

Director: Laurence Bourne
Designer: Michael Young

THE ADVENTURES OF DON QUICK

Science fiction satire based on the character of Don Quixote, with its astronaut anti-hero, Don Quick, tilting at planets instead of windmills.

As a member of the Inter Galactic Maintenance Squad, Quick should only be concerned with nuts and bolts. But he's not satisfied with that role. Each time he and his trusty companion Sgt Sam Czopanser (Sancho Panza, get it?) land on a new planet, he sees himself as the roving ambassador of Earth, and sets about trying to right imaginary wrongs. This penchant for interference invariably ends with him upsetting the balance of whatever society he encounters.

Impressively designed, the six-part series boasted some elaborate sets, rich costumes and clever technical effects – such as Quick being shrunk to a six-inch dwarf by the queen of a matriarchal planet. But it was short on laughs, and though its makers LWT persevered with its prime-time slot (9.00 pm, Fridays), other ITV regions quickly demoted it to a late-evening one.

REGULAR CAST

Captain Don Quick Ian Hendry   *Sgt Sam Czopanser* Ronald Lacey

Executive producer: Peter Wildeblood

London Weekend Television Production

Six colour 60-minute episodes
30 October–4 December 1970

The Benefits of Earth

w Peter Wildeblood

The intrepid Don Quick lands on a planet inhabited by two alien races – one technically advanced but addicted to warfare and human sacrifice, the other living in a dream world of peace and sensitivity.

Babachuk Kevin Stoney
Goolmarg John Woodnutt
Dulcie Margaret Nolan
Grippik Patrick Durkin
Marvana Anouska Hempel
Gezool Donald Sumpter
Chief dreamer Thorley Walters

Director: Mike Newell
Designer: Bryan Bagge

People Isn't Everything

w Kenneth Hill

Astronauts Don and Sam trustingly leave their spaceship in charge of the first friendly face they find on the planet Ophiuchus. But that face belongs to Skip, a robot castaway who likes a drink . . .

Skip Tony Bateman
Dovax Jonathan Elsom
Broul Michael Sheard
Peleen Kate O'Mara
Skander Damien Thomas
Malin Arne Gordon
Ziggs Glenn Williams
Clerk of the court Bryan Mosley
TV announcer John Carlin
Judge Lockwood West
Public prosecutor Dennis Edwards
Physiological expert Victor Platt
Mam Dovax Nan Munro
Bank clerks David Gooderson
James Ware
Rebel Colin Baker

Director: Quentin Lawrence
Designer: Bryan Bagge

The Higher the Fewer

w Peter Wildeblood

When Don and Sam land on the planet Melkior 5, they find themselves in the middle of a huge rubbish dump. The inhabitants have all taken refuge in 2000-storey skyscrapers, with the top people living at the top, and the lower classes at the bottom. Then Don starts turning everything upside down.

Hendenno James Hayter
Guards James Appleby
John Lawrence
Mrs Arborel Hildegard Neil
Arborel Derek Francis
Magdis Maggie Don
Beltane Oliver Cotton
Section leader Neil Wilson
Afghar Kenny Rodway

Director: Cliff Owen
Designer: Rodney Cammish

The Love Reflector

w Keith Miles

The population of the planet Herekos seems to consist wholly of beautiful girls. But there is danger in succumbing to their charms for the Queen Bee has the power to reduce men to six-inch dwarfs. Lieutenant Vasco, the only Spaniard ever to get into orbit, succumbed a generation ago. How will Quick fare?

Angeline Liz Bamber
Oriel Gay Soper
Juno Vicki Woolf
Magda Susan Porrett
Queen Bee Faith Brook
Lt Vasco Michael Aldridge
Iris Anna Brett
Leonie Madeline Smith

Director: Cyril Coke
Designer: John Emery

The Quick and the Dead

w Keith Miles

When the astronauts inadvertently land in the crater of a live volcano, Sgt Sam is convinced that he is dead. He's not much reassured by finding that the volcano houses a strange assortment of ancient gods.

Doris Jacqueline Clarke
Billy, a satyr Louis Mansi
Aphrodite Patricia Haines
Hera Pauline Jameson
Zeus Graham Crowden
Hephaestus Reg Lye
Frigg Gaye Browne

Odin **Arthur Brough**
Krimhilda **Madeleine Mills**
Flosshilda **Yutte Stensgaard**

Director: **Bob Hird**
Designer: **Rodney Camish**

Paradise Destruct

---

w **Charlotte** and **Dennis Plimmer**
To anyone but Don Quick, the planet
Amity would seem a paradise. The girls
are beautiful, the vegetation is lush and
both night and winter have mysteriously
been abolished. But Quick, as usual,
cannot let well alone.

Jonquil **Kara Wilson**
Willow **Lorna Heilbron**
Sycamore **Roy Marsden**
Butternut **Brian Oulton**
Delphinium **Madeleine Newbury**
Oleander **Leigh Lawson**

Director: **Bill Turner**
Designer: **John Emery**

THE ADVENTURES OF SUPERMAN

As American as cowboys or gangsters, Superman took his place in ITV's early schedules alongside such other time-honoured US favourites as *Dragnet*, *Roy Rogers*, *I Love Lucy* and *Rin Tin Tin*.

Billed over here without his US prefix, 'The Adventures Of', Superman has the distinction of being ITV's first science fiction show, arriving here in 1956, albeit three years after the series' American debut.

Youngsters reared on the spectacular big-screen image of Christopher Reeve as the Man of Steel might need some persuading, but to generations of British and American fans Superman will always be George Reeves and yes, they believed *this* man could fly. Week after week they had the message drummed home, as indelibly as the ink on a *Daily Planet* headline: 'Faster than a speeding bullet, more powerful than a locomotive, able to leap tall buildings at a single bound. Look . . . up in the sky . . . it's a bird . . . it's a plane . . . it's Superman!'

Reeves, a 6 ft 2½ in, 13 st 13 lb bachelor who'd succeeded where 200 previous job applicants had failed, was a former light-heavyweight boxer who'd studied acting alongside Victor Mature and Robert Preston. He'd been in love with Vivien Leigh in *Gone With the Wind* and appeared in other movie classics such as *Blood and Sand* and *From Here to Eternity*, and he'd actually first donned the superhero tights and underpants for a 1951 cinema feature *Superman and the Mole Men* (re-edited for the TV series as a two-part story *The Unknown People*).

Superman may have fought tirelessly for 'truth, justice and the American way', but he was, of course, an alien, a survivor of the doomed planet Krypton. He'd been launched into space as an infant by his scientist father Jor El just before the planet exploded, and crash-landed on Earth in a field near Smallville, USA, where he was discovered by a childless farm couple, Jonathan and Martha Kent who adopted him and named him Clark.

Because the boy was from a larger world with a red sun, Earth's yellow sun endowed him with super powers of flight, strength, X-ray vision, hearing and invulnerability, his only weakness being Kryptonite – fragments of his old home planet – which invariably fell into the wrong hands. As a man, Clark moved to Metropolis, working as a reporter on the *Daily Planet*. As Clark, he was bespectacled, meek and mild-mannered, but at the drop of his snap-brimmed hat he became Superman, scourge of the underworld

Other regulars in the series were naive cub reporter Jimmy Olsen, gruff *Planet* editor Perry White, Metropolis police chief Insp. Henderson, and Lois Lane, the *Planet*'s impulsive star reporter, enamoured of Supie but contemptuous of Clark. Lois was played abrasively (in the first 26-week American season) by Phyllis Coates, and toned down for the rest by Noel Neill.

Though Superman's origins were pure science-fiction, the shows were basically crime melodramas, shot on a low budget of 15,000 dollars each, at the rate of roughly two a week, and frequently called for the Man of Steel to rescue Lois, Jimmy or both from mortal danger and clutches of crazed scientists, gangsters, madmen and pirates. Occasionally there was a sci-fi theme to the story, such as *Superman in Exile*, when contamination from gamma rays leads Superman into a self-imposed exile; *Panic in the Sky*, when exposure to Kryptonite in a meteor induces amnesia; *Through the Time Barrier*, in which a scientist's time machine sends him, a crook, Lois, Jimmy, Perry and Clark back to the Stone Age; and *Mr Zero*, in which a small man from outer space who can paralyse people by pointing his finger at them falls among thieves.

Special effects were unsophisticated but effective. Reeves took off via wires, hydraulics and springboards, landed by jumping off a ladder and flew by being filmed lying on a glass table, with the Metropolis skyline (actually Hollywood) matted in later. Imagination did the rest.

When Superman first flew across British screens in 1956, ATV in the Midlands managed a prolonged 18-month run of some 78 episodes. These were culled from the first five US seasons but shown at random, only vaguely following the original seasonal flow. In fact, Noel Neill's Lois Lane was the first to be seen over here, while Phyllis Coates's acid-tongued version occasionally elbowed her milder counterpart out of the schedules for the odd week later in the run.

The last adventure of Superman was made in 1957. Two years later George Reeves, who had been so synonymous with the role that other acting jobs were almost impossible to come by, shot himself. His shows, though, have run and run. In the end nearly all of the 104 episodes were screened somewhere in the UK – and it was still popping up as recently as 1988–9, when BBC1 dusted off a few reels for the Christmas holidays.

REGULAR CAST

Superman/Clark Kent **George Reeves**
Lois Lane **Phyllis Coates** *(US Season One)*, **Noel Neill** *(from Season Two)*
Jimmy Olsen **Jack Larsen**   *Perry White* **John Hamilton**
Insp. Henderson **Robert Shayne**

Producers: **Robert Maxwell, Bernard Luber** *(Season One)* **Whitney Ellsworth** *(the rest)*
Directors: **Thomas Carr** *(33)*, **Lee Sholem** *(11)*, **George Blair** *(26)*, **Harry Gerstad,** *(20)*, **Phil Ford** *(8)*, **Howard Bretherton** *(1)*, **Lew Landers** *(2)*, **George Reeves** *(3)*

Principal writers: **David Chantler, Jackson Gillis, Whitney Ellsworth**

ABC Production
104 30-minute episodes, made in black and white (Seasons 1 & 2), colour (3–6) UK premiere (all b/w): 23 February 1956– 13 September 1957 (ATV Midlands)

ALF

ALF is the latest in a line of American comedy series that set an alien in a typical Earth household so that we can look at our world through his eyes and see how dumb we really are.

It's 1980s insult comedy laced with traditional US morality, a sophisticated line in wisecracking satire, and a lineage that can be traced back through *Mork and Mindy* as far as *My Favourite Martian*.

ALF is a 230-year-old 'alien life form' called Gordon Shumway. He was born on the 'lower east side' of the planet Melmac and he looks like a cross between an aardvark and a dwarf orang-utan. His arrival on Earth is dramatic. His spaceship (a classic sports model called a Phlegm 220) crash lands through the garage roof of a typical American suburban home. ALF takes up residence with the Tanner family and quickly disrupts their lives with his unusual habits (he likes to eat cats!) and assertive personality. ALF doesn't understand simple things like manners. He just blurts out statements and opinions with scant regard for the consequences. Children love him because he's irreverent and clued up on pop culture (all he knows about Earth is what he sees on TV). Naturally there are plenty of conflicts, but the family – even grumpy old dad, Willie Tanner – are protective, loyal and loving.

ALF is the puppet creation of a former comic magician called Paul Fusco, and has become a worldwide star. Britain is one of more than 60 countries showing *ALF*. So far we've seen more than

40 episodes (mostly named after song titles!) with more to come. There's also an *ALF* cartoon series in the wings as well as *ALF: The Movie*.

REGULAR CAST

Willie Tanner **Max Wright**   *Kate Tanner* **Anne Schedeen**
Lynn Tanner **Andrea Elson**   *Brian Tanner* **Benji Gregory**
ALF **Himself! (Paul Fusco)**
Trevor Ochmonek **John La Motta**   *Raquel Ochmonek* **Liz Sheridan**

Created by: **Paul Fusco**
Producer: **Tom Patchett**
Writers: Various, including **Paul Fusco, Tom Patchett, Bob** *and* **Howard Bendetson**
Directors: Various, including **Peter Bonerz, Nancy Heydorn, Tom Patchett, Paul Fusco**

UK: 42 colour 30-minute episodes (and still counting)
UK premiere: 25 April 1987 (ITV)
Still in production

ALIENS IN THE FAMILY

Six-part children's serial about a young alien who comes to Earth on a mission and gets involved with an ordinary British family.

Adapted from the novel by Margaret Mahy, it was a mixture of science fiction and domestic drama for although Bond, the student from the planet Galgonqua, is the obvious alien, there is another alien of sorts *inside* the family – 12-year-old Jacqueline (Jake). She is feeling like an outsider in her new family unit, now that her father, David, is remarried to Pip, who already has a 12-year-old daughter Dora and a younger son, Lewis.

Jake and Dora are not getting on at all well when they first meet Bond, but agree to help him. Bond's mission involves reaching a particular stone circle before his pursuing enemies, the awesome Wirdegens, catch him. The dangerous chase takes the group across country until they finally reach the circle where the Wirdegens show up and congratulate Bond on passing what he suddenly remembers was a test all along.

Special effects in the series were devised by the award-winning team from the 1986 fantasy, *The Box of Delights*.

REGULAR CAST

Bond **Grant Thatcher**   *Jake* **Sophie Bold**   *Dora* **Clare Wilkie**
Lewis **Sebastian Knapp**   *David* **Rob Edwards**   *Philippa* **Clare Gifford**
Solita **Elizabeth Watkins**   *Wirdegen leader* **Granville Saxton**
Wirdegens **Sue Soames, Tony Birch, James Woodward**

Dramatised by: **Allan Baker**, *from the*
story by **Margaret Mahy**
Executive producer: **Paul Stone**
Director: **Christina Secombe**
Video effects: **Robin Lobb**
Music: **Roger Limb, BBC Radiophonic**
Workshop
Designer: **Paul Montague**

A BBC Production
Six colour 25-minute episodes
18 November–23 December 1987
(BBC1)

THE AMAZING SPIDERMAN

Marvel's comic-strip came to life in this American series starring Nicholas Hammond as the superhuman, skyscraper-scaling, web-hurling hero.

Spiderman kicked off with a pilot film (first shown in British cinemas in 1978) which showed how Peter Parker, a student scientist and aspiring news photographer, is bitten by a spider contaminated with highly radioactive material, and acquires the power to climb sheer walls and an arachnid's sixth sense.

Using his scientific know-how, Parker invents an adhesive fluid that can be shot from a special holder, solidifying on contact with the air to form a strong rope. Hiding his true identity behind the distinctive 'Spidey' costume, Parker uses his powers against the forces of crime and evil.

And that was about it. Week after week Spiderman foiled the designs of various crooks, kidnappers or terrorists, but the series never really took off, only occasionally venturing beyond the routine crime format.

REGULAR CAST

Spiderman/Peter Parker **Nicholas Hammond**   *Rita* **Chip Fields**
J. Jonah Jameson **Robert F. Simon**   *Capt. Barbera* **Michael Pataki**

Executive producers: **Charles Fries** *and*
Daniel R. Goodman
Producers: **Robert Janes, Ron Satlof,**
Lionel E. Siegel
Writers: Various
Directors: Various

A Charles Fries and Daniel R. Goodman
Production
12 colour episodes (plus one pilot film), 60
mins unless stated

Spiderman (pilot)
The Deadly Dust (2-part story)

The Curse of Rava
Night of the Clones
The Captive Tower
Photo Finish
Wolfpack
Escort to Danger
The Con Caper
A Matter of State
The Kirkwood Haunting
Chinese Web (90 mins)

4 September–27 November 1981
(ITV, London)

ASTRONAUTS

Two-thirds of *The Goodies*, Bill Oddie and Graeme Garden, wrote this four-handed 1980s ITV sitcom about the first British space mission – a claustrophic affair consisting of two men, one woman and Bimbo the dog.

The astronauts – all temperamentally incompatible – were locked together in a two-roomed skylab for several months. Constantly under surveillance, their only contact with the ground was an abrasive, unsympathetic American mission controller.

Given such a situation, there was no opportunity to, as Bill Oddie put it, 'bring in the funny plumber when things got dull'. *Astronauts* relied on the interaction between the Skylab trio – commander Malcolm Mattocks, an ex-RAF type who was lousy at handling people, posh woman doctor Gentian Foster, and truculent technical officer David Ackroyd – and the controller, Col. Beadle. There were gags about the jargon (Skylab was 'Pooh', mission control 'Piglet'), the tedious routine, going to the loo, homesickness, mysterious messages and space madness with Mattocks assuring the rest of the crew that 'God is my co-pilot'.

Astronauts was not a giant leap for TV comedy, and despite a networked peak-time run on Monday nights, its success was only moderate.

MAIN CAST

Cmdr. Malcolm Mattocks **Christopher Godwin**
Dr Gentian Foster **Carmen Du Sautoy**   *David Ackroyd* **Barrie Rutter**
Col. Beadle **Bruce Boa**

Writers: **Graeme Garden, Bill Oddie**
Director: **Douglas Argent**
Producers: **Tony Charles, Douglas Argent**
Executive Producer: **Allen McKeown**
Designer: **John Hickson**

Developed for television by Witzend Productions
Six colour 13-minute episodes
26 October– 7 December 1981

AUTOMAN

The title character of this American crime adventure series is a hologram – a three-dimensional computer-generated picture who becomes a super sleuth.

Automan starts life as a character in a computer, created by Los Angeles policeman Walter Nebicher. Walter, who'd rather be out on the streets chasing crooks, is stuck with a job on the police computer at headquarters. His boss doesn't think much of Walter – or his computer – until Automan comes along to walk through walls and reach the crimes other cops can't.

The result: the pair become Los Angeles Police Department's brightest crimefighting duo.

REGULAR CAST

Automan **Chuck Wagner**   *Walter Nebicher* **Desi Arnaz Jr**
Lt Jack Curtis **Robert Lansing**   *Roxanne Caldwell* **Heather McNair**
Capt. E.G. Boyd **Gerald S. O'Loughlin**

Created by: **Glen A. Larson**
Producer: **Glen A. Larson**
Writers: Various, including **Glen A. Larson, Doug Heyes Jr**
Directors: Various, inc. **Lee Katzin, Rick Kolbe, Kim Manners**

A Glen A. Larson Production
13 colour episodes
(one × 70 mins, 12 × 50 mins)

Pilot
The Biggest Game in Town
Staying Alive While Running a High Flash Dance Fever

The Great Pretender
Ships in the Night
Unreasonable Facsimile
Flashes and Ashes
Renegade Run
Murder MTV
Murder, Take One
Death by Design
Club Ten
Zippers

12 May–28 August 1984
(BBC1)

THE AVENGERS

Taking a literal definition, *The Avengers* was not a 'science-fiction show', but then neither was it a show to be taken literally . . .

One of the most potent cocktails of fantasy and adventure that television has seen, *The Avengers* began as a straight crime thriller, evolved into a stylish secret agent romp and hit its peak in the mid-1960s as an outlandish, tongue-in-cheek extravaganza that pitted its hero and heroine against some of the most outlandish villains the underworld – or any world – could muster.

Like few other long-running series, *The Avengers* moved with the times – more than that, it helped shape them. From the high boots and black leather of Honor Blackman to the catsuits of Diana Rigg, the show quickly became an innovative frontrunner in 1960s style culture. It was adored in America for its cultivated 'British-ness', and adored in Britain for its creation of a sophisticated fantasy world. Brian Clemens, a co-producer on the series once said, 'We admitted to only one class – and that was the upper.

Because we were a fantasy, we have not shown policemen or coloured men. And you have not seen anything as common as blood. We have no social conscience at all.'

Running through the series, from the first episode in 1961 to the 161st in 1969 was the debonair figure of old Etonian adventurer John Steed, played to the hilt of urbane charm by Patrick Macnee. Originally he was the sidekick, a foil for Ian Hendry as the main star, Dr David Keel. When Hendry departed, Macnee moved to centre stage where he was joined by a succession of lovely, liberated ladies – Cathy Gale (Honor Blackman), Emma Peel (Diana Rigg), Tara King (Linda Thorson) and then, in *The New Avengers*, Purdey (Joanna Lumley).

(Author's note: as this *is* a science fiction guide, it would be inappropriate to include a full episode rundown since the sf streak didn't really emerge until the Emma Peel era when almost every week, it seemed, a mad scientist or some such evil genius with a chip on his shoulder would unleash a bizarre bid for power or fortune. So I've covered, in brief, the early years featuring Ian Hendry and Honor Blackman, and lingered over the later ones. Anyone seeking further information should check out *The ITV Encyclopedia of Adventure* by Dave Rogers or his other books on the series such as *The Avengers Anew* or *The Complete Avengers*. Meanwhile . . .)

Season One
AVENGING TIME!

REGULAR CAST

Dr David Keel Ian Hendry   *John Steed* Patrick Macnee
Carol Wilson (Keel's receptionist) Ingrid Hafner

Young doctor David Keel teams up with a mysterious undercover agent John Steed to avenge the death of his fiancée when she is shot by a drugs gang. Steed then recruits Keel for his crusade against crime and they tackle an assortment of villains from diamond thieves, protection racketeers and arsonists to industrial spies and political assassins. However, they also hunt a killer who uses a radioactive isotope as a murder weapon (*The Radioactive Man*), foil a doctor who is deep-freezing patients as part of his suspended animation experiments (*Dead of Winter*) and run down saboteurs at an atomic research station working on a radiation shield for astronauts (*Dragonsfield*).

Format: Sydney Newman *and* Leonard White
Producer: Leonard White
Principal directors: Don Leaver, Peter Hammond
Writers: 21 used, including Brian Clemens, Richard Harris, Terence Feely, Dennis Spooner, John Lucarotti, Eric Paice

An ABC Weekend Network Production
26 60-minute episodes, black and white

Hot Snow
Brought to Book
Square Root of Evil
Nightmare

Crescent Moon
Girl on the Trapeze
Diamond Cut Diamond
The Radioactive Man
Ashes of Roses
Hunt the Man Down
Please Don't Feed the Animals
Dance with Death
One for the Mortuary
The Springers
The Frighteners
The Yellow Needle
Death on the Slipway

Double Danger
Toy Trap
The Tunnel of Fear
The Far Distant Dead
Kill the King
Dead of Winter
The Deadly Air
A Change of Bait
Dragonsfield

7 January–30 December 1961
(ABC – Northern)

Season Two
FOUR PLAY . . .

REGULAR CAST

John Steed **Patrick Macnee**   *Cathy Gale* **Honor Blackman**

Exit Dr Keel, enter Cathy Gale . . . and others. The second series saw Steed enlist three new companions for his war on crime – nightclub singer Venus Smith, idealistic doctor Martin King and Cathy Gale, anthropologist and judo expert. Venus featured in six episodes, King in just three. It was Cathy Gale who helped redefine *The Avengers* and set the trend for the years to come.

Plotwise, the set-up was much the same. Fast-paced crime thrillers, laced with humour but with a growing rapport between the principals. Mostly, adversaries were assassins, smugglers, spies or saboteurs, but one story (*The White Dwarf*) had Earth apparently threatened by a rogue star, while another (*The Golden Eggs*) featured a deadly virus, sealed inside two gold-plated eggs.
Venus Smith **Julie Stevens**
Martin King **John Rollason**

Producers: **Leonard White** *(1–14),* **John Bryce** *(15–26)*
Principal directors: **Richmond Harding, Jonathan Alwyn, Don Leaver, Peter Hammond, Kim Mills**
Writers: 19 used, including **Martin Woodhouse, Eric Paice, Malcolm Hulke** *and* **Terrance Dicks, Roger Marshall**

An ABC Television Network Production
26 60-minute episodes, black and white

Mr Teddy Bear
Propellant 23
The Decapod
Bullseye
Mission to Montreal
The Removal Men
The Mauritius Penny
Death of a Great Dane
The Sell-Out
Death on the Rocks
Traitor in Zebra
The Big Thinker
Death Dispatch
Dead on Course
Intercrime
Immortal Clay
Box of Tricks
Warlock
The Golden Eggs
School for Traitors
The White Dwarf
Man in the Mirror
Conspiracy of Silence
A Chorus of Frogs
Six Hands Across a Table
Killerwhale

29 September 1962–23 March 1963
(ABC – Northern)

Season Three
GALE FORCE . . .

REGULARS

Patrick Macnee, Honor Blackman

In which Steed acquires a past (*Brief for Murder*) and Cathy gets a trendy new wardrobe . . .

Season Three saw *The Avengers* production team crystallise the series' sophisticated appeal, with increasingly offbeat situations, and dialogue that swung effortlessly between suspense and humour. Among the regular battalions of crooks, spies and killers, the odd fanatic was popping up. In *November Five*, a politician threatens to blow up the House of Commons with a stolen nuclear warhead; in *The Grandeur That Was Rome*, a Caesar-fixated nutter tries to take over the world by spreading bubonic plague in food grain. A New Year episode was the most fantasy-filled yet, with Steed trying to winkle out a killer at a fancy dress party (*Dressed to Kill*). This was also the first series to be sold abroad.

Producer: John Bryce
Story editor: Richard Bates
Principal directors: Peter Hammond, Bill Bain, Kim Mills
Writers: 13 used, including Brian Clemens, Malcolm Hulke, Roger Marshall, Eric Paice

An ABC Television Network Production 26 60-minute episodes, black and white

Brief for Murder
The Undertakers
The Man with Two Shadows
The Nutshell
Death of a Batman
November Five
The Gilded Cage
Second Sight
The Medicine Men
The Grandeur That Was Rome
The Golden Fleece
Don't Look Behind You
Death à la Carte
Dressed to Kill
The White Elephant
The Little Wonders
The Wringer
Mandrake
The Secrets Broker
The Trojan Horse
Build a Better Mousetrap
The Outside-In Man
The Charmers
Concerto
Esprit De Corps
Lobster Quadrille

28 September 1963–21 March 1964
(ATV)

Season Four
M-APPEAL

REGULAR CAST

John Steed Patrick Macnee   *Emma Peel* Diana Rigg

Honor Blackman had dropped out after two seasons. With the arrival of the new female lead, *The Avengers* reached new heights of fantasy, with a string of science fiction orientated plots. Among the most bizarre were the killer robots, the Cybernauts, a man-eating plant from outer space and a machine that created torrential downpours out of thin air. Invariably, these fantastic situations arose out of ordinary, innocent-seeming locations, heightening the feeling of surrealism. This also became the first series to be sold to America where it secured a prime-time network slot. *The Avengers* had hit the big time.

(With the series now centred firmly in a fantasy world of exaggerated Englishness, I've included a brief rundown of all the Emma Peel episodes)

The Town of No Return

w Brian Clemens
Steed and Emma find that a remote remote Norfolk village has been overrun by subversives training a pocket army to take over the country.
Brandon Alan MacNaughtan
Smallwood Patrick Newell
Piggy Warren Terence Alexander
Vicar Jeremy Burnham

Director: Roy Baker

The Grave-Diggers

w Malcom Hulke
Steed digs up a bizarre plot to jam the nation's early-warning radar system
Sir Horace Winslip Ronald Fraser
Johnson Paul Massie
Miss Thirlwell Caroline Blakiston
Nurse Spray Wanda Ventham
Dr Marlowe Lloyd Lamble

Director: Quentin Lawrence

The Cybernauts

w Philip Levene
The Avengers' best remembered adversaries – unstoppable killer robots, controlled by a power-mad crippled scientist.
Dr Armstrong Michael Gough
Benson Frederick Jaeger
Jephcott Bernard Horsfall
Tusamo Bert Kwouk

Director: Sidney Hayers

Producer: Julian Wintle
Associate producer: Brian Clemens
New theme: Laurie Johnson

An ABC Television Network Production
26 one-hour episodes, black and white
28 September 1965–25 March 1966
(Rediffusion, London)

Death at Bargain Prices

w Brian Clemens
A tycoon known as King Kane plots to hold Britain to ransom by converting an entire department store into a giant atomic bomb.
Horatio Kane André Morell
Wentworth T. P. McKenna
Farthingale Allan Cuthbertson
Professor Popple Peter Howell
Massey George Selway
Marco Harvey Ashby
Jarvis John Cater

Director: Charles Crichton

Castle De'ath

w John Lucarotti
Beneath a Scottish castle, the laird and his gillie plan to corner the fish market by driving them into their underground base with three midget submarines.
Ian Gordon Jackson
Angus Robert Urquhart
McNab Jack Lambert
Robertson James Copeland

Director: James Hill

The Master Minds

w Robert Banks Stewart
A club for intellectuals is the cover for a fiendish plan to hypnotise top people.
Sir Clive Todd Laurence Hardy
Holly Trent Patricia Haines
Desmond Leeming Bernard Archard
Dr Campbell Ian McNaughton
Davinia Todd Georgina Ward

Director: Peter Graham Scott

The Murder Market

w Tony Williamson
A marriage bureau runs a murder racket on the side.
Mr Lovejoy Patrick Cargill
Dinsford Peter Bayliss
Barbara Suzanne Lloyd
Robert Stone John Woodvine

Director: Peter Graham Scott

A Surfeit of H₂O

w Colin Finbow
A scientist develops a rain-making device which he plans to sell as a weapon.
Jonah Noel Purcell
Dr Sturm Albert Lieven
Joyce Jason Sue Lloyd
Eli Barker Talfryn Thomas

Director: Sidney Hayers

The Hour That Never Was

w Roger Marshall
An oscilloscope and a brain-washing drug are being used to discover military secrets.
Ridsdale Gerald Harper
Philip Leas Dudley Foster
Hickey Roy Kinnear
Porky Purser Roger Booth

Director: Gerry O'Hara

Dial a Deadly Number

w Roger Marshall
A hi-tech murder device is accounting for a series for deaths in the financial world.
Henry Boardman Clifford Evans
Ruth Boardman Jan Holden
Fitch John Carson
John Harvey Peter Bowles
Frederick Yuill Gerald Sim

Director: Don Leaver

Man-Eater of Surrey Green

w Philip Levene
Steed and Emma trace several missing scientists to a research establishment where a man-eating plant from outer space is growing to dangerous size.
Sir Lyle Peterson Derek Farr
Dr Sheldon Athene Seyler
Laura Burford Gillian Lewis

Director: Sidney Hayers

Two's a Crowd

w Philip Levene
Battling a quartet of spies, Steed finds himself facing some lethal toys – from a midget sub to model aircraft.
Brodny Warren Mitchell
Pudeshkin Wolfe Morris
Vogel Julian Glover
Ivenko John Bluthal

Director: Roy Baker

Too Many Christmas Trees

w Tony Williamson
A Dickensian party is a cover for the hosts' mindbending attempts to unlock secret information in Steed's head.
Brandon Storey Mervyn Johns
Dr Felix Teasel Edwin Richfield
Janice Crane Jeanette Sterke

Director: Roy Baker

Silent Dust

w Roger Marshall
Steed and Emma investigate how whole areas of the countryside are being laid to waste – and uncover another bizarre plot to take over the country.
Omrod William Franklyn
Mellors Conrad Phillips
Croft Norman Bird
Clare Prendergast Isobel Black

Director: Roy Baker

Room Without a View

w Roger Marshall
A fanatical hotelier tries to use kidnapped

scientists to realise his plans for a chain of luxury hotels around the world.
Chessman **Paul Whitsun-Jones**
Varnals **Peter Jeffrey**
Carter **Philip Latham**
Pushkin **Vernon Dobtcheff**

Director: **Roy Baker**

Small Game for Big Hunters

w **Philip Levene**
Another dastardly plot – this time to use a new species of tsetse fly to take over a tropical country.
Col. Rawlings **Bill Fraser**
Simon Trent **James Villiers**
Swain **Liam Redmond**
Fleming **Peter Burton**

Director: **Gerry O'Hara**

The Girl from Auntie

w **Roger Marshall**
Emma gets held captive in a cage and Steed has to bid at auction to release her.
Georgie Price-Jones **Liz Fraser**
Gregorio Auntie **Alfred Burke**
Arkwright **Bernard Cribbins**
Ivanov **David Bauer**

Director: **Roy Baker**

The Thirteenth Hole

w **Tony Williamson**
Steed and Emma uncover a satellite spy ring – in a secret chamber beneath the 13th green of a golf course.
Reed **Patrick Allen**
Col. Watson **Hugh Manning**
Dr Adams **Peter Jones**
Collins **Francis Matthews**

Director: **Roy Baker**

Quick-Quick-Slow Death

w **Robert Banks Stewart**
A dance school is being used to infiltrate foreign spies into the country.

Lucille Banks **Eunice Gayson**
Ivor Bracewell **Maurice Kaufmann**
Nicki **Carole Gray**
Chester Read **Larry Cross**

Director: **James Hill**

The Danger Makers

w **Roger Marshall**
Trying to infiltrate a secret society whose members crave mortal danger, Emma has to negotiate a metal ring along a tortuous course of live electrical poles where one touch would mean instant death by electrocution.
Maj. Robertson **Nigel Davenport**
Dr Long **Douglas Wilmer**
Col. Adams **Fabia Drake**
Peters **Moray Watson**

Director: **Charles Crichton**

A Touch of Brimstone

w **Brian Clemens**
Steed and Emma unmask the notorious Hellfire Club – a replica of an 18th-century organisation dedicated to over-throwing the government.
John Cartney **Peter Wyngarde**
Lord Darcy **Colin Jeavons**
Sara **Carol Cleveland**
Horace **Robert Cawdron**

Director: **James Hill**

What the Butler Saw

w **Roger Marshall**
Steed poses as a butler to expose an association which is selling vital defence plans.
Hemming **Thorley Walters**
Benson **John Le Mesurier**
Group Capt. Miles **Dennis Quilley**
Maj. Gen. Goddard **Kynaston Reeves**

Director: **Bill Bain**

The House That Jack Built

w **Brian Clemens**
Emma is imprisoned in a house that is a

huge machine – the posthumous revenge of a crazed, embittered scientist who once worked for her father.
Prof. Keller Michael Goodliffe
Burton Griffith Davies
Withers Michael Wynne
Pennington Keith Pyott

Director: Don Leaver

A Sense of History

w Martin Woodhouse
A fascist group try to eliminate the last surviving founder of a plan to eradicate world poverty – at a Robin Hood theme rag ball.
Richard Carlyon Nigel Stock
Dr Henge John Barron
Grindley John Glyn-Jones
Duboys Patrick Mower
Marianne Jacqueline Pearce

Director: Peter Graham Scott

How to Succeed . . . at Murder

w Brian Clemens
A keep-fit school is the cover for a group of modern-day suffragettes intent on the elimination of all men.
Mary Merryweather Sarah Lawson
Sara Penny Angela Browne
Gladys Murkle Anne Cunningham
Henry Throgbottom Artro Morris
Joshua Rudge Jerome Willis

Director: Don Leaver

Honey for the Prince

w Brian Clemens
Steed and Emma foil an organisation called Quite Quite Fantatic Ltd which helps create people's fantasies – including assassination.
Ponsonby-Hopkirk Ron Moody
Prince Ali Zia Mohyeddin
Arkadi George Pastell
B Bumble Ken Parry

Director: James Hill

Seasons Five/Six
Regular cast as for Season Four

With the American market now open, the next Emma Peel series was *The Avengers'* first to be filmed in colour – a vital clause in the US deal. The humour was as offbeat as ever, but the hazards and plots became even more way-out, reflecting the audience's growing fascination with the fantasy aspects of the series.

Executive producer: Julian Wintle
Producers: Albert Fennell *and* Brian Clemens

An ABC Television Network Production

Season Five

16 colour 60-minute episodes
13 January–5 May 1967
(Rediffusion, London)

From Venus With Love

w Philip Levene
Steed and Emma tangle with the British Venusian Society whose members are being fried by laser beams.
Venus Browne Barbara Shelley
Promble Philip Locke
Brigadier Whitehead Jon Pertwee
Crawford Derek Newark
Bertram Smith Jeremy Lloyd

Director: Robert Day

The Fear Merchants

w Philip Levene
Rival industrialists are being eliminated by a strange organisation that exposes its victims to their greatest fear until they are driven out of their minds.
Pemberton Patrick Cargill
Raven Brian Wilde
Gilbert Garfield Morgan
Dr Voss Annette Cavell
Crawley Andrew Keir

Director: Gordon Flemyng

Escape in Time

w Philip Levene
A time machine, which apparently enables criminals to escape into the past, turns out to be a series of perfectly furnished rooms in a large mansion.
Thyssen Peter Bowles
Clapham Geoffrey Bayldon
Vesta Judy Parfitt
Anjali Imogen Hassall

Director: John Krish

The See-Through Man

w Philip Levene
Steed and Emma expose an invisible enemy agent as an elaborately staged series of tricks.
Elena Moira Lister
Brodny Warren Mitchell
Quilby Roy Kinnear
Ackroyd Jonathan Elsom

Director: Robert Asher

The Bird Who Knew Too Much

w Brian Clemens, *based on a story by* Alan Pattillo
Top secret information about a new missile base is being smuggled East – in the mind of a trained parrot!
Jordan Ron Moody
Samantha Ilona Rodgers
Tom Savage Kenneth Cope
Cunliffe Anthony Valentine

Director: Roy Rossotti

The Winged Avenger

w Richard Harris
A deranged cartoonist believes he is the hero of his own cartoon strip 'The Winged Avenger', and has been killing evil, ruthless men.
Sir Lexius Cray Nigel Green
Prof. Poole Jack MacGowran
Arnie Packer Neil Hallett
Stanton Colin Jeavons

Directors: Gordon Flemyng & Peter Duffell

The Living Dead

w Brian Clemens, *based on a story by* Anthony Marriott
Steed and Emma go ghosthunting and unearth a vast underground city built to house 20,000 people after a nuclear bomb has been dropped on Britain.
Masgard Julian Glover
Mandy Pamela Ann Davy
Geoffrey Howard Marion Crawford
Rupert Edward Underdown

Director: John Krish

The Hidden Tiger

w Philip Levene
PURRR, an organisation of cat lovers, is plotting to overthrow the entire country by using an electronic device that will make cats attack at a given signal.
Cheshire Ronnie Barker
Dr Manx Lyndon Brook
Angora Gabrielle Drake
Nesbitt John Phillips

Director: Sidney Hayers

The Correct Way To Kill

w Brian Clemens
Steed and Emma join forces with a pair of enemy agents to trap a murderer.
Olga Anna Quayle
Nutski Michael Gough
Ivan Philip Madoc
Ponsonby Terence Alexander
Percy Peter Barkworth

Director: Charles Crichton

Never, Never Say Die

w Philip Levene
A scientist has created computerised duplicates which he wants to use to keep great minds alive.
Prof. Stone Christopher Lee
Dr Penrose Jeremy Young
Dr James Patricia English
Eccles David Kernan

Director: Robert Day

Epic

w Brian Clemens
A crazed Hollywood veteran film director wants Emma to star in his latest epic – *The Destruction of Emma Peel*.
Stewart Kirby Peter Wyngarde
Damita Syn Isa Miranda
ZZ Von Schnerk Kenneth J. Warren

Director: James Hill

The Superlative Seven

w Brian Clemens
Steed joins a group of invited specialists who are taken to a deserted island and told only one of them will leave . . .
Hana Wilde Charlotte Rampling
Mark Dayton Brian Blessed
Jason Wade James Maxwell
Max Hardy Hugh Manning
Jessel Donald Sutherland

Director: Sidney Hayers

A Funny Thing Happened on the Way to the Station

w Bryan Sherriff
Steed and Emma foil a plot to blow up the Prime Minister's train.
Crewe John Laurie
Groom Drewe Henley
Bride Isla Blair
Salt Tim Barrett
Admiral Richard Caldicott
Ticket collector James Hayter

Director: John Krish

Something Nasty in the Nursery

w Philip Levene
The Guild of Noble Nannies are nobbling noblemen and stealing vital secrets.
Mr Goat Dudley Foster
Miss Lister Yootha Joyce
Beaumont Paul Eddington
Sir George Patrick Newell
Gordon Trevor Bannister
Martin Clive Dunn
Nanny Brown Penelope Keith

Director: James Hill

The Joker

w Brian Clemens
Prendergast, a deranged vicious criminal, stages an elaborate plot to kill Emma.
Prendergast Peter Jeffrey
Ola Sally Nesbitt
Strange young man Ronald Lacey

Director: Sidney Hayers

Who's Who???

w Philip Levene
An enemy agent uses his latest invention to transfer the minds of two assassins into the bodies of Steed and Emma.
Lola Patricia Haines
Basil Freddie Jones
Major B Campbell Singer
Krelmar Arnold Diamond

Director: John Moxey

Season Six
8 colour 60-minute episodes
28 September–17 November 1967
(Rediffusion, London)

Return of the Cybernauts

w Philip Levene
Back come the killer robots controlled by a rich art collector who wants to dispose of Steed and Emma by the most gruesome means possible.
Paul Beresford Peter Cushing
Benson Frederick Jaeger
Dr Neville Charles Tingwell
Prof. Chadwick Fulton Mackay
Rosie Aimi MacDonald

Director: Robert Day

Death's Door

w Philip Levene
Enemy agents try to sabotage a conference by manipulating the participants' dreams.
Boyd Clifford Evans
Stapley William Lucas
Lord Melford Allan Cuthbertson
Becker Marne Maitland

Director: Sidney Hayers

The £50,000 Breakfast

w Roger Marshall, *from a story by* Roger Marshall *and* Jeremy Scott
Plotters try to benefit by concealing a financier's death.
Glover Cecil Parker
Miss Pegram Yolande Turner
Sir James Arnet David Langton
Judy Anneke Wills
Minister Cardew Robinson

Director: Robert Day

The Positive–Negative Man

w Tony Williamson
The head of a shelved research project takes his revenge – using phenomenal electrical charges as his weapon.
Cresswell Ray McAnally
Haworth Michael Latimer
Cynthia Caroline Blakiston
Mankin Peter Blythe
Jubert Sandor Elès

Director: Robert Day

Dead Man's Treasure

w Michael Winder
Emma is wired to a racing car simulator that goes faster and faster to force her to offer a clue to lost treasure.
Mike Norman Bowler
Penny Valerie Van Ost
Alex Edwin Richfield
Carl Neil McCarthy
Benstead Arthur Lowe

Director: Sidney Hayers

Murdersville

w Brian Clemens
Steed and Emma discover that the townsfolk of a small, sleepy village operate a discreet service – murder!
Mickle Colin Blakeley
Hubert John Ronane
Dr Haynes Ronald Hines
Prewitt John Sharp
Jenny Sheila Fearn

Director: Robert Asher

You Have Just Been Murdered

w Philip Levene
A blackmailer makes 'mock' attempts on the life of millionaires to force them to pay – and kills them for real if they don't.
Unwin Barrie Ingham
Lord Maxted Robert Flemyng
Needle George Murcell
Rathbone Leslie French
Jarvis Geoffrey Chater

Director: Robert Asher

Mission . . . Highly Improbable

w Philip Levene
Steed and Emma are among several people cut down to size by a scientist's reducing ray.
Shaffer Ronald Radd
Susan Jane Merrow
Prof. Rushton Noel Howlett
Chivers Francis Matthews
Gifford Nicholas Courtney

Director: Robert Day

Season Seven
TARA, MRS PEEL

REGULAR CAST

John Steed Patrick Macnee   *Tara King* Linda Thorson
Mother Parick Newell   *Rhonda* Rhonda Parker

And so to Tara King . . . the least distinctive Avengers girl, who entered the scene in the opening handover episode which also featured the departure of Emma Peel (Diana Rigg, who had left the show, had agreed to do one last episode).

Linda Thorson was a controversial choice as her replacement – she came to the series fresh out of drama school. And there was to be no special fighting technique for Tara – she'd simply use whatever came to hand. The Seventh Season also introduced two other new characters with the American market in mind – Steed's outsize boss Mother and his Amazonian secretary Rhonda. A running gag had Mother's 'office' turning up in the most unexpected places – the top deck of a London bus, the middle of a field, even a swimming pool.

The plots shifted their stance now, with more emphasis on far-fetched secret agent-style plots.

Executive producer: Gordon L. T. Scott
Producers: Albert Fennell *and* Brian Clemens
Music: Laurie Johnson *and* Howard Blake

An ABC Television Production
33 colour 60-minute episodes
25 September 1968–21 May 1969
(Thames, London)

The Forget-Me-Knot

w Brian Clemens
Emma is kidnapped . . . there's a traitor in Mother's section . . . and Steed winds up with a new partner – Agent 69, Tara King.
Emma Peel Diana Rigg
Sean Mortimer Patrick Kavanagh
George Burton Jeremy Young
Karl Alan Lake

Director: James Hill

Game

w Richard Harris
A vengeful games king, Bristow, forces Steed to play a bizarre game 'Super Agent' to save the life of Tara who is trapped in a giant hour-glass.
Bristow Peter Jeffrey
Manservant Garfield Morgan
Prof. Witney Aubrey Richards
Wishforth-Browne Anthony Newlands

Director: Robert Fuest

Super-Secret Cypher Snatch

w Tony Williamson
A window-cleaning firm, Classy Glass Cleaning, is the front for a group of hypnotic thieves.
Peters John Carlisle
Maskin Simon Oates
Lather Nicholas Smith
Webster Allan Cuthbertson

Director: John Hough

You'll Catch Your Death

w Jeremy Burnham
Steed sniffs out a plot to gain power using a deadly concentrated cold virus that makes its victims sneeze to death.
Col. Timothy Roland Culver
Butler Valentine Dyall
Glover Fulton Mackay
Matron Sylvia Kay
Dexter Dudley Sutton

Director: Paul Dickson

Split!

w Brian Clemens *(and* Dennis Spooner *– uncredited)*
An enemy mastermind tries to transfer a killer's personality to Tara's mind.
Lord Barnes Nigel Davenport
Peter Rooke Julian Glover
Dr Constantine Bernard Archard
Harry Mercer Maurice Good

Director: Roy Baker

Whoever Shot Poor George Oblique XR40

w Tony Williamson
A computer is given a 'brain transplant' by a cybernetic surgeon to discover the identity of a traitor.
Jason Dennis Price
Pelley Clifford Evans
Loris Judy Parfitt
Tobin Frank Windsor

Director: Cyril Frankel

False Witness

w Jeremy Burnham
Steed and Tara face a problem – how to unmask a traitor when it seems everyone is lying. It must be something in the milk.
Land Rio Fanning
Melville Barry Warren
Lord Edgefield William Job
Sloman Dan Meaden
Sykes John Bennett
Sir Joseph Tony Steedman

Director: Charles Crichton

All Done With Mirrors

w Leigh Vance
Steed is under house arrest at Mother's swimming pool and Tara is sent to unravel a mystery centred on a lighthouse.
Watney Dinsdale Landen
Sparshott Peter Copley
Barlow Edwin Richfield
Col. Withers Michael Trubshawe
Pandora Joanna Jones

Director: Ray Austin

Legacy of Death

w Terry Nation
An ornate dagger is the key to a secret treasure, and elderly Henley Farrar will go to great lengths to hang on to it.
Farrer Richard Hurndall
Sidney Stratford Johns
Humbert Ronald Lacey
Baron Von Orlak Ferdy Mayne
Dickens Kynaston Reeves
Oppenheimer Peter Swanwick

Director: Don Chaffey

Noon Doomsday

w Terry Nation
Gerald Kafta, head of Murder International, is out of jail and bent on revenge against the man who put him there – John Steed.
Farrington Ray Brooks
Grant T.P. McKenna

Kafta Peter Bromilow
Sunley Anthony Ainley
Perrier Peter Halliday

Director: Peter Sykes

Look (Stop me if you've heard this one) But There Were These Two Fellers . . .

w Dennis Spooner
Steed and Tara pose as a pantomime horse to deliver the knockout blow to Mr Punch and his vaudevillian killers.
Maxie Martin Jimmy Jewel
Jennings Julian Chagrin
Bradley Marler Bernard Cribbins
Marcus Pugman John Cleese
Seagrave John Woodvine
Fiery Frederick Talfryn Thomas

Director: James Hill

Have Guns . . . Will Haggle

w Donald James
Steed and Tara double in ballistics in their duel with some gun-runners.
Col. Nsonga Johnny Sekka
Adriana Nicola Pagett
Conrad Jonathan Burn
Spencer Timothy Bateson

Director: Ray Austin

They Keep Killing Steed

w Brian Clemens
A group of villains hatch a plot to provide one of their agents with a replica of Steed's face so he can plant a bomb at a peace conference.
Baron Von Court Ian Ogilvy
Arcos Ray McAnally
Zerson Norman Jones
Capt. Smythe Bernard Horsfall

Director: Robert Fuest

The Interrogators

w Richard Harris, Brian Clemens
Col. Mannering sets up a brilliant plan to

extract information from secret agents – in a dentist's waiting room.

Col. Mannering Christopher Lee
Minnow David Sumner
Caspar Philip Bond
Blackie Glynn Edwards

Director: Charles Crichton

The Rotters

w Dave Freeman
A madman threatens to unleash a highly contagious dry-rot virus on Europe.

Kenneth Gerald Sim
George Jerome Willis
Pym Eric Barker
Palmer John Nettleton

Director: Robert Fuest

Invasion of the Earthmen

w Terry Nation
The fanatical head of the strange Alpha Academy is training his students for the conquest of outer space.

Brett William Lucas
Huxton Christian Roberts
Emily Lucy Fleming
Bassin Christopher Chittell

Director: Don Sharp

Killer

w Tony Williamson
Steed and his fellow agents are threatened by a deadly assassin called REMAK (Remote Electro-Matic Agent Killer), a computer programmed for murder.

Lady Diana Forbes-Blakeney Jennifer Croxton
Mirridon Grant Taylor
Brinstead William Franklyn
Clarke Richard Wattis

Director: Cliff Owen

The Morning After

w Brian Clemens
With the help of quadruple agent Merlin, Steed and Tara foil a brigadier's plot to hold the government to ransom with a nuclear bomb.

Merlin Peter Barkworth
Jenny Penelope Horner
Brig. Hansing Joss Ackland
Sgt Hearn Brian Blessed

Director: John Hough

The Curious Case of the Countless Clues

w Philip Levene
Countless clues suggest that the murder in Dawson's flat was committed by press tycoon William Burgess – but Steed isn't so sure.

Earle Anthony Bate
Gardiner Kenneth Cope
Stanley Tony Selby
Doyle Peter Jones
Burgess George A. Cooper
Flanders Edward de Souza

Director: Don Sharp

Wish You Were Here

w Tony Williamson
A holiday hotel proves an unusual prison for Tara and her uncle, while their captors take over his vast business empire.

Charles Merrydale Liam Redmond
Maxwell Robert Urquhart
Basil Brook Williams
Parker Dudley Foster
Mellor Richard Caldicott

Director: Don Chaffey

Love All

w Jeremy Burnham
Civil servants are leaking secrets after reading a book that's hypnotising them to fall in love with the next person they see.

Martha Veronica Strong
Bromfield Terence Alexander
Sir Rodney Robert Harris
Thelma Patsy Rowlands

Director: Peter Sykes

Stay Tuned

w Tony Williamson
Steed is hypnotised and conditioned to kill Mother.
Proctor Gary Bond
Lisa Kate O'Mara
Father Iris Russell
Kreer Roger Delgado

Director: Don Chaffey

Take Me To Your Leader

w Terry Nation
Mother is suspected of defecting to the enemy and to clear his name, Steed and Tara have to track the destination of an unusual talking briefcase.
Stonehouse Patrick Barr
Capt. Tim John Ronane
Cavell Michael Robbins
Audrey Long Penelope Keith

Director: Robert Fuest

Fog

w Jeremy Burnham
Steed and Tara are on the trail of the Gaslight Ghoul, a murderer who is killing off delegates to a peace conference with the Victorian style of Jack the Ripper.
President Nigel Green
Travers Guy Rolfe
Carstairs Terence Brady
Sanders Paul Whitsun-Jones

Director: John Hough

Who Was That Man I Saw You With?

w Jeremy Burnham
Tara is accused of being a double agent and Steed has just 24 hours to clear her name.
Fairfax William Marlowe
Gen Hesketh Ralph Michael
Zaroff Alan Browning
Gilpin Alan MacNaughtan
Dangerfield Alan Wheatley
Phillipson Bryan Marshall

Director: Don Chaffey

Homicide and Old Lace

w Malcolm Hulke *and* Terrance Dicks
Mother tells a story . . . of how Steed and Tara thwarted the Great Great Britain Crime – the theft of every art treasure in the country.
Harriet Joyce Carey
Georgina Mary Merrall
Col. Corf Gerald Harper
Dunbar Keith Baxter

Director: John Hough

Thingumajig

w Terry Nation
Steed and Tara do battle with a killer black box that feeds on electricity.
Teddy Jeremy Lloyd
Kruger Ian Cuthbertson
Truman Willoughby Goddard
Major Star Hugh Manning

Director: Leslie Norman

My Wildest Dream

w Philip Levene
A psychiatrist is conditioning patients to kill their enemies and Steed is in danger from a jealous rejected suitor of Tara's.
Jaeger Peter Vaughan
Tobias Derek Godfrey
Chilcott Edward Fox
Slater Philip Madoc
Nurse Owen Susan Travers

Director: Robert Fuest

Requiem

w Brian Clemens
Steed is assigned to protect Miranda Loxton, key witness in a case against Murder International.
Miranda Angela Douglas
Firth John Cairney
Wells John Paul
Murray Denis Shaw
Rista Terence Sewards

Director: Don Chaffey

Take-Over

w Terry Nation
A gang of crooks takes over a country house intending to train a long-range weapon on a nearby conference.
Grenville Tom Adams
Laura Elisabeth Sellars
Bill Michael Gwynn
Circe Hilary Pritchard
Sexton Garfield Morgan

Director: Robert Fuest

Pandora

w Brian Clemens
Tara is brainwashed into believing she is a senile man's old flame by two brothers out to steal his hidden fortune.
Rupert Lasindall Julian Glover
Henry Lasindall James Cossins
Juniper John Laurie
Miss Faversham Kathleen Byron
Uncle Gregory Peter Madden

Director: Robert Fuest

Get-A-Way!

w Philip Levene
A 'chameleon' liquid enables three Russian agents to escape from an impregnable monastery and carry out their mission to kill three British agents – including Steed.
Col. James Andrew Keir
Rostov Vincent Harding
Neville Terence Langdon
Lubin Robert Russell
Ezdorf Peter Bowles

Director: Don Sharp

Bizarre

w Brian Clemens
Steed and Tara try to get to the bottom of the mystery of the disappearing bodies at Happy Meadows Cemetery.
Capt. Cordell James Kerry
Jonathan Jupp John Sharp
Happychap Roy Kinnear
The Master Fulton Mackay

Director: Leslie Norman

THE NEW AVENGERS

REGULAR CAST

John Steed Patrick Macnee   *Purdey* Joanna Lumley
Mike Gambit Gareth Hunt

1976 saw the return of John Steed with two '*New Avengers*' – Joanna Lumley as the long-legged, high-kicking Purdey, and Gareth '*Upstairs Downstairs*' Hunt as the dour, kung-fu champ and weapons expert Mike Gambit.

The plots were similar to the Tara King *Avengers* era, with plenty of spy-type mysteries and less sf, but still stamped with the familiar fantasy style. The Cybernauts returned for one more crack at Steed and Co. in *The Last of the Cybernauts . . . ?*, a disease-carrying man whose touch spelt instant death stalked Purdey in *The Midas Touch*, and a man with the power to control birds was intent on taking over the world with his feathered army in *Cat Amongst the Pigeons*.

Despite massive press hype (much of it centring on Joanna Lumley's stockings) *The New Avengers* never achieved the renown of their 1960s predecessors though the series did good business round the world.

Producers: Albert Fennell *and* Brian Clemens
Writers: Brian Clemens, Dennis Spooner, Terence Feely, John Goldsmith

Directors: 12 used, principally **Ray Austin, Sidney Hayers**
Music: **Laurie Johnson**

An Avengers (Film and TV) Enterprises Ltd Production and IDTV TV Productions, Paris
26 colour 60-minute episodes

Season One

The Eagle's Nest
House of Cards
The Last of the Cybernauts . . . ?
The Midas Touch
Cat Amongst the Pigeons
Target!
To Catch a Rat
The Tale of the Big Why
Faces
Gnaws
Dirtier By the Dozen
Sleeper
Three Handed Game

19 October 1976–19 January 1977
(Thames)

Season One

Dead Men Are Dangerous
Angels of Death
Medium Rare
The Lion and the Unicorn
Obsession
Trap
Hostage
K is for Kill (A 2-part story)
Complex
Forward Base
The Gladiators
Emily

8 September–1 December 1977
(Thames)

NB: The last four episodes are also known collectively as *The New Avengers in Canada*.

BATMAN

'I make absolutely no excuses for *Batman*. It's not meant to be a contribution to the culture of the world. It's not meant to contain deep messages . . .'

(William Dozier, executive producer)

Any show that includes the immortal refrain 'Holy Priceless Collection of Etruscan Snoods' can't be all lowbrow, but there have been few greater champions of comic-book culture than the caped crusader.

Here was a superhero who didn't fly, climbed buildings the hard way rather than leap them at a single bound, and clunk-clicked every trip in his Batmobile. A hero who faced death with as much dignity as anyone could muster in a fancy dress costume, but who always won in the end.

It was a carefully contrived camp formula that gave the kids a serious hero and presented knowing adults with a send-up of all the old radio serials and Saturday morning picture shows they'd ever known and loved. Nearly all the stories were two-parters, with the first episode ending in a cliffhanger. As Batman and his trusty sidekick, Robin the Boy Wonder, seemed doomed to a diabolical death at the hands of some nefarious villain, the alarmed voice of a narrator urged viewers to tune in for the conclusion 'same bat-time, same bat-channel'. In part two, a stroke of ingenuity – or sometimes luck – enabled the dynamic duo to escape, defeat their foe in a glorious fist-fight and make Gotham City a safer place . . . until the next week, at least.

Behind the masks and capes, Batman and Robin were, of course, millionaire philanthropist Bruce Wayne and his youthful ward Dick Grayson, but while the bad guys did *their* best to put two and two together, the top guys on the side of the law, Commissioner Gordon and Chief O'Hara, never looked like coming up with the right answer.

Week after week, they'd get on the Batphone to stately Wayne Manor where Bruce and Dick, aided by loyal butler Alfred would slide down the batpoles behind the drawing room bookcase, emerging at the bottom in their crimebusting clothes, leap into the Batmobile and roar off to fight some of the most eccentric crooks ever invented.

Among Batman's regular nemeses were the Joker (the Clown Prince of Crime), the Riddler (the Prince of Puzzles), the Penguin (that Pompous Perpetrator of Foul Play) and Catwoman (the Felonious Feline). And the high-powered stars of Hollywood queued up to play the low-life of *Batman*. Vincent Price, Cesar Romero, Burgess Meredith, Otto Preminger, Roddy McDowall, Van Johnson, Ethel Merman, Tallulah Bankhead, Liberace, Zsa Zsa Gabor, Eartha Kitt, Shelley Winters and even Joan Collins all wore outlandish costumes and roguish grins as they consigned Batman to another fiendish fate.

And what fates. In their ceaseless campaign against crime, the dynamic duo have been frozen into ice lollies, tied above a vat of bubbling wax, roasted on a spit, sealed in a sand-filled hourglass, trapped in a giant coffee cup beneath a percolator filled with acid, served up to carnivorous plants and corrugated into slabs of cardboard. But apart from the ghoulish voyeurism of watching them face more perils than Pauline, there was little actual violence. The fight scenes were carefully choreographed with comic-book style effects – BIFF! . . . ZAP! . . . BAM! – superimposed over the action.

Even in black and white Britain, circa 1966, the series caught on instantly, and *Batman* has never looked back. Although production stopped in 1969 after 120 episodes and one feature film, (now two!) as recently as 1988 the shows were still playing in 106 countries with a worldwide audience of 400 million. And when daily doses of

Batman were transmitted by a beleagured TV-am during its 1988 technicians' strike, the station actually increased its ratings. Holy Anne Diamonds!

Some Bat-facts . . .

- Adam West was a virtual unknown outside the industry before he became Batman. His acting credits include roles in *77 Sunset Strip*, *Cheyenne*, *Maverick*, *Perry Mason*, *Bonanza*, *Rifleman*, *The Detectives*, *The Outer Limits* (see separate entry), *Bewitched* and *The Virginian*.

- Burt Ward was 20 when he landed the role of 15-year-old Robin. A brown belt in karate, he convinced the producers that he was right for the part by cracking a brick with his bare hand at the screen test.

- The Batmobile weighed 2½ tons and was 17 ft long. Its windscreen bubbles were made of aircraft glass.

- Batman was originally created by Bob Kane for a cartoon strip in *Detective Comics* in 1939. Four years later Columbia Pictures turned it into a film serial, also called *Batman*.

- Alan Napier, who played Alfred, thought the idea of being a butler was a bit of a comedown after years of playing dukes, earls and viscounts, until someone told him: 'Hang it all, man. Don't you realise you are going to be the most famous butler of all time?'

BAT-CAST

Batman/Bruce Wayne **Adam West**   *Robin/Dick Grayson* **Burt Ward**
Alfred **Alan Napier**   *Aunt Harriet* **Madge Blake**
Commissioner Gordon **Neil Hamilton**   *Chief O'Hara* **Stafford Repp**
Batgirl **Yvonne Craig** *(Season Three)*   *Narrator* **William Dozier**

Executive producer: **William Dozier**
Producer: **Howie Horowitz**
Story consultant: **Lorenzo Semple Jr**
Make-up: **Ben Nye**
Music: **Neal Hefti** *(theme)*, **Nelson Riddle**

A Greenaway Production for 20th Century-Fox Television
120 colour 30-minute episodes
UK premiere: 21 May 1966

Season One
34 half-hour episodes
21 May–11 September 1966
(Northern: ABC Television)

Hi Diddle Riddle/Smack in the Middle

---

w **Lorenzo Semple Jr**

The twisted trail of the Riddler leads Batman to break the law and dance the Batusi with Molly, the Molehill Mob moll.
The Riddler **Frank Gorshin**
Molly **Jill St John**
Harry **Allen Jaffe**
Insp. Basch **Michael Fox**

Director: **Robert Butler**

Fine Feathered Finks/The Penguin's a Jinx

w Lorenzo Semple Jr
Bruce Wayne is caught trying to plant a bug in the Penguin's Umbrella factory and is sentenced to die in the feathered felon's furnace.
The Penguin Burgess Meredith
Dawn Robbins Leslie Parrish
Sparrow Walter Burke
Hawkeye Lewis Charles

Director: Robert Butler

The Joker is Wild/Batman Gets Riled

w Robert Dozier
Batman and Robin are nearly unmasked by the Joker when he fashions his own devilish utility belt.
The Joker Cesar Romero
Queenie Nancy Kovack
Museum attendant Jonathan Hole
Asst Warden Merritt Bohn

Director: Don Weiss

Instant Freeze/Rats Like Cheese

w Max Hodge
The notorious Mr Freeze tries to turn the dynamic duo into ice-pops with his deadly ice-gun.
Mr Freeze George Sanders
Princess Sandra Shelby Grant
Chill Troy Melton
Nippy Guy Way

Director: Robert Butler

Zelda the Great/A Death Worse Than Fate

w Lorenzo Semple Jr
Supersexy escape artiste Zelda kidnaps Aunt Harriet and holds her to ransom, then locks Batman and Robin in her inescapable doom-trap.
Zelda the Great Anne Baxter
Eivol Ekdal Jack Kruschen
Hilary Stonewin Barbara Heller

Director: Robert Butler

A Riddle a Day Keeps the Riddler Away/When the Rat's Away, the Mice will Play

w Fred De Gorter
The Prince of Puzzles tries to finish off the caped crusaders by shackling them to giant generator wheels.
Riddler Frank Gorshin
Mousey Susan Silo
Fangs Marc Cavell
Whiskers Tim Herbert
Ambassador Tristram Coffin

Director: Tom Gries

The Thirteenth Hat/Batman Stands Pat

w Charles Hoffman
The Mad Hatter plots to uncowl Batman and kidnap the jury that once convicted him.
The Mad Hatter David Wayne
Cappy Roland La Starza
Dicer Gil Perkins
Babette Sandra Wells

Director: Norman Foster

The Joker Goes to School/He Meets His Match, the Grisley Ghoul

w Lorenzo Semple Jr
The Joker plots to recruit high-school dropouts and tries to electrocute our heroes.
The Joker Cesar Romero
Susie Donna Loren
Nick Kip King
Two-Bits Greg Benedict

Director: Murray Golden

True or False-Face/Super Rat Race

w Stephen Kandel
The devil of disguise, False-Face glues the dynamic duo to the subway tracks, but is finally out-phonied by Batman.
False-Face Malachi Throne
Blaze Myrna Fahey
Midget Billy Curtis

Director: William A Graham

The Purr-Fect Crime/Better Luck Next Time

w Stanley Ralph Ross & Lee Orgel
The Catwoman nearly feeds Batman and Robin to her feline friends, before the dynamic duo deduct one of her nine lives.
Catwoman Julie Newmar
Leo Jock Mahoney
Felix Ralph Manza

Director: James Sheldon

The Penguin Goes Straight/Not Yet, He Ain't

w Lorenzo Semple Jr *and* John Cardwell
The mocking mountebank sets up his own Penguin Protective Agency and strings up the dynamic duo in a shooting gallery.
The Penguin Burgess Meredith
Sophia Starr Kathleen Crowley
Eagle-Eye Harvey Lembeck

Director: Les Martison

The Ring of Wax/ Give 'Em The Axe

w Jack Paritz *and* Bob Rodgers
Batman and Robin nearly meet a waxy fate as they stop Riddler from stealing an ancient Incan treasure.
Riddler Frank Gorshin
Moth Linda Scott
Matches Michael Greene
Tallow Joey Tata

Director: James B. Clark

The Joker Trumps an Ace/Batman Sets the Pace

w Francis *and* Marian Cockrell
In their efforts to save a visiting Maharajah from the Joker's clutches, the peerless pair are locked into a high chimney which begins to fill with lethal gas.
The Joker Cesar Romero
Jill Jane Wald
Maharajah Dan Seymore

Director: Richard C Sarafian

The Curse of Tut/The Pharoah's in a Rut

w Robert C. Dennis *and* Earl Barret
A latter-day King of the Nile claims Gotham City as his kingdom and inflicts an ancient pebble torture on Batman.
King Tut Victor Buono
Nefertiti Ziva Rodann
Grand Vizier Don Barry

Director: Charles R. Rondeau

The Bookworm Turns/While Gotham City Burns

w Rik Vollaerts
Holy Batstew! The dynamic duo are trapped inside a giant cookbook.
The Bookworm Roddy McDowall
Lydia Francine York
Major Byron Keith

Director: Larry Peerce

Death in Slow Motion/The Riddler's False Notion

w Dick Carr
The Riddler makes a silent film comedy of Batman and Robin and the Boy Wonder nearly gets sawn in half.
Riddler Frank Gorshin
Pauline Sherry Jackson
Van Jones Francis X Bushman
Von Bloheim Theo Marcuse

Director: Charles R Rondeau

Fine Finny Fiends/ Batman Makes the Scenes

w Sheldon Stark
Are Batman and Robin doomed to be vanquished by a vacuum as the Penguin lets the air out of their lungs?
Penguin Burgess Meredith
Finella Julie Gregg
Octopuss Victor Lundin
Shark Dal Jenkins
Swordfish Louie Elias

Director: Tom Gries

Season two
60 half-hour episodes
17 September 1966–2 April 1967
(Northern: ABC Television)

Shoot a Crooked Arrow/Walk the Straight and Narrow

w **Stanley Ralph Ross**
A latter-day Robin Hood who robs from the rich but doesn't always give to the poor strings up Batman and Robin for some jousting practice.
The Archer **Art Carney**
Maid Marilyn **Barbara Nichols**
Crier Tuck **Doodles Weaver**
Big John **Archie Moore**
Alan A Dale **Robert Cornthwaite**

Director: **Sherman Marks**

Hot off the Griddle/The Cat and the Fiddle

w **Stanley Ralph Ross**
Catwoman leaves Batman and Robin out to fry in the midday sun – but a timely eclipse enables them to escape and overcome the feline fiend who's trying to steal two priceless violins.
Catwoman **Julie Newmar**
Jack O'Shea **Jack Kelly**
Driver **James Brolin**
John **Buck Kartalian**
Hostess **Edy Williams**

Director: **Don Weiss**

The Minstrel's Shakedown/ Barbecued Batman

w **Francis** *and* **Marian Cockrell**
A lute-strumming melodic fiend has the peerless pair hoisted on a spit to be roasted until well done.
The Minstrel **Van Johnson**
Amanda **Leslie Perkins**
Treble **Norman Grabowski**
Bass **Remo Pisani**
Courtland **John Gallaudet**
Scrub woman **Phyllis Diller**

Director: **Murray Golden**

The Spell of Tut/Tut's Case is Shut

w **Robert C Dennis** *and* **Earl Barrett**
Abu raubu simbu tu . . . King Tut plots to take over Gotham City with an ancient paralysing potion. Batman foils him by drinking buttermilk to coat his stomach.
King Tut **Victor Buono**
Cleo **Marianna Hill**
Lapidary **Peter Mamakos**
Amenophis Tewfik **Michael Pataki**

Director: **Larry Peerce**

The Greatest Mother of Them All/ Ma Parker

w **Henry Slesar**
Infamous Ma Parker and her children try to blow up the dynamic duo by rigging the Batmobile to explode at 60 mph – but naturally Batman sticks to the speed limit . . .
Ma Parker **Shelley Winters**
Legs **Tisha Sterling**
Mad Dog **Michael Vandever**
Pretty Boy **Robert Biheller**
Machine Gun **Peter Brooks**
Warden Crichton **David Lewis**

Director: **Oscar Rudolph**

The Clock King's Crazy Crimes/ Clock King Gets Crowned

w **Bill Finger** *and* **Charles Sinclair**
Batman and Robin are captured by Clock King and his Second Hands and imprisoned in a giant hour glass. They escape by toppling the glass and running like hamsters inside so that it rolls into a truck!
The Clock King **Walter Slezak**
Car Hop **Linda Lorimer**
Millie Second **Eileen O'Neill**
Parkhurst **Ivan Triesault**

Director: **James Neilson**

An Egg Grows in Gotham/The Yegg Foes in Gotham

w **Stanley Ralph Ross** *and* **Ed Self**
Egghead gains legal control of Gotham City and attaches a truth machine to

Bruce Wayne, suspecting him to be Batman. But the tables are turned in an eggstraordinary battle.
The Egghead Vincent Price
Chicken Edward Everett Horton
Miss Bacon Gail Hire
Foo Yung Ben Welden
Benedict Gene Dynarski

Director: George Waggner

The Devil's Fingers/The Dead Ringers

w Lorenzo Semple Jr
A crooked pianist named Chandell (Fingers) woos Aunt Harriet, while Batman and Robin are nearly perforated on a music roll cutter for a player piano.
Fingers Liberace
Doe Marilyn Hanold
Rae Edy Williams
Mimi Sivi Aberg

Director: Larry Peerce

Hizzoner the Penguin/Dizzoner the Penguin

w Stanford Sherman
The Penguin runs for Mayor against Batman – and nearly wins.
The Penguin Burgess Meredith
Mayor Linseed Byron Keith
Rooper Woodrow Parfrey
Themselves Paul Revere and The Raiders
Gallus George Furth
Klondike Don Wilson

Director: Oscar Rudolph

Green Ice/Deep Freeze

w Max Hodge
Mr Freeze embarks on a campaign to disredit the dynamic duo and tries to turn them into human popsicles in his Frosty Freezie Factory.
Mr Freeze Otto Preminger
Miss Iceland Dee Hartford
Shivers Nicky Blair
Chill Kem Dibbs
Mayor Byron Keith

Director: George Waggner

The Impractical Joker/The Joker's Provokers

w Jay Thompson *and* Charles Hoffman
The Joker's new time device causes havoc in Gotham City; the Boy Wonder is sprayed with wax and Batman is trussed up on a giant duplicator.
The Joker Cesar Romero
Cornelia Kathy Kersh
Latch Luis Quinn

Director: James B Clark

Marsha, Queen of Diamonds/Marsha's Scheme with Diamonds

w Stanford Sherman
Holy Matrimony! Marsha schemes to steal the Batjewels that power the Batcomputer by becoming Mrs Batman!
Marsha Carolyn Jones
Grand Mogul Woody Strode
Sgt O'Leary James O'Hara
Aunt Hilda Estelle Winwood

Director James B. Clark

Come Back, Shame/It's the Way You Play the Game

w Stanley Ralph Ross
A crooked car-rustling cowboy unleashes a herd of stampeding cattle at the dynamic duo, but Batman draws them away by waving h s cape like a matador.
Shame Cliff Robertson
Okie Annie Joan Staley
Messy James Timothy Scott

Director: Oscar Rudolph

The Penguin's Nest/The Bird's Last Jest

w Lorenzo Semple Jr
Penguin tries every trick he knows to get sent to prison so that he can collaborate with jailed forger Ballpoint Baxter.
The Penguin Burgess Meredith
Chickadee Grace Gaynor
Cordy Blue Lane Bradford
Maty Dee Vitto Scotti

Director: Murray Golden

The Cat's Meow/The Bats Kow Tow

w Stanley Ralph Ross
Using a voice-eraser, Catwoman steals the singing voices of Chad and Jeremy and demands a ransom after locking Batman and Robin in a giant echo chamber.
Catwoman Julie Newmar
Chad Chad Stuart
Jeremy Jeremy Clyde
Moe Ric Roman
Meanie Tom Castronova
Eenie Sharyn Winters
Miney Chuck Henderson

Director: James B. Clark

Puzzles Are Coming/The Duo Is Slumming

w Fred De Gorter
The Puzzler casts the duo adrift in a balloon rigged to drop at 20,000 feet – but Robin jams the altimeter with a piece of chewing gum.
The Puzzler Maurice Evans
Rocket Barbara Stuart
Artie Knab Paul Smith
Blimpy Robert Miller Driscoll

Director: Jeff Hayden

The Sandman Cometh/The Catwoman Goeth

w Ellis St Joseph *and* Charles Hoffman
A European crook, Sandman, double-crosses Catwoman to steal all of a noodle queen's fortune for himself.
Sandman Michael Rennie
Catwoman Julie Newmar
J. Pauline Spaghetti Spring Byington
Cameo Don Ho
Female Newscaster Gypsy Rose Lee

Director: George Waggner

The Contaminated Cowl/The Mad Hatter Runs a Foul

w Charles Hoffman
The Mad Hatter sprays Batman's cowl with radioactive fumes in an effort to add it to his chapeau collection.

Mad Hatter (Jervis Tetch) David Wayne
Polly Jean Hale
Hattie Hatfield Barbara Morrison

Director: Oscar Rudolph

The Zodiac Crimes/The Joker's Hard Time/The Penguin Declines

w Stanford Sherman *and* Steve Kandel
Batman and Robin are nearly devoured by a giant clam in this three-part tale in which the Penguin and the Joker join forces in a series of astrological capers.
The Joker Cesar Romero
The Penguin Burgess Meredith
Venus Terry Moore

Director: Oscar Rudolph

That Darn Catwoman/ Scat, Darn Catwoman

w Stanley Ralph Ross
Catwoman's hypnotic drug turns Robin into a criminal.
Catwoman Julie Newmar
Pussycat Leslie Gore
Pat Pending J. Pat O'Malley

Director: Oscar Rudolph

Penguin is a Girl's Best Friend/ Penguin Sets a Trend/Penguin's Disastrous End

w Stanford Sherman
Pengy and Marsha, Queen of Diamonds team up in a caper to turn gold bullion into guns, while the other dynamic double-act get tied to a huge catapult.
Penguin Burgess Meredith
Marsha Carolyn Jones
Aunt Hilda Estelle Winwood
Beasley Bob Hastings
Gen. MacGruder Alan Reed

Director: James Clark

Batman's Anniversary/A Riddling Controversy

w W.P. D'Angelo
It's Batman's anniversary as a crime-

fighter – but the Riddler prepares a giant cake with quicksand icing.
The Riddler John Astin
Anna Gram Deanna Lund

Director: James Clark

The Joker's Last Laugh/The Joker's Epitaph

w Lorenzo Semple Jr and Peter Rabe
Batman is ordered to arrest Bruce Wayne for collaborating with the Joker's latest scheme.
The Joker Cesar Romero
Josie Phyllis Douglas

Director: Oscar Rudolph

Catwoman Goes to College/ Batman Displays His Knowledge

w Stanley Ralph Ross
Catwoman takes a course in criminology and nearly cooks Batman and Robin in a cup of sulphuric acid.
Catwoman Julie Newmar
Cornell Paul Mantee
Cameo Art Linkletter

Director: Robert Sparr

A Piece of the Action/Batman's Satisfaction

w Charles Hoffman
Batman and Robin combine with Green Hornet and Kato to foil the rare stamp forging of Colonel Gumm.
Col. Gumm Roger C. Carmel
The Green Hornet Van Williams
Kato Bruce Lee
Pinky Pinkston Diane McBain

Director: Oscar Rudolph

King Tut's Coup/ Batman's Waterloo

w Stanley Ralph Ross
Tut seals Batman into a jewelled casket and drops it into a vat of water.

King Tut Victor Buono
Lisa Lee Meriweather
Neila Grace Lee Whitney

Director: James B. Clark

Black Widow Strikes Again/Caught in the Spider's Den

w Robert Mintz
Batman and Robin are caught in a giant web with two black widow spiders.
The Black Widow Tallulah Bankhead
Cameo George Raft
Tarantula Donald Barry

Director: Oscar Rudolph

Pop Goes the Joker/ Flop Goes the Joker

w Stanford Sherman
Robin is turned into a 'Bat-mobile' as he is strung up in a moving display of giant palette knives. (First shown: 16/17 May 1967)
The Joker Cesar Romero
Baby Jane Towser Diana Ivarson
Bernie Park Reginald Gardiner

Director: George Waggner

Ice Spy/The Duo Defy

w Charles Hoffman
Batman tries to track down the notorious Mr Freeze who threatens to return the country to the ice age. (This story was absent from the original first UK run and was first shown: 8/9 June 1968)
Mr Freeze Eli Wallach
Glacia Glaze Leslie Parrish
Prof. Isaacson Elisha Cook

Director: Oscar Rudolph

Season Three
26 half-hour episodes
14 September 1974–8 March 1975
(London Weekend Television)

(For this season, the format changed, with more complete stories and fewer cliff-hangers)

Enter Batgirl, Exit Penguin

w Stanford Sherman
Penguin schemes to marry Barbara
Gordon, the Commissioner's daughter,
but she turns out to be a third secret
crimefighter, called Batgirl – and only
Alfred knows . . .
The Penguin Burgess Meredith
Drusilla Elizabeth Harrower
Rev. Hazlitt Jonathan Troy

Director: Oscar Rudolph

Ring Around the Riddler

w Charles Hoffman
The Riddler schemes to take over the fight
game in Gotham City – and calls in The
Siren to help.
The Riddler Frank Gorshin
The Siren Joan Collins
Betsey Boldface Peggy Ann Garner
Kid Gulliver James Brolin

Director: Sam Strangis

The Wail of the Siren

w Stanley Ralph Ross
Commissioner Gordon and Bruce Wayne
both fall under the spell of Lorelei Circe,
the world-famous chanteuse who's determined to discover Batman and Robin's
true identities.
The Siren Joan Collins
Allegro Mike Mazurki
Andante Cliff Osmond

Director: George Waggner

The Sport of Penguins/A Horse of Another Colour

w Charles Hoffman
Penguin and racehorse owner Lola
Lasagne plot to win the Bruce Wayne
Handicap – but Batgirl and Robin are
riding in the same race.
Penguin Burgess Meredith
Lola Lasagne Ethel Merman
Glu Gluten Horace McMahon

Director: Sam Strangis

The Unkindest Tut of All

w Stanley Ralph Ross
Villainous King Tut nearly unmasks Bat-
man in his brazen efforts to become
master of the Universe.
King Tut Victor Buono
Osiris James Gammon
Shirley Patti Gilbert

Director: Sam Strangis

Louie, the Lilac

w Dwight Taylor
Louie plots to control the flower-children
of Gotham City and tries to feed the caped
crusaders to a man-eating lilac!
Louie the Lilac Milton Berle
Lila Lisa Seagram
Arbutus Richard Bakalyan
Primrose Schuyler Aubrey

Director: George Waggner

The Ogg Couple

w Stanford Sherman
Egghead with Olga and her Cossacks
begin a series of well-planned raids
leading up to a plot to steal 500 lbs of
caviar.
Egghead Vincent Price
Olga Anne Baxter
Old lady Violet Carlson

Director: Oscar Rudolph

The Ogg and I/How to Catch a Dinosaur

w Stanford Sherman
Egghead kidnaps the commissioner then
he and Olga baffle Batman and Co. with
onion-gas before scheming to hatch a 40-
million-year-old dinosaur egg.
Egghead Vincent Price
Olga Anne Baxter
Mike Alan Hale
Omar Orloff Alfred Dennis

Director: Oscar Rudolph

Surf's Up! Joker's Under!

w Charles Hoffman
Batman, Robin and Batgirl foil the Joker's plot to become surfing champion of the world by draining the knowledge of a top young surfer.
The Joker Cesar Romero
Skip Parker Ronnie Knox
Hot Dog John Mitchum

Director: Oscar Rudolph

The Londoninium Larcenies/The Foggiest Notion/The Bloody Tower

w Elkan Allan *and* Charles Hoffman
Batman, Robin and Batgirl answer 'Ireland's Yard's call for help in solving a baffling series of fog-bound thefts.
Lord Ffogg Rudy Vallee
Lady Penelope Peasoup Glynis Johns
Prudence Lyn Peters
Supt. Watson Maurice Dallimore

Director: Oscar Rudolph

The Funny Feline Felonies/The Joke's on Catwoman

w Stanley Ralph Ross
The Joker and Catwoman team up to steal a huge haul of dynamite.
The Joker Cesar Romero
Catwoman Eartha Kitt
Lucky Pierre Pierre Salinger

Director: Oscar Rudolph

Catwoman's Dressed to Kill

w Stanley Ralph Ross
Catwoman sets a pattern-cutting machine to bisect Batgirl and tries to steal a cloth-of-gold coat.
Catwoman Eartha Kitt
Angora Dirk Evans
Manx James Griffith

Director: Sam Strangis

Louie's Lethal Lilac Time

w Charles Hoffman
The terrific trio spoil Louie's smelly scheme to corner the lilac perfume market.
Louie Milton Berle
Sassafras Ronald Knight
Saffron John Dennis

Director: Sam Strangis

Nora Clavicle and the Ladies' Crime Club

w Stanford Sherman
A suffragette bent on destroying Gotham City ties the terrific trio into a terrific Siamese human knot.
Nora Clavicle Barbara Rush
Mayor Linseed Byron Keith
Mrs Linseed Jean Byron

Director: Oscar Rudolph

The Joker's Flying Saucer

w Charles Hoffman
The Joker builds a flying saucer, hoping to conquer the world by seeming to have come from outer space.
The Joker Cesar Romero
Emerald Corinne Calvert
Mayor Linseed Byron Keith
Prof Greenleaf Fritz Feld
Mrs Green Ellen Corby

Director: Sam Strangis

Penguin's Clean Sweep

w Stanford Sherman
Penguin contaminates Gotham City's money with germs of a rare disease to make everyone throw it away.
Penguin Burgess Meredith
Miss Clean Monique Van Vooren
Doctor John Beradino

Director: Oscar Rudolph

The Entrancing Dr Cassandra

w Stanley Ralph Ross
The Bat-Brigade are baffled by the 'non-appearance' of two invisible adversaries who plan to release Gotham City's arch-fiends and reduce Batman and his pals to one-dimensional beings.
Dr Cassandra Ida Lupino
Cabala Howard Duff
Warden Crichton David Lewis

Director: Sam Strangis

The Great Escape/The Great Train Robbery

w Stanley Ralph Ross
Cowboy crook Shame sprays the Bat-gang with fear gas, turning them into snivelling cowards.
Shame Cliff Robertson
Calamity Jan Dina Merrill
Frontier Fanny Hermione Baddeley

Director: Oscar Rudolph

I'll Be a Mummy's Uncle

w Stanley Ralph Ross
King Tut discovers the secret of the Batcave while digging for a rare metal near Wayne Manor.
King Tut Victor Buono
Suleiman Joey Tata
Florence of Arabia Angela Dorian

Director: Sam Strangis

Minerva, Mayhem and Millionaires

w Charles Hoffman
The Bat-bunch match wits with glamorous thief Minerva who tries to cook the caped crusaders in a giant pressure cooker.
Minerva Zsa Zsa Gabor
Adonis Bill Smith
Monroe William Dozier
Customer Howie Horowitz

Director: Oscar Rudolph

BATTLESTAR GALACTICA

Billed as TV's most expensive series ever, *Battlestar Galactica* was derided by the critics and fought over by the lawyers, but still became a phenomenon.

Forgoing the big finish, this series *began* with the virtual destruction of the human race. In a distant galaxy, the 12 colonial tribes of Man come together to end a 1000-year war with a robot race called Cylons. But the Cylons spring a trap, devastating the humans' home planets and attacking their vast battlestar spaceships.

The remnants of mankind reassemble under the leadership of the final remaining battlestar, the *Galactica*, commanded by Adama, last member of the shattered colonial government. Forming a cumbersome caravan of some 220 assorted spacecraft, from shuttles to freighters, taxis to tankers, the survivors head off into deep space in search of the 'lost' 13th colony – Earth. Naturally, the Cylons don't let it go at that and relentlessly pursue them through the galaxy.

Aside from the paternalistic Adama, the series' other main characters were his son Apollo who led the *Galactica*'s elite squadron of one-man Viper fighters; his handsome but impetuous buddy Starbuck; Adama's beautiful daughter Athena who was in charge of the ship's communications equipment; Starbuck's fancy,

Cassiopea; Adama's second in cammand, Col. Tigh; Sgt Boomer, fighter pilot pal of Apollo and Starbuck; Apollo's adopted son Boxey; and the villain of the piece, Count Baltar, a human traitor now in league with the Cylons.

Battlestar Galactica was the subject of eager lawsuits from 20th Century Fox who complained it was a steal from *Star Wars*; for Apollo and Starbuck read Solo and Skywalker, for the Cylons read stormtroopers, for the Imperius Leader read Darth Vader, etc. Galactica creator Glen A. Larson claimed his script was in the pipeline before *Star Wars* came out, and that if anything it was a lift from the Bible, with Adama as Moses leading the lost tribes to the Promised Land, pursued by the Egyptians, sorry, Cylons. Others have called it *Wagon Train* in space, with the Cylons replacing the marauding Indians and Lorne Greene reprising his famous father figure role of *Bonanza*'s Ben Cartwright.

The ace up Galactica's sleeve was its dazzling special effects, masterminded by John Dykstra who also did the tricks for *Star Wars*. But impressive though these were, they were diminished by the small screen and ultimately proved an expensive substitute for the lack of convincing characters and imaginative plotting.

By the time *Battlestar Galactica* reached British TV screens in 1980, American audiences had already seen off its successor, *Galactica 1980*. This was not down to UK reluctance to screen the series. ITV wanted to show it in 1979, hard on the heels of the American network, and with *Star Wars* still burning brightly in the hearts and minds of film fans. But Universal Studios insisted on a cinema release to squeeze precious box-office bucks from its costly £5 million pilot before the series could be screened in Britain and Europe.

So it was that *Battlestar Galactica* finally reached our screens in September 1980, starting in the London region, but its possible impact was dissipated by the lack of a network run. Other ITV regions were slow to follow. Some, for example, didn't show it until 1984, by which time *Galactica 1980* had arrived elsewhere (see separate entry). Once ITV had had its turn, the BBC picked up the series for a BBC2 run in autumn 1987.

MAIN CAST

Commander Adama Lorne Greene   *Capt. Apollo* Richard Hatch
Lt Starbuck Dirk Benedict   *Col. Tigh* Terry Carter
Lt Bomer Herb Jefferson Jr   *Athena* Maren Jensen
Boxey Noah Hathaway   *Cassiopea* Laurette Spang
Flight Sgt Jolly Tony Swartz   *Count Baltar* John Colicos
with:
Flight Corp. Rigel Sarah Rush   *Light Officer Omega* David Greenan
Sheba Anne Lockhart   *Voice of Imperious Leader* Patrick Macnee
Imperious Leader Dick Durock   *Voice of Lucifer* Jonathan Harris

Creator/Executive producer: **Glen A. Larson**
Producers: **Don Bellisario, John Dykstra, Paul Playdon, David O'Connell**
Special effects co-ordinator: **John Dykstra**
Music: **Stu Phillips**

A Glen Larson Production in association with Universal Television
UK: 24 colour 60-minute episodes
4 September 1980–30 April 1981
(Thames Television)

Saga of a Star World

(US: one three-hour episode, UK: three X 60 mins)
w **Glen A. Larson**
When their peace mission to end a 1000-year war with the robot Cylon race is all but wiped out by the treacherous enemy, the remnants of the 12 colonies of man gather under the protection of their last surviving battlestar, the *Galactica*. Led by Commander Adama, the rag-tag 'wagon train' of 220 assorted spacecraft sets off in search of the lost 13th colony – Earth. Needing to refuel, the *Galactica* heads for the ore planet Carillon where it finds a vast resort complex populated by humans and faces another mass Cylon attack.
Serina **Jane Seymour**
Uri **Ray Milland**
Adar **Lew Ayres**
Anton **Wilfrid Hyde White**
Sandell **David Tress**

Director: **Alan Levi**

Lost Planet of the Gods

w **Glen A. Larson, Don Bellisario** *(A 2-part story)*
Striving to escape the relentless Cylon pursuit, the *Galactica* heads for a magnetic void which will scramble all navigational signals. Emerging, they are led by a mysterious pulsating star to Kobol, the lost planet of the Gods, where human life began. But the traitor Baltar is lying in wait and in the resulting Cylon attack Apollo's new bride, Serina, is killed.
Giles **Larry Manetti**
Sorell **Janet Lynn Curtis**
Brie **Janet Louise Johnson**
Sgt Greenbean **Ed Begley Jr**

Director: **Christian Nyby**

The Lost Warrior

w **Don Bellisario**
Crash-landing on a remote Western-style planet, Apollo helps a beautiful young widow and her fellow homesteaders in their fight against a ruthless land baron whose Cylon gunslinger Red-Eye confronts Apollo in a deadly laser shootout.
Vella **Kathy Cannon**
Puppis **Johnny Timko**
Bootes **Lance LeGault**
La Certa **Claude Earl Jones**
Marco **Red West**
Red-Eye **Rex Cutter**

Director: **Rod Holcomb**

The Long Patrol

w **Don Bellisario**
Starbuck, while testing a new ultrafast spaceship, loses the craft to a renegade convict and finds himself marooned on a mysterious planet where the prisoners serve terms for the crimes of their ancestors. Determined to escape, Starbuck incites a revolt.
Waiter **John Holland**
Robber **James Whitmore Jr**
Croad **Ted Gehring**
Assault **Sean McClory**
Adultress **Tasha Martell**
Forger **Ian Abercrombie**

Director: **Christian Nyby**

The Gun on Ice Planet Zero

w **Leslie Stevens, Michael Sloan, Don Bellisario** *(A 2-part story)*
With the *Galactica* threatened by a giant, mountain-based laser on the ice planet Arcta, Apollo must lead a dangerous band

of prisoners to the planet's surface to destroy the Cylon stronghold. The *Galactica* team discovers and joins forces with an enslaved clone society to defeat the Cylons.
Croft Roy Thinnes
Thane James Olson
Dr Ravashol Dan O'Herlihy
Leda Christine Belford
Wolfe Richard Lynch
Tenna Britt Ekland
Ser Five Nine Danny Miller
Cadet Bow Alex Hyde-White
Killian Richard Milholland

Director: Alan Levi

The Magnificent Warriors

w Glen A. Larson
To save the fleet from starvation, Adama finds himself trapped into a compromising courtship of an old flame; and a fast-dealing card game leaves Starbuck the unwilling sheriff in a rugged farming community which he is forced to defend against vicious pig-like creatures called Borays.
Belloby Brett Somers
Carmichael Olane Soule
Bogan Barry Nelson
Dipper Eric Server
Duggy Dennis Fimple

Director: Christian Nyby

The Young Lords

w Don Bellisario, Frank Lupo, Paul Playdon
After crash-landing on the planet Trillion, Starbuck is rescued by a band of children who decide to ransom the Galactican warrior to the Cylons in exchange for their imprisoned father.
Kyle Charles Bloom
Miri Audrey Landers
Ariadne Brigitte Muller
Nilz Adam Mann
Megan Bruce Glover

Director: Don Bellisario

Mission Galactica: The Cylon Attack (aka The Living Legend)

w Glen A. Larson *(A 2-part story)*
Humanity is threatened with annihilation when Adama clashes with the hot-blooded, glory-hungry Cain, commander of the lost battlestar *Pegasus*, who is obsessed with leading both ships in a suicidal attacks on the Cylon forces. (This story was shown *last* by some ITV regions.)
Commander Cain Lloyd Bridges
Bojay Jack Stauffer
Tolen Rod Haase
Pegasus officer Junero Jennings

Director: Vince Edwards

Fire in Space

w Jim Carlson, Terrence McDonnell
Adama is critically injured when a Cylon kamikaze raid on the *Galactica* causes a fire to spread through the ship. Meanwhile Boomer races against time to save Athena and Boxey from a fiery death.
Dr Salik George Murdock
Fireleader William Bryant

Director: Christian Nyby

War of the Gods

w Glen A. Larson *(A 2-part story)*
The *Galactica* encounters the mysterious Count Iblis who claims to be the last survivor of an alien culture. He is taken aboard the battlestar where he charms the fleet with his omnipotent powers and promises to lead them safely to Earth. He grants the Council three wishes in return for its blind allegiance and delivers them Baltar as their first! But then Adama discovers the stranger's true identity and a life-or-death struggle ensues between the mortals and . . . the Prince of Darkness.
Iblis Patrick Macnee
Dr Salik George Murdock
Dr Wilker John Dullaghan
Statesman John Williams
Brie Janet Louise Johnson

Director: Dan Haller

The Man With Nine Lives

w Don Bellisario
Starbuck must save an ageing conman named Chameleon, who he believes to be his father, from bloodthirsty Borellian henchmen.
Chameleon Fred Astaire
Siress Blassie Anne Jeffreys
Zed Frank Parker
Zara Patricia Stich
Maga Lance LeGault
Bora Robert Feero

Director: Rod Holcomb

Murder on the Rising Star

w Don Bellisario, James Carlson, Terence McDonnell
Apollo uncovers a blackmail operation and finds his own life threatened as he works against time to clear Starbuck, who has been accused of murdering Ortega, a fellow Viper pilot.
Ortega Frank Ashmore
Pallon Lyman Ward
Elias Newell Alexander
Barton W.K. Stratton
Solon Brock Peters
Zara Patricia Stich

Director: Rod Holcomb

Greetings From Earth

(US: Two-hour special, UK: Two × 60 mins)
w Glen A. Larson
Apollo and Starbuck intercept a primitive spaceship containing a family of six humans in suspended animation who are believed to be from Earth. When it is discovered that they cannot survive in the Galactica's atmosphere, Adama gets Apollo, Starbuck and Cassiopea to accompany the travellers to their final destination, the planet Paradeen.
Geller Murray Matheson
Michael Randy Mantooth
Sarah Kelly Harmon
Hector Bobby Van
Vector Ray Bolger
Aggie Lesley Woods

Director: Rod Holcomb

Baltar's Escape

w Don Bellisario
Baltar leads a prison revolt aboard the Galactica, taking many hostages including Adama and other council members. To rescue them, Apollo and Starbuck pose as Cylon robots and stage their own surprise attack.
Leiter Lloyd Bochner
Maga Lance LeGault
Bora Robert Feero
Taba Anthony DeLongis
Domra John Hoyt
Siress Tinia Ina Balin

Director: Rick Kolbe

Experiment in Terra

w Glen A. Larson
Apollo is recruited by an angelic stranger to help rescue the inhabitants of the planet Terra from nuclear destruction at the hands of the evil Eastern Alliance, but is unable to prevent the start of a holocaust.
Brenda Melody Anderson
Dr Horning Kenneth Lynch
President Peter D. MacLean
John Edward Mulhare
Supreme commandant Nehemiah Persoff
Max-Well Ken Swofford
Stone Sidney Clute

Director: Rod Holcomb

Take the Celestra

w Jim Carlson, Terrence McDonnell
When Starbuck enlists Apollo's aid in rekindling an old flame, their mission becomes embroiled in a struggle for control of a battlestar ruled by the iron-fisted Commander Kronus.
Kronus Paul Fix
Charka Nick Holt
Aurora Ana Alicia
Damon Randy Stumpf
Hermes Richard Styles

Director: Dan Haller

The Hand of God

w Don Bellisario

Weary of evading their Cylon pursuers, the *Galactica* crew decides to take on a Cylon base star in a fight to the death.

Starbuck and Apollo take off in a captured enemy craft to try to infiltrate the base star and give the *Galactica* a fighting chance. (No guest cast.)

Director: Don Bellisario

BENJI, ZAX AND THE ALIEN PRINCE

American children's series about the adventures of 10-year-old alien Prince Yubi who arrives on Earth as a refugee. Pursued by enemies from his own planet, he tries to keep his identity secret, but comes to rely on two friends – a stray dog called Benji and Zax, the guardian robot.

REGULAR CAST
Prince Yubi **Chris Burton**

Executive producers: **Joseph Barbera, Margaret Loesch**
Director: **Joe Camp**

13 colour 20-minute episodes
5 October–28 December 1984
(BBC1)

BEYOND WESTWORLD

As far as the UK was concerned, there was very little life *Beyond Westworld*. This five-part American series, inspired by the 1973 *Westworld* movie, made very small localised dents in ITV's schedules from 1980 onwards.

Briefly, Westworld was an amusement park where superhuman androids helped visitors fulfil their Wild West fantasies. In *Beyond Westworld*, the powerful robots are sprung from the amusement park and sent out into the big wide world by their megalomaniac scientist creator, Simon Quaid, as the advance guard for his vision of a perfectly programmed society.

Ranged against them are John Moore and Pam Williams, the top agents of Delos, the giant corporation behind Westworld. They must expose and prevent the android threat whenever and wherever it occurs. Helping them out at Delos headquarters is computer genius Prof. Oppenheimer.

Beyond Westworld was the brainchild of writer-producer Lou Shaw (the man who created *Quincy!*)

REGULAR CAST

Simon Quaid **James Wainwright**   *John Moore* **Jim McMullan**
Pamela Williams **Connie Sellecca**   *Prof. Oppenheimer* **William Jordan**

Creator/Executive producer: **Lou Shaw**
Writers: Various, including **Lou Shaw, Martin Roth**
Directors: Various, including **Ted Post**
Five colour 60-minute episodes
Westworld Destroyed (pilot)
Takeover
The Lion

My Brother's Keeper
Sound of Terror

UK premiere: 31 August–21 September 1980
1 January 1981
(Grampian/Granada)

THE BIG PULL

Six-part 1962 BBC serial of the 'something is out there and it ain't friendly' variety. A tale of alien invasion by stealth rather than direct confrontation, it boasted an absence of monsters, relying on man's inability to see beyond the end of his nose to carry the story through to its end.

Briefly, American astronaut Mike Sklorski completes a single Earth orbit, passing through the deadly Van Allen belts of radioactive particles encircling the planet, and returns safely with both man and capsule apparently free from any trace of cosmic radiation. Yet soon after the capsule is opened, Sklorski dies from an unknown cause. Then the rocket's designer Dr Weatherfield – the first man to inspect the capsule – disappears following nightmares in which he has 'absorbed' Sklorski's memory. When Sklorski is seen alive, space research head Sir Robert Nailer believes the two have become one body, one personality, and concludes that the astronaut returned contaminated by something from beyond the Van Allen belts. It's the start of a series of 'attacks' in which men are targeted in pairs – one being killed and one going missing – with each attack doubling the number of victims. Nailer's hopes rest with the capture of one of the 'fusions' . . .

The Big Pull's producer was Terence Dudley – a first association with TV sci-fi for the man who later produced *Doomwatch* and *Survivors*. And the serial had a huge cast of more than 90 players, one of the biggest ever assembled for any such spin-off serial, headed by William Dextor as Nailer.

Transmission of *The Big Pull* (in an early Saturday evening slot) overlapped the start of the BBC's second *Andromeda* tale.

MAIN CAST

Sir Robert Nailer William Dexter   *Lady Nailer* June Tobin
Janet Nailer Susan Purdie   *Dr Alan Tullis* Ray Robert
Anderson (Eps 1–3)/Bruton- Anderson (Eps 4–5) Frederick Treves
Mrs Stone Joan Frank   *Jeff Murray* Raymond Mason
Det. Chief Supt. Allison Fred Ferris   *Van Heusen* Keith Anderson
Pam Laura Graham   *Gen. Nant* Paul Bacon   *Dr Weatherfield* Felix Deebark
Sklorski Frank Fenter   *Air Vice Marshal Collins* Keith Pyott
Royston Ian Clark

Writer: Robert Gould
Producer: Terence Dudley
Designer: Lionel Radford
Film sequences . . .
Cameraman: A.A. Englander
Editor: Seymour Logie

Music/special effects: The Radiophonic
   Workshop

A BBC Production
Six 30-minute episodes, black and white
9 June–14 July 1962

THE BIONIC WOMAN

*T*he Bionic Woman, alias Jaime Somers, first appeared as Steve Austin's childhood sweetheart in a two-part story of *The Six Million Dollar Man* in which she became his 'jogging partner' after a terrible sky-diving accident.

When she was killed off at the end of the story, Americans howled in sorrow and protest and Jaime was brought back to life for another double dose with the explanation that she'd been deep-frozen until bionic surgery was possible. *The Bionic Woman*'s staying power was confirmed, and a second bionic series was born.

Jamie Sommers also had bionic legs and a bionic arm, but instead of a new eye she got a bionic ear, enabling her to hear conversations over a mile away – or talking at the back of the airbase classroom where she worked as a teacher when she wasn't gallivanting off on dangerous missions for Oscar Goldman's OSI agency. These involved such weighty tasks as flying down to South America to rescue an ambassador (*Angel of Mercy*), teaming up with Steve Austin to avert a missile threat to Los Angeles (*The Deadly Missiles*), saving a pet lion from angry farmers (*Claws*), or posing as a beauty queen to uncover a spy ring (*Bionic Beauty*).

Alien plots weren't neglected either. Jaime was called on to tame the mysterious power of a living meteorite in *The Vega Influence*; in *The Pyramid*, she was trapped within an underground structure with an alien who insisted that Earth was about to be destroyed; and in *Sanctuary Earth*, she discovered a 14-year-old girl from another planet inside a satellite which unexpectedly returned to Earth. And Jaime also faced an army of deadly female robots bent on capturing an energy ray weapon in *Fembots in Las Vegas*.

Moreover, after we'd had the bionic man, the bionic woman and the bionic boy (see *The Six Million Dollar Man*), the nuclear family was completed by Max, *The Bionic Dog* – able to chew rifle barrels and outrun a motorbike.

Finally, Jaime bowed out of bionic duty with a splendid spoof of *The Prisoner*, called *On the Run*, in which she resigned and was sent to a special camp for ex-agents.

When *The Bionic Woman* was first aired over here she actually topped the ratings, and the show ran for about three years on ITV – its runs varying from region to region.

REGULAR CAST

Jaime Sommers **Lindsay Wagner**   *Oscar Goldman* **Richard Anderson**
Dr Rudy Wells **Martin E. Brooks**
Jim Elgin **Ford Rainey**   *Helen Elgin (Steve Austin's mum)* **Martha Scott**

Executive producer: **Harve Bennett**
Producer: **Ken Johnson**
Writers: **Various**
Directors: **Various**
Music supervision: **Hal Mooney**

An MCA Television Production
57 colour 60-minute episodes
UK premiere: 1 July 1976

(Author's note: ITV's regionalisation meant that after the initial concerted launch, the series' fate was left to the whims of the individual companies, thus the length and composition of its various UK runs varied considerably around the nation. So, for ease of reference, I've listed the episodes in their original American seasons.)

Season One
Welcome Home, Jaime (Part 2)*
Angel of Mercy
Thing of the Past
Claws
The Deadly Missiles
Bionic Beauty
Jaime's Mother
Winning is Everything
Canyon of Death
Fly Jaime
The Jailing of Jaime
Mirror Image
The Ghosthunter

Season Two
The Return of Bigfoot (Part 2)**
In This Corner, Jaime Sommers
Assault on the Princess
Road to Nashville
Kill Oscar (Part 1 & 3)***
Black Magic
Sister Jaime
The Vega Influence
Jaime's Shield (two-parter)
Biofeedback
Doomsday Is Tomorrow (two-parter)
Deadly Ringer (two-parter)
Jaime and the King

* ITV's 'premiere' episode of *The Bionic Woman* was actually a repackaged instalment of *The Six Million Dollar Man*. Thus, the *second* half of the 'two-part' opening story 'Welcome Home, Jaime' was the true *first* episode of *The Bionic Woman*! Confused? Try the next one!)

** In America this was the second half of a two-part story – the first half being an episode of *The Six Million Dollar Man*. Both parts were shown in Britain as *The Six Million Dollar Man* (December 1976 – Thames).

*** This was actually a three-part story, but although all three episodes were screened over here as *The Bionic Woman*, in fact only parts one and three were true *Bionic Woman* episodes. Part two was a *Six Million Dollar Man* and *that's* the way they played it in America.

Beyond the Call
The De Jon Caper
The Night Demon (aka The Daemon Creature)
Iron Ships and Dead Men
Once a Thief

Season Three
The Bionic Dog (two-parter)
Fembots in Las Vegas (two-parter)
Rodeo
African Connection
Motorcycle Boogie
Brain Wash

Escape to Love
Max
Over the Hill Spy
All for One
The Pyramid
The Antidote
The Martians Are Coming, The Martians Are Coming
Sanctuary Earth
Deadly Music
Which One Is Jaime?
Out of Body
Long Live the King
Rancho Outcasts
On the Run

BLAKE'S 7

Blake's 7 was an attempt to mount a serious space opera, to occupy the middle ground between the frolics of *Doctor Who* and the class of an *Out of the Unknown*. It might have been the beginning of a new creed of television science fiction – instead it became one of the last of a dying breed.

The series was created by Terry Nation, father of the Daleks, one-time gag writer for Tony Hancock, and deviser of *Survivors*, who infused it with his own characteristically gloomy vision of the future.

Set in the 'third century of the second calendar', it showed a near-omnipotent totalitarian government, the Federation, stifling freedom and creative endeavour, filling the air and water with tranquillising drugs, and ruthlessly eliminating opponents either by killing them or shipping them out to a galactic penal colony.

Such is to be the fate of Roj Blake, former resistance leader, who is convicted on false charges and put aboard a prison ship. Escaping with some fellow prisoners in an abandoned alien spaceship, renamed *Liberator*, Blake becomes an intergalactic Robin Hood, leading his dogged band of raffish outlaws against a tyrannical empire with the same persistence that made his Sherwood counterpart a thorn in the Sheriff's side.

The original seven were: Blake, cold computer genius Kerr Avon, cowardly thief Vila Restal, gentle giant Olag Gan, smuggler Jenna Stannis, Auron telepath Cally, and Zen – the *Liberator*'s almost-human computer.

As some of these heroes went, others came – the mercenary Del Tarrant, weapons expert Dayna Mellanby and blonde gunslinger

Soolin. Plus, of course, the two other computer stars, the testy box of tricks, Orac, and *Scorpio*'s obsequious Slave.

Leading the Federation pursuit of Blake and his crew were chief villainess Servelan and her hate-filled, obsessive huntsman Travis.

The series rapidly built up a huge and devoted cult following, and remains one of the most popular television series transmitted; its final episode was watched by more than 10 million viewers.

Nation himself wrote the entire first season of scripts and six subsequent stories, but his heroic ideals began to shift towards the end of Season Two. As Blake started to feel the pinch of revolutionary zeal, so the other characters began to emerge more forcefully, particularly Avon and Vila whose sniping relationship was a pivotal feature of the series. And as Blake disappeared by the start of the third season, it was Avon who assumed control.

Blake's 7's greatest strength – and its enduring appeal – lay in its characterisations. These are not stereotype heroes who win every time. They frequently lose and show an alarming tendency to get killed off, a trend which reached its climax in the last episode when most of the surviving outlaws are shot down with indulgent, slow-motion savagery. Also, there's little sanctimonious moralising. The line between right and wrong is often shown as a thin one and even the good guys are flawed – Blake becomes fanatical, Avon is paranoid and arrogant, Vila is spineless and Tarrant is conceited.

In the face of such humanity, fans happily overlooked the low-budget limitations of the series – the shaky sets and recycled props.

Blake's 7 started in Britain on the night *Star Wars* premiered in London. It was a good year for science fiction.

REGULAR CAST

Blake **Gareth Thomas** *(Seasons 1–2)*   *Avon* **Paul Darrow**
Villa **Michael Keating**   *Cally* **Jan Chappell** *(Seasons 1–3)*
Jenna **Sally Knyvette** *(Seasons 1–2 only)*
Gan **David Jackson** *(Seasons 1–2)*   *Zen* **Peter Tuddenham** *(Seasons 1–3)*
Dayna **Josette Simon** *(Seasons 3–4)*   *Orac* **Peter Tuddenham** *(Seasons 2–4)**
Tarrant **Steven Pacey** *(Seasons 3–4)*   *Soolin* **Glynis Barber** *(Season 4 only)*
Servelan **Jacqueline Pearce**
Travis **Stephen Greif** *(Season 1)/***Brian Croucher** *(Season 2)*
Slave **Peter Tuddenham** *(Season 4)*

Creator: **Terry Nation**
Script editor: **Chris Boucher**
Producers: **David Maloney** *(Seasons 1–3)*, **Vere Lorrimer** *(Season 4)*
Music: **Dudley Sipson**

A BBC Production
52 colour 50-minute episodes

Season One:
2 January–27 March 1978
Season Two:
9 January–3 April 1979
Season Three:
7 January–31 March 1980
Season Four:
28 September–31 December 1981

* In 'Orac', the voice is by **Derek Farr** (uncredited)

Season One
(all stories written by Terry Nation)

The Way Back

Roj Blake, a former resistance leader who has been 'reprogrammed' by the Federation, is falsely convicted on a series of trumped-up charges and sentenced to transportation to the prison planet Cygnus Alpha. Waiting to board, he meets Jenna and Vila for the first time . . .
Bran Foster Robert Beatty
Glynd Robert James
Tarrant Jeremy Wilkin
Varon Michael Halsey
Maja Pippa Steel
Ravella Gillian Bailey
Richie Alan Butler
Arbiter Margaret John
Dr Havant Peter Williams
Alta Morag Susan Field

Director: Michael E. Briant
Designer: Martin Collins

Space Fall

Aboard the prison ship bound for Cygnus Alpha, Blake attempts a mutiny. It fails, but when a mysterious unmanned space vessel appears alongside, Blake, Avon and Jenna are sent to investigate. After a struggle with a mind-blowing hallucinatory device, the rebels gain control of the ship and escape.
Avon Paul Darrow *(intro)*
Gan David Jackson *(intro)*
Leylan Glyn Owen
Raiker Leslie Schofield
Artix Norman Tipton
Teague David Hayward
Krell Brett Forrest
Nova Tom Kelly
Dainer Michael Mackenzie
Garton Bill Weston
Wallace Clinton Morris

Director: Pennant Roberts
Designer: Roger Murray-Leach

Cygnus Alpha

In the alien spaceship which they have named the *Liberator*, Blake, Jenna and Avon plan to free the prisoners on Cygnus Alpha. Blake teleports down but is captured by the planet's ruler, Vargas, who demands that he hand over the ship.
Vargas Brian Blessed
Leylan Glyn Owen
Artix Norman Tipton
Kara Pamela Salem
Laran Robert Russell
Arco Peter Childs
Selman David Rydall
Zen Peter Tuddenham *(intro)*

Director: Vere Lorrimer
Designer: Robert Berk

Time Squad

En route to attack a Federation communications complex, the *Liberator* crew take on board a mysterious drifting projectile. While Blake, Avon and Vila proceed with the raid – ambushed then helped by Cally – the projectile's alien passengers cause problems back on the ship.
Cally Jan Chappell (intro)
Aliens Tony Smart, Mark McBride, Frank Henson

Director: Pennant Roberts
Designer: Roger Murray-Leach

The Web

Outlawed members of Cally's race use their telepathic powers to force her to sabotage the *Liberator* and lure it into a gossamer-like web surrounding an unknown planet where they plan to use the ship's energy for their own ends.
Sayman Richard Beale
Geela Ania Marson
Novara Miles Fothergill
Decimas Deep Roy, Gilda Cohen, Ismet Hassam, Marcus Powell, Molly Tweedley, Willie Sheara

Director: Michael E. Briant
Designer: Martin Collins

Seek – Locate – Destroy

Stepping up his war against the Federation, Blake plans to steal a message decoder from a top security installation on the planet Centero. But things go badly wrong and Cally is taken prisoner by Travis and Servalan.

Travis **Stephen Greif** *(intro)*
Servalan **Jacqueline Pearce** *(intro)*
Rontaine **Peter Miles**
Bercol **John Bryans**
Escon **Ian Cullen**
Prell **Peter Craze**
Rai **Ian Oliver**
Eldon **Astley Jones**

Director: **Vere Lorrimer**
Designer: **Robert Berk**

Mission to Destiny

Blake and his companions become involved in murder and intrigue surrounding a crippled spaceship which was on a mission to save its home planet, Destiny.

Kendall **Barry Jackson**
Sara **Beth Morris**
Mandrian **Stephen Tate**
Sonheim **Nigel Humphreys**
Levett **Kate Coleridge**
Grovane **Carl Forgione**
Rafford **Brian Capron**
Pasco **John Leeson**
Dortmunn **Stuart Fell**

Director: **Pennant Roberts**
Designer: **Martin Collins**

Duel

On an uncharted planet the last survivors of an ancient alien race force Blake and Travis to fight a duel so that they can learn about their kind.

Sinofar **Isla Blair**
Giroc **Patsy Smart**
Mutoid **Carol Royle**

Director: **Douglas Camfield**
Designer: **Roger Murray-Leach**

Project Avalon

Travis devises a plan to destroy Blake's crew *and* capture the *Liberator* using a plague-carrying android of Avalon, a captured resistance leader. But Avon's

talents help Blake turn the tables – to Servalan's fury.

Avalon **Julia Vidler**
Chevner **David Bailie**
Mutoid **Glynis Barber**
Scientist **John Baker**
Terloc **John Rolfe**

Director: **Michael E. Briant**
Designer: **Chris Pemsel**

Breakdown

The limiter implant in Gan's brain malfunctions and he becomes unusually aggressive. The crew seek help from a research station neurosurgeon, Professor Kayn. But Kayn alerts the Federation . . .

Kayn **Julian Glover**
Farren **Ian Thompson**
Renor **Christian Roberts**

Director: **Vere Lorrimer**
Designer: **Peter Brachacki**

Bounty

While Blake and Cally try to inspire a planet's rejected president to return to help his people, the *Liberator* is lured into a trap by a phoney distress call from a group of bounty hunters.

Sarkoff **T.P. McKenna**
Tyce **Carinthia West**
Cheney **Mark York**
Tarvin **Marc Zuber**
Amagon guard **Derrick Branche**

Director: **Pennant Roberts**
Designer: **Roger Murray-Leach**

Deliverance

A spaceship crashes on the planet Cephlon. A *Liberator* search party finds one fatally injured survivor, Ensor, and Blake learns of Ensor's father's greatest creation – Orac.

Ensor **Tony Caunter**
Meegat **Suzan Farmer**
Maryatt **James Lister**

Director: **Michael E. Briant** *(and David Maloney – uncredited)*
Designer: **Robert Berk**

Orac

Despite competition from Travis and Servalan, Blake and his companions get to Orac first, and its dying creator, Ensor Sr, gives them the super-computer. Back on the ship Orac makes its first prediction – the destruction of the *Liberator* . . .
Ensor Derek Farr
Phibians James Muir
Paul Kidd

Director: Vere Lorrimer
Designer: Martin Collins

Season Two

Redemption

w Terry Nation
The *Liberator* is attacked and boarded by aliens – the original owners of the ship come to reclaim their property. With Orac's help the crew are able to escape, pursued by an identical sister ship which then blows up – thus confirming Orac's 'prediction'.
Alta One Sheila Ruskin
Alta Two Harriet Philpin
Norm One Roy Evans

Director: Vere Lorrimer
Designer: Sally Hulke

Shadow

w Chris Boucher
Blake tries to enlist the help of the Terra Nostra, an interplanetary crime syndicate, in his fight against the Federation, but finds them more dangerous than he'd bargained.
Largo Derek Smith
Bek Karl Howman
Hanna Adrienne Burgess
Chairman Vernon Dobtcheff
Enforcer Archie Tew

Director: Jonathan Wright Miller
Designer: Paul Allen

Weapon

w Chris Boucher
Blake and his crew set out to find a stolen

secret weapon – a 'delayed-effect' gun which can be triggered over great distances and many years after the victim has been shot. But Servalan is also after it in a plot involving a Blake clone.
Coser John Bennett
Rashel Candace Glendenning
Travis Brian Croucher *(intro)*
Fen Kathleen Byron
Carnell Scott Fredericks
Officer Graham Simpson

Director: George Spenton Foster
Designer: Mike Porter

Horizon

w Allan Prior
Fleeing from pursuit ships, the exhausted *Liberator* crew head out towards the edge of the galaxy. But they find the Federation has long arms – and on a planet called Horizon they are captured by the empire's puppet regime.
Kommissar William Squire
Ro Darien Angadi
Selma Souad Faress
Assistant Brian Miller
Chief guard Paul Haley

Director: Jonathan Wright Miller
Designer: Paul Allen

Pressure Point

w Terry Nation
Blake declares his intention of returning to Earth to attack Control – the computer complex which runs the entire Federation. But the raid ends in failure, and death for Gan after a clash with Travis deep underground.
Kasabi Jane Sherwin
Veron Yolande Palfrey
Arle Alan Halley
Berg Martin Connor
Mutoid Sue Bishop

Director: George Spenton Foster
Designer: Mike Porter

Trial

w Chris Boucher
Travis stands trial at Space HQ where

Servalan is anxious to cover up her own failings. And a guilt-stricken Blake decides to desert his crew. But both men live to fight another day . . .

Zil Claire Lewis
Samor John Savident
Thania Victoria Fairbrother
Bercol John Bryans
Rontane Peter Miles
Par Kevin Lloyd
Lye Graham Sinclair
Guard commander Colin Dunn

Director: Derek Martinus
Designer: Gerry Scott

Killer

w Robert Holmes
On the planet Fosforon, Avon tries to persuade an old ally to help steal a vital component in the Federation cypher machine. On the *Liberator*, Blake and the others watch the salvage of a 700-year-old Earth ship and Cally senses great danger. Her fears are confirmed when a virulent plague breaks out.

Bellfriar Paul Daneman
Tynus Ronald Lacey
Gambril Colin Farrell
Wiler Morris Barry
Tak Colin Higgins
Bax Michael Gaunt

Director: Vere Lorrimer
Designer: Sally Hulke

Hostage

w Allan Prior
Although he himself is now an outlaw, Travis is still determined to kill Blake and lures him into a trap, using the rebel's cousin Inga as a hostage.

Ushton John Abineri
Inga Judy Buxton
Joban Kevin Stoney
Space commander Andrew Robertson
Molok James Coyle
Mutoid Judith Porter

Director: Vere Lorrimer
Designer: Steve Brownsey *and* Gerry Scott

Countdown

w Terry Nation
Blake's crew arrive on the newly liberated planet Albian, to find the population facing destruction from a radiation device activated by the defeated garrison commander.

Grant Tom Chadbon
Cauder James Kerry
Provine Paul Shelley
Ralli Lindy Alexander
Tronos Geoffrey Snell
Selson Robert Arnold
Vetnor Sidney Arnold
Arrian Nigel Gregory

Director: Vere Lorrimer
Designers: Stephen Brownsey *and* Gerry Scott

Voice from the Past

w Roger Parkes
A mysterious telepathic signal forces Blake to reroute the *Liberator* to an isolated asteroid where a heavily disguised Travis is waiting to spring yet another trap.

Glynd Richard Bebb
Le Grand Frieda Knorr
Nagu Martin Read

Director: George Spenton Foster
Designer: Ken Ledsham

Gambit

w Robert Holmes
The search for Docholli, the man believed to know the secret location of Star One, the Federation's main control complex, brings the Liberator to Freedom City, a vast gambling town. But Travis and Servalan are on the same trail.

Krantor Aubrey Woods
Docholli Denis Carey
Chenie Nicolette Roeg
Croupier Sylvia Coleridge
Cevedic Paul Grist
Toise John Leeson
Jarriere Harry Jones
Zee Michael Halsey
Klute Deep Roy

Director: George Spenton Foster
Designer: Ken Ledsham

The Keeper

w Allan Prior

One of the tribal chiefs on the planet Goth unknowingly holds the key to Star One. By the time he finds out which one, Blake discovers Travis has also learned the secret . . .

Gola Bruce Purchase
Tara Freda Jackson
Rod Shaun Curry
Fool Cengiz Saner
Old man Arthur Hewlett
Patrol Leader Ron Tarr

Director: Derek Martinus
Designer: Eric Walmsley

Star One

w Chris Boucher

Blake finally reaches Star One and determines to destroy it. But aliens from Andromeda are gathering for a galactic invasion, and after a shootout in which Travis seriously wounds Blake before being killed by Avon, the *Liberator* is left standing alone against their battle fleet until the Federation ships can arrive.

Lurena Jenny Twigge
Stot David Webb
Parton Gareth Armstrong
Durkin John Bown
Marcol Paul Toothill
Leeth Michael Maynard

Director: David Maloney
Designers: Ray London, Ken Ledsham

Season Three

Aftermath

w Terry Nation

The war is won, but the *Liberator* is severely damaged. The crew escape in one-man capsules and Avon lands on a tribal planet where he is rescued by Dayna and her fugitive father. But Servalan arrives there, too . . .

Dayna Josette Simon *(intro)*
Hal Mellanby Cy Grant
Chel Alan Lake
Lauren Sally Harrison

Tarrant Steven Pacey *(intro)*
Troopers Richard Franklin
Michael Melia

Director: Vere Lorrimer
Designer: Don Taylor

Powerplay

w Terry Nation

Back on the *Liberator*, Avon and Dayna find 'Federation Space Captain' Tarrant is not all he seems to be. Meanwhile Vila and Cally fight their own battle for survival in a hospital which is not all *it* seems either.

Klegg Michael Sheard
Harman Doyne Byrd
Lom John Hollis
Mall Michael Crane
Zee Primi Townsend
Barr Julia Vidler
Nurse Catherine Chase
Receptionist Helen Blatch

Director: David Maloney
Designer: Gerry Scott

Volcano

w Allan Prior

For the *Liberator*'s new crew, the planet Obsidian offers the prospect of allies and a safe base from which to strike at the Federation. But it also holds a traitor, and a deadly secret of its own.

Hower Michael Gough
Bershar Malcolm Bullivant
Mori Ben Howard
Commander Allan Bowerman
Mutoid Judy Matheson
Milus Russell Denton

Director: Desmond McCarthy
Designer: Gerry Scott

Dawn of the Gods

w James Follett

The *Liberator* is mysteriously drawn off-course, landing on an artificial planet where the crew fall into the clutches of

The Thaarn, a creature from Cally's Auron legends.
Caliph **Sam Dastor**
Groff **Terry Scully**
Thaarn **Marcus Powell**

Director: **Desmond McCarthy**
Designer: **Ray London**

The Harvest of Kairos

w **Ben Steed**
A mysterious death awaits anyone who remains on the planet Kairos after the harvest week. And when Servalan finally captures the *Liberator*, it's on Kairos that she strands the crew.
Jarvik **Andrew Burt**
Dastor **Frank Gatliff**
Shad **Anthony Gardner**
Carlon **Sam Davies**
Guard **Charles Jamieson**

Director: **Gerald Blake**
Designer: **Ken Ledsham**

City of the Edge of the World

w **Chris Boucher**
Sent to open a strange vault in return for some crystals, Vila finds love and a temporary idyll on a bizarre odyssey that takes him 3000 light years away.
Kerril **Carol Hawkins**
Baybon **Colin Baker**
Norl **Valentine Dyall**
Sherm **John J. Carney**

Director: **Vere Lorrimer**
Designer: **Don Taylor**

Children of Auron

w **Roger Parkes**
Servalan engineers a deadly virus which strikes the planet Auron. Cally is telepathically summoned home to help her people but though Servalan is lying in wait, the *Liberator* crew succeed in saving the planet's gene banks.
Deral **Rio Fanning**
Franten **Sarah Atkinson**
Ginka **Ric Young**
C A One **Ronald Leigh-Hunt**

C A Two **Beth Harris**
Patar **Jack McKenzie**
Pilot Four-Zero **Michael Troughton**

Director: **Andrew Morgan**
Designer: **Ray London**

Rumours of Death

w **Chris Boucher**
Avon returns to Earth to seek revenge on the Federation torturer who killed his girlfriend Anna Grant, but finds the past was not what it seemed and the present holds only grief.
Sula (Anna Grant) **Lorna Heilbron**
Shrinker **John Bryans**
Chesku **Peter Clay**
Grenlee **Donald Douglas**
Forres **David Haig**
Balon **Philip Bloomfield**
Hob **David Gillies**

Director: **Fiona Cumming**
Designer: **Paul Munting**

Sarcophagus

w **Tanith Lee**
After investigating an unmanned alien spaceship, Cally is taken over by a strange entity that assumes her form and begins to drain all energy from the *Liberator*. Only Avon is able to stand up to it and help Cally defeat the creature. (No guest cast.) Dayna's Song by Tanith Lee.

Director: **Fiona Cumming**
Designer: **Ken Ledsham**

Ultraworld

w **Trevor Hoyle**
The Liberator encounters the strange artificial planet of Ultraworld which turns out to be a giant computer whose thirst for knowledge includes wiping clean the brains of new visiting species.
Relf **Ronald Govey**
Ultras **Peter Richards, Stephen Jenn, Ian Barritt**

Director: **Vere Lorrimer**
Designer: **Jan Spoczynski**

Moloch

w Ben Steed
The *Liberator* crew trail Servalan to Sardos where both are captured by Federation renegades who are aiming to harness the planet's advanced technology for their own ends. Then Sardos's supreme power shows itself as Moloch, a computer creature from the future.
Doran Davyd Harries
Grose John Hartley
Lector Mark Sheridan
Moloch Deep Roy
Chesil Sabina Franklyn
Poola Debbi Blythe

Director: Vere Lorrimer
Designer: Jan Spoczynski

Death-Watch

w Chris Boucher
The ritual war fought by two professional champions seems like the ultimate spectator sport – until the crew of the *Liberator* discover that Tarrant's brother Deeta is one of the combatants and a scheming Servalan the 'neutral' judge.
Deeta Steven Pacey
Vinni Mark Elliott
Max Stewart Bevan
Commentator David Sibley
Karla Kathy Iddon

Director: Gerald Blake
Designer: Ken Ledsham

Terminal

w Terry Nation
Responding to secret instructions he believes are from Blake, Avon heads for Terminal, an old artificial planet originally in orbit round Mars. But it's just an illusion created by Servalan to lure and capture the *Liberator*. With the crew stranded on Terminal, she departs in her prize only to be cheated when the ship – which had earlier passed through a strange particle field – begins to break up completely . . .
Blake Gareth Thomas
Kostos Gillian McCutcheon

Reeval Heather Wright
Toron Richard Clifford

Director: Mary Ridge
Designer: Jim Clay

Season Four

Rescue

w Chris Boucher
Cally dies in a series of explosions on Terminal. Avon and the rest are 'rescued' by a stranger called Dorian whose sinister purpose is revealed when they arrive on the planet Xenon where they also meet his associate, Soolin.
Soolin Glynis Barber *(intro)*
Dorian Geoffrey Burridge
Creature Rob Middleton
Slave Peter Tuddenham *(intro)*

Director: Mary Ridge
Designer: Roger Cann

Power

w Ben Steed
Having killed Dorian, the outlaws try to get back to his spaceship, *Scorpio* – but first they become embroiled in a war between the planet's two tribes, the male-dominated Hommiks and the female Seska. When they finally make their escape they are joined by Soolin.
Gunn Sar Dicken Ashworth
Pella Juliet Hammond-Hill
Kate Alison Glennie
Nina Jenny Oulton
Cato Paul Ridley
Luxia Linda Barr

Director: Mary Ridge
Designer: Roger Cann

Traitor

w Robert Holmes
Using Xenon as their new base, Avon needs to know why the Federation are suddenly making such easy territorial gains. They find the answer – a new pacifying drug – on the newly subdued planet, Helotrix. And they also learn that

Servalan did not die in the destruction of the *Liberator*.

Leitz Malcolm Stoddard
Colonel Quute Christopher Neame
Major Hunda Robert Morris
Practor John Quentin
Forbus Edgar Wreford
General Nick Brimble
The Tracer David Quilter
Avandir Neil Dickson
Igin George Lee
Sgt Hask Cyril Appleton

Director: David Sullivan Proudfoot
Designer: Nigel Curzon

Stardrive

w Jim Follett
Collision with an asteroid damages *Scorpio*'s main drives. The need to replace them is urgent enough to warrant a trip to the lair of the Space Rats – psychotic 'Hell's Angels' of space.

Dr Plaxton Barbara Shelley
Atlan Damien Thomas
Bomber Peter Sands
Napier Leonard Kavanagh

Director: David Sullivan Proudfoot
Designers: Nigel Curzon, Roger Cann

Animals

w Allan Prior
Dayna goes in search of her former tutor, Justin, a genetic engineer whose knowledge Avon now needs. She finds a horrifying genetic experiment – and is also captured by Servalan.

Justin Peter Byrne
Captain William Lindsay
Borr Max Harvey
Ardus Kevin Stoney
Og David Boyce

Director: Mary Ridge
Designers: Nigel Curzon, Roger Cann

Headhunter

w Roger Parkes
Avon sets out to recruit a cybernetics genius called Muller – but instead winds up with a homicidal android who plans to use Orac to dominate the galaxy.

Muller John Westbrook
Vena Lynda Bellingham
Technician Douglas Fielding
Android Nick Joseph
Voice Lesley Nunnerley

Director: Mary Ridge
Designer: Graham Lough

Assassin

w Rod Beacham
Servalan hires a feared assassin, Cancer, to kill the *Scorpio* crew. Orac advises that they take the fight to Cancer, but no one knows what he – or she – looks like.

Verlis Betty Marsden
Nebrox Richard Hurndall
Cancer John Wyman
Piri Caroline Holdaway
Benos Peter Attard
Tok Adam Blackwood
Servalan's captain Mark Barratt

Director: David Sullivan Proudfoot *(and*
  Vere Lorrimer – *uncredited)*
Designer: Ken Ledsham

Games

w Bill Lyons
The planet Mecron is a vital source of Feldon, a rare and valuable energy crystal. The mining is controlled by Belkov, a renowned games player – and to reach his illicit private cache, the *Scorpio* crew must play a series of dangerous games.

Belkov Stratford Johns
Gambit Rosalind Bailey
Gerren David Neal
Computer Michael Gaunt
Guard James Harvey

Director: Vivienne Cozens
Designers: Eric Walmsley, Ken
  Ledsham

Sand

w Tanith Lee
Following up Federation concern over a lost expedition, Tarrant finds himself

alone with Servalan on a planet where the sand is alive – and deadly.
Reeve **Stephen Yardley**
Chasgo **Daniel Hill**
Servalan's assistant **Peter Craze**
Keller **Jonathan David**
Computer **Michael Gaunt**

Director: **Vivienne Cozens**
Designers: **Eric Walmsley, Ken Ledsham**

Gold

w **Colin Davis**
Stealing a gold shipment from an undefended pleaure cruiser en route to Earth seems to be too good an opportunity to miss. But the *Scorpio* crew have been set up by Servalan who for once has the Midas touch . . .
Keiller **Roy Kinnear**
Doctor **Anthony Brown**
Woman passenger **Dinah May**
Pilot **Norman Hartley**

Director: **Brian Lighthill**
Designer: **Ken Ledsham**

Orbit

w **Robert Holmes**
Egrorian, a renegade Federation scientist, offers Avon the ultimate weapon. But in return he wants Orac. Once again, Servalan is quietly manipulating the situation – but this time fails to get what she wants.
Egrorian **John Savident**
Pinder **Larry Noble**

Director: **Brian Lighthill**
Designer: **Ken Ledsham**

Warlord

w **Simon Masters**
Avon attempts to establish an anti-Federation alliance to spread the antidote to the empire's pacifying drug. He needs the co-operation of the most powerful warlord, Zukan – but he gets only treachery.
Zukan **Roy Boyd**
Zeeona **Bobbie Brown**
Finn **Dean Harris**
Boorva **Simon Merrick**
Chalsa **Rick James**
Lod **Charles Augins**
Mida **Brian Spink**

Director: **Viktors Ritelis**
Designer: **Paul Allen**

Blake

w **Chris Boucher**
Avon reveals that Orac has found Blake on the lawless planet Gauda Prime where he has seemingly become a bounty hunter. *Scorpio* crashlands on the planet, and when he meets Blake, Tarrant is convinced he has betrayed them. Avon is unsure of the truth but is forced to shoot Blake before Federation guards appear for the final shootout in which Dayna, Tarrant, Vila and Soolin are all gunned down . . . and the guards move in for Avon.
Blake **Gareth Thomas**
Deva **David Collings**
Arlen **Sasha Mitchell**
Klyn **Janet Lees Price**

Director: **Mary Ridge**
Designer: **Roger Cann**

BRAVE NEW WORLD

Bland US adaptation of Aldous Huxley's classic 1932 novel set 600 years in the future in a plastic world where Henry Ford is worshipped as God and babies are hatched in batches and conditioned to want only what they can have.

Individuality, art and free expression have been sacrificed for the sake of stability and a drug-induced happiness. A strict caste system is rigorously maintained by an assembly line of test-tube babies ranging from high-intelligence Alphas through Betas, Deltas and Gammas to the sub-moron Epsilons. Promiscuity is in, procreation is taboo and mother and father are dirty words.

Keir Dullea (of *2001: A Space Odyssey*) starred as the director of Central Hatcheries whose trip to the 'savage reservation' – the ultimate in exclusive holidays – has unforeseen consequences, namely a son, John, who is 'rediscovered' years later by Alpha malcontent Bernard Marx, and introduced to civilisation. But John, versed in Shakespeare and romance, is unable to adapt and when he falls in love events move to a tragic conclusion.

This *Brave New World* was not a great success. Instead of Huxley's blackly comic vision it offered futuristic beautiful people who looked more like refugees from a disco.

CAST

Linda Lysenko Julie Cobb   *Bernard Marx* Bud Cort
Thomas Grahmbell Keir Dullea   *Mustapha Mond* Ron O'Neal
Lenina Disney Marcia Strassman   *John Savage* Kristoffer Tabori
Helmholtz Watson Dick Anthony Williams
High priestess Delia Salvi   *Maoina Krupps* Tricia O'Neill
Miss Trotsky Carole Mallory   *Henry Exxon* Reb Brown
Chief dispenser Sam Chew Jr   *Hochina* Sheree Brewer
Chief warden Valerie Curtin   *Gamma male* Patrick Cronin
Gamma female Beatrice Colen

Screenplay: Robert E. Thompson
Producer: Jacqueline Babbin
Director: Burt Brinckerhoff

An NBC/Universal/Milton Sperling Production
Two colour 95-minute episodes
12–19 March 1981
(BBC1)

BUCK ROGERS IN THE 25TH CENTURY

Buck Rogers is a look at our world five centuries from now, laced with a lot of fun, mischief and colour'

(Glen A. Larson)

Purists blanched, but *Buck Rogers in the 25th Century* was really a hero of the 1980s. Gone was the serious character of the original comic strip. This young Buck was a brash, fun-loving man who refused to take the computerised society of the future seriously.

The series, too, didn't take itself seriously – it aimed at escapist entertainment with a glossy, slick package packed with special effects. And Buck Rogers had one other weapon to fight the ratings war – sex, mainly in the slinky form of actress Erin Gray who played Buck's sidekick Wilma Deering in alluring jumpsuits one size too small.

The premise behind the original 1929 comic strip (which ran for nearly 40 years) was that Buck Rogers, an ex-Air Force pilot, was overcome by a strange, noxious gas while surveying an abandoned mine shaft near Pittsburgh, and spent 500 years in a state of suspended animation.

In this series, however, Buck was an American astronaut who, in 1987, is launched on a deep space probe. His rocket is blown out of trajectory and Buck is frozen for 500 years, returning to Earth in the 25th century and becoming involved in a conflict between Earth and the Draconians, ruled by the evil (but beautiful) Princess Ardala.

All that happened in the pilot episode, *The Awakening*, but over here the series reached TV *before* the pilot, which had a cinema release, so Buck was already thawed, integrated and ready for further action.

Besides Buck and Wilma, other regulars were scientist Dr Huer and Twiki, a vibrating-voiced little robot. Season Two saw the departure of Huer and the arrival of some new characters: Dr Goodfellow (played with long-suffering dignity by Wilfrid Hyde-White), Admiral Asimov (presented as a descendant of author Isaac Asimov) and the tragic figure of Hawk, last survivor of a race of man-birds.

And there were plenty of guest stars, led by Buster Crabbe – who played Buck in the 1930s film serial – who came out of retirement, aged 71, to play an ageing space pilot. Other notables were *My Favourite Martian* star Ray Walston, *Batman* villains Frank Gorshin, Cesar Romero and Julie Newmar, plus Woody Strode, Roddy McDowall, Jamie Lee Curtis and Jack Palance.

The series premiered here in August 1980, with ITV – in a concerted network move – scheduling it against the BBC's *Doctor Who*. After just nine weeks, Buck was pulling an average audience of 9.9 million against the doctor's 9 million (this was the last season of Tom Baker and Lalla Ward). It was a short-lived success, however. The series ended in mid-1981, though episodes were rerun on BBC2 in 1989.

(NB: Buck Rogers *had* appeared on British TV screens before this series. In 1967, Grampian screened the 1939 movie serial starring Buster Crabbe. And the BBC showed it again in April 1982 – while some ITV regions were catching up on the last few episodes of *Buck Rogers in the 25th Century*.)

MAIN CAST

Capt. Buck Rogers Gil Gerard   *Col. Wilma Deering* Erin Gray
Dr Huer Tim O'Connor   *Twiki* Felix Silla
Voice of Twiki Mel Blanc   *Hawk* Thom Christopher
Dr Goodfellow Wilfrid Hyde-White   *Adm. Asimov* Jay Garner
Princess Ardala Pamela Hensley   *Kane* Michael Ansara
Dr Theopolis (computer) Eric Server   *Voice of Crichton* Jeff David

---

Executive producers: Glen A. Larson, John Mantley *(Season Two)*
Producers: Leslie Stevens, Jock Gaynor, David O'Connell, Dick Caffey, Bruce Lansbury, John G. Stephens, Calvin Clements

A Glen A. Larson Production in association with Universal Television

34 colour episodes 60-minute (unless stated otherwise), plus pilot: The Awakening
UK premiere: 30 August 1980 (LWT)

Pilot episode

The Awakening

(120 mins)
w Glen A. Larson, Leslie Stevens
In the year 1987, astronaut Buck Rogers is launched on a deep space probe, but his rocket is blown off course and its lone passenger frozen for 500 years. When Buck awakens from his slumber, he is aboard the flagship of the Draconian fleet, en route to a peace conference on Earth. The lovely Princess Ardala is strongly attracted to him, but her earthly adviser Kane suspects he is a spy.
Kane Henry Silva
Draco Joseph Wiseman
Tigermen Duke Butler, H.B. Haggerty

Director: Daniel Haller

(This pilot episode was not originally shown on British television, getting a cinema release instead. However, it has subsequently found its way on to the small screen as a TV movie. The following episodes are grouped in their American running order, for ease of reference. Following the initial 16-week network run, the series was subjected to the usual quirks of ITV regionalisation.)

Season One

Planet of the Slave Girls (aka Flight to Sorcerer's Mountain)

(105 mins)
w Steve Greenberg, Aubrey Solomon, Cory Applebaum
When Dr Huer suspects that poison in Earth's food supply is depleting the planet's fighting forces, he sends Buck and Wilma to Vistula, an agricultural planet which grows most of Earth's veg. There, Buck confronts a sorcerer named Kaleel and discovers a massive fleet poised to attack Earth.
Brigadier Gordon Buster Crabbe
Kaleel Jack Palance
Governor Saroyan Roddy McDowall
Duke Danton David Groh
Ryma Brianne Leary
Dr Mallory Macdonald Carey

Director: Michael Caffey

Vegas in Space (aka Flight from Sinaloa)

w Anne Collins
Buck races against time to rescue a kidnapped girl from Sinaloa, an orbiting gambling paradise devoted to the pursuit of pleasure and vice.
Armat Cesar Romero
Falina Ana Alicia

Tangie **Pamela Shoop**
Velosi **Richard Lynch**
Marla **Juanine Clay**
Morphus **Joseph Wiseman**

Director: **Sig Neufeld**

The Plot to Kill a City (aka Death Squad 2500)

w **Alan Brennert** *(A 2-part story)*
Buck goes undercover to infiltrate the Legion of Death, a bizarre band of killers which plans to wipe out New Chicago, Buck's hometown and his last link with 20th-century Earth. But his true identity is discovered by the group's scientist leader, Kellogg. (Originally shown in the UK as a 105-minute episode.)
Sherese **Nancy DeCarl**
Argus **Victor Argo**
Quince **John Quade**
Kellogg **Frank Gorshin**
Varek **Anthony James**
Markos **Robert Tessier**
Barney **James Sloyan**
Joella **Markie Post**

Director: **Dick Lowry**

Return of the Fighting 69th

w **David Bennett Carren**
Noah Cooper, an ageing starfighter pilot, is brought out of retirement to help Buck and Wilma blast through a treacherous asteroid belt to the stronghold of deadly Commander Corliss and his ally Roxanne.
Noah Cooper **Peter Graves**
Roxanne Trent **Elizabeth Allen**
Commander Corliss **Robert Quarry**
'Big Red' Murphy **Woody Strode**
Harriet Twain **K.T. Stevens**
Clayton **Robert Hardy**

Director: **Phil Leacock**

Unchained Woman (aka Escape from Zeta)

w **Bill Taylor**
Buck masquerades as a ruthless convict to help a beautiful female prisoner, Jen Burton, break out of jail. But they are pursued by Hugo, an indestructible android.
Jen Burton **Jamie Lee Curtis**
Malary Pantera **Michael Delano**
Sergio Sanwiler **Bert Rosario**
Ted Warwick **Robert Cornthwaite**
Majel **Tara Buckman**
Hugo **Walter Hunter**

Director: **Dick Lowry**

Planet of the Amazon Women

w **D.C. Fontana, Richard Fontana**
Legendary space hero Buck is put up for auction after being kidnapped by two conniving women and taken to Zantia – a planet ruled by women.
Nyree **Liberty Godshall**
Ariela **Ann Dusenberry**
Linea **Teddi Siddell**
Cassius Thorne **Jay Robinson**
Prime Minister **Anne Jeffreys**
Flight controller **Sean Garrison**

Director: **Phil Leacock**

Cosmic Whiz Kid

w **Alan Brennert, Anne Collins**
Hieronymus Fox is a child genius, frozen in the 20th century and revived in the 25th to become president of the planet Genesia. When he is kidnapped by a ruthless criminal, Buck risks life and limb to rescue him.
Hieronymus Fox **Gary Coleman**
Roderick Zale **Ray Walston**
Lt Dia Cyrton **Melody Rogers**
Koren **Albert Popwell**
Toman **Lester Fletcher**
Selmar **Earl Boen**

Director: **Lesley Martinson**

Escape from Wedded Bliss

w **Cory Applebaum, Patrick Hoby Jr**
The beautiful but deadly Draconian Princess Ardala promises not to destroy Earth with her new ultimate weapon if granted one small request – to marry Buck Rogers.

Princess Ardala Pamela Hensley *(re-intro)*
Kane Michael Ansara *(intro)*
Tigerman H.B. Haggerty

Director: David Moessinger

Cruise Ship to the Stars

w Ann Collins, Alan Brennert
Aboard a luxury space yacht, Buck is assigned to protect Miss Cosmos, a genetically perfect woman, from a mysterious kidnapper with strange powers.
Alison Kimberly Beck
Sabrina Trisha Noble
Jalor Leigh McCloskey
Miss Cosmos Dorothy Stratten
Captain Brett Halsey
Tina Patty Maloney

Director: Sig Neufeld

Space Vampire

w Kathleen Barnes, David Wise
The Vorvon, a galactic creature that steals souls and turns people into walking zombies, marks Wilma as his next victim.
The Vorvon Nicholas Hormann
Royko Christopher Stone
Dr Ecbar Lincoln Kilpatrick
Nelson Phil Hoover
Twiki Patty Maloney *(this ep. only)*

Director: Larry Stewart

Happy Birthday, Buck

w Martin Pasko
A vengeful assassin capable of turning people into solid marble plans to eliminate Dr Huer who is planning his own surprise – a party to celebrate Buck's 534th birthday.
Col. Traeger Peter MacLean
Dr Delora Batliss Tamara Dobson
Raylyn Derren Morgan Brittany
Carew Chip Johnson
Rorvik Bruce Wright
Niles Tom Gagen

Director: Sig Neufeld

A Blast for Buck

w John Gaynor, Dick Nelson, Alan Brennert
Buck submits himself to a mind probe to discover if a villain from his past is responsible for a sinister plot that threatens Earth. He summons up memories of his greatest adventures – and the beautiful women he has encountered in the 25th century.
Hieronymus Fox Gary Coleman
Kaleel Jack Palance
Noah Cooper Peter Graves
Kellogg Frank Gorshin
Ardala Pamela Hensley
Zale Ray Walston
Brig. Gordon Buster Crabbe
Ryma Brianne Leary
Tangie Pamela Susan Shoop
Jen Burton Jamie Lee Curtis

Director: David Phinney

Ardala Returns

w Chris Bunch, Allan Cole
Buck is forced into a dogfight in space – against himself – when he once again falls into the clutches of Princess Ardala who has created four duplicates of him.
Tigerman H.B. Haggerty

Director: Larry Stewart

Twiki is Missing

w Jaron Summers
Twiki the robot is seized by three treacherous women known as the Omni Guard who become omnipotent when they join hands. Meanwhile Wilma fights to prevent a giant spaceberg from igniting the Earth's atmosphere.
Kerk Belzak John P. Ryan
Stella Eddie Benton
Clare Janet Louie
Dawn Eugenia Wright
Pinchas David Darlow

Director: Sig Neufeld

Olympiad

w Craig Buck

Buck helps a defecting athlete during the 25th century's intergalactic Olympics – but the athlete has a powerful explosive implanted in his head. (Six top US athletes appeared in this episode, including Olympic pole vault champion Bob Seagren and boxer Jerry Quarry.)

Jorex Leet Barney McFadden
Alaric Nicholas Coster
Lara Judith Chapman
Karl Paul Mantee
Rand Sorgon Bob Seagren
Quarod Jerry Quarry

Director: Larry Stewart

A Dream of Jennifer (aka Jennifer)

w Alan Brennert

Buck is startled by the mysterious appearance of his 20th-century girlfriend in 25th-century Chicago and tracks her down at a futuristic Mardi Gras. But before he can determine her true identity, he falls victim to a sinister alien plot.

Jennifer/Leila Anne Lockhart
Reev Paul Koslo
Merlin Gino Conforti
Nola Mary Woronov
Lt Rekoff Jessie Lawrence Ferguson
Toby Kaplin Cameron Young

Directors: Harvey Laidman, David
    Phinny

Space Rockers

w Chris Bunch, Allan Cole

Buck infiltrates the orbiting satellite Musicworld to stop sinister rock group manager Mangros from seizing power in the galaxy by exerting sonic mind-control over billions of youngsters listening to a galactic rock concert.

Lars Mangros Jerry Orbach
Joanna Judy Landers
Karana Nancy Frangione
Cirus Leonard Lightfoot
Rambeau Jesse Goina
Tarkas Paul LeClair

Director: Guy Magar

Buck's Duel to the Death

w Robert W. Gilmer

The people of the planet Katar turn to Buck to fulfil a prophecy that a 500-year-old man will defeat their cruel dictator, the Trebor.

Darius Keith Andes
The Trebor William Smith
Kelan Fred Sadoff
Dr Doctor Robert Lussier
Vionne Elizabeth Stack
Neil Edward Power

Director: Bob Bender

Flight of the War Witch

w Robert W. Gilmer, William Mageean
    based on a story by David Chomsky *(A
    2-part story)*

Buck makes a daring pioneer journey through a black hole into an alternative universe. There he is coerced into joining forces with his arch-enemy Ardala to save a peaceful planet from being destroyed by a deadly dictator called Zarina.

The Keeper Sam Jaffe
Tora Vera Miles
Zarina Julie Newmar
Chandar Kelly Miles
Pantherman Tony Carroll
Spirot Sid Haig
Kodus Donald Petrie

Director: Larry Stewart

Season Two

Time of the Hawk (aka Hawk)

w Norman Hudis *(A 2-part story)*

Buck Rogers battles a powerful foe, Hawk, a man-bird who has vowed vengeance on the human race after his people have been wiped out by marauding pirates. But it is a duel that ends not in death, but in friendship.

Koori Barbara Luna
Simmons Susan McIver
Thordis Andre Harvey
Flagg Lance LeGault
Pratt Sid Haig

Dr Goodfellow Wilfrid Hyde-White *(intro)*
Hawk Thom Christopher *(intro)*
Adm. Asimov Jay Garner *(intro)*

Director: Vincent McEveety

Journey to the Oasis

w Robert *and* Esther Mitchell *(A 2-part story)*
Wilma falls in love with an alien ambassador, unaware that he has a shocking secret which jeopardises a vital peace conference.
Ambassador Duvoe Mark Lenard
Odee-X Felix Silla
Rolla Mike Stroka
Admiral Zite Len Birman
Zykarian Jr Donn White

Director: Daniel Haller

The Guardians

w Paul *and* Margaret Schneider
A dying man entrusts Buck with a mysterious glowing jade box which causes the *Searcher*'s crew to have visions from the past and future. For Buck, it's lunch with mom on her front porch . . .
Lt Devlin Paul Carr
Boy Shawn Stevens
Janovus Harry Townes
Buck's mum Rosemary DeCamp
Koori Barbara Luna
Mailman Howard Culver

Director: Jack Arnold

Mark of the Saurian (aka The Unseen)

w Francis Moss
Buck, feverish with the flu, insists that a high-ranking ambassador is really a terrifying lizard creature plotting to destroy the starship *Searcher*. But his friends say he is just hallucinating.
Major Elif Barry Cahill
Ambassador Sorens Linden Chiles
Dr Moray Vernon Weddle
Nurse Paulton Kim Hamilton
Crewman Andi Pike
Lt Martin Alex Hyde-White

Director: Barry Crane

The Golden Man

w Calvin Clements, Stephen McPherson
When the *Searcher* is grounded on an asteroid, the crew's only hope for survival rests with a strange golden-skinned boy who has the power to alter molecular structure.
Alphie Bob Elyea
Velis David Hollander
Relcos Russell Wiggins
Hag Diane Chesney
Loran Bruce M. Fischer
Graf Anthony James

Director: Vincent McEveety

The Crystals

w Robert *and* Esther Mitchell
A young woman with no memory of her past has a terrifying vision of her future, and a strange mummified creature threatens Buck, Wilma and Hawk.
Laura Amanda Wyss
Hall Sandy Alexander Champion
Kovick James R. Parkes
Johnson Gary Bolen
Petrie Leigh Kim
Lt Martin Alex Hyde-White

Director: John Patterson

The Satyr

w Paul *and* Margaret Schneider
Buck is mysteriously transformed into a dangerous goat-horned satyr-like creature when he tries to rescue a mother and her young son on an abandoned planet.
Delph Bobby Lane
Syra Anne E. Curry
Pangor Dave Cass
Midshipman Dennis Freeman

Director: Victor French

Shgoratchx!* (aka The Derelict Equation)

w William Keys
The *Searcher* crew discovers a centuries-

(* Pronounced Sagoratek)

old derelict spaceship with a peculiar crew aboard – seven little men who call themselves the Zeerdonians. But their cargo consists of extremely volatile solar bombs.
Ensign Moore Alex Hyde-White
General Xces Tommy Madden
General Zoman John Edward Allen
General Yoomak Billy Curtis
General Sothoz Harry Monty

Director: Vincent McEveety

The Hand of the Goral

w Francis Moss
Buck, Hawk and Wilma return from a survey of a bizarre planet and find the starship *Searcher* and its human crew strangely altered.
Goral John Fujioka
Reardon Peter Kastner
Cowan William Bryant
Parsons Dennis Haysbert

Director: David Phinney

Testimony of a Traitor

w Stephen McPherson
Buck goes on trial for his life when he's accused of being responsible for the nuclear holocaust that devasted 20th-century Earth – and a probe of his own memory seems to prove his guilt.
Commissioner Bergstrom Ramon Bieri
US president Walter Brooks
Gen. Arnheim David Hooks
Maj. Peterson John O'Connell
Gen. Myers William Sylvester
Col. Turner Bill Andes

Director: Bernard McEveety

The Dorian Secret

w Stephen McPherson
Buck rescues a beautiful stowaway called Asteria Eleefa who is facing a death sentence. But the powerful warlord pursuing her suffocates the *Searcher* crew with deadly heat rays as he demands the woman's return.
Asteria Devon Ericson
Koldar Walker Edmiston
Saurus Denny Miller
Demeter William Kirby Cullen
Falgor Thomas Bellin
Chronos Eldon Quick

Director: Jack Arnold

CAPTAIN SCARLET AND THE MYSTERONS

Supermarionation reached twin peaks of sophistication and expense in Gerry Anderson's fifth sci-fi puppet series. With his company now flying the flag of Century 21, Anderson's latest show maintained his optimistic vision of a 21st century where nations are united under a benevolent world government.

It followed the efforts of a secret organisation, Spectrum, to defend Earth against powerful Martian foes, the Mysterons, who have sworn vengeance on mankind after misinterpreting a peaceful Spectrum mission to Mars as an unprovoked attack. Week by week the Mysterons' war of attrition continued, always with a taunting warning of where they would strike next. They were tough adversaries, too, possessing the power of retrometabolism, whereby they could kill, then reconstruct their victim as an agent under their control.

To lead the fight, Gerry and Sylvia Anderson created a new breed of TV hero – the indestructible Captain Scarlet. The man in red acquired his own mysterious regenerative power during his first close encounter with the Mysterons. It enabled him to take on the missions impossible, facing and surviving hazards from car and plane crashes to nuclear blasts.

A colourful supporting cast was assembled around the lead figure of Scarlet – a team of colour-coded Spectrum agents and a quintet of glamorous pilots called Angels. All came complete with detailed 'pasts', some of which preserved a continuity with earlier Supermarionation shows. The full line-up was:

Captain Scarlet: Spectrum's no. 1 agent; English, with a brilliant army career behind him.

Col. White: English ex-navy man, now Spectrum's commander-in chief.

Captain Blue: American ex-test pilot and brilliant scholar who accompanies Scarlet on many of his missions.

Captain Grey: American ex-WASP who worked on the proto-type Stingray.

Captain Ochre: American flyer and crack crimefighter.

Captain Magenta: Irishman who became New York's top gang boss. Recruited by Spectrum as their man inside their underworld.

Lt Green: Col. White's Trinidadian right-hand man. Another ex-WASP.

Dr Fawn: Aussie medic. The 'Bones' of Spectrum.

The Angels – **Symphony**, **Melody**, **Rhapsody**, **Harmony** and **Destiny** all combine courage and beauty. Rhapsody's 'biography' described her as a Chelsea deb who once worked with Lady Penelope!

Principal villain was the elusive **Captain Black**, a Spectrum agent who becomes the Mysterons' Earth agent when they take him over. The Mysterons themselves are heard but never seen, save for two roving eyes that seek out their targets.

After the success of the *Thunderbirds*, there was again a heavy accent on hardware. Spectrum itself operated from a flying aircraft carrier, Cloudbase, and the ground agents relied on a range of hi-tech vehicles, including the ten-wheeled Spectrum Pursuit Vehicle (SPV), and the Maximum Security Vehicle (MSV).

Captain Scarlet and the Mysterons cost £1,500,000 to make, but significantly advanced the Supermarionation cause. The figures were perfectly proportioned, with the equipment that worked the eye, lip and hand movements housed in the body, so ending the 'big-headed' marionette tradition. And if the eyes seemed uncannily real, that's because, in a sense, they were real. They were the eyes of Century 21 employees – production assistants, cameramen, continuity girls and secretaries – photographed, then superimposed on to plastic eyeballs.

The cast of voices was headed by Francis Matthews as Captain Scarlet, South African Donald Gray as Col. White and the menacing Mysterons, Ed Bishop as Captain Blue and *Emergency Ward 10* star Charles Tingwell as Dr Fawn. Paul Maxwell, previously heard as Steve Zodiac in Fireball XL5, was Captain Grey, while Jeremy Wilkin (Virgil in the second series of Thunderbirds) voiced Captain Ochre and many of the guest characters.

The quirks of ITV regionalisation meant that Captain Scarlet was denied a nationwide launch. The series premiered in the Midlands area on 29 September 1967 and in London on 1 October (ironically in black and white), with the rest of the country trailing in soon after. It still crops up here and there. *Night Network*, the weekend 'small hours' service for the London, TVS and Anglia regions, ran 25 of the 32 episodes from August 1987 to February 1988.

VOICE CAST:

Captain Scarlet **Francis Matthews**   *Col. White/Mysteron voice* **Donald Gray**
Captain Grey/World President **Paul Maxwell**   *Captain Blue* **Ed Bishop**
Captain Ochre **Jeremy Wilkin**   *Captain Magenta* **Gary Files**
Lt Green **Cy Grant**   *Dr Fawn* **Charles Tingwell**
Melody Angel **Sylvia Anderson**   *Symphony Angel* **Janna Hill**
Harmony Angel **Lian-Shin**   *Rhapsody Angel/Destiny Angel* **Liz Morgan**

Created by: **Gerry** *and* **Sylvia Anderson**
Producer: **Reg Hill**
Script editor: **Tony Barwick**
Special effects: **Derek Meddings**
Characterisation: **Sylvia Anderson**
Music: **Barry Gray**

A Century 21 Production for ITC
32 colour 30-minute eposides
29 September 1967–14 May 1968
(ATV, Midlands)

The Mysterons

w **Gerry** *and* **Sylvia Anderson**
Mistakenly believing themselves the victims of an unprovoked Spectrum attack, the Mysterons begin their war of attrition by taking over the mind of Captain Black and vowing to assassinate the World President. Captain Scarlet meets with a car accident that has astonishing consequences.

Director: **Desmond Saunders**

Winged Assassin

w **Tony Barwick**
Col. White assigns Captains Scarlet and Blue to protect an Asian leader from another Mysteron death threat. When that threat emerges in the form of a Mysteron-controlled jet, Captain Scarlet finds he must put his invincibility to the test.

Director: **David Lane**

Big Ben Strikes Again

w **Tony Barwick**
The Mysterons threaten to destroy London by hijacking a nuclear device. Spectrum's only clue – to find the spot where the mugged driver heard Big Ben strike 13 times. With no time to defuse it,

Captain Scarlet must take the bomb deep underground where only he could survive the explosion.

Director: Brian Burgess

Manhunt

w Tony Barwick
Captain Black is detected while breaking into an atomic plant and only avoids capture by hiding in a radioactive room. Col. White has his first proof that the Mysterons control one of his men – and the net closes in on Black.

Director: Alan Perry

Avalanche

w Shane Rimmer
The Mysterons try to sabotage the Outer Space Defence System in northern Canada, but Captain Scarlet finds snow his best weapon – triggering a vast avalanche to bury the opposition.

Director: Brian Burgess

White as Snow

w Peter Curran *and* David Williams
Singled out as the Mysterons' next target, Col. White seeks refuge in a submarine. But the Mysterons have a man on board. To protect his commander, Captain Scarlet must first attack him – laying himself open to a court martial where the sentence is death!

Director: Robert Lynn

The Trap

w Alan Pattillo
The Mysterons warn that they will 'clip the wings of the world' and set a trap to wipe out the World Air Force Supreme Command. Trapped in a castle dungeon by Mysteron agents, Scarlet must escape in time to avert the plot.

Director: Alan Perry

Operation Time

w Richard Conway, Stephen J. Mattick
Spectrum is puzzled by the latest Mysteron threat: 'to kill time', until a newspaper report reveals that a General 'Tiempo' is to undergo a brain operation. The Mysterons have turned the surgeon into their agent, but Scarlet plays a substitution trick of his own.

Director: Ken Turner

Spectrum Strikes Back

w Tony Barwick
A seemingly innocent waiter is unexpectedly identified as a Mysteron reconstruction by a secret new detector device, and poses a pressing threat to a high-level Spectrum group.

Director: Ken Turner

Special Assignment

w Tony Barwick
Scarlet goes undercover when the Mysterons threaten to destroy North America. Forced to 'resign' from Spectrum over heavy gambling debts, he is recruited by Captain Black who plans to use an SPV to carry a nuclear device into Nuclear City and start a deadly chain reaction. But first he orders Scarlet to shoot Captain Blue to prove his loyalty . . .

Director: Bob Lynn

The Heart of New York

w Tony Barwick
Thieves use a Mysteron threat to destroy the heart of New York as an opportunity to plan a multi-million dollar bank raid.

Director: Alan Perry

Lunarville 7

w Tony Barwick
Moon settlement Lunarville 7 declares its neutrality in the war between Earth and

the Mysterons. Sent to investigate, Scarlet discovers a strange Mysteron-style complex is being built on the far side of the moon.

Director: Bob Lynn

Point 783

w Peter Curran *and* David Williams
The Mysterons kill and then duplicate two Earth Forces officers, using them in a double plot to assassinate the Supreme Commander of Earth Forces. But each time Captain Scarlet is on hand to foil their attempts.

Director: Bob Lynn

Model Spy

w Bill Hedley
Angels Destiny and Symphony pose as models, with Captain Scarlet as PR man and Captain Blue as his photographer, when they are told to protect the famous French fashion designer André Verdain from the latest Mysteron death threat.

Director: Ken Turner

Seek and Destroy

w Peter Curran *and* David Williams
Three Mysteron-controlled Angel aircraft attack Destiny Angel as she is returning to Cloudbase with Captains Blue and Scarlet. Melody, Rhapsody and Harmony are immediately launched to combat the enemy and a fierce dogfight ensues.

Director: Alan Perry

The Traitor

w Tony Barwick
Captain Scarlet is accused of being a traitor when mystery explosions wreck several hovercraft, following a Mysteron warnng that the Spectrum organisation will be sabotaged from within.

Director: Alan Perry

Renegade Rocket

w Ralph Hart
The Mysterons gain control of a Spectrum rocket. Col. White scrambles the Angels to intercept the enemy agent, while Cap'ns Scarlet and Blue must stop the rocket hitting an unidentified target.

Director: Brian Burgess

Crater 101

w Tony Barwick
Captains Scarlet and Blue and Lt Green embark on a hazardous mission to destroy a Mysteron moonbase unaware that the nuclear bomb they are carrying has been set to go off two hours earlier than they think.

Director: Ken Turner

Shadow of Fear

w Tony Barwick
Three astrologers are assigned to help in a Spectrum plan to discover the secrets of the Mysterons, using a satellite on Phobos, the Martian moon. But the Mysterons strike back and when the satellite starts transmitting, there is no equipment to receive its pictures.

Director: Bob Lynn

Dangerous Rendezvous

w Tony Barwick
Using a Mysteron diamond pulsator which Captain Scarlet has brought back from the moon, Col. White contacts the Mysterons and asks for an end to the war of nerves. But when Scarlet goes to keep the agreed rendezvous, he encounters only treachery.

Director: Brian Burgess

Fire at Rig 15

w Bryan Cooper
A Mysteron-reconstructed oil rig expert sets out to destroy the refinery which

supplies Spectrum, with Captain Scarlet in hot pursuit. In the breakneck chase Scarlet wrecks his SPV, but gets his man.

Director: Ken Turner

Treble Cross

w Tony Barwick
The Mysterons reconstruct a man they believe to have been drowned. But his life has been saved and Spectrum use him to set a trap for Captain Black.

Director: Alan Perry

Flight 104

w Tony Barwick
Captain Scarlet foils a Mysteron attempt to wreck a plane carrying a leading astrophysicist – but it means taking the full force of a crashlanding himself.

Director: Bob Lynn

Place of the Angels

w Leo Eaton
A Mysteron-reconstructed research assistant steals a phial containing a deadly liquid and Scarlet faces a desperate race to reach her before she contaminates the Los Angeles water supply.

Director: Leo Eaton

Noose of Ice

w Tony Barwick
Captains Scarlet and Blue fly to the North Pole to try to prevent a Mysteron plot to destroy a unique Tritonium mine – source of an alloy vital to the world space programme.

Director: Ken Turner

Expo 2068

w Shane Rimmer
A nuclear reactor is hijacked and the Mysterons threaten a disaster along the Eastern seaboard. Spectrum trace it to the site of Expo 2068 and discover a vital safety valve has been removed. With the reactor overheating, only Captain Scarlet can withstand the fierce temperatures. Can he deactivate it in time?

Director: Leo Eaton

The Launching

w Peter Curran and David Willams
A Mysteron-reconstructed newsman is used in a presidential assassination attempt at the launch of an atomic liner. The traditional champagne bottle has been laced with an extra kick – high explosive.

Director: Brian Burgess

Codename Europa

w David Lee
Captain Scarlet finds that a simple device is his best weapon when he uses a trip wire to overcome a Mysteron agent who has employed the full range of his electronic wizardry in a triple assassination plot.

Director: Alan Perry

Inferno

w Shane Rimmer, Tony Barwick
An irrigation plant in South America is targeted for destruction by the Mysterons. Spectrum teams are sent to guard the complex but discover too late that Captain Black has planted a homing device in an ancient Aztec statue that brings a Mysteron-controlled spacecraft on a crash course.

Director: Alan Perry

Flight to Atlantica

w Tony Barwick
Tampered champagne gives Spectrum personnel an unexpected kick – and results in the partial destruction of the World Navy Complex by Captains Blue and Ochre.

Director: Leo Eaton

Attack on Cloudbase

w Tony Barwick

An all-out attack on Cloudbase seems to bring victory to the Mysterons. Even Captain Scarlet has been killed for the last time. It all looks hopeless . . . until Symphony Angel awakes to realise it has all been a terrible dream!

Director: Ken Turner

The Inquisition

w Tony Barwick

Captain Blue drinks drugged coffee and revives to find himself facing an interrogation from a stranger who claims to be from Spectrum Intelligence. Blue is asked to reveal cipher codes to prove his identity but refuses and makes a desperate escape bid, only to find he has been held in a mock-up of Cloudbase. But help is on the way . . .

Director: Ken Turner

CAPTAIN ZEP – SPACE DETECTIVE

Unusual BBC children's programme that was a kind of 'Doctor Whodunnit', involving viewers in solving various intergalactic crimes played out in different weekly dramas.

The series was set in the year 2095 at the SOLVE Academy for student space detectives. Each week, Captain Zep – 'the most famous space detective of all time' – showed the students (young viewers) a video of a famous crime, featuring himself and his loyal crew.

He then asked questions and the students tried to guess whodunnit before the solution was revealed. Viewers at home were invited to answer a supplementary question about the action, with SOLVE badges as prizes.

Captain Zep ran for two series of six 'cases' and was a novel, if lightweight, contribution to science fiction TV.

REGULAR CAST

Captain Zep Paul Greenwood *(Season One)*/Richard Morant *(Season Two)*
Jason Brown Ben Ellison   *Prof. Spiro* Harriet Keevil *(Season One only)*
Prof. Vana Tracey Childs *(Series Two)*

Writers: Dick Hills *(Series One)*
Colin Bennett *(Series Two)*
Producer: Christopher Pilkington
Directors: Christopher Pilkington
 (Series One) Michael Forte *(Series Two)*
Graphic designers: Ray Ogden, Dick Bailey

A BBC Production
12 colour 30-minute episodes
Series One:
5 January–9 February 1983
Series Two:
9 March–13 April 1984

Series One:

Case 1: Death on Delos

Captain Zep, in his spaceship *Zep One*, answers an urgent call to save the lives of the gentle plant people of the planet Delos.

Case 2: The Lodestone of Space

Zep is called upon to supervise the security arrangements on the planet Synope – seemingly a straightforward assignment.

Case 3: The Plague of Santos

Zep goes looking for a fellow SOLVE agent who has gone missing on the planet Santos.

Case 4: The G and R 147 Factor

Zep is called up to investigate the space hijacking of freight crafts carrying valuable supplies of the G and R 147 enzyme.

Case 5: The Tinmen of Coza

Captain Zep investigates a murder on the robot planet of Coza.

Case 6: The Warlords of Armageddia

While investigating the murder of Marshall Pax on the violent planet of Armageddia, Zep stumbles across a threat to Earth itself.

Series Two

Case 1: Death Under the Sea

The 'new' Zep, Jason Brown and stunning new scientific adviser Vana, are sent to investigate the murder of the President of Aquabeta – a vast underwater city.

Case 2: The Missing Agent of Ceres

Capt. Zep is sent to contact SOLVE's secret agent at the intergalactic fair on Ceres. But he's missing – either kidnapped or murdered!

Case 3: The Small Planet of Secrets

The people on Planet X are dying. They've run out of water. The old president knows the whereabouts of secret supplies but he is assassinated just as he's about to reveal the location.

Case 4: The Sands of Sauria

On the famous resort planet of Sauria, Zep gets caught up in a terrifying 'meteor' attack which kills hundreds of tourists.

Case 5: The Tree of Life

Zep is called up to find out why the Tree of Yath is dying. Without the fruit from this one tree the people will starve. Is it natural causes or is it sabotage?

Case 6: Death by Design

117 travellers die in space, all of whom were wearing new spacesuits checked and stamped by Zep. Can Zep clear his name?

CATWEAZLE

TV has seen some odd time travellers, but few as eccentric as the scrawny old 11th-century wizard who becomes trapped in the 20th century – twice!

This children's comic fantasy was created by actor/writer Richard Carpenter, later to script ITV's *Robin of Sherwood*, and ran for two seasons, giving its star Geoffrey Bayldon one of his most memorable roles, albeit clothed in rags and sporting a straggly goatee beard.

Trying to discover the secret of flight, using his powers of magic, Catweazle accidentally jumps through time into 20th-century England, where he is quickly bewildered by his new environment. He thinks the electric light is the sun in a bottle and puts everything from the TV to the telephone (or 'telling bone') down to magic.

In the first series, Catweazle is befriended by farmer's son Carrot and the two share a succession of chaotic misadventures before the wizard succeeds in returning to his own time.

Series Two repeated the formula but gave Catweazle a new young companion – Cedric, 12-year-old son of Lord and Lady Collingford – as he searched for the 13th sign of the zodiac that would help him get back to Norman times.

REGULAR CAST

Catweazle **Geoffrey Bayldon**
plus, Season One:
Carrot **Robin Davies**   *Mr Bennett (his father)* **Charles Tingwell**
Sam (a farmhand) **Neil McCarthy**
Season Two:
Cedric **Gary Warren**   *Groome* **Peter Butterworth**
Lord Collingford **Moray Watson**   *Lady Collingford* **Elspet Gray**

Created by **Richard Carpenter**
Writer: **Richard Carpenter**
Directors: **Quentin Lawrence** *(Season One)* **David Reed, David Lane** *(Season Two)*

Producers: **Quentin Lawrence** *(Season One)* **Carl Mannin (Season Two)**

Executive Producer (Season One): **Joy Whitby**
Associate producer (Season One): **Carl Mannin**

A London Weekend Television Production
26 colour 30-minute episodes

Season One
(13 episodes)

The Sun in a Bottle
Castle Saburac
The Curse of Rapkyn
The Witching Hour
The Eye of Time
The Magic Face
The Telling Bone
The Power of Adamcos
The Demi Devil
The House of the Sorcerer
The Flying Broomsticks

The Wisdom of Solomon
The Trickery Lantern

15 February–10 May 1970
(LWT)

Season Two
(13 episodes

The Magic Riddle
Duck Halt
The Heavenly Twins
The Sign of the Crab
The Black Wheels

The Wogle Stone
The Enchanted King
The Familiar Spirit
The Ghost Hunters
The Walking Trees

The Battle of the Giants
The Magic Circle
The Thirteenth Sign

10 January–4 April 1971
(LWT)

THE CHAMPIONS

'Craig Stirling, Sharron Macready, and Richard Barrett . . . *The Champions*. Endowed with the qualities and skills of super humans . . . qualities and skills, both physical and mental, to the peak of human performance. Gifts given to them by the unknown race of people from a lost city in Tibet. Gifts that are a secret to be closely guarded . . . a secret that enables them to use their powers to their best advantage . . . as . . . *The Champions* of Law, Order and Justice. Operators of the International Agency of Nemesis!

That opening narration said it all, really. *The Champions* were not superheroes in the comic-strip tradition, nor hi-tech heroes like *The Six Million Dollar Man* or *The Bionic Woman* (in 1968–9 who could afford the technology?). Rather they were three souped-up humans, whose physical and mental senses were heightened in the series' opening episode *The Beginning*, giving them phenomenal stamina, computer-like brainpower and dazzling insight, plus an ESP that bound them together like triplets.

Their organisation, Nemesis, was a small but powerful agency supported by all countries of the world but answerable to none, dedicated to preserving the balance of power. Thus, the Champions' missions were never trivial, dealing only with situations that might blossom into an international incident – from major-league crime, assassinations, power-politics, even the odd loopy scientist.

A cut above the regular adventure series of the day, *The Champions* also boasted three personable stars in American Stuart Damon, William Gaunt (a sitcom star of the 1980s) and the lovely Alexandra Bastedo. The fourth regular character was the trio's imperturbable boss Tremayne.

The men behind the series were Monty Berman, a producer with series such as *The Saint*, *Gideon's Way* and *The Baron* to his name; and Dennis Spooner, a prolific scriptwriter whose credits include Gerry Anderson's *Fireball XL5*, *Stingray* and *Thunderbirds* as well as a year as script editor on *Doctor Who*. He was also co-deviser of another contemporary thriller series, *Man in a Suitcase*.

The Champions ran for one 30-episode season and was still being repeated until well into the 1980s.

REGULAR CAST

Craig Stirling **Stuart Damon** Richard Barrett **William Guant**
Sharron Macready **Alexandra Bastedo**
Tremayne **Anthony Nicholls**

Created by: **Monty Berman** and **Dennis Spooner**
Producer: **Monty Berman**
Script editor: **Dennis Spooner**
Music: **Edwin Astley**

An ITC Production
30 colour 60-minute episodes
(originally shown in black and white)
25 September 1968–30 April 1969
(ATV-Midlands)

The Beginning

w **Dennis Spooner**
A trio of Nemesis agents are sent to steal a lethal bacteria from the Chinese. Their mission is successful but while trying to escape, their plane is damaged and crashes in the remote peaks of Tibet. There, mysterious rescuers heal the agents and endow them with greatly increased mental and physical powers.
Old man **Felix Aylmer**
Whittaker **Kenneth J. Warren**
Chislenkan **Joseph Furst**
Ho Ling **Eric Young**
Chinese major **Burt Kwouk**

Director: **Cyril Frankel**

The Invisible Man

w **Donald James**
Nemesis is tipped off that the proceeds of a vast bank robbery are to be placed in a Swiss bank. They must find out where the money is to be stolen from.
Hallam **Peter Wyngarde**
Sumner **James Culliford**
Sir Frederick **Basil Dignam**
Van Velden **Aubrey Morris**
Boursin **Steve Plytas**

Director: **Cyril Frankel**

Reply Box No. 666

w **Philip Broadley**
The Nemesis trio jet to the Caribbean to solve a mystery involving a Greek-speaking parrot and the murder of a French businessman.

Jules **Anton Rodgers**
Nikko **George Murcell**
Bourges **Brian Worth**
Corinne **Nike Arrighi**
Clive **Linbert Spencer**
Semenkin **George Roubicek**
Cleo **Imogen Hassall**

Director: **Cyril Frankel**

The Experiment

w **Tony Williamson**
A power-mad scientist experimenting with his own methods of creating super-powered humans, takes a special interest in Craig, Sharon and Richard.
Dr Glind **David Bauer**
Cranmore **Allan Cuthbertson**
Dr Margaret Daniels **Madalene Nicol**
Marion Grant **Caroline Blakiston**
Officer **Philip Bond**
Barman **Russell Waters**
Dr Farley **Nicholas Courtney**
Susan **Nita Lorraine**
Jean **Jonathan Burn**
Paul **Peter J. Elliott**

Director: **Cyril Frankel**

Happening

w **Brian Clemens**
An enemy organisation plots to destroy vast tracts of Australia, including Sydney, by coupling a second atom bomb to one being tested.
Banner **Jack MacGowran**
Gen. Winters **Grant Taylor**
Joss **Michael Gough**
Aston **Bill Cummings**

Director: **Cyril Frankel**

Operation Deep-Freeze

w Gerald Kelsey
Sent to Antarctica to investigate an atomic
blast, Craig and Richard are captured and
left to die in an icy underground chamber
by a tyrannical general who has set up a
secret missile base.
Gen. Gomez Patrick Wymark
Hemmings Robert Urquhart
Jost Walter Gotell
Margoli Peter Arne
Ship's captain Dallas Cavell
Col. Santos George Pastell
Mendoza Michael Godfrey
Gregson Martin Boddey
Zerilli Derek Sydney
Hoffner Alan White

Director: Paul Dickson

The Survivors

w Donald James
The Nemesis agents have to solve the
mystery of three murders in the Austrian
Alps believed to be linked with buried
Nazi treasure.
Emil Bernard Kay
Franz/Col. Reitz Clifford Evans
Richter Donald Houston
Schmeltz John Tate
Mine attendant Frederick Schiller
Hans John Porter Davison
Pieter Stephen Yardley
Heinz Hugo Panczak

Director: Cyril Frankel

To Trap a Rat

w Ralph Smart
The Champions follow a tricky trail to
track down the suppliers of tainted drugs.
Walter Pelham Guy Rolfe
Sandra Edina Ronay
Edwards Michael Standing
Peanut vendor Toke Townley
Jane Purcell Kate O'Mara
Ambulance doctor John Lee
Ambulanceman Michael Guest

Director: Sam Wanamaker

The Iron Man

w Philip Broadley
Sharron becomes a secretary to a deposed
dictator whose life is in jeopardy.
El Gaudillo George Murcell
Pedraza Patrick Magee
Callezon Robert Crewdson
Gen. Tornes Michael Mellinger
Carlos Stephen Berkoff
Cabello Norman Florence

Director: John Moxey

The Ghost Plane

w Donald James
A frustrated scientist's clash with official-
dom leads to him selling his secrets to a
foreign power – secrets that will provide
supremacy in the air.
Doctor John Newman Andrew Keir
Vanessa Hilary Tindall
Coates Michael Wynne
Bridges Dennis Chinnery
Hardwick Tony Steedman
Admiral Derek Murcott
Pilot Paul Grist
Crolic John Bryans

Director: John Gilling

The Dark Island

w Tony Williamson
The Champions investigate a fiendish plan
to sabotage the advance warning systems
of the superpowers and launch missiles
which threaten world peace.
Max Kellor Vladek Sheybal
Admiral Alan Gifford
Controller Bill Nagy
Perango Benito Carruthers
Kai Min Andy Ho
Radar operator Richard Bond

Director: Cyril Frankel

The Fanatics

w Terry Nation
Richard Barrett infiltrates a band of
dedicated assassins and learns that his

boss Tremayne is one of their intended victims.
Croft Gerald Harper
Col. Banks Donald Pickering
Anderson Julian Glover
Roger Carson David Burke
Krasner David Morrell
Faber Barry Stanton
Collings John Robinson

Director: John Gilling

Twelve Hours

w Donald James
A visiting politician is the victim of a bomb explosion in a submarine – and with the oxygen running out, Sharron must operate to save his life.
Raven Mike Pratt
Adm. Cox Peter Howell
Lt Cdr Street John Turner
Captain John Stone
Madame Drobnic Viola Keats
Drobnic Henry Gilbert
Jackson Laurie Asprey
Telegraphist Rio Fanning

Director: Paul Dickson

The Search

w Dennis Spooner
The Champions face the task of saving London from atomic destruction when a nuclear submarine is stolen.
Kruger Haller John Woodvine
Conrad Schultz Reginald Marsh
Dr Mueller Joseph Furst
Suzanne Taylor Patricia English
Allbrecht Ernst Walder
Innkeeper Gabor Baraker

Director: Leslie Norman

The Gilded Cage

w Philip Broadley
Richard Barrett is forced to break a code to save the life of a beautiful fellow prisoner.
Symons John Carson
Samantha Jennie Linden
Lovegrove Clinton Greyn

Orley Charles Houston
Brandon Tony Caunter
Haswell Sebastian Breaks
Manager Vernon Dobtcheff

Director: Cyril Frankel

Shadow of the Panther

w Tony Williamson
A voodoo mystery for the Champions in Haiti where a Nemesis scientist has died – apparently from fear.
Prengo Zia Mohyeddin
David Crayley Donald Sutherland
Riley Tony Wall
Charters Hedger Wallace
Doctor Christopher Carlos
Waiter Kenneth Gardiner

Director: Freddie Francis

A Case of Lemmings

w Philip Broadley
Nemesis investigates the apparent suicides of three Interpol agents.
Del Marco Edward Brayshaw
Umberto John Bailey
Claudine Jeanne Roland
Jacquet Michael Graham
Pillet Michael Slater
Madame Carnot Olive McFarland
Frenchman Jacques Cey
Frenchwoman Madge Brindley

Director: Paul Dickson

The Interrogation

w Dennis Spooner
Craig Stirling is caught up in a nightmare to which there seems no end. But is he dreaming or is it really happening?
Interrogator Colin Blakely

Director: Cyril Frankel

The Mission

w Donald James
A mission for tramps provides cover for a macabre organisation running escape routes for war criminals.

Hogan Dermot Kelly
Pederson Anthony Bate
Sophia Patricia Haines
George Harry Towb
Maltman Robert Russell
Emil Boder Paul Hansard

Director: Robert Asher

The Silent Enemy

w Donald James
The Champions go to sea on a macabre mission to reconstruct the voyage of a nuclear sub which has been found with its entire crew dead.
Capt. Baxter Paul Maxwell
Adm. Parker Warren Stanhope
Stanton James Maxwell
Minoes Marne Maitland
Minister Esmond Knight
Lighthouse keepers David Blake Kelly
Rio Fanning

Director: Robert Asher

The Body Snatchers

w Terry Nation
The Champions encounter eerie drama in Wales and defeat a strange spy plot.
Squires Bernard Lee
Inge Kalmutt Ann Lynn
Yeats Philip Locke
Frank Nicols J.G. Devlin
David Fenton Gregory Phillips
Lee Rogers Christine Taylor
White Fredric Abbott

Director: Paul Dickson

Get Me Out of Here

w Ralph Smart
The Nemesis trio are called in to rescue a girl doctor who is being held against her will.
Anna Maria Martes Frances Cuka
Commandante Ronald Radd
Angel Martes Philip Madoc
Minister Eric Pohlmann
Cuevos Anthony Newlands
Josef Godfrey Quigley

Police captain Norman Florence
Detective Richard Montez

Director: Cyril Frankel

The Night People

w Donald James
The superhumans come up against the supernatural in a mystery with sinister implications.
Douglas Trennick Terence Alexander
Mrs Trennick Adrienne Corri
Porth David Lodge
Jane Soames Anne Sharp
Dan Michael Bilton
George Whetlor Walter Sparrow
Hoad Jerold Wells
Clerk Frank Thornton

Director: Robert Asher

Project Zero

w Tony Williamson
Nemesis investigates when one scientist is murdered and many others disappear – victims of a remarkable series of kidnappings.
Voss Rupert Davies
Antrobus Peter Copley
Forster Geoffrey Chater
Grayson Reginald Jessup
Miss Davies Jan Holden
Postmaster Nicholas Smith
Sloane Donald Morley
Travis John Moore
Wittering Maurice Browning
Chairman John Horsley
Hedges Eric Lander
Stewardess Jill Curzon
Pilot Bruce Beeby

Director: Don Sharp

Desert Journey

w Ian Stuart Black
Danger in the desert for the superhumans who try to restore a young Arab to his throne.
The Bey Jeremy Brett
Yuseff Roger Delgado
Said Nik Zaran

Curtis Reg Lye
Branco Henry Soskin
Sheikh Peter Madden
Major Tuat Tony Cyrus
Sonia Yole Marinelli

Director: Paul Dickson

Full Circle

w Donald James
Craig poses as a prisoner and embarks on an escape plan with a fellow internee. But it leads to torture, not freedom.
Westerman Patrick Allen
Garcian Martin Benson
Booker John Nettleton
Sarah Gabrielle Drake
Carrington Jack Gwillim
Pickering James Donnelly
Sergeant Fairfax Lawrence James
Collins Victor Brooks

Director: John Gilling

The Nutcracker

w Philip Broadley
The Champions are called in to test security at a vault – but the vault is programmed to kill.
Duncan William Squire
Lord Mauncey David Langton
Manager Michael Barrington
Warre John Franklyn-Robbins
Walcott John Bown
Travers David Kelsey
Guard Dervis Ward
Assistant Robert Mill

Director: Roy Ward Baker

The Final Countdown

w Gerald Kelsey
Nemesis is charged with finding a World War Two atom bomb which could launch another major war.
Von Splitz Alan MacNaughtan
Dr Neimann Wolf Frees
Kruger Derek Newark
Wilf Eisen Basil Henson
Schultz Morris Perry
Anna Hannah Gordon
Heiden Norman Jones
Tom Brooks Michael Lees

Director: John Gilling

The Gun-Runners

w Dennis Spooner
Murder in the Burmese jungle takes the Champions into a gun-running mystery.
Hartington William Franklyn
Guido Selvamenti Paul Stassino
Filmer David Lodge
Schroeder Guy Deghy
Police captain Eric Young
Nadkarni Wolfe Morris
Clerk Nicolas Chagrin

Director: Robert Asher

Autokill

w Brian Clemens
The top men in Nemesis get the killing bug – even Tremayne is affected – and Richard finds himself programmed to kill Craig.
Barka Eric Pohlmann
Klein Paul Eddington
Doctor Amis Harold Innocent
George Brading Richard Owens
Loretta Brading Rachel Herbert
Mechanic Conrad Monk
American colonel Bruce Boa

Director: Roy Ward Baker

THE CHANGES

This ten-part BBC children's serial trod the same sort of ground as *Survivors*, but predated its adult cousin by four months.

Based on a trilogy of books by Peter Dickinson, it was a gripping story of a world overtaken by an (initially) unexplained pheno-

menon which makes people destroy the trappings of the technological age – televisions, phones, cars, etc – flee the cities and
revert to a less civilised existence.

Only a few people seem unaffected by the destructive com-
pulsion, including teenager Nicky Gore and a band of Sikhs.
Villain of the piece is Davy Gordon, a would-be feudal ruler who
attacks them and accuses Nicky of being a witch. She escapes with a
boy, Jonathan, on a barge, pursued by Gordon who drowns after a
tussle on the boat.

Finally, after being 'drawn' to a cavern, Nicky finds what has
caused *The Changes*. An eccentric inventor, Mr Furbelow, has
woken up the Necromancer, a 'living stone' which dates from the
age of Merlin. Roused from its centuries-long sleep, the Necromancer didn't like what it saw and sent out shock waves that forced
people to destroy the modern world. Nicky, being a naive,
innocent soul, is able to persuade the Necromancer to go back to
sleep, so that the world can 'return' to normal.

The Changes had an unusual start for a children's series: before
the first episode, the BBC broadcast a warning that it might not be
suitable for very young children. Shot entirely on location on
colour film, its style and content certainly set it apart from most
traditional kids' drama.

Main Cast

Nicky Gore **Vicky Williams**   *Jonathan* **Keith Ashton**
Davy Gordon **David Garfield**   *Chacha* **Rafiq Anwar**
Grandmother **Sahab Qizilbash**   *Kewal* **Marc Zuber**
Gopal **Rugby Brar**   *Ajeet* **Rebecca Mascarenhas**
Maxie **James Ottoway**   *Margaret* **Zuleika Robson**
Michael **Tom Chadbon**   *Mary* **Merelina Kendall**
Mr Furbelow **Oscar Quitak**

With

*Bernard Horsfall, Sonia Graham, Jeremy Conrad,
Clyde Pollitt, Bartlett Mullins, Arthur Hewlett,
David King, Nancy Gabrielle, Edward Brayshaw,
Derek Ware, Stella Tanner, Jack Watson,
Tony Hughes, Kenneth Gilbert, John D. Collins,
Roy Evans, Daphne Neville, Godfrey Jackman*

Writer: **Peter Dickinson**
Adapted by: **Anna Home**
Producer: **Anna Home**
Director: **John Prowse**
Music: **Paddy Kingsland**

A BBC Production
Ten colour 25-minute episodes

The Noise*
The Bad Wires

—

The Devil's Children
Hostages!
Witchcraft!
A Pile of Stones
Heartsease
Lightning!
The Quarry
The Cavern

6 January–10 March 1975

* (NB: The titles were billed in *Radio Times*, but were not seen on screen.)

CHILDREN OF THE DOG STAR

Six-part mystery thriller from New Zealand, described by its author as a 'kidult' series – meaning that it's light years away from the Famous Five.

Filmed entirely on location in South Auckland, New Zealand, it's the story of three children who discover various pieces of a prehistoric space probe and reassemble it – with electrifying results. Tied up with the mystery is a primeval swamp which ancient Maori legend holds to be 'tapu' – forbidden – warning that evil will befall whoever breaks the tapu.

The probe, called Kolob, had come to Earth 7000 years before, from the planet Sirius B in the constellation of Cannus Major. It was one of three remote-controlled argonauts despatched to monitor the progress of Man and, when the time was right, to teach him. The others had done their stuff, in Africa and the Americas. But Kolob had crashed in an area where humans came late to the land. Now, its memory banks warped and traumatised by the long centuries of inaction, it must find a way of putting itself back together, and seeks a mind open enough to be contacted, young enough to be controlled and powerful enough to be used . . . the mind of a child.

That child is Gretchen, an unusually bright 12-year-old with a consuming interest in astronomy. She comes to stay at her uncle's remote farm while her career scientist parents are overseas. With her two new-found friends, Ronny, a streetwise urban Maori boy, and Bevis, a shy bird-watcher, she becomes drawn into the mystery of Kolob. Ultimately, they confront the alien's probe master, the Siri-usians, and gain a brief, tantalising insight into life among the stars.

Also bound up in the tale is the conflict between the townspeople who want to develop the land around the swamp and the Maori population who want it to remain undisturbed.

Children of the Dog Star is an atmospheric series, engagingly underplayed with the extra-terrestrial adventures of the children neatly contrasted with the down-to-earth lives of the adults. Made in 1984 and first shown over here in a twice-weekly format in 1985, with a weekly repeat in 1988, the series won a Golden Gate Award (in America) for the Best Children's Programme of 1985.

It was author Ken Catran's second sci-fi 'kidult' series. He also adapted the novel *Under the Mountain* by Maurice Gee for Television New Zealand, and that series, not shown in Britain, was also directed by 'Dog Star' director Chris Bailey.

CAST

Gretchen Kierney **Sarah Dunn**   *Ronny Kepa* **Jason Wallace**
Bevis Elliott **Hamish Bartle**   *Donald Kierney* **Roy Billing**

Kathleen Kierney **Susan Wilson**   Helen Elliott **Catherine Wilkin**
Herbert Mitchell **Ray Hawthorne**   Vic Mitchell **David McKenzie**
Mataui Kepa **Zac Wallace**   Hemi **Whatanui Skipwith**
Constable Ben Willis **John Mellor**
Siriusians **Rodney Newman/Dennis Gubb** (Ep. 6 only)

Writer: **Ken Catran**
Producer: **Caterina de Nave**
Director: **Chris Bailey**
Designer: **Donald Sutherland**
Music: **Matthew Brown**

A Television New Zealand Production in association with Thames Television International
Six colour 30-minute episodes

The Brass Daisy
Power Stop
Swamp Light
Alien Summons
Kolob
Alien Contact

31 August–14 September 1985

CHILDREN OF THE STONES

Iain Cuthbertson, Gareth Thomas and Freddie Jones headed the cast of this 1977 seven-part mystery serial from HTV, centring on a 4000-year-old stone circle that hides a secret power.

The story is of a whole village held in curious mental slavery by the psychic forces that seem to be generated by a huge Neolithic stone circle. Scientist Adam Brake and his son Matthew arrive in Milbury and quickly notice that all the villagers are docile and placid, greeting each other with the soon-familiar 'Happy Day'. The only ones unaffected are a handful of newcomers such as themselves, and a half-crazed tramp called Dai who lives in an ancient earth-barrow, called The Sanctuary.

One by one, the new arrivals – Margaret the museum curator and her daughter Sandra, Dr Lyle and son Kevin, and a farmer, Browning, and his son Jimmo – are lured into the same state of euphoric happiness. At the centre of this bizarre web of psychic power is the village squire Hendrick, an astronomy professor who has discovered 'Hendrick's Nova', now simply a black hole, a mass of powerful gravitational force.

Soon, Adam realises that he and Matthew are the only 'untreated' people left in Milbury. They try to drive out of the stone circle, but their car inexplicably crashes. They recover in Hendrick's house where they discover that the secret of his psychic domination depends on the supernova being in line with the stone circle – a primitive power-house. Precise timing is essential but by upsetting that timing, Adam is able to break the spell and free the village.

Children of the Stones maintained HTV's reputation for quality children's drama. It was an intelligent, gripping mystery with serious, credible performances from the adult stars.

CAST

Hendrick Iain Cuthbertson   *Adam Brake* Gareth Thomas
Dai Freddie Jones   *Margaret* Veronica Strong
Matthew Peter Demin   *Sandra* Katharine Levy
Mrs Crabtree Ruth Dunnig   *Miss Clegg* June Barrie
Bob Ian Donnolly   *Kevin* Darren Hatch
Jimmo Gary Lock   *Mrs Warner* Peggy Ann Wood
Dr Lyle Richard Matthews   *Link* John Woodnutt

Writers: Jeremy Burnham, Trevor Ray
Director/Producer: Peter Graham Scott
Executive producer: Patrick Dromgoole
Designer: Ken Jones

An HTV Production
Seven colour 30-minute episodes

Into the Circle
Circle of Fear
Serpent in the Circle
The Narrowing Circle
Charmed Circle
Squaring the Circle
Full Circle

10 January–21 February 1977

CHOCKY

The *Chocky* stories were evidence that British-made television science fiction was alive and well, if somewhat hard to find in the 1980s.

Chocky was a highly intelligent alien who befriends Matthew, an ordinary English boy, existing, at first, as a voice inside his head. Chocky's presence unsettles Matthew and his family and leads eventually to a startling revelation.

The original story was written by John Wyndham and was the last work published before his death in 1969. Television writer Anthony Read updated the setting and gave Chocky a visual shape – a ball of glowing green energy. Following the success of the first series which topped the children's ratings, Wyndham's family gave their approval for the character to be developed. That led to the second and third series, *Chocky's Children* and *Chocky's Challenge*, which established the existence of other 'befriended' children around the world and then set about finding a solution to the world's energy problems.

REGULAR CAST

Matthew Gore Andrew Ellams   *David Gore (his father)* James Hazeldine
Mary Gore (his mother) Carol Drinkwater *(Series 1 and 2)*
Polly Gore (his sister) Zoe Hart *(Series 1 and 2)*

Albertine Meyer **Anabel Worrell** *(Series 2 and 3)*
Arnold Meyer **Prentis Hancock** *(Series 2 and 3)*
Chocky's voice **Glynis Brooks**

Producers: **Vic Hughes** *(Series 1 and 2),*
   Richard Bates *(Series 3)*
Executive producers: **Pamela Lonsdale**
   (Series 1 and 2), **Brian Walcroft**
   (Series 3)

Thames Television Productions
18 colour 30-minute episodes
Series One:
9 January–13 February 1984
Series Two:
7 January–11 February 1985
Series Three:
29 September–16 October (twice-weekly)

Series One:

Chocky

w **Anthony Read,** *from the novel by*
John Wyndham, *(A 6-part story)*
Twelve-year-old Matthew suddenly starts
talking to himself and doing things he
couldn't do before, such as binary code
maths. His parents think it's just a 'passing
phase' but Matthew tells them about
Chocky 'who lives inside his head'. The
family becomes increasingly unsettled –
especially when a holiday incident brings
unwelcome publicity and interest. Only
after Matthew has been hypnotised,
mysteriously kidnapped and interrogated,
does Chocky reveal her 'mission' – to
bring a new form of unlimited cosmic
power to Earth.
Mr Trimble **James Greene**
Colin **Devin Stanfield**
Jane **Kelita Groom**
Mark **Jonathan Jackson**
Roger **Peter John Bickford**
Susan **Catherine Elcombe**
Miss Blayde **Lynne Pearson**
Landis **Jeremy Bulloch**
Alan **Colin McCormack**
Phyl **Penny Brownjohn**
Sir William **John Grillo**

Directors: **Christopher Hodson, Vic**
   Hughes
Designer: **David Richens**

Series Two:

Chocky's Children

w **Anthony Read** *(A 6-part story)*
It's nearly a year since Chocky said goodbye to Matthew, and life appears to have
returned to normal for the Gore family.
But mysterious men are eavesdropping on
their telephone conversations and further
trouble lies ahead. Matthew goes on holiday to his Aunt Cissie's and while
exploring a nearby windmill meets an
unusual girl, Albertine. As their friendship grows, it becomes clear that Chocky
is involved and is seeking their help. But
the sinister Dr Deacon is out to learn their
secret and takes Albertine to his clinic.
Matthew goes to find her and the scene is
set for Chocky's Children from all over
the world to 'mentally' come to their
rescue.
Deacon **Ed Bishop**
Luke **Michael Crompton**
Landis **Jeremy Bulloch**
Aunt Cissie **Angela Galbraith**
Doctor **Brian de Salvo**

Directors: **Victor Hughes, Peter Duguid**
Designer: **David Richens**

Series Three:

Chocky's Challenge

w **Anthony Read** *(A 6-part story)*
Matthew and Albertine have continued
their studies, Matthew in art and Albertine
in maths at Cambridge. Chocky now feels
she can tell them about her seret plans to
solve the planet's energy problems. Under
her supervision, Albertine is to build the
world's first cosmic energy collector – a
source of unlimited power. But she will
need help, so Chocky brings in other
young children and they successfully
complete a prototype. But other, more

dangerous parties are interested, including the mysterious Mrs Gibson who offers to finance the work. Her true motive becomes clear when she traps Chocky and Paul inside the cosmic power pack.
Prof. Ferris **Richard Wordsworth**
Dr Liddle **Illona Linthwaite**
Prof. Draycott **Roy Boyd**
Prof. Wade **Kristine Howarth**

Mrs Gibson **Joan Blackham**
Mike **Freddie Brooks**
Su Lin **Karina Wilsher**
Paul **Paul Russell**
Chocky's parent **Norma Ronald**

Director: **Bob Blagden**
Designer: **Peter Elliott**

CITY BENEATH THE SEA

This seven-part children's serial took the stars of ITV's *Pathfinders* series on a new voyage – this time to 'inner space' and the subterranean city of Aegira.

Gerald Flood and Stewart Guidotti once again assumed the roles of science reporter Mark Bannerman and his assistant Peter Blake, which they'd played in the 1961 adventure story *Plateau of Fear* (see separate entry).

Aboard the atomic sub *Cyana* to observe the trials of a new underwater transmitter, Bannerman and Blake are captured by a pirate sub and taken to Aegira, the creation of fanatical scientist Professor Ludwig Ziebrecken who dreams of conquering the world by threatening to devastate its capital cities with rockets launched from his hidden base. Ziebrecken has a number of kidnapped scientists working for him including Dr Ann Boyd (Caroline Blakiston) who helps the resourceful duo to free Aegira and its people from the tyrant's rule.

The script was by John Lucarotti, later a regular contributor to *Doctor Who* and *The Avengers*, and also reunited *Plateau of Fear* director Kim Mills and producer Guy Verney. Playing a supporting role in the cast was Barry Letts before he found greater fame on the other side of the camera as a BBC director and producer, steering *Doctor Who* through its successful Jon Pertwee era.

(See also *Secret Beneath the Sea*.)

MAIN CAST

Mark Bannerman **Gerald Flood**   *Peter Blake* **Stewart Guidotti**
Dr Ann Boyd **Caroline Blakiston**   *Prof. Westfield* **Haydn Jones**
Prof. Ludwig Ziebrecken **Aubrey Morris**
Kurt Swendler (a pirate) **Dennis Goacher**   *Capt. Payne* **Peter Williams**
Radio operator **Morris Perry**   *Commander Bell* **Richard Clarke**
with: Commander Lennard **Barry Letts**   *Helmsman* **John Trenaman**
RN radio operators **Peter Gill, Clive Baxter**
Guards **Marshall Jones, Robert Hunter**   *Engineer* **Ian Parsons**

Writer: John Lucarotti
Producer: Guy Verney
Director: Kim Mills
Settings: James Goddard
Special effects: Derek Freeborn
Programme adviser: Mary Field

An ABC Television Network Production
Seven 30-minute episodes, black and
white

The Pirates
Escape to Aegira
Tide of Evil
Cellar of Fear
Power to Destroy
Operation Grand Design
Three Hours to Doomsday

17 November–29 December 1962

COME BACK MRS NOAH

Sitcom in space, from the creators of *'Allo, 'Allo* and *Are You Being Served*, which starred Mollie Sugden as a prize-winning, no-nonsense 21st-century housewife who wins a trip round Britain's new space station and gets accidentally launched into orbit along with a motley crew including 'roving reporter' Clive Cunliffe (Ian Lavender).

Jokes centred on Mrs Noah regarding the spaceship as no more complicated than a vacuum cleaner, as she and the others adjust to life in the 35,000 mph fast lane, and await the efforts of mission control to rescue them.

REGULAR CAST

Mrs Noah **Molly Sugden**   *Clive Cunliffe* **Ian Lavender**
Carstairs **Donald Hewlett**   *Fanshaw* **Michael Knowles**
Garstang **Joe Black**   *Garfield Hawk* **Tim Barrett**
Scarth Dare **Ann Michelle**   *TV presenter* **Gorden Kaye**
Technician **Jennifer Lonsdale**

Writers: Jeremy Lloyd, David Croft
Producer: David Croft
Director: Bob Spiers
Designers: Don Giles, Paul Trerise,
　Tony Snoaden

A BBC Production
Six colour 30-minute episodes
10 July–14 August 1978
(BBC1)
Episode One also shown as 'pilot',
13 December 1977

COUNTERSTRIKE

'A distant star. A dying planet. A race of
desperate men seeking another home, another
world to take over. One man is trying to stop
them. A man not of this world . . .'

Low-budget 1969 BBC series which relied on psychological thrills rather than hi-tech frills for its *Invaders*-style story of an alien threat to take over Earth.

Centauran refugees from a doomed planet have come to Earth where, for about 15 years, they've been preparing to destroy the human race to make room for their own people. Their approach is covert and based on acts of subversion, rather than on outright open warfare (thus obviating the need for expensive spacecraft, elaborate costumes and lavish effects).

But they've reckoned without the Inter Galactic Council, a kind of United Nations of Space, which sends one of its agents to Earth in the guise of Simon King. King, who comes from the same Centauran star system, possesses acute physical and mental attributes to help him counter the Centauran plots. He's aided in his campaign by Mary, a woman doctor who discovers his secret when she treats him after he's been injured in the first episode. And King's reference points back to his base are the various faces of 'Control', seen only on a triangular screen in his apartment.

The series was created by Tony Williamson, a well-known ITC contributor and previously script editor on *Adam Adamant Lives!*, and was one of the last of its kind to be recorded in black and white. The show was consistently rated in the top 20, but ended – with just nine of its ten episodes having been shown – one week before colour came to BBC1.

REGULAR CAST

Simon King Jon Finch   *Mary* Sarah Brackett

Created by: Tony Williamson
Producer: Patrick Alexander
Script editor: David Rolfe

A BBC Production
Ten 50-minute episodes, made in black and white
8 September–10 November 1969
(BBC1)

King's Gambit

w Patrick Alexander

Two apparently respectable businessmen running an electronics factory are investigated by a journalist called Simon King. But the businessmen turn out to be far from respectable aliens plotting to take over the Earth by paralysing the population. And King is an intergalactic agent sent to stop them.
Idris Evans Clive Merrison
Jill Angela Vincent
Sir Charles Cuttle Charles Durant

Jeffries Reg Whitehead
Armstrong Bernard Shine
Baldock Noel Johnson
Scaife Tom Kempinski
Dr Webber Brian Badcoe
Control Katie Fitzroy

Director: Vere Lorrimer
Designer: John Hurst

Joker One

w Ray Jenkins

Every war has its flashpoint. The

Centaurans think they've found one in a plane permanently stationed with a warhead on board, waiting for the attack command. They plan to send it off and so trigger an atomic war.

Paston **Alexis Chesnakov**
Pinot **Robert Beatty**
General **Bruce Boa**
Elaine Pinot **Barbara Shelley**
Flemyng **Tim Seely**
Control **Katie Fitzroy**

Director: **Henri Safran**
Designer: **Ian Rawnsley**

On Ice

w **Max Marquis**
Three scientists are mysteriously lost on a sledging party that sets out from a polar research station.

Garvin **David Jackson**
Dr Richards **Norman Claridge**
Dr Barker **Donald Pelmear**
Taffy Sadler **David Jason**
Dr Cross **Alexander John**
Len Bryant **Tom Watson**

Director: **Malcom Taylor**
Designer: **Ian Watson**

Nocturne

w **Anthony Skene**
Simon finds himself living in a nightmare between fantasy and reality when he is put to sleep and his dreams manipulated by the Centaurons who programme him to kill a scientist. (This was a reworking of Skene's own script for *The Prisoner* episode 'A, B & C'.)

Inspector **Neil Hallett**
Chairman **John Horsley**
Mother **Maria Aitken**
Jacey **Jenny McCracken**
Plunkett **Kevin Stoney**
Beavis **John Abineri**
Control **Fraser Kerr**
President **Jack Lambert**
Policeman **Keith James**
Secretary **April Walker**

Director: **Cyril Coke**
Designer: **Ian Watson**

Monolith

w **Anthony Skene**
A Centauran plot to murder the richest man in the world is centred on the biggest tower block in the centre of London, where the aliens run the dead man's business empire.

Outram **John Baskcomb**
Miss Roberts **Daphne Newton**
Mr Bentley **Colin Gordon**
Control **Anne Rutter**
Charwoman **Betty Woolfe**
Shaughnessy **Peter Bayliss**
Boland **Douglas Jones**
Carole **Carole Mowlam**

Director: **Henri Safran**
Designer: **Ian Rawnsley**

Out of Mind

w **David Cullen**, *from a story by* **Patricia Hooker**
Mary, visiting a village where she stayed as a child, finds that the woman who used to look after her, Hannah Webley, is now regarded by the superstitious villagers as a witch. Mary is soon caught up in the ensuing witch-hunt.

Hannah Webley **Hilary Mason**
Harry Carter **Michael Beint**
Control **Katie Fitzroy**
John Rossiter **Patrick Bedford**
PC Brookfield **Howard Goorney**
Jerry Randall **Freddie Earlle**
Chief of Control **Edward Brayshaw**

Director: **Henri Safran**
Designer: **Ian Rawnsley**

(This episode was dropped by the BBC in a late programme change but was not rescheduled. It remains unscreened – and the tape has since been erased.)

The Lemming Syndrome

w **Cyril Abraham**
A total of 143 people in one small seaside town commit suicide by drowning. Or were they under some strange and alien influence? Simon decides they were . . .

Control **Katie Fitzroy**
Sir George Halkyn **Anthony Sharp**

Everett **Denis Cleary**
Wyatt **James Villiers**
Pythian **Robert James**
Margo **Deirdre Costello**
Dr Merrow **Sonia Graham**
Norman **Bill Straiton**

Director: **Vere Lorrimer**
Designer: **Ian Watson**

Backlash

w **Paul Wheeler**
During a period of student riots, strong calls for a return to 'law and order' are made by General Falcon, a blood and guts Korean war veteran. As he starts to emerge as an important political figure capable of swaying public and government opinion, Simon King senses the hand of the Centaurans at work.
Jonathan Fry **Mark Edwards**
Housing minister **John Dawson**
Gold **James Beck**
Evans **Morris Perry**
Student **David Simeon**
Lord Falcon **Richard Hurndall**
Johnson **Roy Boyd**
Control **Katie Fitzroy**

Director: **Viktors Ritelis**
Designer: **David Spode**

All That Glistens

w **Adele Rose**
Adults start acting childishly – a grown man plays hopscotch and another falls off a rocking horse. Is there any connection between this and the Centauran plan to take over Earth? It seems unlikely, but Centauran plans usually do – until they start to work . . .
Dr Tate **Lindsay Campbell**
Mrs Sengupta **Nina Baden-Semper**
Bessie Collier **Mary Hignett**
Gwen Gilbert **Wendy Gifford**
Control **Fraser Kerr**
Tom Gilbert **Ian Dewar**
Josh Tetley **Frederick Arle**
Bill Pearce **Roy Pattison**
Esmé Hooper **Daphne Goddard**
Observer Africa **Oscar James**

Director: **Viktors Ritelis**
Designer: **John Hurst**

The Mutant

w **Dick Sharples**
A deadly new germ gets loose at a biological warfare laboratory. Can an antidote be found before the germs spread into a killer plague?
Fenton **Derrick Gilbert**
Alice Cranshaw **Marion Reed**
Brixham **Craig Hunter**
Grant **Arnold Diamond**
MacAllister **Sydney Conabere**
Henley **David Garth**
Lawson **Hedger Wallace**
Charlesworth **John Rapley**
Dr Leonard **David Rowlands**
Control **Meriel Fairburn**

Director: **William Sterling**
Designer: **John Hurst**

THE DAY OF THE TRIFFIDS

John Wyndham's deeply humanistic stories were a popular choice for television in the 1980s. ITV developed *Chocky* in 1984, and three years earlier the BBC turned in this successful six-part adaptation of *The Day of the Triffids*.

Wyndham's classic tale of evil plants taking over the world had been filmed before, as a melodramatic movie in 1963. The TV version was more low-key, almost sober in its approach, bringing out the author's main theme of mankind's response to a holocaust.

The story is told through the eyes of ex-triffid farmer Bill Masen (played by John Duttine, a popular BBC star after his central role in *To Serve Them All My Days*). It begins with Masen in a hospital ward, his eyes bandaged after a near miss from a triffid sting, waiting to know if his sight has been saved. Meanwhile a dazzling cosmic phenomenon in the night sky blinds the watching millions. Masen wake to find himself one of the few 'seeing' people in a world of blindness and panic increasingly menaced by the triffids which now start to roam the streets. He rescues a girl, Jo, from a street attack and they try to find others who are able to oppose the triffids.

A gang of blind scavengers led by Jack Coker provides an additional menace before Masen, Jo and their friends find refuge in a Sussex farmhouse where they prepare for their final confrontation with the triffids.

The monsters themselves were variously described as 'scarily effective' and 'a bunch of outsized plastic orchids left over from a Muppet show', but the series was generally well received.

MAIN CAST

Bill Masen John Duttine   *Jo* Emma Relph
Jack Coker Maurice Colbourne   *Dr Soames* Jonathan Newth
John Stephen Yardley   *Beadley* David Swift
Miss Durrant Perlita Neilson   *Torrence* Gary Olsen
Mary Brent Jenny Lipman   *Dennis Brent* Desmond Adams
Susan Emily Dean/Lorna Charles

Written by: John Wyndham
Adapted by: Douglas Livingstone
Producer: David Maloney
Director: Ken Hannam
Designer: Victor Meredith
Visual effects: Steve Drewett
Music: Christopher Gunning

A BBC Production
Six colour 30-minute episodes
10 September–15 October 1981

DIMENSION OF FEAR

Four-part ITV serial set in a peaceful English village, that took the favourite sci-fi theme of the extraordinary unsettling the ordinary to spin a tale of inter-dimensional menace.

Secrecy at the nearby research establishment, where the problems of feeding astronauts in space are being studied, has raised no more reaction among the villagers than idle gossip. Then the inexplicable deaths of two men – one the village carpenter, the other an astronaut in a space probe – raise the spectre of a threat to the world by powers of a fourth-dimensional world.

John Lucarotti scripted the tale which was shown on Saturday or Sunday nights – depending on which part of the country you lived in.

MAIN CAST

Dr Barbara Finch Katharine Blake   *Prof. Meredith* Peter Copley
Col. Alan Renton Robin Bailey   *Inspector Truick* Richard Coleman
Dolly Cheevers Jo Rowbottom   *Miss Reynolds* Margaret Ashcroft
Dr Leosser Mark Eden   *Dr Read* Peter Vaughan
with: *PC Dumphy* Michael Robbins   *Dr Bender* Hugh Dickson
Astronaut Michael Graham Cox   *Nurse* Mary Kay
Ferris Bruce Montague   *Police Sgt* Frank Peters
George Martin Donald Webster   *Ben Agnew* Neil Wilson
Locals Royston Tickner, Michael Darlow   *Technician* Richard Pescud
Police driver William Kendrick

Writer: John Lucarotti, *based on a story by* Berkely Mather
Settings: Patrick Downing
Story editor: George Kerr
Producer: Guy Verney
Director: Don Leaver

An ABC Television Network Production
Four 45-minute episodes, black and white

Thoughts of Death
Diagram of Death
Deltas of Death
Garden of Death

5–26 January 1963 (ATV, London)

DOCTOR WHO

'If you could touch the alien sand and hear the cries of strange birds, and watch them wheel in another sky – would that satisfy you?'

(The Doctor)

When a grouchy Time Lord, tired of the discipline and order of his home planet, Gallifrey, first stole a clapped-out TARDIS and fled with his granddaughter, he started a myth that has become embedded in television history.

Doctor Who has been the backbone of British TV science fiction for 26 years, an amazing legend of heroes and villains that has touched the dawn of time and peered over the edge of the universe.

It has been the mother ship for much of the creative talent to emerge in television fantasy over the past three decades – nearly everyone who's anyone has worked on the show – and it is now attracting the new writers and directors that will be vital if it is to survive, and thrive, into the 1990s.

Doctor Who was created in 1963 by the BBC's new Head of Drama, Sydney Newman. He had come to the Corporation from ABC Television where he had produced the successful *Armchair Theatre*, activated *The Avengers* and launched the ITV Sunday space sagas, *Target Luna* and *Pathfinders* (see separate entries).

As the new serial was to be for children, Newman wanted *Doctor Who* to have a high educational content in which the Doctor's travels would unroll the tapestry of history for his young audience. The space stories, too, had to be based on factual knowledge. And, quite definitely, no BEMs (Bug-Eyed Monsters). Almost immediatley, producer Verity Lambert and script editor David Whitaker turned up with Terry Nation's Daleks and *another* legend was born, with as much carpet worn out behind the country's sofas as in front of them.

By turns frightening and cosy, bleak and humorous, innovative and traditional, silly and cerebral, *Doctor Who* has evolved a format which allows it to do anything, go anywhere, with only the mode of transport unchanged – the TARDIS (Time and Relative Dimension in Space), still frozen as an old-fashioned police box.

The series' flexibility is at the heart of its success and longevity, and crucial to that is the changing face of the Doctor himself. When William Hartnell, the original Doctor, became too ill to play the part, the show faced a crisis – adapt or die. It adapted, by bringing in a new actor and explaining the change as a process of 'regeneration'. So far the Doctor is in his seventh incarnation and is allowed six more by the series' own Time Lord mythology. After that? Who knows.

Seven so far, though, and all different:

William Hartnell made him a man of mystery, a rather forbidding, tetchy Edwardian eccentric.
Patrick Troughton turned him into a Chaplinesque hobo in a funny hat and baggy check trousers, given to bursts of irrational behaviour to confound his foes.
Jon Pertwee brought a dash of the flamboyant dandy, all swirling cloaks and ruffled shirts as he raced to the rescue in his yellow roadster, Bessie.
Tom Baker took him back on the galactic road as a wide-eyed, curly-haired, grinning Gallifreyan rebel, an intellectual Bohemian in a floppy hat and flowing scarf.
Peter Davison was the most vulnerable – mild-mannered and sensitive, he wore his hearts on his Regency-coated sleeves and listened to his conscience.
Colin Baker's sixth Doctor was deliberately pitched to the other

extreme – arrogant, brash and abrasive – in a self-conscious effort to be different.

Sylvester McCoy is energetically steering the character out of the show's most troubled period since it was nearly axed by Michael Grade back in 1985. But with seasons now lasting just 14 episodes, it's much harder to establish a presence than in the old days when *Doctor Who* ran for up to ten months of the year.

But however often he appears, the Doctor has never travelled alone. Right from the start he has shared his adventures with one or more companions, many of whom have become nearly as famous as the Time Lord himself.

At first there were the schoolteachers, Ian and Barbara, plus his granddaughter, Susan. Then the accent settled firmly on youth – mostly attractive and female. The Who Girls have included the orphaned Victoria, brainy Zoe, scientist Liz Shaw, leggy Jo Grant, liberated Sarah Jane, the warrior Leela, Time Lady Romana, gentle aristocrat Nyssa, the Aussie 'mouth on legs' Tegan, curvy Peri, strident Mel and the streetwise Ace. They've run the gamut of female stereotypes from the screamers and ankle sprainers to the stubborn, independent misses.

There have been far fewer male companions, but the best have been the young Scot Jamie, the artful dodger Adric and the ambivalent alien Turlough. Not forgetting, of course, the loyal men of UNIT, led by Brigadier Lethbridge-Stewart, and the canine robot, K9.

And the show has spawned many memorable villains and monsters in its 26 years. Top of the list are the Daleks 'little green blobs in bonded polycarbite armour' and their creator Davros; others include the Cybermen, the Sontarans, the Ice Warriors, the Yeti, the Autons, the Sea Devils, the Terileptils, the Tractators, the slug-like Sil and the confectioner's nightmare, the Kandyman.

Then there are the humanoid villains, led by the Doctor's indestructible nemesis, the Master. He's one of several renegade Time Lords who have troubled the Doctor – others have been Omega, Borusa, the Rani and the Valeyard.

Danger has also come from without: in its time *Doctor Who* has been derided by critics, vilified by squeamish watchdogs and seen its audience ebb and flow. Its highest average viewing figure was 14.5m for the 1979 story *City of Death* (peaking at 16.1m for episode four), the lowest just 3.1m for the first episode of the season 26 opener, *Battlefield*.

The programme has undoubtedly declined in importance – yet rarely has its presence been more significant. It is, at the time of going to press, the only British science fiction series in production.

REGULAR CAST
(See episode guide)

Created by: **Sydney Newman**
Original theme: **Ron Grainer**

A BBC Production
To date: 695 episodes (25-minute unless stated)
black and white (Seasons 1–6)
colour (from Season 7)
UK premiere: 23 November 1963

Current producer: *John Nathan-Turner*
(since Season 18)

(Author's note: Stories up to and including *The Gunfighters* in Season Three were originally identified by their separate episode titles, but for means of easy reference, have since become known collectively by the titles given here.)

The First Doctor: **WILLIAM HARTNELL**

(1963–1966)

Season One
(23 November 1963–12 September 1964)

REGULAR CAST
The Doctor **William Hartnell**   *Susan Foreman* **Carole Ann Ford**
Ian Chesterton **William Russell**   *Barbara Wright* **Jacqueline Hill**

Producer: **Verity Lambert**
Associate producer: **Mervyn Pinfield**
Story editor: **David Whitaker**

An Unearthly Child/The Tribe of Gum

w **Anthony Coburn, C.E. Weber** *(Ep. 1 only) (A 4-part story)*
Curious about the knowledge displayed by one of their pupils, Susan Foreman, two teachers go to investigate her home – the TARDIS – and meet her grandfather. So begins an adventure in space and time which takes them back to the Stone Age and a tribal power struggle over the secret of fire.
Za **Derek Newark**
Hur **Alethea Charlton**
Kal **Jeremy Young**
Horg **Howard Lang**
Old mother **Eileen Way**

Director: **Waris Hussein**
Designers: **Peter Brachaki** *(Ep. 1)*, **Barry Newbery** *(Eps 2–4)*

An Unearthly Child

The Cave of Skulls
The Forest of Fear
The Firemaker

(23 November–14 December 1963)
NB: There also exists a pilot version, recorded but never transmitted, of 'An Unearthly Child'.

The Daleks (aka The Dead Planet)

w **Terry Nation** *(A 7-part story)*
The TARDIS lands on the planet Skaro where the travellers become involved in the conflict between opposing survivors of centuries of neutronic war – the aryan Thals and the dreadfully mutated Daleks. (Filmed as *Doctor Who and the Daleks*, with Peter Cushing.)
Temmosus **Alan Wheatley**
Ganatus **Philip Bond**
Alydon **John Lee**
Antodus **Marcus Hammond**

Elyon Gerald Curtis
Dyoni Virginia Wetherell
Dalek voices David Graham, Peter
Hawkins

Directors: Christopher Barry *(Eps 1–2,
4–5)*, Richard Martin *(Eps 3, 6, 7)*
Designers: Raymond Cusick *(Eps 1–5,
7)*, Jeremy Davies *(Ep. 6)*

The Dead Planet
The Survivors
The Escape
The Ambush
The Expedition
The Ordeal
The Rescue

(21 December 1963–1 February 1964)

The Edge of Destruction (aka Beyond the Sun or Inside the Spaceship)

w David Whitaker *(A 2-part story)*
The Doctor juggles with the controls and
the TARDIS is hurled back to the dawn of
time.
(Regular cast only.)

Directors: Richard Martin *(Ep. 1)*,
Frank Cox *(Ep. 2)*

The Edge of Destruction
The Brink of Disaster

(8–15 February 1964)

Marco Polo

w John Lucarotti *(A 7-part story)*
Landing in medieval China, the travellers
join Marco Polo on his way to the court of
Kublai Khan where the Doctor gambles
away the TARDIS.
Marco Polo Mark Eden
Tegana Derren Nesbitt
Ping-Cho Zienia Merton
Kublai Khan Martin Miller
Ling-Tau Paul Carson
Chenchu Jimmy Gardner
Empress Claire Davenport

Directors: Waris Hussein *(Eps 1–3, 5–7)*,
John Crockett *(Ep. 4)*
Designer: Barry Newbery

The Roof of the World
The Singing Sands
Five-Hundred Eyes
The Wall of Lies
Rider from Shang-tu
Mighty Kublai Khan
Assassin at Peking

(22 February–4 April 1964)

The Keys of Marinus

w Terry Nation *(A 6-part story)*
On the strange world of Marinus, the
Doctor and his companions become in-
volved in a quest for four lost keys to the
Conscience of Marinus – which are also
sought by the evil Voord.
Arbitan George Coulouris
Altos Robin Phillips
Sabetha Katharine Schfield
Voice of Morpho Heron Carvie
Darrius Edmund Warwick
Vasor Francis de Woolf
Yartek Stephen Dartnell

Director: John Gorrie
Designer: Raymond P. Cusick

The Sea of Death
The Velvet Web
The Screaming Jungle
The Snows of Terror
Sentence of Death
The Keys of Marinus

(11 April–16 May 1964)

The Aztecs

w John Lucarotti *(A 4-part story)*
The TARDIS lands in Mexico – at the
height of the beautiful but bloodthirsty
Aztec empire, and Barbara is mistaken for
the reincarnation of a high priest.
Autloc Keith Pyott
Tlotoxl John Ringham
Ixta Ian Cullen
Cameca Margot van der Burgh
Tanila Walter Randall
Perfect victim André Boulay
Warrior captain David Anderson

Director: John Crockett
Designer: Barry Newbery

The Temple of Evil
The Warriors of Death
The Bride of Sacrifice
The Day of Darkness

(23 May–13 June 1964)

The Sensorites

w Peter R. Newman *(A 6-part story)*
After landing on the deck of a spaceship from Earth in the 28th century, the travellers help a telepathic race, the Sensorites, overcome an illness which is striking their planet.
John Stephen Dartnell
Carol Ilona Rodgers
Maitland Lorne Cossette
Senorites: Ken Tyllsen, Joe Greig, Peter Glaze, Arthur Newall
First Elder Eric Francis
Second Elder Bartlett Mullins

Directors: Mervyn Pinfield *(Eps 1–4)*, Frank Cox *(Eps 5–6)*
Designer: Raymond P. Cusick

Strangers in Space
The Unwilling Warriors
Hidden Danger
A Race Against Death
Kidnap
A Desperate Venture

(20 June–1 August 1964)

The Reign of Terror

w Dennis Spooner *(A 6-part story)*
Spy story set in the time of the French Revolution with the Doctor and his associates getting involved in a 'Pimpernel' style plot to save people from the guillotine.
Lemaitre James Cairncross
Jean Roy Herrick
Jules Renan Donald Morley
Robespierre Keith Anderson
Physician Ronald Pickup
Jailer Jack Cunningham
Leon Colbert Edward Brayshaw
Rouvray Laidlaw Dalling
Judge Howard Charlton
Webster Jeffrey Wickham
Danielle Caroline Hunt
Napoleon Tony Wall

Director: Henric Hirsch
(Ep. 6 directed, uncredited, by Tim Coombe *when Hirsch collapsed before recording)*
Designer: Roderick Laing

A Land of Fear
Guests of Madame Guillotine
A Change of Identity
The Tyrant of France
A Bargain of Necessity
Prisoners of Conciergerie

(8 August–12 September 1964)

Season Two
(31 October 1964–24 July 1965)

REGULAR CAST

As Season One, plus: Vicki Maureen O'Brien *(from Story 3)*

Producer: Verity Lambert
Associate producer: Mervyn Pinfield *(to Story 4)*

Story editors: David Whitaker *(Stories 1–2)*, Dennis Spooner *(Stories 3–8)*, Donald Tosh *(Story 9)*

Planet of Giants

w Louis Marks *(A 3-part story)*
The travellers find themselves miniaturised and thwart the crooked scheme of an insecticide manufacturer.
Forester Alan Tilvern
Farrow Frank Crawshaw
Smithers Reginald Barrat
Hilda Rowse Rosemary Johnson
Bert Rowse Fred Ferris

Directors: Mervyn Pinfield, Douglas Camfield *(Ep. 3)*

Designer: Raymond P. Cusick

Planet of Giants
Dangerous Journey
Crisis

(31 October–14 November 1964)

The Dalek Invasion of Earth

w Terry Nation *(A 6-part story)*
Landing on Earth in 2167, the Doctor and
his companions confront the conquering
Daleks who have turned Bedfordshire
into a vast mine, from which they plan to
extract the Earth's core. At the end,
Susan elects to remain behind with the
victorious freedom-fighters. (Filmed as
Daleks: Invasion Earth 2150AD.)
Carl Tyler Bernard Kay
David Campbell Peter Fraser
Dortmun Alan Judd
Jenny Ann Davies
Larry Madison Graham Rigby
Wells Nicholas Smith
Robomen Martyn Huntley, Peter
   Badger

Director: Richard Martin
Designer: Spencer Chapman

World's End
The Daleks
Day of Reckoning
The End of Tomorrow
The Waking Ally
Flashpoint

(21 November–26 December 1964)

The Rescue

w David Whitaker *(A 2-part story)*
On the planet Dido, the Doctor en-
counters two survivors of a crashed space-
ship and unmasks a murderer.
Vicki Maureen O'Brien *(intro)*
Bennett/Koquillion Ray Barrett *(alias
   Sydney Wilson)*
Space captain Tom Sheridan

Director: Christopher Barry
Designer: Raymond P. Cusick

The Powerful Enemy
Desperate Measures

(2–9 January 1965)

The Romans

w Dennis Spooner *(A 4-part story)*
The TARDIS trips back to ancient Rome
where the Doctor's meeting with Nero
results in the Great Fire of Rome.
Sevcheria Derek Sydney
Ascaris Barry Jackson
Delos Peter Diamond
Tavius Michael Peake
Nero Derek Francis
Poppaea Kay Patrick

Director: Christopher Barry
Designer: Raymond P. Cusick

The Slave Traders
All Roads Lead to Rome
Conspiracy
Inferno

(16 January–6 February 1965)

The Web Planet

w Bill Strutton (A 6 part-story)
To the planet Vortis . . . and a war
between the ant-like Zarbi and the butter-
fly creatures, the Menoptra.
Vrestin Roslyn de Winter
Hrostar Arne Gordon
Prapillus Jolyon Booth
Hlynia Jocelyn Birdsall
Hilio Martin Jarvis
Animus voice Catherine Fleming
Zarbi Robert Jewell, Jack Pitt, Gerald
   Taylor, Hugh Lund, Kevin Manser,
   John Scott Martin

Director: Richard Martin
Designer: John Wood

The Web Planet
The Zarbi
Escape to Danger
Crater of Needles
Invasion
The Centre

(13 February–20 March 1965)

The Crusades

w David Whitaker *(A 4-part story)*
Into the past . . . to the 12th-century crusades and the conflict between Richard the Lionheart and the Saracens.
El Akir Walter Randall
Richard the Lionheart Julian Glover
Ben Daheer Reg Pritchard
William de Tornebu Bruce Wightman
Saphadin Roger Avon
Saladin Bernard Kay
Joanna Jean Marsh
Chamberlain Robert Lankesheer

Director: Douglas Camfield
Designer: Barry Newbery

The Lion
The Knight of Jaffa
The Wheel of Fortune
The Warlords

(27 March–17 April 1965)

The Space Museum

w Glyn Jones *(A 4-part story)*
The TARDIS lands on the planet Xeros which has been turned into a space museum by the Moroks, and the travellers aid the rebelling Xerons.
Sita Peter Sanders
Dako Peter Craze
Lobos Richard Shaw
Tor Jeremy Bulloch
Morok commander Ivor Salter
Dalek voice Peter Hawkins

Director: Mervyn Pinfield
Designer: Spencer Chapman

The Space Museum
The Dimensions of Time
The Search
The Final Phase

(24 April–15 May 1965)

The Chase

w Terry Nation *(A 6-part story)*
Experimenting with a space-time visual-
iser taken from Xeros, the Doctor sees the Daleks in pursuit and a frantic chase through time ensues, ending with a battle on the planet of the Mechonoids, where the Doctor loses two companions (Ian and Barbara, who return to their own time) and gains a new one . . .
Dalek voices Peter Hawkins, David Graham
Rynian Hywel Bennett
Morton Dill Peter Purves
Capt. Briggs David Blake Kelly
Grey Lady Roslyn de Winter
Robot Dr Who Edmund Warwick
Mechonoid voice David Graham
Steven Taylor Peter Purves *(intro)*

Director: Richard Martin
Designers: Raymond P. Cusick, John Wood

The Executioners
The Death of Time
Flight Through Eternity
Journey Into Terror
The Death of Doctor Who
The Planet of Decision

(22 May–26 June 1965)

The Time Meddler

w Dennis Spooner *(A 4-part story)*
Materialising on the Northumbrian coast in 1066, the travellers come up against the Monk, another time traveller from the Doctor's planet, who is planning to change the outcome of the Battle of Hastings.
Steven Taylor Peter Purves
The Monk Peter Butterworth
Edith Alethea Charlton
Eldred Peter Russell
Wulnoth Michael Miller
Ulf Norman Hartley
Sven David Anderson

Director: Douglas Camfield
Designer: Barry Newbery

The Watcher
The Meddling Monk
A Battle of Wits
Checkmate

(3–24 July 1965)

Season Three
(11 September 1965–16 July 1966)

REGULAR CAST

The Doctor **William Hartnell**   Vicki **Maureen O'Brien** (exit Story 3)
Steven Taylor **Peter Purves**   Dodo Chaplet **Jackie Lane** (from Story 5)

Producers: **Verity Lambert** (Stories 1–2), **John Wiles,** (Stories 3–6), **Innes Lloyd** (from Story 7)

Story editors: **Donald Tosh** (to Story 5, Ep. 3), **Gerry Davis** (from Story 5, Ep. 4)

Galaxy Four

w **William Emms** (A 4-part story)
The Doctor, Steven and Vicki land on a doomed planet where they help the peace-loving Rills and their robots, the Chumblies, defeat the evil, women-dominated Drahvins.
Maaga **Stephanie Bidmead**
Drahvin One **Marina Martin**
Drahvin Two **Susanna Carroll**
Drahvin Three **Lyn Ashley**
Chumblies **Jimmy Kaye, William Shearer, Angelo Muscat, Pepi Poupee, Tommy Reynolds**
Rill voice **Robert Cartland**
Garvey **Barry Jackson**

Director: **Derek Martinus**
Designer: **Richard Hunt**

Four Hundred Dawns
Trap of Steel
Air Lock
The Exploding Planet

(11 September–2 October 1965)

Mission to the Unknown

w **Terry Nation** (One episode)
No regulars – this episode served as a one-act hint of things to come. On the planet Kembel, agent Marc Cory of the Space Special Security Service discovers that the Daleks are plotting a concerted alien attack on the Solar System. He is killed, but a tape of his findings survives . . .
Marc Cory **Edward de Souza**
Jeff Garvey **Barry Jackson**
Gordon Lowery **Jeremy Young**

Malpha **Robert Cartland**
Dalek voices **David Graham, Peter Hawkins**
Daleks **Robert Jewell, Kevin Manser, John Scott-Martin, Gerald Taylor**

Director: **Derek Martinus**
Designers: **Richard Hunt, Raymond P. Cusick**

(9 October 1965)

The Myth Makers

w **Donald Cotton** (A 4-part story)
Landing in the midst of the Trojan War, the Doctor helps Achilles defeat Hector, is taken for a god, and masterminds the fall of Troy. Vicki falls in love with Troilus and stays behind.
Achilles **Cavan Kendall**
Odysseus **Ivor Salter**
Agamemnon **Francis de Woolf**
Menelaus **Jack Melford**
Cyclops **Tutte Lemkow**
King Priam **Max Adrian**
Paris **Barrie Ingham**
Cassandra **Frances White**
Troilus **James Lynn**
Katarina **Adrienne Hill** (intro)

Director: **Michael Leeston-Smith**
Designer: **John Wood**

Temple of Secrets
Small Prophet, Quick Return
Death of a Spy
Horse of Destruction

(16 October–6 November 1965)

The Dalek Masterplan

w Terry Nation, Dennis Spooner *(Eps 6, 8–12) (A 12-part story)*
The TARDIS lands in the jungles of Kembel in the year 4000. The doctor finds Cory's tape and meets another Earth agent, Bret Vyon. They discover that Mavic Chen, Guardian of the Solar System, has betrayed Earth to the Daleks, enabling them to build an awesome weapon, the Time Destructor. In a protracted struggle, the Doctor, aided by Vyon's sister, Sara Kingdom, is impeded by an old foe, the Meddling Monk. Fatalities: Katarina, Sara and Bret Vyon. (Nicholas Courtney, who played Vyon, reappeared three years later as the Brigadier.)
Bret Vyon Nicholas Courtney
Mavic Chen Kevin Stoney
Sarah Kingdom Jean Marsh
Katarina Adrienne Hill
The Meddling Monk Peter Butterworth
Trantis Roy Evans
Malpha Bryan Mosley

Director: Douglas Camfield
Designers: Raymond P. Cusick *(Eps 1–2, 5–7, 11)* Barry Newbery *(Eps 3–4, 8–10, 12)*

The Nightmare Begins
Day of Armageddon
Devil's Planet
The Traitors
Counter-Plot
Coronas of the Sun
The Feast of Steven*
Volcano
Golden Death
Escape Switch
The Abandoned Planet
Destruction of Time

(13 November 1965–29 January 1966)

* This episode was a Christmas story, set on Earth.

The Massacre of St Bartholomew's Eve

w John Lucarotti *(Eps 1–4)*, Donald Tosh *(Ep. 4) (A 4-part story)*
The travellers land in the middle of the bitter 16th-century feud between the Catholics and Protestants in France – culminating in the bloody massacre of St Bartholomew's Eve.
Nicholas David Weston
Anne Annette Robertson
Abbot of Amboise William Hartnell
Marshal Tavannes André Morell
Admiral de Coligny Leonard Sachs
Catherine de Medici Joan Young
Toligny Michael Bilton
Dodo Jackie Lane *(intro, Ep. 4)*

Director: Paddy Russell
Designer: Michael Young

War of God
The Sea Beggar
Priest of Death
Bell of Doom

(5–26 February 1966)

The Ark

w Paul Erickson, Lesley Scott *(A 4-part story)*
Having picked up Dodo on a brief stop in Wimbledon at the end of the previous story, the TARDIS now materialises on a gigantic space ark in the far future, carrying the human population of a doomed Earth (the Guardians) and their slaves (the Monoids) to a new planet. In a tale of two halves, spanning 700 years, the Doctor teaches the two groups to live in peace together and finds a cure for the common cold.
Commander Eric Elliott
Zentos Inigo Jackson
Manyak Roy Spencer
Monoids Edmund Coulter, Frank George
Rhos Michael Sheard
Maharis Terence Woodfield
Dassuk Brian Wright

Director: Michael Imison
Designer: Barry Newbery

The Steel Sky
The Plague
The Return
The Bomb

(5–26 March 1966)

The Celestial Toymaker

w Brian Hayles (uncredited additional material by Gerry Davis) *(A 4-part story)*
The Doctor and his companions materialise in the domain of the malevolent mandarin The Celestial Toymaker who forces them to play some bizarre games for their freedom.
The Toymaker Michael Gough
Clowns Campbell Singer, Carmen Silvera
The Hearts Peter Stephens, Reg Lever
Cyril Peter Stephens

Director: Bill Sellars
Designer: John Wood

The Celestial Toyroom
The Hall of Dolls
The Dancing Floor
The Final Test

(2–23 April 1966)

The Gunfighters

w Donald Cotton *(A 4-part story)*
Back in time again, to the Wild West and the gunfight at the OK Corral between the Earps and the Clantons.
Ike Clanton William Hurndell
Phineas Clanton Maurice Good
Billy Clanton David Cole
Seth Harper Shane Rimmer
Wyatt Earp John Alderson
Doc Holliday Anthony Jacobs
Bat Masterson Richard Beale
Pa Clanton Reed de Rouen
Johnny Ringo Laurence Payne

Director: Rex Tucker
Designer: Barry Newbery

A Holiday for the Doctor
Don't Shoot the Pianist
Johnny Ringo
The OK Corral

(30 April–21 May 1966)

The Savages

w Ian Stuart Black *(A 4-part story)*
Arriving on a distant planet, the travellers find an advanced civilisation, the Elders, formed by transferring the life-force of the primitive, cave-dwelling Savages to their people. After helping to bring the two races together, Steven elects to stay on as their leader.
Chal Ewen Solon
Tor Patrick Godfrey
Capt. Edal Peter Thomas
Exorse Geoffrey Frederick
Jano Frederick Jaeger
Nanina Clare Jenkins
Senta Norman Henry
Wylda Edward Caddick

Director: Christopher Barry
Designer: Stuart Walker

(28 May–18 June 1966)

The War Machines

w Ian Stuart Black, *from an idea by* Kit Pedler *(A 4-part story)*
In London, the Doctor fights the menace of WOTAN, a highly sophisticated computer housed in the Post Office Tower, which plans to take over the world with mobile computers called War Machines. He loses Dodo, but gains two new companions – cockney seaman Ben and dolly secretary Polly. This was the first story set in the present day.
Prof. Brett John Harvey
Major Green Alan Curtis
Polly Anneke Wills *(intro)*
Ben Michael Craze *(intro)*
Sir Charles Summer William Mervyn
Prof. Krimpton John Cater
Kitty Sandra Bryant
Newsreader Kenneth Kendall

Director: Michael Ferguson
Designer: Raymond London

(25 June–16 July 1966)

Season Four
(10 September 1966–1 July 1967)

REGULAR CAST

The Doctor **William Hartnell** *(Stories 1–2)/***Patrick Troughton** *(from Story 3)*
Polly **Anneke Wills** *(to Story 8)*   *Ben* **Michael Craze** *(to Story 8)*
Jamie **Frazer Hines** *(from Story 4)*

Producer: **Innes Lloyd**
Associate producer: **Peter Bryant**
  (Story 8)

Story editors: **Gerry Davis** *(to Story 9,*
  Ep. 3), **Peter Bryant** *(Story 9, Eps 4–7)*

The Smugglers

w **Brian Hayles** *(A 4-part story)*
Landing on a remote stretch of the Cornish coast in the 17th century, the Doctor and Co. find themselves in conflict with treasure-hunting pirates and local smugglers.
Cherub **George A. Cooper**
Squire **Paul Whitsun-Jones**
Capt. Pike **Michael Godfrey**
Blake **John Ringham**
Jacob Kewper **David Blake Kelly**
Tom **Mike Lucas**

Director: **Julia Smith**
Designer: **Richard Hunt**

(10 September–1 October 1966)

The Tenth Planet

w **Kit Pedler, Gerry Davis** *(Eps 3–4) (A 4-part story)*
The TARDIS materialises at the South Pole in the late 1980s and the Doctor confronts a new enemy – the Cybermen, invaders from the tenth planet, Mondas, who want to destroy Earth and turn its people into Cybermen, too. The Cybermen are defeated, but the Doctor is worn out and begins to change . . .
General Cutler **Robert Beatty**
Dyson **Dudley Jones**
Barclay **David Dodimead**
Wigner **Steve Plytas**
Radar technician **Christopher Matthews**
Cybermen voices **Roy Skelton, Peter Hawkins**

Director: **Derek Martinus**
Designer: **Peter Kindred**

(8–29 October 1966)

THE SECOND DOCTOR: **PATRICK TROUGHTON**
(1966–1969)

The Power of the Daleks

w **David Whitaker** *(plus uncredited additional material by* **Dennis Spooner)** *(A 6-part story)*
On the Earth colony of Vulcan in the distant future, the Doctor finds apparently servile Daleks, but the treacherous beings have set up a secret reproduction plant.
Quinn **Nicholas Hawtrey**

Bragen **Bernard Archard**
Lesterson **Robert James**
Janley **Pamela Ann Davy**
Hensell **Peter Bathurst**
Valmar **Richard Kane**
Kebble **Steven Scott**

Director: **Christopher Barry**
Designer: **Derek Dodd**

(5 November–10 December 1966)

The Highlanders

w Elwyn Jones, Gerry Davis (A 4-part story)

Landing at Culloden in 1746, The Doctor, Ben and Polly get caught up with a group of Highlanders fleeing from the Redcoats and avoid a one-way ticket on a prison ship to the West Indies. Piper Jamie McCrimmon turns the Tardis trio into a quartet . . .

The Laird Donald Bisset
Jamie Frazer Hines (intro)
Kirsty Hannah Gordon
Lt Algernon ffinch Michael Elwyn
Sergeant Peter Welch
Solicitor Grey David Garth
Perkins Sydney Arnold
Trask Dallas Cavell

Director: Hugh David
Designer: Geoff Kirkland

(17 December 1966–7 January 1967)

The Underwater Menace

w Geoffrey Orme (A 4-part story)

Materialising on an extinct volcano in the middle of the ocean, the travellers are captured and taken far underground to the lost city of Atlantis. There they meet Prof. Zaroff, a scientist who is planning to drain the Atlantic Ocean into the white-hot core of the Earth.

Ara Catherine Howe
Ramo Tom Watson
Lolem Peter Stephens
Damon Colin Jeavons
Zaroff Joseph Furst
Jacko Paul Anil
Sean P.G. Stephens

Director: Julia Smith
Designer: Jack Robinson

(14 January–4 February 1967)

The Moonbase

w Kit Pedler (A 4-part story)

On the Moon, in the year 2070, the Doctor discovers that the Cybermen are determined to tamper with the Gravitron – a machine which controls the weather on Earth – to wreak climatic havoc on the planet.

Hobson Patrick Barr
Benoit André Maranne
Nils Michael Wolf
Sam John Rolfe
Dr Evans Alan Rowe
Cybermen John Wills, Peter Greene, Keith Goodman, Reg Whitehead, Sonnie Willis

Director: Morris Barry
Designer: Colin Shaw

(11 February–4 March 1967)

The Macra Terror

w Ian Stuart Black (A 4-part story)

On a planet run like a holiday camp, the Doctor and his friends meet a man called Medok who tells them the paradise is being infiltrated by a mysterious race of giant crabs.

Pilot Peter Jeffrey
Sunnaa Jane Enshawe
Medok Terence Lodge
Ola Gertan Klauber
Controller Graham Leaman
Control voice Denis Goacher
Macra operator Robert Jewell

Director: John Davies
Designer: Kenneth Sharp

(11 March–1 April 1967)

The Faceless Ones

w David Ellis, Malcolm Hulke (A 6-part story)

The TARDIS lands at Gatwick Airport in 1966, and the Doctor uncovers a plot by an alien race, the Chameleons, to take over the identities of humans using special charter flights to spirit away their victims. (Exit: Ben and Polly)

Commandant Colin Gordon
Meadows George Selway
Jean Rock Wanda Ventham
Spencer Victor Winding
Blade Donald Pickering
Jenkins Christopher Tranchell
Crossland Bernard Kay

Samantha Briggs **Pauline Collins**
Ann Davidson **Gilly Fraser**

Director: **Gerry Mill**
Designer: **Geoff Kirkland**

(8 April–13 May 1967)

The Evil of the Daleks

w **David Whitaker** *(A 7-part story)*
An adventure which starts with the
TARDIS being stolen, sees the Doctor
and Jamie whisked back to Victorian
Canterbury and thence to Skaro, where
the Daleks try to turn the Doctor into a
Dalek. Instead he makes some Daleks

almost human. The result: civil war – and
a new passenger in the TARDIS.
Edward Waterfield **John Bailey**
Victoria Waterfield **Deborah Watling**
  (intro)
Mollie Dawson **Jo Rowbottom**
Theodore Maxtible **Marius Goring**
Ruth Maxtible **Brigit Forsyth**
Toby **Windsor Davies**
Kemel **Sonny Caldinez**

Director: **Derek Martinus**
Designer: **Chris Thompson**

(20 May–1 July 1967)
NB: Repeat of Episode One on 8 June
1968 contained additional footage and
voice-over.

Season Five
(2 September 1967–1 June 1968)

REGULAR CAST

The Doctor **Patrick Troughton**   *Jamie* **Frazer Hines**
Victoria Waterfield **Deborah Watling**

Producers: **Peter Bryant** *(Stories 1, 5–7),*
  Innes Lloyd *(Stories 2–4)*

Story editors: **Victor Pemberton** *(Story 1)*
Peter Bryant *(Stories 2–4)*
Derrick Sherwin *(Stories 5–7)*

The Tomb of the Cybermen

w **Kit Pedler, Gerry Davis** *(A 4-part story)*
The TARDIS arrives on the planet Telso
where an Earth expedition is excavating
the tomb of the last Cybermen. The
Doctor is soon up against his old foes –
plus the Cybermats, deadly little robot
creatures trained to attack by homing in
on brain waves.
Toberman **Roy Stewart**
Prof. Parry **Aubrey Richards**
John Viner **Cyril Shaps**
Jim Callum **Cliver Merrison**
Kaftan **Shirley Cooklin**
Eric Klieg **George Pastell**
Capt. Hopper **George Roubicek**
Cyberman controller **Michael Kilgarriff**

Director: **Morris Barry**
Designer: **Martin Johnson**

(2–23 September 1967)

The Abominable Snowman

w **Mervyn Haisman, Henry Lincoln** *(A 6-
  part story)*
In Tibet, the Doctor and his friends meet
an explorer, Travers, and discover the
Yeti – fur-covered robots controlled by a
malevolent alien entity called the
Intelligence.
Travers **Jack Watling**
Khrisong **Norman Jones**
Thonmi **David Spencer**
Rinchen **David Grey**
Sapan **Raymond Llewellyn**
Songsten **Charles Morgan**
Padmasambhava **Wolfe Morris**
Ralpachan **David Baron**
Yeti **Reg Whitehead**

Director: **Gerald Blake**
Designer: **Malcolm Middleton**

(30 September–4 November 1967)

The Ice Warriors

w **Brian Hayles** *(A 6-part story)*
The far future: England is in the grip of a new, ever-encroaching ice age. Arriving at a scientific base, the Doctor and his companions are on hand when a Martian ice warrior is found trapped in the ice. Once revived, leader Varga has world conquest on his mind.
Miss Garrett **Wendy Gifford**
Clent **Peter Barkworth**
Arden **George Waring**
Walters **Malcolm Taylor**
Storr **Angus Lennie**
Penley **Peter Sallis**
Varga **Bernard Bresslaw**

Director: **Derek Martinus**
Designer: **Jeremy Davies**

11 November–16 December 1967

The Enemy of the World

w **David Whitaker** *(A 6-part story)*
Double trouble for the Doctor when he tangles with Salamander – a would-be world dictator who looks exactly like him.
Astrid **Mary Peach**
Giles Kent **Bill Kerr**
Donald Bruce **Colin Douglas**
Benik **Milton Johns**
Salamander **Patrick Troughton**
Swann **Christopher Burgess**
Colin **Adam Verney**
Mary **Margaret Hickey**

Director: **Barry Letts**
Designer: **Christopher Pemsel**

(23 December 1967–27 January 1968)

The Web of Fear

w **Mervyn Haisman, Henry Lincoln** *(A 6-part story)*
The Doctor again fights the Yeti and 'the Intelligence' – this time in the London Underground. His ally: Col. Lethbridge-Stewart, later to form a special anti-alien task force, UNIT.
Prof. Travers **Jack Watling**
Anne Travers **Tina Packer**
Corp. Lane **Rod Beacham**
Corp. Blake **Richardson Morgan**
Capt. Knight **Ralph Watson**
Harold Chorley **Jon Rollason**
Staff Sgt Arnold **Jack Woolgar**
Col. Lethbridge-Stewart **Nicholas Courtney**

Director: **Douglas Camfield**
Designer: **David Myerscough-Jones**

(3 February–9 March 1968)
(NB: Inside one of the Yeti costumes was **John Levene**, later a cast regular as UNIT's Sgt Benton)

Fury From the Deep

w **Victoria Pemberton** *(A 6-part story)*
At a gas refinery on the North East coast of England, the Doctor, Jamie and Victoria tangle with a parasitic seaweed that turns people into weed creatures.
Robson **Victor Maddern**
Harris **Roy Spencer**
Price **Graham Leaman**
Maggie Harris **June Murphy**
Chief engineer **Hubert Rees**
Van Lutyens **John Abineri**
Quill **Bill Burridge**
Oak **John Gill**

Director: **Hugh David**
Designer: **Peter Kindred**

(16 March–20 April 1968)

The Wheel in Space

w **David Whitaker,** *from a story by* **Kit Pedler** *(A 6-part story)*
Having left Victoria behind on Earth, the TARDIS now materialises in an abandoned rocket, in the orbit of a giant space station. There, they again fight off invading Cybermen – helped by a new companion, Zoe.
Zoe **Wendy Padbury** *(intro)*
Leo Ryan **Eric Flynn**
Dr Gemma Corwyn **Anne Ridler**
Tanya Lernov **Clare Jenkins**
Jarvis Bennett **Michael Turner**
Enrico Casali **Donald Sumpter**
Armand Vallance **Derrick Gilbert**
Sean Flannigan **James Mellor**

Director: **Tristan de Vere Cole**
Designer: **Derek Dodd**

(27 April–1 June 1968)

Season Six
(10 August 1968–21 June 1969)

REGULAR CAST

The Doctor **Patrick Troughton**   *Jamie* **Frazer Hines**
Zoe **Wendy Padbury**

Producers: **Peter Bryant** *(Stories 1–6),*
   Derrick Sherwin *(Story 7)*
Story editors: **Derrick Sherwin** *(Stories 1–2, 6)*, **Terrance Dicks** *(Stories 3–5, 7)*

The Dominators

w **Norman Ashby** *(alias* **Mervyn Haisman** *and* **Henry Lincoln)** *(A 5-part story)*
The Doctor hopes for a peaceful holiday on the planet Dulkis but finds the island he lands on has been taken over by the cruel Dominators and their deadly robots, the Quarks, with the aim of turning the world into a radioactive power source.
Rago **Ronald Allen**
Toba **Kenneth Ives**
Cully **Arthur Cox**
Kando **Felicity Gibson**
Teel **Giles Block**
Balan **Johnson Bayly**
Senex **Walter Fitzgerald**

Director: **Morris Barry**
Designer: **Barry Newbery**

(10 August–7 September 1968)

The Mind Robber

w **Peter Ling, Derrick Sherwin** *(Ep. 1 only – uncredited) (A 5-part story)*
The crew of the TARDIS find themselves in a bizarre white void, and then the Land of Fiction, populated by strange white robots, mythical monsters and fictional characters, and ruled by an aged Master who wants the Doctor to take his place.
The Master **Emrys Jones**
A stranger/Gulliver **Bernard Horsfall**
Rapunzel **Christine Pirie**
The Medusa **Sue Pulford**
Karkus **Christopher Robbie**

D'Artagnan/Sir Lancelot **John Greenwood**

Director: **David Maloney**
Designer: **Evan Hercules**

(14 September–12 October 1968)

The Invasion

w **Derrick Sherwin**, *from an idea by* **Kit Pedler** *(An 8-part story)*
With the help of Brigadier Lethbridge-Stewart's newly-formed task force, UNIT, the Doctor foils the Cybermen's latest plot to invade Earth – after first paralysing the population.
Isobel Watkins **Sally Faulkner**
Benton **John Levene**
Tobias Vaughn **Kevin Stoney**
Packer **Peter Halliday**
Brigadier Lethbridge-Stewart **Nicholas Courtney**
Sgt Walters **James Thornhill**
Capt. Turner **Robert Sidaway**
Prof. Watkins **Edward Burnham**

Director: **Douglas Camfield**
Designer: **Richard Hunt**

(2 November–21 December 1968)

The Krotons

w **Robert Holmes** *(A 4-part story)*
The Doctor and Zoe try out the Kroton Teaching Machine, and their combined brain power reawakens a dormant – and dangerous – crystalline race.
Selris **James Copeland**

Vana Madeleine Mills
Thara Gilbert Wynne
Eelek Philip Madoc
Axus Richard Ireson
Beta James Cairncross
Kroton voices Roy Skelton, Patrick Tull

Director: David Maloney
Designer: Ray London

(28 December 1968–18 January 1969)

Maj. Ian Warne Donald Gee
Technician Penn George Layton
Milo Clancey Gordon Gostelow
Madeleine Issigri Lisa Daniely
Dom Issigri Esmond Knight
Lt. Sorba Nick Zavan

Director: Michael Hart
Designer: Ian Watson

(8 March–12 April 1969)

The Seeds of Death

w Brian Hayles *(A 6-part story)*
The Ice Warriors prepare for an attack on Earth by sending Martian seed pods containing a deadly fungus along the T-Mat, an instantaneous travel device linking the Moon with the Earth.
Gia Kelly Louise Pajo
Brent Ric Felgate
Radnor Ronald Leigh-Hunt
Fewsham Terry Scully
Phipps Christopher Coll
Eldred Philip Ray
Slaar Alan Bennion
Computer voice John Witty
Ice Warriors Tony Harwood, Sonny Caldinez

Director: Michael Ferguson
Designer: Paul Allen

(25 January–1 March 1969)

The Space Pirates

w Robert Holmes *(A 6-part story)*
Materialising on a space beacon, the TARDIS travellers are caught up in a raid by Space Pirates, and join forces with space miner Milo Clancey to end their thieving ways.
Dervish Brian Peck
Caven Dudley Foster
Gen. Hermack Jack May

The War Games

w Terrance Dicks *and* Malcolm Hulke *(A 10-part story)*
On an Earth-like planet, the Doctor and his companions become involved in the war games of aliens who have captured and brainwashed soldiers from different periods of Earth's history, to train an invincible army. With a handful of Resistance fighters, the Doctor opposes the War Lord and his assistant, the War Chief, but finally has to call on his own people, the Time Lords to help. After ending the 'games', the Time Lords bring the Doctor to trial for 'intervening' and exile him to Earth – with a changed appearance. Jamie and Zoe are sent back to their own eras. (This story did more than end an era – it introduced the Time Lords and 'filled in' the Doctor's own history.)
Lady Jennifer Buckingham Jane Sherwin
Lt Carstairs David Savile
War Chief Edward Brayshaw
Gen. Smythe Noel Coleman
Von Weich David Garfield
War Lord Philip Madoc
Scientist Vernon Dobtcheff
Russell Graham Weston
Security chief James Bree
Time Lords Bernard Horsfall, Trevor Martin, Clyde Pollitt
Moor David Troughton

Director: David Maloney
Designer: Roger Cheveley

(19 April–21 June 1969)

THE THIRD DOCTOR: JON PERTWEE
(1970–1974)

Season Seven
(3 January–20 June 1970)
REGULAR CAST

The Doctor Jon Pertwee Liz Shaw Caroline John
Brigadier Lethbridge-Stewart Nicholas Courtney
Sgt Benton John Levene (from Story 3)

Producers: Derrick Sherwin (Story 1),
Barry Letts (Stories 2–4)

Script editor: Terrance Dicks

Spearhead from Space

w Robert Holmes (A 4-part story)
Exiled to Earth, the Doctor agrees to help
UNIT investigate strange meteorites
which have landed. He comes up against
the Nestene – an alien intelligence which
is planning – to use Autons, plastic replicas
of human beings, to replace key figures in
the government. (First colour story.)
Seeley Neil Wilson
Capt. Munro John Breslin
Channing Hugh Burden
Hibbert John Woodnutt
Maj. Gen Scobie Hamilton Dyce
Ransome Derek Smee

Director: Derek Martinus
Designer: Paul Allen

(3–24 January 1970)

Doctor Who and The Silurians

w Malcolm Hulke (A 7-part story)
The Silurians, an intelligent prehistoric
race, are revived by work at an atomic
research centre and plan to recapture the
world by unleashing a deadly disease and
destroying the Van Allen belt.
Dr Lawrence Peter Miles
Maj. Baker Norman Jones
Miss Dawson Thomasine Heiner
Capt. Hawkins Paul Darrow
Silurian scientist Pat Gorman
Masters Geoffrey Palmer
Young Silurian Nigel John
Dr Quinn Fulton Mackay

Director: Timothy Combe
Designer: Barry Newbery

(31 January–14 March 1970)

The Ambassadors of Death

w David Whitaker, Malcolm Hulke (un-
credited rewrites) (A 7-part story)
A manned space probe returns to Earth –
but with an alien crew aboard. The Doctor
flies into space in search of the real
astronauts.
Taltalian Robert Cawdron
Van Lyden Ric Felgate
Ralph Cornish Ronald Allen
Gen. Carrington John Abineri
Quinlan Dallas Cavell
Reegan William Dysart
Sgt Benton John Levene (intro)
Astronauts Steve Peters, Neville
Simons

Director: Michael Ferguson
Designer: David Myerscough-Jones

(21 March–2 May 1970)

Inferno

w Don Houghton (A 7-part story)
The Doctor clashes with Prof Stahlman,
head of a project to release a new energy
source from the Earth's core. His own
efforts to reactivate the TARDIS console
hurl him into a parallel world where his

friends are enemies and Stahlman's Inferno project has a terrifying outcome.
Prof. Stahlman Olaf Pooley
Bromley Ian Fairbairn
Sir Keith Gold Christopher Benjamin
Petra Williams Sheila Dunn
Greg Sutton Derek Newark
Primords Dave Carter, Peter Thompson, Pat Gorman, Walter Henry, Philip Ryan

Directors: Douglas Camfield, Barry Letts*
Designer: Jeremy Davies

(9 May–20 June 1970)

* Took over later episodes when Camfield fell ill.

Season Eight
(2 January–19 June 1971)

REGULAR CAST
The Doctor Jon Pertwee   *Jo Grant* Katy Manning
The Brigadier Nicholas Courtney
Capt. Mike Yates Richard Franklin *(except Story 4)*   *Sgt Benton* John Levene
(except Story 4)
The Master Roger Delgado

Producer: Barry Letts

Script editor: Terrance Dicks

Terror of the Autons

w Robert Holmes *(A 4-part story)*
With a new companion, Jo Grant, an over-keen, newly fledged UNIT agent, the Doctor faces his newest and trickiest foe . . . the Master, a villainous renegade Time Lord, who arrives on Earth to pave the way for a Nestene invasion with the Autons.
Rossini John Baskcomb
Prof. Philips Christopher Burgess
Rex Farrel Michael Wisher
Mrs Farrel Barbara Leake
McDermott Harry Towb
Auton leader Pat Gorman
Auton policeman Terry Walsh

Director: Barry Letts
Designer: Ian Watson

(2–23 January 1971)

The Mind of Evil

w Don Houghton *(A 6-part story)*
The Doctor exposes the Master's deadly scheme to wreck a world peace conference using an alien mind parasite that feeds on

criminal evil – and a stolen nerve-gas missile.
Prison Governor Raymond Westwell
Dr Summers Michael Sheard
Barnham Neil McCarthy
Cpl. Bell Fernanda Marlowe
Capt. Chin Lee Pik-Sen Lim
Vosper Haydn Jones
Mailer William Marlowe

Director: Timothy Combe
Designer: Ray London

(30 January–6 March 1971)

The Claws of Axos

w Bob Baker *and* Dave Martin *(A 4-part story)*
The Doctor uses the TARDIS to save Earth from an alien parasite creature, Axos, by forcing it into a time-loop.
Chinn Peter Bathurst
Bill Filer Paul Grist
Sir George Hardiman Donald Hewlett
Axon man Bernard Holley
Winser David Savile
Minister Kenneth Benda
Capt. Harker Tim Pigott-Smith
Cpl. Bell Fernanda Marlowe

Director: **Michael Ferguson**
Designer: **Kenneth Sharp**

(13 March–3 April 1971)

Colony in Space

w **Malcolm Hulke** *(A 6-part story)*
The Time Lords restore the TARDIS'
ability to move through time and space,
and send the Doctor (and Jo) to a bleak
alien world where they help colonist
farmers overcome an exploitative mining
corporation, and prevent the Master from
gaining control of the most deadly weapon
in the galaxy.
Ashe **John Ringham**
Winton **Nicholas Pennell**
Mary Ashe **Helen Worth**
Norton **Roy Skelton**
Primitive **Pat Gorman**
Caldwell **Bernard Kay**
Dent **Morris Perry**
Morgan **Tony Caunter**
The Guardian **Norman Atkyns**

Director: **Michael Briant**
Designer: **Tim Gleeson**

(10 April–15 May 1971)

The Daemons

w **Guy Leopold** (*alias* **Robert Sloman**
and **Barry Letts**) *(A 5-part story)*
An archaeological dig near the village of
Devil's End starts a series of terrifying
events as the Master releases the power of
Azal, last survivor of an ancient alien race
called the Daemons.
Miss Hawthorne **Damaris Hayman**
Winstanley **Rollo Gamble**
Dr Reeves **Eric Hillyard**
Bert **Don McKillop**
Tom Girton **Jon Croft**
Bok **Stanley Mason**
Azal **Stephen Thorne**

Director: **Christopher Barry**
Designer: **Roger Ford**

(22 May–19 June 1971)

Season Nine
(1 January–24 June 1972)

REGULAR CAST

As Season Eight, except:
The UNIT men (Stories 1 and 5 only), The Master (Stories 3 and 5 only)

Producer: **Barry Letts**

Script editor: **Terrance Dicks**

Day of the Daleks

w **Louis Marks** *(A 4-part story)*
The Doctor and Jo fight to prevent the
death of diplomat Sir Reginald Styles and
a war that will deliver Earth's future to the
Daleks and their ferocious, gorilla-like
slaves, the Ogrons.
Sir Reginald Styles **Wilfrid Carter**
Ogron **Rick Lester**
Chief Dalek **John Scott Martin**
Controller **Aubrey Woods**
Anat **Anna Barry**
Shura **Jimmy Winston**
Boaz **Scott Fredericks**
Monia **Valentine Palmer**

Director: **Paul Bernard**
Designer: **David Myerscough-Jones**

(1–22 January 1972)

The Curse of Peladon

w **Brian Hayles** *(A 4-part story)*
On the planet Peladon, the Doctor
exposes a plot by High Priest Hepesh to
sabotage his king's bid to join the Galactic
Federation.
King Peladon **David Troughton**
Hepesh **Geoffrey Toone**
Grun **Gordon St Clair**
Aggedor **Nick Hobbs**

Alpha Centauri **Stuart Fell**
Arcturus **Murphy Grumbar**
Ssorg **Sonny Caldinez**
Izlyr **Alan Bennion**
Voice of Alpha Centauri **Ysanne Churchman**
Voice of Arcturus **Terry Bale**

Director: **Lennie Mayne**
Designer: **Gloria Clayton**

(29 January–19 February 1972)

The Sea Devils

w **Malcolm Hulke** *(A 6-part story)*
The Master, supposedly held captive on a small island, plots to revive a machine which with he can control underwater lizard creatures called Sea Devils and conquer the world.
Capt. Hart **Edwin Richfield**
Trenchard **Clive Morton**
Third Officer Jane Blythe **June Murphy**
Sea Devil **Pat Gorman**
Cmdr Ridgeway **Donald Sumpter**
Lt Cmdr Mitchell **David Griffin**
Chief Sea Devil **Peter Forbes-Robertson**
Ldg Telegraphist Bowman **Alec Wallis**

Director: **Michael Briant**
Designer: **Tony Snoaden**

(26 February–1 April 1972)

The Mutants

w **Bob Baker** *and* **David Martin** *(A 6-part story)*
A summons from the Time Lords takes the Doctor and Jo to the planet Solos where they help its mutant inhabitants realise their destiny – against the wishes of the cruel Earth Marshal.

Marshal **Paul Whitsun-Jones**
Stubbs **Christopher Coll**
Cotton **Rick James**
Varan **James Mellor**
Ky **Garrick Hagan**
Jaeger **George Pravda**
Sondergaard **John Hollis**
Administrator **Geoffrey Palmer**
Mutt **John Scott Martin**

Director: **Christopher Barry**
Designer: **Jeremy Bear**

(8 April–13 May 1972)

The Time Monster

w **Robert Sloman** *(A 6-part story)*
In his unceasing quest for power, the Master unleashes Kronos, an entity that feeds on time, and causes the destruction of Atlantis.
Dr Ruth Ingram **Wanda Moore**
Stuart Hyde **Ian Collier**
Krasis **Donald Eccles**
Hippias **Aidan Murphy**
Kronos **Marc Boyle**
Dalios **George Cormack**
Galleia **Ingrid Pitt**
Lakis **Susan Penhaligon**
Minotaur **David Prowse**

Director: **Paul Bernard**
Designer: **Tim Gleeson**

(20 May–24 June 1972)

Season Ten
(30 December 1972–23 June 1973)

Regular Cast

As Season Eight, except:
The Brigadier, Sgt Benton (Stories 1 and 5 only)
Capt. Yates (Story 5 only), The Master (Story 3 only)

Producer: **Barry Letts**   *Script editor:* **Terrance Dicks**

The Three Doctors

w Bob Baker *and* Dave Martin *(A 4-part story)*
The Time Lords are under siege, their energy being drained through a black hole by Omega, an embittered Time Lord trapped in a world of anti-matter. The Doctor is joined by his two previous selves and together they succeed in defeating Omega. The grateful Time Lords lift their exile sentence.
Omega Stephen Thorne
Doctor Who William Hartnell
Doctor Who Patrick Troughton
President of the Council Roy Purcell
Time Lord Graham Leaman
Ollis Laurie Webb
Dr Tyler Rex Robinson
Chancellor Clyde Pollitt

Director: Lennie Mayne
Designer: Roger Liminton

(30 December 1972–20 January 1973)

Carnival of Monsters

w Robert Holmes *(A 4-part story)*
Free to roam the cosmos again, the Doctor sets off for Metebelis 3, but winds up trapped in the Scope, an alien peep-show containing various galactic lifeforms – including the Drashigs, ferocious swamp dragons.
Kalik Michael Wisher
Orum Terence Lodge
Shirna Cheryl Hall
Vorg Leslie Dwyer
Major Daly Tenniel Evans
Claire Daly Jenny McCracken
Andrews Ian Marter
Pletrac Peter Halliday

Director: Barry Letts
Designer: Roger Liminton

(27 January–17 February 1973)

Frontier in Space

w Malcolm Hulke *(A 6-part story)*
The Doctor and Jo are caught up in a power struggle between Earth and Draconia – with the Master manipulating both sides to provoke space war, and the Daleks standing by to cash in.
Draconian Prince Peter Birrel
President of Earth Vera Fusek
Gen. Williams Michael Hawkins
Gardiner Ray Lonnen
Prof. Dale Harold Goldblatt
Draconian Captain Bill Wilde
Draconian Emperor John Woodnutt
Chief Dalek John Scott Martin

Director: Paul Bernard
Designer: Cynthia Kljuĉo

(24 February–31 March 1973)

Planet of the Daleks

w Terry Nation *(A 6-part story)*
On the planet Spiridon, the Doctor and Jo help a group of Thals prevent thousands of dormant Daleks from being revived to conquer the galaxy.
Taron Bernard Horsfall
Vaber Prentis Hancock
Codal Tim Preece
Wester Roy Skelton
Rebec Jane How
Latep Alan Tucker
Dalek voices Michael Wisher, Roy Skelton

Director: David Maloney
Designer: John Hurst

(7 April–12 May 1973)

The Green Death

w Robert Sloman *(A 6-part story)*
A mysterious death near the site of a new chemicals refinery brings UNIT to Wales, and the Doctor faces a twin threat – a plague of giant green maggots caused by industrial pollution, and the BOSS, a maniac computer. Jo leaves to marry an ecologist.
Clifford Jones Stewart Bevan
Stevens Jerome Willis
Hinks Ben Howard
Elgin Tony Adams

Dave Talfryn Thomas
BOSS's voice John Dearth
Nancy Mitzi McKenzie

Director: Michael Briant
Designer: John Borrowes

(19 May–23 June 1973)

Season Eleven
(15 December 1973–8 June 1974)

REGULAR CAST

The Doctor Jon Pertwee: *Sarah Jane Smith* Elisabeth Sladen
plus:
The Brigadier (Stories 1, 2 & 5), Sgt Benton, Capt. Yates (Stories 2 & 5)

Producer: Barry Letts

Script editor: Terrance Dicks

The Time Warrior

w Robert Holmes *(A 4-part story)*
With stowaway journalist Sarah Jane
Smith, the Doctor follows the trail of
missing scientists back to the Middle Ages
– and into the hands of an alien warrior,
the Sontaran Linx.
Irongron David Daker
Bloodaxe John J. Carney
Meg Sheila Fay
Linx Kevin Lindsay
Prof. Rubeish Donald Pelmear
Eleanor June Brown
Edward of Wessex Alex Rowe
Hal Jeremy Bulloch

Director: Alan Bromly
Designer: Keith Cheetham

(15 December 1973–5 January 1974)

Invasion of the Dinosaurs*

w Malcolm Hulke *(A 6-part story)*
The Doctor battles Operation Golden
Age – an MP and a scientist's bizarre plot
to reverse time and return Earth to a pre-
technological era.
Charles Grover, MP Noel Johnson
Butler Martin Jarvis
Prof. Whitaker Peter Miles
Gen. Finch John Bennett
Mark Terence Wilton
Adam Brian Badcoe

* Episode One titled 'Invasion' only

Director: Paddy Russell
Designer: Richard Morris

(12 January–16 February 1974)

Death to the Daleks

w Terry Nation *(A 4-part story)*
The time travellers are involved in a
struggle between Daleks, Exxilons and
humans for the antidote to a space plague.
Lt Dan Galloway Duncan Lamont
Lt Peter Hamilton Julian Fox
Jill Tarrant Joy Harrison
Bellal Arnold Yarrow
Dalek voices Michael Wisher
Capt. Richard Railton John Abineri

Director: Michael Brant
Designer: Colin Green

(23 February–16 March 1974)

The Monster of Peladon

w Brian Hayles *(A 6-part story)*
Returning to Peladon, the Doctor finds
the planet torn by civil war, with the Ice
Warriors imposing their own rule of terror,
with a monster-making machine.
Ettis Ralph Watson
Eckersley Donald Gee
Thalira Nina Thomas
Ortron Frank Gatliff
Alpha Centauri Stuart Fell
Alpha Centauri's voice Ysanne
  Churchman

Gebek **Rex Robinson**
Aggedor **Nick Hobbs**
Sskel **Sonny Caldinez**
Azaxyr **Alan Bennion**

Director: **Lennie Mayne**
Designer: **Gloria Clayton**

(23 March–27 April 1974)

Planet of the Spiders

---

w **Robert Sloman** (A 6-part story)
An alien crystal is the key to a web of
invasion and revolution as the Doctor
clashes with the Spiders of Metebelis 3.
Mortally wounded, his dying body goes
through another regeneration . . .

Lupton **John Dearth**
Moss **Terence Lodge**
Keaver **Andrew Staines**
Barnes **Christopher Burgess**
Land **Carl Forgione**
Cho-je **Kevin Lindsay**
Tommy **John Kane**
Tuar **Ralph Arliss**
Arak **Gareth Hunt**
Queen Spider **Kismet Delgado**
Lupton's Spider **Ysanne Churchman**
The Great One **Maureen Morris**

Director: **Barry Letts**
Designer: **Rochelle Selwyn**

(4 May–8 June 1974)

THE FOURTH DOCTOR: **TOM BAKER**
(1974–1981)

Season Twelve
(28 December 1974–10 May 1975)

REGULAR CAST

The Doctor **Tom Baker**   Sarah Jane Smith **Elisabeth Sladen**
Harry Sullivan **Ian Marter**

Producers: **Barry Letts** (Story 1) **Philip**
  Hinchcliffe (Stories 2–4)

Script editor: **Robert Holmes**

Robot

---

w **Terrance Dicks** (A 4-part story)
Still recovering from his latest change, the
Doctor combats a group of unscrupulous
scientists planning to start a Third World
War, and a rampaging giant robot, and
gains a second companion.
Harry Sullivan **Ian Marter** (intro)
Jellicoe **Alec Linstead**
Miss Winters **Patricia Maynard**
Prof. Kettlewell **Edward Burnham**
Robot **Michael Kilgarriff**
The Brigadier **Nicholas Courtney**
Sgt Benton **John Levene**

Director: **Christopher Barry**
Designer: **Ian Rawnsley**

(28 December 1974–18 January 1975)

The Ark in Space

---

w **Robert Holmes** (A 4-part story)
Aboard a space station in the future, an
insect race, the Wirrn, threaten to devour
and absorb the human race as it lies in
cryogenic suspension.
Vira **Wendy Williams**
Noah **Kenton Moore**
Rogan **Richardson Morgan**
Wirrn operators **Stuart Fell, Nick Hobbs**
Libri **Christopher Masters**
Voices **Gladys Spencer,**
  Peter Tuddenham

Director: **Rodney Bennett**
Designer: **Roger Murray-Leach**

(25 January–15 February 1975)

The Sontaran Experiment

w Bob Baker, Dave Martin *(A 2-part story)*

Leaving the ark, the Doctor goes to Earth where he finds and defeats a Sontaran officer, Styre, who is conducting cruel experiments on humans.

Styre/The Marshal Kevin Lindsay
Erak Peter Walshe
Krans Glyn Jones
Roth Peter Rutherford
Vural Donald Douglas

Director: Rodney Bennett
Designer: Roger Murray-Leach

(22 February–1 March 1975)

Genesis of the Daleks

w Terry Nation *(A 6-part story)*

The Time Lords send the Doctor to Skaro where the war between the Thals and the Kaleds is in its final stage. His mission: to prevent the birth of the Daleks, created by the crippled Kaled genius, Davros.

Davros Michael Wisher
Nyder Peter Miles
Gharman Dennis Chinnery
Sevrin Stephen Yardley

Ronson James Garbutt
Kavell Tom Georgeson
Bettan Harriet Philpin

Director: David Maloney
Designer: David Spode

(8 March–12 April 1975)

Revenge of the Cybermen

w Gerry Davis *(A 4-part story)*

Returning to the Ark to recover the TARDIS, the Doctor and his companions are plunged into a fight to the death between the Cybermen and the Vogans, inhabitants of a planet of gold – a substance deadly to the Cybermen.

Lester William Marlowe
Commander Stevenson Ronald Leigh-Hunt
Kellman Jeremy Wilkin
Vorus David Collings
Magrik Michael Wisher
Cyberleader Christopher Robbie
Tyrum Kevin Stoney
Sheprah Brian Grellis

Director: Michael E. Briant
Designer: Roger Murray-Leach

(19 April–10 May 1975)

Season Thirteen
(30 August 1975–6 March 1976)

REGULAR CAST

The Doctor Tom Baker   *Sarah Jane Smith* Elisabeth Sladen
Harry Sullivan Ian Marter*   *RSM Benton* John Levene*

Producer: Philip Hinchcliffe

Script editor: Robert Holmes

Terror of the Zygons

w Robert Banks Stewart *(A 4-part story)*

The Doctor solves the riddle of the Loch Ness monster – it's a half-creature, half-machine called the Skarasen, created by an alien race, the Zygons, as part of their plan to take over the world.

* Stories 1, 4 only

Duke of Forgill/Broton John Woodnutt
The Caber Robert Russell
Sister Lamont Lillias Walker
Angus Angus Lennie
Zygons Keith Ashley, Ronald Gough
The Brigadier Nicholas Courtney

Director: Douglas Camfield
Designer: Nigel Curzon

(30 August–20 September 1975)

Planet of Evil

w Louis Marks *(A 4-part story)*
A mayday call brings the Doctor and Sarah to Zeta Minor, a planet on the edge of the known universe where he battles with a man who becomes an anti-matter monster.
Sorenson Frederick Jaeger
Vishinsky Ewen Solon
Salamar Prentis Hancock
Morelli Michael Wisher
De Haan Graham Weston
Reig Melvyn Bedford

Director: David Maloney
Designer: Roger Murray-Leach

(27 September–18 October 1975)

Pyramids of Mars

w Stephen Harris (alias Lewis Greifer, Robert Holmes) *(A 4-part story)*
An inexplicable force draws the TARDIS to an old priory in 1911, where the Doctor finds Egyptologist Marcus Scarman has been possessed by the spirit of Sutekh, a malevolent god-like being seeking to escape from his Egyptian tomb.
Marcus Scarman Bernard Archard
Namin Peter Mayock
Dr Warlock Peter Copley
Laurence Scarman Michael Sheard
Sutekh Gabriel Woolf

Director: Paddy Russell
Designer: Christine Ruscoe

(25 October–15 November 1975)

The Android Invasion

w Terry Nation *(A 4-part story)*
The TARDIS lands in a replica of an English village on the planet of the Kraals, an alien race plotting to conquer Earth with android copies of humans.
Corporal Adams Max Faulkner
Morgan Peter Welch
Guy Crayford Milton Johns
Styggron Martin Friend

Kraal Stuart Fell
Col. Faraday Patrick Newell

Director: Barry Letts
Designer: Philip Lindley

(22 November–13 December 1975)

The Brain of Morbius

w Robin Bland *(alias* Terrance Dicks) *(A 4-part story)*
On the storm-lashed planet of Karn, the Doctor has a brush with the witch-like Sisterhood of the Flame, and grapples with the mind of an evil Time Lord, Morbius, whose brain has been installed in a monstrous new body by a disreputable surgeon, Solon.
Solon Philip Madoc
Condo Colin Fay
Chica Gilly Brown
Maren Cynthia Grenville
Voice of Morbius Michael Spice

Director: Christopher Barry
Designer: Barry Newbery

(3–24 January 1976)

The Seeds of Doom

w Robert Banks Stewart *(A 6-part story)*
In which the Doctor faces the 'growing' menace of the Krynoid – an alien plant form which incites a vegetable revolution against the animal kingdom, aided by demented millionaire botanist, Harrison Chase.
Richard Dunbar Kenneth Gilbert
Hargreaves Seymour Green
Harrison Chase Tony Beckley
Scorby John Challis
Sir Colin Thackeray Michael Barrington
Amelia Ducat Sylvia Coleridge
Arnold Keeler/Voice of the Krynoid Mark Jones

Director: Douglas Camfield
Designers: Roger Murray-Leach *(Eps 1–6)*, Jeremy Bear *(Eps 1–2 only)*

(31 January–6 March 1976)

Season Fourteen
(4 September–20 November 1976)
(1 January–2 April 1977)

REGULAR CAST

The Doctor **Tom Baker**　*Sarah Jane Smith* **Elisabeth Sladen** *(exit Story 2)*
Leela **Louise Jameson** *(from Story 4)*

Producer: **Philip Hinchcliffe**　　　　*Script editor:* **Robert Holmes**

The Masque of Mandragora

w **Louis Marks** *(A 4-part story)*
In Renaissance Italy, the travellers get involved in family intrigue, a secret sect – the Brothers of Demnos – and an alien energy force, the Mandragora Helix, which seeks to plunge Earth back into the Dark Ages. (Filmed in and around Portmeirion.)
Count Federico **Jon Laurimore**
Capt. Rossini **Antony Carrick**
Giuliano **Gareth Armstrong**
Marco **Tim Pigott-Smith**
Hieronymous **Norman Jones**
High Priest **Robert James**
Brother **Brian Ellis**

Director: **Rodney Bennett**
Designer: **Barry Newbery**

(4–25 September 1976)

The Deadly Assassin

w **Robert Holmes** (A 4-part story)
Returning alone to Gallifrey, the Doctor witnesses the murder of the President and finds his old foe the Master plotting to use the power of a black hole to destroy the Time Lords. (The Doctor's only 'solo' story.)
The President **Llewellyn Rees**
Cmdr Hilred **Derek Seaton**
Castellan Spandrell **George Pravda**
Co-ordinator Engin **Erik Chitty**
Chancellor Goth **Bernard Horsfall**
Commentator Runcible **Hugh Walters**
Cardinal Borusa **Angus Mackay**
The Master **Peter Pratt**

Director: **David Maloney**
Designer: **Roger Murray-Leach**

(30 October–20 November 1976)

The Hand of Fear

w **Bob Baker** *and* **Dave Martin** *(A 4-part story)*
The Doctor and Sarah tangle with Eldrad, an alien criminal regenerated by the power of a nuclear explosion, before the companions have to part, when the Doctor is summoned back to Gallifrey.
Dr Carter **Rex Robinson**
Prof. Watson **Glyn Houston**
Miss Jackson **Frances Pidgeon**
Driscoll **Roy Boyd**
Eldrad **Judith Paris**

Director: **Lennie Mayne**
Designer: **Christine Ruscoe**

(2–23 October 1976)

The Face of Evil

w **Chris Boucher** *(A 4-part story)*
The Doctor is captured by the primitive Sevateem tribe, befriended by a warrior girl, Leela, and threatened by a mad computer – the legacy of his own age-old mistake.
Leela **Louise Jameson** *(intro)*
Calib **Leslie Schofield**
Tomas **Brendan Price**
Neeva **David Garfield**
Jabel **Leon Eagles**
Gentek **Mike Elles**

Director: **Pennant Roberts**
Designer: **Austin Ruddy**

(1–22 January 1977)

The Robots of Death

w Chris Boucher *(A 4-part story)*
A warped scientist raised by robots, incites a 'robot rebellion' aboard a mobile mining factory, the Sandminer.
Dask David Bailie
Borg Brian Croucher
Toos Pamela Salem
Uvanov Russell Hunter
Poul David Collings
SV7 Miles Fothergill
D84 Gregory de Polney

Director: Michael E. Briant
Designer: Kenneth Sharp

(29 January–19 February 1977)

The Talons of Weng-Chiang

w Robert Holmes *(A 6-part story)*
The Doctor plans to take Leela to an authentic Music Hall – but they wind up fighting a war criminal from the future and his body-snatching Chinese Tong of the Black Scorpion in the sewers of Victorian London.
Weng-Chiang Michael Spice
Li H'sen Chang John Bennett
Mr Sin (an homunculus) Deep Roy
Henry Jago Christopher Benjamin
Casey Chris Gannon
Prof. Litefoot Trevor Baxter
Lee Tony Then

Director: David Maloney
Designer: Roger Murray-Leach

(26 February–2 April 1977)

Season Fifteen
(3 September 1977–11 March 1978)

REGULAR CAST

The Doctor Tom Baker   *Leela* Louise Jameson
Voice of K9 John Leeson *(from Story 2, but except Story 3)*

Producer: Graham Williams

Script editors: Robert Holmes *(Stories 1–4)*, Anthony Read *(Stories 5–6)*

Horror of Fang Rock

w Terrance Dicks *(A 4-part story)*
A deadly alien entity, the Rutan, stalks a turn-of-the-century lighthouse at Fang Rock where the survivors of a shipwreck have come ashore.
Vince John Abbott
Reuben Colin Douglas
Lord Palmerdale Sean Caffrey
Skinsale Alan Rowe
Adelaide Annette Woollett
Harker Rio Fanning

Director: Paddy Russell
Designer: Paul Allen

(3–24 September 1977)

The Invisible Enemy

w Bob Baker, and Dave Martin *(A 4-part story)*
When the nucleus of a malignant virus lodges in the Doctor's brain, cloned micro-copies of the Time Lord and Leela journey into his brain to confront it.
Safran Brian Grellis
Lowe Michael Sheard
Prof. Marius Frederick Jaeger
Voice of the Nucleus/Voice of K9 John Leeson
Opthalmologist Jim McManus

Director: Derrick Goodwin
Designer: Barry Newbery

(1–22 October)

Image of the Fendahl

w Chris Boucher *(A 4-part story)*
Dr Fendelman's experiments on a skull eight million years older than man, revives the Fendahl, a powerful life-sapping force that materialises through his psychic assistant, Thea.

Adam Colby Edward Arthur
Thea Ransome Wanda Ventham
Maximillian Stael Scott Fredericks
Dr Fendelman Denis Lill
Ted Moss Edward Evans
David Mitchell Derek Martin
Martha Tyler Daphne Heard
Jack Tyler Geoffrey Hinsliff

Director: George Spenton Foster
Designer: Anne Ridley

(29 October–19 November 1977)

The Sun Makers

w Robert Holmes *(A 4-part story)*
Landing on Pluto, the Doctor and Leela help a band of rebels overthrow the corrupt and oppressive rule of Gatherer Hade and the Collector.

Cordo Roy Macready
Hade Richard Leech
Marn Jonina Scott
Goudry Michael Keating
Mandrel William Simons
Veet Adrienne Burgess
Collector Henry Woolf
Bisham David Rowlands
Synge Derek Crewe

Director: Pennant Roberts
Designer: Tony Snoaden

(26 November–17 December 1977)

Underworld

w Bob Baker *and* Dave Martin *(A 4-part story)*
Materialising aboard a spaceship at the edge of the universe, the travellers become involved in its crew's quest to find the long-lost race banks of their home planet, Minyos.

Jackson James Maxwell
Tala Imogen Bickford-Smith
Orfe Jonathan Newth
Herrick Alan Lake
Idmon Jimmy Gardner
Idas Norman Tipton
Tarn Godfrey James
Rask James Marcus

Director: Norman Stewart
Designer: Dick Coles

(7–28 January 1978)

The Invasion of Time

w David Agnew *(alias* Anthony Read, Graham Williams) *(A 6-part story)*
Returning to Gallifrey, the Doctor poses as a traitor to lure a powerful alien race, the Vardans, into a time loop, only to face an even greater threat from the Sontarans. He gains a victory, but loses his companion Leela who falls in love!

Andred Chris Tranchell
Castellan Kelner Milton Johns
Cardinal Borusa John Arnatt
Vardan leader Stan McGowan
Rodan Hilary Ryan
Nesbin Max Faulkner
Presta Gai Smith
Stor Derek Deadman

Director: Gerald Blake
Designer: Barbara Gosnold

(4 February–11 March 1978)

Season Sixteen
(2 September 1978–24 February 1979)

REGULAR CAST

The Doctor Tom Baker   *Romana* Mary Tamm   *Voice of K9* John Leeson *(except Story 5)*

Producer: Graham Williams   *Script editor:* Anthony Read

The Ribos Operation

w Robert Holmes *(a 4-part story)*
With a new companion, graduate Time
Lady Romanadvoratrelundar (Romana),
and a new Mark II K9, the Doctor is
assigned a new quest by the White
Guardian – to gather the six scattered
segments of the Key of Time. The first is
hidden on the planet Ribos which a con-
man called Garron is trying to sell to
warlord Graff Vynda-K.
The Guardian Cyril Luckham
Garron Iain Cuthbertson
Unstoffe Nigel Plaskitt
Graff Vynda-K Paul Seed
Sholakh Robert Keegan
Captain Prentis Hancock

Director: George Spenton Foster
Designer: Ken Ledsham

(2–23 September 1978)

The Pirate Planet

w Douglas Adams *(A 4-part story)*
Searching for the second segment to the
Key of Time, the Time Lords land on a
planet-draining hollow world manned by a
half-man, half-machine called the Captain.
The Captain Bruce Purchase
Mr Fibuli Andrew Robertson
Mentiad Bernard Finch
Pralix David Sibley
Mula Primi Townsend
Kimus David Warwick
Queen Xanxia Rosalind Lloyd

Director: Pennant Roberts
Designer: Jon Pusey

(30 September–21 October 1978)

The Stones of Blood

w David Fisher *(A 4-part story)*
The trail of the third key segment leads
the Doctor and Romana to Earth and a
struggle with a 3,000-year-old pagan
goddess and her bloodthirsty stone
creatures, the Orgi. (This was the 100th
Doctor Who story.)
Prof. Rumford Beatrix Lehmann

Vivien Fay (the Cailleach) Susan Engel
Dr Vries Nicholas McArdle
Martha Elaine Ives-Cameron
Megara voices Gerald Cross, David
McAlister

Director: Darrol Blake
Designer: John Stout

(28 October–18 November 1978)

The Androids of Tara

w David Fisher *(A 4-part story)*
Finding the fourth key segment is easy.
Getting it gives the Doctor and Romana
an identity crisis involving android
doubles, the Crown Prince of Tara and a
wicked nobleman.
Count Grendel Peter Jeffrey
Prince Reynart Neville Jason
Zadek Simon Lack
Farrah Paul Lavers
Lamia Lois Baxter
Till Declan Mulholland
Archimandrite Cyril Shaps
Kurster Martin Matthews

Director: Michael Hayes
Designer: Valerie Warrender

(25 November–16 December 1978)

The Power of Kroll

w Robert Holmes *(A 4-part story)*
The Time Lords are caught up in a feud
between refinery technicians and green-
skinned Swampies, and menaced by a
giant squid-like monster, the Kroll, which
has swallowed the fifth segment!
Fenner Philip Madoc
Thawn Neil McCarthy
Dugeen John Leeson
Rohm-Dutt Glyn Owen
Varlik Carl Rigg
Ranquin John Abineri
Skart Frank Jarvis

Director: Norman Stewart
Designer: Don Giles

(23 December 1978–13 January 1979

The Armageddon Factor

w Bob Baker *and* Dave Martin *(A 6-part story)*
After narrowly averting Armageddon between two warring planets, the Doctor completes the Key to Time, but when confronted by the Black Guardian, decides it's too dangerous to be allowed to remain intact.
The Marshal John Woodvine
Princess Astra Lalla Ward
Merak Ian Saynor
Shapp Davyd Harries
The Shadow William Squire
Drax Barry Jackson
The Black Guardian Valentine Dyall

Director: Michael Hayes
Designer: Richard McManan-Smith

(20 January–24 February 1979)

Season Seventeen
(1 September 1979–12 January 1980)

REGULAR CAST
The Doctor Tom Baker   *Romana* Lalla Ward
Voice of K9 David Brierley *(from Story Three)*

Producer: Graham Williams
Script editor: Douglas Adams

Destiny of the Daleks

w Terry Nation *(A 4-part story)*
With Romana now regenerated in the likeness of Princess Astra, the travellers land on Skaro where they find the Daleks searching for Davros to give them an edge in their war with the ruthless Movellans.
Tyssan Tim Barlow
Cmdr Sharrel Peter Straker
Agella Suzanne Danielle
Lan Tony Osoba
Veldan David Yip
Jall Penny Casdagli
Davros David Gooderson
Dalek voice Roy Skelton

Director: Ken Grieve
Designer: Ken Ledsham

(1–22 September 1979)

City of Death

w David Agnew *(alias* David Fisher, Douglas Adams, Graham Williams)
(A 4-part story)
A plot to steal the Mona Lisa alerts the Doctor to an alien creature's scheme to prevent the explosion that scattered him throughout history – and created life on Earth.
Count Julian Glover
Countess Catherine Schell
Kerensky David Graham
Duggan Tom Chadbon
Hermann Kevin Flood
Art gallery visitors John Cleese, Eleanor Bron

Director: Michael Hayes
Designer: Richard McManan-Smith

(29 September–20 October 1979)

The Creature from the Pit

w David Fisher *(A 4-part story)*
The travellers answer a distress call from the planet Chloris and fall into the hands of its despotic ruler Adrasta.
Adrasta Myra Frances
Karela Eileen Way
Torvin John Bryans
Edu Edward Kelsey
Organon Geoffrey Bayldon
Ainu Tim Munro

Director: Christopher Barry
Designer: Valerie Warrender

(27 October–17 November 1979)

Nightmare of Eden

w Bob Baker *(A 4-part story)*
A space liner is overrun with monsters released from a naturalist's crystal 'recordings' of the planet Eden.
Tryst Lewis Fiander
Rigg David Daker
Dymond Geoffrey Bateman
Della Jennifer Lonsdale
Stott Barry Andrews
Fisk Geoffrey Hinsliff
Costa Peter Craze

Directors: Alan Bromly *(plus* Graham Williams *– uncredited)*
Designer: Roger Cann

(24 November–15 December 1979)

The Horns of Nimon

w Anthony Read (A 4-part story)
The Doctor prevents a bull-like alien race from invading a planet via a black hole in space.
Teka Janet Ellis
Seth Simon Gipps-Kent
Sorak Michael Osborne
Soldeed Graham Crowden

Co-pilot Malcolm Terris
Voice of the Nimons Clifford Norgate

Director: Kenny McBain
Designer: Graeme Story

(22 December 1979–12 January 1980)

Shada

w Douglas Adams *(A 6-part story)* *
The Doctor and Romana visit a Time Lord living 'in retirement' as Cambridge don Professor Chronotis, to retrieve a book *The Ancient Law of Gallifrey*. Also after the book is a power-crazy mind-thief, Skagra, who wants to use it to free a powerful Time Lord, Salyavin, from the prison planet Shada. But Chronotis is really Salyavin and a galactic chase ensues before the Doctor defeats Skagra and leaves Chronotis in peace on Earth.
Chronotis Denis Carey
Skagra Christopher Neame
Clare Keightley Victoria Burgoyne
Chris Parsons Daniel Hill

Director: Pennant Roberts
Designer: Victor Meredith

* This story was never transmitted, as filming was interrupted by a strike, and the adventure was shelved by the BBC.

Season Eighteen
(30 August 1980–21 March 1981)

REGULAR CAST

The Doctor Tom Baker   *Romana* Lalla Ward   *Voice of K9* John Leeson
(both exit Story 5)
Adric Matthew Waterhouse *(from Story 3)*
Nyssa Sarah Sutton *(from Story 6)*

Producer: John Nathan-Turner
Executive producer: Barry Letts

Script editor: Christopher H. Bidmead

The Leisure Hive

w David Fisher (A 4-part story)
The Time Lords visit an artificial galactic entertainment centre, the Leisure Hive, and become embroiled in a struggle for control between the native Argolians and their reptilian enemies, the Foamosi.
Mena Adrienne Corri
Pangol David Haig
Brock John Collin
Vargos Martin Fisk

Hardin Nigel Lambert
Klout Ian Talbot
Guide Roy Montague

Director: Lovett Bickford
Designer: Tom Yardley-Jones

(30 August–20 September 1980)

Meglos

w John Flanagan, Andrew McCulloch
(A 4-part story)
A prickly, cactus-like character called Meglos impersonates the Doctor to steal the Dodecahedron, a crystal which powers the underground civilisation of Tigella.
Caris Colette Gleeson
Deedrix Crawford Logan
Zastor Edward Underdown
Lexa Jacqueline Hill
Gen. Grugger Bill Fraser
Lt Brotadac Frederick Treves
Earthling Christopher Owen

Director: Terence Dudley
Designer: Philip Lindley

(27 September–18 October 1980)

Full Circle

w Andrew Smith *(A 4-part story)*
The TARDIS enters E-Space where, on the planet Alzarius, the Doctor finds a divided human community, learns the secret of Mistfall and picks up a new young passenger, Adric, who stows away in the Time Lord's craft.
Adric Matthew Waterhouse *(intro)*
Varsh Richard Willis
Login George Baker
Tylos Bernard Padden
Keara June Page
Nefred James Bree
Garif Alan Rowe
Omril Andrew Forbes
Dexeter Tony Calvin

Director: Peter Grimwade
Designer: Janet Budden

(25 October–15 November 1980)

State of Decay

w Terrance Dicks *(A 4-part story)*
On a medieval planet, the Doctor helps a group of rebels oppressed by their tyrannical rulers, a trio of vampires living in a lost spaceship and, using a scout ship, he literally 'drives' a stake through the stirring Great Vampire, last survivor of a race believed destroyed by the Time Lords.
Aukon Emrys James
Zargo William Lindsay
Camilla Rachel Davies
Kalmar Arthur Hewlett
Tarak Thane Bettany
Veros Stacy Davies
Ivo Clinton Greyn

Director: Peter Moffatt
Designer: Christine Ruscoe

(22 November–13 December 1980)

Warriors' Gate

w Steve Gallagher *(A 4-part story)*
The TARDIS is 'hijacked' by Biroc, a time-sensitive Tharil who departs into a white void where E-Space and N-Space intersect. While the Doctor follows Biroc to a mirrored Gateway, his friends encounter a trader, Capt. Rorvik, who is trapped in the void with his cargo of Tharils and intends to blast his way out – a potentially catastrophic manoeuvre. After the Doctor foils him, Romana elects to remain with the Tharils while the TARDIS returns to N-Space.
Rorvik Clifford Rose
Packard Kenneth Cope
Sagan Vincent Pickering
Aldo Freddie Earlle
Royce Harry Waters
Lane David Kincaid
Lazlo Jeremy Gittins
Biroc David Weston

Director: Paul Joyce
Designer: Graeme Story

(3–24 January 1981)

The Keeper of Traken

w Johnny Byrne *(A 4-part story)*
Intrigue threatens the peaceful harmony of Traken – and the Doctor finds the evil influence of the Master is at work again, in the form of a statue-like creature called Melkur.
The Keeper Denis Carey
Consul Kassia Sheila Ruskin
Consul Tremas Anthony Ainley
Nyssa Sarah Sutton *(intro)*
Seron John Woodnutt
Katura Margot Van der Burgh
Luvic Robin Soans
Melkur Geoffrey Beevers
Neman Roland Oliver

Director: John Black
Designer: Tony Burrough

(31 January–21 February 1981)

Logopolis

w Christopher H. Bidmead *(A 4-part story)*
When the Master's meddling with the mathematical calculations of Logopolis threatens to unravel the Universe, it takes the combined power of the two Time Lords to avert catastrophe. But the Master's treachery prompts a fight in which the Doctor falls to his death – and a new regeneration.
The Master Anthony Ainley
Tegan Jovanka Janet Fielding *(intro)*
Aunt Vanessa Dolores Whiteman
The Monitor John Fraser
Detective Inspector Tom Georgeson
The Doctor Peter Davison *(intro)*

Director: Peter Grimwade
Designer: Malcolm Thornton

(28 February–21 March 1981)

THE FIFTH DOCTOR: **PETER DAVISON**

(1982–1984)

Season Nineteen
(4 January–30 March 1982)

REGULAR CAST
The Doctor Peter Davison   *Tegan* Janet Fielding
Nyssa Sarah Sutton   *Adric* Matthew Waterhouse

Producer: John Nathan-Turner

Script editors: Eric Saward *(Stories 1, 3, 5, 7)*, Anthony Root *(Stories 2, 4, 6)*

Castrovalva

w Christopher H. Bidmead *(A 4-part story)*
The Doctor's latest regeneration is the least successful and he needs the recuperative powers of his TARDIS Zero Room. However, the Master, who has kidnapped Adric, causes the loss of the Zero Room and draws the Doctor to the apparently calm planet of Castrovalva.
The Master/Portreeve Anthony Ainley *(alias Neil Toynay!)*
Shardovan Derek Waring

Ruther Frank Wylie
Mergrave Michael Sheard
Head of security Dallas Cavell

Director: Fiona Cumming
Designer: Janet Budden

(4–12 January 1982)

Four to Doomsday

w Terence Dudley *(A 4-part story)*
Aboard an alien starship, the TARDIS crew encounter the frog-like Urbankans

who are travelling to Earth, apparently in peace. However, their leader, Monarch, believes he is God and is planning to travel faster than light to meet himself face to face.

Monarch Stratford Johns
Enlightenment Annie Lambert
Persuasion Paul Shelley
Bigon Philip Locke
Lin Fitu Burt Kwouk
Kurkutji Illario Bisi Pedro
Villagra Nadia Hamman

Director: John Black
Designer: Tony Burrough

(18–26 January 1982)

Kinda

w Christopher Bailey *(A 4-part story)*
Arriving on Deva Loka, the Doctor is caught up in the reappearance of the Mara. An Earth expedition to assess Deva Loka as a potential new home find their numbers reducing as they confront the mystical powers of an ancient evil.

Sanders Richard Todd
Hindle Simon Rouse
Todd Nerys Hughes
Panna Mary Morris
Karunna Sarah Prince
Anatta Anna Wing
Dukkha Jeffrey Stewart

Director: Peter Grimwade
Designer: Malcolm Thornton

(1–9 February 1982)

The Visitation

w Eric Saward *(A 4-part story)*
The Terileptils have come to Earth in the 17th century and are responsible for the spread of the Great Plague. Their explosive attempts to return home won't endear them to humanity either . . .

Richard Mace Michael Robbins
Terileptil leader Michael Melia
Squire John John Savident
Charles Anthony Calf
Ralph John Baker

Elizabeth Valerie Fyfer
Android Peter Van Dissel

Director: Peter Moffatt
Designer: Ken Starkey

(15–23 February 1982)

Black Orchid

w Terence Dudley *(A 2-part story)*
Heroic exploits on the cricket field and murderous events off it test the Doctor as the TARDIS team get involved with the Cranleigh family in 1925 England. The attic hides a dark family secret and Nyssa sees double. (This was the first purely historical story since *The Highlanders* in 1966.)

Lady Cranleigh Barbara Murray
Charles Cranleigh Michael Cochrane
Sir Robert Muir Moray Watson
George Cranleigh (The Unknown) Gareth Milne
Latoni Ahmed Khalil
Ann Talbot Sarah Sutton

Director: Ron Jones
Designer: Tony Burrough

(1–2 March 1982)

Earthshock

w Eric Saward *(A 4-part story)*
In the 25th century, the Cybermen once again attack Earth and the ensuing battle costs the Doctor dearly as a foolhardy Adric allows himself to be trapped on a doomed spaceship spiralling back through time on a collision course with an Earth populated by . . . dinosaurs.

Prof. Kyle Clare Clifford
Lt. Scott James Warwick
Briggs Beryl Reid
Berger June Bland
Cyber leader David Banks
Ringway Alec Sabin

Director: Peter Grimwade
Designer: Bernard Lloyd

(8–16 March 1982)

Time-Flight

w Peter Grimwade *(A 4-part story)*
The Master is trapped on primordial Earth and is trying to rebuild his TARDIS engines using the alien powers of the feuding Xeraphin. He succeeds in dragging Concorde and the Doctor's TARDIS back along the time contour. Whilst one Xeraphin aids the Doctor, his nemesis utilises the metamorphic powers of the other.

The Master/Kalid Anthony Ainley *(alias Leon Ni Taiy)*
Capt. Stapley Richard Easton
First Officer Bilton Michael Cashman
Flight Engineer Scobie Keith Drinkel
Prof. Hayter Nigel Stock
Angela Clifford Judith Byfield
Anithon Hugh Hayes

Director: Ron Jones
Designer: Richard McManan-Smith

(22–30 March 1982)

Season Twenty
(3 January–16 March 1983, 25 November 1983)

REGULAR CAST
The Doctor Peter Davison   *Tegan* Janet Fielding
Nyssa Sarah Sutton *(to Story 4)*   *Turlough* Mark Strickson *(from Story 3)*

Producer: John Nathan-Turner

Script editor: Eric Saward

Arc of Infinity

w Johnny Byrne (A 4-part story)
Hedin, a treacherous Time Lord on Gallifrey, is helping the renegade and long-believed dead Omega to re-enter this universe from his anti-matter prison by 'bonding' him with the Doctor. But the process is incomplete and a bitter Omega determines to take the universe down with him.
The Renegade/Omega Ian Collier
President Borusa Leonard Sachs
Councillor Hedin Michael Gough
Commander Maxil Colin Baker
Castellan Paul Jerricho
Chancellor Thalia Elspet Gray
Ergon Malcolm Harvey

Director: Ron Jones
Designer: Marjorie Pratt

(3–12 January 1983)

Snakedance

w Christopher Bailey *(A 4-part story)*
The Doctor takes Tegan, still affected by the influence of the snake-like creature, the Mara, to its home planet Manussa. There, local festivities draw the powerful evil back into the real world for another dangerous confrontation. (A sequel to *Kinda*.)
Ambril John Carson
Tahna Colette O'Neil
Lon Martin Clunes
Chela Jonathan Morris
Dojjen Preston Lockwood
Dugdale Brian Miller

Director: Fiona Cumming
Designer: Jan Spoczynski

(18–26 January 1983)

Mawdryn Undead

w Peter Grimwade *(A 4-part story)*
The Black Guardian seeks revenge on the Doctor for cheating him out of the Key to Time in his previous incarnation. He uses Turlough, a young alien trapped on Earth, as his agent. By chance, one of Turlough's teachers is an old friend of the Doctor – but with an alarming memory loss.
The Black Guardian Valentine Dyall

Brigadier Lethbridge Stewart **Nicholas Courtney**
Mawdryn **David Collings**
Dr Runciman **Roger Hammond**
Headmaster **Angus MacKay**
Matron **Sheila Gill**
Ibbotson **Stephen Garlick**

Director: **Peter Moffatt**
Designer: **Stephen Scott**

(1–9 February 1983)

Terminus

w **Steven Gallagher** *(A 4-part story)*
Arriving on an alien spaceship carrying plague victims, the Doctor and his friends are separated. Whilst Turlough, prompted by the Black Guardian, tries to find more ways of killing the Doctor, Nyssa finds her destiny with the hapless Lazars and remains to sort out a cure.
Kari **Liza Goddard**
Valgard **Andrew Burt**
Eirak **Martin Potter**
Black Guardian **Valentine Dyall**
Olvir **Dominic Guard**
Sigurd **Tim Munro**
Bor **Peter Benson**
The Garm **R.J. Bell**

Director: **Mary Ridge**
Designer: **Dick Coles**

(15–23 February 1983)

Enlightenment

w **Barbara Clegg** *(A 4-part story)*
The Doctor, Tegan and Turlough find themselves part of a race being run by the Eternals, beings who utilise the emotions and attributes of mortals to find pleasure in their incessant existence. Turlough finally discovers the good within himself, banishing both Guardians from the Doctor's life – for now.
White Guardian **Cyril Luckham**
Black Guardian **Valentine Dyall**
Wrack **Lynda Baron**

Striker **Keith Barron**
Jackson **Tony Caunter**
Marriner **Christopher Brown**

Director: **Fiona Cumming**
Designer: **Colin Green**

(1–9 March 1983)

The King's Demons

w **Terence Dudley** *(A 2-part story)*
Whilst King Richard fights the Crusades, the Doctor faces Kamelion, a shape-changing android posing as King John, controlled by the Master. After a fierce battle of wills, Kamelion sides with the Doctor.
The Master/Sir Gilles **Anthony Ainley** *(alias James Stoker [Master's Joke])*
The King (Kamelion) **Gerald Flood**
Ranulf **Frank Windsor**
Isabella **Isla Blair**
Hugh **Christopher Villiers**
Sir Geoffrey **Michael J. Jackson**

Director: **Tony Virgo**
Designer: **Ken Ledsham**

(15–16 March 1983)

The Five Doctors

w **Terrance Dicks** *(90 minute special)*
Doctors and companions past and present are brought together by a renegade Time Lord to play the lethal Game of Rassilon in the Death Zone. President Borusa seeks immortality and will stop at nothing to achieve it – including treachery, murder and breaking more than one of the legendary Laws of Time. (This 20th anniversary story featured footage from the 'lost' tale *Shada*.)
With **Tom Baker, Jon Pertwee, Patrick Troughton, William Hartnell** and . . .
Richard Hurndall as *the First Doctor*
Borusa **Philip Latham**
Castellan **Paul Jerricho**
Rassilon **Richard Matthews**
The Master **Anthony Ainley**
Chancellor Flavia **Dinah Sheridan**

The Old Companions:
**Nicholas Courtney, Elisabeth Sladen,
Lalla Ward, Carole Ann Ford,
Caroline John, Richard Franklin,
Frazer Hines, Wendy Padbury**

Director: **Peter Moffatt**
Designer: **Malcolm Thornton**

(25 November 1983)

Season Twenty-one
(5 January–30 March 1984)

REGULAR CAST
The Doctor **Peter Davison**   *Tegan* **Janet Fielding** *(exit, Story 4)*
Turlough **Mark Strickson** *(Exit, Story 5)*
Perpugillian Brown (Peri) **Nicola Bryant** *(from Story 5)*
The Doctor **Colin Baker** *(intro, Story 5)*

Producer: **John Nathan-Turner**   *Script editor:* **Eric Saward**

Warriors of the Deep

w **Johnny Byrne** *(A 4-part story)*
Earth, 2084. Two global powers rule the planet, an uneasy truce awaiting one slip that might spark armageddon. On an underwater base, Sea Base Four, a group of spies might be that slip – or it could be the invasion force of the Doctor's old foes the Silurians and the Sea Devils.
Vorshak **Tom Adams**
Solow **Ingrid Pitt**
Nilson **Ian McCulloch**
Bulic **Nigel Humphreys**
Karina **Nitza Saul**
Maddox **Martin Neil**
Preston **Tara King(!)**
Sauvix **Christopher Farries**
Icthar **Norman Comer**

Director: **Pennant Roberts**
Designer: **Tony Burrough**

(5–13 January 1984)

The Awakening

w **Eric Pringle** *(A 2-part story)*
Tegan's wish to visit her English uncle turns disastrously wrong during his village's annual re-enactment of the English Civil War. The Malus, an evil force that has lain in the Church crypt, reawakes to exert its powers over time and people with lethal results.

Sir George **Denis Lill**
Jane Hampden **Polly James**
Joseph Willow **Jack Galloway**
Col. Wolsey **Glyn Houston**
Will Chandler **Keith Jayne**

Director: **Michael Owen Morris**
Designer: **Barry Newbery**

(19–20 January 1984)

Frontios

w **Christopher H. Bidmead** *(A 4-part story)*
In the far future, on the newly colonised planet of Frontios, the human inhabitants find themselves repeatedly and illogically bombarded by asteroids brought down by the gravitational powers of the malicious Tractators.
Range **William Lucas**
Norna **Lesley Dunlop**
Brazen **Peter Gilmore**
Plantagenet **Jeff Rawle**
Gravis **John Gillett**
Cockerill **Maurice O'Connell**

Director: **Ron Jones**
Designer: **David Buckingham**

(26 January–3 February 1984)

Resurrection of the Daleks

w Eric Saward *(Two 45-minute episodes)*
On a prison ship in deep space sits
Davros, evil creator of the Daleks. After
losing their war against the Movellans
(*Destiny of the Daleks*), the Daleks, using
mercenaries led by the sadistic Lytton,
come in search of their creator. But
Davros does not trust his 'children' and a
terrible battle ensues. Sickened by the
carnage, Tegan decides to leave . . .
Lytton Maurice Colbourne
Davros Terry Molloy
Stien Rodney Bewes
Styles Rula Lenksa
Col. Archer Del Henney
Prof. Laird Chloe Ashcroft
Kiston Les Grantham

Director: Matthew Robinson
Designer: John Anderson

(8–15 February 1984)

Planet of Fire

w Peter Grimwade *(A 4-part story)*
Resting in Lanzarote, Turlough finds an
alien artifact from his home planet in the
possession of Peri, an American student
he saves from drowning. As the Master
repossesses Kamelion, the Doctor takes
Turlough to meet his own people, and
after Kamelion is destroyed and the
Master defeated, Turlough leaves the
Doctor in the care of Peri.

The Master Anthony Ainley
Timanov Peter Wyngarde
Voice of Kamelion Gerald Flood
Malkon Edward Highmore
Sorasta Barbara Shelley
Prof. Howard Foster Dallas Adams
Amyand James Bate

Director: Fiona Cumming
Designer: Malcolm Thornton

(23 February–2 March 1984)

The Caves of Androzani

w Robert Holmes *(A 4-part story)*
The Doctor and Peri are caught up in the
political battles being waged on the twin
planets of Androzani. While Peri is
captured by the disfigured Jek, the Doctor
battles the gunrunner Stotz. But both
travellers contract a lethal disease to
which there is only enough cure for one.
As Peri recovers, the Doctor changes
before her eyes.
Sharaz Jek Christopher Gable
Stotz Maurice Roeves
Salateen Robert Glenister
Morgus John Normington
Krepler Roy Holder
Chellak Martin Cochrane
President David Neal

Director: Graeme Harper
Designer: John Hurst

(8–16 March 1984)

THE SIXTH DOCTOR: **COLIN BAKER**
(1984–1986)

The Twin Dilemma

w Anthony Steven *(and Eric Saward –*
uncredited) (A 4-part story)
The new Doctor throws himself into the
mystery of the missing Sylveste twins
which takes him and a frightened, distrustful Peri to the planet Jaconda where he
confronts the evil, slug-like Gastropods
and finally defeats them.

Edgeworth Maurice Denham
Mestor Edwin Richfield
Hugo Kevin McNally
Drak Oliver Smith
Romulus Gavin Conrad
Remus Andrew Conrad

Director: Peter Moffatt
Designer: Valerie Warrender

(22–30 March 1984)

Season Twenty-two
(45-minute episodes)
(5 January–30 March 1985)

REGULAR CAST
The Doctor Colin Baker   *Peri* Nicola Bryant

Producer: John Nathan-Turner   *Script editor:* Eric Saward

Attack of the Cybermen

w Paula Moore *(alias* Paul Wolsey *and* Eric Saward*) (A 2-part story)*
Earth, 1985: The Doctor and Peri become involved in a plot by the Cybermen to destroy the planet by diverting Halley's Comet. Travelling to the Cyber-world, Telos, with the mercenary Lytton, the Doctor discovers the Cybermen have another foe – the Cryons.
Lytton Maurice Colbourne
Griffiths Brian Glover
Russell Terry Molloy
Cyber leader David Banks
Cyber controller Michael Kilgarriff
Bates Michael Attwell
Stratton Jonathan David
Varne Sarah Greene
Flast Faith Brown

Director: Matthew Robinson
Designer: Marjorie Pratt

(5–12 January 1985)

Vengeance on Varos

w Philip Martin *A 2-part story*
On the planet Varos, entertainment is supplied by videos of torture and mutilation, and rulers are voted in by their ability to survive torturous elections! Into this scenario comes the repellent alien trader Sil, trying to gain a financial foothold – and enjoying the torture, too.
The Governor Martin Jarvis
Sil Nabil Shaban
Jondar Jason Connery
Arak Stephen Yardley
Etta Sheila Reid
Quillam Nicholas Chagrin

Areta Geraldine Alexander
Chief Forbes Collins

Director: Ron Jones
Designer: Tony Snoaden

(19–26 January 1985)

The Mark of the Rani

w Pip *and* Jane Baker *(A 2-part story)*
At Lord Ravensworth's mine, the Doctor discovers his old academy foe the Rani is inspiring 19th-century Luddite attacks as she seeks chemicals needed to restore harmony on her chosen base planet Miasimia Goria. When the Master joins in, the havoc really starts.
The Rani Kate O'Mara
The Master Anthony Ainley
Lord Ravensworth Terence Alexander
George Stephenson Gawn Grainger
Jack Ward Peter Childs
Luke Ward Gary Cady
Tim Bass William Ilkley

Director: Sarah Hellings
Designer: Paul Trerise

(2–9 February 1985)

The Two Doctors

w Robert Holmes *(A 3-part story)*
The Doctor meets up with a former self when a Space Station is destroyed by the Sontarans. Trailing the aliens to Spain, the Two Doctors also find themselves menaced by the cannibalistic Androgum, Shockeye.
The Doctor Patrick Troughton
Jamie Frazer Hines

Chessene **Jacqueline Pearce**
Shockeye o' the Quancing Grig **John Stratton**
Dastari **Laurence Payne**
Oscar Botcherby **James Saxon**
Stike **Clinton Greyn**
Varl **Tim Raynham**

Director: **Peter Moffatt**
Designer: **Tony Burrough**

(16 February–2 March 1985)

Timelash

w **Glen McCoy** *(A 2-part story)*
The Doctor and Peri arrive on the planet Karfel, where he was once an honoured guest (in his third incarnation). Since the Borad took over, though, life there has changed, with dissenters hurled into the destructive Timelash.
Tekker **Paul Darrow**
Borad **Robert Ashby**
Mykros **Eric Deacon**
Android **Dean Hollingsworth**
Brunner **Peter Robert Scott**
Katz **Tracy Louise Ward**
Vena **Jeananne Crowley**
Sezon **Dicken Ashworth**

Director: **Pennant Roberts**
Designer: **Bob Cove**

(9–16 March 1985)

Revelation of the Daleks

w **Eric Saward** *(A 2-part story)*
On the planet Necros, Davros is hailed as The Great Healer, a galactic saviour. However, the Doctor uncovers his real plan as one of universal carnage involving his creations, the Daleks. But not all Daleks are Davros fans . . .
Davros **Terry Molloy**
Kara **Eleanor Bron**
Orcini **William Gaunt**
Jobel **Clive Swift**
DJ **Alexei Sayle**
Vogel **Hugh Walters**
Takis **Trevor Cooper**
Tasambeker **Jenny Tomasin**
Lilt **Colin Spaull**

Director: **Graeme Harper**
Designer: **Alan Spaulding**

(23–30 March 1985)

Season Twenty-three

THE TRIAL OF A TIME LORD

(14 25-minute episodes)
(6 September–6 December 1986)

REGULAR CAST

The Doctor **Colin Baker**   *Peri* **Nicola Bryant** *(exit, Story 2)*
Mel **Bonnie Langford** *(from Story 3)*
The Valeyard **Michael Jayston**   *The Inquisitor* **Lynda Bellingham**

Producer: **John Nathan-Turner**

Script editor: **Eric Saward** *(Eps 1–8, 13)*

(Parts 1–4)

The Mysterious Planet*

w **Robert Holmes**
The Doctor is on trial again. His crime: breaking the laws of time, and he sits

* See note at end of Season.

condemned before his own people. He cannot recall how he got there, so the malicious prosecutor, the Valeyard, shows him a recent exploit involving the planet Ravlox and a pair of con men Dibber and Glitz.
Katryca **Joan Sims**
Glitz **Tony Selby**

Dibber **Glen Murphy**
Merdeen **Tom Chadbon**
Broken Tooth **David Rodigan**
Humker **Billy McColl**
Tandrell **Siôn Tudor Owen**
Drathro **Roger Brierley**

Director: **Nick Mallett**
Designer: **John Anderson**

(6–27 September 1986)

(Parts 5–8)

Mindwarp*

w **Philip Martin**
Aware that Peri is not 'in court' with him, the Doctor wonders where she is. The Valeyard then shows 'recent' events on Thoros Beta involving the sluggish Sil and a series of brain transplants by the scientist Crozier. Peri becomes the final host for Sil's master, Kiv – and is 'seemingly' destroyed by the Warrior King Yrcanos.
Yrcanos **Brian Blessed**
Sil **Nabil Shaban**
Kiv **Christopher Ryan**
Crozier **Patrick Ryecart**
The Lukoser **Thomas Branch**
Matrona Kani **Alibe Parsons**
Frax **Trevor Laird**
Tuza **Gordon Warnecke**

Director: **Ron Jones**
Designer: **Andrew Howe-Davies**

(4–25 October 1985)

* See note at end of Season.

(Parts 9–12)

Terror of the Vervoids*

w **Pip** *and* **Jane Baker**
At last the Doctor is able to present evidence in his defence: an adventure from his future in which he and a new companion, Mel, save the passengers aboard the space-liner *Hyperion III* from the genetically engineered killer plant people, the Vervoids.
Prof. Lasky **Honor Blackman**
Janet **Yolande Palfrey**
Commodore **Michael Craig**
Rudge **Denys Hawthorne**
Grenville/Enzu **Tony Scoggo**
Bruchner **David Allister**
Doland **Malcolm Tierney**

Director: **Chris Clough**
Designer: **Dinah Walker**

(1–22 November 1986)

* See note at end of Season.

(Parts 13–14)

The Ultimate Foe*

w **Robert Holmes** *(Part 13),* **Pip** *and* **Jane Baker** *(Part 14)*
The trial is exposed as a charade by the Master who is within the Time Lords' Martrix. He brings Mel and Glitz out of time as witnesses in the Doctor's favour – and shows the Valeyard to be an evil future interim incarnation of the Doctor. The Doctor then battles and defeats his evil self within the Matrix.
The Master **Anthony Ainley**
Keeper of the Matrix **James Bree**
Glitz **Tony Selby**
Mr Popplewick **Geoffrey Hughes**

Director: **Chris Clough**
Designer: **Michael Trevor**

(29 November–6 December 1986)

---

* All these identifications are purely *working* titles which were never used officially on screen or in *Radio Times*.

THE SEVENTH DOCTOR: **SYLVESTER McCOY**

(1987–?)

Season Twenty-four
(7 September–7 December 1987)

REGULAR CAST

The Doctor Sylvester McCoy   *Mel* Bonnie Langford
Ace Sophie Aldred *(from Story 4)*

Producer: John Nathan-Turner   *Script editor:* Andrew Cartmell

---

Time and the Rani

w Pip *and* Jane Baker *(A 4-part story)*
The TARDIS is forced down on the planet Lakertya by the Rani who needs the Doctor's mental powers to control her latest creation. The crash transforms the Doctor into his new form and, though confused, he and Mel overcome the Rani, leaving her to the mercy of her slaves, the Tetraps.
The Rani Kate O'Mara
Beyus Donald Pickering
Faroon Wanda Ventham
Ikona Mark Greenstreet
Urak Richard Gauntlett

Director: Andrew Morgan
Designer: Geoff Powell

(7–28 September 1987)

Paradise Towers

w Stephen Wyatt *(A 4-part story)*
Arriving at the apparently palatial Paradise Towers, the Doctor and Mel find those that live there under threat. The Rezzies, Kangs and caretakers have only one thing in common – something is killing them off.
Chief Caretaker Richard Briers
Deputy Chief Caretaker Clive Merrison
Tabby Elizabeth Spriggs
Tilda Brenda Bruce
Maddy Judy Cornwell
Pex Howard Cooke

Bin Liner Annabel Yuresha
Fire Escape Julie Brennon
Blue Kang Leader Catherine Cusack

Director: Nicholas Mallett
Designer: Martin Collins

(5–26 October 1987)

Delta and the Bannermen

w Malcolm Kohll *(A 3-part story)*
The Doctor and Mel win a chance to join a party of aliens who are due to holiday in Disneyland, Earth. A stray satellite sends the group crashing to a Welsh holiday camp in the 1950s, where the evil Bannermen are pursuing the Chimeron queen, Delta.
Gavrok Don Henderson
Goronwy Hugh Lloyd
Delta Belinda Mayne
Burton Richard Davies
Weismuller Stubby Kaye
Tollmaster Ken Dodd
Billy David Kinder
Hawk Morgan Deare

Director: Chris Clough
Designer: John Asbridge

(2–16 November 1987)

Dragonfire

w Ian Briggs *(A 3-part story)*
On the planet Svartos, the Doctor and

Mel go dragon hunting with Glitz and a young Earth girl, Ace. They discover that the dragon contains a key to a prison – a key which the evil Mr Kane will stop at nothing to find.
Kane Edward Peel
Glitz Tony Selby
Belazs Patricia Quinn

Kracauer Tony Osoba
McLuhan Stephanie Fayerman
Bazin Stuart Organ

Director: Chris Clough
Designer: John Asbridge

(23 November–7 December 1987)

Season Twenty-five
(5 October 1988–4 January 1989)

REGULAR CAST

The Doctor Sylvester McCoy   *Ace* Sophie Aldred

Producer: John Nathan-Turner

Script editor: Andrew Cartmell

Remembrance of the Daleks

w Ben Aaronovitch *(A 4-part story)*
The 25th anniversary story takes the Doctor back to Earth, November 1963, to retrieve the Hand of Omega – a powerful Gallifreyan weapon he had left behind previously. But Davros and his Daleks are after it, too – and so is the Dalek Supreme and his faction. In the conflict, the Doctor goads Davros into using the device which he has programmed to fly into Skaro's sun and turn it into a super nova.
Davros Terry Molloy
(alias Emperor Dalek Roy Tromelly)
Rachel Pamela Salem
Gilmore Simon Williams
Ratcliffe George Sewell
Mike Dursley McLinden
Harry Harry Fowler
Allison Karen Gledhill
Headmaster Michael Sheard

Director: Andrew Morgan
Designer: Martin Collins

(5–26 October 1988)

The Happiness Patrol

w Graeme Curry *(A 3-part story)*
On Terra Alpha, the Doctor and Ace find that to be a killjoy is fatal – the Happiness Patrol see to that. Whilst Helen A rules the planet, the Kandyman rules the kitchen.

Helen A Sheila Hancock
Joseph C Ronald Fraser
Gilbert M Harold Innocent
Susan Q Lesley Dunlop
Daisy K Georgina Hale
Trevor Sigma John Normington
Earl Sigma Richard D. Sharp
Kandyman David John Pope

Director: Chris Clough
Designer: John Asbridge

(2–16 November 1988)

Silver Nemesis

w Kevin Clarke *(A 3-part story)*
The Doctor and Ace try to thwart the multiple threats of a mad 17th-century noblewoman, a team of Fourth Reich activists and the Cybermen over control of Nemesis, a statue made of a living metal, which has returned to Earth 350 years after the Doctor himself launched it into space.
De Flores Anton Diffring
Lady Peinforte Fiona Walker
Richard Gerard Murphy
Karl Metin Yenal
Cyber Leader David Banks

Director: Chris Clough
Designer: John Asbridge

(23 November–7 December 1988)

The Greatest Show in the Galaxy

w Stephen Wyatt *(A 4-part story)*
The Psychic Circus has a reputation throughout the galaxy. The Doctor persuades Ace to visit but the circus is a death-trap run by the vile Three Gods of Ragnarok.
The Captain T.P. McKenna
Mags Jessica Martin
Ringmaster Ricco Ross

Stallslady Peggy Mount
Chief Clown Ian Reddington
Whizzkid Gian Sammarco
Nord Daniel Peacock
Deadbeat Chris Jury
Morgana Deborah Manship

Director: Alan Wareing
Designer: David Laskey

(14 December 1988–4 January 1989)

Season Twenty-six
(6 September–6 December 1989)

REGULAR CAST
The Doctor Sylvester McCoy   *Ace* Sophie Aldred

Producer: John Nathan-Turner

Script editor: Andrew Cartmell

Battlefield

w Ben Aaronovitch *(A 4-part story)*
An Arthurian legend, a nuclear convoy and a reunion with an old friend, as Cornwall becomes the battlefield for warriors from another dimension.
The Brigadier Nicholas Courtney
Morgaine Jean Marsh
Mordred Christopher Bowen
Peter Warmsley James Ellis
Doris Angela Douglas
Brigadier Bambera Angela Bruce

Director: Michael Kerrigan
Designer: Martin Collins

(6–27 September 1989)

The Curse of Fenric

w Ian Briggs *(A 4-part story)*
Vampires walk, and an ancient Viking curse comes to roost at an isolated World War Two research station.
Dr Judson Dinsdale Landen
Commander Millington Alfred Lynch
Mr Wainwright Nicholas Parsons
Jean Joanne Kenny
Phyllis Joanne Bell
Kathleen Corey Pulman
Vershinin Marek Anton

Director: Nicholas Mallett
Designer: David Laskey

(25 October–15 November 1989)

Ghost Light

w Marc Platt *(A 3-part story)*
The Doctor takes Ace to Victorian Perivale and the scene of her greatest nightmare.
Josiah Samuel Smith Ian Hogg
Mrs Pritchard Sylvia Syms
Nimrod Carl Forgione
Insp. MacKenzie Frank Windsor
Control Sharon Duce

Director: Alan Wareing
Designer: Nick Somerville

(4–18 October 1989)

Survival

w Rona Munro *(A 3-part story)*
A search for friends in Perivale turns up cats – and an old foe.
The Master Anthony Ainley
Patterson Jilian Holloway
Karra Lisa Bowerman
Midge William Barton
Harvey Gareth Hale
Len Norman Pace

Director: Alan Wareing
Director: Nick Somerville

(22 November–6 December 1989)

DOOMWATCH

Doomwatch was the first 'green' television drama series. It caught the stirrings of ecological awareness in the early 1970s and hit the target with a string of prophetic bullseyes.

The advances of science and technology promised a bright future, but here was a show that pointed out clouds not silver linings. As a word, *Doomwatch* quickly entered the national vocabulary; newspapers learning the new language of ecology saw in it a ready-made banner headline.

The programme title stood – loosely – for the Department for the Observation and Measurement of Science, a fictional government department set up to watch and control advances in science. *Doomwatch* was headed by Dr Spencer Quist, an abrasive but incorruptible scientist who didn't give a damn for the vested interests of politicians and businessmen. He ran a highly strung and independent team, including the dashing duo, Dr John Ridge and Tobias 'Toby' Wren, who were constantly clashing with the authorities.

The series was devised by Gerry Davis and Dr Kit Pedler and evolved out of their private obsession with the inherent dangers to mankind in scientific progress. The two had worked together on *Doctor Who* and, finding common cause, kept tabs on each new, devastating hazard, filling scrapbooks with examples on pesticides, defoliation, chemical and atomic waste, pollution, genetic experiments, noise and so on.

They called their new series 'sci-fact' and, indeed, many of the issues it raised became mirrored in real headlines over the coming months and years.

It soon gained a huge following and its first series audience of 12 million was the record for a first run. There were other surprises, too. The death of Toby Wren, blown up while trying to defuse a bomb on a South Coast pier, astonished viewers who weren't used to seeing their TV heroes die.

But it couldn't last. New faces came and went – including Dr Fay Chantry, brought in to give women a higher profile, but increasing emphasis on character conflicts was pushing the show away from its roots, and towards more conventional drama.

By the third season Pedler and Davis had left and were soon publicly disassociating themselves from the programme. After the third series' opening episode in which Ridge held the world to ransom with phials of anthrax, Pedler said he was 'absolutely horrified'.

'When we started it,' he commented, 'the clear object of the series was to make serious comment about the dangerous facts of science which should be drawn to the public. They have made a total travesty of the programme.'

Producer Terence Dudley defended the show, insisting that the third series *was* confronting the issues, and it did cover such subjects as lead poisoning, the population explosion, pesticides and river pollution. But the end was nigh and *Doomwatch* didn't come up for a fourth time.

REGULAR CAST

Dr Spencer Quist John Paul   *Dr John Ridge* Simon Oates*
Toby Wren Robert Powell *(Season One only)*
Colin Bradley Joby Blanshard   *Pat Hunisett* Wendy Hall *(Season One only)*
Barbara Mason Vivien Sherrard *(Seasons Two and Three only)*
Geoff Hardcastle John Nolan *(Season Two only)*
Dr Fay Chantry Jean Trend *(Season Two only)*
Dr Anne Tarrant Elizabeth Weaver *(Season Three regular)*
Minister John Barron *(Season Three regular)*
Cmdr Neil Stafford John Bown *(Season Three only)*

Series devised by: Gerry Davis and Kit Pedler
Producer: Terence Dudley
Script editor (Seasons One and Two): Gerry Davis
Script consultant (Season Three): Anna Kaliski
Music: Max Harris

A BBC Production
37 colour 50-minute episodes
Season One:
9 February–11 May 1970
Season Two:
14 December 1970–22 March 1971
Season Three:
5 June–14 August 1972
(BBC1)

Season One

The Plastic Eaters

w Kit Pedler *and* Gerry Davis
A plane dissolves in mid-air, its plastic components eaten away . . . Doomwatch faces its first challenge – to halt the disastrous spread of a man-made virus with the power to melt all plastic.
Minister John Barron
Miss Wills Jennifer Wilson
Jim Bennett Michael Hawkins
Hal Symonds Kevin Stoney

Director: Paul Ciappessoni
Designers: Ian Watson, Barry Newbery

Friday's Child

w Harry Green
Doomwatch is unwillingly drawn into a controversy which confronts Quist with a fundamental ethical question, when a scientist breeds a human embryo which he plans to bring to life in a flask.
Dr Patrick Alex Scott
Mrs Patrick Mary Holland
Mrs Norman Delia Paton
Det. Sgt. Bill Straiton
Gwilliam Richard Caldicott
Prosecuting solicitor John Graham
Defending solicitor Margaret John

Director: Paul Ciappessoni
Designer: Ian Watson

* NB: In Season Three, Ridge appears in just four episodes – 1, 4, 7, 10.

Burial at Sea

w Dennis Spooner

Deaths occur on a luxury yacht owned by a famous pop group which strays close to a secret dumping ground for surplus chemical weapons, including a defoliant.

Angela Connor Nova Sainte-Claire
Cobie Vale Julian Barnes
Peter Hazlewood Brian Spink
Tranton Peter Copley
Dr Collinson Gerald Sim
Johnny Clive John Stone
Astley John Horsley
The Minister John Savident

Director: Jonathan Alwyn
Designer: Moira Tait

Tomorrow, the Rat

w Terence Dudley

Geneticist Dr Mary Bryant's experiment in rat-breeding gets out of hand, and London is plagued with a new mutant breed of intelligent killer with a taste for human flesh.

Dr Mary Bryant Penelope Lee
Joyce Chambers Eileen Helsby
Dr Hugh Preston Robert Sansom
Fred Chambers Ray Roberts
Reporter John Berryman
Minister Hamilton Dyce
Small boy Stephen Dudley

Director: Terence Dudley
Designer: John Hurst

Project Sahara

w Gerry Davis, *additional dialogue by* N.J. Crisp

A state computer programmed with highly personal information on its citizens . . . The electronic invasion of privacy becomes an issue for the Doomwatch team who fall under the baleful eye of a newly established security section.

Commander Keeping Nigel Stock
Dr Stella Robson Hildegard Neil
Barker Robert James
Computer technician Margaret Pilleau
Computer voice Peter Hawkins

Jack Foster Philip Brack
Old man Erik Chitty

Director: Jonathan Alwyn
Designer: Moira Tait

Re-Entry Forbidden

w Don Shaw

A new nuclear-powered rocket is being tested, with the first British astronaut aboard. The smallest error could turn it into a flying nuclear bomb, spreading radioactive fallout over a wide area of Europe. And an error occurs . . .

Bill Edwards Craig Hunter
Max Friedman Noel Sheldon
Dick Larch Michael McGovern
Charles Goldsworthy Joseph Furst
Carol Larch Veronica Strong
BBC man, London James Burke
BBC man, Houston Michael Aspel
Gus Clarke Kevin Scott
Col Kramer Grant Taylor

Director: Paul Ciappessoni
Designer: Ian Watson

The Devil's Sweets

w Don Shaw

A new chocolate liqueur mix contains a drug which makes people susceptible to subliminal advertising. But it's also potentially lethal and when Doomwatch secretary Pat Hunnisett takes a give-away choc, the results involve the team in a desperate race to save her life.

Jack Jack Comer
Shipton Maurice Roëves
Scott William Fox
Mrs Tyler Bay White
Pegg John Law
Benson John Young
Dr Gray Mary Loughran
Dr Green Patrick Connell

Director: David Proudfoot
Designer: John Hurst

The Red Sky

w Kit Pedler *and* Gerry Davis

The rising crescendo of everyday sound

becomes more than an irritant, when noise from a high-flying aircraft actually kills . . .

Capt. Gort Edward Kelsey
Dana Colley Jennifer Daniel
Bernard Colley Aubrey Richards
Dr O'Brien Dudley Jones
Reynolds Paul Eddington
Mrs Knott Sheila Raynor
Duncan Michael Elwyn

Director: Jonathan Alwyn
Designer: Moira Tait

Spectre at the Feast

w Terence Dudley
Quist convenes a conference of top scientists to make recommendations about pollution. Many of the delegates become victims of what is thought to be food poisoning. Are they being got at?
Fielding William Lucas
Whitehead Richard Hurndall
Bau Oscar Quitak
Egri George Pravda
Royston David Morrell
Mrs Bonenti Karen Ford
Laura Lindsay Helen Downing

Director: Eric Hills
Designer: Moira Tait

Train and De-Train

w Don Shaw
Doomwatch investigates a mass extermination of wildlife in Somerset and finds the trail apparently leading to field trials of a new pesticide.
Branston Bill Wilde
Ellis David Markham
Mitchell George Baker
Miss Sephton Patricia Maynard
Miss Jones Rosemary Turner
Stephens Brian Badcoe
Ministry inspector Peter Whitaker

Director: Vere Lorrimer
Designer: Ian Watson

The Battery People

w Elwyn Jones
Tough ex-miners in South Wales drinking gin instead of beer and giving their wives the cold shoulder . . . A village's odd behaviour puts Doomwatch on the trail of a new hormone that is turning factory workers impotent.
Col. Smithson Emrys Jones
Vincent Llewellyn Jeremy Young
Dai Edward Evans
Bryn Michael Newport
Davies David Davies
Elizabeth Llewellyn Eliza Ward
Jones Ray Mort
Mrs Adams Mary Hignett

Director: David Proudfoot
Designer: Stuart Walker

Hear No Evil

w Gerry Davis
One northern firm's answer to unofficial strikes is to use the latest scientific discoveries to manipulate the lives of their employees. Quist is forced to fight them with their own methods.
Falken Griffith Jones
Operator Derrick O'Connor
Cook Peter Miles
Owen Brian Cox
Reid Michael Ripper
Mrs Reid Tessa Shaw

Director: Frank Cox
Designer: Tim Gleeson

Survival Code

w Kit Pedler *and* Gerry Davis
An object which falls into the sea near a south coast pier is identified as a nuclear device and must be defused. Toby Wren thinks he has succeeded – then finds another wire . . .
Air Commodore Parks Donald Morley
Wing Commander Colin Rix
Geoff Harker Ray Brooks
Toni Harker Stephanie Turner
Sam Billings Tommy Godfrey
Commander Sefton Robert Cartland
Minister Hamilton Dyce
Len White Edwin Brown
Chief Supt Charles John Dawson

Director: Hugh David
Designer: Ian Watson

Season Two

You Killed Toby Wren

w Terence Dudley *(pre-title sequence by* Kit Pedler *and* Gerry Davis*)*
In the aftermath of the death of Toby Wren, Quist – already riddled with self-doubt – finds himself under attack on all fronts. Meanwhile, Ridge is out to stop some human/animal embryo experiments.
Air Commodore Parks Donald Morley
Len White Edwin Brown
Minister John Barron
Permanent Secretary Macdonald Hobley
Dr Anne Tarrant Elizabeth Weaver
Dr Judith Lennox Shirley Dixon
Sam Billings Tommy Godfrey
Dr Warren Robert Gillespie
Prof. Eric Hayland Graham Leaman
Tribunal chairman Edward Underdown

Director: Terence Dudley *(pre-title sequence:* Hugh David)
Designer: Graham Oakley

Invasion

w Martin Worth
Two boys go missing while exploring caves beneath a mansion that houses deadly chemical weapons, and Ridge is held for 24 hours by a mysterious army unit in a remote Yorkshire village.
Dave David Lincoln
Joe Bates Victor Platt
Sandy Larch Arthur Brough
Sgt Harris Anthony Sagar
Tom Hedley Peter Welch
Mrs Smith Sheila Raynor
Mrs Hunter Joyce Windsor
Major Sims Geoffrey Palmer
Duncan Michael Elwyn

Director: Jonathan Alwyn
Designer: Jeremy Davies

The Islanders

w Louis Marks
The 200 inhabitants of the idyllic Pacific island of St Simon are evacuated following earth tremors. A return to their island home is dangerous – but the islanders question the kind of future they have in an increasingly polluted Britain.
Thomas George A. Cooper
Isaac David Buck
Inspector Charles Rea
Joan Shelagh Fraser
Alice Geraldine Sherman
Mullery Geoffrey Chater
Miss Marshall Rachel Treadgold
Busby George Waring
Dr Somerville Robert Sansom

Director: Jonathan Alwyn
Designer: Stanley Morris

No Room for Error

w Roger Parkes
Doomwatch investigates allegations that children have died after taking a new 'wonder drug'.
Senior House Officer Anthony Ainley
Dr Ian Phelps Anthony Sharp
Nigel Waring John Wood
Prof. Lewin Angus Mackay
Minister's PPS Michael Culver
Hilda Freda Dowie
Elliott Norman Scace
Gillian Blake Sheila Grant

Director: Darrol Blake
Designer: Graham Oakley

By the Pricking of My Thumbs . . .

w Robin Chapman
Sixteen-year-old Stephen Franklin is expelled from school because, his father says, he has an obscure genetic defect – an extra 'Y' chromosome.
Stephen Franklin Barry Stokes
Oscar Franklin Bernard Hepton
Mary Franklin Patsy Byrne
Judy Franklin Sally Thomsett
McPherson David Janson
Painton Robert Yetzes
Ensor Olaf Pooley
Botting Colin Jeavons
Avery David Jarrett
Jenkins Martin Howells

Director: Eric Hills
Designer: Tim Gleeson

The Iron Doctor

w Brian Hayles

An electronic watchdog that constantly monitors the health of the patients, diagnoses any change in their condition and prescribes treatment. 'A great step forward' claim the hospital governors. But is it?

Dr Carson Barry Foster
Dr Whittaker James Maxwell
George Harold Bennett
Mr Faber Frederick Schiller
Dr Godfrey Keith Grenville
Sister Trewin Amanda Walker
Mr Kemp Frank Littlewood
Mr Tearson Raymond Young

Director: Joan Kemp Welch
Designer: Ian Watson

Flight Into Yesterday

w Martin Worth

The effects of jet-lag acquire a personal significance for Quist when he is ordered home by the Prime Minister on the eve of addressing a major ecological conference in Los Angeles.

Minister John Barron
Duncan Michael Elwyn
Secretary John Quarmby
Miss Wills Jennifer Wilson
Thompson Desmond Llewellyn
Ainslie Robert Urquhart

Director: Darrol Blake
Designer: Christine Ruscoe

The Web of Fear

w Gerry Davis

The Scilly Isles are sealed off following an outbreak of Yellow Fever and Doomwatch is drawn into a virus hunt involving spiders.

Minister John Savident
Duncan Michael Elwyn
Patterson Desmond Cullum-Jones
Dr Seaton Walter Horsbrugh
Jenson John Lee
Griffiths Glyn Owen
Janine Stephanie Bidmead
Dr George Anthony Newlands

Director: Eric Hills
Designer: Jeremy Davies

In the Dark

w John Gould

A man called McArthur is threatened by a crippling disease that will eventually turn him blind, dumb and deaf. He's being kept alive by computers, but Quist convinces him that he should have the machines turned off.

Flora Seton Alethea Charlton
Andrew Seton Simon Lack
McArthur Patrick Troughton
Journalist David Purcell
Naval officer Michael Ellison
Dr Jackson Joseph Greig

Director: Lennie Mayne
Designer: John Hurst

The Human Time Bomb

w Louis Marks

A new age demands a new architecture . . . and a study into urban neurosis caused by living in tower blocks imposes its own stresses on Fay Chantry.

Mrs Hetherington Joan Phillips
Hetherington Talfryn Thomas
Cavendish John Quayle
Mrs Frank Ursula Hirst
Donovan Ray Armstrong
Grant Patrick Godfrey
Scobie Roddy McMillan
Sir Billy Langley Kevin Brennan

Director: Joan Kemp Welch
Designer: Colin Shaw

The Inquest

w Robert Holmes

'Every dog within a five mile radius of Silby must be destroyed' – the death of a ten-year-old schoolgirl from rabies brings a shock recommendation from Doomwatch scientist Colin Bradley.

Dr Fane Frederick Treves
Philips David Spurling
Mary Lincoln Judith Furse
Pritchard Frederick Hall
Marge Jean Marlow
McAlister Robert Cawdron
Harry Garry Smith
Coroner Edward Evans

Director: Lennie Mayne
Designer: Graham Oakley

The Logicians

w Dennis Spooner

Industrial spies are blamed for a break-in at a chemicals factory in which vital papers are stolen.

Malcolm Priestland Robin Davies
David Wagstaffe Stuart Knee
Colin Tredget Peter Duncan
Richard Whetlor Robert Barry Jr
Withers John Kelland
Priestland Noel Johnson
Kelsey Michael Grover

Director: David Proudfoot
Designer: Graham Oakley

Public Enemy

w Patrick Alexander

A clash between ideals and economics as Doomwatch probes 'revolting, dangerous and now deadly' pollution at a metals firm.

Arnold Payne Derek Benfield
Lewis Trevor Bannister
Gerald Marlowe Glyn Houston
Jimmy Brookes John Trayhorn
Dr Barton Roy Purcell
Nicholls Bill Weston
Donovan Norman Florence
Duncan Michael Elwyn

Director: Lennie Mayne
Designer: Graham Oakley

Season Three

Fire and Brimstone

w Terence Dudley

Ridge, disillusioned by the world about him, holds mankind to ransom by planting phials of anthrax in Moscow, Paris, Rome, New York, Berlin and London, and demanding that the governments tell the truth about environmental dangers.

Dr Richard Poole Henry Knowles
Julie Caroline Rogers
Duncan Michael Elwyn
Police sgt John Drake
Prison officer Clarke Eric Longworth
Warren Talfryn Thomas
PCs Jonathan Pryce/David Waterman

Director: Terence Dudley
Designer: Graham Oakley

High Mountain

w Martin Worth

In the wake of the Ridge affair, the Government wants to close down Doomwatch. Quist's integrity is questioned when he is offered a private 'Doomwatch' to lend respectability to a giant industrial combine.

Ian Drummond Ronald Hines
Cowley John Scott
Barman Kedd Senton
Manservant Ian Elliott
Drummond Moultrie Kelsall
Mrs Bell Betty Cardno
Gillie David Grahame

Director: Lennie Mayne
Designer: Graham Oakley

Say Knife, Fat Man

w Martin Worth

Anarchist students steal plutonium and threaten to make an atomic bomb. Then a group of gangsters try to muscle in on the action.

Lawson Alan Hockey
Eddie Peter King
David Adrian Wright
Sarah Elisabeth Sladen
Susan Maria O'Brien
Rafael Peter Halliday
Chief Supt Mallory Geoffrey Palmer
Prof. Holman Hugh Cross
Williams Sean Lynch

Director: Eric Hills
Designer: Graham Oakley

Waiting for a Knighthood

w Terence Dudley

A vicar's mental breakdown is found to be due to lead poisoning, and industrialist Richard Massingham becomes drawn into the pollution debate.

Rev. Frank Simpson Anthony Oliver
Mrs Simpson Margaret John
Richard Massingham Frederick Jaeger
Peggy Massingham Ann Firbank
Stephen Massingham Stephen Dudley
Josie Julie Neubert
Joan Sylvester Glen Walford

Det. Chief Insp. Logan Don McKillop
Norman Sylvester Bruce Purchase

Director: Pennant Roberts
Designer: Ray London

Without the Bomb

w Roger Parkes
A doctor invents a contraceptive which can be sold in the form of a lipstick. But it has an odd side effect – it's also an aphrodisiac.
Dr James Fulton Brian Peck
Mrs Joan Fulton Antonia Pemberton
Harry Brooke Charles Hodgson
Clive Hughes Kenneth Benda
Lady Holroyd Katherine Kath
Amanda Fulton Sally Anne Marlowe
Roger Halls John Gregg

Director: Darrol Blake
Designer: Jeremy Davies

Hair Trigger

w Brian Hayles
Anne Tarrant is horrified when she visits a research unit which is controlling psycho-paths and epileptics, using temporal lobotomies.
Beavis Michael Hawkins
Dr McEwan Barry Jackson
Prof. Hetherington Morris Perry
Miss Abrahams Pamela Saire
Robbie Damon Sanders
Emily Gillian Lewis
Police inspector Victor Platt

Director: Quentin Lawrence
Designer: Oliver Bayldon

Deadly Dangerous Tomorrow

w Martin Worth
An Indian family living in a tent in St James's Park – one of them suffering from malaria – draws Doomwatch into the problems of homeless immigrants, and Ridge into a protest against the horrors of widespread DDT use.
Duncan Michael Elwyn
Hanif Khan Madhav Sharma
Senator Connell Cec Linder

Miss Brandon Lorna Lewis
Susan Maria O'Brien
His Excellency Renu Setna
Indian family Ahmad Nagi, Farhat, Talib and Rahat Shamsi

Director: Darrol Blake
Designer: Jeremy Davies

Enquiry

w John Gould
Doomwatch discovers that a new aerosol nerve gas designed to defeat an enemy army without inflicting any casualties on them or the civilian population, is not as safe as is claimed.
Mike Clark Jack Tweddle
Dr Evans Michael Forrest
Dr Margery Becker Margaret Ashcroft
Dr O'Dell Eddie Doyle
Col. Jones Barrie Cookson
Susan Lewis Ann Curthoys
Stephen Grigg Michael Keating
Mr Clark James Ottaway

Director: Pennant Roberts
Designer: Ray London

Flood

w Ian Curteis
'One more inch! A mere inch! And we would have had a full-scale disaster in the very heart of London.' A freak tide threatens to flood the capital.
BBC reporter Tim Nicholls
Critchley Raymond Mason
Ericson Wensley Pithey
Dr Ridley Derek Benfield
General Robert Raglan
GLC man Robert James
Minister of Defence Michael Lees
Lt Cmdr Morrison Patrick Jordan

Director: Quentin Lawrence
Designer: (not known)

Cause of Death

w Louis Marks
Headlines allege euthanasia at a clinic run by Dr Cordell. And Ridge's geriatric father is a patient there.

Dr Cordell John Lee
Susan Maria O'Brien
Edna Jennifer Wilson
Phillip Nicholas Courtney
Wilfred Ridge Graham Leaman
Hospital sisters Margaret Ford, Patsy Trench

Director: Lennie Mayne
Designer: (not known)

The Killer Dolphins

w Roy Russell
Quist hears about dolphins being trained by the Navy to attach explosives to the hulls of enemy ships.
Professore Fillippo Balbo Angelo Infanti
Susan Maria O'Brien
Guila Rita Giovannini
Paola Maria Totti Viviane Ventura
Bill Manzero Richardson Morgan
Commodore Aylward Frank Duncan
Cavalli Bruno Barnabe

Director: Darrol Blake
Designer: Jeremy Davies

Unbroadcast episode:

Sex and Violence

w Stuart Douglass
An extreme right-wing politician tries to win power under the cloak of a women's clean-up campaign which is fostering an atmosphere of outrage and intolerance. Quist's team are called in to probe a suspected conspiracy of corruption. (Though recorded for the third series, this episode was declared too dodgy over its use of real footage of a military execution.)
Arthur Ballantyne Nicholas Selby
Mrs Catchpole June Brown
Lord Purvis Donald Eccles
Steven Granger Bernard Horsfall
Mrs Hastings Angela Crow
Mrs Angela Cressy Noel Dyson
Prof. Fairbairn Brian Wilde

Director: Darrol Blake
Designer: Jeremy Davies

DRAMARAMA

As a series of plays for children, *Dramarama* could roam far and wide for its styles and ideas. In the event, although the supernatural has been a regular theme, science fiction has only cropped up a few times, generally as light-hearted fantasy. For example . . .

Mr Stabs

w Trevor Preston
Mr Stabs is summoned to the City of Shadows by the sinister cardinals and is chosen to win the Black Glove of Melchisedek, the powerful sorcerer. He has to defeat the beautiful but evil Polandi and then seek the Raven Stone which will unlock the Great Gates leading to Earth. There, he will face Melchisedek in mortal, magical combat. (The character of Mr Stabs had first appeared in the ITV series *Ace of Wands*, in 1971.)

Mr Stabs David Jason
Luko David Rappaport
Melchisedek John Woodnutt
Polandi Lorna Heilbron
Visitor Patrick Malahide
Dog Derrick Branche

Director: John Woods
Producer: Pamela Lonsdale

Thames Television Production
2 July 1984
colour, 30 minutes

The Universe Downstairs

w Tessa Krailing
When bored teenager Vincent falls down the cellar steps of his new home, he's amazed to find himself on another planet, Cosmo, where his neighbours are fascinated by *his* world. On Cosmo, an old-fashioned mangle is considered more modern than a washing machine.
Beryl Rosemary Leach
Hervey Brian Peck
Vincent Jay Simpson
Dollbaby Cassie Stuart
Sky David Collings
Star Eileen Nicholas

Director: Michael Kerrigan
Producer: John Dale

TVS Production
20 May 1985
colour, 30 minutes

The Come-Uppance of Captain Katt

w Peter Grimwade
It is the year 3001. Captain Katt, the Robin Hood of space, roams the universe in his ancient spaceship, the *Salamander*, robbing the rich to help the poor, rescuing alien damsels in distress, fighting against galactic tyranny. (This episode was actually a play *about* the making of a long-running science-fiction show. Peter Grimwade had 'seen out' the Tom Baker *Doctor Who* in 1981.)
Katt/Ludovic French Alfred Marks
The Professor/Frank Lucas Derek Royle
Lt. Rook/Louise Jobling Janet Behan
Desmond Gibb Simon Rouse
Margot Clare Clifford
Pat Sarah James

Director: Peter Grimwade
Producer: John Dale

TVS Production
30 June 1986
colour, 30 minutes

Flashback

w Dennis Spooner
A child is caught in a time warp and transported back to the early 1940s.
Jeremy Dorian MacDonald
Elaine Charlotte Chatton
Simpkins Graham Stark
Parminter Noel Williams
Curator Stella Riley
Schoolteacher John Hartoch
Terry Roach Oliver Powers

Director: Terry Miller
Producer: Peter Miller

HTV Production
11 August 1986
colour, 30 minutes

Now You See Them

w Nick McCarty
Two badly behaved children, Ben and Lucy, visit a fair with their parents where they watch a magic show given by a magician The Great Callisto. But when the kids touch a magic box they are suddenly transported to a mysterious world of magic. When they eventually return, they are small enough to keep in a shoebox . . .
The Great Callisto Don Henderson
Evelyn Deborah Grant
Ben Lewis Turner
Lucy Joanna Clarke
Mum Liz Gebhardt
Dad Ian Talbot
Mr Birkett Peter O'Farrell
Soldier Ross Boatman
Dowager Vivienne Burgess
Sawn lady Lowri-Ann Richards
Clown Jo-Jo
Man in audience Howard Lew Lewis

Director/producer: Alistair Clarke

TVS Production
18 July 1988
colour, 30 minutes

EDGE OF DARKNESS

Gripping political thriller given an apocalyptic twist by some haunting mystical symbolism and its chilling nuclear theme.

On the surface, it begins as a murder investigation with Yorkshire police detective Ronald Craven facing his most harrowing case – the death of his own daughter. But as he uncovers her mysterious involvement in an ecological group called Gaia, Craven reveals what author Troy Kennedy Martin called the 'silhouette' of modern British politics and Whitehall's relationship with America, and he opens a sinister can of worms concerning defence, nuclear waste and the environornment.

Helping him lever off the lid is a burly American secret agent, Darius Jedburgh, who, with Craven, breaks into a nuclear reprocessing plant, Northmoor, where he steals some plutonium. This he subsequently unveils to startling dramatic effect in a speech to a NATO conference. Throughout the series, Craven is driven by conversations with his dead daughter Emma, who keeps appearing to him as a pretty substantial spectre.

Kennedy Martin's inspiration for *Edge of Darkness* was the image of Gaia, the name of the Greek Earth Goddess and, more recently, the theory of former NASA scientist James Lovelock that the Earth is a sort of self-regulating living being maintaining the planet's inhabitable environment.

Central to his story was the idea of 'man v planet' and the 'betrayal of Gaia' – evocatively captured in the series' final image of the black flowers, symbol of the Earth's preparation for the apocalypse.

MAIN CAST

Ronald Craven **Bob Peck**   *Darius Jedburgh* **Joe Don Baker**
Emma Craven **Joanne Whalley**   *James Godbolt* **Jack Watson**
Grogan **Kenneth Nelson**   *Bennett* **Hugh Fraser**
Pendleton **Charles Kay**   *Det. Chief Supt Ross* **John Woodvine**
Harcourt **Ian McNeice**   *Terry Shields* **Tim McInnerny**
Clemmy **Zoë Wanamaker**   *Chilwell* **Allan Cuthbertson**
Childs **Trevor Bowen**

Writer: **Troy Kennedy Martin**
Producer: **Michael Wearing**
Director: **Martin Campbell**
Designer: **Graeme Thomson**
Photography: **Andrew Dunn**
Music: **Eric Clapton** *and* **Michael Kamen**

Compassionate Leave
Into the Shadows
Burden of Proof
Breakthrough
Northmoor
Fusion

A BBC Production
Six colour 55-minute episodes

4 November–9 December 1985
(BBC2)

ERASMUS MICROMAN

A cross between a mad professor and *Doctor Who*, *Erasmus Microman* first burst onto the screen when he dragged two bored children inside his TV lair and led them on a time trip to meet history's greatest scientists.

A second series saw the 1005-year-old Microman return from a sojourn as Inspector of Black Holes for the Universal Space Federation to chase through time the deranged Dr Dark, an interloper from a parallel universe who sought to plunge the planet into a new dark age.

REGULAR CAST

Erasmus Microman **Ken Campbell**   *Dr Dark* **Lee B. McPlank** *(Series Two)*

Writers: **Stephen Trombley** *(Series One),* **Gary Hopkins** *(Series Two)*
Producers: **John Slater, Stephen Trombley**
Director: **David Richards**
Designer: **Rod Stratfold**

A Mirageland Production for Granada Television
14 colour 25-minute episodes
Series One:
3 March–14 April 1988
Series Two:
3 November–15 December 1989

THE ESCAPE OF R.D.7

TV science fiction took a giant stride forward in 1961 with the provocative *A for Andromeda*, but immediately shuffled back with *The Escape of R.D.7*. This five-part BBC serial which filled the Saturday-night void was a totally different concoction.

It concerned a dedicated but fanatical virologist, Anna Hastings, who believes she has developed a myxamatosis-like virus (R.D.7) that could wipe out rats and so end the scourge of the plague. Success would bring her international recognition, but when a young lab cleaner, Peter Warner, is accidentally bitten by a virus-infected rat, Anna is ordered to halt her experiments.

Somewhat miffed, the lady doctor rebels, drugging her hapless assistant and carting him off to a remote boathouse on the Essex marshes where she tries to win his trust by injecting herself, too, with the virus. Alas, she falls ill and with conventional sources of help now out of bounds, she is forced to seek the advice of Patrice Constantine, a sinister financier operating on the fringe of medicine. Then she learns that she may not be the only one infected. Tortured by fears that she has caused a nationwide epidemic and deserted by Warner, she accepts the dubious assistance of Constantine in a bid to turn the tide.

Barbara Murray starred as Anna Hastings, with Patrick Cargill as Constantine, Derek Waring as her officious boss David Cardosa, and Ellen Pollock as a colleague, Dr Mary Carter. The serial was produced by James Ormerod who had himself been involved in scientific research during the war.

MAIN CAST

Dr Anna Hastings **Barbara Murray** *Peter Warner* **Roger Croucher**
Tucker **Eddie Malin** *David Cardosa* **Derek Waring**
Dr Mary Carter **Ellen Pollock** *Mrs Warner* **Joan Newell**
Peggy Butler **Jennifer Wright** *George Warner* **Victor Platt**
Cafe proprietor **Doel Luscombe** *Mackie* **Nigel Arkwright**
Glass **Tony Bronte** *Dr Blenkinsop* **Philip Holles**
Dr Harrington **William Fox** *Dr Protheroe* **John Dearth**
Patrice Constantine **Patrick Cargill** *Michael Rabinowitz* **Paul Eddington**
Sir Charles Delman **Austin Trevor** *Mr Bannard* **Alec Ross**

Writer: **Thomas Clarke,** *from an original idea by* **James Parish**
Producer: **James Ormerod**
Designer: **Stephen Bundy**
Film cameraman: **Peter Hamilton**
Film editor: **Agnes Spear**
Music: **Eric Spear**

A BBC Television Production
Five 30-minute episodes, black and white
Out of Hand
The Glass Is Shattered
Twice Bitten
The Trap
A Matter of Business
21 November–19 December 1961

THE FANTASTIC JOURNEY

One of the more fanciful theories about the Bermuda Triangle has been that it contains a time-space warp that projects victims into some other dimension – and that was the basis for this fanciful American adventure series.

A small scientific expedition sets off across the Caribbean to study a natural phenomenon known as 'red tide'. On board a yacht run by Ben Wallace and his mate Carl Johanson are science professor Paul Jordan, his teenage son Scott, Eve Costigan, Dr Fred Walters, medical adviser Jill Sands and a pair of scientific assistants Andy and George.

Soon after setting sail they are enveloped by a green cloud, to the accompaniment of clanging bells, and a sudden violent storm capsizes the boat. The two assistants are drowned and the others washed up on a strange island where they encounter Varian, a man from the 23rd Century whose spaceship had crashed, marooning him here. They have a run in with Sir James Camden and his band of Elizabethan privateers before the group splits up, with Varian, Scott and Dr Fred going it alone into the ensuing series where, with the addition of two new regulars, a half-human, half-alien called Liana and a 1960s scientist, Willoway (from episode 3), they cross various time zones in search of a way home.

REGULAR CAST

Varian Jared Martin   *Dr Fred Walters* Carl Franklin
Scott Jordan Ike Eisenmann   *Liana* Katie Saylor
Dr Jonathan Willoway Roddy McDowall *(from Ep. 3)*

Executive producer: Bruce Lansbury
Producer: Leonard Katzman
Story consultants: Dorothy (D.C)
  Fontana, Calvin Clements
Music: Robert Prince

*Bruce Lansbury Productions, in assoc.
with Columbia Pictures Television*
10 colour episodes; pilot × 70 minutes,
rest × 50 minutes
5 March–6 May 1977
(BBC1)

Vortex (pilot)

w Michael Michaelian, Katharyn
  Michaelian Powers, Merwin Gerard,
  from a story by Merwin Gerard
A scientific team in the Bermuda Triangle
stumbles on a time warp into a different
dimension where they encounter Varian,
a man from the 23rd century who opens
their eyes to wonders beyond the dreams
of science.
Ben Wallace Leif Erickson
Sir James Camden Ian McShane
Carl Johanson Scott Brady
Prof. Jordan Scott Thomas
Eve Susan Howard
Jill Karen Somerville

Director: Andrew V. McLaglen

Atlantium

w Katharyn Michaelian Powers
All seems well at the gleaming white city
of the Atlantians, but the Source – a
master brain which controls all around it –
is in need of energy and Scott is singled
out as the supply.
Dar-L Gary Collins
Rhea Mary Ann Mobley
Atar Jason Evers
Itar Albert Stratton

Director: Barry Crane

Beyond the Mountain

w Howard Livingstone
Separated from her friends, Liana finds
herself in a village of beautiful men and
women led by Jonathan Willoway. Mean-

while Varian, Fred and Scott are lost in a
swamp and captured by green-skinned
aliens who claim they are the rightful
owners of Willoway's people – a race of
androids.
Cyrus John David Carson
Rachel Marj Dusay
Aren Joseph Della Sorte
Willoway Roddy McDowall *(intro)*

Director: Irving Moore

The Children of the Gods

w Leonard Katzman
Resting in the ruins of a Grecian temple,
the travellers are captured by children
with strange powers who hate the older
generation.
Alpha Mark Lambert
Sigma Bobby Eilbacher
Delta Cosie Costa
Beta Stanley Clay

Director: Alf Kjellin

A Dream of Conquest

w Michael Michaelian
Varian and his companions cross another
time zone and find would-be conqueror
Consul Tarant plotting to invade the other
time zones.
Tarant John Saxon
Argon Morgan Paull
Lara Lenore Stevens
Luther Robert Patten
Nikki Johnny Doran
Neffring Bobby Porter

Director: Vincent McEveety

An Act of Love

w Richard Fielder

Secretly injected with Cupid's arrow, Varian falls deeply in love with Gwenith, an alien whose people are living in a geologically unstable zone.

Gwenith Christina Hart
Maera Ellen Weston
Zaros Jonathan Goldsmith
Baras Vic Mohica
Arla Belinda Balaski

Director: Virgil Vogel

Funhouse

w Michael Michaelian

Varian and his companions come across a deserted carnival where Appolonius, a powerful sorcerer, offers to entertain them. (Unscreened in UK, after being scheduled, then withdrawn.)

Appolonius Mel Ferrer
Roxanne Mary Frann
Barker Richard Lawson

Dirctor: Art Fisher

Turnabout

w D.C. Fontana, Ken Kolb

Liana is imprisoned in a society where men treat women as slaves. But Queen Halyana has plans for a revolution.

Halyana Joan Collins
Morgan Paul Mantee
Adrea Julie Cobb
Connell Beverly Todd

Director: Victor French

Riddles

w Katharine Michaelian Powers

Varian and his fellow wanderers learn of a mysterious stone – the key to a doorway back to their own times.

Kedryn Dale Robinette
Krysta Carole Demas
The Rider Dax Xanos
Simkin William O'Connell

Director: David Moessinger

The Innocent Prey

w Robert Hamilton

The travellers befriend two survivors from a crashed spacecraft. But the two men are criminals and their arrival has a disturbing effect on a group of people who cannot understand the concept of evil.

Tye Nicholas Hammond
York Richard Jaeckal
Rayat Lew Ayres
Natica Cheryl Ladd
Roland Jim Payner

Director: Vincent McEveety

FIREBALL XL5

With *Fireball XL5*, Gerry Anderson's Supermarionation took its giant leap into space fantasy. Set in the year 2063, the series charted the interplanetary adventures of a spacecraft and its crew: handsome blond pilot Steve Zodiac, glamorous blonde space doctor Venus, maths genius Professor Mat Matic, and a transparent 'auto pilot', Robert the Robot. There was also a pet – a strange creature called the Lazoon, who had a habit of imitating sounds and a hungry passion for Martian Delight.

XL5 was part of a World Space Fleet based at Space City, an island in the Pacific Ocean, run by Commander Zero and Lieutenant 90. Its mission: to patrol sector 25 of the universe, beyond the solar system. The biggest craft of its kind, the 300-foot long XL5 had a detachable nose cone called Fireball Junior, used for landings while the mother ship stayed in orbit. Other equipment included hoverbikes called jetmobiles. (These were reused in Gerry Anderson's next series, *Stingray*.)

The Fireball shows contained an imaginative array of detailed space models and miniature sets, both terrestrial and alien – all given an extra atmospheric twist by the black and white photography. The special effects were again masterminded by Derek Meddings who later graduated from the Anderson studio floor to become an Oscar-winning creator of dazzling effects for such films as *Moonraker* and *Superman*.

The voice of Steve Zodiac was provided by Paul Maxwell; John Bluthal, a renowned character actor, was Commander Zero; while Sylvia Anderson played all the female characters, including Venus.

Fireball XL5's impact was tremendous. It is still the only Gerry Anderson production to have been fully networked on American television (NBC, 1963), and in its modest way stands as a role model for series such as *Star Trek*. It has always been fondly remembered by its contemporary audience though a revival on the ITV network in 1985–6 achieved disappointing ratings. Today's young audience were not as impressed as their parents had been.

CHARACTER VOICES

Steve Zodiac **Paul Maxwell**   *Venus* **Sylvia Anderson**
Prof. Mat Matic **David Graham**   *Cmdr Zero* **John Bluthal**
Robert the Robot **Gerry Anderson**   *Lt 90* **David Graham**

Created by: **Gerry** and **Sylvia Anderson**
Producer: **Gerry Anderson**
Associate producer: **Reg Hill**
Music: **Barry Gray**
Title song sung by: **Don Spencer**
Special effects: **Derek Meddings**

An AP Films Production for ATV/ITC
39 30-minute episodes, made in black and white

28 October 1962–23 June 1963 (eps 1–35)
6–27 October 1963 (eps 36–39)*
(ATV, London region)

Planet 46

w **Gerry** and **Sylvia Anderson**
Steve Zodiac and his crew intercept a planetomic missile on a course to destroy Earth. Seeking out the source of the attack, on Planet 46, Steve and Venus are captured by a race of Subterrains who launch another missile – with Venus on board as a hostage.

Director: **Gerry Anderson**

The Doomed Planet

w **Alan Fennell**
A flying saucer leads to Steve Zodiac saving a planet which is doomed to be destroyed because it is in the path of another planet which has broken orbit.

Director: **Alan Pattillo**

* The last four episodes were immediately followed by repeats of earlier episodes.

Space Immigrants

w Anthony Marriott

A spaceship, the *Mayflower III*, piloted by Venus, is carrying pioneers to a new planet. But they are unaware of the danger that awaits them from an evil race of little people called the Lilliputians.

Director: Alan Pattillo

Plant Man From Space

w Anthony Marriott

The World Space Patrol foils a fiendish plan hatched by Prof. Matic's old friend Dr Rootes, to overcome Earth by strangling it with a strange kind of plant life.

Director: John Kelly

Spy in Space

w Alan Fennell

Refuelling at a space station, Steve and the Fireball crew walk into a trap laid by the notorious Mr and Mrs Spacespy who plan to seize Fireball, holding Venus as hostage. All seems lost until an ingenious device of Mat Matic's sends Mr Space Spy screaming into orbit.

Director: Alan Pattillo

The Sun Temple

w Anthony Marriott

On the planet Rejusca, Steve and Zoonie must save Venus from a pair of sun worshippers who plan to make her a sizzling sacrifice to their god.

Director: John Kelly

XL5 to H₂O

w Alan Fennell

Fireball responds to an urgent distress call from the last two survivors of a planet menaced by a weird fish man armed with a poisonous smoke gun.

Director: John Kelly

Space Pirates

w Anthony Marriott

The Fireball crew get involved in a complicated game of bluff and double bluff to outwit a gang of space pirates plundering freighters from the mineral-rich planet Minera. The final bluff is that this whole saga is a bedtime story Venus is telling to Cmdr Zero's son Jonathan.

Director: Bill Harris

Flying Zodiac

w Anthony Marriott

Steve nearly falls victim to sabotage at a Space City circus as part of a scheme by Mr and Mrs Spacespy to help alien nomads take over Earth. Then Venus wakes up . . . it was only a dream. (Dreams provided a recurring source of storylines for APF scriptwriters!)

Director: Bill Harris

Space Pen

w Dennis Spooner

Posing as criminals, the Fireball crew head for the prison planet Conva in pursuit of two Space City raiders, and wind up facing death in Mr and Mrs Spacespy's lethal water chamber.

Director: John Kelly

Space Monster

w Gerry Anderson

Zoonie's talent for mimicry gets the Fireball folk out of a tight spot when they investigate the disappearance of patrol ship *XL2* and find themselves menaced by a space monster.

Director: John Kelly

The Last of the Zanadus

w Anthony Marriott

Zoonie falls sick – victim of a plot by the evil Kudos, lone inhabitant of the planet

Zanada, to destroy all lazoons with a deadly virus. Fireball flies to Zanada where Steve defeats Kudos and obtains the antidote.

Director: Alan Pattillo

Planet of Platonia

w Alan Fennell
Sent to bring the King of the Platinum Planet back to Earth for trade talks, the Fireball crew foil a bomb plot by the King's aide, Volvo, to kill his ruler and plunge the two planets into war.

Director: David Elliott

The Triads

w Alan Fennell
Steve, Venus and Mat encounter Graff and Snaff, a couple of friendly giants, on Triad – a planet three times the size of Earth, and help them in their efforts to explore space.

Director: Alan Pattillo

Wings of Danger

w Alan Fennell
Investigating strange signals coming from Planet 46 – the home of the subterrains – Steve Zodiac is unknowingly poisoned by a robot bird equipped with deadly radium capsules. Swift surgery by Venus saves his life, but the bird is waiting to 'pounce' again . . .

Director: David Elliott

Convict in Space

w Alan Fennell
Mr and Mrs Spacespy pull the old 'can you help, our spaceship has broken down' routine to trick Steve into releasing convicted space robber Grothan Deblis who is being taken to Planet Conva, the prison planet. They want Deblis to lead them to where he has hidden his stolen plans.

Director: Bill Harris

Space Vacation

w Dennis Spooner
A quiet, relaxing vacation on the rich and beautiful planet of Olympus turns into a race against time for Steve when he and the Fireball crew become caught up in an interplanetary feud.

Director: Alan Pattillo

Flight to Danger

w Alan Fennell
To win his astronaut's wings Lt 90 must complete a solo orbit of the moon. But disaster strikes when his rocket catches fire, and he is feared lost until Mat picks up a drifting object on his spacemanscope. Lt 90's wings are well-earned!

Director: David Elliott

Prisoner on the Lost Planet

w Anthony Marriott
Answering a distress call from uncharted space, Steve finds himself on a misty planet, dominated by a giant smouldering volcano, where he meets a beautiful Amazonian exile who threatens to activate the volcano if she is not helped to escape.

Director: Bill Harris

The Forbidden Planet

w Anthony Marriott
Prof Matic's new invention, the ultra-scope, picks out the planet Nutopia – never before seen by eyes from Earth, and reputed to be the perfect planet. But the Nutopians are watching *them*, and decide to kidnap the Earthlings using their travel transmitter.

Director: David Elliott

Robert to the Rescue

w Dennis Spooner
Steve, Mat and Venus are imprisoned on an Unknown Planet by two domeheads,

Magar and Proton, who propose to wipe their Earth memories and keep them there forever. Before his brainwashing begins Steve orders Robert to rescue them . . . Coming out of a trance later, the crew find they are bound for home, but remember nothing.

Director: Bill Harris

Dangerous Cargo

w Dennis Spooner
On a mission to destroy an unstable ghost planet, Steve and Mat set the explosives, then find they've been trapped in a mineshaft by Subterrains. With the seconds ticking away, they struggle to escape before the planet blasts into a blazing inferno.

Director: John Kelly

Mystery of the TA2

w Dennis Spooner
When the Fireball team find the wreck of a spaceship that disappeared 48 years before, their search for the lost pilot, Col. Denton, leads them to Arctan where they discover Denton is living happily as King of the planet's Ice People.

Director: John Kelly

Drama at Space City

w Anthony Marriot
Jonathan Zero's midnight exploration of *Fireball XL5* turns into a terrifying adventure when Zoonie orders Robert to take off. Racing in pursuit, Cmdr Zero and Lt 90 are horrified to see *XL5* on fire. Boarding the ship they find Jonathan out cold and Zoonie, also unconscious, but holding a fire extinguisher. The brave little Lazoon has saved the day.

Director: Alan Pattillo

1875

w Anthony Marriott
Mat Matic's new time machine whisks Steve, Venus and Commander Zero back to the wild west of 1875, where Steve becomes a sheriff and Venus and Zero bank robbers! (This episode utilised leftovers from Anderson's puppet western *Four Feather Falls*).

Director: Bill Harris

The Granatoid Tanks

w Alan Fennell
Scientists on a glass-surfaced planet radio for help when they are menaced by six Granatoid tanks. *Fireball XL5* responds but is powerless to halt the assault until a surprise stowaway, Ma Doughty, turns out to be wearing Plyton pearls – the only substance that can repel the Granatoids.

Director: Alan Pattillo

The Robot Freighter Mystery

w Alan Fennell
Steve Zodiac resorts to subterfuge to prove that an unscrupulous pair of space salvage contractors, the Briggs Brothers, are sabotaging robot supply freighters so that they can pick up the pieces.

Director: David Elliott

Whistle for Danger

w Dennis Spooner
A plant disease has wiped out all vegetation on the jungle planet Floran. Fireball explodes an Ellvium bomb to kill the disease and restore the plant life – but the inhabitants are suspicious and imprison Steve, Mat and Venus in a 100 ft high tower.

Director: John Kelly

Trial by Robot

w Alan Fennell
Robots have vanished from four planets – and the disappearances are linked to visits by a famous robot scientist Prof. Himber. Then Robert also goes missing, but Steve

and Mat are prepared and follow their robot on a three-month journey to Planet 82 where they are captured and put on trial by the mad professor – ruler of his own robot race.

Director: Alan Pattillo

The Day in the Life of a Space General

w Alan Fennell
Lt 90 is promoted to General and his erratic commands trigger confusion and finally disaster as *XL5* crashes into Space City, setting it ablaze. What a nightmare . . . and that's just what poor old Lt 90 is having!

Director: David Elliott

Invasion Earth

w Dennis Spooner
A strange cloud hangs in the space sky and two Fireball craft sent to investigate explode with a blinding flash. *XL5*, returning to Space City, discovers that the cloud hides an alien invasion fleet poised to take over.

Director: Alan Pattillo

Faster Than Light

w Anthony Marriott
An out-of-control Fireball breaks the light barrier and the crew find they have emerged in a sea of air.

Director: Bill Harris

The Day the Earth Froze

w Alan Fennell
Icemen from the ice planet Zavia work to destroy Earth by deflecting the sun's rays using a giant disc, so lowering the temperature and causing even the sea to freeze solid. After escaping from an ice jail, Fireball's crew manage to destroy the deflector and the thermometer begins to rise again.

Director: David Elliott

The Fire Fighters

w Alan Fennell
Real fireballs are plunging to Earth, from a mysterious gas cloud. Steve and his crew must contain the cloud before it reaches the atmosphere. Their plan goes smoothly until a technical fault means Steve must complete the work by hand.

Director: John Kelly

Space City Special

w Dennis Spooner
Astronaut of the Year Steve Zodiac needs all his skills to talk Venus down after she takes over the controls of a supersonic airliner whose pilot has been sent into a trance by Subterrains. And it's awards all round as Venus and Mat pick up plaudits for bravery, service and courage.

Director: Alan Pattillo

Ghosts of Space

w Alan Fennell
A seemingly deserted planet . . . electric rocks . . . weird, poltergeist-like happenings . . . all part of a mystery that unravels after Steve takes a geologist to the Planet Electon.

Director: John Kelly

Hypnotic Sphere

w Alan Fennell
Steve, Venus and Prof. Matic are thrown into a trance by a mysterious sphere that has already immobilised a series of space tankers. Luckily, Robert the Robot is unaffected and, after saving the ship from disaster, provides the videotape clue that helps the Fireball crew defeat their evil assailant.

Director: Alan Pattillo

Sabotage

w Anthony Marriott

A neutroni bomb planted aboard XL5 is detonated by remote control. As the craft pitches helplessly, a sinister Gamma spaceship moves in to stun the crew with its gamma rays and 'beams' them aboard the vessel.

Director: John Kelly

Space Magnet

w Anthony Marriott

Fireball XL5 becomes trapped in the powerful gravitational pull of the planet Magneton and the crew discover that its invisible inhabitants the Solars are plotting to bring the Moon into their orbit.

Director: Bill Harris

FIRST BORN

Three-part BBC saga about the birth, life and violent death of a man/gorilla hybrid, based on the futuristic novel *Gorsaga* by Maureen Duffy.

Genetic scientist Edward Forester dreams of creating a new species, one with man's intelligence but without his homicidal aggression. The crowning achievement of his experiments is the birth of a human/gorilla hybrid, secretly using his own sperm. The baby, born with a temporary top-to-toe covering of body hair, is named Gordon and eventually grows up to be almost everything Forester could have wished for.

Almost, but not quite, for shortly before Gordon discovers his true origins he beds Forester's fanciable daughter Nell. Then, after angrily confronting 'dad', Gor demands to meet his 'mum', Mary the gorilla, who pounds her hybrid offspring to death in a frenzy of rage. The inevitable epilogue has Forester watching the christening of his daughter's baby boy, his benevolent smile turning to a look of horror as the baby's simian cry leaves us in no doubt that it is Gor's child . . .

Coming from the producer/director team responsible for *The Lives and Loves of a She-Devil*, this tale of genetic science-fiction was assured of a fair hearing. And though it began promisingly enough it was ultimately savaged by the critics for eschewing credibility in favour of melodrama.

CAST

Edward Forester Charles Dance *Ann Forester (his wife)* Julie Peasgood
Lancing (his boss) Philip Madoc *Chris Knott* Peter Tilbury
Nancy Knott Rosemary McHale *Dr Graham* Roshan Seth
Marais Marc de Jonge *Jessop* Niven Boyd *Emily Jessop* Sharon Duce
Gerry Nina Zuckerman *Gor* Jamie Foster *Young Gor* Peter Wiggins
Nell Forester Gabrielle Anwar *Young Nell* Beth Pearce
Priest Rob Dixon *Old priest* Ralph Michael *Lucy* Francesca Brill
Doctor Susan Beresford

Screenplay: **Ted Whitehead**, from the
   novel **Gorsaga** by **Maureen Duffy**
Producer: **Sally Head**
Director: **Philip Saville**
Music: **Hans Zimmer**

*A BBC Television Production in associa-
tion with the Australian Broadcasting
Corporation and Television New Zealand*
Three colour 50-minute episodes
30 October–13 November 1988

GALACTICA 1980

Hastily produced sequel to *Battlestar Galactica*, this series was voted third worst science fiction show of all-time by American critics.

First shown over here in 1984 on ITV where it steered a wayward course around the regional companies – many of whom were clearly without the proper assembly instructions as the series was rarely billed under its correct title – it usually went out as further episodes of *Battlestar Galactica*. It got a slightly more coherent nationwide run in 1988 when BBC2 played it back to back with the original Battlestar series.

The premise was straightforward. Having fled from the robot Cylon race that destroyed their homeworlds at the start of the original series, the Battlestar fleet reaches Earth after a 30-year odyssey with the Cylons still dogging their trail. Joy at finding the home of their long-lost 13th tribe turns to dismay when they realise Earth is not sufficiently advanced to help them repel the Cylon hordes. Determined not to expose the planet to the robot warriors, the Galacticans decide to try to speed up Earth's technology. A sub-plot involved a group of Galactican children on Earth, with an air force colonel trying his darnedest to prove they were aliens, and there was a brief flurry of Cylon conflict before the series fizzled out.

Lorne Greene recreated his role as Adama, avuncular commander of the *Galactica*, and there were a couple of new space heroes in Kent McCord as the untempestuous Troy (Adama's grown-up grandson), and Barry Van Dyke as his impulsive pal Dillon. Also hanging around was TV reporter Jamie Hamilton (Robyn Douglass) who became the only Earthling to board the Galactica. Villainy was taken care of by Richard Lynch and then Jeremy (Sherlock Holmes) Brett as the renegade Xavier. Masterminding the new campaign was a mysterious boy wonder, Dr Zee, a 14-year-old genius whose origins were belatedly revealed in the last episode.

In America, ABC had wanted *Galactica 1980* produced quickly to fill a gap in early evening schedules, so the shows were tailored to a 'family' audience. Violence was toned down and morality/educational angles played up. But the critics were cruel and the audiences unreceptive. Battlestar fans deserted the ship which sank in the ratings. Even a late re-entry by Dirk Benedict (later Face in *The A-Team*), to re-create his *Battlestar Galactica* role of Starbuck, failed to save the show which was scuppered after just ten episodes.

Main Cast

Commander Adama Lorne Greene   *Capt. Troy* Kent McCord
Lt Dillon Barry Van Dyke   *Jamie Hamilton* Robyn Douglass
Dr Zee Robbie Rist *(Galactica Discovers Earth)* Patrick Stuart *(all other episodes)*
Col Boomer Herb Jefferson Jr   *Col. Sydell* Alan Miller
Brooks Fred Holliday   *Xavier* Richard Lynch, Jeremy Brett *(Spaceball)*

Creator/Executive producer: Glen A. Larson
Theme: Stu Phillips *and* Glen Larson
Director of photography: Frank P. Beascoechea
Miniatures and special photography: Universal Hartland, *supervisors* David M. Garber, Wayne Smith

ABC TV Production in association with Glen A. Larson Productions and Universal MCA Ltd
Ten 60-minute colour episodes
UK premiere: 1 September–20 October 1984 (Seven episodes)*
(Grampian)

* Until the BBC's run in 1988, all ITV regional runs began with episode four, *The Super Scouts*.

Galactica Discovers Earth

w Glen A. Larson *(A 3-part story)**
Finding Earth ill-equipped to meet the Cylon menace, the Galacticans despatch teams to try to speed up its technological advance. Troy and Dillon become entangled with newsgirl Jamie Hamilton who tags along when they are recalled to the *Galactica* where renegade Xaviar, impatient with the slow progress, has decided to use time travel to bestow Galactican secrets on an earlier Earth generation. Unwisely he plumps for Nazi Germany so Troy, Dillon and Jamie pursue him back in time.
Gen. Cushing Richard Eastham
Prof. Mortinson Robert Reed
Carlyle Pamela Susan Shoop
Willy Brion James
Sheriff Ted Gehring
German commander Curt Lowens
Stockwell Christopher Stone

Director: Sidney Hayers

The Super Scouts

w Glen A. Larson *(A 2-part story)*
A surprise Cylon attack forces Troy and Dillon to take a group of Galactican children to Earth where they pose as a scout troop on a camping trip. But three of the kids become critically ill after drinking polluted water and with Air Force Col. Sydell's net closing in, Adama and Dr Zee must stage an emergency rescue mission.

Stockton Mike Kellin
Sheriff Ellsworth John Quade
Spencer George Deloy
Nurse Valerie Carlene Watkins
Moonstone Eric Larson
Starla Michelle Larson
Jason Eric Taslitz

Directors: Vince Edwards, Sig Neufeld

* First shown in the UK on 7 May 1984 as a TV movie, *Conquest of Earth*, which combined the first part of this story with footage from the later episodes *The Night the Cylons Landed* and *So This is New York*. The three original first episodes were finally shown in their 'proper' form in the BBC's run (17–31 March 1988).

Spaceball

w Frank Lupo, Jeff Freilich, Glen A.
   Larson

Treacherous Xaviar, now in disguise (as Jeremy Brett!), sends Troy and Dillon on a phoney mission in a sabotaged Viper spacecraft, so that he can kidnap the earthbound Galactican children. However, they're taken by Jamie Hamilton to a baseball camp for under-privileged kids where, with both Xaviar and Col. Sydell waiting to pounce, they play ball . . . Galactican style!

Hal Bert Rosario
Billy Paul Koslo
Tommy Wayne Morton
Stratton Trent Dolan
Red Bill Molloy

Director: Barry Crane

The Night the Cylons Landed

w Glen A. Larson

A Cylon craft, damaged by a Galactican Viper, crashes on America's East Coast. Luckily for its survivors, lookalike humanoid Andromus and Centurion Andromidus, it's Hallowe'en and they have *no* trouble blending in. While Troy and Dillon pursue them, the Cylon duo plot to take over a New York radio station and call up the Cylon fleet.

Andromus Roger Davis
Norman William Daniels
Col. Briggs Peter Mark Richman
Shirley Lara Parker
Andromidus Neil Zevnik

Director: Sig Neufeld

So This is New York

w Glen A. Larson

Troy and Dillon don tuxedos for an onstage dance with a star, elude Central Park thugs and rescue a girl trapped in a blaze started by the Cylons who've been hanging out at a media costume party. But can they stop the Cylon pair broadcasting to their hostile space fleet?

Guest cast as previous episode plus:
Arnie Val Bisoglio
Mildred Marj Dusay
Star Heather Young
Himself Wolfman Jack

Director: Barry Crane

Space Croppers (aka Harvest Home)

w Robert L. McCullogh

Desperate to replenish the space fleet's food supplies after a Cylon attack destroys their farm ship, Troy and Dillon team up with a farmer who faces his own threat – from a powerful land baron. Dealing with that *and* getting the crop planted, calls for a little help from their friends in space . . .

Hector Ned Romero
Steadman Dana Elcar
Trent Bill Cort
Louise Anna Navarro
Gloria Ana Alicia
Maze Andy Jarrell
Barrett Bill McKinney

Director: Dan Haller

The Return of Starbuck

w Glen A. Larson

The fate of space warrior Lt Starbuck is revealed in a vivid dream of teenage genius Dr Zee in which Starbuck crashes on a desolate planet where he reassembles a Cylon robot for company and encounters a mysterious (and pregnant) woman. When his story is told, Dr Zee finally learns the truth about the identity of the woman's baby.

Starbuck Dirk Benedict
Centurion Rex Cutter
Angela Judith Chapman

Director: Ron Satloff

GALLOPING GALAXIES!

Wacky space comedy from the team behind *Rentaghost*, Bob Block and Jeremy Swan. Set in the 25th century, it followed the interplanetary merchant ship *Voyager* as it boldly went through asteroid belts, time warps and black holes, supposedly under the control of SID (Space Investigation Detector), a bossy computer.

Manning the spaceship was a crew of three – Captain Pettifer, Second Officer Morton and Communications Officer Webster (replaced in Season Two by Mr Elliott), who were joined by an assortment of odd aliens and by Miss Mabel Appleby who arrived by accident after a time-warp wobble. They were pursued by a notorious space pirate and his disintegrating robots.

REGULAR CAST

Voices of SID and Junior **Kenneth Williams**   *Capt. Pettifer* **Robert Swales**
Morton **Paul Wilce**   *Webster* **Nigel Cooke** *(Season One only)*
Mabel Appleby **Priscilla Morgan**   *Elsie Appleby* **Josie Kidd**
Space Pirate Chief Murphy **Sean Caffrey** *(Season One)*, **Niall Buggy** *(Season Two)*
Robot 7 **Michael Deeks**   *Robot 20* **Matthew Sim**
Robot 35 **Julie Dawn Cole**   *Dinwiddy Snurdle* **James Bree**
Mr Elliott **James Mansfield** *(Season Two only)*

Created and written by: **Bob Block**
Producer: **Jeremy Swan**
Designer: **Alan Spalding, Nick Somerville** *(Season One)*, **John Asbridge, Jonathan Taylor** *(Season Two)*
Music: **Jonathan Cohen**

A BBC Production
Ten colour 25-minute episodes
1–29 October 1985
20 November–18 December 1986
(BBC1)

GEMINI MAN

Originally billed here in Britain as *The Invisible Man Becomes The Gemini Man*, this 1976 pilot and subsequent one-season series were an attempt to turn an invisible flop into a visible success.

Ben Murphy (alias wisecracking outlaw Kid Curry from *Alias Smith & Jones*) starred as Sam Casey, an investigator for a government organisation called Intersect. During an underwater salvage operation he is caught in a radiation explosion that alters his body's molecular structure. Casey can now disappear at will – a knack exploited by his no-nonsense boss Leonard Driscoll who turns him into his new secret agent, assigned to such tasks as guarding an Olympic swimmer, driving a truck-load of chemicals and fighting a mad scientist's computerised robot.

But there is a catch. Casey can stay invisible for a total of just 15 minutes each day. If he miscalculates and allows his brief moments out of sight to add up to more than that in any 24-hour period, he will vanish for good.

Presumably someone, somewhere wasn't counting, because the *Gemini Man* did disappear after just one season.

It was produced by Harve Bennett who was also responsible for *The Six Million Dollar Man* and *The Bionic Woman*.

REGULAR CAST

Sam Casey **Ben Murphy**   *Dr Abigail Lawrence* **Katherine Crawford**
Leonard Driscoll **Richard Dysart** *(in pilot)/***William Sylvester**

Executive producer: **Harve Bennett**
Writer/Producer: **Leslie Stevens** *(pilot)*
Director: **Alan Levi** *(pilot)*

A Harve Bennett Production in association with Universal TV and NBC TV
11 colour 50-minute episodes
plus one 95-minute pilot
12 October–28 December 1976
(BBC1)

THE GEORGIAN HOUSE

Seven-part 1975 drama from HTV that followed the adventures through time of two children in a beautiful Georgian house in Bristol.

Two students, Dan and Abbie, take a holiday job at a museum which, 200 years earlier, was the home of the wealthy Leadbetter family. The pair are attracted by an African carving which suddenly emits a strange sound, and a voice commands them back in time to 1772. There Dan is transformed into a kitchen boy and Abbie becomes a member of the Leadbetter household.

The reason for their trip back in time? Ngo, a negro slave boy with strange powers, who is threatened with an enforced return to the misery of the sugar plantations, has manipulated a time tunnel that links the 18th and 20th centuries to bring Abbie and Dan back to help him return to Sierra Leone.

For one of the series' stars, Spencer Banks, time travel was not a novel experience. He'd played Simon Randall in the much admired 1970 children's series *Timeslip*.

CAST

Dan **Spencer Banks**   *Abbie* **Adrienne Byrne**
Ngo **Brinsley Forde**   *Ellis (Curator)* **Jack Watson**
Mistress Anne **Constance Chapman**   *Leadbetter* **Peter Schofield**
Ariadne **Janine Duvitski**   *Maid* **Monica Lavers**
Miss Humphreys **Anna Quayle**   *Lady Cecilia* **Valeria Lush**
Sir Jeremy **Michael Gover**

WITH

Cook **Ruth Kettlewell**   *Footman* **Stephen Holton**
Madame Lavarre **Anne Blake**   *Hezekiah Allsop* **Dudley Jones**

Writers: **Jill Laurimore, Harry Moore**
Producer: **Leonard White**
Executive producer: **Patrick Dromgoole**
Directors: **Derek Clark** *(Eps 1–2)*,
  Sebastian Robinson *(Ep. 3)*, **Terry**
  Harding *(Eps 4, 6)*, **Leonard White**
  (Eps 5, 7)
Designer: **Ken Jones**

An HTV Production
Seven colour 30-minute episodes
2 January–13 February 1976
(ITV)

GOLIATH AWAITS

Two-part American drama about a colony of survivors living for more than 40 years in a sunken liner.

A routine underwater exploration discovers the wreck of the *Goliath*, a 1000-ton luxury cruise liner, sunk by a German U-boat in 1938. Diving down to investigate, Peter Cabot is startled to see the face of a pretty young woman staring out at him through a porthole.

The US Navy is brought in to check out his story and discovers a community of more than 300 people who, under the 'benevolent dictatorship' of Third Engineer John McKenzie and his aide Wesker, have managed to live and flourish, building an apparently Utopian society in which they grow food in hydroponic gardens, obtain oxygen from seawater through electrolysis and create light from algae.

But the society has flaws, not least of which are the attacks of a group of ragged outcasts called 'bow people' led by a rebellious youth, Ryker. In the end, amidst chaos and conflict, most of *Goliath*'s inhabitants choose to leave the sunken ship and find a new life above the waves.

Location filming took place in the Firth of Forth and aboard the *Queen Mary* at Long Beach, California, and the 51-strong cast was headed by Christopher Lee, Mark Harmon, Emma Samms and Frank Gorshin.

Goliath Awaits was shown over two nights on ITV in June 1982.

MAIN CAST

Peter Cabot **Mark Harmon**   John McKenzie **Christopher Lee**
Adm Sloan **Eddie Albert**   Ronald Bentley **John Carradine**
Dr Sam Marlowe **Alex Cord**   Cmdr Jeff Selkirk **Robert Forster**
Dan Wesker **Frank Gorshin**   Dr Goldman **Jean Marsh**
Senator Bartholomew **John McIntire**   Mrs Bartholomew **Jeanette Nolan**
Lea McKenzie **Emma Samms**   Lew Bascomb **Alan Fudge**
Paul Ryker **Duncan Regehr**   Bill Sweeney **John Ratzenberger**

Writers: **Richard Bluel, Pat Fielder,** from an idea by **Hugh Benson** and **Richard Bluel**
Producers: **Hugh Benson, Richard Bluel**
Executive producer: **Lawrence R. White**
Director: **Kevin Connor**
Director of photography: **Al Francis**

A Larry White and Hugh Benson Production in association with Columbia Pictures Television
Two colour 90-minute episodes
10–11 June 1982

THE GUARDIANS

Television has frequently embraced the 'what if?' strand of science fiction to offer ideas about the kind of society the future might hold. *The Guardians* was such a series.

A political thriller, it unravelled an uncomfortable scenario for a not-too-distant future. After a general strike, galloping inflation, massive unemployment and the failure of a coalition government, England is run by a committee of dedicated experts and their sinister paramilitary police, The Guardians.

Peace and order have been restored from the chaos. But the price exacted is a high one – individual freedom. The 13-part series follows the growing conflict between those representing order and those dedicated to its overthrow who adopted the name of their unseen leader Quarmby.

Among the leading characters were Tom Weston, a Guardian officer who becomes a pawn in the struggle between resistance and government; his wife Clare; Dr Benedict, a psychiatrist who emerges as one of the leading rebels; Sir Timothy Hobson, the prime minister, and his son Christopher; and Norman, a sinister and powerful civil servant.

The Guardians was welcomed by most critics as entertaining and thought-provoking, raising questions about the nature of democracy and suggesting, in the end, the idea that self-government is better than 'strong' government.

The series was fully networked by ITV in 1971, except in Northern Ireland where Ulster Television deemed it 'not appropriate at this time'. They showed *The Comedians* instead . . .

MAIN CAST

Tom Weston **John Collin**   *Clare Weston* **Gwyneth Powell**
Sir Timothy Hobson **Cyril Luckham**
Christopher Hobson **Edward Petherbridge**
Dr Benedict **David Burke**   *Norman* **Derek Smith**
Eleanor **Lynn Farleigh**

Created by: **Rex Firkin** *and* **Vincent Tilsley**
Producer: **Andrew Brown**
Theme music: **Wilfred Josephs**

London Weekend Television Production
13 colour 60-minute episodes
10 July–2 October 1971

The State of England

w **Vincent Tilsley**
The Guardians have brought order to the land. But the people, oppressed by the new regime, begin to react. Dissenters appear.
First worker **Windsor Davies**
Peter Lee **Robin Ellis**
Receptionist **Patricia Dermott**
First minister **Garth Watkins**

Director: **Robert Tronson**
Designer: **Colin Pigott**

Pursuit

w **Hugh Whitemore**
As the Prime Minister, Sir Timothy Hobson, is leaving a Cabinet meeting he narrowly avoids an assassin's bullet, and is rushed to safety by a squad of Guardians.
Assassin **Peter Hutchins**
Newscaster **Michael Smee**
Interrogator **Richard Kane**
Sir Francis Wainwright **Richard Hurndall**

Director: **James Goddard**
Designer: **Colin Pigott**

Head of State

w **John Bowen**
An embarrassing diplomatic situation develops when the French president, due in London for important defence talks, refuses to come unless he meets the true Head of State. But who is *really* in charge?
Geoff Hollis **Peter Howell**
Bullmore **John Bryans**

Felicien de Bastion **André Maranne**
Cockney Guardian **Stephen Yardley**
Birmingham Guardian **Ray Lonnen**
The General **Kenneth Benda**

Director: **Robert Tronson**
Designer: **John Emery**

The Logical Approach

w **John Bowen**
Using his skill and acumen, Sir Timothy Hobson finally usurps power and becomes an effective rather than a nominal Prime Minister.
Gary Wilson **Jimmy Ray**
Paula Hollis **Monica Grey**
Steve **Brian Deacon**
Lady Sarah **Mary Merrall**
Sam Wilson **Ken Jones**
Quarmby **William Simons**

Director: **Tony Wharmby**
Designer: **Bryan Bagge**

Quarmby

w **John Bowen**
After the stabbing of Hollis, the Home Secretary, an immediate investigation is made by the PM and Norman to discover who shot the murderer, Sam Wilson. It reveals that the shot came from a hidden sniper. But who is the mastermind behind the killings?
Miss Quarmby **Joan Heal**
Detective **David Cook**
CID officer **Geoffrey Morris**
M15 officer **Leon Eagles**

Capt. Gerald Barclay Laurence Carter
Peter Petra Davies

Director: Robert Tronson
Designer: John Emery

Appearances

w Monty Poole
Having killed a detective in cold blood, Benedict now turns back to the routine business of causing chaos for the Guardians and the Government.
Dr Thorn Dinsdale Landen
Dr Banks Richard Moore
Man in clock shop Derrick Gilbert
Jordan Martin Fisk
Miss Quarmby Joan Heal
Newscaster Michael Smee

Director: Mike Newell
Designer: Andrew Drummond

This Is Quarmby

w Arden Winch
Quarmby has struck many times against the regime with bomb attacks and assassinations. But now the resistors launch a new campaign to get their message across, reaching the man in the street and confusing Norman and the Guardians.
Dace Richard Vernon
Gibb Robert Russell
TV presenter Christine Shaw
First Guardian John Rhys-Davies

Director: Brian Parker
Designer: Bryan Bagge

The Dirtiest Man in the World

w John Bowen
Guardians officer Tom Weston is still 'confined' to the rehabilitation centre and making no effort to escape. Benedict sees his value as a pawn in the struggle against the government and the Guardians but must encourage him to break out.
Dirtiest man Graham Crowden
Quarmby Peter Barkworth
Male nurse Ian Stirling

Director: Derek Bailey
Designer: Frank Nerini

I Want You To Understand Me

w John Bowen
Hobson's government is stronger than ever, with the Guardians clamping down on personal freedom. But the more repressive their measures, the more ruthless the resistance.
Det. Sgt Arnold Robert Morris
Paul Michael Culver
Jenny Ann Curthoys
Andy Christopher Martin
Barbara Barbara Ewing
Bob John White
Henryson Norman Bird
Ernest Fred McNaughton
Major Raymond Adamson
Quarmby Artro Morris

Director: Robert Tronson
Designer: John Emery

The Nature of the Beast

w Jonathan Hales
Clare has problems. Her husband Tom, now a drug addict, is still at large and being hunted by the Guardians. She turns to Benedict for help, but he plans to use Tom as a scapegoat for Quarmby.
Young Guardian lieutenant Nikolas Simmonds
Guardian private Richard Borthwick
Barry Anthony Bate
Carole Pamela Roland
First man Jonathan Hales
Barbara Hilda Kriseman

Director: Mike Newell
Designer: Andrew Drummond

The Roman Empire

w John Bowen
Dissatisfaction with Hobson's government is spreading – from sinister events in public to unrest and plotting in the Cabinet.
Ruth Elizabeth Adare
Patience Kathleen Michael
Hobbs James Grout
Industrialist Keneth Thornett
Steve John Rapley
Announcer Richard Grant
Major Eric McCaine
Insp. Arnold Robert Morris

Whittaker **Brian Worth**
Hawkins **Brian Badcoe**

Director: **Moira Armstrong**
Designer: **Colin Pigott**

The Killing Trade

w **Jonathan Hales**
Tom is still lying in a coma at Benedict's flat. Every hour he remains there means increased danger for the others if the Guardians discover him. So Quarmby must dispose of Tom. (No guest cast.)

Director: **Derek Bailey**
Designer: **Bryan Bagge**

End in Dust

w **John Bowen**
No one in England is safe any more – not even the disillusioned PM. The Guardians have not been disbanded and Quarmby terrorists continue their attacks. As conflict grows inside and outside the Cabinet the stage is set for a showdown. But where does Norman stand? Who will Chris Hobson side with?
Sgt Arnold **Robert Morris**

Director: **Robert Tronson**
Designer: **John Emery**

HELPING HENRY

Unusual series that uses the device of showing the world through alien eyes to inform and entertain pre-school children. Henry, though, is not your everyday run-of-the-mill space traveller – he's come to check out Earth disguised as a dining room chair. Guided by a young friend, Stephen, he makes hopelessly confused reports back to his superiors on the distant planet of Holgon, Cosmics 1 and 2 – a clear case of upholstering the truth.

The 13 15-minute episodes, shown on Channel 4 covered aspects of Earth Life such as pets and animals, shopping, transport, clothes and household appliances – 'just because the fridge is cold doesn't mean it's not well'. Deadpan comedian Jeremy Hardy co-wrote the shows and supplied the voice of Henry. Richard Vernon (Slartibartfast in *The Hitch-Hiker's Guide to the Galaxy*) played the ill-informed Cosmic 1.

CAST

Henry **Jeremy Hardy**   *Cosmic 1* **Richard Vernon**
Cosmic 2 **Martin Wimbush**   *Stephen* **Ian Harris**
Tricia **Miranda Borman**

Writers: **'Chips' Hardy, John Henderson**
Producer: **Madeleine French**
Director: **Philip Casson**
Puppeteer: **Roman Stefanski**
Puppet by: **Jim Hennequin, Peter Fluck**

Chips Hardy and Co Production
13 colour 15-minute episodes
28 February–19 May 1988
(Channel 4)

THE HITCH-HIKER'S GUIDE TO THE GALAXY

'The history of *The Hitch-Hiker's Guide to the Galaxy* is one of idealism, despair, struggle, passion, success, failure and enormously long lunch-breaks'

(Hurling Frootmig, 17th acting editor)

The Hitch-Hiker's Guide began life in the cultural ghetto of a Radio 4 serial, and by expressing ideas above its station rose through the ranks of repeats, a book and a record until it finally materialised before our square eyes in 1981, when it was hailed as the first inter-galactic multi-media epic.

Making a visual version of a cult radio show carried the huge risk that the result might not live up to listeners' preconceptions. But it did, and the series, created by Douglas Adams, is widely held to be the funniest science fiction TV show ever.

Neither did it squander the opportunities TV provided, stamping its own visual ID in the innovative use of computer graphics to accompany narrator Peter Jones's guide entries (a style adapted some seven or eight years later by *The Daily Telegraph* for its own TV ad campaign).

The Hitch-Hiker's Guide to the Galaxy is part satire, part fantasy, in which Arthur Dent, a typical, nonplussed Englishman still in his dressing gown, is swept up into galactic events of far-ranging magnitude, dealt with in a down-to-earth, prosaic manner which turns everyone and everything into a cosmic joke.

The basic plot – as if it really mattered – begins with Ford Prefect, a field researcher for the Guide (the standard reference for information on the universe), on Earth to update the entry on our world. With his human friend Arthur, he narrowly escapes the planet's destruction to make way for a hyperspace bypass.

They eventually find themselves aboard a stolen starship with two-headed con-man Zaphod Beeblebrox, his pilot girlfriend Trillian, and Marvin the Paranoid Android, a manic-depressive robot whose capacity for mental activity is as boundless as the infinite reaches of space, but whose capacity for happiness could be fitted into a matchbox, without even taking the matches out first . . .

Other stars of the shows are the Vogons, fat, ugly, green aliens who write the worst poetry in the Universe; Slartibartfast, designer of the Fjords; the Dish of the Day, a talking dinner; and a pair of pan-dimensional beings disguised as white mice who are searching for the Ultimate Question to Life, the Universe and Everything. They already have the answer – 42.

REGULAR CAST

Arthur Dent **Simon Jones**   *Ford Prefect* **David Dixon**
Voice of the Book **Peter Jones**
Zaphod Beeblebrox **Mark Wing-Davey** *(from Ep. 2)*
Trillian **Sandra Dickinson** *(from Ep. 2)*
Marvin **David Learner** *(Eps 2–3, 5–6)*
Voice of Marvin **Stephen Moore** *(Eps 2–3, 5–6)*

Writer/creator: **Douglas Adams**
Producer: **Alan J.W. Bell**
Associate producer: **John Lloyd**
Designers: **Andrew Howe-Davies** *(Eps 1–3, 5–6)*, **Tom Yardley-Jones** *(Ep. 4)*
Animated sequences: **Rod Lord**
Radiophonic music: **Paddy Kingsland**

A BBC Production
Six colour 35-minute episodes
5 January–9 February 1981
(BBC2)
first rpt: 4 June–9 July 1981
(BBC1)

Episode One

Arthur Dent is not convinced when his best friend Ford Prefect tells him that the world is about to end in 12 minutes, particularly when Ford reveals that he is an alien from the planet Betelgeuse and not from Guildford after all . . .
Mr Prosser **Joe Melia**
Barman **Steve Conway**
Vogon Captain **Mark Benson**

Episode Two

Rescued from Earth, moments before its destruction to make way for a hyperspace bypass, Arthur and Ford are on board the actual demolition spacecraft of the Vogons. Should they face certain death by being flung into the cold vacuum of space? Or should they tell the Vogon captain how good they think his poetry is?
Vogon Captain **Martin Benson**
Vogon Guard **Michael Cule**
Newscaster **Rayner Bourton**
Gag Halfrunt **Gil Morris**
Eddie the computer **David Tate**

Episode Three

Zaphod Beeblebrox heads the stolen spaceship *Heart of Gold* for the legendary planet of Magrathea whose business is building other planets. Arthur continues his search for a good cup of tea.
Voice of Eddie **David Tate**
Slartibartfast **Richard Vernon**

Episode Four

Arthur is astonished to learn that Earth was not what it had seemed and neither were the mice – and he's quite put out to learn that they are after his brain.
Slartibartfast **Richard Vernon**
Lunkwill **Antony Carrick**
Fook **Timothy Davey**
Majikthise **David Leland**
Vroomfondel **Charles McKeown**
Shooty **Matt Zimmerman**
Bang Bang **Marc Smith**

Episode Five

Having been blown to smithereens when a computer exploded on the planet Magrathea, the travellers find themselves in the restaurant at the end of the Universe.
Garkbit (head waiter) **Jack May**
Bodyguard **Dave Prowse**
Max Quordlepleen **Colin Jeavons**
Zarquon **Colin Bennett**
Dish of the Day **Peter Davison**

Episode Six

As a spectacular finale to his Disaster Area rock concert, megabig superstar Hotblack Desiato crashes an unmanned black spacecraft into the sun – unmanned, that is, apart from Arthur, Ford, Trillian and Zaphod . . .

Newscaster **Rayner Bourton**
Captain **Aubrey Morris**
No. 1 **Matthew Scurfield**
No. 2 **David Neville**
No. 3 **Geoffrey Beevers**
Marketing girl **Beth Porter**
Management consultant **Jon Glover**
Hairdresser **David Rowlands**

HOLMES AND YOYO

American comedy series about a bungling, accident-prone detective who is assigned a new partner – Yoyo, a six-foot electronic robot who's not much brighter than he is, despite a computer brain.

From Leonard Stern, the man who gave the world *Get Smart*, it starred Walter Matthau lookalike Richard B. Shull and John Schuck, best remembered as Rock Hudson's stooge in *MacMillan and Wife*.

REGULAR CAST

Alexander Holmes **Richard B. Shull**   *Gregory 'Yoyo' Yoyonovitch* **John Schuck**

Executive producer: **Leonard Stern**

A Universal Production

13/16 colour 25-minute episodes
29 October 1976–9 February 1977
(BBC1)

THE INCREDIBLE HULK

'Philosophically the show reaches out to an even broader point – how can man learn to control the demon within him'

(MCA TV press handout)

'It did not seem possible that there could be a sillier series than *The Man From Atlantis* . . .'

(*The Sun*, June 1978)

The *Incredible Hulk* was introduced to British TV viewers in 1978, as the latest product off the conveyor belt of sf-based heroes to emerge from America in the 1970s.

We'd had *The Six Million Dollar Man*, *The Bionic Woman* and *Man From Atlantis*, now there was Dr David Banner, a sensitive, compassionate scientist whose search for a way to unleash man's secret source of strength had a bizarre result.

Banner's desire to find a way of tapping some kind of super-strength is triggered by his failure to rescue his wife from a blazing car. Experimenting with gamma rays, he accidentally receives an overdose, bringing about a Jekyll and Hyde personality he cannot control. Every time anger and frustration overpower his normally placid emotions, Banner is transformed into the Hulk – a 7 ft tall, green-skinned man-beast with phenomenal strength. His shirt splits, his shoes vanish, but, as this was a family show, his trousers stay on.

After a couple of 90-minute pilot films, the series took on the familiar mantle of *The Fugitive*, a 'lumbering man' show with Banner/Hulk searching for the scientific answers and antidote to his plight. Each week he encountered various strangers who tried to help, hinder or understand him. The usual format was: Banner meets good guy/girl. They get in trouble. Banner gets cross and turns into the Hulk who stomps the bad guys. His anger subsides and he becomes mild-mannered David Banner again.

The regular 'villain' of the show was nosy, headline-hunting reporter Jack McGee who believes the Hulk is a killer and trails him round the country, desperate to expose Banner's secret.

Bill Bixby, familiar to TV fans as *The Magician*, starred as David Banner, and former Mr World and Mr Universe, Lou Ferrigno was the Hulk. Ferrigno, whose first major acting role was in Arold Schwarzenegger's *Pumping Iron* film, was anxious not to portray the Hulk as a simple beast, but as a man striving to control the beast within him. Whatever the motivation, this TV Hulk bore little resemblance to the Marvel Comics original.

One in-joke, partly lost on younger fans, was the guest appearance of Ray 'Uncle Martin' Walston as an ageing magician (with Bixby as his assistant) in an episode called . . . *My Favourite Magician*.

Note: The Hulk never spoke in the TV series, but almost uttered his first words in a British TV commercial – for *TV Times*. However, studio chiefs at Universal in Hollywood were afraid that if the Hulk spoke it would ruin his image, so the green giant was gagged and the ad went out with subtitles. The line: 'Gee, I never knew there was so much in it!'

(See also *The Incredible Hulk* cartoon.)

REGULAR CAST

Dr David Banner **Bill Bixby**   *The Hulk* **Lou Ferrigno**
Jack McGee **Jack Colvin**

Executive producer: Ken Johnson
Producers: Chuck Bowman, Jim
  Parriott, Nicholas Corea, James G.
  Hirsch, Bob Steinhauer, Karen
  Harris, Jill Sherman
Directors: Various, inc. Ken Johnson,
  Sig Neufeld, Reza Badiyi, Jeff
  Hayden
Writers: Various, inc. Ken Johnson,
  Richard Matheson, Nick Corea, Jill
  Sherman *and* Karen Harris

An MCA Television Production
80 colour episodes (55 mins except where
stated) plus two pilot films
UK premiere: 26 May 1978

(Author's note: As with most American
series, the UK running order for *The
Incredible Hulk* deviated from the US
original – and differed in the length and
composition of various runs around the
ITV regions. So for ease of reference I've
listed the episodes in their original
American order.)

Pilot films

The Incredible Hulk (120 mins)*
Death in the Family (aka Return of the
Incredible Hulk) (120 mins)*

Season One

The Final Round
The Beast Within
Of Guilt, Models and Murder
Terror in Time Square
747
The Hulk Breaks Las Vegas
Never Give a Trucker An Even Break
Life and Death
Earthquakes Happen
The Waterfront Story

Season Two

Married (aka Bride of the Incredible
Hulk) (120 mins)†
The Autowuk Horror
Ricky
Rainbow's End
A Child in Need
Another Path
Alice in Disco Land
Killer Instinct
Stop the Presses
Escape from Los Santos
Wildfire
A Solitary Place
Like a Brother
The Haunted
Mystery Man (A 2-part story)
The Disciple (sequel to Another Path)

* UK running time: 90 mins
† UK running time: 105 mins

No Escape
Kindred Spirits
The Confession
The Quiet Room
Vendetta Road (aka Vendetta)

Season Three

Metamorphosis
Blind Rage
Brain Child (aka Odyssey)
The Slam
My Favourite Magician
Jake
Behind the Wheel
Homecoming
The Snare
Babalao
Captive Night (aka Hostage Night)
Broken Image
Proof Positive (aka Nightmare)
Sideshow
Long Run Home
Falling Angels
The Lottery
The Psychic
A Rock and a Hard Place
Death Mask
Equinox (aka Masquerade)
Nine Hours
On the Line

Season Four

Prometheus (A 2-part story)
Free Fall
Dark Side
Deep Shock
Bring Me the Head of the Hulk
Fast Lane
Goodbye, Eddie Cain

King of the Beach
Wax Museum
East Winds
The First (A 2-part story)
The Harder They Fall
Interview With the Hulk
Half Nelson
Danny
Patterns

Season Five

The Phenom
Two Godmothers
Veteran
Sanctuary
Triangle
Slaves
A Minor Problem

INTO THE LABYRINTH

HTV had carried the flag of television fantasy for ITV during the late 1970s – and it raised the standard again in the 1980s.

Into the Labyrinth combined magic and time travel in three moderately successful series depicting a world of suspended time and a never-ending duel between good and evil.

At the heart of the story was the white sorcerer Rothgo (played by Ron Moody) who, down through time, has been constantly got at by the beautiful but evil witch Belor (Pamela Salem). Three teenagers get caught up in their struggle and a quest for the Nidus – a source of magical power which has protected Rothgo until it is stolen by Belor. The third series saw Rothgo 'substituted' by a new magician, a bit of a bungler called Lazlo, but the battle went on, up and down the centuries. Each week, the protagonists would pop up as different characters from history or mythology.

Into the Laybrinth was devised by Bob Baker and Peter Graham Scott and utilised the scriptwriting talents of such writers as John Lucarotti, Christopher Priest, Robert Holmes, and Baker himself.

REGULAR CAST

Rothgo Ron Moody*   *Belor* Pamela Salem   *Phil* Simon Beal
Terry Simon Henderson*   *Helen* Lisa Turner*
Lazlo Chris Harris†   *Bram* Howard Goorney†

Devisors: Bob Baker, Peter Graham Scott
Producer: Peter Graham Scott
Executive producer: Patrick Dromgoole
Designer: John Reid
Music: Sidney Sagar

* Series One & Two only
† Series Three only

An HTV Production
21 30-minute colour episodes
Series One:
13 May–24 June 1981
Series Two:
3 August–21 September 1981
Series Three:
28 July–8 September 1982

Series One

w Bob Baker *(Ep. 1)* Andrew Payne *(Eps 2, 4)*, Anthony Read *(Eps 3, 7)*, Ray Jenkins *(Eps 5–6) (A 7-part story)*

A sudden thunderstorm drives Terry and his sister Helen to seek shelter in a cave. There they meet another boy, Phil, and are led by mysterious voices to discover Rothgo, a magician from another age, trapped in the rock. After releasing him, the teenagers become involved in the search for the stolen Nidus. The quest spans thousands of years and they encounter Rothgo and Belor in the pagan times of the druids; in medieval England; old Baghdad; the fields of the Civil War; revolutionary France; and finally to ancient Greece.

Robin of Loxley Tony Wright
Maid Marian Patricia Driscoll
Sheriff of Nottingham Conrad Phillips
Ali Derrick Branche
Colonel Ewen Solon

with:
Paul Lavers, Edwina Ford,
Peewee Hunt, Suzanne Wright,
Philip Manikum, David Trevena,
Adele Saleem, William Byers,
June Barrie, Simeon Andrews,
Tim Bannerman, John Abineri,
Jeremy Arnold

Director: Peter Graham Scott

Seven episodes:
Rothgo
The Circle
Robin
Masrur
Conflict
Revolution
Minotaur

Series Two

w Bob Baker *(Ep. 1)*, Christopher Priest *(Ep. 2)*, John Lucarotti *(Eps 3, 6)*, Ivan Benbrook *(Ep. 4)* Robert Holmes *(Ep. 5)*, Martin Worth *(Ep. 7) (A 7-part story)*

Once again the powers of goodness and light are challenged by Belor. This time she holds the Albedo, an energy source strong enough to neutralise the Nidus and so destroy Rothgo. In a catastrophic collision between the Albedo and the Nidus, Rothgo's power source is split into five fragments, each pursuing its own course through time and space. Rothgo recalls Phil, Terry and Helen to help retrieve them and sends them to the Wagnerian world of the Nibelung; the dangerous days of the Gunpowder Plot; the Alamo; ancient India (where Belor appears as the goddess Kali); Victorian London; and the Great Siege of Malta. The final confrontation comes at the burial of Tutankhamen.

Loke Howard Goorney
King James I Patrick Malahide
Davey Crockett Jack Watson
Jim Bowle Norman Bowler
Kadru Cyril Shaps
La Valette Ewen Solon

with:
David Trevena, Peter Burroughs,
Stephen Lyons, Ian Mackenzie,
Laura Cairns, April Johnson,
Jon Glentoran, Paul Nicholson,
Rita McKerrow, Roger Snowden,
Dino Shafeek, Jacob Witkin,
Michael O'Hagan, Edwina Ford,
Brian Coburn, Ian Brimble,
Jo Anderson, Suzi Arden,
Mark Buffery, Simeon Andrews

Director: Peter Graham Scott

Seven episodes:
The Calling
Treason
Alamo
Cave of Diamonds
Shadrach
Siege
Succession

Series Three

w Bob Baker, Robert Holmes, Ivan Benbrook, Jane McCloskey, Gary Hopkins, Moris Farhi, David Martin *(one episode each!) (A 7-part story)*

The unreliable magician Lazlo draws Phil into Delta Time where history is turned upside down. There they must seek and find the Scarabeus missing from the magician's ornate bracelet – or be devoured by a creeping green slime. They encounter

Long John Silver, Dr Jekyll and Mrs Hyde (guess who's Mrs Hyde), Incas and Conquistadores, treachery during the Great Fire of London, the Phantom of the Opera, Kubla Khan, and King Arthur's Knights of the Round Table. Their footsteps along the dangerous Delta timetrack are dogged by Belor and her odious 'familiar' Bram. In the final battle with Belor, in the shape of Morgan Le Fay, Lazlo – as Merlin – recaptures the Scarabeus and fastens it to his bracelet. He and Phil are released from Delta Time (and the creeping green slime) and Phil returns to his own time possessing his own magical power source.

Long John Silver **Godfrey James**
Mayor Thomas Bloodworth **Frank Windsor**
Phantom of the Opera **Conrad Phillips**
Kubla Khan **Peter Copley**
King Arthur **Ewen Solon**

with:
Walter Sparrow, Sara Markland, Geoff Serle, Hubert Tucker, Nick Chilvers, Tim Bannerman, June Marlow, Mhairi Harkens, John Abineri, Mark Buffery, Lily Kar, Jason Lake, Jo Crawford, Phillip Manikum, Michael Feldman, Shireen Shah, Pavel Douglas, Barry Jackson, Paul Nicholson, Bobby Collins, Paddy Joyce

Directors: **Peter Graham Scott** *(Eps 1–3, 6–7)* **Ken Price** *(Ep. 4)* **Alex Kirby** *(Ep. 5)*

Seven episodes:
Lazlo
Dr Jekyll and Mrs Hyde
Eye of the Sun
London's Burning
The Phantom
Xanadu
Excalibur

THE INVADERS

'How does a nightmare begin? For David Vincent it began at four in the morning, looking for a short cut he never found. What he found instead were creatures from another world . . .'

The Invaders was pure paranoia and its hero, David Vincent, the TV embodiment of the graffiti cliché: 'Just because you're paranoid, doesn't mean they're *not* out to get you.'

The premise was simple. Alien beings from a dying planet have landed on Earth. Their ultimate goal is to take over our world. With their ability to assume human form, they have already begun to infiltrate all the strata of Earth society – government, police and media. Eventually, they will control the planet. One man, architect David Vincent, has seen them land, knows they are here. Somehow he must convince a sceptical world that he is not crazy, that they really are out to get us . . .

In the 1950s, film-makers had exploited McCarthyist America's fears of Communist subversion with allegorical tales of insidious alien takeover such as *Invasion of the Body Snatchers* (1956). But in 1967, *The Invaders* had no political implications. Its intention was simply to scare.

Vincent's nightmare begins when he stops to rest while driving along a remote road. He is awakened by a strange noise and sees a flying saucer land. Returning to the scene later, he finds only a honeymoon couple who claim to have seen nothing. Vincent notices that the little fingers of the newlyweds protrude at an odd angle. But no one believes him.

And that's the way the series goes. Vincent responds to any call, any sighting, repeating his story to anyone who will listen. And sometimes people do. But they invariably turn out to be other invaders, until Vincent no longer knows who he can trust. The aliens themselves were amorphous beings who needed recharging every 10–12 days in special regeneration chambers to retain their disguises, otherwise they reverted to their natural form and died. But Vincent couldn't even show the authorities a dead alien – when they were killed they disintegrated, leaving behind nothing but ashes and a scorched outline.

Towards the end of the second season, Vincent's solo crusade did turn into a team effort of sorts, with the addition of a group called The Believers, led by businessman Edgar Scoville, who provided cash aid and connections. But by that time, the repetitive format of the series had begun to pall with American audiences and it ended after just 43 episodes – a short run by contemporary US standards.

A Quinn Martin production, many critics dubbed *The Invaders* as just another 'running man' show like Martin's other famous series *The Fugitive*. There were undoubtedly similarities – both men crossed and recrossed the country in pursuit of their quarry – but there was one vital difference. Richard Kimble got his man. David Vincent never did. No matter how many aliens he killed he couldn't get them all . . .

'So maybe they're here now. Take a look around you. Casually. No sense letting them know you're suspicious. That guy opposite on the bus . . . can you *really* be sure he's not one of them?'

REGULAR CAST

David Vincent **Roy Thinnes**   *Edgar Scoville* **Kent Smith** *(from Season Two episode* The Believers*)*

Creator: **Larry Cohen**
Executive producer: **Quinn Martin**
Producer: **Alan Armer**
Music: **Dominic Frontière**

A Quinn Martin Production
43 colour 60-minute episodes
UK premiere: 21 January 1967

(*The Invaders* was rare for an American series, in that it debuted over here at the same time as it started over there, running simultaneously, for a few weeks at least, in ITV's London region, though the first coherent run was on Granada Television in the north. Overall, though, the show's run round the ITV regions was typically sporadic and uncoordinated; it achieved a UK network run only when the rights were taken up by the BBC in 1984.)

Season One
17 one-hour episodes
20 February–10 July 1967
(Granada Television)

Beachhead

w Anthony Wilson
David Vincent sights a flying saucer landing but when he returns to the scene with the police and his business partner Alan Landers the ship is gone and Vincent is considered a crackpot. So begins his quest to convince the world that the aliens have arrived.
Alan Landers James Daly
Ben Holman J.D. Cannon
Kathy Adams Diane Baker
Carver John Milford
Old lady Ellen Corby
Mr Kemper Vaughn Taylor

Director: Joseph Sargent

The Experiment

w Anthony Spinner
Famed astrophysicist Dr Curtis Lindstrom also discovers proof of the presence of aliens. Vincent tries to keep him alive so that he can expose the invaders at an international conference.
Lloyd Lindstrom Roddy McDowall
Dr Curtis Lindstrom Laurence Naismith
Dr Paul Mueller Harold Gould
Minister Dabbs Greer
Lt James Willard Sage

Director: Joseph Sargent

The Mutation

w David Chandler *and* George Eckstein
Vincent investigates a landing in Mexico unaware that he is being led into an alien trap.
Vikki Suzanne Pleshette
Mark Evans Edward Andrews
Fellows Lin McCarthy
Alien Roy Jenson
Miguel Rudolfe Hoyes

Director: Paul Wendkos

The Leeches

w Dan Ullman
Following the disappearance of several leading scientists, Vincent is contacted by an electronics expert who fears he is next in line to be abducted by the aliens.
Warren Doneghan Arthur Hill
Tom Wiley Mark Richman
Eve Doneghan Diana van der Vlis
Hastings Robert H. Harris
Noel Markham Theo Marcuse

Director: Paul Wendkos

Genesis

w John W. Bloch
Vincent's search leads him to a sea lab where life is being created in a secret project.
Selene Lowell Carol Rossen
Sgt Hal Corman Phillip Pine
Joan Corman Louise Latham
Steve Gibbs Tim McIntire
Dr Ken Harrison William Sargent
Dr Grayson Frank Overton

Director: Richard Benedict

Vikor

w Don Brinkley
A dying telephone operator's incredible account of what he has seen draws David Vincent to a vast industrial plant owned by a famous war hero.
George Vikor Jack Lord
Nexus Alfred Ryder
Sherri Vikor Diana Hyland
Police Sgt Richard O'Brien
Hank Sam Edwards

Director: Paul Wendkos

Nightmare

w John Kneubuhl
Vincent discovers terrifying evidence that the aliens are turning insects into carnivores.
Ellen Woods Kathleen Widdoes
Mr Ames Robert Emhardt

Miss Havergill **Jeanette Nolan**
Ed Gidney **James Callahan**
Constable Gabbard **William Bramley**

Director: **Paul Wendkos**

Doomsday Minus One

w **Louis Vittes**
Vincent's help is requested when a saucer is seen near the site of an underground nuclear test.
Major Rick Graves **William Windom**
General Beaumont **Andrew Duggan**
Tomkins **Wesley Addy**
Carl Wyeth **Robert Osterloh**
Spencer **Tom Palmer**

Director: **Paul Wendkos**

Quantity Unknown

w **Don Brinkley**
While investigating a mysterious cylinder found in a plane crash, Vincent himself is accused of being an alien.
Harry Swain **James Whitmore**
Col. Griffith **William Talman**
Diane Oberly **Susan Strasberg**
A.J. Richards **Milton Selzer**
Walt Anson **Barney Phillips**

Director: **Sutton Roley**

The Innocents

w **John W. Bloch**
Vincent is kidnapped and taken aboard an alien flying saucer.
Nat Greely **William Smithers**
Magnus **Michael Rennie**
Sgt Ruddell **Robert Doyle**
Edna Greely **Patricia Smith**
Capt. Ross **Dabney Coleman**

Director: **Sutton Roley**

The Ivy Curtain

w **Don Brinkley**
Vincent uncovers an alien indoctrination centre in an Ivy League school.
Cahill **Jack Warden**

Stacy **Susan Oliver**
Mr Burns **David Sheiner**
Dr Reynard **Murray Matheson**
Lt Alvarado **Barry Russo**

Director: **Joseph Sargent**

The Betrayed

w **John W. Bloch**
Vincent finds computer controls and a mysterious tape that could be proof of an invasion.
Simon Carver **Ed Begley**
Susan Carver **Laura Devon**
Evelyn Bowers **Nancy Wickwire**
Neal Taft **Norman Fell**
Joey Taft **Victor Brandt**

Director: **John Meredyth Lucas**

Storm

w **John Kneubuhl**
A meteorologist calls in Vincent after a bizarre hurricane that has veered erratically to spare a fishing village.
Father Joe **Joseph Campanella**
Lisa **Barbara Luna**
Dr Malcolm Gantley **Simon Scott**
Luis Perez **Carlos Romero**
Danny **Paul Comi**

Director: **Paul Wendkos**

Panic

w **Robert Sherman**
In the woods of West Virginia, Vincent pursues Nick Baxter, an ailing invader whose touch freezes humans to death.
Nick Baxter **Robert Walker**
Madeline Flagg **Lynn Loring**
Gus Flagg **R.G. Armstrong**
Deputy Wallace **Len Wayland**
George Grundy **Ford Rainey**

Director: **Robert Butler**

Moonshot

w **Alan Armer**
Vincent investigates the death of two lunar astronauts in a strange red fog.

Gavin Lewis **Peter Graves**
Hardy Smith **John Ericson**
Angela Smith **Joanne Linville**
Stan Arthur **Kent Smith**
Tony LaCava **Anthony Eisley**
Charlie Coogan **Strother Martin**

Director: **Paul Wendkos**

Wall of Crystal

w **Don Brinkley**
The aliens kidnap Vincent's brother and
pregnant wife to force him to keep quiet
about his latest discoveries.
Theodore Booth **Burgess Meredith**
Dr Bob Vincent **Linden Chiles**
Grace Vincent **Julie Sommars**
Taugus **Edward Asner**
Joe McMullen **Lloyd Gough**

Director: **Joseph Sargent**

The Condemned

w **Robert Sherman**
Vincent is framed by the aliens for the
apparent death of Morgan Tate, an
industrialist who had stolen an important
alien file.
Morgan Tate **Ralph Bellamy**
Carol Tate **Marlyn Mason**
Lewis Dunhill **Murray Hamilton**
Det. Carter **Larry Ward**
John Finney **John Ragin**

Director: **Richard Benedict**

Season Two
26 one-hour stories
7 November 1967–9 February 1968*
(Granada Television)

Condition: Red

w **Laurence Heath**
Alien infiltration of an Air Defence
Command unit poses a new problem for
Vincent.
Laurie Keller **Antoinette Bower**
Dan Keller **Jason Evers**

* See subsequent note, after 'The Captive'.

Dr Rogers **Roy Engel**
Mr Arius **Mort Mills**
Gen. Winters **Robert Brubaker**
Capt. Connors **Burt Douglas**
Capt. Albertson **Forrest Compton**

Director: **Don Medford**

The Saucer

w **Dan B. Ullman**
Vincent manages to capture tangible
proof of the alien invasion – a flying
saucer.
Annie Rhodes **Anne Francis**
Robert Morrison **Charles Drake**
John Carter **Dabney Coleman**
Joe Bonning **Robert Knapp**
Sam Thorne **Kelly Thorsden**

Director: **Jesse Hibbs**

The Watchers

w **Jerry Sohl, Earl Hamner Jr**
A blind girl helps Vincent find the link
between an electronic wizard and the
aliens. (This episode also features Kevin
McCarthy, star of *Invasion of the Body
Snatchers*.)
Margaret Cook **Shirley Knight**
Paul Cook **Kevin McCarthy**
Ramsey **Leonard Stone**
Danvers **Walter Brooke**
Simms **Robert Yuro**
General **John Zaremba**

Director: **Jesse Hibbs**

Valley of the Shadow

w **Howard Merrill, Robert Sabaroff**
Vincent tries to convince a small town
community that the man they've locked
up on a murder charge is really an alien.
Sheriff Clements **Ron Hayes**
Maria McKinley **Nan Martin**
Will Hale **Harry Townes**
Capt. Taft (alien) **Joe Maross**
Major **Ted Knight**
Capt. Taft (human) **James B. Sikking**

Director: **Jesse Hibbs**

The Enemy

w John W. Bloch
A nurse witnesses an alien's horrifying transformation to his natural state.
Gale Frazer Barbara Barrie
Blake Richard Anderson
Sheriff Russell Thorson
Vern Hammond Paul Mantee
Sawyer Gene Lyons

Director: Robert Butler

The Trial

w George Eckstein, David W. Rintels
A friend of Vincent's goes on trial for the 'murder' of an alien.
Charlie Gilman Don Gordon
Janet Wilk Lynda Day
Allen Slater Harold Gould
Fred Wilk John Rayner
Bert Wisnofsky William Zuckert

Director: Robert Butler

The Spores

w George Eckstein, David W. Rintels
Vincent searches for a suitcase full of experimental spores, each capable of producing a full-grown alien upon brief exposure to the Earth's atmosphere.
Tom Jessup Gene Hackman
Ernie Goldhaver John Randolph
Hal James Gammon
Mavis Judee Morton
Roy Kevin Coughlin
Mattson Wayne Rogers

Director: William Hale

Dark Outpost

w Jerry Sohl
Investigating the aliens' vulnerability to minor human diseases, Vincent finds himself aboard a flying saucer.
Dr John Devin William Sargent
Hal Tim McIntire
Vern Andrew Prine
Eileen Dawn Wells
Col. Harris Whit Bissell

Director: George McCowan

Summit Meeting

w George Eckstein *(2-part story)*
Vincent is alerted to an alien plot to assassinate world leaders at the testing of an experimental rocket. But he must rely on an attractive alien informer to help him warn the authorities in time.
Michael Tressider William Windom
Ellie Markham Diana Hyland
Per Alquist Michael Rennie
Thor Halvorsen Eduard Franz
Jonathan Blaine Ford Rainey

Director: Don Medford

The Prophet

w Warren Duff *and* Jerry De Bono
An alien evangelist begins to glow as he prophesies the coming of a 'host from the skies'.
Brother Avery Pat Hingle
Sister Claire Zina Bethune
Bill Shay Roger Perry
Brother John Richard O'Brien
Brother James Byron Keith

Director: Robert Douglas

Labyrinth

w Art Wallace
Vincent takes chest X-rays of an alien to the head of a UFO research project as proof of their existence.
Dr Samuel Crowell Ed Begley
Laura Crowell Sally Kellerman
Dr Harry Mills James Callahan
Prof. Edward Harrison John Zaremba
Argyle Martin Blaine

Director: Murray Golden

The Captive

w Laurence Heath
An alien held captive by a communist UN delegation convinces his captors that David Vincent is a spy.
Dr Katherine Serret Dana Wynter
Peter Borke Fritz Weaver
Sanders Don Dubbins
Josef Lawrence Dane
Leo Peter Coe

Director: William Hale

(The following remaining second season episodes were treated as a 'third' season in Britain.)
25 June–17 September 1970,
Granada Television

The Believers

w Barry Oringer
The series undergoes a format change as David Vincent organises a small group of 'Believers' to help in his battle against the aliens.
Edgar Scoville Kent Smith *(intro)*
Elyse Reynolds Carol Lynley
Torberg Than Wyenn
Harland Donald Davis
Lt Sally Harper Kathleen Larkin
Prof. Hellman Rhys Williams

Director: Paul Wendkos

The Ransom

w Robert Collins
Vincent captures an important alien leader but Earth is threatened with massive reprisals if he is not released.
Alien leader Alfred Ryder
Bob Torin Anthony Eisley
Cyrus Stone Laurence Naismith
Claudia Stone Karen Black
Garth Lawrence Montaigne
Kant John Ragin

Director: Lewis Allen

Task Force

w Warren Duff
The aliens plot to take over the nation's news media by exploiting the weakness of the heir to a powerful publishing empire.
William Mace Martin Wolfson
Jeremy Mace Linden Chiles
June Murray Nancy Kovack

Director: Gerald Mayer

The Possessed

w John W. Bloch
Following up a lead from an old friend, Vincent discovers the aliens are using radio implants to programme human beings.
Ted Willard Michael Tolan
Martin Willard Michael Constantine
Janet Garner Katherine Justice
Adam Lane William Smithers
Burt Newcomb Charles Bateman

Director: William Hale

Counterattack

w Laurence Heath
The Believers plan to attack the aliens' spaceships using radio navigational beams. Meanwhile, Vincent is falsely accused of murder and ridiculed in the press.
Joan Surrat Anna Capri
Archie Harmon Lin McCarthy
Jim Bryce John Milford
Lt Conners Ken Lynch
Lucian Warren Vanders

Director: Robert Douglas

The Pit

w Jack Miller
A scientist belonging to Vincent's group who claims he has proof of alien infiltration is declared insane.
Prof. Julian Reed Charles Aidman
Pat Reed Joanne Linville
Jeff Brower Donald Harron

Director: Lewis Allen

The Organisation

w Franklin Barton
Vincent learns that a crime syndicate is hunting the aliens to recover stolen narcotics.
Peter Kalter J.D. Cannon
Mike Calvin Chris Robinson

Director: William Hale

The Peacemakers

w David W. Rintels
A top military man asks Vincent to set up peace talks with the aliens.

Gen. Concannon James Daly
Sarah Concannon Phyllis Thaxter

Director: Robert Day

The Vice

---

w Robert Sabaroff *and* William Blinn
Vincent tries to stop the appointment of a
Negro alien to a vital post in the space
programme by turning to other negroes
for help.
James Baxter Raymond St Jacques
Arnold Warren Roscoe Lee Browne
Celia Baxter Janet MacLachlan

Director: William Hale

The Miracle

---

w Robert Collins
A young girl witnesses the fiery death of
an alien near a religious shrine and
believes it was a vision.
Beth Ferguson Barbara Hershey
Ferguson Edward Asner

Director: Robert Day

The Life Seekers

---

w Laurence Heath
Two aliens contact Vincent saying they
wish to stop the invasion of Earth.
(Missing from first UK run.)
Keith Barry Morse
Claire Diana Muldaur

Director: Paul Wendkos

The Pursued

---

w Don Brinkley
An attractive alien loses control of her
synthetic emotions and turns to David
Vincent for help.
Anne Gibbs Suzanne Pleshette

Director: William Hale

Inquisition

---

w Barry Oringer
A zealous government official tries to pin
the explosive death of a senator on
Vincent and his 'group of fanatics'.
Andrew Hatcher Mark Richman
Joan Seeley Susan Oliver

Director: Robert Glatzer

(NB: BBC2's reruns ran from 7
September 1984 to 22 August 1985, but
excluded the two-part story *Summit
Meeting* and the episodes *The Prophet* and
The Captive.)

THE INVISIBLE MAN (1958–9)

H.G. Wells's famous creation has inspired three television series
and this underrated 1958–9 British version, more properly known
as *H.G. Wells' Invisible Man*, was the first.

It owes nothing to Wells but its name, being set in Fifties Britain
with a hero, Peter Brady, who remains a 'good guy' throughout.

While successfully testing his theory of optical density – a
principle that every form of matter could be reduced to invisibility
through total refraction – promising young scientist Brady turns
unexpectedly invisible when an experiment misfires. Unable to
reverse the process, Brady becomes stuck as *The Invisible Man*. At
first pursued and imprisoned by the men from the ministry, he
proves his loyalty, allowing subsequent episodes to follow his

adventures as he takes on an assortment of villains for both friends and country. Underlying the series, however, is Brady's search for an antidote, a way to restore his 6 ft 3 in frame to full visibility.

The series' star was kept anonymous. The most viewers ever saw was a suit of clothes and a bandaged head. On the whole, Brady remained completely invisible – even down to his goosepimples! His presence, however was conveyed through his actions and mannerisms. While sitting at a desk, for example, he would pick up a paper-knife, twirling it in unseen fingers or tapping it on the desk. He sipped wine and puffed cigarettes through invisible lips, drove cars and motorbikes and even enjoyed an invisible kiss with actress Zena Marshall.

All sorts of special effects contributed to the Invisible Man's presence, with many of the delicate tricks still hailed as some of the best effects seen on television. Jack Whitehead, who once pulled the strings for Muffin the Mule, used his skills to raise a glass, suspended on two fine wires, to an invisible mouth, to jerk down the springs on a chair to simulate sitting, and to lift a hat from an invisible head. There were several ways, too, of making the Invisible Man appear to be driving a car. A stuntman lay flat on the floor with the nearside door slightly open so that he could see where he was going, steering with one hand at the bottom of the wheel and using the other hand to operate the foot pedals. Another way was to have the driver 'built into' the upholstery. A false seat was dropped over him with small holes cut out for him to see through. On one occasion, while filming in London's Lincoln's Inn Fields, two pedestrians attempted to wrest control of a 'riderless' motorcycle combination, unaware that a stuntman, concealed in the sidecar, was steering the bike.

The second series also featured more 'subjective' camera work, so that viewers saw the world through the eyes of the Invisible Man.

Because so many people, including stuntmen and technicians, made *The Invisible Man* what he wasn't, producer Ralph Smart (*Danger Man*, *William Tell*) decided not to name the actors who played him and none was ever credited. But his voice was revealed as that of actor Tim Turner, while the man in the overcoat, playing the headless body, was short-built Johnny Scripps who 'saw' through a button in the coat.

The female lead in the series was Lisa Daniely, as Brady's sister, Diane (Dee), and making her ITV debut was Deborah Watling, as his young niece Sally.

The first series of 13 episodes was aired in London, Scotland and the South from September 1958, with the second season following in April 1959. Viewers elsewhere saw both series back to back from June 1959.

In 1989, ITV bought the rights to one rerun of the whole series.

MAIN CAST

Voice of Peter Brady **Tim Turner**   *Diane* **Lisa Daniely**
Sally **Deborah Watling**

Producer: **Ralph Smart**
Music: **Sidney John Key**
Production supervisor: **Aida Young**

An Official Films/ITP (Incorporated Television Programme) Ltd Production for ATV

26 30-minute episodes, made in black and white
Season One:
14 September–14 December 1958
Season Two:
12 April–5 July 1959
(ITV, London region)

Season One

Secret Experiment

w **Michael Connor** *and* **Michael Cramoy**
Scientist Peter Brady becomes invisible following a laboratory accident. He is at first detained as a security risk but escapes and then outwits a fellow scientist, Crompton, who is out to steal his notes.
Dr Hanning **Lloyd Lamble**
Kemp **Bruce Seton**
Sir Charles **Ernest Clark**
Crompton **Michael Goodliffe**

Director: **Pennington Richards**

Crisis in the Desert

w **Ralph Smart**
Colonel Warren, of British Military Intelligence, asks Brady's help in rescuing one of his agents, Jack Howard, from the secret police of a Middle East state. There, Brady meets rebel leader, Yolande.
Yolande **Adrienne Corri**
Hassan **Erich Pohlmann**
Omar **Martin Benson**
Nesib **Peter Sallis**
Jack Howard **Howard Pays**
Col. Warren **Douglas Wilmer**
Corporal **Derren Nesbitt**
Surgeon **Derek Sydney**

Director: **Pennington Richards**

Behind the Mask

w **Stanley Mann** *and* **Leslie Arliss,** *from a story by* **Stanley Mann**

Brady is quite willing to help when horribly disfigured Raphael Constantine asks to be made invisible – but then he realises Constantine is planning an invisible assassination.
Constantine **Dennis Price**
Max **Edwin Richfield**
Marcia **Barbara Chilcott**
Josef **David Ritch**
Juan **Michael Jacques**
President Domecq **Arthur Gomez**
Official **John Wynn Jones**

Director: **Pennington Richards**

The Locked Room

w **Lindsay Galloway,** *from a story by* **Ralph Smart**
A beautiful scientist from behind the Iron Curtain criticises her government while she is in London and efforts are made to 'recall' her. Brady, believing she can help him regain his visibility, attempts to rescue her.
Tania **Zena Marshall**
Dr Hanning **Lloyd Lamble**
Dushkin **Rupert Davies**
Clerk **Emrys Leyshon**
Phillips **Noel Coleman**
Porter **Alexande Doré**

Director: **Pennington Richards**

Picnic with Death

w **Leonard Fincham** *and* **Leslie Arliss,** *from a story by* **Leonard Fincham**
Through his niece Sally, Brady becomes involved with a woman whose husband

and sister-in-law are planning to murder her.

John Norton Derek Bond
Carol Norton Faith Brook
Lindy Norton Margaret McCourt
Janet Norton Maureen Pryor
Sir Charles Ernest Clark
Stableman Michael Ripper

Director: Pennington Richards

Play to Kill

w Leslie Arliss, *from a story by* Robert Westerby

Celebrated actress Barbara Crane is being blackmailed. Was she really to blame for a fatal accident on a lonely clifftop road? Brady sets out to clear her name.

Barbara Crane Helen Cherry
Colonel Colin Gordon
Tom Hugh Latimer
Simon Garry Thorne
Manton Ballard Berkeley
Arthurson Vincent Holman

Director: Peter Maxwell

Shadow on the Screen

w Ian Stuart Black, *from a story by* Ralph Smart *and* Philip Levene

Sonia Vasa, a communist spy, tries to trap the Invisible Man into revealing his secret by posing as a refugee seeking his help in getting her scientist husband into the West.

Stephan Vasa Edward Judd
Sonia Vasa Greta Gynt
Bratski Redmond Phillips
Captain Andre Mikhelson
Commissar Anthony Newlands
Sir Charles Ernest Clark
Woman in lift Irene Handl

Director: Pennington Richards

The Mink Coat

w Ian Stuart Black, *from a story by* Leonore Coffee

When Penny Page flies to France, she is unaware that vital stolen atomic secrets are hidden in the lining of her mink coat, making her the target for the thieves. Luckily, Brady and his sister are among her fellow passengers.

Penny Page Hazel Court
Walker Derek Godfrey
Bunny Harold Behrens
Marcel Murray Kash
Customs officer Keith Rawlings
Madame Dupont Joan Hickson
Photographer John Ruddock

Director: Pennington Richards

Blind Justice

w Ralph Smart

Peter Brady becomes a blind woman's 'eyes' when trying to trap the drug-smuggling gang responsible for framing and murdering her husband.

Katherine Holt Honor Blackman
Arthur Holt Philip Friend
Sandy Mason Jack Watling
Simmons Julian Somers
Sparrow Leslie Phillips
Det. Insp. Heath Robert Raglan
Det. Sgt. Desmond Llewellyn

Director: Pennington Richards

Jailbreak

w Ian Stuart Black

Joe Green, jailed for robbery with violence, protests his innocence and makes repeated escape attempts. Believing his story, Brady helps him prove his alibi.

Joe Green Dermot Walsh
Doris Denny Dayvis
Brenner Michael Brennan
Governor Ralph Michael
Sharp Ronald Fraser
Taylor Charles Farrell
Robson Maurice Kaufman

Director: Pennington Richards

Bank Raid

w Doreen Montgomery *and* Ralph Smart

Brady's niece Sally is kidnapped and held hostage by a gang of crooks who force him to rob a bank to save her life.

Crowther **Willoughby Goddard**
Williams **Brian Rawlinson**
Headmistress **Patricia Marmont**

Director: **Ralph Smart**

Odds Against Death

w **Ian Stuart Black**, *from a story idea by*
  Stanley Mann
Brady uses his invisibility to manipulate
the casino tables in Italy as he tries to help
a brilliant scientist who is gambling his
daughter's life away.
Prof. Owens **Walter Fitzgerald**
Suzy Owens **Julia Lockwood**
Lucia **Colette Wilde**
Caletta **Alan Tilvern**
Bruno **Peter Taylor**
Croupier **Peter Elliott**
Manager **Olaf Pooley**

Director: **Pennington Richards**

Strange Partners

w **Michael Cramoy**
Brady discovers that being The Invisible
Man is a defence against detection by
humans – but not by a dog, when he is
tricked into visiting the home of Lucian
Currie who wants him to murder his ailing
partner, Vickers.
Insp. Quillan **Victor Platt**
Collins **Jack Melford**
Vickers **Patrick Troughton**
Ryan **Robert Cawdron**
Doctor **Reginald Hearne**
Lucian Currie **Griffith Jones**

Director: **Pennington Richards**

Season Two

Point of Destruction

w **Ian Stuart Black**
When four test pilots are killed in plane
crashes while experimenting with a new
fuel diffuser, Brady steps in to investigate
and finds one of the team is in league with
an enemy agent.
Scotty **Duncan Lamont**
Dr Court **John Rudling**

Katrina **Patricia Jessel**
Stefan **Derren Nesbitt**
Jenny **Jane Barrett**
Control officer **Barry Letts**

Director: **Quentin Lawrence**

Death Cell

w **Michael Connors**
A beautiful but frightened young woman
escapes from a mental home to seek The
Invisible Man's help, claiming she has
been held there as she is the only person
who can prove the innocence of her
fiancé, George Wilson, who is awaiting
execution for murder.
Ellen Summers **Lana Morris**
Dr Trevor **Ian Wallace**
George Wilson **William Lucas**
Sir Charles **Bruce Seton**
Prison Governor **Jack Lambert**
Miss Beck **Bettina Dickson**
Mrs Willis **Patricia Burke**

Director: **Peter Maxwell**

The Vanishing Evidence

w **Ian Stuart Black**
Peter Thal, an international spy, murders
Prof. Harper and steals vital papers. MI5
send Brady to Amsterdam to track him
down.
Prof. Harper **James Raglan**
Thal **Charles Gray**
Col. Ward **Ernest Clark**
Jenny Reyden **Sarah Lawson**
Porter **Michael Ripper**
Insp. Strang **Peter Illing**
Superintendent **Ewen Solon**

Director: **Peter Maxwell**

The Prize

w **Ian Stuart Black**
Arriving in Scandanavia to collect a prize
for his contribution to science, Brady finds
the guest of honour, Russian writer Tania
Roskoff, has been arrested at the border.
Tania **Mai Zetterling**
Gunzi **Anton Diffring**
Prof. Kenig **Tony Church**

General **Tom Gill**
Sentry **Clive Baxter**
Capt. Bera **Richard Clarke**
Agasha **Ruth Lodge**

Director: **Quentin Lawrence**

Flight Into Darkness

w **Ian Stuart Black,** *from a story by*
   William H. Altman
Talked into believing that his remarkable
new anti-gravity discovery will endanger
mankind, Dr Stephens destroys his papers
and disappears. Brady promises Pat
Stephens he will try to find her father.
Dr Stephens **Geoffrey Keen**
Wilson **Esmond Knight**
Wade **John Harvey**
Sir Jasper **Michael Shepley**
Pat Stephens **Joanna Dunham**
Sewell **Colin Douglas**
Fisher **Alex Scott**

Director: **Peter Maxwell**

The Decoy

w **Brenda Blackmore**
Identical twins Terry and Toni Trent, an
American stage musical act, are on tour in
Britain when one of them disappears. The
Invisible Man volunteers to solve the
mystery.
Toni and Terry Trent **Betta St John**
Capt. Rubens **Robert Gallico**
Stavros **Philip Leaver**
Andreas **Wolf Morris**
Giorgio **Barry Shawzin**
General **Lionel Murton**
First Secretary **Bruno Barnabe**

Director: **Quentin Lawrence**

The Gun Runners

w **Ian Stuart Black**
Brady is sent to investigate gun-running in
the Mediterranean state of Bay Akim,
accompanied by government agent Zena
Fleming.
Col. Grahame **Bruce Seton**
Zena Fleming **Lousie Allbritton**
Sardi **Paul Stassino**

Arosa **Charles Hill**
Hotel manager **Josef Attard**
Malia **Laurence Taylor**
Ali **James Booth**
Airport clerk **Morris Sweden**
Receptionist **Ann Dimitri**

Director: **Peter Maxwell**

The White Rabbit

w **Ian Stuart Black**
After a terrified rabbit materialises before
a young French doctor's eyes, French
Security call in Brady to investigate a
château where Monsieur Rocher is plotting
to gain world power by creating an
invisible army.
Suzanne Dumasse **Marla Landi**
Hugo **Austin Trevor**
Rocher **Paul Daneman**
Valois **Arnold Marle**
Prof. Blaire **Arnold Diamond**
Max **Reed de Rouen**
Louise **Myrtle Reed**
Dr Dumasse **Keith Pyott**
Colette **Isobel Black**
Brun **André Cherisse**
Chauffeur **Andrée Muller**

Director: **Quentin Lawrence**

Man in Disguise

w **Brenda Blackmore** *from a story by*
   Leslie Arliss
Brady is tricked by a beautiful girl in Paris
and loses his passport. When the girl's
accomplice, Nick, uses it to impersonate
him on a drugs run, Brady finds himself
involved in an international drugs-
smuggling racket.
Nick **Tim Turner**
Madeleine **Leigh Madison**
Matt **Lee Montague**
Det. Insp. **Robert Raglan**
Sgt Day **Howard Pays**
Sgt Winter **Jeanette Sterke**
Victor **Robert Rietty**
Club manager **Denis Shaw**
Aylmer **Felix Felton**

Directors: **Quentin Lawrence, Peter**
   Maxwell

Man in Power

w Ian Stuart Black

A Middle East king is murdered by his power-crazy Army chief and Brady becomes involved in thwarting a dangerous plot to install a dictatorship.

General Shafari André Morell
King Rashid Vivian Matalon
Princess Taima Nadia Regin
Prince Jonetta Gary Raymond
Hassan Andrew Keir
Col. Fayid Derek Sydney
Ambassador Ivan Craig

Director: Peter Maxwell

The Rocket

w Michael Pertwee

Brady's ingenuity is tested when gambling losses prompt one of his aides, Smith, to sell rocket secrets to a foreign power.

Smith Glyn Owen
Reitter Russell Waters
Prof. Howard Robert Brown
Det. Insp. Robert Raglan
Mrs Smith Jennifer Wright
Evans Harold Goodwin
Sgt Maurice Durant
Bill Colin Croft

Director: Quentin Lawrence

Shadow Bomb

w Tony O'Grady *(alias* Brian Clemens*)* and Ian Stuart Black

Brady risks his life trying to save his friend Barry Finch from being blown up by a new type of bomb detonator that will be triggered the moment even a shadow falls on it.

Capt. Barry Finch Conrad Phillips
Betty Jennifer Jayne
Lloyd Walter Gotell

Lt Daniels Ian Hendry
General Martin Anthony Bushell

Director: Quentin Lawrence

The Big Plot

w Ian Stuart Black, *from a story by* Tony O'Grady *(alias* Brian Clemens*) and* Ralph Smart.

When a plane crash reveals that a canister of Uranium 235, used to make atomic bombs, was being smuggled into England, Brady must break a plot to start World War Three, involving atomic bombs hidden in every major world capital.

Waring William Squire
Helen Barbara Shelley
Lord Peversham John Arnatt
Officers Richard Warner, Derrick Sherwin
Macbane Edward Hardwicke
Minister Basil Dignam
Sir Charles Ewen MacDuff
Hanstra Terence Cooper

Director: Peter Maxwell

Unbroadcast first pilot:

(Title Unknown)

w Doreen Montgomery *and* Ralph Smart

Peter Brady becomes invisible in a laboratory accident. He goes home to his sister, Jane, and niece Sally. When Sally is kidnapped, Brady must break into a bank to buy her freedom. (This version had different music and inferior effects, but elements of the story emerged in *Secret Experiment* and *Bank Raid*.)

Brady's voice Robert Beatty
Jane Lisa Daniely
Sally Deborah Watling
Crowther Willoughby Goddard
Williams Brian Rawlinson

Director: Ralph Smart

THE INVISIBLE MAN (1975)

The 1975 American version of *The Invisible Man* was a short-lived action-adventure series starring ex-UNCLE hero David McCallum as invisible scientist Dr Daniel Weston.

In the pilot TV film, Weston discovers how to make himself invisible and must then try to keep the secret from unscrupulous agents who want to use it as a means of achieving world power. He has a friend Nick Maggio (Henry Darrow) who makes a lookalike mask for him to wear so that he can appear in public (and we can get to see the star once in a while).

In the series, Weston and his visible wife Kate take on various assignments for the government such as testing out a security system (*The Fine Art of Diplomacy*), unmasking a fake spiritualist (*Man of Influence*), helping a scientist defector to return home (*Barnard Wants Out*), rescuing the kidnapped daughter of a vital mob trial witness (*Sight Unseen*) and secretly returning stolen money (*Pin Money*).

Melinda Fee played Kate (some viewers were wryly concerned that she spent so much time with a naked – if invisible – man!), and their boss Carlson was played by Jackie Cooper in the pilot and Craig Stevens in the series.

Despite its personable stars and some good special effects, *The Invisible Man* never caught on in America and ended after its first season run of just 13 episodes. It was screened three times by the BBC, in autumn 1975, summer 1976 and autumn 1989.

REGULAR CAST

Dr Daniel Weston **David McCallum**   *Kate Weston* **Melinda Fee**
Walter Carlson **Craig Stevens** (Jackie Cooper *in the pilot*)

Pilot credits:
Teleplay: Steven Bochco
Director: Robert Michael Lewis
Producer: Steven Bochco
Executive producer: Harve Bennett
Music: Richard Clements

A Harve Bennett Production in association with Universal/NBC
13 colour episodes,
(one × 80 mins, 12 × 50 mins)

The Invisible Man (pilot: 80 mins)
The Klae Resource

The Fine Art of Diplomacy
Man of Influence
Eyes Only
Barnard Wants Out
Go Directly to Jail
Pin Money
Stop When the Red Lights Flash
Sight Unseen
The Klae Dynasty
Attempt to Save Face
Power Play

26 September–22 December 1975
(BBC1)

THE INVISIBLE MAN (1984)

The third of television's *Invisible Man* series was, in effect, the first – a stylishly staged six-part BBC adaptation of H.G. Wells's original 1897 novel.

Pip Donaghy starred as the heavily bandaged 'mad scientist' Dr Griffin who turns his scientific brilliance to bad ends, for power and destruction. Embarking on a personal reign of terror, he becomes a homicidal maniac, invisible morally as well as physically. A fugitive, a lonely and pathetic outcast, his acts lead ultimately to his own self-destruction.

Frank Middlemass co-starred as Griffin's unwilling and untrustworthy helper, the tramp Thomas Marvel, and David Gwillim appeared as the Invisible Man's old colleague Dr Samuel Kemp who is forced to shelter Griffin and listens, horrified and fascinated, to the story of how he discovered the secret of invisibility.

Originally intended as a Sunday teatime serial, *The Invisible Man* was upgraded from the family classics slot to a weekday mid-evening one, where it became a solid success for the former *Doctor Who* combo of producer Barry Letts and script editor Terrance Dicks.

MAIN CAST

The Invisible Man **Pip Donaghy**   *The Rev. Bunting* **Michael Sheard**
Thomas Marvel **Frank Middlemass**   *Dr Samuel Kemp* **David Gwillim**
Dr Cuss **Gerald James**   *Mr Hall* **Ron Pember**   *Mrs Hall* **Lila Kaye**
Teddy Henfrey **Jonathan Adams**   *Sandy Wadgers* **Roy Holder**
Mrs Roberts **Anna Wing**   *Constable Jaffers* **John Quarmby**
Lucy **Merelina Kendall**   *Colonel Adye* **Frederick Treves**

Dramatised by: James Andrew Hall, from the novel by H.G. Wells
Producer: Barry Letts
Director: Brian Lighthill
Script editor: Terrance Dicks
Visual effects designer: John Brace
Video effects supervisor: Dave Jervis
Designer: Don Giles
Music: Stephen Deutsch

A BBC Production
Six colour 30-minute episodes

The Strange Man's Arrival
The Unveiling of the Stranger
Mr Marvel's Visit to Iping
Dr Kemp's Visitor
Certain First Principles
The Hunting of the Invisible Man

4 September–9 October 1984
(BBC1)

JAMIE

Jamie was a 13-year-old boy who travelled through time on a magic carpet, meeting such notable historical characters as Guy Fawkes, Nelson, Samuel Pepys, Robert the Bruce and William the Conqueror.

Jamie discovers his carpet in a junk shop and learns its secret from the mysterious Mr Zed who prompts him to make his journeys back into the past. Jamie would sit on his carpet which would rise then whirl round faster and faster, flipping back through time.

Mr Zed remained an enigma. Nobody could say what age he was – sometimes he was young, sometimes he was incredibly old. But he was certainly 'not of this world' . . .

In the course of the 13-part series (which filled a corner of ITV's Sunday teatime schedules), Jamie tries to warn the Gunpowder plotters of impending treachery, joins Nelson's crew at the Battle of Trafalgar, meets his father as a young boy, travels to old Baghdad and 19th-century London, fights the Great Fire of London, learns the legend of Robert the Bruce and the spider and, finally, goes back to 1066. On some of his sorties he was joined by his best friend Tink.

REGULAR CAST

Jamie Dodger **Garry Miller**   *Molly Dodger (his mum)* **Jo Kendall**
David Dodger (his dad) **Ben Aris**   *Mr Zed* **Aubrey Morris**
Tink Bellow **Nigel Chivers**

Writer: **Denis Butler**
Producer: **Antony Kearey**
Executive producer: **Francis Coleman**
Directors: **Antony Kearey, Geoffrey Nethercott, Brian Izzard, John Reardon, David Coulter**

London Weekend Television Production
13 colour 30-minute episodes

The Carpet
Remember, Remember
The Sugar Islands

England Expects
Summer Holiday
Prince of Fire
The Climbing Boy
The Devil's Rookery
London Bridge Is Falling Down
New Lamps for Old
Buttercap
The Last Adventure
Dragon's Wake

6 June–5 September 1971
(LWT)

JASON OF STAR COMMAND

Half-baked live-action kids' series about the exploits of ace space pilot Jason and his comrades in Star Command as they fight the never-ending fight against the villainous galactic gangster, Dragos.

Notable mainly for the presence in some episodes of James 'Scotty' Doohan as Jason's commander, the series' general format was three-part stories with a cliffhanger ending to each episode.

In America it originally didn't even merit its own slot and was seen as part of the animated series *Tarzan and the Super Seven*. Over here it limped through the children's schedules in just three ITV regions, Central, Yorkshire and Tyne Tees.

REGULAR CAST

Jason **Craig Littler**   *Dragos* **Sid Haig**

A Filmation Production
UK: 28 colour 30-minute episodes

UK premiere:
21 January 1982
(Central)

JET JACKSON, FLYING COMMANDO

Early American foray into science fiction which followed the daredevil exploits of Jet Jackson, hero of his nation's 'Secret Squadron' of top agents who fought to thwart the evil designs of foreign powers and other nefarious influences.

Jet had two regular companions – a mechanic pal called Ikky, and an inventive scientist friend Tut. Their adventures were played out against a cold war-type background with threats of radiation, nuclear weapons and missile warfare never far away.

The series was seen in the UK by ITV viewers in Wales and the West of England, where it was the first sf-based show to emerge on the new channel run by TWW, collaring a regular early Monday evening slot until it ran out of steam towards the end of a 39-episode run, skipping weeks and changing days.

REGULAR CAST

Jet Jackson **Richard Webb**   *Ikky* **Sid Melton**
Tut **Olan Soule**

Producer: **George Bilson**
Director: **D. Ross Lederman**

39 black and white 30-minute episodes
20 April 1959–23 February 1960
(TWW)

JOE 90

Gerry Anderson's ninth TV puppet show – and the sixth of the Supermarionation series – *Joe 90* marked a conscious change of style and pace.

Gone were the hi-tech hardware and jut-jawed heroes of *Thunderbirds* and *Captain Scarlet*. In their place . . . a bespectacled nine-year-old boy.

A normal, adventure-loving schoolboy, Joe was the adopted son of brilliant electronics engineer, Professor Ian McClaine, creator of BIG RAT (Brain Impulse Galvanoscope Record and Transfer), a sophisticated device which recorded the brain patterns of one person and transferred them to another. At the behest of Shane Weston, Deputy Head of the World Intelligence Network (an organisation dedicated to maintaining the balance of power throughout the world), Prof. McClaine used his brainchild on Joe, giving him the specialist attributes of an appropriate highly skilled adult, and making him WIN's Most Special Agent, on the assumption that Joe could boldly go where no man could venture – and get away with it.

At the outset of each mission, Joe sat in a special chair that rose up into a circular cage which revolved as the BIG RAT tape was run, amid electronic noises and a psychedelic light show. Once the transfer was complete, Joe donned a pair of 'electrode glasses' to trigger the knowledge. In the course of the series he became an astronaut, test pilot, racing driver, aquanaut, computer boffin and a brain surgeon, among others.

Joe carried with him an ordinary-looking schoolboy's case which appeared to contain the usual scholarly paraphernalia. But when he flipped the case over and pressed two small studs, secret lids opened revealing compartments containing his electrode glasses, his WIN badge, pistol, pocket transmitter, ammo and secret reports. What more could a boy wish for?

Joe 90 premiered, in ITV's Midlands area (ATV), on 29 September 1968, running for 30 episodes, with reruns coming as recently as 1983. But the series failed to catch on in the way its illustrious predecessors had done. Among the voices behind the puppets were TV's *Maigret*, Rupert Davies, and Keith Alexander,

another 1960s puppet celebrity – Topo Gigio. But there was less to attract adult viewers this time.

Joe 90 was intended to be the fulfilment of every schoolboy's fantasies. So it was perhaps unfortunate, then, that in his glasses, Joe looked more like the class swot than the classy hero.

CHARACTER VOICES

Joe 90 **Len Jones**   *Prof. McClaine* **Rupert Davies**
Shane Weston **David Healy**   *Sam Loover (his deputy)* **Keith Alexander**
Mrs Ada Harris (the professor's housekeeper) **Sylvia Anderson**

Format: **Gerry** *and* **Sylvia Anderson**
Executive producer: **Reg Hill**
Producer: **David Lane**
Script editor: **Tony Barwick**
Music: **Barry Gray**

A Century 21 Production for ITC
(Presented by ATV)
30 colour 30-minute episodes
29 September 1968–20 April 1969
(ATV – Midlands)

Most Special Agent

w **Gerry** *and* **Sylvia Anderson**
Professor McClaine gives his adopted son Joe amazing powers via a pair of special glasses, enabling him to become an invaluable agent of the World Intelligence Network. Joe's first mission: to steal a new Russian prototype plane.

Director: **Desmond Saunders**

Most Special Astronaut

w **Tony Barwick**
Joe acquires the brain pattern of a top astronaut to save two men in a space station who are without an air supply.

Director: **Peter Anderson**

Project 90

w **Tony Barwick**
Prof. McClaine is kidnapped by spies anxious to learn more about Big Rat. Joe saves his father using the brain pattern of a balloonist.

Director: **Peter Anderson**

Hijacked

w **Tony Barwick**
Joe has himself nailed into a crate so he can catch a dangerous gun-runner and smuggler red-handed.

Director: **Alan Perry**

Colonel McClaine

w **Tony Barwick**
Joe delves into the brain patterns of an explosives expert and a top driver to transport a dangerous cargo across Africa.

Director: **Ken Turner**

The Fortress

w **Shane Rimmer**
A microfilm hidden in a remote jungle could blow the cover of every WIN agent in the area if it falls into the wrong hands. Joe has to find it first.

Director: **Leo Eaton**

King for a Day

w **Shane Rimmer**
Joe impersonates the heir to a Middle East throne who has been kidnapped to prevent his enthronement. Then Joe is kidnapped himself.

Director: **Leo Eaton**

International Concerto

w Tony Barwick
Wonder-boy Joe 90 receives the brain patterns of a top pianist who is also a secret agent.

Director: Alan Perry

Splashdown

w Tony Barwick
Joe acquires the skills of a top test pilot to investigate the deaths of two electronics experts.

Director: Leo Eaton

The Big Fish

w Shane Rimmer
Joe becomes one of the world's leading aquanauts and prevents an international incident when a sub breaks down in enemy waters.

Director: Leo Eaton

Relative Danger

w Shane Rimmer
Joe is given the brain pattern of a leading underground explorer in an effort to save the lives of three men trapped in an old silver mine.

Director: Peter Anderson

Operation McClaine

w Gerry Anderson *and* David Lane
Joe becomes a brilliant brain surgeon and performs a life-or-death operation on a famous writer.

Director: Ken Turner

The Unorthodox Shepherd

w Tony Barwick
Joe is given the persona of a World Bank president to investigate a flood of forged notes – an investigation which leads him to a supposedly haunted church. (This episode featured the first-ever location work for any Anderson series sowing the seeds for *The Secret Service* – see separate entry.)

Director: Ken Turner

Business Holiday

w Tony Barwick
Joe becomes a 'colonel' to ensure that a former World Army base is destroyed to prevent it becoming a threat to world peace.

Director: Alan Perry

Arctic Adventure

w Tony Barwick
A secret nuclear bomb is buried in the icy waters of the Arctic. Joe is sent to retrieve it.

Director: Alan Perry

Double Agent

w Tony Barwick
Joe's life is in danger when he is given the brain patterns of a double agent.

Director: Ken Turner

Three's a Crowd

w Tony Barwick
Joe receives the brain patterns of a lovely girl who has attracted his father's attention but who is suspected of being a spy.

Director: Peter Anderson

The Professional

w Gerry *and* Sylvia Anderson
Joe receives the skills of a burglar to help him break into a castle to recover some stolen gold.

Director: Desmond Saunders

The Race

w Tony Barwick
The brain patterns of a Monte Carlo rally winner help Joe take up a challenge WIN must win to ensure its own future.

Director: Alan Perry

Talkdown

w Tony Barwick
Joe becomes a test pilot to find out why a hypersonic fighter plane crashed.

Director: Alan Perry

Breakout

w Shane Rimmer
Two Canadian convicts escape from jail and threaten the life of their Prime Minister. Joe, on holiday, and using the brain patterns of a bobsleigh champion, goes to the rescue.

Director: Leo Eaton

Child of the Sun God

w John Lucarotti
Joe discovers a lost jungle tribe and has to prove that he is a god, to save his life.

Director: Peter Anderson

See You Down There

w Tony Barwick
Joe uses a variety of brain patterns to make a ruthless businessman, who operates by fraud, believe he is going mad.

Director: Leo Eaton

Lone-Handed 90

w Desmond Saunders *and* Keith Wilson
Joe dreams of becoming a sheriff and taking part in a rip-roaring Western adventure.

Director: Ken Turner

Attack of the Tiger

w Tony Barwick
The code name of 'tiger' hides the identity of Joe when he is sent on a hazardous mission, against an Eastern Alliance rocket base.

Director: Peter Anderson

Viva Cordova

w Tony Barwick
Joe becomes a Mexican president's bodyguard – without the president knowing.

Director: Peter Anderson

Mission X–41

w Pat Dunlop
Joe parachutes into an enemy research station in a daring search for a new formula.

Director: Ken Turner

Test Flight

w Donald James, Gerry *and* Sylvia Anderson
The brain pattern of a computer specialist and an explosives expert (again) helps Joe avert a sabotage threat.

Director: Peter Anderson

Trial at Sea

w Donald James
Joe races against time to prevent a new hoverliner from being blown up.

Director: Leo Eaton

The Birthday

w Tony Barwick
At a special celebration to mark his tenth birthday, Joe and his friends look back over some of the exciting moments of his young life.

Director: Leo Eaton

JOURNEY TO THE UNKNOWN

This 1968 Anglo-American hybrid can only marginally be counted as science fiction – even though it has been lumped into the sf category in America.

Produced by Joan Harrison, a former associate of Alfred Hitchcock, it was more a collection of psychological suspense dramas – encompassing devil worship, reincarnation, the supernatural, murder and revenge.

But it did touch on science fiction – in *Stranger in the Family*, a remake of an *Out of the Unknown* episode; in *The Madison Equation*, where a jealous husband programmes a computer to kill his errant wife; and in *Jane Brown's Body*, in which a suicide victim is brought back to life by a new experimental drug.

The anthology of 17 stories was made in Britain by Hammer Films and marked that company's first TV venture. It has since notched up two more series – *Hammer House of Horror* in 1980 and *Hammer House of Mystery and Suspense* in 1984. However, the series' £12m budget (£70,000 an episode) was all-American, the cash coming from ABC-TV and 20th Century Fox. And *Journey to the Unknown* premiered in America in September 1968, several weeks prior to its British debut. Here, screenings were patchy. London viewers were first to see episodes, with other ITV regions following in 1969 and 1970, and it's cropped up, too, in late-night schedules in the 1980s.

REGULAR CAST

None

Executive producers: **Joan Harrison, Norman Lloyd**
Executive consultant: **Jack Fleischmann**
Producer: **Anthony Hinds**
Main theme: **Harry Robinson**

Hammer Film Productions Ltd/20th Century Fox Television
17 colour 60-minute episodes
UK premiere: 16 November 1968
(LWT)

The New People

w **Oscar Millard and John Gould**, *from a story by* **Charles Beaumont**
Luther Ames, rich, charming and bored, plays Mephistopheles in his small circle and condemns to death any who break his unwritten laws.
Hank Prentiss **Robert Reed**
Anne Prentiss **Jennifer Hilary**
Luther Ames **Patrick Allen**

Helen Ames **Melissa Stribling**
Matt Dystal **Milo O'Shea**
Terry Lawrence **Adrienne Corri**
David Redford **Damian Thomas**
Susan Redford **Suzanne Mokler**
Ben **Anthony Colby**
Rhoda **Beryl Richardson**
Manservant **Robert Webber**

Director: **Peter Sasdy**

Somewhere in a Crowd

w Michael J. Bird

TV commentator William Searle is disturbed by the appearance of five strangely familiar faces at a series of tragic happenings, and discovers that the five were killed in a train crash two years earlier which he survived.

William Searle David Hedison
Ruth Searle Ann Bell
Max Newby Jeremy Longhurst
Marielle Jane Asher
Douglas Bishop Ewen Solon
Hugh Baillie Tenniel Evans
The Watchers George McGrath, Frank Cousins, Kaplan Kaye, Ann King, Elizabeth Robillard

Director: Alan Gibson

Matakitas Is Coming

w Robert Heverley

A young researcher, June Wiley, is trapped in a closed library where she discovers that she has been pledged to the devil.

June Wiley Vera Miles
Ken Talbot Dermot Walsh
Sylvia Ann Gay Hamilton
Matakitas Leon Lissek

Director: Michael Lindsay-Hogg

Jane Brown's Body

w Anthony Skene, *based on a story by* Cornell Woolrich

A young girl is brought back to life by Dr Ian Denholt's experimental serum, but has no memory of the past. However, she learns, remembers – and then follows the path that led to her death.

Jane Brown Stefanie Powers
Paul Amory David Buck
Dr Ian Denholt Alan McNaughtan
Pamela Denholt Sarah Lawson
Receptionist Arthur Pentelow
Robert Clive Graham
Mrs Brown Yvonne Gilan
Butler Lewis Fiander

Director: Alan Gibson

Do Me a Favour – Kill Me!

w Stanley Miller, *based on a story by* Frederick Rawlings

Fading actor Jeff Wheeler asks a friend to kill him to spare his obscurity, telling him to ignore any requests to call it off. Then he changes his mind . . .

Jeff Wheeler Joseph Cotten
Faith Wheeler Judy Parfitt
Harry Vantese Douglas Wilmer
Dirk Brogan Kenneth Haigh
Betty Joyce Blair
Chris David Warbeck
Asst director David Baxter
Wardrobe dresser Hugh Futcher
Lisa Carol Cleveland
Golfer Tom Gill

Director: Gerry O'Hara

Poor Butterfly

w Jeremy Paul, *from a story by* William Abney

Commercial artist Steven Miller receives a costume party invitation that takes him back 40 years, into a tragic past.

Steven Miller Chad Everett
Rose Beacham Susan Brodrick
Robert Sawyer Edward Fox
Ben Loker Bernard Lee
Mrs Loker Susan Richards
Friar Tuck Norman Chappell
Nelson Anthony Webb
Queen Victoria Fay Compton
Lady Hamilton Linda Cole
Guest Martin Lyder
Diana Marty Cruikshank

Director: Alan Gibson

The Madison Equation

w Michael J. Bird

A jealous husband programmes a highly sophisticated computer to electrocute his unfaithful wife. But instead, it kills him . . .

Inga Madison Barbara Bel Geddes
Ralph Madison Alan Cuthbertson
Stuart Crosbie Paul Daneman
Barbara Rossiter Sue Lloyd
Adam Frost Jack Hedley

Sir Gerald Walters **Richard Vernon**
Gen Wannamaker **Lionel Murton**
Frederick Shea **Aubrey Morris**
Insp Bridges **Lloyd Lamble**

Director: **Rex Firkin**

Girl of my Dreams

w **Robert Bloch** and **Michael J. Bird,**
   from a story by **Richard Matheson**
Opportunist Greg Richards tries to exploit
the psychic dreams of a shy young cashier,
Carrie, who is able to predict people's
deaths.
Carrie Clark **Zena Walker**
Greg Richards **Michael Callan**
Sue Tarleton **Justine Lord**
Mrs Wheeler **Jan Holden**
Mr Thwaite **David Lampton**

Director: **Peter Sasdy**

The Last Visitor

w **Alfred Shaughnessy**
Barbara King, a young girl in need of rest,
is terrorised by a mysterious prowler at a
seaside hotel.
Barbara King **Patty Duke**
Mrs Walker **Kay Walsh**
Mr Plimmer **Geoffrey Bayldon**
Mrs Plimmer **Joan Newell**
Butler **Blake Butler**
Mitchell **John Bailey**
Fred **Michael Craze**

Director: **Don Chaffey**

Eve

w **Paul Wheeler** and **Michael Ashe,** from
   a story by **John Collier**
A lonely misfit, Albert Baker, falls in love
with a wax window-display mannequin,
and steals her to make her his own.
Eve **Carol Lynley**
Albert **Dennis Waterman**
Mrs Kass **Hermione Baddeley**
George Esmond **Errol John**
Jennifer **Angela Lovell**
Royal **Michael Gough**
Miller **Peter Howell**
Loverley-Smith **Nicolas Phipps**

Girl in cinema **Elna Pearl**
Tovey **Frank Forsyth**
First Detective **Barry Linehan**
Kim **Barry Fantoni**
Youths **John Nightingale, Marcus
   Hammond**

Director: **Robert Sevens**

The Indian Spirit Guide

w **Robert Bloch**
Jerry Crown, an unscrupulous private
detective, tries to set himself up for life
with a wealthy widow, Leona Gillings,
who wants to contact her late husband in
the spirit world. But he fails to reckon
with the powers of the world beyond.
Leona Gillings **Julie Harris**
Jerry Crown **Tom Adams**
Chardur **Marne Maitland**
Joyce **Tracy Reed**
Miss Sarah Prinn **Catherine Lacey**
Mrs Hubbad **Dennis Ramsden**
Bright Arrow **Julian Sherrier**
Knife thrower **Geoff Winslip**

Director: **Roy Ward Baker**

The Killing Bottle

w **Julian Bond,** from a story by **L.P.
   Hartley**
Jimmy Rintoul, a young man hopeful of
becoming a composer, is caught in a trap
of madness and murder when he tries to
have his agent's brother, Randolph,
committed to an asylum so that he can
claim the family fortune.
Rollo Verdew **Roddy McDowall**
Vera Verdew **Ingrid Brett**
Jimmy Rintoul **Barry Evans**
Randolph Verdew **William Marlowe**
Policeman **Eddie Byrne**
Hodgson **John Rudling**

Director: **John Gibson**

Stranger in the Family

w **David Campton**
Charles Wilson and his family are
hounded from place to place because his
son, Boy, is a mutant with dangerous

powers to command the minds of others. (Remake of an episode of *Out of the Unknown*.)
Boy Anthony Corlan
Paula Janice Rule
Sonny Maurice Kaufmann
Charles Wilson Phil Brown
Margaret Wilson Jane Hylton
Dr Evans Gerald Sim
Wally Gold Ronald Radd
Brown Glynn Edwards
Miss Payne Ann Wrigg
Drunk James Donelly

Director: Peter Duffell

The Beckoning Fair One

w William Woods *and* John Gould, *from a story by* Oliver Onions
A young artist recovering from a mental breakdown falls under the spell of a long-dead coquette whose portrait exerts a hold over him.
Jon Holden Robert Lansing
Kit Beaumont Gabrielle Drake
Derek Wilson John Fraser
Mr Barrett Larry Noble
Mrs Barrett Gretchen Franklin
Crichton Clive Francis

Director: Don Chaffey

One on a Desert Island

w Oscar Millard
Alec Worthing, a young man dominated by his mother, buys a boat to sail round the world when she dies. He is ship-wrecked on a desert island where a young woman walks out of the sea . . .
Alec Worthing Brandon de Wilde
Uncle George David Bauer

Vickie Suzanna Leigh
Joe Hallum Robert Sessions
Preston John Ronane
Baker Victor Maddern

Director: Noel Howard

Paper Dolls

w Oscar Millard, *from a story by* L.P. Davies
American exchange teacher Craig Miller tries to solve the mystery of a group of psychically linked quadruplets, in which the most powerful, Steven, directs his three brothers in evil deeds.
Craig Miller Michael Tolan
Jill Collins Nanette Newman
Rodney Blake Roderick Shaw
Bart Brereton John Welsh
Mrs Latham Dorothy Alison
Joe Blake Kenneth J. Warren
Dr Yarrow Edward Hardwicke
Albert Cole Michael Ripper
The Vicar George Benson
Emily Blake June Jago

Director: James Hill

Miss Belle

w Sarett Rudley, *from a story by* Charles Beaumont
A rejected spinster takes her bitterness out on her small nephew by dressing him as a girl. Then a roguish American comes to the house and asks Miss Belle for work . . .
Drake George Maharis
Miss Belle Watson Barbara Jefford
Robert Kim Burfield
Girl Adrienne Posta

Director: Robert Stevens

KING OF THE CASTLE

Lurking behind this nightmarish fantasy was the story of a young teenager's nervous breakdown.

Shy, sensitive Roland Wright's mind snaps under the strain of living at the top of a council tower block. He clashes wth his parents, his teachers and the local bullies, and retreats into a fantasy world in which all the people he knows are transformed into nightmarish doubles. His headmaster, Spurgeon, becomes a mad scientist, his stepmother, June, becomes a witch and bully leader Ripper turns into a fully armed Samurai warrior.

Roland enters this fantasy world when he plunges down a lift shaft. While in reality a rescue operation is being mounted, Roland lives out a fantasy. He meets Vein, the keeper of the keys, and discovers that he must earn certain keys to escape. He becomes 'King of the Castle' but discovers that all the dirty rascals are plotting against him and he is put on trial . . .

King of the Castle was written by Bob Baker and Dave Martin who were also responsible for the previous year's HTV science fiction series, *Sky* (see separate entry). It was originally scheduled for a weekday children's slot early in 1977 but ITV's Network Planning Committee deemed it 'too scary' for children to watch alone, so it was postponed for four months and moved to a Sunday teatime slot.

CAST

Roland Philip Da Costa   *Spurgeon/Hawkspur* Fulton Mackay
Hawker/Ergon Milton Johns   *Vine/Vein* Talfryn Thomas
Voss/Voysey Derek Smith   *Ripper/Warrior* Jamie Foreman
June/Lady Angela Richards   *Ron/Lord* Sean Lynch
First engineer/Chef Patrick Durkin   *Second engineer/Sous chef* David Trevena
Sgt Tarr/Governor Edward Dentith   *PC Briggs/Guard* Paul Nicholson
Alf/Alfie Kevin Hudson   *Betty/Beattie* Georgina Keen
Della/Delta Majelia Dennehy

Writers: Bob Baker, Dave Martin
Director: Peter Hammond
Producer: Leonard White
Executive producer: Patrick Dromgoole
Designer: John Biggs

An HTV Production
Seven colour 30-minute episodes
8 May–19 June 1977

KINVIG

Whimsical science fiction comedy series from *Quatermass* creator Nigel Kneale that took the mickey out of the 'I was taken for a ride by Venusians' brigade of UFO freaks.

The hero of this seven-part series was Des Kinvig, an ineffectual dreamer who runs a backstreet electrical repair shop. Fussed over by his mumsy wife Netta and saddled with a huge dog called Cuddley, Des finds escape from his humdrum life in the passions of his pal Jim, a fully paid-up UFO fanatic.

One night, while walking his dog, Des's fantasies are apparently fulfilled when he comes across a spaceship and discovers that one of his customers, bossy Miss Griffin, is really a dishy woman from Mercury (played by Prunella Gee in some of the sexiest costumes imaginable – from silver catsuit to pink leather bikini!). Des is whisked off to Mercury where he meets the 500-year-old Buddo and learns that a race of ant-like creatures called Xux are secretly plotting to invade Earth by replacing people with humanoid robots, and indiscriminately handing out the power to bend cutlery.

It was Kneale's intent that *all* Des's experiences with the delectable Miss Gee (dubbed 'Quatermiss' by one national newspaper) were the product of his fanciful imagination. But this was not made crystal clear in the production and a lot of people didn't know what to make of it. But it was a welcome change from the usual sit-com fare.

MAIN CAST

Des Kinvig **Tony Haygarth**   *Netta Kinvig* **Patsy Rowlands**
Jim Piper **Colin Jeavons**   *Miss Griffin* **Prunella Gee**
Mr Horsley **Patrick Newell**   *Buddo* **Simon Williams**
Sagga **Danny Schiller**   *Loon* **Stephen Bent**   *Bat* **Alan Bodenham**

Creator/writer: **Nigel Kneale**
Producer: **Les Chatfield**
Directors: **Les Chatfield** *(Eps 1–7),* **Brian Simmons** *(Ep. 1 only)*
Designer **Mike Oxley**

A London Weekend Television Production
Seven colour 30-minute episodes

Contact
Creature of Xux
Double, Double
The Big Benders
Where Are You, Miss Griffin?
The Humanoid Factory
The Mystery of Netta

4 September–16 October 1981

KNIGHTS OF GOD

Ambitious 1987 adventure serial from TVS set in a future devastated by Civil War.

It is the year 2020. The country is split between North and South, London has been destroyed and replaced by Winchester as the capital. The Royal Family has been deposed and no one knows whether the King of England is still alive.

Out of the carnage has arisen a new ruling order – a brutal military and religious governing elite called the Knights of God, led by Prior Mordrin, a ruthless dictator who sends rebels to be brainwashed at special re-education camps.

Meeting at one of these camps are teenagers Gervase Edwards, who has been through the Knights' mind-altering programme, and Julia, who has not. They fall in love and escape, joining the growing resistance to the evil regime as they set out to find the rightful King of England and help restore him to the throne.

The quest element helped foster the semi-medieval style of *Knights of God*, with the grim, rundown future offset by some high-tech elements such as the Knights' crow-like black helicopters. But the 13-part series – which carried a £1 million price tag – caused jitters among ITV network bosses, worried that the serial might prove too gritty for family viewing in its Sunday teatime slot.

An impressive cast of nearly 50 included John Woodvine as Mordrin, Julian Fellowes as his scheming henchman Hugo, Patrick Troughton, Gareth Thomas, Anne Stallybrass and Don Henderson as rebels.

MAIN CAST

Gervase George Winter *Julia* Claire Parker *Mordrin* John Woodvine
Owen Gareth Thomas *Arthur* Patrick Troughton
Hugo Julian Fellowes *Beth* Shirley Stelfox *Colley* Don Henderson
Simon Nigel Stock *Brigadier Clarke* Barrie Cookson
Williams John Vine *Tyrell* Peter Childs *Nell* Anne Stallybrass
Dai Owen Teale *Dafydd* Tenniel Evans *Fr Gregory* Frank Middlemass
Helicopter pilot Christopher Bowen

Writer: Richard Cooper
Directors: Andrew Morgan, Michael
 Kerrigan
Producer: John Dale
Executive producer: Anna Home
Designer: Christine Ruscoe

TVS Production
13 colour 30-minute episodes
6 September–6 December 1987

KOLCHAK: THE NIGHT STALKER

'Ancient, fabled monsters stalk 20th-century America. They lurk in the dark corners of cities, alleyways, abandoned buildings, scientific research centres, within sewers, sports stadia, high-rise flats and hospitals . . . all set to pounce on their next unsuspecting victim.'

(Central TV press handout)

Where monsters tread, only Carl Kolchak dares to follow. A walking pastiche of newshound clichés, Kolchak is an unorthodox, down-at-heel reporter with a gift for snappy patter and nose for the supernatural.

Barely tolerated by his ulcer-ridden editor, and despised by the cops and politicians, Kolchak works a lonely beat, his only companions a camera and a tape recorder into which he narrates his findings. And though he always gets his monster he never gets his scoop as the lid is slammed down on his story.

Kolchak, played by Darren McGavin, first appeared in a brace of US TV movies, *The Night Stalker* and *The Night Strangler* (both seen on British TV). The first, about a vampire on the loose in Las Vegas, broke all ratings records. The second explored the strange underground world of old Seattle, lair for an alchemist who is murdering women to retain his youthful looks.

Convinced that his character was a winner, McGavin himself co-produced the series, retaining the movies' narrative style, but adding more character humour and toning down the violence.

Each story featured a new monster – from Jack the Ripper, a bloodthirsty werewolf and a succubus (female demon) to a rampaging robot, a legendary swamp monster and an invisible space force. but in the best horror tradition, McGavin kept his monsters in the shadows, favouring the power of suggestion over grisly and explicit shocks.

With so much wishy-washy television about, it is a pleasure to be able to report that this very scary horror-fantasy series will at last find a prime place on British TV. To date, Kolchak has stalked the late-night schedules of only one ITV region, Central, which proudly announced the series' UK premiere in October 1983, though, of the 20 episodes made, only 13 were screened. Now it's been bought by the BBC. Watch this space . . .

REGULAR CAST

Carl Kolchak **Darren McGavin**   *Tony Vincenzo* **Simon Oakland**
Ron Updyke **Jack Grinnage**   *Edith Cowles* **Ruth McDevitt**

Creator: **Jeff Rice**
Executive producer: **Darren McGavin**
Producers: **Paul Playdon, Cy Chermak**
Music: **Gil Melle**

Francy Productions for Universal TV
20 colour 60-minute episodes
UK: 15 October–10 December 1983
14 November 1984–4 March 1985
(Central)

Episodes marked* not yet transmitted in UK

The Ripper

w **Rudolph Borchert**
The shocking murders of several young women leave Chicago stunned and lead

crime reporter Carl Kolchak to a man he believes is the original Jack the Ripper.
Jane Plumm **Beatrice Colen**

Director: **Allen Baron**

The Zombie

w Zekial Markal
Kolchak covers a gangland war and finds himself face to face with an avenging killer – a zombie.
Capt. Winwood Charles Airdman
Benjamin Sposate Joseph Sirola
Victor Friese Val Bisoglio

Director: Alex Grasshoff

U.F.O. (aka They Have Been, They Are, They Will Be . . .)

w Rudolph Borchert
Kolchak unravels a series of mysterious murders to discover an invisible alien force is draining the bone marrow from animals and humans.
Capt. Quill James Gregory
Dr Winestock Mary Wickes
Alfred Brindle Dick Van Patten
Gordy John Fiedler
Monique Carol Anne Susi

Director: Allen Baron

The Vampire

w David Chase
A trail of bloodless bodies sets Kolchak on the track of a female vampire stalking the city of Los Angeles.
Kaye Kruger Kathleen Nolan
Catherine Rawlins Suzanne Clarney
Lt Matteo Williams Daniels
Gingrich Milt Kamen

Director: Don Weiss

The Werewolf

w David Chase, Paul Playdon
The last cruise of an old luxury liner turns into a voyage of horrors when the full moon brings out a bloodcurdling werewolf.
Capt. Wells Henry Jones
Paula Griffin Nita Talbot
Bernhardt Stiegliz Eric Braeden

Director: Don Weiss

Firefall (aka The Doppelganger)

w Bill S. Ballinger
Kolchak fights fatigue as he challenges the satanic powers that threaten the life of a famous Chicago pianist.
Ryder Bond Fred Beir
Sgt Mayer Philip Carey
Maria Madlyn Rhue

Director: Don Weiss

The Devil's Platform*

w Donn Mullally
A scheming politician in league with the Devil transforms himself into a 'hound from hell' to kill off his rivals.
with: Tom Skerritt, Ellen Weston, Julie Gregg

Director: Allen Baron

Bad Medicine

w L. Ford Neale
Kolchak discovers a creature stalking Chicago that takes eerie animal form and uses its hypnotic eyes to transfix and kill wealthy matrons for their jewels.
Capt. Joe Baker Ramon Biere
with: Richard Kiel, Alice Ghostley, Victor Jory

Director: Alex Grasshoff

The Spanish Moss Murders

w Al Friedman
Kolchak is earmarked for death by a legendary Bayou swamp monster that shrouds its victims in slimy moss.
Capt. Siska Keenan Wynn
Dr Aaron Pollack Severn Darden
Michelle Kelly Roberta Dean
Henry Villon Maurice Marsac

Director: Alex Grasshoff

The Energy Eater (aka Matchemonedo)

w Arthur Rowe, Rudolph Borchert
A new hospital becomes a monument to horror when a bizarre invisible creature begins creating destruction within its walls.
with: William Smith, Michael Strong, John Alvin

Director: Alex Grasshoff

Horror in the Heights (aka The Rakshasah)*

w Jimmy Sangster
Elderly ghetto-dwellers are gnawed to death by an alien monster which appears to each of its victims as a figure of trust.
with: Phil Silvers, Abraham Sofaer

Director: Michael T. Caffey

Mr R.I.N.G.

w L. Ford Neale
A rampaging robot breaks out of a scientific institute and terrorises the community.
with: Julie Adams, Corrine Michaels

Director: Gene Levitt

The Primal Scream (aka The Humanoids)

w Bill B. Ballinger, David Chase
Prehistoric oil cells from the Arctic grow into a primitive, ape-like creature.
with: Pat Harrington, Katherine Woodville, Lindsay Workman

Director: Robert Scherer

The Trevi Collection*

w Rudolph Borchert
Kolchak stalks a beautiful witch who brings to life some wooden mannequins.
with: Nina Foch, Lara Parker

Director: Don Weiss

Chopper*

w Steve Fisher, David Chase
A headless corpse on a motorbike is slaying members of a gang of hoodlums.
with: Larry Linville, Jim Backus, Sharon Farrell

Director: Bruce Kessler

Demon in Lace

w Stephen Lord, David Chase
Kolchak uncovers a succubus, a female demon that takes over attractive young women and lures men into an embrace with death.
with: Andrew Prine, Keenan Wynn

Director: Michael Kozoll

Legacy of Terror*

w Arthur Rowe
Aztec sun-worshippers set about acquiring fresh human hearts to revive a centuries-old mummy.
with: Ramon Bieri, Pippa Scott, Sorrell Booke, Victor Campos

Director: Don McDougall

The Knightly Murders

w Michael Kozoll, David Chase
Chicago is menaced by a 12th-century knight.
with: John Dehner, Hans Conreid, Robert Emhart, Jeff Donnell

Director: Vincent McEveety

The Youth Killer*

w Rudolph Borchert
Kolchak tries to solve the mystery of why perfectly fit young men die from old age.
with: Cathy Lee Crosby, Dwayne Hickman

Director: Don McDougall

The Sentry

w L. Ford Neale, John Huff

A reptilian creature threatens an underground establishment when scientists there take away its eggs.

with: Kathie Brown, Tom Bosley

Director: Seymour Robbie

LAND OF THE GIANTS

The fourth and final chapter of Irwin Allen's television science fiction quartet was a mix of *Lost in Space* and *Gulliver's Travels*.

In the year 1983, the spaceship *Spindrift*, with its roll call of seven passengers and crew, is on a routine sub-orbital flight from California to London when it passes through a mysterious white cloud, emerging over a world where everything is 12 times larger. In this *Land of the Giants* they find a society that exactly mirrors theirs, complete with political and social upheavals and a highly advanced scientific community. Indeed, it appears the giants are aware of Earth and had been probing our atmosphere, which is what caused the *Spindrift* to drift into their world in the first place.

The space travellers find friends and make enemies – notably a giant detective, Inspector Kobick – and encounter a range of menaces from the expected (giant cats and insects) to the sinister (sadistic children and inquisitive scientists) and the totally bizarre (*Lost in Space* star Jonathan Harris as a 'pied piper' figure).

At the time, the show was Allen's most expensive so far, costing more than £250,000 dollars per episode, most of the cost being swallowed up by the elaborate props, optical and photographic effects. Allen's stable of regular writers and directors brought their final total over his four shows to some 274 episodes in six years.

Though Allen's third series, *The Time Tunnel*, had appeared – and disappeared – on the BBC, *Land of the Giants* followed *Voyage to the Bottom of the Sea* and *Lost in Space* onto ITV. It debuted in the London area in 1968, for the first of two seasons, with other ITV areas following – or not – according to the whims of regionalisation. Channel 4 picked up the series to replace *Lost in Space* starting in autumn 1989.

REGULAR CAST

THE 'LITTLE PEOPLE'

Steve Burton **Gary Conway**   *Dan Erickson* **Don Marshall**
Betty Hamilton **Heather Young**   *Mark Wilson* **Don Matheson**
Alexander Fitzhugh **Kurt Kasznar**   *Valerie Scott* **Deanna Lund**
Barry Lockridge **Stefan Arngrim**

GIANT

Insp. Kobick **Kevin Hagen** *(semi-regular)*

Creator/Executive producer: **Irwin Allen**
Director of Photography: **Howard Schwartz**
Special effects: **L.B. Abbott, Art Cruickshank, Emil Kosa Jr**
Music: **Johnny Williams**

An Irwin Allen Production for 20th Century Fox Television
51 colour 60-minute episodes

UK premieres:
Season One (26 episodes)
7 December 1968–31 May 1969
(London Weekend Television)
Season Two (25 episodes)
24 January–12 October 1972
(Thames Television – run included repeats from first season.)

Season One
26 episodes

The Crash

w **Anthony Wilson**
1983: Passengers and crew on a London-bound spaceship crash-land after passing through a mysterious cloud and find themselves in a land of giants – a society similar to Earth, but 12 times bigger!
with: **Anne Dore, Don Watters, Pat Michenaud**

Director: **Irwin Allen**

Ghost Town

w **Gil Ralston, William Welch**
Marooned in the land of the giants, the space travellers find that even the giant children can be dangerous.
with: **Percey Helton, Amber Flower, Raymond Guth**

Director: **Nathan Juran**

Framed

w **Mann Rubin**
The 'little people' clear a giant tramp of the murder of a photographer's model.
with: **Paul Carr, Doodles Weaver, Linda Peck, Dennis Cross**

Director: **Harry Harris**

Underground

w **Ellis St Joseph**
The travellers help an underground leader

to destroy papers that could cost the lives of his associates.
with: **John Abbott, Lance Le Gault, Jerry Catron, Paul Trinka**

Director: **Sobey Martin**

Terror-Go-Round

w **Charles Bennett**
A gypsy giant captures the travellers and plans to sell them to a circus as performing midgets.
with: **Joseph Ruskin, Arthur Batanides, Gerald Michenaud, Arch Whiting**

Director: **Sobey Martin**

Flight Plan

w **Peter Packer**
A miniaturised giant and his two friends try to use the space travellers to glean powerful knowledge from Earth.
with: **Linden Charles, William Bramley, Myron Healey, John Pickard**

Director: **Harry Harris**

Manhunt

w **J. Selby, Stanley Silverman**
The travellers risk their lives to save a giant convict who becomes bogged down in quicksands as he attempts to flee pursuing guards.
with: **John Napier**

Director: **Sobey Martin**

The Trap

w Jack Turley
When a giant scientist imprisons Betty and Valerie in a specimen jar, the travellers must sacrifice some of their precious fuel to save them.
with: Morgan Jones, Stewart Bradley

Director: Sobey Martin

The Creed

w Bob and Esther Mitchell
When young Barry gets appendicitis, unexpected aid is offered by a giant doctor.
with: Paul Fix, Henry Corden, Harry Lauter, Grant Sullivan

Director: Sobey Martin

Double-Cross

w Bob and Esther Mitchell
The travellers become involved with two giant thieves who plan to steal a valuable ruby.
with: Willard Sage, Lane Bradford, Howard Culver, Ted Jordan

Director: Harry Harris

The Weird World

w Ellis St Joseph
The Spindrift group encounter the nearly-mad survivor of an earlier space flight.
with: Glenn Corbett, Don Gazzaniga

Director: Harry Harris

The Golden Cage

w Jack Turley
Mark is nearly tricked into betraying his friends when the giants send out a beautiful girl as bait.
with: Celeste Yarnall, Douglas Bank, Dawson Palmer, Page Slattery

Director: Sobey Martin

The Lost Ones

w Bob and Esther Mitchell
The travellers meet up with four teenage boys, victims of a space-wreck two years earlier.
with: Tommy Webb, Jack Chaplain, Lee Jay Lambert, Zalman King, Dave Dunlop

Director: Harry Harris

Brainwash

w William Welch
Steve is brainwashed and nearly destroys a new-found means of contacting Earth.
with: Warren Stevens, Leonard Stone, Len Lesser, Robert Dowdell

Director: Harry Harris

The Bounty Hunter

w Dan Ullman
A reward is offered for the capture of the Spindrift folk.
with: Kimberley Beck, Paul Sorenson

Director: Harry Harris

Deadly Lodestone

w William L. Stuart
Hiding in a storm drain, two of the travellers hear a giant detective outline a new method of finding them.
with: Kevin Hagen, Paul Fix, Bill Fletcher, Robert Emhardt, Sheila Mathews, Gene Dynarski

Director: Harry Harris

On a Clear Night You Can See Earth

w Sheldon Stark, Anthony Wilson
Two of the titchy group are captured by Murtrah, a mad giant scientist.
with: Michael Ansara

Director: Sobey Martin

The Night of Thrombeldinar

w Bob and Esther Mitchell
While searching for food, Fitzhugh is captured by two giant orphans who think he is a magic elf who brings gifts to children.
with: Teddy Quinn, Michael A. Freeman, Jay Novello, Miriam Schiller, Alfred Ryder

Director: Sobey Martin

Seven Little Indians

w Bob and Wanda Duncan
When four of the spacefolk are captured, the others effect a courageous rescue from the zoo.
with: Kevin Hagen, Cliff Osmond, Chris Alcald

Director: Harry Harris

Genius at Work

w Bob and Esther Mitchell
A scientific formula which enables Fitzhugh to become giant-sized creates problems for the others.
with: Ronny Howard, Jacques Aubuchon, Kevin Hagen, Vic Perrin

Director: Sobey Martin

Target Earth

w Arthur Weiss
Mark's knowledge is needed to help the giants perfect a guidance system. In return, the travellers will be returned to Earth.
With: Dee Hartford, Arthur Franz, Kevin Hagen, Peter Mamakos

Director: Sobey Martin

Return of Inidu

w Bob and Esther Mitchell
The Earthlings must prove that a giant magician is innocent of a murder.
With: Jack Albertson, Tony Benson, Peter Haskell

Director: Sobey Martin

The Shell Game

w William Welch, Bob and Esther Mitchell
The travellers build a hearing aid for a giant deaf boy.
with: Gary Dubin, Larry Ward, Jan Shepard, Tol Avery

Director: Harry Harris

Sabotage

w Bob and Esther Mitchell
The Spindrift crew become involved in a struggle between a sympathetic giant senator and the power-mad chief of the Police Bureau.
with: Robert Colbert, John Marley, Elizabeth Rogers, Parley Baer, Keith Taylor, Douglas Bank

Director: Harry Harris

Rescue

w Bob and Esther Mitchell
Two giant children are trapped in an abandoned drain shaft after chasing the travellers. With other giants unable to reach the youngsters, Steve devises an ingenious but hazardous plan to rescue them.
with: Kevin Hagen, Lee Meriwether, Don Collier, Buddy Foster, Blair Ashley, Michael J. Quinn, Tom Reese, Roy Rowan

Director: Harry Harris

The Chase

w Arthur Weiss, William Welch
Insp. Kobick forces the little people to help him trap some underground freedom fighters – but the Earthlings turn the tables on him.
with: Kevin Hagen, Erik Nelson, Timothy Scott, Robert F. Lyons, Patrick Sullivan Burke, Norman Burton, Cecile Ozorio, Robert Donner

Director: Sobey Martin

Season Two
26 episodes

Six Hours to Live

w Dan Ullman
The Earth group risk their safety to prove the innocence of a young giant awaiting execution for murder.
with: George Mitchell, Anne Seymour, Richard Anderson, Bill Quinn, Larry Pennell, Michael J. Quinn

Director: Sobey Martin

Collector's Item

w Sidney Marshall, Bob *and* Wanda Duncan
A penniless giant kidnaps Valerie and puts her in a fancy costume, in a music box.
with: Guy Stockwell, Robert H. Harris, Susan Howard, George Sperdakos

Director: Sobey Martin

Chamber of Fear

w Arthur Weiss
While trying to rescue Fitzhugh, the travellers become involved with jewel thieves who operate a wax museum.
with: Cliff Osmond, Christopher Cary, Joan Feeman, Robert Tiedeman

Director: Sobey Martin

Deadly Pawn

w Arthur Weiss
Fitzhugh, Valerie and Barry become pawns on a giant's chessboard.
with: Alex Dreier, John Zaremba, Charlie Briggs

Director: Nathan Juran

The Unsuspected

w Bob *and* Esther Mitchell
Steve becomes a dangerous madman when he accidentally swallows poison and tries to turn his friends over to Insp. Kobick
with: Kevin Hagen, Leonard Stone

Director: Harry Harris

A Place Called Earth

w William Welch
The adventurers encounter Earth people from the future who prove more of a threat than the giants.
with: Warren Stevens, Jerry Douglas, Jerry Quarry *(the US heavyweight boxer)*

Director: Harmon Jones

The Mechanical Man

w William L. Stuart
A giant scientist enlists Mark's help in solving a problem with a super-robot he has built.
with: Broderick Crawford, Stuart Margolin, James Daris *(as the robot)*

Director: Harry Harris

Every Boy Needs a Dog

w Jerry Thomas
Barry takes his dog Chipper to a giant vet and endangers the lives of all his fellow travellers.
with: Michael Anderson Jr, Oliver McGowan, Bob Shayne

Director: Harry Harris

The Inside Rail

w Richard Shapiro
Fitzhugh leads his friends into danger at a racetrack because of his love of the gee-gees.
with: Arch Johnson, Ben Blue, Joe Turkel, Vic Tayback

Director: Harry Harris

Land of the Lost

w William Welch
When four of the Earth group are accidentally carried away by a giant's balloon, they discover a new land, ruled by a despot.
with: Nehemiah Persoff, Clint Ritchie, Peter Canon, Brian Nash

Director: Harmon Jones

Giants and All That Jazz

w Richard Shapiro
Dan, a talented jazz trumpeter, uses his skill to save his friends and help a kindly giant.
with: Sugar Ray Robinson, William Bramley, Mike Mazurki, Diana Chesney

Director: Harry Harris

Home, Sweet Home

w William Welch
After finding a space capsule, Steve and Fitzhugh return briefly to Earth but are forced to go back to the giants' planet.
with: William H. Bassett, William Benedict, Robert Adler, Pete Kellett

Director: Harry Harris

Nightmare

w William Welch
When the space travellers are accidentally exposed to radiation from a new power device, they become invisible to the giants.
with: Torin Thatcher, Yale Summers, Kevin Hagen

Director: Nathan Juran

Panic

w Bob *and* Wanda Duncan
Kirmus, a giant scientist, promises to return the travellers to Earth.
with: Jack Albertson *(Kirmus)*, Mark Richman, Diane McBain

Director: Sobey Martin

Our Man O'Reilly

w Jackson Gillis
The Earth people get unexpected help from a superstitious giant who thinks they are leprechauns.
with: Alan Hale, Alan Bergmann, Billy Halop, Michael J. Quinn

Director: Sobey Martin

Pay the Piper

w Richard Shapiro
The travellers are lured away by a giant Pied Piper.
with: Jonathan Harris *(the Piper)*, Peter Leeds, Michael-James Wixted

Director: Harry Harris

The Secret City of Limbo

w Bob *and* Esther Mitchell
The Earth people help prevent a war between the surface-dwelling giants and a race from below the ground.
with: Malachi Throne, Joseph Ruskin, Peter Jason, Whit Bissell

Director: Sobey Martin

The Deadly Dart

w William L. Stuart
Mark is accused of murdering a giant policeman.
with: Christopher Dark, Kent Taylor, Madlyn Rhue, John Dehner, Donald Barry, Willard Sage

Director: Harry Harris

Doomsday

w Dan Ullman
The Earth travellers uncover a bomb plot and help to trap a saboteur.
with: Francine York, Ed Peck, Kevin Hagen

Director: Harry Harris

A Small War

w Shirl Hendryx
The Earth people are unwillingly drawn into a war with a giant boy and his toy soldiers.
with: Sean Kelly, Charles Drake

Director: Harry Harris

The Marionettes

w William Welch
The travellers are able to help improve the act of a giant puppeteer who has aided them.
with: Frank Ferguson, Bob Hogan, Victoria Vetri, Sandra Giles, Carl Carlsson

Director: Sobey Martin

The Clones

w Oliver Crawford, Bob and Esther Mitchell
An evil scientist makes exact copies of Valerie and Barry.
with: William Schallert, Sandra Giles

Director: Nathan Juran

Comeback

w Richard Shapiro
The travellers meet a kindly but ugly giant who was once a famous star of the monster movies, and try to help him make a comeback.
with: John Carradine, Janos Prohaska, Jesse White, Fritz Feld

Director: Harry Harris

Graveyard of Fools

w Sidney Marshall
To aid their ambitions, three power-mad giant transport four of the little people to a strange, distant land inhabited by giant insects.
with: Albert Salmi, John Crawford, Michael Stewart

Director: Sobey Martin

Wild Journey

w William Welch
Steve and Dan are given the chance to relive the hours before their space flight.
with: Bruce Dern, Yvonne Craig, Martin Liverman, Erik Nelson

Director: Harry Harris

LEGEND OF DEATH

Five-part reworking of the Theseus/Minotaur Greek legend given a modern setting and a sci-fi twist.

King Aegeus became E.G., a tycoon whose crowning achievement was to have been Icarus III, the first nuclear-powered aircraft. But the project has come to sicken him because of its cost in human lives: each year 14 volunteers are sent to the sinister atomic plant on the island of Mitremos and none has ever returned.

Enter Theseus, or rather Theodore, E.G.'s illegitimate son who goes to Mitremos and discovers the 'Minotaur' – actually a power-crazy scientist called Minolti who is running the Icarus project but also using the island for a series of experiments of his own into the effects of radiation on humans. Avoiding a similar fate, Theodore destroys the beast and his den, and returns to claim his inheritance.

MAIN CAST

Theodore **David Andrews** *Edward Gargan (E.G.)* **John Phillips**
Myra Gargan **Sarah Lawson** *Finn* **Victor Brooks**
Irwin **James Cossins** *Edgarsund* **Gerald Sim** *Dr Zemaron* **Andrew Sachs**
Minolti **John Hollis** *Adela* **Stephanie Randall** *Francesca* **Sheila Hammond**
Joseph Dugascin **Robert Cartland** *Yvonne* **Felicity Mason**
Daniel Spencer **Christopher Tranchell** *Arnold* **Brian Cant**

Writer: **Brian Hayles**
Director: **Gerald Blake**
Producer: **Alan Bromly**
Designer: **Peter Seddon**

A BBC Production
Five 25-minute episodes, black and white

The Golden Intruder
Journey Into Danger
The Moving Maze
The Black Return
The Death Switch

19 July–16 August 1965
(BBC2)

LOGAN'S RUN

A futuristic version of *The Fugitive*, Logan ran for just 14 episodes (including the obligatory movie-length pilot) with his companions Jessica and Rem the android.

Set in the 23rd century, some 200 years after a nuclear holocaust, the series depicted a world of pocket civilisations – each an isolated law unto itself, with its inhabitants largely unaware of the alternatives. One of these closed societies is the City of Domes, a precisely programmed world where population control is achieved by people voluntarily submitting to a youthful euthanasia. On their 30th birthday – known as Lastday – all inhabitants must undergo the spectacular extermination ceremony of Carousel. Those who refuse and opt to run from the city are hunted and killed by Sandmen, the Domed City's elite police.

Logan is a Sandman who is persuaded by Jessica, a member of the underground, to run with her in search of a mythical place in the Outside World, known as Sanctuary, where people can grow old gracefully. On the run (in a dinky little hovercraft) they encounter other groups and societies – some friendly, some threatening. But always their goal remains Sanctuary where they hope to find other runners and, ultimately, return to the Domed City to disprove the institution of Carousel. Early on, they stumble upon a Mountain City where they meet Rem, an android who becomes their trusted companion.

The trio are relentlessly pursued by Sandmen, led by Logan's one-time partner and best friend Francis who has been promised a life beyond 30 as a city elder if he can bring back the fugitives.

The series, based on the novel and 1976 feature film of the same name, was brought to television by Ivan Goff and Ben Roberts (whose track record included *Charlie's Angels*), and described as human dramas projected into the future. 'Psychologically', said Goff, 'Logan and Jessica face the same concerns that baffled Adam and Eve.'

In the end, despite some enjoyable sequences, *Logan's Run* was a fairly antiseptic series, aimed firmly at the family audience. The relationship between Logan and Jessica was more like brother and sister than Adam and Eve, despite the wispy little mini-dress Jessica *always* wore (and which never looked dirty or crumpled), and the whimsical Rem was the only character with a sense of humour.

ITV screened the series in Britain, starting in the Midlands (Central) region in January 1978, with other areas a few weeks behind.

REGULAR CAST

Logan **Gregory Harrison**   *Jessica* **Heather Menzies**
Rem **Donald Moffat**   *Francis* **Randy Powell**

Based on the novel by **William F. Nolan** *and* **George Clayton Johnson**
Executive producers: **Ivan Goff** *and* **Ben Roberts**
Producer: **Leonard Katzman**

An MGM Television Production
14 colour episodes (one × 80 mins, 13 × 60 mins)
7 January–2 April 1978
(Central)

Logan's Run (pilot)

w **William F. Nolan, Saul David**
Logan and Jessica flee the 'utopian' world of the Domed City, pursued by Francis and his Sandmen. In a mountain city they are 'captured' by two robots, Draco and Siri, who need someone to serve, and rescued by Rem who joins their search for Sanctuary.
Siri **Lina Raymond**
Draco **Kenne Curtis**
Riles **Ron Hajek**
Akers **Gary Dontzig**
Ketcham **Anthony De Longis**

Director: **Robert Day**

The Collectors

w **James Schmerer**
Jessica and Logan are captured by alien invaders who manipulate their minds into believing they have found Sanctuary. Rem finds other captives from yet another planet and devises a plan that could free them all.
John **Linden Chiles**
Joanna **Leslie Parrish**
Karen **Angela Cartwright**
Martin **Lawrence Casey**

Director: **Alexander Singer**

Capture

w **Michael Edwards**
After Francis captures Logan, Jessica and Rem, they in turn are seized by James Borden, a collector of antique weapons who also makes a sport of hunting men. He selects Logan and Francis as his next quarry – but the Sandmen unite to turn the tables.
Borden **Horst Bucholz**
Irene **Mary Woronov**
Benjamin **Stan Stratton**

Director: **Irving J. Moore**

The Innocent

w Ray Brenner, D.C. Fontana
The fugitives meet a beautiful young woman who was left by her parents to live alone in a clinical, computerised atmosphere with only two robots for company. When the girl, Lisa, develops a crush on Logan she schemes to eliminate her rival – Jessica.
Lisa Lisa Eilbacher
Strong Lou Richards
Jeremy Barney McFadden
Patrick Brian Kerwin
Friend Gene Tyburn

Director: Michael Preece

Man Out of Time

w Noah Ward
Logan and his companions meet up with a scientist from 200 years before who has travelled into the future to find a way of preventing the holocaust.
David Eakins Paul Shenar
Analog Mel Ferrer
Lab Tech One Woodrow Chambliss
Comp Tech Four Gene Tyburn
Gold Hank Brandt

Director: Nicholas Colasanto

Half Life

w Shimon Wincelberg
Logan, Jessica and Rem encounter a society able to divide its people physically into two halves – The Positives (goodies) and the Castouts (baddies). When Jessica herself is processed, Logan and Rem must try to reunite the two halves.
Patron/Modok William Smith
Positive 14/Brawn Leon Birman
Rama II Kim Cattrall
Rama I Jeanne Sorel
Woman positive Betty Jinette

Director: Steven Stern

Crypt

w Al Hayes, Harlan Ellison
The runners discover the frozen bodies of six people in a ruined city and a serum to bring them back to life permanently. But after reviving them initially, one vial of serum accidentally breaks, leaving only enough to keep three alive . . .
David Pera Christopher Stone
Rachel Greenhill Ellen Weston
Dexter Kim Soon-Teck Oh
Victoria Mackie Neva Patterson
Frederick Lyman Liam Sullivan
Sylvia Reyna Adrienne Larussa

Director: Michael Caffey

Judas Goat

w John Meredyth Lucas
The fugitives meet Hal 14 who claims to be a runner but is really a Sandman sent to lure Logan's heroes back to the Domed City.
Hal 14 Nicholas Hammond
Matthew Lance Le Gault
Jonathan Wright King
Garth Spencer Milligan
Morgan Morgan Woodward

Director: Paul Krasny

Fear Factor

w John Sherlock
Logan, Jessica and Rem are trapped by strange scientists experimenting to produce a master race by removing the ability to experience emotion from the minds of their 'patients'.
Dr Rowan Ed Nelson
Dr Paulson Jared Martin
Psychiatrists William Wellman Jr, Peter Brandon, Carl Byrd

Director: Gerald Mayer

Futurepast

w Katharyn Michaelian Powers
Logan and Jessica finds their lives in peril when a beautiful android woman tries dream analysis on them.
Ariana Mariette Hartley
Clay Michael Sullivan
Sandmen Ed Couppee, Joey Fontana
The woman Janis Jamison

Director: Michael O'Herlihy

Carousel

w D.C. Fontana, Richard L. Breen Jr

When Logan is shot with a dart that erases his memory, he is captured by Francis and taken back to the Domed City. Rem and Jessica must rescue him before he is sent to Carousel.

Diane Rosanne Katon
Michael Ross Bikell
Jonathan Wright King
Morgan Morgan Woodward
Sheila Melody Anderson
Darrel Regis J. Cordic

Director: Irving J. Moore

Night Visitors

w Leonard Katzman

The three fugitives are welcomed into a strange house which Rem, searching his memory bank, decides is haunted and their hosts are ghosts from the spirit world.

Gavin George Maharis
Marianne Barbara Babcock
Barton Paul Mantee

Director: Paul Krasny

Turnabout

w Michael Michaelian, Al Hayes

When Logan, Jessica, Rem *and* Francis are all captured by desert horsemen and sentenced to death, Logan finds himself trying to save his arch enemy.

Gera Gerald McRaney
Asa Nehemiah Persoff
Samuel Harry Rhodes
Mia Victoria Racimo
Phillip John Furey

Director: Paul Krasny

Stargate

w Dennis O'Neill

When they encounter strange people from a planet much hotter than Earth, Logan and Jessica have to fight to save Rem who's being dismantled to provide spare parts for the aliens' spaceship.

Timon Eddie Firestone
Xorah Paul Carr
Pata Darrell Fetty
Arcana Ian Tanza

Director: Curtis Harrington

LOST IN SPACE

After launching the Poseidon adventures of *Voyage to the Bottom of the Sea* in 1964, producer Irwin Allen looked for further fortunes in the stars and found himself *Lost in Space*.

This folksy saga of a family of galactic castaways first appeared in 1965. Over here it wandered through the ITV schedules, flitting haphazardly from region to region, until it disappeared in the mid-Seventies. Filed under 'c' for cult, it remained lost to sight until Channel 4 resurrected the series in 1988.

Set in 1997, *Lost in Space* charted the adventures of the Space Family Robinson, selected from more than two million volunteers to embark on a 5½-year voyage to colonise a distant planet in the Alpha Centauri system. Enemy agent Dr Zachary Smith sneaks aboard the *Jupiter 2* spaceship and reprogrammes their robot to destroy it. But his sabotage backfires when he becomes trapped aboard and by the time they regain control the ship is far off course.

Astrophysicist John Robinson (played by Walt Disney's ex-Zorro star Guy Williams), his down-to-earth biochemist wife Maureen, and children Judy, Penny and Will, are the pioneering family. Aided by handsome geologist/pilot Major Don West, they set about trying first to survive and then to escape from their galactic desert island, hindered by the self-centred desires of the idle, whingeing scoundrel Dr Smith. Despite the wholesome nature of the family, it was Smith who became the star of the show, along with the robot, a 7 ft 'bubble-headed booby' who was forever warning of imminent danger.

Young actor Billy Mumy already had a list of more than 50 film and TV credits by the time he was cast as Will, including pivotal roles in three *Twilight Zone* stories (*Long Distance Call*, 1960; *It's a Good Life*, 1961; and *In Praise of Pip*, 1963). Angela Cartwright, who played Penny, had the dubious credential of being one of the Von Trapp children in *The Sound of Music*, while Jonathan Harris (Dr Smith) had enjoyed a three-year run with Michael Rennie in *The Third Man*.

Although the series degenerated into increasingly camp comic fantasy – in which a carrot monster was the final straw! – the early black and white shows had a hard edge of serious science fiction, occasionally sustaining a decent level of suspense. This was mildly heightened by the use of cliffhanger endings to each episode – though these were always the first moves in a *new* story, that week's adventure having been safely resolved. The early shows in particular also took a high moral tone, stressing the virtues of family unity and handing out lessons in prejudice, social behaviour, loyalty, responsibility and manners. In one episode Will is even told to take his elbows off the table!

REGULAR CAST

Prof. John Robinson Guy Williams   *Maureen Robinson* June Lockhart
Judy Marta Kristen   *Penny* Angela Cartwright   *Will* Billy Mumy
Don West Mark Goddard   *Dr Zachary Smith* Jonathan Harris
Robot Bob May

Creative/Executive producer: Irwin Allen
Story editor: Anthony Wilson
Music: Johnny Williams
Director of photography: Gene Polito
   (Season One), Frank Carson
Special effects: L.B. Abbott, Hal
   Lydecker

CBS/An Irwin Allen Production in association with Jodi Production Inc, Van Bernard Productions Inc for 20th Century Fox Television

83 60-minute episodes (1965–68)
Black and white (Season One)
Colour (from Season Two)
UK premiere: 2 October 1965
(Incomplete run in Northern region by ABC Weekend Television.)

Dates on the following Season guides are 'first complete run' dates for the UK. Other regions followed – in their own time.

Season One
29 episodes
9 October 1965–24 April 1966
(Southern Television)

The Reluctant Stowaway

w Shimon Wincelberg
16 October 1997: the Robinson family
blast off in their *Jupiter 2* spaceship bound
for Alpha Centauri. The unexpected
presence on board of a saboteur, Dr
Smith, sends the ship off course, becoming
'lost in space'.
TV Commentator Don Forbes
General Hal Torey

Director: Tony Leader

The Derelict

w Peter Packer, *story* Shimon
Wincelberg
Searching for a clue as to their whereabouts, the *Jupiter 2* crew is drawn into a
cavernous spaceship where they discover
the wonders of an advanced alien civilisation.
TV Commentator Don Forbes
Giant Dawson Palmer

Director: Alex Singer

Island in the Sky

w Norman Lessing, *story* Shimon
Wincelberg
After John has plummeted to the unknown planet's surface, Smith tampers
with the *Jupiter 2*'s rockets and the ship
crash-lands. The party begin the search
for John in the space chariot.

Director: Tony Leader

There Were Giants in the Earth

w Carey Wilber, *story* Shimon
Wincelberg
Alarmed by the prospect of a 150 degree
drop in temperature, the Robinsons head
south and encounter cyclopean giants.
Giant Dawson Palmer

Director: Leo Penn

The Hungry Sea

w William Welch, *story* Shimon
Wincelberg
Data from the robot warns that the planet's
elliptical orbit will bring it perilously close
to the sun. Barely escaping a fiery death,
the Robinsons decide to head back to
their spaceship – but the elements haven't
finished with them yet!

Director: Sobey Martin

Welcome Stranger

w Peter Packer
A long-lost astronaut lands on the Robinsons' planet and after helping to repair his
ship, both the family and Smith see him as
a ticket back to Earth – John and Maureen
for the children, Smith for himself!
Jimmy Hapgood Warren Oates

Director: Alvin Ganzer

My Friend, Mr Nobody

w Jackson Gillis
Penny befriends a cosmic force which she
encounters in a secret cave.
Voice William Bramley

Director: Paul Stanley

Invaders from the Fifth Dimension

w Shimon Wincelberg
Luminous aliens invade the Robinson
space colony and capture Smith, planning
to use his brain to replace their burnt-out
computer. But sly old Smith talks them
into letting him bring them Will instead.
Alien Ted Lehmann
Luminary Joe Ryan

Director: Leonard Horn

The Oasis

w Peter Packer
Dr Smith samples some untested alien
fruit and grows into a giant.

Director: Sutton Roley

The Sky Is Falling

w Barney Slater and Herman Groves
Unable to understand each other, mutual
mistrust grows between the Robinsons
and a visiting alien family until Will and
the aliens' son find a way to achieve
friendship.
Rethso Don Matheson
Moela Francoise Ruggieri
Lunon Eddie Rosson

Director: Sobey Martin

Wish Upon a Star

w Barney Slater
A typical *Lost in Space* morality tale. Will
finds a thought machine that can turn
wishes into reality, but it begins to arouse
selfish emotions in the family. When
Smith's greed gets too great, a strange
creature comes to reclaim the device.
Rubberoid Dawson Palmer

Director: Sutton Roley

The Raft

w Peter Packer
The Robinsons build a small space craft
from parts of the Jupiter, planning to send
Don back to Earth for help. But Dr Smith
plots to hijack it.
Bush creature Dawson Palmer

Director: Sobey Martin

One of Our Dogs Is Missing

w William Welch
A 20-year-old space dog lands on the
planet and helps rescue Judy from the
clutches of a great hairy mutant (another
addition to the Dawson Palmer monster
club!)

Director: Sutton Roley

Attack of the Monster Plants

w William Read Woodfield and Allan
  Balter
Giant cyclamen plants that can duplicate

anything fed into them create a replica of
Judy and devour a vital fuel supply.

Director: Justis Addis

Return from Outer Space

w Peter Packer
Will uses a discarded matter transfer unit
to make a Christmas trip back to Earth.
But no one there will believe his story.
Aunt Clara Reta Shaw
Sheriff Baxendale Walter Sande
Davey Sims Donald Losby
Ruth Templeton Sheila Mathews

Director: Jerry Juran

The Keeper (Part 1)

w Barney Slater
An alien beast-collector threatens to add
Will and Penny to his bizarre menagerie.
(This story reunited the 'Third Man'
partnership of Jonathan Harris and
Michael Rennie.)
The Keeper Michael Rennie
Lighted head Wilbur Evans

Director: Sobey Martin

The Keeper (Part 2)

While trying to steal the alien's spaceship
Smith accidentally releases the Keeper's
animals. The Keeper threatens to let his
beasts overrun the planet unless Will and
Penny are turned over to him.
(Guest cast as Part 1)

Director: Harry Harris

The Sky Pirate

w Carey Wilbur
Tucker, a grizzled old space pirate,
kidnaps and then befriends Will, raising
everybody's hopes of rescue.
Tucker Albert Salmi

Director: Sobey Martin

Ghost in Space

w Peter Packer
A turbulent 'ghost' threatens the cast-aways' camp and Dr Smith, convinced it's the troubled spirit of his Uncle Thaddeus, sets out to exorcise it.
Presence Dawson Palmer

Director: Sobey Martin

The War of the Robots

w Barney Slater
Will repairs a highly advanced robotoid that pretends to help the Robinsons while secretly plotting to capture them for its alien master. (The 'guest villain' is none other than Robby the Robot – mechanical star of sci-fi film classic *Forbidden Planet*.)

Director: Sobey Martin

The Magic Mirror

w Jackson Gillis
Penny and her pet bloop fall through a magic mirror into a strange dark world inhabited by a lonely alien boy.
Boy Michael J. Pollard

Director: Nathan Juran

The Challenge

w Barney Slater
A ruler from another planet and his son try to prove their superiority by challenging Will and his father to a test of strength and courage. (Guest role here for a young Kurt Russell, while Guy Williams gets to relive his 'Zorro' days in a swordfight.)
Ruler Michael Ansara
Quano Kurt Russell

Director: Donald Richardson

The Space Trader

w Barney Slater
Smith sells the robot to a dodgy space trader for a 12-day food supply, then tries to buy it back by offering himself in exchange believing that the trader won't 'collect' for 200 years.
Trader Torin Thatcher

Director: Jerry Juran

His Majesty Smith

w Carey Wilbur
Dr Smith schemes his way into becoming king of a mysterious alien civilisation – but is horrified when he discovers he has been chosen for his uselessness and is due to be skinned and stuffed in a primitive ritual.
Nexus Liam Sullivan
Alien Kevin Hagen

Director: Harry Harris

The Space Croppers

w Peter Packer
Once again sensing a chance to get back to Earth, Smith decides to marry the matri-archal head of a space clan whose strange crop threatens to devour all life on the Robinsons' planet.
Sybilla Mercedes McCambridge
Effra Sherry Jackson
Keel Dawson Palmer

Director: Sobey Martin

All That Glitters

w Barney Slater
Using a space thief's magic key, Dr Smith finds a strange neck-ring that turns every-thing he touches into platinum – including Penny!
Bolix Werner Klemperer
Ohan Larry Ward

Director: Harry Harris

Lost Civilisation

w William Welch
Exploring an underground world, Will awakens a sleeping Princess, and triggers an alien civilisation's plans to conquer the Universe with its 'frozen' army.
Princess Kym Karath
Major Domo Roy Dano

Director: Don Richardson

A Change of Space

w Peter Packer

Will climbs aboard an alien spacecraft and shoots off into the sixth dimension, returning as an intellectual giant. When Smith tries it he returns as a decrepit old man.
Alien Frank Graham

Director: Sobey Martin

Follow the Leader

w Barney Slater

Trapped in a cave by a rock fall, John Robinson is possessed by the unseen spirit of an alien warrior. But Will's love for his father overcomes the spirit and drives it away.
Alien voice Gregory Norton

Director: Don Richardson

Season Two
(30 episodes)
25 October 1966–27 May 1967
(Grampian Television)

Blast Off Into Space

w Peter Packer

Despite Smith's rascally dealings with intergalactic prospector Nerim, the Robinsons manage to get *Jupiter 2* into space before the mining blasts cause the planet to disintegrate.
Nerim Strother Martin

Director: Jerry Juran

Wild Adventure

w William Read Woodfield, Allan Balter

Jupiter 2 almost returns to Earth, but Smith is lured out into space by a seductive Lorelei, Athena, the green girl, and the ship must change course to rescue him.
Athena Vitina Marcus

Director: Don Richardson

The Ghost Planet

w Peter Packer

Fooled into thinking it's Earth, Smith causes the ship to land on an alien planet run by Cyborgs who try to enslave the travellers.
Automaton voice Sue England
Summit voice Michael Fox

Director: Jerry Juran

The Forbidden World

w Barney Slater

The *Jupiter 2* is forced down on another alien planet where Smith drinks some unusual nectar which turns him into a human bomb.
Tiabo Wally Cox
Monster Janos Prohaska

Director: Don Richardson

Space Circus

w Bob *and* Wanda Duncan

Will nearly joins Dr Marvello's intergalactic circus to save his family from the troupe's monster. Smith also tries to join, singing *Tiptoe Through the Tulips*.
Dr Marvello James Westerfield
Fenestra Melinda Fee
Vicho Harry Varteresian
Nubu Michael Greene
The Monster Dawson Palmer

Director: Harry Harris

The Prisoners of Space

w Barney Slater

The Robinsons are tried by a mysterious tribunal for committing space crimes. All are vindicated except Smith who is found guilty but insane and released into the custody of the robot.
Monster Dawson Palmer

Director: Jerry Juran

The Android Machine

w **Bob** *and* **Wanda Duncan**
The Robinsons help a simple android develop into a higher grade model by teaching her the meaning of love.
Verda **Dee Hartford**
Mr Zumdish **Fritz Feld**

Director: **Don Richardson**

The Deadly Games of Gamma 6

w **Barney Slater**
Smith and the Robinsons become embroiled in an alien's intergalactic gladiatorial fights – with the losers incurring invasion of their home planets.
Myko **Mike Kellin**
Geoo **Harry Monty**
Gromack **Ronald Weber**
Alien leader **Peter Brocco**
Alien giant **Chuck Robertson**

Director: **Harry Harris**

The Thief of Outer Space

w **Jackson Gillis**
Will helps a futuristic Arab chieftain to find his long-lost princess.
Thief **Malachi Throne**
Slave **Ted Cassidy**
Fat Princess **Maxine Gates**

Director: **Don Richardson**

The Curse of Cousin Smith

w **Barney Smith**
A low plausibility reading even by *Lost in Space* standards . . . Smith's equally rascally cousin arrives on the Robinson's planet and tries to do Zachary out of his inheritance.
Jeremiah Smith **Henry Jones**

Director: **Justis Addiss**

The Dream Monster

w **Peter Packer**
Sesmar, a white-haired space scientist,
tries to drain the Robinsons' human emotions to bolster his android creation.
Sesmar **John Abbott**
Raddison **Dawson Palmer**
Midgets **Harry Monty, Frank Delfino**

Director: **Don Richardson**

The Golden Man

w **Barney Slater**
A galactic morality tale . . . Penny and the family become involved in a war between the leaders of two alien civilisations – one a handsome Golden Man called Keema, the other a big ugly frog. Guess which one turns out to be a prince of a guy?
Keema **Dennis Patrick**
Frog alien **Ronald Gans**
Handsome alien **Bill Troy**

Director: **Don Richardson**

The Girl from the Green Dimension

w **Peter Packer**
Smith gets involved again with Athena, the Green-skinned girl.
Athena **Vitina Marcus**
Ursuk **Harry Raybould**

Director: **Jerry Juran**

The Questing Beast

w **Carey Wilbur**
Penny and Will become embroiled in a bumbling futuristic knight's lifelong quest for a fire-breathing female beast.
Sagramonte **Hans Conried**
Que Track voice **Sue England**
Gundemar **Jeff County**

Director: **Don Richardson**

The Toymaker

w **Bob** *and* **Wanda Duncan**
Will and Dr Smith are imprisoned in a fourth dimensional toyland and meet up again with Zumdish of the Celestial Department Store.

Zumdish Fritz Feld
O M Walter Burke
Security guard Tiger Joe Marsh
Monster Dawson Palmer
Wooden soldier Larry Dean

Director: Robert Douglas

Mutiny in Space

w Peter Packer
Will, Smith and the Robot are shanghaied by a renegade space ship admiral.
Admiral Zahrk Ronald Long

Director: Don Richardson

The Space Viking

w Margaret Brookman Hill
It's off to Valhalla as Dr Smith finds himself pitted against the mighty Thor.
Brynhilde Sheila Mathews
Thor Bern Hoffman

Director: Ezra Stone

Rocket to Earth

w Barney Slater
Smith nearly makes it back to Earth in a rocket he steals from a bungling space magician.
Zalto Al Lewis

Director: Don Richardson

The Cave of the Wizards

w Peter Packer
A chance to get to Alpha Centauri is blown when Smith is seduced by the luxurious powers of a computer – the relic of a lost civilisation. (No guest cast)

Director: Don Richardson

Treasure of the Lost Planet

w Carey Wilbur
Smith and Will are reunited with space pirate Tucker – first seen in Season One –

and get involved in his bizarre treasure hunt.
Tucker Albert Salmi
Deek Craig Duncan
Smeek Jim Boles

Director: Harry Harris

Revolt of the Androids

w Bob *and* Wanda Duncan
Smith dreams of transforming a rundown android into an all-powerful machine – but reckons without the tender loving care of female 'droid Verda.
Verda Dee Hartford
Idak Don Matheson
Monster Dawson Palmer

Director: Don Richardson

The Colonists

w Peter Packer
With the Robinsons enslaved by a real Amazon, Will and the Robot must find a way to defeat her.
Niolani Francine York

Director: Ezra Stone

Trip Through the Robot

w Barney Slater
When the Robot, with a failing power-pack, stumbles into a misty valley, an ionic reversal enlarges him to the size of a house, and Will and Smith have to crawl inside – à la *Fantastic Voyage* – to fix him. (No guest cast.)

Director: Don Richardson

The Phantom Family

w Peter Packer
An alien scientist makes android copies of Smith, Don and the girls, then forces Will and the Robot to teach them to act like their human counterparts.
Lemnoc Alan Hewitt

Director: Ezra Stone

The Mechanical Men

w Barney Slater
When tiny mechanical men want the Robot as their leader, they improve him by trading the voice and personality of Smith for his. (No guest cast.)

Director: S. Robbie

The Astral Traveller

w Carey Wilbur
Will stumbles through a space warp and finds himself in a haunted Scottish castle with a monster in the loch . . .
Hamish Sean McClory
Angus Dawson Palmer

Director: Don Richardson

The Galaxy Gift

w Barney Slater
Penny is given a magic amulet but aliens enlist Smith's help to make her give it up, promising to return him to Earth.
Arcon John Carradine
Saticon Jim Mills

Director: Ezra Stone

The Wreck of the Robot

w Barney Slater
The robot becomes the blueprint for an alien machine that could threaten the entire universe.
Alien Jim Mills

Director: Jerry Juran

A Visit to Hades

w Carey Wilbur
Smith's greed lands him in a Hell-like place, a prison for a devilish political revolutionary called Morbus.
Morbus Gerald Mohr

Director: Don Richardson

West of Mars

w Michael Fessier
Smith is mistaken for his double – a notorious intergalactic gunslinger.
Enforcer Allan Melvin
Dee Mickey Manners
Photo DBL Charles Arthur
Pleiades Pete Lane Bradford
Bartender Eddie Quillan

Director: Jerry Juran

Season Three

(24 episodes)
3 August 1968–24 January 1969
(Grampian Television)
all except episodes marked * which were first shown in the *London* region, April–May 1970, at end of complete Season Three run.

The Condemned of Space

w Peter Packer
The *Jupiter 2* stops at a space-station to refuel and finds it's a computerised space prison.
Phanzig Marcel Hillaire

Director: Jerry Juran

Visit to a Hostile Planet

w Peter Packer
The Robinsons are taken for dangerous aliens when they land on Earth 50 years before their own time.
Grover Pitt Herbert
Cragmire Robert Foulk
Craig Robert Pine
Charlie Norman Leavitt
Stacy Clair Wilcox

Director: Sobey Martin

Kidnapped in Space

w Robert Hamner
The Robot turns surgeon when mechanical men kidnap the Robinson party to make him operate on their leader.
Aliens Grant Sullivan, Carol Williams
Young Smith Joey Russo

Director: Don Richardson

Hunter's Moon

w Jack Turley
Scouting out a strange planet, John is regarded as a prize quarry by a hunter.
Megazor Vincent Beck

Director: J. Richardson

The Space Primevals

w Peter Packer
The space family is menaced by a primitive race controlled by a mammoth computer.
Rangah Arthur Batanides

Director: Jerry Juran

The Space Destructors

w Robert Hamner
Smith discovers a Cyborg manufacturing machine and dreams of conquering the universe with his own army.
Cyborg Tommy Farrell

Director: Don Richardson

The Haunted Lighthouse

w Jackson Gillis
The *Jupiter 2*, with a strange young passenger, J-5, aboard takes off, but encounters an American lighthouse in space.
J-5 Lou Wagner
Col. Fogey Woodrow Parfrey
The zaybo Kenya Coburn

Director: Sobey Martin

Flight Into the Future

w Peter Packer
Landing on an unknown green planet, Will, Dr Smith and the Robot experience strange adventures of illusions in time.
Sgt Smith Don Eitner
Cmdr Fletcher Lew Gallo

Director: Sobey Martin

Collision of the Planets

w Peter Packer
Aliens planning to destroy an erratic planet the Robinsons are on, refuse to give them time to prepare their ship for lift-off. (Early role for *Hill Street Blues* star Daniel J. Travanti.)
Ilan Dan Travanti
Aliens Linda Gaye Scott, Joey Tata

Director: Don Richardson

The Space Creature

w William Welch
After everyone vanishes from the *Jupiter 2*, Will faces a fearsome blue misty spectre. (No guest cast.)

Director: Sobey Martin

Deadliest of the Species

w Robert Hamner
The Robot falls in love with an evil alien female super-robot and helps her in her quest to rule the Universe.
Alien leader Ronald Gans
Female robot Sue England
Mechanical men Lyle Waggoner, Ralph Lee

Director: Sobey Martin

A Day at the Zoo

w Jackson Gillis
Penny is abducted and placed on display at a zoo by galactic showman Farnum B.
Farnum Leonard Stone
Oggo Gary Tigerman
Mort Ronald Weber

Director: I. Moore

Two Weeks in Space

w Robert Hamner
A disguised quartet of monsters, on the run from the galactic cops, give Smith the idea to turn the *Jupiter 2* into a holiday hotel.

Zumdish Fritz Feld
MXR Richard Krisher
QZW Eric Matthews
Non Edy Williams
Tat Carroll Roebke

Director: Don Richardson

Castles in Space

w Peter Packer
When a ferocious bandit threatens to abduct an Ice Princess in the Robinsons' care, the Robot fights like a bull to save her.
Chavo Alberto Monte
Reyka Corinna Tsopei

Director: Sobey Martin

The Anti-Matter Man

w Barney Slater *and* Robert Hamner
John Robinson's evil counterpart from an anti-matter world tries to take the prof's place in the family circle.
Drun Mark Goddard

Director: Sutton Roley

Target: Earth

w Peter Packer
Will foils a plot by shapeless aliens to duplicate the Robinsons and use the Robot to help them conquer Earth.
Gilt Proto James Gosa
Mike officer Brent Davis
2nd officer Thant Brann

Director: Jerry Juran

Princess of Space

w Jackson Gillis
An old space captain thinks Penny is a lost princess of his planet and grooms her for a royal visit.
Kraspo Robert Foulk
Fedor Arte Johnson
Aunt Gamma Sheila Mathews

Director: Don Richardson

The Time Merchant

w Bob *and* Wanda Duncan
Smith tricks a time merchant, Dr Chronos, into returning him to Earth just before Jupiter's flight, but in doing so risks changing the course of the past and imperilling the lives of the Robinsons.
Dr Chronos John Crawford
General Byron Morrow
Sergeant Hoke Howell

Director: Ezra Stone

The Promised Planet

w Peter Packer
The *Jupiter 2* lands on a turned-on planet populated solely by hippie youngsters.
Bartholomew Gil Rogers
Edgar Keith Taylor

Director: Ezra Stone

Fugitives in Space*

w Robert Hamner
Smith and Don are framed and jailed on a prison-planet. Will and the Robot go to the rescue.
Creech Michael Conrad
Warden Tol Avery
Guard Charles Horvath

Director: Ezra Stone

Space Beauty

w Jackson Gillis
Judy wins a galactic beauty contest and is nearly carted off to a planet of fire.
Farnum Leonard Stone
Nancy Dee Hartford
Miss Teutonium Miriam Schiller

Director: I. Moore

The Flaming Planet*

w Barney Slater
A plant-creature grows fond of Smith, then comes close to engulfing the ship

until a home is found for it on a war-ravaged planet.
Sobram **Abraham Sofaer**

Director: **Don Richardson**

The Great Vegetable Rebellion*

w **Peter Packer**
The travellers land on a lush planet and fall into the hands of a carrot monster who proposes to turn them all into plants.
Tybo **Stanley Adams**

Director: **Don Richardson**

The Junkyard of Space*

w **Barney Slater**
The Robinsons encounters a mechanical junk man who acquires the Robot's memory banks and nearly makes off with the Jupiter but is stopped by Will's emotional appeal.
Junk Man **Marcel Hillaire**

Director: **Ezra Stone**

THE LOST PLANET

While television was in its infancy during the 1950s, radio drama still held a powerful hold over the imagination of its younger audience who tuned in week after week for the exploits of their adventurous heroes. *The Lost Planet* was one such radio serial which made the transition to the new medium in 1954, as six fortnightly episodes in the BBC's Children's Television slot – immediately before the early evening shutdown which existed as a kind of truce between broadcasters and parents!

Adapted by Angus MacVicar (alias André Norton) from her own 1952 radio production, the story charted the voyage of an assorted group of travellers to the lost planet of Hesikos in a spaceship powered by an atomic motor firing charged droplets of water from a bank of six enormous jets. On board were intrepid scientist Lachlan McKinnon, his assistant Lars Bergman, engineer Spike Stranahan, pretty secretary Janet Campbell, cockney cook Madge Smith, and McKinnon's 16-year-old nephew Jeremy Grant.

Besides the perils of space travel, such as a shower of meteorites, the crew also had to deal with the rival ambition of the villainous Hermanoff, before reaching their goal. (See also *Return to the Lost Planet*.)

CAST

Dr Lachlan McKinnon **John Stuart**   *Lars Bergman* **Geoffrey Lumsden**
Spike Stranahan **John Springett**   *Janet Campbell* **Mary Law**
Madge Smith **Joan Allen**   *Jeremy Grant* **Peter Kerr**
Hermanoff **Van Boolen**

Writer: **Angus MacVicar**
Producer: **Kevin Sheldon**
Settings: **John Cooper**

Special effects: **Reginald Jeffreys**
Director (credited Ep. 6): **Bill Hitchcock**

A BBC Production
Six 30-minute episodes, black and white

Mystery at Inverard
Zero Hour
Vermin of the Skies

The Voice of Hesikos
The Creeping Mist
Through Corridors of Space

16 January–27 March 1954

LUNA

'Tedium tocks in the viron prompt Jo-oy to
programme habitel limbs at the saline'

Futuristic ITV children's comedy series of the 1980s with a
language all its own that emerged as a cross between Orwellian
doublespeak and Stanley Unwin's gobbledygook.

Created by ex-Monkees drummer and *Metal Mickey*-taker
Michael Dolenz, *Luna* was set 50 years in the future, when animals
have been replaced by furry little robots and speech has evolved
into 'techno talk'. This was a language designed for the computer
age when words have to be abbreviated, linked or even lost in
favour of numbers to allow more speedy electronic processing.

So, there are 'dimi males' and 'dimi females' (children) and
families are divided into 'habiviron groups', each person possessing
an 'egothenticity' card which they lose at their peril. Time is
measured in 'ticks', 'tocks' and 'tacks'; and for birthday, read
'batch day'. The episode titles alone reached sublime heights of
techno talk.

Main characters in the series were Gramps, teenagers Brat and
Luna (played in the first series by actress/pop star Patsy Kensit),
Andy the robot and bureaucrat beings 80H and 40D.

Writer Colin Bennett, who also starred in the series, described
Luna as a kind of morality play, conveying the idea that in future
human ethics would still have to be observed – that the silicon chip
would not be the answer to everything.

Luna lasted for two six-part series, in 1983 and 1984.

REGULAR CAST

Luna **Patsy Kensit** *(Series One)*, **Joanna Wyatt** *(Series Two)*
Brat **Aaron Brown**   *Gramps* **Frank Duncan**
Andy **Colin Bennett**   *80H* **Roy Macready**   *40D* **Natalie Forbes**
Mother **Linda Polan**   *Jazzmine* **Hugh Spight**
Mr Efficiecity **David Gretton**

Created by: Michael Dolenz
Producer: Michael Dolenz
Directors: Michael Dolenz, Chris
  Tookey *(Series Two)*
Executive producer: Lewis Rudd
Writers: Colin Bennett, Colin Prockter
Designer: Tony Ferris

Central Production
12 colour 30-minute episodes

Series One:
Habiviron Sweet Habiviron
The Clunkman Cometh
All the World's a Teletalk Linkup
Happy Batch Day, Dear Luna
Environmental Ambience Stable, Wish
You Were Here

When Did You Last See Your Pater
Batch Mix Donor?

22 January–26 February 1983

Series Two:
You Can't Judge A Videotalker By Its
Blurb
Go Forth and Quadruplicate
The Happiest Earth Revolves of Your
Span
It Isn't How You Vict or Flunk But How
You Co-Participate
A Bureaubureau in the Hand is Worth a
Pension
You're Only as Multi-Tocked as You
Perceive

11 February–17 March 1984

MAN DOG

Little-known BBC drama series from 1972, about a trio of present-day children who become involved in a conflict between opposing groups from the future.

A group of renegades from the 26th century – known simply as The Group – escape to the present where they meet schoolkids Kate, her brother Duncan and friend Sammy. Forcing the children to keep quiet about their presence, they transfer the mind of their leader, Levin, into Sammy's dog Radnor.

But The Group are being pursued by Gala, a secret police from the future, led by Halmar, and the children find themselves helping the runaways to obtain a vital piece of equipment they need before they can return to the future.

The six-part series was produced by Anna Home, latterly head of BBC Children's Television, who also shared directing chores with Paul Stone.

MAIN CAST

Kate Carol Hazell   *Sammy* Jane Anthony   *Duncan* Adrian Shergold
Levin Christopher Owen   *Halmar* Jonathan Hardy
Mrs Morris Mollie Sugden   *Mr Morris* John Rapley
Henry Roy Boyd   *Gala One* Derek Martin   *Gala Two* Ray Taylor

WITH
Valerie Georgeson, Sebastian Graham-Jones, David Millett,
David Pelton, Roger Marston, Arnold Peters, Tony Cerasoli,
Elizabeth Adare, Muriel Hunte, Christopher Jobling, Ian Sharp,
Edna Goodyear, Daryl Grove

Writer: Peter Dickinson
Producer: Anna Home
Directors: Anna Home (Eps 1–3), Paul
   Stone (Eps 4–6)

A BBC Production
Six colour 25-minute episodes

The Man Who Could Walk Through
Doors

Mister Makes His Mark
There Is No Duncan
The Consignment
On the Run
You Have 30 Seconds . . .

30 January–7 February 1972
(BBC1)

MAN FROM ATLANTIS

Soggy series that started well but ended up as just another TV also-swam.

Man From Atlantis, played by *Dallas* star Patrick Duffy in his first major TV series, had piercing green eyes, gills, webbed hands and feet and could outswim a dolphin. The last survivor of the lost city of Atlantis, he first appeared in a set of four TV movies.

Washed up on a California beach after a storm, this half-dead amphibian is rushed to a naval hospital where a beautiful woman doctor, Elizabeth Merrill, saves his life by popping him back in the water after X-rays have shown he has gills where his lungs should be.

Dr Merrill christens the submariner Mark Harris and recruits him to the Foundation for Oceanic Research. While helping Dr Merrill and her colleagues in the supersub *Cetacean*, he hopes to find out if he is indeed the sole survivor of his race. The quartet of TV movie-episodes combined some exploration of the character with stories about a missing submarine, alien invasion, space spores and a crazy scientist, but once the 'series proper' began, the quest for the Atlantean's origins ebbed away as the plots trod the same deep water as the tail-end of *Voyage to the Bottom of the Sea*, with silly villains, sea monsters, undersea races and time travel stories.

Victor Buono played the lead villain, Mr Schubert, with the same tongue-in-cheek style he'd used as King Tut in *Batman*. The other main regulars were Brent, Schubert's incompetent accomplice, and C. W. Crawford, the director of the research foundation.

Man From Atlantis surfaced on ITV in September 1977 – and sank in January 1978. (In the London area it was ditched two weeks 'early' and replaced by *Logan's Run*.) Each episode was accompanied by a warning to young viewers not to try to copy Mark Harris's underwater feats.

British TV critics poured cold water on the whole venture, either dismissing it as 'puerile rubbish' or taking the mickey out of Patrick Duffy's yellow underpants.

REGULAR CAST

Mark Harris **Patrick Duffy**   Dr Elizabeth Merrill **Belinda J. Montgomery**
C W Crawford **Alan Fudge**   Mr Schubert **Victor Buono**   Brent **Robert Lussier**
WITH

Dr Miller Simon (Eps 2–4) **Kenneth Tigar**
Cetacean crew (From Ep. 5):
Jomo **Richard Williams**   Chuey **J. Victor Lopez**
Jane **Jean Marie Hon**   Alan **Anson Downes**

Executive producer: **Herbert F. Solow**
Producer: **Herman Miller**
Music: **Fred Karlin**
Special effects: **Tom Fisher**

A Solow Production for NBC
17 colour episodes
3 × 100 mins, one × 75 mins, 13 × 60 mins)
24 September 1977–14 January 1978 (ITV)

Man From Atlantis (pilot)

(100 mins)
w **Mayo Simon**
After a storm, a young man is found washed up on a beach. Nearly dead after hours out of the life-sustaining ocean water, he is nursed back to health by Dr Elizabeth Merrill and eventually agrees to undertake a hazardous mission to locate a missing sub. Several miles beneath the sea he finds an underwater habitat where he confronts loopy scientist Mr Schubert for the first time.
Admiral Pierce **Art Lund**
Phil Roth **Larry Pressman**
Ltd Cdr Johnson **Allen Case**
Dr Doug Berkely **Joshua Bryant**
Ernie Smith **Dean Santoro**

Director: **Lee H. Katzin**

The Death Scouts

(100 mins)
w **Robert Lewin**
Now working for the Foundation for Oceanic Research, Dr Merrill and Mark try to discover clues to his origins. Called in by the coastguard to investigate the disappearance of three scuba divers, they encounter two water-breathing humanoids who Mark thinks could be his people, but who turn out to be scouts from an alien civilisation intent on colonising Earth.
Lioa/Dilly **Tiffany Bolling**
Xos/Chazz **Burr DeBenning**

Ginny Mendoza **Annette Cardona**
Grant Stockwood **Alan Mandell**
Herb Wayland **Vincent Deadrick**

Director: **Marc Daniels**

Killer Spores

(100 mins)
w **John D.F. Black**
A NASA space probe returns to Earth contaminated with ectoplasmic matter that is capable of invading humans, placing them in a catatonic stupor or forcing them to do things aaginst their will. The spores, visible only to Harris because of the unique structure of his eyes, communicate with him and demand that he help them return to space or see mankind destroyed.
Edwin Shirley **Ivan Bonar**
Sub captain **Fred Beir**
Col. Manzone **James B. Sikking**

Director: **Reza Badiyi**

The Disappearances

(75 mins)
w **Jerry Sohl, Luther Murdoch**
When Dr Merrill is kidnapped, Mark Harris and Miller Simon must locate a remote island off the coast of South America and penetrate the carefully guarded complex of mad scientist, Dr Mary Smith.

Dr Smith **Darleen Carr**
Jane Smith **Pamela Peters Solow**
Dick Redstone **Dennis Redfield**
Dr Medlow **Ivor Francis**
Sub captain **Fred Beir**

Director: **Charles Dubin**

Melt Down

w **Tom Greene**
Villainous Mr Schubert causes the world's
sea level to rise alarmingly by melting the
polar ice caps, and won't stop unless Mark
submits himself to his genetic study.
Trubshawe **James E. Brodhead**

Director: **Virgil Vogel**

Mudworm

w **Alan Caillou**
Mr Schubert loses control of his latest
invention – a robot-like machine designed
to gather a radioactive mineral from the
sea bed. Discovering that the 'Mudworm'
has taken on 'human' characteristics,
Mark tries to reason with it.

Director: **Virgil Vogel**

The Hawk of Mu

w **David Balkan, Luther Murdoch**
After Mark rescues an ancient stone hawk
from its watery crypt, evil Mr Schubert
steals it for his own malevolent purposes,
unaware that the statue has the power to
come to life and cause worldwide electrical
blackouts.
Juliette Schubert **Vicky Huxtable**
Vicki **Carole Mallory**
Smith **Sydney Lassick**

Director: **Harry Harris**

Giant

w **Michael Wagner**
Investigating a 'leak' in the ocean, Mark is
swept into the inner world where he meets
Thark, a nine-foot tall gold prospector
whose sluice mining is draining the world
of its water. Realising the threat, he and
Mark join forces to close off the sluice
gate. Complicating matters is a gold-
seeking conman called Muldoon.
Thark **Kareem Abdul-Jabbar**
Muldoon **Ted Neeley**

Director: **Richard Benedict**

Man O' War

w **Larry Alexander**
It's the Man from Atlantis v the world's
biggest jellyfish when Mr Schubert plots
to extort money by sabotaging an international swimming gala.
Dashki **Harvey Jason**
Announcer **Gary Owens**

Director: **Michael O'Herlihy**

Shoot-out At Land's End

w **Luther Murdoch**
A time warp in the ocean throws Mark
back to the old West, where he encounters
his twin – desperado Billy Jones – who is
identical in every way, except that he has
scars where his webbing on his hands has
been removed.
Billy **Patrick Duffy**
Clint Hollister **Pernell Roberts**
Bettina Washburn **Jamie Smith Jackson**
Artemus Washburn **Noble Willingham**
Virgil **Bill Zuckert**

Director: **Barry Crane**

Crystal Water, Sudden Death

w **Larry Alexander**
Investigating a disturbance in the Pacific,
Mark finds Mr Schubert trying to get his
hands on some precious crystals located
within a force field. Penetrating the field,
Mark encounters a mysterious white-
skinned, white-suited race called the
Deepspeople, who talk in a strange clicking
language.
Havergal **Rene Auberjonois**
Conrad **Rozelle Gayle**
Click One **Tina Lennert**
Click Two **Flip Reade**
Click Three **Whitney Rydbeck**

Director: **David Moessinger**

The Naked Montague

w Stephen Kandel
Mark travels back in time to 14th-century Italy where he gets involved with Romeo and Juliet 'rewriting' the story to give it a happy ending!
Romeo John Shea
Juliet Lisa Eilbacher
Mercutio Scott Porter

Director: Robert Douglas

The Siren

w Michael Wagner
Mark tangles with a mermaid who can 'capture' humans with her nerve-penetrating wail. She has been kidnapped by a modern-day pirate, Stringer, who is using her to lure mariners to his lair.
Hugh Trevanian Michael Strong
Amanda Laurette Spang
Stringer Neville Brand
Caine Timothy Scott
Jenny Lisa Blake Richards
Siren Carol Miyaoka

Director: Ed Abroms

C W Hyde

w Stephen Kandel
C.W. Crawford accidentally swallows a deep-sea enzyme which alters his appearance and mind, resulting in Jekyll and Hyde personalities.
Lew Calendar Val Avery
Belle Michele Carey
Sarah Pamela Peters Solow

Director: Dann Cahn

Deadly Carnival

w Larry Alexander
Mark infiltrates an oceanside carnival where a government agent was working before he was found mysteriously drowned, and foils a plot to steal a priceless Egyptian artefact from a museum.
Moxie Bill Barty
Summersday Anthony James
Charlene Baker Sharon Farrell

Director: Dennis Donnelly

Imp

w Shimon Wincelberg
Mark and his friends tangle with Moby, a water-breathing imp whose magic touch makes his victims revert to their childhood – with sometimes fatal results.
Moby Pat Morita

Director: Paul Krasny

Scavenger Hunt

w Peter Allan Fields
Investigating a loss of five poisonous gas canisters, Mark Harris re-encounters con-man Jake Muldoon and his tame, two-legged, two-headed giant sea monster, called Oscar.
Jack Muldoon Ted Neeley
Oscar Tony Urbano
Canja Ted Cassidy
Toba Yabo O'Brien
Trivi Eugenia Wright

Director: David Moessinger

THE MAN FROM U.N.C.L.E.

'It all began with the idea of a never-never world in which an international group where everybody is good works together to beat the hell out of whoever is bad. I picked UNCLE simply as a bunch of letters I could make a name out of.'

(Sam Rolfe, producer)

The Man From U.N.C.L.E. was a 1960s escapist fantasy about the far-fetched exploits of a pair of super-spies, Napoleon Solo and Illya Kuryakin, role models for every young boy with a ballpoint pen to talk to . . .

UNCLE stood for United Network Command for Law and Enforcement, and existed to protect the world from all forms of disruption, terror and exploitation. Its never-never world was entered via a hidden door in a New York tailor's shop (Del Floria's), unlocked by a steamy squeeze on the trouser press.

It was the cue for a series of all-action, tongue-in-cheek spy adventures involving futuristic hardware, glamorous girls, complex plots, exotic locations and cliff hanging climaxes. Science fiction? Well . . . there was always THRUSH.

THRUSH were the bad guys, forever plotting to rule the world by foul means rather than fair. Modelled on the SPECTRE organisation of the Bond movies, they were prompted by a diabolical computer into inflicting a variety of space-age perils such as a death ray (The Maze Affair), a human vaporiser (The Arabian Affair), invisible killer bees (The Birds and the Bees Affair), a radiation projector (The Moonglow Affair), even a volcano-activating device (The Cherry Blossom Affair).

Other weeks Napoleon and Illya found themselves up against lone madmen, from the crazy sea captain hijacking the world's brightest brains as a hedge against the holocaust, to an industrial tycoon hoping to further his ambitions with a willpower-sapping gas.

The coveted hardware included radios disguised as pens or cigarette packets, guns disguised as canes, nerve-paralysing bombs and the all-purpose UNCLE gun – a combination rifle, pistol and submachine gun which also fired sleep darts. A distinctive touch about the THRUSH gun was its infra-red sight which 'branded' its target with a thrush a second before the gun was fired.

As for the main characters, the head of UNCLE was Mr Alexander Waverly, an amiable Englishman played by Leo G. Carroll, but the series really made stars out of Robert Vaughn as Napoleon Solo (the sophisticated, extrovert bachelor who nearly always got the girl) and David McCallum as Illya Kuryakin (the enigmatic, introspective Slav who never let personal relationships get in the way of his work).

The BBC screened 90 *Man From U.N.C.L.E.* episodes (or 'Affairs') – all in black and white – in two long seasons spanning three years from 1965–8.

ITV picked up the rights in the 1970s and many regions showed selected episodes in colour. The series still enjoys reruns in different ITV areas even now.

(A spin-off series, *The Girl From U.N.C.L.E.*, ran for just one year on BBC1, alternating each week with her male colleagues. Stefanie Powers starred as feisty April Dancer, with Noel Harrison [son of Rex] as English agent Mark Slate.)

REGULAR CAST

Napoleon Solo Robert Vaughn   *Illya Kuryakin* David McCallum
Mr Waverly Leo G. Carroll   *Del Floria* Mario Siletti

Creator/producer (Season One): Sam Rolfe
Producer (Season Two): David Victor
Executive producer: Norman Felton
Writers: Various, including Alan Caillou, Peter Allan Field, Dean Hargrove
Directors: Various, including Richard Donner, Joseph Sargent, Alvin Ganzer

An Arena Production for MGM Television
UK: 90 (out of 105) colour 50-minute episodes (first shown in black and white)
24 June 1965–22 March 1968
(BBC1)

(Author's note: the BBC stuck devotedly to the UNCLE cause, screening 90 episodes in two bumper runs between 24 June 1965 and 19 May 1966, and 20 October 1966 to 22 March 1968. The second run also included the 29 episodes of *The Girl From U.N.C.L.E.*, which alternated with 'The Man' until November 1967.

The episode guide below lists *both* series in their original US order, with details of the episodes not transmitted in Britain.)

Season One
29 50-minute episodes, black and white

The Vulcan Affair
(not transmitted in UK. Cinema release with additional material as *To Trap a Spy*)
The Iowa Scuba Affair
The Quadripartite Affair
The Shark Affair
The Deadly Games Affair
The Green Opal Affair
The Giuoco Piano Affair (sequel to *The Quadripartite Affair*)
The Double Affair
(not transmitted in UK. Cinema release with additional material as *The Spy With My Face*)
The Project Strigas Affair
The Finny Foot Affair
The Neptune Affair
The Dove Affair
The King of Knaves Affair
The Terbuf Affair
The Deadly Decoy Affair
The Fiddlesticks Affair
The Yellow Scarf Affair
The Mad, *Mad* Tea Party Affair
The Secret Sceptre Affair
The Bow-Wow Affair

The Four Steps Affair
(not transmitted in UK. Compiled of additional material made for cinema features *To Trap a Spy* and *The Spy With My Face*)
The See Paris and Die Affair
The Brain Killer Affair
The Hong Kong Shilling Affair
The Never Never Affair
The Love Affair
The Gazebo in the Maze Affair
The Girls from Nazarone Affair
The Odd Man Affair

Season Two
30 colour 50-minute episodes

The Alexander the Greater Affair
(a 2-part story, not transmitted in UK. Released theatrically as *One Spy Too Many*)
The Ultimate Computer Affair
The Foxes and Hounds Affair
The Discotheque Affair
The Recollectors Affair
The Arabian Affair
The Tigers are Coming Affair
The Deadly Toys Affair
The Cherry Blossom Affair
The Virtue Affair

The Children's Day Affair
The Adriatic Express Affair
The Yukon Affair (sequel to *The
Gazebo in the Maze Affair)*
The Very Important Zombie Affair
The Dippy Blonde Affair
The Deadly Goddess Affair
The Birds and the Bees Affair
The Waverly Ring Affair
The Bridge of Lions Affair
(a 2-part story, not transmitted in UK.
Released theatrically as *One of Our Spies
is Missing)*
The Foreign Legion Affair
The Moonglow Affair
(pilot for *The Girl From U.N.C.L.E.)*
The Nowhere Affair
The King of Diamonds Affair
The Project Peephole Affair
The Round Table Affair
The Bat-Cave Affair
The Minus X Affair
The Indian Affairs Affair

Season Three
30 colour 50-minute episodes

The Her Master's Voice Affair
The Sort of Do-It-Yourself Dreadful
Affair
The Galatea Affair
(with Noel Harrison as Mark Slate)
The Super Colossal Affair
The Monks of St Thomas Affair
The Pop Art Affair
The Thor Affair
The Candidate's Wife Affair
The Come With Me to the Casbah
Affair
The Off-Broadway Affair
The Concrete Overcoat Affair
(a 2-part story, not transmitted in UK.
Released theatrically as *The Spy in the
Green Hat)*
The Abominable Snowman Affair
The My Friend the Gorilla Affair
The Jingle Bells Affair
The Take Me To Your Leader Affair
The Suburbia Affair
The Deadly Smorgasbord Affair
The Yo-Ho-Ho and a Bottle of Rum
Affair
The Napoleon's Tomb Affair
The It's All Greek to Me Affair
The Hula Doll Affair
The Pieces of Fate Affair

The Matterhorn Affair
The Hot Number Affair
The When in Roma Affair
The Apple-a-Day Affair
The Five Daughters Affair
(a 2-part story, not transmitted in UK.
Released theatrically as *The Karate
Killers)*
The Cap and Gown Affair

Season Four
16 colour 50-minute episodes

The Summit-5 Affair
The Test Tube Killer Affair
The J for Judas Affair
The Prince of Darkness Affair
(a 2-part story, not transmitted in UK.
Released theatrically as *The Helicopter
Spies)*
The Master's Touch Affair
The Thrush Roulette Affair
The Deadly Quest Affair
The Fiery Angel Affair
The Survival School Affair
The Gurnius Affair
The Man from THRUSH Affair
The Maze Affair
The Deep Six Affair
The Seven Wonders of the World Affair
(a 2-part story, not transmitted in UK.
Released theatrically as *How To Steal The
World)*

NB: The Men from UNCLE also came
out of retirement for a 1983 TV movie,
'The Fifteen Years Later Affair' shown
over here by most of the ITV network on
21 April 1984 as *Return of the Man from
U.N.C.L.E.* This also starred Patrick
Macnee as the organisation's 'new'
director.

(An unbroadcast UNCLE pilot called
Solo also exists. This is identical to The
Vulcan Affair but features Will Kuluva as
Mr Allison instead of Leo G. Carroll as
Mr Waverly.)

The Girl from U.N.C.L.E.

*29 colour 50-minute episodes
(shown in UK in black and white)*

The Dog-Gone Affair
The Prisoner of Zalimar Affair

The Mother Muffin Affair *(with Robert Vaughn as Napoleon Solo)*
The Mata Hari Affair
The Montori Device Affair
The Horns-of-the-Dilemma Affair
The Danish Blue Affair
The Garden of Evil Affair
The Atlantis Affair
The Paradise Lost Affair
The Lethal Eagle Affair
The Romany Lie Affair
The Little John Doe Affair
The Jewels of Topango Affair
The Faustus Affair

The UFO Affair
The Moulin Ruse Affair
The Catacomb and Dogma Affair
The Drublegratz Affair
The Fountain of Youth Affair
The Carpathian Caper Affair
The Furnace Flats Affair
The Low Blue C Affair
The Petit Prix Affair
The Phi Beta Killer Affair
The Double-O-Nothing Affair
The UNCLE Samurai Affair
The High and Deadly Affair
The Kooky Spook Affair

MANIMAL

Short-lived American adventure series about a professor of criminology with the inherited powers to transform himself at will into any animal he chooses.

It could have been the premise for an interesting, original fantasy – instead it was little more than *Magnum* in an animal suit, with the hero Jonathan Chase using his powers to solve crimes from an arms heist to smuggling, murder and espionage. His secret is shared by police detective Brooke McKenzie.

The transformation scenes were well done, though their credibility was spoilt by the fact that when Chase changed back he was always fully clothed on the spot. But the series, a product of the Glen A. Larson conveyor belt, stuck closely to the tried and trusted action formula.

REGULAR CAST

Jonathan Chase Simon MacCorkindale *Brooke McKenzie* Melody Anderson
Ty Michael D. Roberts *Lt Rivera* Reni Santoni

Created by: Glen A. Larson
Producer: Glen A. Larson
Writers: Various, including Glen A. Larson, Michael Berk
Directors: Various, including Russ Mayberry, Dan Haller

A Glen A. Larson Production
One colour 70-minute pilot episode
Seven colour 50-minute episodes

Manimal (pilot)
Illusion
Night of the Scorpion
Female of the Species
High Stakes
Scrimshaw
Breath of the Dragon
Night of the Beast

4 June–23 July 1984
(BBC1)

THE MARTIAN CHRONICLES

Ray Bradbury's subtle, elegant fantasy of man's earliest experiences on an alien planet was given the big treatment in this three-part American adaptation.

Rock Hudson starred as the pivotal character of Col. John Wilder, leader of a successful expedition to Mars who finds his sympathies torn, but who is helpless to prevent the planet bring raped by American culture.

Hudson wore his usual stolid expression of bemusement throughout – a feeling largely shared by audience and critics alike.

MAIN CAST

Col. John Wilder **Rock Hudson**   Ruth Wilder **Gayle Hunnicutt**
Sam Parkhill **Darren McGavin**   Father Stone **Roddy McDowall**
Elma Parkhill **Joyce Van Patten**

Teleplay: **Richard Matheson**, based on the book by **Ray Bradbury** (first published as **The Silver Locusts**)
Producers: **Andrew Donally, Milton Subotsky**

Director: **Michael Anderson**

A Charles Fried Production
Three colour 95-minute episodes
9–23 August 1980
(BBC1)

The Expeditions

January 1999: The Zeus Project makes its first manned flight to Mars. Its ultimate goal: colonisation. On Mars, Ylla dreams of the coming astronauts and her husband, Mr K, plots their doom . . . The second expedition lands and finds Mars a deceptively familiar but deadly home from home. Finally, Col. Wilder's Zeus III expedition arrives to find the Martians dead, wiped out by chicken-pox. For one crew member, Spender, the thought of Earth culture tearing the planet apart is too much to bear . . .
Jeff Spender **Bernie Casey**
Captain Black **Nicholas Hammond**
General Halstead **Robert Beatty**
Mr K **James Faulkner**
Ylla **Maggie Wright**
Briggs **John Cassady**
Conover **Richard Heffer**
York **Richard Oldfield**

The Settlers

February 2004. The colonisation of Mars proceeds rapidly, the rockets arriving like 'silver locusts'. Settlers pour in, each in search of a dream – Fr Peregrine wants to meet Christ; the Lustigs want to find their missing son; the Parkhills want to make their fortune; and Wilder himself wants to meet a Martian . . .
Fr Peregrine **Fritz Weaver**
Anna Lustig **Maria Schell**
David Lustig **Michael Anderson Jr**
Jesus Christ **Jon Finch**
Lafe Lustig **Wolfgang Reichmann**

The Martians

November 2006. Earth is an amber cinder, all life annihilated by total nuclear war. A handful of settlers left on Mars are the sole survivors of the human race, facing a desolate future, cut off and isolated even from each other. Wilder finally meets his Martian 'counterpart'.
Alice Hathaway **Nyree Dawn Porter**
Hathaway **Barry Morse**
Ben Driscoll **Christopher Connelly**
Genevieve **Bernadette Peters**
Martian Elder **Terence Longdon**

THE MASTER

From his granite fortress on the isle of Rockall, a 150-year-old, Shakespeare-quoting, telepathic madman plots to take over the world.

But this was *not* your everyday story of world domination . . . this was *The Master*, one of television's creepiest villains, and the man who dragged ITV children's drama out of the shadow of the BBC. The six-part serial, shown in 1966, made history for its makers, Southern Television. It was the first big drama the company had produced for the ITV network and cost around £6000 an episode – more pro rata than other ITV companies were spending on their children's drama. And it reached no. 2 in the kids' ratings – relegating *Doctor Who* to third, but denied the top spot by *Pinky and Perky*!

The Master was adapted by Rosemary Hill, later head of single plays at the BBC, from the final novel of T. H. White, author of *The Sword in the Stone*. It began with two children, Nicky and Judy, and their dog, Jokey, becoming marooned on the isle of Rockall while out sailing off the west coast of Scotland. There they encounter a community under the sway of a despotic 150-year-old ruler who calls himself *The Master*. This sinister villain, aided by an inscrutable Chinaman, is plotting to hold the world to ransom by targeting high-powered destructive lasers on major cities.

A highly developed intellect, The Master controls people's minds by telepathy. Sensing that Nicky is also telepathic, he decides to groom the boy as his successor. But Nicky gets wise to his plotting and he and Judy, plus a handy squadron leader called Frinton determine to thwart his diabolical schemes. This doesn't prove easy as The Master has a nasty habit of telepathically compelling his enemies to stand in the path of his lasers where they are instantaneously vaporised – a particularly vivid end met by several of the cast including eccentric scientist Dr McTurk (a terrific crazy-eyed role for John Laurie).

Underlying the story is the issue of whether it's right to kill for good, as the children decide that the only way to stop The Master is to kill him. In the final episode, with the fiend's world ultimatum delivered, Nicky lures him up to the top of the island intending to shoot him. In the event, though, the question is dodged as The Master slips and breaks a leg – a seemingly innocuous injury, but a fatal one for his brittle body. As the Marines arrive on the island, the kids and Frinton escape by helicopter seconds before The Master's fortress blows up.

Rockall being in reality an inhospitable lump of rock in the Atlantic, the location sequences were shot around Swanage and Portland. Veteran actor Olaf Pooley endured an hour-long make-up session to emerge as the old man in the rubber mask, while 16-year-old Adrienne Posta was 'strapped up' for her part as 12-year-old Judy. TV astronomer Patrick Moore made a guest appearance as himself.

CAST

The Master Olaf Pooley   *Chinaman* Terence Soall
Nicky Paul Guess   *Judy* Adrienne Posta   *Frinton* George Baker
McTurk John Laurie   *Pinkie* Thomas Baptiste
Jim John Woodnutt   *Father* Richard Vernon   *Bert* Anthony Eady

WITH:

Skipper: Roy Patrick   *Pierrepoint* John Brown   *Jo* Morris Perry
Sub-editor Leonard Woodrow   *Reporter* Frank Jarvis
TV man Lewis Jones   *Himself* Patrick Moore   *Fish fryer* Margaret Ashcroft
Customer Jennifer Stuart   *Newscaster* John McGavin
Newsagent Joe Gibbons   *Customer* Yvonne Walsh
TV reporter Alex Macintosh   *Woman* Zena Blake
Teacher Rowena Torrance   *Office worker* Ian Lindsay
Jokey trained by John Holmes

Adapted by: Rosemary Hill, *from the*
novel by T. H. White
Producer: John Braybon
Directors: John Braybon, John Frankau
Designer: John Dilly
Title sequence directed by: Fred Tucker

The Yellow Hands
Totty McTurk
Behind the Antlers
The Squadron Leader
World of Disbelief
Death by Misadventure

A Southern Independent Television
Network Production
Six 30-minute episodes, black and white

11 January–15 February 1966

MAX HEADROOM

*M*ax Headroom began as a stylish satire on television culture and became a phenomenon.

The world's first computer-generated TV presenter turned into one of the 1980s most charismatic media celebrities, moving from video linkman to chat-show host, Coca Cola salesman and star of an American adventure series from the makers of *Dallas*. In the end, over-exploitation may have killed the video star, but the Max Headroom effect has been felt worldwide.

Max's genesis started in 1982, with a commitment by Chrysalis Records executive Peter Wagg and C4's commissioning editor Andy Park to find a new way of linking pop videos. The name and characterisation came from advertising copywriter George Stone, and visualisation from directors Rocky Morton and Annabel Jankel. The result was a £750,000 television film, *Max Headroom*, written by Steve Roberts, first screened on Channel 4 in April 1985.

Set '20 minutes into the future', it depicts a decaying urban environment where television is the only growth industry. A fierce ratings battle is raging and Network 23 is winning, thanks to its use of 'blipverts' – a form of subliminal selling where 30 seconds of commercials are condensed into a three-second burst, giving viewers no time to change channels. But the blipverts, created by the station's teenage computer whiz-kid Bryce Lynch, have a lethal side-effect – they cause some viewers literally to explode. Anxious to preserve profits and ratings, Network 23 president Grossman is determined to keep the lid on the story. But when the station's own star investigative reporter Edison Carter uncovers disturbing evidence, Grossman and Bryce unleash two disreputable body-snatchers to bring him in. After a remarkable pursuit in which Carter's 'guide' Theora Jones and Bryce vie for control of the building's computer-operated systems, Carter comes a nasty cropper on a car park barrier. Bryce proposes to keep Carter's disappearance quiet by translating his memory and physical appearance into data, and computer generate him onto a TV screen. Thus Max Headroom is born, taking his name from the last words Carter saw on the car park sign before he blacked out.

Ultimately, Carter gets his man and Max winds up in the hands of a hard-up pirate TV channel called Big-Time Television where his scratch-style stammer and razor wit make him a megastar . . .

Once the Max Headroom character was established, the media machine took over. The film was followed by the video and chatshow series, *The Max Headroom Show*, lucrative ad campaigns, records, books, computer games and even cosmetics. In America, Lorimar produced a multi-million dollar adventure series for the ABC network, beginning with a reworking of the original film story. Some 14 episodes were made, spanning two seasons from March 1987, but failed to secure high enough ratings to justify any more.

Canadian actor Matt Frewer reprised the role which had called for a four-and-a-half hour make-up job to transform him into his alter ego (and an equally uncomfortable one-and-a-half hours to take it all off again), while Amanda Pays was also back as Theora Jones. Among new faces in the series were Chris Young as Bruce Lynch – now more of a good guy – and Jeffrey Tambor as Carter's producer, Murray.

Steve Roberts remained with the show – as executive story editor, a regular writer, and co-producer of the second season.

The classic 'coals to Newcastle' deal finally took place when the *Max Headroom* series was screened back where it all began, on Channel 4, in 1989.

MAX HEADROOM – THE MOVIE

CAST

Edison Carter/Max Headroom **Matt Frewer**   *Grossman* **Nickolas Grace**
Dominique **Hilary Tindall**   *Blank Reg* **Morgan Shepherd**
Theora Jones **Amanda Pays**   *Bryce Lynch* **Paul Spurrier**
Breugal **Hilton McRae**   *Mahler* **George Rossi**   *Murray* **Roger Sloman**
Gorrister **Anthony Dutton**   *Ben Cheviot* **Constantine Gregory**
Edwards **Lloyd McGuire**   *Ms Formby* **Elizabeth Richardson**
Ashwell **Gary Hope**   *Body bank receptionist* **Joane Hall**
ENG reporter **Howard Samuels**   *Helipad reporter* **Roger Tebb**
Eye witness **Val McLane**   *Exploding man* **Michael Cule**

Screenplay: **Steve Roberts**, *from an original idea by* **George Stone, Rocky Morton, Annabel Jankel**
Directors: **Rocky Morton** *and* **Annabel Jankel**
Producer: **Peter Wagg**
Executive producer: **Terry Ellis**
Designer: **Maurice Gain**
Director of photography: **Phil Meheux**

Music: **Midge Ure** *and* **Chris Cross**
Max dialogue: **Paul Owen** *and* **David Hansen**
Special make-up: **Coast to Coast**

Chrysalis Production for Channel Four
70 minutes, colour
4 April 1985
(Channel 4)

MAX HEADROOM – THE SERIES

REGULAR CAST

Edison Carter/Max Headroom **Matt Frewer**   *Theora Jones* **Amanda Pays**
Ben Cheviot **George Coe**   *Bryce Lynch* **Chris Young**
Murray **Jeffrey Tambor**   *Ms Formby* **Virginia Kiser** *(Season One only)*
Ashwell **Hank Garrett** *(except eps 4, 10, 12)*
Edwards **Lee Wilkof** *(except eps 4, 8, 10, 12)*
Blank Reg **William Morgan Sheppard** *(except eps 1–2, 5, 8–9, 13)*
Dominique **Concetta Tomei** *(Eps 3–4, 6–7, 10, 12 and 14 only)*

Executive producers: **Philip De Guere** *(Ep. 1)*, **Peter Wagg** *(Eps 2–14)*
Producers: **Peter Wagg, Brian Frankish, Steve Roberts** *(Season Two only)*
Executive story editors: **Steve Roberts** *(Season One)*, **Michael Cassutt** *(Season Two)*
Music: **Cory Lerios** *(Season One)* **Michael Hoenig** *(Season Two, main theme)*
Designer: **Richard B. Lewis**

Director of photography: **Paul Goldsmith, Robert Stevens** *(Eps 1, 3 only)*

A Chrysalis/Lakeside Production in association with Lorimar Telepictures
14 colour 60-minute episodes
US premiere: 31 March 1987
UK first run: 2 March–14 June 1989
(Channel 4)

Season One (US)

Blipverts

w Joe Gannon, Steve Roberts *and*
   Philip DeGuere, *based on the British*
   screenplay by Steve Roberts
Initially a reworking of the British film,
with Edison Carter investigating blipverts,
the episode deviates after Carter hits the
car-park barrier. It is Grossberg (Grossman in the original) who uses newly
created Max Headroom as a Network 23
gimmick, before his chicanery is exposed
by Carter at a press conference Grossberg
calls to announce Edison's 'tragic death'.
Breughel Jere Burns
Mahler Rick Ducommon
Grossberg Charles Rocket
Martinez Ricardo Gutierrez *(plus eps*
   2–5, 8)
Gorrister Ken Swofford
Florence Billie Bird

Director: Farhad Mann

Rakers

w Steve Roberts, James Crocker
Theora is told that her young brother
Shawn is involved in 'raking', a high-speed
gladiatorial contest between two youths
on motorised skateboards who wear
spiked gloves and try to score 'rakes', or
hits, on their opponent. Zik-Zak, Network 23's main sponsor, is keen to see
raking televised – if the sport can be
legalised. Can Carter expose the vicious
truth – and save Shawn?
Shawn Peter Cohl
Jack Friday Wortham Krimmer
Rik J.W. Smith
Peller Howard Sherman
Promoter Joseph Ruskin
Ped Zing Arsenio 'Sonny' Trinidad

Director: Thomas J. Wright

Body Banks

w Steve Roberts
Bodysnatchers Breughel and Mahler kid-
nap a Fringer girl, Rayna, for a corrupt
Body Bank, and her friend Mel threatens

Theora's life unless Edison helps him find
her. While Edison seeks the help of Blank
Reg at Big Time TV, a man called
Plantaganet blackmails Ms Formby into
giving him Bryce and Max Headroom.
Breughel Jere Burns
Mahler Rick Ducommon
Rik J.W. Smith
Mel Scott Kraft
Plantaganet John Winston

Director: Francis De Lia

Security Systems

w Michael Cassutt
Edison probes a take-over of Security
Systems Inc – part of a bid to set up a
worldwide security monopoly. But he
finds himself branded a credit fraudster by
a computer, A-7, and lands up a prisoner
in a freezer.
Valerie Towne Carol Mayo Jenkins
Rik J.W. Smith
Voice of A-7 Sally Stevens

Director: Tommy Lee Wallace

War

w Michael Cassutt *and* Steve Roberts,
   from a story by Martin Pasko *and*
   Rebecca Parr
Network 23 is losing ratings when it is
offered exclusive rights to film a guerrilla
war as it happens in their own city.
Cheviot declines, but when a rival net-
work starts to notch up impressive figures,
Edison investigates the sinister tie-up
between TV and terrorists.
Janie Crane Lisa Niemi
Braddock Gary Swenson
Ped Zing Arsenio 'Sonny' Trinidad
Croyd Hauser Robert O'Reilly
Lucian J. Michael Flynn
Hewett Richard Lineback

Director: Thomas J. Wright

The Blanks

w Steve Roberts
Network 23's politician, Peller, has the
Blanks – those without computer records

– rounded up by the Metrocops. Then computers start to go down and a Blank, Bruno, threatens to disable the city by sunset unless the captured Blanks are released.

Janie Crane Lisa Niemi
Peller Howard Sherman
Bruno Peter Crook

Director: Tommy Lee Wallace

Season Two (US)

Academy

w David Brown
Blank Reg is arrested for 'zipping' – hijacking network frequencies – and goes on a TV trial series called *You, the Jury*. But Theora and Edison trace the real culprits to Bryce's old school, the Academy of Computer Sciences.

Sidney Harding James Greene
Lauren Sharon Barr
Shelley Keeler Maureen Teefy

Director: Victor Lobl

Deities

w Michael Cassutt
Edison is reluctant to investigate the Church of Entropic Science which is offering 'immortality' to people by having their personality stored on computer to await future resurrection, as he was once very close to its leader, Vanna Smith.

Vanna Smith Dayle Haddon

Director: Thomas J. Wright

Grossberg's Return

w Steve Roberts
Arch-villain Grossberg resurfaces at Network 66, a rival station clocking up huge ratings with its new VuDoze system that allows people to sleep and view simultaneously. He is determined to take over Network 66 and bring down Network 23.

Grossberg Charles Rocket
Harriet Garth Caroline Kava
Lauren Sharon Barr
Thatcher Stephen Elliott

Director: Janet Greek

Dream Thieves

w Steve Roberts, *from a story by* Charles Grant Craig
The death of an old reporting rival, Paddy Ashton, and Network 66's new concept Dream-Vu, which offers amazing, dream-like shows, leads Carter to the Mind's Eye – a place where derelict fringers are paid for their sleep in special cubicles.

Paddy Ashton Mark Lindsay Chapman
Breughel Jere Burns
Greig Ron Fassler
Bella Jenette Goldstein
Finn Vernon Weddle

Director: Todd Holland

Whacketts

w Arthur Sellers, *from a story by* Dennis Rolfe
Big Time TV has a hit on its hands with *Whacketts* – an old-style game show which is so addictive that people are stealing sets to watch it, causing a tower block literally to collapse under the weight of stolen sets. Naturally, the Networks want a piece of the action . . .

Grossberg Charles Rocket
Lauren Sharon Barr
Ziskin Bert Kramer
Haskel Bill Maher
Biller Richard Frank

Director: Victor Lobl

Baby Grobags

w Chris Ruppenthal
Carter investigates the Ovu-Vat Grobag centre which allows working women to have their babies grown in bags in front of TV monitors. He finds a distressed couple claiming their baby has been stolen. Meanwhile, Network 66 airs its new show *Prodigies* – a debate between brilliant babies.

Grossberg Charles Rocket
Breughel Jere Burns
Lauren Sharon Barr
Helen Amanda Hillwood
Cornelia Firth Millicent Martin

Director: Janet Greek

Neurostrim

w Arthur Sellars

Zik-Zak's sales are up by 700 per cent – thanks to a Neurostim bracelet which feeds adverts directly into the consumer's mind by stimulating the brain. When Edison's investigations threaten to expose them, Zik-Zak prepare a special bracelet to make him a complete addict of their products.

Lauren Sharon Barr
Edison's dream girl Joan Severance

Director: Maurice Phillips

Lessons

w Adrian Hein, Steve Roberts, *from a story by* Colman Dekay *and* Howard Brookner

Carter and Theora witness a raid by Metrocops and the Network 23 censor on a secret school for Fringer children. Edison's overt sympathies bring him into direct conflict with the Network censor.

Lauren Sharon Barr
Frances Laura Carrington
Traker Mike Preston
Dragul John Durbin
Blank Bruno Peter Crook

Director: Victor Lobl

MEN INTO SPACE

Semi-educational American series about the adventures of a space pioneer, Col. Edward McCauley, and his crew in and around their small moon colony.

The series, made in 1959, prided itself on its authenticity and an absence of monsters or little green men. Each script was said to have been sumitted to the American Defence Department and anything which couldn't possibly happen was then ruled out.

The BBC screened a season of 13 stories in its Saturday 5.00 pm teatime slot (usually home to western series such as *Range Rider*) and followed it with *Billy Bunter*!

REGULAR CAST
Col. Edward MacCauley William Lundigan

A United Artists Production for CBS
US: 28 25-minute episodes, black and white

UK premiere: 9 July–1 October 1960 (BBC)

METAL MICKEY

Advance publicity called it a 'children's science fiction comedy series', but really, *Metal Mickey* was never more than a sitcom with a robot as its star.

Mickey (always billed as 'playing himself') was a 5 ft tall robot with magical powers and a metallic catchphrase 'boogie, boogie'. He was built by scientific whiz-kid Ken Wilberforce to help around the house, but naturally brought more chaos than order. Various episodes had him getting kidnapped, getting hiccups, becoming a pop star, communicating with aliens, travelling into the future, teleporting people and shrinking. Everyday stuff.

The ITV series, which first appeared in 1980, also attracted attention for its other 'Mickey' – former Monkee Mickey Dolenz who produced and directed.

REGULAR CAST

Father Michael Stainton   *Mother* Georgina Melville
Granny Irene Handl   *Ken* Ashley Knight
Haley Lucinda Bateson   *Janey* Lola Young
Steve Gary Shail . . .and Metal Mickey *as himself*

Writer: Colin Bostock-Smith
Producer: Michael Dolenz
Directors: Michael Dolenz, David Crossman, Nic Phillips
Designers: Mike Oxley, Rae George, David Catley, James Dillon, Phil Coulter
Music: Phil Coulter

A London Weekend Television Production
39 colour 30-minute episodes
Season One:
6 September–25 October 1980
Season Two:
4 April–9 May 1981
Season Three:
5 September–26 December 1981
(including Christmas episodes)
Season Four:
18 September 1982–15 January 1983

Season One

Metal Mickey Lives
School Master Mickey
Mickey Makes Money
Taking the Mickey
Hiccy Mickey
Top Secret Mickey
Mickey in Love
Music Man Mickey

Season Two

Caveman Mickey
Mickey the Demon Barber
Hard Man Mickey
Many a Mickey
Mickey Plays Cupid

Season Three

It Came From Outer Mickey

A Girlfriend for Mickey
Goodbye Mickey (postponed from Season Two)
Mickey and the Future
Football Crazy Mickey
Medical Mickey
Fair Godmother Mickey
Marshal Mickey

Merry Christmas Mickey
Pantomickey

Season Four

Maturity Mickey
A Night Out With Mickey
Go Away Mickey
Video Mickey
His Worship the Mickey
Fancy Mickey
Mickey Meets Mumsie
Mickey Under Siege

The Incredible Shrinking Mickey   Detective Mickey
Mickey Pops the Question   Mickey to the Rescue
Somebody Stop Mickey   The Confessions of Mickey
Mickey Saves the World   Mickey and the Magic Wishbone

THE MONSTERS

Four-part tale that took a honeymooning zoologist in search of a fabled 'Loch Ness' style monster and ended with him uncovering an even greater mystery surrounding the survival of mankind.

Newlywed John Brent has his curiosity aroused while staying in a small north England hotel by a lake in which, over the centuries, local people have claimed to have seen strange creatures. When the body of a government agent, Charles Pulford, is found floating in the water, Brent wonders if there might be a connection. The trail leads to the mysterious Prof. Cato and his enemy mini-subs, but Brent eventually discovers that the monsters really do exist, and that the fate of man is affected by their survival.

The story, co-written by playwright Evelyn Frazer (*The Critical Point, Virus X*) and Vincent Tilsley, was inspired by a *Panorama* report about the Loch Ness Monster and a subsequent conversation in a BBC canteen. The director, Mervyn Pinfield, became better known for his work on the early seasons of *Doctor Who*.

MAIN CAST

John Brent William Greene   *Felicity Brent* Elizabeth Weaver
Hopkins Mark Dignam   *Howard Milroy* Clifford Cox
Van Halloran Alan Gifford   *Prof. Cato* Robert Harris
Meissonier Gordon Whiting   *Esmee Pulford* Helen Lindsay
Sgt Oakroyd Norman Mitchell   *Wilf Marner* Howard Douglas
Richard Philip Madoc   *Smetanov* George Pravda
Edward Kenneth Mackintosh   *Col. Swinton* Clive Morton
PC Mills Stuart Hoyle   *Holt* Arthur Skinner

WITH

Charles Pulford Geoffrey Colville   *Jess Milroy* Joyce Wright
Parsons John Barrett   *Harris* Edward Harvey
Adamson John DeVaut

AND

Cameron Miller, Ronald Mayer, Michael Earl, Martin Gordon, Jonathan Field, Clifford Earl, Malcolm Ward, Rodney Cardiff, John McLaren, Alexis Chesnakov

Writers: Evelyn Frazer, Vincent Tilsley
Producer: George R. Foa
Director: Mervyn Pinfield
Designer: Stewart Marshall
Special effects: Bernard Wilkie *and* Stewart Marshall
Music: Humphrey Searle, *played by members of the* Sinfonia of London Orchestra

A BBC Television Production
Four episodes (Eps 1–3 45 minutes, Ep. 4 50 minutes)
Black and white
8–29 November 1962

MOONBASE 3

The early 1970s saw the culmination of the US manned moon missions, with Skylab expected to be the next giant leap for mankind. Against such a background of *real* exploration, *Moonbase 3* took the space race a step further in a six-part series based on scientific probability rather than pure fancy.

The year is 2003. Men and women are at last living on the moon in small, enclosed communities set up by the various world power blocs. But it's a tenuous foothold in a hostile environment, operating on shoestring budgets and an overdraft of Earthly goodwill. No one has it easy, with psychological problems ranking alongside technical ones.

Central figures in a large cast of regular or semi-regular characters were scientific troubleshooter and new European Moonbase director David Caulder, his deputy Michel Le Brun, technical director Tom Hill and team psychiatrist Dr Helen Smith.

The series set out to provide intelligent, realistic drama rather than science fantasy. As such, it was a change in pace for its creators, producer Barry Letts and script editor Terrance Dicks, who were currently steering the resurgent *Doctor Who* through some of his most testing adventures. *Moonbase 3* also attracted attention for its scientific advisor – the BBC's own high-profile resident science buff James Burke, doyen of the corporation's Apollo coverage and star of his own *Burke Special* series of applied science programmes.

MAIN CAST

David Caulder **Donald Houston**   *Tom Hill* **Barry Lowe**
Michel Lebrun **Ralph Bates**   *Dr Helen Smith* **Fiona Gaunt**

PLUS

Rao **Madhav Sharma** *(Eps 1, 4–5)*   *Director General* **Peter Bathurst** *(Eps 1, 3, 5)*
Ingrid **Christine Bradwell** *(Eps 1–2, 4–5)*
Stephen Partness **Tom Kempinski** *(Eps 1–2, 4)*
Peter Conway **John Hallam** *(Eps 1–2, 4)*
Bruno Bertoli **Garrick Hagon** *(Eps 2, 4, 6)*
Per Bengtson **Jurgen Anderson** *(Eps 1–2)*

Producer: **Barry Letts**
Script editor: **Terrance Dicks**
Designer: **Roger Liminton**
Music: **Dudley Simpson**
Scientific advisor: **James Burke**

A BBC Production
Six colour 50-minute episodes
9 September–14 October 1973

Departure and Arrival

w **Terrance Dicks** *and* **Barry Letts**

'We're only hanging on to the moon by an eyebrow. Do you really think we'll survive a scandal like that?' In a tiny, enclosed society a spark of temperament can mean disaster. New Moonbase director David

Caulder's first task is to investigate the death of his predecessor.
Jenny Patsy Tench
Tony Ransome Michael Lees
Harry Sanders Michael Wisher
Madame Carnac Elma Soiran
Sandy Mary Ann Severne
Walters Jonathan Sweet
Heinz Laubenthal Peter Miles
Bill Jackson Robert La Bassiere

Director: Ken Hannam

Behemoth

w John Brason
Fear and panic spread through Moonbase after a mysterious attack. Is there something alive in Mare Frigoris – the frozen sea?
Guido Mirandelli Denis De Marne
Juan Benavente John Moreno
Dr Robertson Derek Anders
Cheng Anthony Chinn
Heinz Laubenthal Peter Miles
Bill Jackson Robert La Bassiere
Technician Cy Town
Foreman Ken Haward

Director: Ken Hannam

Achilles Heel

w John Lucarotti
A demented astronaut causes trouble on the Moonbase.
Adam Blaney Edward Brayshaw
Bill Knight Malcolm Reynolds
Jane Joanna Ross
Lisa Anne Rosenfeld
Kate Weyman Anne Ridler
Dodi Knight Nancie Watt
Astronaut Oliver Ford-Davies

Director: Christopher Barry

Outsiders

w John Brason
Helen Smith becomes involved in the problems facing two Moonbase men, Conway and Partness, one of whom is heading for disaster.
Macadam Edmund Pegge
Franz Hauser Victor Beaumont
Jenny Patsy Trench
Walters Jonathan Sweet
Juan Benavente John Moreno
Technician Cy Town

Director: Ken Hannam

Castor and Pollux

w John Lucarotti
A freak accident leaves a man stranded in a space capsule with little hope of rescue.
Mather Perry Soblosky
Gen. Trenkin George Pravda
Col. Gararov Milos Kirek
Sandy Mary Ann Severne

Director: Christopher Barry

Views of a Dead Planet

w Arden Winch
'They will explode a hydrogen bomb above the weakest point in the Earth's armour' . . . Will the Arctic Sun Project be the disaster that Sir Benjamin Dyce predicts? When contact with Earth is lost, the Moonbase people fear the worst.
Disc jockey Ed Stewart
Paula Renner Magda Miller
Sir Benjamin Dyce Michael Gough
José Joe Santo
Quizmaster Leonard Gregory
Hopkirk Aubrey Danvers-Walker
Lisa Anne Rosenfeld

Director: Christopher Barry

MORK & MINDY

Mork from Ork first landed on Earth in an episode of *Happy Days* called 'My Favourite Orkan'. He made such an impact that he was given his own series and by the end of 1978 America's kids were twisting their ears, chirruping 'Nanu, nanu', and offering each other split-fingered handshakes. The *Mork & Mindy* cult had taken hold.

There hadn't been a TV alien like Mork since Uncle Martin in *My Favourite Martian* (and, really, Mork was nothing like him) and there hasn't been a TV alien like him since until *ALF* (and Mork was nothing like him, either). Mork may be part of the same lineage but he was a one-off, the lunatic creation of stand-up comedian Robin Williams.

As Mork, Williams took the classic 'stranger in a strange land' theme and literally stood it on its head. Totally unaccustomed to the ways of Earth, alien Mork sits on his head, drinks with his fingers, talks to eggs, wears suits backwards, grows down not up and wears a watch on his ankle. Williams dominated the show. His lightning improvisation, funny voices, frenetic rubber-faced clowning and relentless stream of ad-libbed one-liners gave the one-gag variants their velocity and momentum. His co-star, Pam Dawber (Mindy) admitted: 'He is the show. I'm lucky I got my name in the title'.

A misfit in his own world because of his sense of humour, Mork was sent to observe Earth's primitive society whose customs were beyond Orkan understanding. Landing in his giant eggshell near Boulder, Colorado, he was befriended by Mindy McConnell, a clerk at her father's music store and came to live with her family where he tried to adjust to Earth's ways while everyone else tried to get used to his.

Mork and Mindy's relationship started out platonic. But three seasons and 93 shows is a long time and eventually, after Mindy had graduated as a journalism student and become a TV reporter, they fell in love and married, honeymooning on Ork. Then Mork discovered *he* was pregnant, and laid an egg from which hatched their middle-aged son Mearth – who will grow younger each year.

The series introduced various regular characters over the three seasons, including Exidor, a crazy UFO prophet, grouchy neighbour Mr Bickley, brother and sister Remo and Jean da Vinci from the Bronx, Mindy's ambitious cousin Nelson and her TV station boss Miles Sternhagen. And, of course, Mearth, played by Williams's childhood hero Jonathan Winters.

Williams himself found *Mork & Mindy* launched him into movies, with a succession of star roles including *Popeye* (1980) *The World According to Garp* (1982) and *Good Morning Vietnam* (1988).

Mork & Mindy was popular with parents as well as kids, for behind the off-the-wall insanity, it was one of the most moral shows on television – part of a long US tradition of blending comedy and pathos to teach simple lessons about life. These were spelt out by

Mork at the end of each episode when he would report back to the Orkan leader Orson what he had learned about Earthlings.

Britain wasn't slow to pick up *Mork & Mindy*, with the pilot getting its first showing here on ITV, on 10 March 1979 though the series didn't reach some parts of the country until much later. It played around the regions until 1984 and was revived by Channel 4 in June 1988.

MAIN CAST

Mork Robin Williams   *Mindy McConnell* Pam Dawber
Frederick McConnell Conrad Janis   *Cora Hudson* Elizabeth Kerr
Eugene Jeffrey Jacquet   *Voice of Orson* Ralph James
Exidor Robert Donner   *Franklin Delano Bickley* Tom Poston
Remo da Vinci Jay Thomas   *Jean da Vinci* Gina Hecht
Nelson Flavor Jim Staahl   *Mearth* Jonathan Winters
Miles Sternhagen Foster Brooks

Created by: Garry K. Marshall, Dale McRaven, Joe Gauberg
Producers: Garry K. Marshall
Principal writers: Dale McRaven, April Kelly, Tom Tenowich, Ed Scharlach, Bruce Johnson
Principal directors: Howard Storm, Bob Claver

Miller-Milkis Productions Inc and Henderson Production Co Inc in associa-tion with Paramount Television
93 colour episodes (pilot: 60 minutes; rest: 30 minutes)
UK premiere: 10 March 1979 (London)

MY FAVOURITE MARTIAN

Forget H.G. Wells . . . forget Orson Welles, come to that. As far as TV is concerned, Martians are just regular people with not the slightest intention of waging war on any world.

My Favourite Martian was one of the 1960s' biggest hit comedies and a forerunner of *Mork & Mindy* and *ALF* in its premise of a lone alien visitor living among human beings.

The Martian, played totally straight by veteran actor Ray Walston, crash-lands on Earth during one of his regular recon-naissance trips. His arrival is witnessed by Tim O'Hara (Bill Bixby), a young reporter for the Los Angeles Sun. Rescued and befriended by O'Hara, the Martian goes to stay with him, as his 'Uncle Martin', establishing a situation ripe for comic exploitation. And audiences quickly warmed to the extraterrestrial who com-bined folksy wisdom with alien magic – Martin sported a pair of retractable antennae, could become invisible at will, read minds and talk to animals.

TV's favourite Martian was created by John L. Greene, an American TV writer who first began toying with the idea of a stranded alien in 1955. Control of Uncle Martin's destiny eventually passed to producer Jack Chertok, with Greene one of a team of scriptwriters working on the project (though when one episode called for Martin to get 'involved' with a striptease dancer called Peaches, Greene felt as lost as any parent might feel). Mostly, the humour was mischievous but comfortable, with Martin game to help Tim in his career and domestic life . . . but only up to a point. Special effects were gentle rather than spectacular; Uncle Martin's antennae were strapped to Walston's back and push-button controlled by the actor himself, and when Martin flew, it was courtesy wires and harness.

The series' only other regular characters were O'Hara's landlady Mrs Brown and, occasionally, her teenage daughter Angela, and O'Hara's editor, Harry Burns.

My Favourite Martian premiered in America in September 1963 and was on British screens within two months, becoming a regular – and repeated – visitor over the next few years.

REGULAR CAST

Uncle Martin (The Martian) **Ray Walston**
Tim O'Hara **Bill Bixby**   *Mrs Brown* **Pamela Britton**
Angela Brown **Ann Marshall**   *Harry Burns* **J. Pat O'Malley**

Created by: **John L. Greene**
Writers: various (and numerous)
Directors: various, including **Sheldon Leonard, Sidney Miller, Alan Rafkin**
Music: **George Greeley**
Producer: **Jack Chertok**

A Jack Chertok Production
107 30-minute episodes (75 black and white; 32 colour)
UK premiere run:
7 November 1963–16 September 1964
(Rediffusion, London)

NB: Trying to ascertain exactly how many episodes of this series have been shown in the UK is a tricky business, given ITV's fragmented state at the time. I have definite transmission dates for 67 episodes (all b/w) between November 1963 and May 1968, based on several different regional schedules. It seems likely, though, that all 75 of the b/w episodes did find their way over here. I have no record of any colour episodes transmitted in the UK.

NIGHT GALLERY

'*Night Gallery* – like a huge diamond turning slowly in the bony grasp of a skeleton – dazzles with the reflection of at least 100 stories which might – just might – generate a nightmare or two . . .'

(publicity release)

Night Gallery – or to give it its full title, *Rod Serling's Night Gallery* – only occasionally ventured into the realm of science fiction. The main stamping ground of this American anthology series from the creator of *The Twilight Zone* was the occult, the supernatural and sheer horror – reflecting the dark side of Serling's imagination.

Each segment was introduced by Rod Serling in an art gallery where he invited us to view a painting that depicted the coming tale as a moment of nightmare frozen on canvas.

Of the 100 or so stories, Serling himself wrote about a third, and the series utilised top Hollywood talent behind and in front of the camera.

Tales that had an sf angle included *The Nature of the Enemy*, in which a mission controller (Joseph Campanella) monitors the efforts of an astronaut (Richard Van Vleet) to investigate the strange disappearance of a team that landed on the Moon. In *The Little Black Bag*, Burgess Meredith played a discredited physician and skid row wino who discovers a medical bag and its contents that have accidentally returned to the 20th century from the 21st, enabling him to effect miraculous cures. *The Different Ones* starred Dana Adnrews as a father who sends his misfit son to another planet in accordance with the Federal Conformity Act of 1993; *Camera Obscura* had a heartless moneylender hurled through time by a most unusual camera; *Class of '99* featured Vincent Price as a futuristic instructor in bigotry addressing a strange graduating class; *You Can Come Up Now, Mrs Millikan* had an inventor's wife agreeing to be the subject of his latest experiment.

Two of the Serling stories were nominated for Emmys: *They're Tearing Down Tim Riley's Bar* in which a lonely widower saw the story of his life paralleled in the destruction of his favourite bar; and *The Messiah of Mott Street* which starred Edward G. Robinson as a sick old Jew waiting to see the coming of the Messiah before he dies.

In America, the first two seasons (1970–1) featured hour-long episodes, each with two or three playlets. The third and final season was reduced to half-hours.

In Britain, ITV first screened individual episodes in 1973, but they have never been networked and the series has never been given a really coherent run, switching days, times and duration, skipping weeks and generally failing to establish a settled format. It ran through the 1970s, into the 1980s and still shows up occasionally in late-night schedules.

Serling himself is said to have become increasingly disillusioned by the studio's heavy-handed treatment of his idea and retired from television when the series ended, dying two years later in 1975, aged 50.

REGULAR CAST
Host/narrator **Rod Sterling**

Created by: **Rod Serling**
Producer: **Jack Laird**
Directors: Various, including **Steven Spielberg, John Badham, Jeannot Szwarc, Leonard Nimoy, Gene Kearney, Jeff Corey**

Writers: Various, including **Rod Serling, Jack Laird, Gene Kearney**

A Jack Laird Production for Universal
94 colour episodes (durations vary)
UK premiere: 18 April 1973*
(Thames Television, London)

* The three-in-one TV movie premiere, showcasing three stories – one directed by Steven Spielberg – was screened on 4 August 1970 on BBC2.

THE NIGHTMARE MAN

This atmospheric 1981 BBC thriller combined brutal murder, Russian agents and a secret experiment in a tale of a killer on the loose on a remote Scottish island.

Adapted by Robert Holmes from the novel *Child of Vodyanoi* by David Wiltshire, it toned down the graphic horror, but remained a gripping, suspenseful drama.

The Scottish isle of Inverdee is preparing for its usual long hard winter when the dismembered body of a woman tourist is found. Local dentist Michael Gaffikin and Insp. Inskip are baffled by the ferocity of the murder – and their alarm increases when an ornithologist, Dr Symonds, suffers a similar fate. When he was attacked, his camera had been running and the film reveals a shadowy, monster-like creature. This, and the sleek capsule found washed-up on the beach leads Michael to suspect that the murderer could be something alien . . .

And, in a sense, it is, for the killer turns out to be the result of a secret Russian experiment called the Vodyanoi in which a man's brain is linked to a mini-sub's controls. In his panic to get out, the Russian submariner had half his brain ripped away, turning him into a grotesque 'Nightmare Man'.

The Russians duly turn up, disguised as a British army unit, but their cover is blown when a soldier salutes with the wrong hand! In the end, after the killer has also attacked a coastguard station, the Russians track down and kill him.

A good cast featured James Warwick, Maurice Roëves and Celia Imrie, with the mainly half-glimpsed killer played by Pat Gorman, a veteran of many a *Doctor Who* monster costume.

Tautly directed by Douglas Camfield, the series included several sequences shot from the killer's point of view, and filmed through a red filter.

CAST

Michael Gaffikin **James Warwick**	*Fiona Patterson* **Celia Imrie**
Insp. Inskip **Maurice Roëves**	*Dr Goudry* **Tom Watson**
Col. Howard **Jonathan Newth**	*Sgt. Carch* **James Cosmo**
PC Malcolmson **Fraser Wilson**	*Dr Symonds* **Tony Sibbald**
Mrs Mackay **Elaine Wells**	*McGrath* **Jon Croft**
Campbell **Ronald Forfar**	*Drummond* **Jeffrey Stewart**
Lt Carey **Robert Vowles**	*The killer* **Pat Gorman**

Dramatised by: **Robert Holmes,** *from the novel* **Child of Vodyanoi** *by* **David Wiltshire**
Producer: **Ron Craddock**
Director: **Douglas Camfield**
Designer: **Allan Anson**

Script editor: **Jenny Sheridan**

A BBC Production
Four colour 30-minute episodes
1–22 May 1981
(BBC1)

1990

This BBC drama series from 1977 looked just a few years into the future and saw a population overwhelmed by bureaucracy, and the country practically a police state.

Parliament is just a cypher; the rights of the individual sublimated in a concept of the common good which is maintained by the Home Office's Public Control Department, using rationing, identity cards and electronic surveillance.

These tyrannical bureaucrats have turned the Channel and the North Sea into a watery equivalent of the Berlin Wall – and illegal immigration has given way to undercover emigration as doctors and scientists try to escape.

Devised by Wilfred Greatorex, creator of ITV's *The Power Game*, the series starred Edward Woodward as dissident journalist Jim Kyle, Home Affairs correspondent for one of the three remaining newspapers. He aids a growing resistance movement which smuggles people out of the country, runs an underground press and generally hinders the PCD at every turn. Ranged against him are Herbert Skardon, ruthless controller of the PCD and his deputies Delly Lomas (Season One) and Lynn Blake (Season Two).

The series was born out of Greatorex's own 'suffering' at the hands of zealous VATmen and his resentment at the growing power of the burgeoning bureaucracy of the 1970s – a sentiment shared by many for whom the memory of overkill VAT raids on small shopkeepers still rankled. Greatorex played on this paranoia to take the powers of the administrators a stage or two further.

Some critics carped, but *1990* was essentially a thriller series, not a solemn political statement, and retained the adventure motifs of car chases, tight spots and close shaves.

REGULAR CAST

Jim Kyle **Edward Woodward**   *Herbert Skardon* **Robert Lang**
Dave Brett **Tony Doyle**   *Faceless* **Paul Hardwick**

SEASON ONE ONLY

Delly Lomas **Barbara Kellerman**   *Dan Mellor* **John Savident**
Henry Tasker **Clifton Jones**   *Greaves* **George Murcell**
Jack Nichols **Michael Napier Brown**   *Tommy Pearce* **Mathias Kilroy** *(Eps 1–3)*
Marly **Honor Shepherd** *(Eps 1, 5, 7)*

SEASON TWO ONLY

Lynn Blake **Lisa Harrow**   *Kate Smith* **Yvonne Mitchell**
PCD Insp Macrae **David McKail**   *Tony Doran* **Clive Swift** *(Eps 1–2, 4)*
Digger Radford **Stanley Lebor** *(Eps 3–5)*

Devised by: **Wilfred Greatorex**
Producer: **Prudence Fitzgerald**
Theme music: **John Cameron**

A BBC Production
16 colour 55-minute episodes
Season One:
18 September–31 October 1977
Season Two:
20 February–10 April 1978
(BBC2)

Season One

Creed of Slaves

w **Wilfred Greatorex**
Newspaperman Jim Kyle, a resolute opponent of the Public Control Department's repressive bureaucracy, tries to help a doctor who has been trying in vain to get his asthmatic daughter out of the country.
Dr Vickers **Donald Gee**
Mrs Vickers **Eileen Davies**
Tina Vickers **Sophie Coghill**
PCD Inspector **Stacy Davies**
Randall **Paul Chapman**
Grey **Luke Hanson**
Mrs Grey **Lynn Dalby**
Wilkie **Robert Swales**
Emigration officer **Malcolm Rennie**
Nolan **Willie Johah**
Harper **Bruce Lidington**
Burnley **Desmond Jordan**
Emigrant **Bill Rourke**

Director: **Alan Gibson**
Designer: **Rochelle Selwyn**

When Did You Last See Your Father?

w **Wilfred Greatorex**
Kyle learns that the Home Secretary is about to abolish all exit visa appeals and redoubles his efforts to help Dr Vickers.
Henry Duncan **Reginald Jessup**
Chairperson **Gillian Raine**
Norton **John Hamill**
Ian Cursley **Peter Attard**
Carol Harper **Alix Kirsta**
Randall **Paul Chapman**

Director: **David Sullivan Proudfoot**
Designer: **Judy Steele**

Health Farm

w **Edmund Ward**
Kyle is assigned to investigate an Adult Rehabilitation Centre where murderers and political dissidents alike are treated with drugs that 'reshape' their minds.
Dr Gelbert **Donald Douglas**
Charles Wainwright **Ray Smith**

Halloran Howard Bell
Agnes Culmore Mitzi Rogers
Ivor Griffith John Rhys-Davies

Director: Kenneth Ives
Designer: Robert Berk

Decoy

w Edmund Ward
Dr Sondeberg, the power behind many presidential desks, pays a state visit to Britain. Meanwhile Kyle plans to use a motorised caravan to help top brains flee the country.
Dr Sondeberg Graham Crowden
Sammy Calhoun Victor Maddern
Kingston Antony Scott
Carr George Mallaby
Bowden Alan Tucker

Director: Alan Gibson
Designer: Rochelle Selwyn

Voice From the Past

w Arden Winch
'The age of the common man seems to be degenerating in the age of the common denominator.'
Avery Richard Hurndall
Mitchell Esmond Knight
Brian Simon Chandler
Baker Michael Graham Cox
Luff Simon Lack
Sefton Raymond Mason
Bland John Quarmby
Williams Joby Blanshard

Director: David Sullivan Proudfoot
Designer: Judy Steele

Whatever Happened to Cardinal Wolsey?

w Wilfred Greatorex
An outraged attorney general orders the PCD to intimidate the pregnant wife of a judge who is upholding appeals and trying to dispense justice fairly.
Philip Carter John Castle
Attorney General John Phillips
Susie Carter Anna Cropper
PCD Inspector Frank Mills

Lena Janie Booth
Ed Burbank Ed Bishop
PCD Supervisor James Lister

Director: David Sullivan Proudfoot
Designer: Judy Steele

Witness

w Wilfred Greatorex
'We'll get Kyle . . . He's an enemy of the State . . . and of this Department.' The PCD net begins to close in around Jim Kyle.
Bingham Peter Myers
Paul Mark Heath
Technician Michael Cashman
Maggie Kyle Patricia Garwood
Bevan Jonathan Scott-Taylor
Prosecutor John Bennett
Defence counsel Yvonne Gillian

Director: Alan Gibson
Designer: Rochelle Selwyn

Non-Citizen

w Edmund Ward
Kyle is punished for his 'misdeeds' by being stripped of his citizenship, but still succeeds in turning the tables on the PCD and the nation's Privilege Card holders.
Agnes Culmore Mitzi Rogers
Auckland Edward Judd
Woman non-citizen Julia Sutton
Prof. Cheever Vernon Dobtcheff
Sammy Calhoun Victor Maddern
'Nutter' Stonebridge Colin Edwynn
Frank Woodcock Tony Sympson

Director: Bob Hird
Designer: Robert Berk

Season Two

Pentagons

w Wilfred Greatorex
A pentagon, one of a growing army of dissent groups, prepares to take on the hated PCD.
Everton Oscar James
Tomson John Nolan
Green Paul Beech

Sewell Norman Mitchell
Frank Fenton Barry Lowe
Perez Edward de Souza

Director: Peter Sasdy
Designer: Paul Joel

The Market Price

w Wilfred Greatorex
The government of Kate Smith turns its attention to the black marketeers providing food when official supplies in the supermarkets begin to run low. Peter Greville from the Ministry of Food tries to keep Kyle informed of the PCD's movements but soon suspicion falls on him and his family.
Peter Greville Lyndon Brock
Rev. Newgate Max Harvey
Mrs Greville Ann Curthoys
Jodie Greville Jane Foster
Alf Turner Michael Cassidy
Charles Graydon John Ronane

Director: Roger Tucker
Designer: John Hurst

Trapline

w Edmund Ward
Kyle falls into the hands of Police Commissioner Hallam.
Richard Hallam John Paul
William Grainger John Carson
Tony Borden Norman Eshley
Harry Blaney Donald Burton
Barbara Fairlie Sandra Payne

Director: Peter Sasdy
Designer: Judy Steele

Ordeal by Small Brown Envelope

w Edmund Ward
When the comments in the press by Kyle and Doran again annoy Skardon, he decides to implement ASH – Automatic Systematic Harrassment. Confronted by a stream of bailiffs, bills and official nightmares, 'the noiseless steamroller of the State', Doran and his wife soon reach a crisis.
Jane Doran Hermione Gregory
Arthur Hayes Jim Norton

Harry Blaney Donald Burton
Carter John Saunders

Director: Kenneth Ives
Designer: Michael Young

Hire and Fire

w Edmund Ward
An extortionist network collecting money from repressed workers causes trouble for both Kyle and Skardon.
George Molloy David Buck
Johnny Rolfe Ken Kitson
Gerald Arnold James Greene
James Conrad John Bolt
Ernest Harrison Joseph Brady
Robert Jessup Simon Cadell
Mrs Hutchinson Sally Travers
Joe Hutchinson Colin Douglas

Director: Alan Gibson
Designer: John Hurst

You'll Never Walk Alone

w Wilfred Greatorex
'The authorities have refused me an exit visa for the Chess Championship because they fear I might not come back.'
Alan Adam Bareham
Philip Ross David Rintoul
Cyrus Asher Geoffrey Burridge
Nancy Skardon Joyce Carey
Abe James Murray
Annie Sue Woodley

Director: David Sullivan Proudfoot
Designer: Judy Steele

Young Sparks

w Jim Hawkins
Dissident groups are growing and sinking their differences in the battle against the PCD.
Alan Adam Bareham
Pallin George Pravda
Liz Julia Schofield
Riley William Wilde
Mayers Peter Clay
Sanders Martin Fisk

Director: Kenneth Ives
Designer: Michael Young

What Pleases the Prince

w Wilfred Greatorex
'We always said there'd be Peace Crimes
Trials one day . . . We're winning now'.
The PCD begins to divide against itself.
John Brooks Michael Tarn

Robert Brooks Michael Osborne
Verna Wells Primi Townsend
Mrs Brooks Jenny Laird
Barbara Fairlie Sandra Payne

Director: Alan Gibson
Designer: John Hurst

OBJECT Z

A mystery object hurtling through space on a collision course with good old Earth. In the chaos that follows, traditional enemies combine to save mankind from annihilation. That was the theme of a pair of children's serials of the mid-Sixties, *Object Z* and its sequel, the aptly named *Object Z Returns*. Central figures in the unfolding dramas were TV commentator/reporter Peter Barry, his assistant Diana Winters, a mysterious scientist, Professor Ramsay, and a supporting cast of world leaders and boffins.

The first serial was originally written by Christopher McMaster as an adult programme, but adapted to meet Rediffusion's need for a children's drama. Star Trevor Bannister is perhaps better known as Mr Lucas in the BBC sitcom, *Are You Being Served?*

REGULAR CAST

Peter Barry Trevor Bannister   *Professor Ramsay* Ralph Nossek
Diana Winters Celia Bannerman *(Series One only)*
June Challis Margaret Neale   *Robert Duncan* Denys Peek
Brian Barclay Brandon Brady   *Keeler* Arthur White
Ian Murray (Home Secretary) William Abney
Sir John Chandos (Prime Minister) Julian Somers
Terry Toni Gilpin *(Series Two only)*

Writer: Christopher McMaster
Director/Producer: Daphne Shadwell
Designer: Andrew Drummond

Rediffusion Network Production

Object Z

When a mystery object is detected hurtling towards Earth, anxious world leaders prepare to launch a rocket to destroy the unknown projectile. Are aliens coming? If so, what do they want? Or is it all a hoax perpetrated by scientist Professor Ramsay and his colleagues to frighten the world into peace? (You bet it is!)

Capt. Wade Terrence J. Donovan
President McCone Robert O'Neil
Dr Baranov Jeffrey Wickham
Dr Rickover Lindsay Campbell
Premier Yeremenko Dmitri Makaroff
with: David Munro, Terence Woodfield,
  Penny Morrell, Roger Rowland,
  Hugh Munro, John Newman,
  Roy Herrick, Bernard Kay,
  Richard Bidlake, Milton Johns

Six 30-minute episodes, black and white

The Meteor
The World in Fear
Flight from Danger
The Aliens
Too Late
The Solution

19 October–23 November 1965
(ITV)

Object Z Returns

Scientists spot three more objects on their screens, moving in formation towards Earth at tremendous speed. Are they out-of-control asteroids or space ships? Prof. Ramsay is freed from jail to work out the truth with his assistants Robert Duncan

and June Challis. This time it's no hoax, as the alien craft – from a water-covered world – land in Earth's oceans and the world begins to freeze.
Premier Petrov **Paul Armstrong**
The Voice **Terence Woodfield**
Dr O'Toole **Barry Lowe**
Dallier **David Saire**
Radio operator **Roy Herrick**

Six 30-minute episodes, black and white

The Voice From Space
The Machine
The Monsters
The Menace from the Depths
The Big Freeze
The Eleventh Hour

22 February–29 March 1966
(ITV)

ONE STEP BEYOND

'What you are about to see is a matter of human record. Explain it? We cannot. Disprove it? We cannot. We simply invite you to explore with us the amazing world of the unknown, to take that *One Step Beyond*.'

Neither science nor, by its own assertion, fiction, *One Step Beyond* dealt with the realm of psychic phenomena. Technically that puts it one step beyond the province of this volume.

Yet this vintage anthology series, which did as much as any to blur the edges of reality, repeatedly crops up in genre guides and has long been accepted into the hearts of television fantasy fans.

Created in America, it ran there for two years (1959–61) and 94 episodes (as *Alcoa Presents . . .*). But what isn't widely known is that 13 of those episodes, all for the third and final season, were made in Britain – and *that's* why the series is in *this* book.

The UK 13 were made at the now long-lost MGM film studios in Borehamwood by Lancer Films, and were hailed as the first time British Television production had gone into an association with an established American network show. Using mainly British scripts, they featured British casts, with Anton Rodgers, Peter Wyngarde, Donald Pleasence, Christopher Lee, Adrienne Corri, Roger Delgado and a young Michael Crawford among the stars.

Like the rest of the series, the stories dealt with various psychic phenomena – supernatural visitations, ESP, dreams that are portents of disaster, hallucinations of the future, reincarnations of the past. These episodes – and the series as a whole – were directed and hosted by American actor John Newland who took a sardonic delight in introducing what became renowned as a genuinely spooky glimpse of the paranormal.

The UK 13 were bought by Associated-Rediffusion and given a network run from November 1961, at peak time.

The rest of the series didn't fare quite as well. Granada was the first ITV company to screen American-made episodes, showing 13 between October 1962 and January 1963. Rediffusion and Southern TV have also given it reasonable air-time. Invariably, though, all have played to the late-night audience, and overall, little more than half the 94 episodes have been seen in this country.

(Author's note: a full episode guide would be space-consuming and probably inappropriate, given the series' general stamping ground, so I've plumped for a rundown of the British-made episodes, the UK 13.)

REGULAR CAST
Host John Newland

Series creator: Merwin Gerard
Series producer: Collier Young
Director: John Newland
Music: Harry Lubin

A Collier Young Production
94 30-minute episodes, black and white

The UK 13

Director: John Newland
Executive producer: Collier Young
Producer: Peter Marriott
Story supervisor: Martin Benson

A Lancer Films Production
13 30-minute episodes, black and white
29 November 1961–28 February 1962

Eye Witness

w Derry Quinn
Henry Soames, night news editor of the *Boston Globe*, experiences the 1883 Krakatoa earthquake in the quiet of his office and while unconscious writes an exclusive 'eyewitness' account.
Henry John Meillon

Nora Rose Alba
Mark Anton Rodgers
Jake Robin Hughes
Frank John Phillips
Leo J.G. Devlin
Richards Robert Ayres
Danny Howard Knight
with Gordon Stern, Janet Blandes, Patricia English

Nightmare

w Martin Benson
Artist Paul Roland, haunted by the face of a girl he has never met, feels compelled to keep painting her portrait.
Paul Peter Wyngarde
Jill Mary Peach
Lady Diana Ambrosine Phillpotts
Heathcote Ferdy Mayne

Stapleton Richard Caldicott
Meg Jean Cadell
Doctor Patrick Holt

The Confession

w Larry Marcus
Harvey Laurence, an old man on a Hyde
Park soapbox, constantly tells the story of
his guilt in allowing a man to die for the
murder of a woman he knew was still
alive . . . but no one ever listens.
Laurence Donald Pleasence
Sarah Adrienne Corri
Policeman Robert Raglan
KC Raymond Rollett
Mrs Evans Eileen Way
Martha Carmel McSharry
Locksmith Jack Newmark
with Douglas Ives, Gerald James,
   Julian Orchard, Brenda Dunrich

The Avengers

w Martin Benson
A general's replica of an old 18th century
tyrant's party stirs up spirits of the ancient
gathering and the consequences are
chillingly similar.
General André Morell
Marianne Lisa Gastoni
Priest Stanley van Beers
Doctor Carl Jaffe
Orderly Richard Leech
Gardener Steve Plytas
Sergeant Walter Gotell
Musicians Carl Duering, Jan Conrad,
   Charles Russell, Robert Crewdson

The Stranger

w Larry Marcus
The fingerprints of a man who helped
keep three earthquake victims alive until
their rescue 11 days later, show he had
'died' in prison some time ago.
Cole Bill Nagy
Hadley Peter Dyneley
Warden Patrick McAlliney
Peter Graham Stark
Teacher Harold Kasket
Guard Ken Wayne
Barber Mark Baker

Signal Received

w Derry Quinn
Three sailors on HMS *Hood* are given
separate glimpses of the future – revealing
their own fates and that of the ship. (One
of the three, Robin Hughes, subsequently
became an actor and appeared in the *One
Step Beyond* story *Eye Witness*).
Watson Mark Eden
Breed Terry Palmer
Hughes Richard Gale
Mrs Breed Viola Keats
with Patrick McLoughlin, Patrick
   Jordan, Anne Ridler, Sally Layng,
   Garrard Green, Jennifer Daniel, John
   Downing, Susan Richards, Mark
   Burns, Charles Lamb

The Prisoner

w Larry Marcus
Concentration camp survivor Ruth Gold-
man kills a German soldier in retribution
for Nazi atrocities, but her doctor insists
the man has been dead for six years.
German Anton Diffring
Ruth Catherine Feller
Nurse Faith Brook
Samuel Sandor Elès
Doctor Gerard Heinz
Woman Annette Carell

The Sorcerer

w Derry Quinn
A farmer's supernatural powers enable a
German officer, anxious about his fiancée's
faithfulness, to visit her flat 800 miles
away in Berlin.
Reitlinger Christopher Lee
Klaus Martin Benson
Elsa Gabrielli Licudi
Scholl Alfred Burke
Letterhaus George Pravda
Landlord Peter Swanwick
Johann Frederick Jaeger
with Edwin Richfield, Richard Shaw

That Room Upstairs

w Merwin Gerard *and* Larry Marcus
An American couple rent a large house in
London. When the wife hears the voice of

a child calling for help she goes to one of the upstairs rooms where she finds a wasted girl crying in pain. To her horror her surroundings change into an old nursery . . .

Esther Lois Maxwell
Will David Knight
Hudson Anthony Oliver
Child Gilda Emmanueli
Man David Markham
Woman Jane Hylton
Doctor Carl Bernard

The Tiger

w Ian Stuart Black
A neglected child 'wishes' up an unusual way to drive out her unwanted governess.

Pamela Pauline Challenor
Miss Plum Pamela Brown
Mrs Murphy Elspeth March
Cleaning lady Patsy Smart
Solicitor Brian Parker
Inspector Michael Collins

The Villa

w Derry Quinn
Mary sees a beautiful villa while taking part in a hypnotic experiment. The next day she accompanies her husband to Milan . . . and to the beautiful villa.

Mary Elizabeth Sellars
Jim Geoffrey Toone
Stella Marla Landi
Mr Hudson David Horne
Tony Michael Crawford
Lionel Kenneth Cope
Bertollini Robert Rietty
Porter Gertan Klauber

The Face

w Derry Quinn
Haunted since childhood by a seaman's face in a recurring dream of murder, Stephen Bolt hangs around the docks in the hope of recognising the face. One day he gets drunk and wakes up on a Spanish ship where one of the seaman has *that* face.

Stephen Sean Kelly
Mark John Brown
Rosemary Penelope Horner
Isaiah Victor Platt
Hogan Robert Cawdron
Sergeant John Scott
Tattooist Erik Chitty
Norriss Andrew Faulds
Second officer Roger Delgado
Spanish sailor Derek Sydney
with Michael Peake, Leon Cartez, Paula Burne

Justice

w Guy Morgan
A respected bank manager in a little Welsh village confesses to a murder and supplies evidence of his guilt – but witnesses swear he was asleep in a church pew when the crime was committed.

PC Jones Clifford Evans
Mrs Jones Barbara Mullen
Mr Roberts Meredith Edwards
Mrs Roberts Pauline Jameson
Insp. Pugh Edward Evans
Supt Rees Ewan Roberts
Mr Owen Jack Melford
Mrs Owen Helen Sessions
Dr Evans Martin Benson

OTHERWORLD

Lost in Space meets *The Fantastic Journey* in a short-lived series about a family lost in another dimension.

The Sterlings, touted as 'a typical Southern California family', slip into the parallel universe of Otherworld while on a sightseeing tour of the ancient Pyramids, when a strange alignment of the planets opens up a portal between the two universes.

They discover that the Great Pyramid was built, not as the mere tomb of a king, but as a barricade at the portal, and that thousands of years ago it was common for people to pass between the two dimensions.

Not so now, however, and Hal and June Sterling and their three children become fugitives in this alien environment as they strive to reach the Capital Province of Imar where the Supreme Governors have the power to return them to their own world. It's a perilous task, as they are pursued by the Zone Troopers of the Imperial Kommander Nuveen Kroll.

Otherworld's eight episodes ranged from the comic (*Rock and Roll Suicide*) through the blatantly ludicrous (*Village of the Motorpigs*), to the excellent (a beauty and the beast-style story, *Mansion of the Beast*). But they never did make it home.

In the UK, the series has been seen in all ITV regions except the London area.

REGULAR CAST

Hal Sterling Sam Groom   *June Sterling* Gretchen Corbett
Trace Tony O'Dell   *Gina* Jonna Lee
Smith Brandon Crane   *Nuveen Kroll* Jonathan Banks

Executive producers: Philip De Guere
    (pilot only), Roderick Taylor
Producers: Roderick Taylor *(pilot only),*
    Lew Hunter

MCATV International
Eight colour 55-minute episodes

UK premiere:
7 September–2 November 1985
(HTV)

(UK running orders varied around the regions, so the following guide lists the episodes in their original US order.)

Rules of Attraction (pilot)

w Roderick Taylor
The Sterling family are on holiday on Egypt when, while sightseeing at the ancient pyramids, they slip through a dimensional gateway into a parallel universe 'just slightly different from our reality'. There, they becomes fugitives from the authorities in their quest for Capital where lies their only hope of return to their own world.
Nova Amanda Wyss
Bureaucrat Ray Walston
Litten Conrad Bachmann
Prof. Kroyd James Costy

Director: William Graham

The Zone Troopers Build Men

w Coleman Luck, *from a story by*
    Roderick Taylor *and* Bruce A. Taylor
The Sterlings are living quietly for a while in a peaceful town, when Trace is suddenly snatched by Zone Troopers because of low school grades and put through strenuous training. To leave he must become an officer, as only officers can resign.
Hilbird Racks Dominick Brascia
Sightings Mark Lenard

Director: Richard Compton

Paradise Lost

w Josef Anderson, *from a story by*
    Roderick Taylor *and* Bruce A. Taylor
Following a powerful storm, the Sterlings

are washed up on the shores of a beautiful island, setting for a paradise-lost resort. Their host is the equally beautiful and mysterious Scarla who falls in love with Hal.
Scarla Barbara Stock

Director: Tom Wright

Rock and Roll Suicide

w Roderick Taylor *and* Bruce A. Taylor
Gina and Trace introduce rock and roll to the other kids in a Centrex City high school and become instant celebrities but also risk exposing the whole family to the attention of Kroll.
Host Joyce Little
Claxxon Warren Munson
Billy Sunshine Michael Callan

Director: Roderick Taylor

Village of the Motorpigs (aka Tribunal)

w Roderick Taylor
While trying to put as much distance between themselves and the Zone troopers as possible, the Sterlings fall into the hands of a tribe of neo-Barbarians whose social set-up is opposed to the family entity. (This episode was formerly the pilot, Part 2.)
Chalktrauma Marjoe Gortner
Rev Jeff East
Pango Vincent Schiavelli
Pigseye David Katims
Motorface Donald Gibb
Motorpig Jerry Potter

Director: Paul Michael Glaser

I Am Woman, Hear Me Roar (aka You've Come a Long Way, Baby)

w Bruce A. Taylor, Coleman Luck, *from a story by* Roderick Taylor, Bruce A. Taylor, Coleman Luck
The Sterlings wander into a province called Ador where men are second-class citizens and women rule.
Lieutenant Wayne Alexander
Belisama Elaine Giftos
Gretchen Askyou Susan Powell
Sam Askyou Dennis Howard

Director: Tom Wright

Mansion of the Beast

w Roderick Taylor, Coleman Luck, Bruce A. Taylor, *from a story by* R. Taylor, C. Luck
June is held prisoner by a creature – half-man, half-beast – who falls in love with her and tells her she is his only salvation from a terrible fate.
Vorago Alan Feinstein
Aiken John Astin

Director: Corey Allen

Princess Metra

w Douglas Lloyd McIntosh, *from a story by* Roderick Taylor, Bruce A. Taylor
When the Sterlings arrive in Metraplex, Gina is mistaken for a long-lost princess and, seeing this as a way to get closer to home, assumes her new identity.
Zal Philip Simone
Kort Drake Hogestyn
Vertleena Joan Foley

Director: Peter Medak

OUT OF THE UNKNOWN

'Without doubt the best adult science fiction series ever to be written for the small screen.'

(*Daily Express*)

The cause of British adult science fiction was never better served than by this prestigious BBC anthology series of single plays.

Drawn heavily from the written works of top-notch sf writers such as Isaac Asimov, John Wyndham, Ray Bradbury and Frederick Pohl, *Out of the Unknown* ran for four seasons on BBC 2 between 1965 and 1971 – two black and white, two colour – and became a magnet for some of the brightest talent around at the time.

Inspiration came from producer Irene Shubik who already had an enviable track record in the field – as story editor for ABC Television, she had helmed the pioneering 1962 ITV science fiction anthology series *Out of This World*, and had also established a reputation for picking winners for ABC's renowned *Armchair Theatre* series.

Among the dramatists working on the first season were Terry Nation, Leon Griffiths and Bruce Stewart (later to script the first, and best, *Timeslip* stories for ATV), all of whom had worked with Shubik on *Out of This World*. The directorial credits included Philip Saville (*Boys from the Blackstuff*), Alan Bridges and Peter Sasdy, and among the ranks of BBC designers were Barry Learoyd, Peter Seddon and Ridley Scott who, of course, found greater acclaim as director of *Alien* and *Blade Runner*. And the series regularly attracted high-calibre casts with David Hemmings, Milo O'Shea, Warren Mitchell, Donald Houston, Rachel Roberts, George Cole, Anton Rodgers, Ed Begley and Marius Goring among the stars.

Being an anthology, *Out of the Unknown* was never tied to one style of science fiction, though it eschewed membership of the 'bug-eyed monster' club. Some stories were played for suspense (*The Counterfeit Man*, *Time in Advance*, *Lambda 1*, *The World in Silence*), some played on fears (*Some Lapse of Time*, *Frankenstein Mark II*), and others aimed for satire (*The Midas Plague*), black comedy (*Second Childhood*) or whimsy (*Andover and the Android*, *Satisfaction Guaranteed*). Nearly all had *something* to offer the starved intellect.

The third and fourth seasons, produced in colour by Alan Bromly, saw a shift in style towards what Bromly called 'plays of psychological suspense', with mostly supernatural thrills. Only gradual at first, the transition was almost total in the fourth and final season.

Explaining the decision to take the series away from pure science fiction, Bromly told *Radio Times*: 'To do these things really successfully must involve you in spending an enormous amount of money on special effects . . . which is beyond the reach of television.' He added: 'When everybody has seen men walking on the moon and sat through a cliffhanger about getting them back alive, then just setting a story somewhere in space is not, you can see, the automatic thrill it was'.

It wasn't a view shared by everyone and although Bromly's reign included plays by Michael J. Bird and the prolific Nigel Kneale, it was not a series for purists. The era of the science fiction anthology was over.

Producers: **Irene Shubik** *(Seasons One and Two)* **Alan Bromley** *(Seasons Three and Four)*
Script editors: **Irene Shubik** *(Seasons One and Two)* **Roger Parkes** *(Seasons Three and Four)*
Theme music: **Norman Kay**

A BBC Production
49 episodes – 12 × 50 mins (Season One)
37 × 60 mins (Seasons Two–Four)

black and white (Seasons One and Two)
colour (Seasons Three and Four)
Season One:
4 October–20 December 1965
Season Two:
6 October 1966–1 January 1967
Season Three:
7 January–1 April 1969
Season Four:
21 April–30 June 1971
(BBC2)

Season One

No Place Like Earth

w **Stanley Miller,** *from a story by* **John Wyndham**
Wandering on Mars is a lone, homesick Earthman, stranded when Earth exploded. One day he learns of a reborn Earth, and his hope is also rekindled.
Bert **Terence Morgan**
Zaylo **Hannah Gordon**
Annika **Jessica Dunning**
Blane **Alan Tilvern**
Harris **Bill Treacher**
Carter **Vernon Joyner**
Freeman **Joseph O'Conor**
Major Khan **George Pastell**
Spaceship captain **Jerry Stovin**
Chief officer **Geoffrey Palmer**
Security guard **Roy Stewart**

Director: **Peter Potter**
Designer: **Peter Seddon**

(4 October 1965)

The Counterfeit Man

w **Philip Broadley,** *from a story by* **Alan Nourse**
Aboard a spaceship bound for Earth are a crew of tired, edgy explorers, returning from a fruitless mission to the barren planet Ganymede. Then a routine medical check reveals that one man, Westcott, has a blood sugar count of zero – which means he is not human. Some entity has taken over his mind and body.
Dr Crawford **Alex Davion**
Westcott **David Hemmings**
Capt. Jaffe **Charles Tingwell**
Donnie **Peter Fraser**
Jensen **Anthony Wager**
Scotty **Keith Buckley**
Gerry **David Savile**
Dave **Geoffrey Kenion**
Frank **Barry Ashton**
Ken **David Munro**
Commander **Hedger Wallace**
Officer **Lew Luton**
Guard **Derek Martin**

Director: **George Spenton-Foster**
Designer: **Trevor Williams**

(11 October 1965)

Stranger in the Family

w **David Campton**
Boy is a child ahead of his time – a mutant born with amazing mental powers of perception and persuasion. His parents have tried to protect him but he is shadowed by a strange group of men who have their own plans for his future. To 18-year-old Boy, it seems only one person understands him – the lovely Paula. But their relationship is doomed to tragedy.
Boy **Richard O'Callaghan**
Hall **Joby Blanshard**

Paula Justine Lord
Sonny Eric Lander
Lorry driver Peter Thornton
Charles Wilson Peter Copley
Margaret Wilson Daphne Slater
Brown John Paul
Evans Jack May
Mrs Pain Bay White
Director Maurice Podbray
Assistant Clive Graham
Swain Brian Vaughan

Director: Alan Bridges
Designer: Barry Learoyd

(18 October 1965)

The Dead Past

w Jeremy Paul, from a story by Isaac
  Asimov
In the 21st century, historian Arnold
Potterley requests permission from the
World Government to use its Chronoscope – a device able to recapture any
event from the past on screen – to view a
scene from ancient Carthage. It seems a
harmless request, but Araman, the official
in charge of the Chronoscope, no only
forbids it but warns Potterley he risks
'intellectual anarchy' if he pursues the
matter. Determined not to be thwarted,
Potterley persuades a young physicist,
Foster, to build his own private Chrono-
scope. The result is unexpected and
frightening.
Arnold Potterley George Benson
Jonas Foster James Maxwell
Thaddeus Araman David Langton.
Caroline Potterley Sylvia Coleridge
Miss Clements Shirley Cain
Laurel Frances Alger
Ralph Nimmo Willoughby Goddard

Director: John Gorrie
Designer: Norman James

(25 October 1965)

Time in Advance

w Paul Erickson, from a story by William
  Tenn
The future: people with criminal tend-
encies can be licensed to commit a crime –
provided they first serve an appropriate

term of imprisonment. A convict space-
ship is returning to Earth from a penal
colony in outer space. Aboard are
Crandall and Henck, the first men ever to
survive the seven years of rigorous punish-
ment, which ears them the right to commit
a murder. As the ship lands, reporters
press forward to ask the men who their
victims will be.
Chief guard Oliver MacGreevy
Crandall Edward Judd
Henck Mike Pratt
Henson Dyson Lovell
The Examiner Peter Madden
Newsreader Michael Harding
Ryman Jerome Willis
Marie Judy Parfitt
Polly Wendy Gifford
Stephenson Peter Stephens
A captor Patrick Scanlan
Dan Danvers Walker
Police officer Phillip Voss
Ballaskia Ken Parry

Director: Peter Sasdy
Designer: Tony Abbott

(1 November 1965)

Come Buttercup, Come Daisy, Come . . .?

w Mike Watts
A chilling comedy. Fishmonger Henry
Wilkes cultivates carnivorous plants in his
suburban garden, feeding them diced
rabbit and massive doses of vitamins. He
gives them pet names and talks to them.
Henry Wilkes Milo O'Shea
Danny Jack Wild
Monica Wilkes Christine Hargreaves
Anne Lovejoy Patsy Rowlands
Mrs Bryant Ann Lancaster
Norman Eric Thompson
Dr Chambers Desmond Jordan
Mrs Dixon Julie May
Milkman Nigel Lambert
Det. Sgt Crouch Bernard Kay
Det. Con. Fraser Alan Heywood
Mina-Mina trained by Barbara Wood-
  house

Director: Paddy Russell
Designer: John Cooper

(8 November 1985)

Sucker Bait

w Meade Roberts, *from a story by* Isaac Asimov

Time: the far future. Mark Annuncio is a Mnemonic, one of a group of specially selected children rigorously trained to soak up facts and store them in the subconscious and to recall them in association with other facts in a human way no computer can match. Mark and his attendant psychologist, Dr Sheffield, are viewed with mistrust by scientists aboard the spaceship Triple G, hurtling towards the planet Troan to discover why a colony died there within three years. But Mark's insatiable curiosity comes to threaten not only the expedition's purpose, but also the lives of its members.

Captain Bill Nagy
Mark Clive Endersby
Dr Sheffield John Meillan
Cinam David Knight
Novee Burt Kwouk
Fawkes Roger Croucher
Rodriguez Tenniel Evans
Vernadsky David Sumner

Director: Naomi Capon
Designer: William McCrow

(15 November 1965)

The Fox and the Forest

w Terry Nation, *from a story by* Ray Bradbury
Additional material: Meade Roberts

In the year 2165, time travel is a luxury which privileged government workers may use to take holidays in the past. David and Sarah Kirsten chose 1938 and liked it so much they decided to stay. But they are too important to be allowed to escape from the future, so 'hunters' are sent to bring them back – remorseless pursuers who blend in so well, that to the 'hunted' everyone they meet becomes suspect.

David Frederick Bartman
Sarah Liane Aukin
Joe Warren Mitchell
Shaw Marne Maitland
Boy Aziz Resh
Mexican woman Serafina di Leo

Faber Eric Flynn
Dancer Delphine
Guitarist Domingo de Lezaria
American couple Robert MacLeod, Bettine Milne
Mexicans Guido Adorni, Jose Berlinka
Man in mask Dean Francis
Bellboy Steve Georgio
Singer/guitarist Patrick Scanlan
Beth Marcella Markham
Hotel manager George Roderick

Director: Robin Midgley
Designer: Peter Seddon

(22 November 1965)

Andover and the Android

w Bruce Stewart, *from a story by* Kate Wilhelm

Roger Andover's aunt Mathilde wants him to marry and take over the family electronics business. Determined to avoid complicated human relationships, Roger acquires one of the secret new super-androids that he can pass off as his wife – a beautiful 'woman' called Lydia. Despite some anxious moments when she is introduced to the family, Lydia looks like being the perfect wife. She never argues and is always eager to please. Then her circuits become confused.

Sir Felix Ronald Ibbs
Cullen Fulton Mackay
Prof. Tzhilyantsi Robert Eddison
Purvis Robin Parkinson
Charlie David Coote
Phoebe Helen Lindsay
Andover Tom Criddle
French David Conville
Eleanor Lisa Daniely
Patrice John Malcolm
Mathilde Marda Vanne
Lydia Annette Robertson
Bernard Erik Chitty
Barnaby Peter Bathurst
Fred Fred Hugh

Director: Alan Cooke
Designer: Lionel Radford

(29 November 1965)
(repeated 29 December 1965, BBC1)

Some Lapse of Time

w Leon Griffiths, *from a story by* John
  Brunner

Dr Max Harrow is awakened from a
recurrent nightmare in which he is pursued by barbaric accusing figures, to find a
tramp collapsed on his doorstep. The
tramp is suffering from a genetic radiation
disorder that should have killed him in
infancy as it did Harrow's baby son. The
man is the living image of Harrow's
nightmare figures. Clutched in his hand is
a human finger bone and he speaks a
strange, unknown tongue. Why did he
collapse outside Harrow's house? What is
his motive for tracing him?
Max Harrow Ronald Lewis
Diana Harrow Jane Downs
Policeman Peter Bowles
Smiffershon John Gabriel
Dr Gordon Faulkner Richard Gate
Det. Sgt Cloudby George Woodbridge
Prof Leach Moultrie Kelsall
Dr Laura Danville Delena Kidd
Radiographer Laidlaw Dalling
Anderson Blake Butler

Director: Roger Jenkins
Designer: Ridley Scott

(6 December 1965)

Thirteen to Centaurus

w Stanley Miller, *from a story by*
  J. G. Ballard

Thirteen people are living in a steel-
encased, self-sufficient world of their own,
known as 'the Station'. All but one has
been conditioned to accept it as their only
home, their Earth memories carefully
erased to ensure the Station functions
efficiently. The odd man out is psychologist Dr Francis, responsible for maintaining the blocks. Then Abel, a boy born
in the strange community, starts asking
questions. Dr Francis knows he should
stop them, but, curious, gives partial
answers. But Abel is not so docile as the
others.
Capt. Peters Lionel Stevens
Dr Francis Donald Houston
Zenna Peters Carla Challoner
Abel Granger James Hunter

Matthias Granger John Moore
Mrs Granger Joyce Donaldson
Sarah Granger Janet Gallagher
Mrs Peters Wendy Johnson
Matthew Peters Karl Lanchbury
Jeremiah Baker Peter Bennett
Mrs Baker Christine Lander
Mark Baker Roy Hills
Ruth Baker Janet Fairhead
Sgt Burke Robert Russell
Capt. Sanger John Line
Col. Chalmers John Abineri
Gen. Short Noel Johnson
Dr Kersh Robert James

Director: Peter Potter
Designer: Trevor Williams

(13 December 1965)

The Midas Plague

w Troy Kennedy Martin, *from a story by*
  Frederick Pohl

The Robot Age has arrived, producing
more than enough of everything. Man has
only to consume and, in theory, enjoy
himself. But superabundance brings
problems for Morrey who is low on the
social scale in a world where such values
have been reversed and only the rich are
privileged enough to lead the simple life,
while the 'poor' are swamped with more
goods than they can possibly consume.
Morrey Graham Stark
Edward Julian Curry
Wainwright Victor Brooks
Henry Anthony Dawes
George Robert Sidaway
Edwina Anne Lawson
Gideon Graham Lines
Police robot Michael Earl
Counsel Geoffrey Alexander
Judge A.J. Brown
Prisoner Sydney Arnold
Analyst David Nettheim
Fred Sam Kydd
Rebel leader David Blake Kelly
Rebels Richard Davies, Arne Gordon
Sir John John Barron

Director: Peter Sasdy
Designer: William McCrow

(20 December 1965)

Season Two

The Machine Stops

w Clive Donner, Kenneth Cavander, *from a story by* E.M. Forster
An Edwardian vision of a future dominated by machines. A mother and her son struggle to maintain their natural bond of love in a world in which human beings have become tyrannised by machines.
Vashti Yvonne Mitchell
Kuno Michael Gothard
Airship attendant Nike Arrighi
Airship passenger Jonathan Hansen
Voice of friend Jane Jordan Rogers
Girl Lucy Hill

Director: Philip Saville
Designer: Norman James

(6 October 1966, BBC2)
(BBC1 rpt: 15 April 1967)*

Frankenstein Mark II

w Hugh Whitemore
A stranger calls at the home of divorcee Anna Preston, asking to collect some of her ex-husband's belongings. Anna agrees, but is suspicious, and tries to contact her 'ex' at the space-research establishment where he worked. But none of his colleagues can tell her where he is and the authorities block all her efforts to find out. Anna grows more convinced that he is in danger, but the truth is more horrifying than even she can imagine.
Dr Morrison David Langton
Security man Michael Beint
Dr Giddy Bernard Archard
Anna Preston Rachel Roberts
Smithers Wolfe Morris
Mrs Burgoyne Annette Kerr
Insp. Gilliat Richard Carpenter
Nurse Dorothea Phillips
George Preston Basil Henson

Director: Peter Duguid
Designer: Tony Abbott

(13 October 1966)

Lambda 1

w Bruce Stewart, *from a story by* Colin Kapp
In a distant future, a new form of space travel has evolved – travel through the Earth by a system known as Tau whereby the displacement of atoms enables one solid body to pass through another. But it's still experimental, and when a spaceship gets lost, anxiety mounts, especially as the wife of the Senior Controller is on board. The controller and a friend set out on a rescue mission.
Bridie Mary Webster
Julie Kate Story
Ferris Michael Lees
Dantor Charles Tingwell
Alex Geoffrey Frederick
Birch Geoffrey Kenion
Harvey Anthony Wager
Mary Jessica Dunning
American Murray Kash
Brett Danvers Walker
Porter Sebastian Breaks
Benedict Ronald Lewis
Rorsch Jan Conrad
Oriental Andy Ho
Caradus Peter Fontaine

Director: George Spenton-Foster
Designer: Peter Seddon

(20 Octber 1966)

Level 7

w J.B. Priestley, *from a story by* Mordecai Roshwald
After completing his final training on defence computers, 'H' is entitled to three weeks' leave. But his colonel tells him he must first visit certain underground installations. 'H' goes to Level 7, 4500 ft below ground, unaware that he has been sent there for good . . .
X127 ('H') Keith Buckley
Colonel Michael Bird
General Anthony Bate
Doctor Tom Criddle
Woman commandant Jane Jordan Rogers

---

* At the time of their original transmission, BBC2 was still unavailable in parts of the country, so six of the Season Two plays were also showcased on BBC1.

X117 David Collings
R747 Michele Dotrice
New man Sean Arnold
Air supply officer Anthony Sweeny
Radio Man One David Cargill
Radio Man Two Raymond Hardy
Man Glenn Williams
Woman Patricia Denys

Director: Rudolph Cartier
Designer: Norman James

(27 October 1966, BBC2)
(BBC1 rpt: 29 April 1967)

Second Childhood

w Hugh Leonard
Charles Dennistoun, a 60-year-old contestant on 'You Bet a Million' – a quiz show for millionaires – wins the jackpot prize, a course in rejuvenation. But his friends and family have mixed feelings, and the repercussions have blackly comic effects on all concerned.
Charles Dennistoun Nigel Stock
Kenneth Dennistoun Donald Pickering
Joan Dennistoun Geraldine Newman
Betty Dennistoun Betty Cooper
Tom Dennistoun John Horsley
Ronnie Cash Roland Curram
Dr Willi Herstein Robin Phillips
Dr Gerhardt Keppler Hugo Schuster
Dr Odile Keppler Caroline Blakiston
Maid Sybilla Kay

Director: John Gorrie
Designer: Tony Abbott

(10 November 1966, BBC2)
(BBC1 rpt: 6 May 1967)

The World in Silence

w Robert Gould, from a story by John Rankins
College student Sarah Richards is alone in fearing and disliking the new teaching machines but even she does not forsee the terrifying situation that arises when her supervisor, Stephen Kershaw, rearranges the machines to conform with revised fire regulations.
Sarah Deborah Watling
Eric Lonsbury John Baskcomb

George Kenneth Gardiner
Stephen Kershaw Mark Eden
Geoffrey Harrison John Allison
Florrie Nadine George
Harold Stephen Whittaker
Freda Sara Aimson
Mrs Richards Susan Field
Davison Noel Davis
Chief Supt Mailer Richard Hampton
Gen. Harboard Keith Pyott
Dr Hammond Erik Chitty

Director: Naomi Capon
Designer: William McCrow

(17 November 1966)

The Eye

w Stanley Miller, from a story by Henry Kuttner
Julian Clay is accused of murdering Andrew Maddox – a charge he cannot deny because 'The Eye', a device wich records the past, saw him do it. However, the law affords one loophole.
Maddox Leslie Sands
Clay Anton Rodgers
Stevens John Wentworth
Munder Eric Young
Bea Valerie Gearson
Judge Frank Singuineau
Josephine Wanda Ventham
Caller Peter Noel Cook

Director: Peter Sasdy
Designer: Norman James

(24 November 1966)

Tunnel Under the World

w David Campton, from a story by Frederick Pohl
In a world where brain patterns run machinery, and powerful new advertising techniques appear daily, Guy and Mary Birkett live apparently humdrum lives – until one day Guy makes a discovery. (This tale was a satire on advertising and featured miniature 'people' being studied on a table top by an advertising firm.)
Guy Birkett Ronald Hines
Mary Birkett Petra Davies

Swanson Timothy Bateson
Miss Mitkin Fanny Carby
Spelman Peter Madden
Salesman Bryan Hunt
April Dorn Gay Hamilton
Waiter Patrick Parnell

Director: Alan Cooke
Designer: William McCrow

(1 December 1966)

The Fastest Draw

w Julian Bond, *from a story by* Larry Eisenberg

A science fiction western. Millionaire eccentric Amos Handworthy is determined to keep the old west alive and has installed an original Pecos saloon as part of his fully automated electronics factory. When Peter Stenning flies in from England to work in this strange set-up, he becomes irresistibly drawn into conflict with his domineering boss.

Peter Stenning James Maxwell
The Pilot Jerry Stovin
Marie Crane Patricia English
Amos Handworthy Ed Begley
Emma Bowles Annette Carell

Director: Herbert Wise
Designer: Peter Seddon

(8 December 1966, BBC2)
(BBC1 rpt: 13 May 1967)

Too Many Cooks

w Hugh Whitemore, *from a story by* Larry Eisenberg

Dr Andrew Cook, inventor of a process for making living replicas of human beings, has unwittingly duplicated himself and becomes a secret weapon in the Solar System's struggle for economic survival against a powerful alien culture, the Sentients.

Dr Cook Paul Daneman
Wattari Marius Goring
Mrs Emily Cook Jean Aubrey
Brenner John Wood
Dr Duval Cyril Shaps

Easterbrook John Gabriel
Czesni John Hollis

Director: John Gibson
Designer: Raymond Cusick

(15 December 1966)

Walk's End

w William Trevor

Dr Saint's offer of a free place in his comfortable old-folks' home appears entirely philanthropic to Miss Claythorpe. However, he is suspiciously vague about the treatment that goes with it.

Dr Saint John Robinson
Mrs Dakers Brenda de Banzie
Maid Sally Travers
Matron Elizabeth Begley
Miss Claythorpe Susan Richards
Miss Ormsby Mary Hinton
Maj. Gregory Sebastian Shaw
Mr Bone Felix Aylmer
Mrs Hope Ailsa Grahame
Mr Wardle Henry Oscar
Mr Quire Carleton Hobbs
Manservants Sylvester Morand, Christopher Owen

Director: Ian Curteis
Designer: William McCrow

(22 December 1966)

Satisfaction Guaranteed

w Hugh Leonard, *from a story by* Isaac Asimov

First of two Asimov comedies about robots. Larry Belmont, an ambitious executive working for US Robots, embarks on a business trip, leaving his wife Claire to take charge of Tony – a robot which, though indistinguishable from a man, is programmed to do housework 24 hours a day, seven days a week.

Dr Inge Jensen Ann Firbank
K.G. Bullen Bruce Boa
Larry Belmont Barry Warren
Claire Belmont Wendy Craig
Brenda Claffern Helen Horton
Miriam Swann Valerie Colgan
Deirdre Schwartz Patty Thorne

Tony **Hal Hamilton**
Assistant **Rodney Archer**

Director: **John Gorrie**
Designer: **Norman James**

(29 December 1966, BBC2)
(BBC1 rpt: 22 April 1967)

The Prophet

w **Robert Muller,** *from the story* **The Reason** *by* **Isaac Asimov**
Dr Susan Calvin has seen some strange development in her 60 years as a robot psychologist, but none stranger than robot QT-1. (The character of Dr Calvin had also appeared in another Asimov story, *Little Lost Robot*, in the 1962 ITV anthology series *Out of This World*, and appears again in a Season Three episode, *Liar!*)
Dr Susan Calvin **Beatrix Lehmann**
Interviewer **James Cossins**
QT-1 **Tenniel Evans**
Greg Powell **David Healy**
Mike Donovan **Brian Davies**
Martha Powell **Julie Allan**
Abigail Donovan **Judy Keirn**
Van Muller **Michael Wolf**
Robots **Ron Eagleton, Robin Sherringham, Chris Blackwell, Jim Wyatt, Graham Lawson, George Rutland, Tony Barnes, Derek Davis**
Robot voices **David Graham, Haydn Jones, Roy Skelton**

Director: **Naomi Capon**
Designer: **Richard Henry**

(1 January 1967, BBC2)
(BBC1 rpt: 20 May 1967)

Season Three

Immortality Inc

w **Jack Pulman,** *from a story by* **Robert Sheckley**
An ageing man of the future reaches back into the 20th century for a 'young, active body' into which he can transfer his mind; and a young man from 1969 is suddenly transported into a strange and terrifying future.

Mark Blaine **Charles Tingwell**
Dr Cole **Robert MacLeod**
Tom Clarke **Derek Benfield**
Marie Thorne **Dallia Penn**
Earth Blaine **Peter Van Dissel**
Reilly **Peter Swanwick**
Reject **Donald Morley**
Theologian **Christopher Denham**
Sammy **Tom Rowman**
Hull **Peter Copley**
Irma Henderson **Nancie Jackson**
Davis **Tommy Eytle**
Clerk **Dee MacDonald**
Technicians **John Berwyn, Brian Cullingford, Edward Davies, John Gulliver, Tony Handy**

Director: **Philip Dudley**
Designer: **Peter Seddon**

(7 January 1969)

Liar!

w **David Campton,** *from a story by* **Isaac Asimov**
Robot RB34 is to be demonstrated to the press to quieten public concern about possible dangers from the growing number of robots. But RB34 has a fault – it is telepathic. Somehow it has been programmed to read minds – secret schemes, desires and all. And who is without his secrets?
Herbie (RB34) **Ian Ogilvy**
Dr Lanning **Hamilton Dyce**
Dr Susan Calvin **Wendy Gifford**
Dr Bogert **Gerald Sim**
Milton Ashe **Paul Chapman**
Hargreaves **Roy Hanlon**
Kelvin Brooke **Robert James**
Cleaner **Jumoke Debayo**
Brooke's secretary **Anna Perry**
Jamieson **Edwin Richfield**
Mary Curl **Jenny Russell**
Receptionist **Rita Davies**

Director: **Gerald Blake**
Designer: **Martin Johnson**
(14 January 1969)

The Last Lonely Man

w **Jeremy Paul,** *from a story by* **John Brunner**
Time: the future. The government of the

day has won many votes with the introduction of its new Contact Service just before the election. Contact banished the fear of death. A man's body may die, but his mind can now pass into someone still alive – a relative, friend or loved one. But what of the man who is friendless and unloved? He must make Contact with someone – whatever the cost.

James Hale George Cole
Rowena Hale June Barry
Patrick Wilson Peter Halliday
Man Norman Hartley
Girl Annabella Johnston
Ambulanceman Berry Fletcher
Police inspector Guy Standeven
Sir Barrimore Jones Gerald Young
Mary Lillias Walker
Sam Peter Welch
George Bryan Mosley
Young girl Gillian Shed
Young man Albert Lampert
Consultant Eve Ross
Goddard Anthony Woodruff
Jenkins Richard Wardale
Henry Stanley Meadows

Director: Douglas Camfield
Designer: Richard Wilmont
(21 January 1969)

Beach Head

w Robert Muller, *from a story by* Clifford Simak

Commandant Decker, disenchanted veteran of 36 faultless space missions, finds the cause and cure for his dissatisfaction when a new planet subtly defeats the 'infallible' technology which has hitherto overcome all eventualities, however unknown.

Tom Decker Ed Bishop
Cassandra Jackson Helen Downing
Bertrand Le Maitre John Gabriel
Oliver MacDonald James Copeland
A.G. Tiosawa Robert Lee
N.G. Waldron Vernon Dobtcheff
Ensign Warner-Carr Barry Warren

Director: James Cellan Jones
Designer: Tony Abbott

(28 January 1969)

Something in the Cellar

w Donald Bull

Eccentric professor Monty Lafcado, haunted by the powerful memory of his dead mother, builds a monster computer in his cellar.

Lafcado Milo O'Shea
Bettina June Ellis
Fred Murray Melvin
Dr Pugh Clive Morton
Inspector Clifford Cox
Sergeant Brian Grellis
Waitress Nova Sainte-Claire
Taxi driver Lane Meddick
Blonde Priscilla Tanner
Monster John Lawrence

Director: Roger Jenkins
Designer: John Wood

(4 February 1969)

Random Quest

w Owen Holder, *from a story by* John Wyndham

Physicist Colin Trafford is blown up in a laboratory accident and finds himself in a parallel world where he has a ready-made life as a novelist, a new group of friends and business acquaintances, and is married to a beautiful girl who apparently hates him. How can Colin explain that he is not the man she thinks he is?

Colin Trafford Keith Barron
Taxi driver George Lee
Ottilie Tracy Reed
Mrs Walters Beatrice Kane
Dr Harshom Noel Howlett
Munnings Arnold Ridley
George Charles Lamb
Martin Bernard Brown
TV newsreader McDonald Hobley
Gerry Carole Boyer
Trevor Bernard Finch
Bates Reg Peters
Laura Anna Darlington
Nurse Maclean Molly Weir
Mrs Gale Beryl Cooke

Director: Christopher Barry
Designer: Roy Oxley

(11 February 1969)

The Naked Sun

w Robert Muller, *from a story by* Isaac Asimov

Baley, a detective from Earth, is assigned to investigate a murder on the planet Solaria, where all the inhabitants live in isolation attended by a large number of robots, and communicating by a form of three-dimensional viewer.

Baley Paul Maxwell
Minnim Sheila Burrell
Daneel David Collings
Gruer Neil Hallett
Thool Erik Chitty
Attlebish Ronald Leigh-Hunt
Quemot John Robinson
Leebig Frederick Jaeger
Gladia Trisha Noble
Rikaine Paul Stassino
Bik John Hicks
Robots David Cargill, Raymond Hardy, Roy Patrick, John Scott Martin, Gerald Taylor

Director: Rudolph Cartier
Designer: James Weatherup

(18 February 1969)

The Little Black Bag

w Julian Bond, *from a story by* C.M. Kornbluth

An electronic medical kit of the future is accidentally transported back in time to the present day where it falls into the hands of a drunken, disqualified doctor, Roger Full, who builds up a successful practice in cosmetic surgery, while being blackmailed by a vicious young woman, Angie. (Also filmed in America for *Rod Serling's Night Gallery*.)

Dr Gillis Robert Dean
Mike James Chase
Dr Hemingway Dennis Bowen
Al Harvey Hall
Dr Roger Full Emrys Jones
Samuels Leon Cortez
Angie Geraldine Moffatt
First youth Bill Lyons
Second youth Peter King
Johnny Ian Frost
Edna Flannery Elizabeth Weaver
Mallinson Alan Downer

Mr Collins John Dunbar
Kelland John Woodnutt
Receptionist Katherine Kessey
Mrs Coleman Honora Blake

Director: Eric Hills
Designer: Barry Learoyd

(25 February 1969)

1 + 1 = 1.5

w Brian Hayles

Comedy set at the beginning of the next century. Britain is proud of its population control system, based on computer analysis and an anti-fertility factor. But national complacency is rudely shattered when Mary Beldon, the wife of a highly-esteemed population officer, becomes pregnant for the second time, though she is licensed for only one child.

Mary Beldon Julia Lockwood
Henry Beldon Garfield Morgan
John Stewart Bernard Horsfall
TV announcer Bernard Holley
Miss Harvey Lynda Marchal
Mrs Proctor Frances Bennett
Gosford Geoffrey Palmer
Minister Petra Davies
Secretary Clare Shenstone
First man Steve Peters
Second man Derek Chafer
Susanna Cloe Ashcroft
Reporter Juan Moreno
Yates Davyd Harries
Computer voice John Witty

Director: Michael Ferguson
Designer: Barry Learoyd

(4 March 1969)

The Fosters

w Michael Ashe

An old tramp is found dead with signs that someone had tried to operate on his head; a youth disappears; the wife of biochemist Harry Gerwyn falls into a coma which baffles the doctors. Then a caller, intro-ducing himself as Mr Foster, invites Gerwyn to visit him and his sister at a quiet suburban address. The Fosters appear a perfectly ordinary retired couple

– but they possess scientific knowledge far in advance of Gerwyn.

Bob Alan Ross
Geoff Anton Darby
Anne Pauline Cunningham
Miss Foster Freda Bamford
Mr Foster Richard Pearson
Sally Gerwyn Ann Penfold
Harry Gerwyn Bernard Hepton
Mary Gerwyn Yvonne Manners
Calton Kevin Stoney
Digby John Dawson
Geoff's mother Rose Hill
Japhet John Berwyn
Cazalet Richard Pescud

Director: Philip Dudley
Designer: Marilyn Taylor

(11 March 1969)

Target Generation

w Clive Exton, *from a story by* Clifford Simak

A puritan, superstitious, inward-looking community of the future is confined within The Ship. They have been there for generations and have long forgotten why. They know that one day they will feel a tremor in the ship, but only one man, John Hoff, has inherited the secret of what must be done when the tremor comes. (Remake of a version first scripted for ITV's *Out of This World* in 1962.)

Jon Hoff David Buck
Joe Manx Ronald Lacey
Joshua Owen Berry
Jon as a boy Gary Smith
Jon's father Godfrey Kenton
Mary Hoff Suzan Farmer
Martin Toke Townley
Mrs Kane Ruth Kettlewell
George Michael McGovern

Director: Roger Jenkins
Designer: Tony Abbott

(18 March 1969)

The Yellow Pill

w Leon Griffiths, *from a story by* Rog Phillips

Well-known psychiatrist John Frame is ·

asked by the police to examine a murderer. It seems a routine case, but the young man seems to possess startling powers and knows intimate details of the psychiatrist's private life. (This, too, was a remake of a version shown in *Out of This World*.)

John Frame Francis Matthews
Helen Carter Angela Browne
Insp. Slinn Glynn Edwards
Wilfrid Connor Stephen Bradley
Plain-clothes men Steve Peters, James Haswell
Radio voice Carl Conway

Director: Michael Ferguson
Designer: Roy Oxley

(25 March 1969)

Get off My Cloud

w David Climie, *from a story by* Peter Phillips

Science fiction writer Marsham Craswell has had a mental breakdown. Though lying inert on a hospital bed, in his mind he is living through one of his own fantasies. In an effort to bring him back to reality, a doctor uses a new device to link the writer's mind to that of the most level-headed man he knows, Pete, an Irish sports reporter. But when Pete finds himself in Craswell's bizarre world, he wonders if he was wise to take the job.

Young Pete Robert Duncan
Parnell Jon Croft
Pete Donal Donnelly
Stephen Peter Barkworth
Marsham Craswell Peter Jeffrey
Police Sgt Alec Ross
Taxi driver Royston Tickner
Garer Vicki Woolf

Director: Peter Cregeen
Designer: Raymond P. Cusick

(1 April 1969)

Season Four

Taste of Evil

w John Wiles

Stephen Chambers, a new master at Warby Stones school for 'ultra-intelligent boys', finds strange things happening to him. Reason tells him that they must be linked with the boys' Psychic Phenomena Club.

Chambers Maurice Roëves
Mackinley Peter Copley
Bellows Jack Lambert
Maurice Gerry Davis
Andrew John Moulder-Brown
Crabbe Sebastian Abineri
Sinclair Keith Skinner
Boston Martin Howells
Cull Ian Pigot
Matron Katherine Parr
with:
Boys John Ash, Norman Bacon, Paul Frazer, Brent Oldfield, Shane Raggett, David Smith, Mark Wilding

Director: Michael Ferguson
Designer: Paul Allen

(21 April 1971)

To Lay a Ghost

w Michael J. Bird
Young photographer Eric Carver and his bride Diana – a girl with a traumatic past – move into an old house with which she feels a strong affinity. When a ghost appears in pictures he takes of her in their new home, Eric calls in a psychic researcher – and precipitates a crisis.
Eric Carver Iain Gregory
Diana Lesley-Anne Down
Dr Phillimore Peter Barkworth
Ewan Mackenzie Clifford Cox
Police inspector Geoffrey Russell
Thomas Hobbs Walter Randall

Director: Ken Hannam
Designer: Fanny Taylor

(28 April 1971)

This Body Is Mine

w John Tully
Research physicist Allen Meredith discovers a means of transferring his mind into another man's body – but the process is reciprocal.
Jack Gregory Jack Hedley
Allen Meredith John Carson

Ann Meredith Alethea Charlton
Elizabeth Gregory Sonia Graham
George Simpson Hector Ross
Tony Randall Darryl Kavann
Sheila Norma West
John Pinner Anne Kidd
Harvey Bruno Barnabee
Rawlinson John Rolfe

Director: Eric Hills
Designer: Sally Hulke

(5 May 1971)

Deathday

w Brian Hayles, *from a story by* Angus Hall
Adam Crosse seems a normal, well-integrated member of society. But in reality, his marriage is a failure, he is a hypochondriac and a tranquilliser addict, needing only a final nudge to push him over the edge. One morning, his wife tells him she has a lover.
Adam Crosse Robert Lang
Lydia Crosse Lynn Farleigh
Quilter John Ronane
Postman Roy Evans
Stanley Hudson Lindsay Campbell
Dorothy Hudson Valerie Lush
Det. Chief Insp. Schofield Simon Merrick
Det. Sgt Roberts Leslie Schofield
Joanne Susan Glanville
Arnold Douglas Wells
Telephone operator Gina Manicorn
Newsreader Tim Gudgin

Director: Raymond Menmuir
Designer: John Stout

(12 May 1971)

The Sons and Daughters of Tomorrow

w Edward Boyd
The small East Anglian village of Plampton has one distinction – a famous unsolved murder. A cynical journalist decides to go there to see what he can stir up. But Plampton is a community linked by telepathy and led by a witch . . .
Shawlor Gascoyne William Lucas
Simon Willows Malcolm Tierney

Rosa Cavendish **Margery Withers**
Hamilton White **David Griffin**
Jeanette **Pamela Salem**
Wilfrid Russell **Arthur Pentelow**
Isiah **Christopher Reynolds**
PC Wilkes **Chris Tranchell**
Tom Palfrey **Edward Evans**
Dr Lesley Clifford **Brenda Kaye**
Coroner **Les Shannon**
Undertakers **Brian Jacks, Peter Wilson-Holmes**

Director: **Gerald Blake**
Designer: **David Spode**

(19 May 1971)

Welcome Home

w **Moris Farhi**
Psychiatrist Frank Bowers comes home after six months in hospital following an accident, to find another man in his place – a man who looks nothing like him, but who his wife and everyone else says is her husband.
Penny Powers **Jennifer Hilary**
Bowers-One **Anthony Ainley**
Bowers-Two **Bernard Brown**
Det.-Sgt Greene **Gerald Sim**
Dr Liam Moore **Derek Benfield**
Sam Sheppard **David Morrell**
Sheila Sherwood **Margaret Anderson**
John Sherwood **Alan Downer**
Miss Pringle **Pamela Craig**
PC Jones **David Munro**

Director: **Eric Hills**
Designer: **Sally Hulke**

(26 May 1971)

The Last Witness

w **Martin Worth**
A man, Harris, wakes up in a hotel on a small island after a shipwreck. He keeps recognising flashes of what he sees, until he realises his visions are of actions yet to come – culminating in murder.
Harris **Anthony Bate**
Mrs Kemble **Sheila Brennan**
Dr Benson **James Kerry**

Sgt Walker **Lawrence James**
David **Michael McStay**
Ann **Denise Buckley**
Businessman **Brian Sullivan**
Mrs Fane **Joyce Carey**
Barbara **Joanna Ross**
Bus driver **Milton Brehaut**

Director: **Michael Ferguson**
Designer: **Chris Pemsel**

(2 June 1971)

The Man in My Head

w **John Wiles**
A small group of soldiers have been briefed for a dangerous mission. But the briefing has been imprinted on their sub-conscious minds and can only be released by a special signal.
Stock **Martin Thurley**
Sanders **David Whitman**
Fulman **Robert Oates**
Camber **Robert Walker**
Brinson **Tom Chadbon**
Ira **Marianne Benet**
Denman **James Drake**
Lydia **Elizabeth Bell**
Hine **Kenneth Watson**

Director: **Peter Cregeen**
Designer: **Jeremy Davies**

(9 June 1971)

The Chopper

w **Nigel Kneale**
The vengeful spirit of a dead motorcyclist is reluctant to leave his wrecked machine and manifests itself to a woman journalist as motorbike noise.
Jimmy Reed **Patrick Troughton**
Chaser **George Sweeney**
Sandie **Margaret Brady**
Rupert Molloy **David Wood**
Lorna Venn **Ann Morrish**

Director: **Peter Cregeen**
Designer: **Tim Harvey**
(16 June 1971)

The Uninvited

w Michael J. Bird

A middle-aged couple are disturbed during the night by a series of unwelcome visitations.

George Pattison John Nettleton
Millicent Pattison June Ellis
Donald Ramsey Brian Wilde
Frances Mervyn Shirley Cain
Jack Mervyn Geoffrey Palmer
Jessica Ramsey Hilary Mason
Blonde woman Bobbie Oswald
PC Wheeler David Sinclair
Fuller David Allister

Director: Eric Mills
Designer: John Burrowes

(23 June 1971)

The Shattered Eye

w David T. Chantler

A chance meeting with an old tramp brings a violent force into a young painter's life.

Lester Freddie Jones
Alec Richard Warwick
Gwenn Tessa Wyatt
Gavin Peter Arne
Barton John Wentworth
Tony Sebastian Breaks
Randall James Copeland
Perris John Saunders
Jackson Lee Fox
Arcade manager Michael Lynch

Director: Peter Hammond
Designer: Chris Thompson

(30 June 1971)

OUT OF THIS WORLD

Considering ITV's timid approach to adult science fiction over the years, it seems somewhat remarkable to record that they can claim the honour of Britain's first series of science fiction plays. Yet there they were, straddling the summer of 1962, 13 one-hour dramas introduced by the master of the macabre, Boris Karloff.

And through the lineage of its creator, Irene Shubik, this pioneering anthology was also the ancestor of the BBC's prestigious *Out of the Unknown* (see previous entry). At the time, Shubik was ABC Television's story editor and had already established a strong track record in picking plays for *Armchair Theatre*.

For *Out of This World* she tapped the talents of leading sf writers including genre giants Isaac Asimov, Philip K. Dick and Clifford Simak, enlisting notable British TV writers such as Clive Exton and Leon Griffiths to adapt their stories. The series also featured the work of another promising writer – Terry Nation, later to become the creator of the Daleks, *Survivors* and *Blake's 7*.

Being an anthology, *Out of This World* found time and space to explore different styles and moods of science fiction, from the grimmer suspense of *Impostor*, *Botany Bay* and *The Dark Star*, through tender intrigue in *Medicine Show* and the macabre comedy of *Vanishing Act*, to broad satire in *The Tycoons*.

There was no shortage of familiar faces in the casts, with Peter Wyngarde, Jane Asher, Patrick Allen, Maurice Denham, Gerald Harper, Dinsdale Landen, Charles Gray, Geraldine McEwan and Ronald Fraser among the leading men and women.

Producer for the series was Leonard White, and the directors, drawn from ABC's drama stable, included Guy Verney, director of the *Pathfinders* trilogy. The 13 plays went out on Saturday nights at 10.00 pm, from 30 June.

(The principal British script in Shubik and White's original schedule, John Wyndham's *Dumb Martian*, was 'lifted' by ABC's drama boss Sydney Newman and shown in the preceding Sunday's *Armchair Theatre* slot as a curtain raiser to the series proper, with Boris Karloff appearing at the play's end to announce the impending start of the series, six days later. It is listed here, in that context, for ease of reference.)

REGULAR CAST
Host **Boris Karloff**

Story editor: **Irene Shubik**
Producer: **Leonard White**

An ABC Television Network Production
13 60-minute plays, black and white
30 June–22 September 1962

Dumb Martian

adapted from a story by **John Wyndham**
Too old to fly, 35-year-old boorish space pilot Duncan Weaver is drafted as keeper of a remote space station. To offset the loneliness, he buys Lellie, a Martian girl, as wife and housekeeper. Like all 'Marts', Lellie has a totally expressionless face, and Weaver treats her as little better than a dumb animal. But when an intelligent young geologist, Dr Alan Whint, joins them, Lellie becomes a point of conflict between the two men and proves to be not as dumb as her husband thought.
Reception clerk **Garfield Morgan**
Chief **Charles Morgan**
Duncan Weaver **William Lucas**
Harry **Michael Bird**
Mac **Michael Pratt**
Alastair **Morris Perry**
Lellie **Hilda Schroder**
Withers **Raymond Adamson**
Alan Whint **Ray Barrett**

Director: **Charles Jarrott**
Designer: **James Goddard**
Producer: **Sydney Newman**

An ABC Television Network Production
60 minutes, black and white for *Armchair Theatre*

(24 June 1962)

The Yellow Pill

dramatised by **Leon Griffiths**, *from a story by* **Rog Phillips**
An alleged murderer is brought by the police to psychiatrist Dr Frame, claiming that he was born in 1962 and comes from another time. Though a complete stranger, he possesses an uncanny knowledge of the doctor's private life. (Remade for *Out of the Unknown*.)
John Frame **Nigel Stock**
Michael Connor **Richard Pasco**
Insp. Slinn **Peter Dyneley**
Helen Carter (receptionist) **Pauline Yates**
with **Gerald Turner, Robert Pitt**

Director: **Jonathan Alwyn**
Designer: **Robert MacGowan**

(30 June 1962)

Little Lost Robot

dramatised by **Leo Lehman**, *from a story by* **Isaac Asimov**
The time: 2039. The place: Hyper Base 7, near Saturn. Black, an engineer, working on a space project, angrily tells a robot to 'get lost' – and the mechanical man takes him at his word, joining up with a group of 20 others who are in revolt against their

masters. Base commander Maj. Gen. Kallner sends for robot psychologist Susan Calvin who is very fond of robots and treats them like children. She is horrified to hear that the 'lost' robot has been modified.

Black Gerald Flood
Robot Roger Snowden
Peter Bogert Murray Hayne
Maj. Gen. Kallner Clifford Evans
Dr Susan Calvin Maxine Audley
Walensky Haydn Jones

Director: Guy Verney
Settings: Douglas James

(7 July 1962)

Cold Equations

adapted by Clive Exton, *from a story by* Tom Godwin

Teenager Lee Cross stows away on a mercy rocket flight taking life-saving serum to six men on the planet Woden, hoping to see her brother who has been there for eight years. But her extra weight means the rocket doesn't have enough fuel to reach its destination, presenting the pilot, Capt. Barton, with a difficult equation that he and ground control strive desperately to solve.

Bill May William Marlowe
Capt. Barton Peter Wyngarde
Perry Godfrey James
Selfe Patrick Holt
Commander Delhart Peter Williams
Lee Cross Jane Asher
Gerry Cross Richard Gale
Ship's records clerk Piers Keelan

Director: Peter Hammond
Designer: Paul Bernard

(14 July 1962)

Impostor

dramatised by Terry Nation, *from a story by* Philip K. Dick

Earth is at war with the Outspacers. Security officer Maj. Peters believes that an Outspace robot bomb is masquerading as top scientist Roger Carter. Condemned to death, a horrified Carter tries desperately to prove his innocence . . . or is Peters right?

Frank Nelson Glyn Owen
Maj. Peters Patrick Allen
Roger Carter John Carson
Jean Baron (Carter's secretary) Angela Browne
Paul Kirby Keith Anderson
Alan Richards Philip Anthony
Control Colin Rix
Security chief Paul Bacon
Darvi Louida Vaughan
Landon Alec Ross
Mary Carter June Shaw
Mute-O Walter Randall

Director: Peter Hammond
Designer: Robert Fuest

(21 July 1962)

Botany Bay

w Terry Nation

Psychiatry student Bill Sheridan discovers that patients at an institution where he is working are being possessed by aliens. When he reveals his belief he is forced to kill a 'possessed' orderly in self-defence. Convicted of murder, Sheridan is committed to the same clinic. His only hope of convincing the world that a covert invasion is taking place is to persuade his brother Dave and girlfriend Betty that he is not crazy . . .

Bill Sheridan William Gaunt
Pierce Storm Durr
Monroe Norman Johns
Adams Donald Douglas
Garfield Anthony Bate
Miss Hayes Virginia Stride
Dave Sheridan Julian Glover
Janitor Reginald Smith
Betty Madison Ann Lynn
Harding Richard Clarke
Wilson Peter Jesson
Tyler Aubrey Morris
Dr Polk Jerry Stovin

Director: Guy Verney
Designer: Douglas James

(28 July 1962)

Medicine Show

dramatised by Julian Bond, *from a story by* Robert Moore Williams

The close-knit community of a small American town is thrown into hysteria by the arrival of two mysterious medicine men whose remarkable cures seem to originate with a strange machine. Doctor's wife Lil Harmon tries to find out its secret – and why the two strangers ask only for seeds in payment.

Dr Harmon Alan MacNaughtan
Lil Harmon Jacqueline Hill
Sam Barrett Vic Wise
Ellen Madeleine Burgess
Yanvro Carl Bernard
Pienster Peter Madden
Silas Washam Nigel Arkwright
Mrs Washam Natalie Lynn
Donna Culver Elaine Millar
Jason Kemper Ken Wayne
Mrs Culver Margo Cunningham
Culver Rory MacDermot
Dr Lapham Martin Wyldeck
Sheriff Raymond Adamson

Director: Richmond Harding
Designer: Adrian Vaux

(4 August 1962)

Pictures Don't Lie

dramatised by Bruce Stewart *from a story by* Katherine Maclean

Radio research worker Nathen picks up signals coming from a spaceship hovering near Earth and succeeds in communicating with his 'opposite number' aboard the ship. Speech and pictures are received showing that the occupants are humanoid – and friendly. But can *they* trust *us*?

Nathen Gary Watson
Major Race Roger Avon
Butch Judy Cornwell
Col. Ford Reginald Marsh
Parker Blake Butler
Jacob Luke Milo O'Shea
Dr Trayne Madi Hedd
Bud Kenneth Watson
Journalists Richard Wilding, Gordon Sterne, David Hemmings
Commander Frank Gatliff

Aliens Bill Mills, Gary Wyler
Man from the Ministry Norman Claridge

Director: John Knight
Settings: Brian Currah

(11 August 1962)

Vanishing Act

w Richard Waring

Struggling, hen-pecked conjuror Edgar Brocklebank buys a box that once belonged to a famous dead magician, the Great Vorg, and becomes an instant success. But no one, least of all Edgar, can explain away the complete disappearance of his attractive assistants and countless objects and animals that have passed through his box.

Edgar Brocklebank Maurice Denham
Harold William Job
John Philip Grout
Freda Hoggin Jennifer Wilson
Harriet Brocklebank Joan Heath
Maj. Bentley Edward Dentith
Shop assistant Barry Wilsher
Customer Ivor Bean
Mr Hoggin Cameron Miller
Benjy Hoggin Terence Woodfield
Furrier John Frawley
Second furrier Evan Thomas
Reporter William Buck
Reg Herbert Richard Klee
Mr Daventry Robert Lankesheer
Schreiber David Lander
Nancy Sheena Marshe
Youth Donald Webster
Insp. Wright Derek Newark
Vorg Godfrey Quigley

Director: Don Leaver
Designer: Robert Fuest

(18 August 1962)

Divided We Fall

dramatised by Leon Griffiths, *from a story by* Raymond F. Jones

2033: Eddy, the world's most powerful computer, has accused synthetic beings, 'the Syns', of working as fifth columnists for a hostile space power. Syns can be identified by a variation in their brain waves. Tests become compulsory and all detected Syns are arrested. Scientist Arthur Bailey is called on to help. But two years on the planet Cyprian, without automation, have made him distrustful of Eddy and sceptical of the Syns' existence.

Dr Waldron **Ronald Radd**
Col. Tanner **Gerald Harper**
Dr Arthur Bailey **Bernard Horsfall**
Jean Bailey (his wife) **Ann Bell**
Burrows **John Barcroft**
Sheen **Ian Clark**
Passenger **Kenneth Keeling**
Dr Exner **Norman Scace**
'Eddy' **Piers Keelan**
Prison guard **Bill Mills**
Security guard **Marc Ashlyn**
Sir Gerald Christie **Clive Morton**

Director: **John Knight**
Designer: **Ann Spavin**

(25 August 1962)

The Dark Star

adapted by **Denis Butler,** *from the novel* Ape of London *by* **Frank Crisp**
A mysterious disease is sweeping through London, giving its victims superhuman strength in the early stages. Most alarmingly, however, it seems to be selecting targets, with each link in the chain leading a step higher in status. Where will it end and how did it start? Scotland Yard chiefs and scientist Dr Howard must find out – fast.

Joan Thurgood **Rosemary Miller**
Jim Thurgood **John Garvin**
George Chalmers **Michael Hawkins**
Miss Guthrie **Vanessa Thornton**
Commander Delabo **Bruce Beeby**
John Irvine **Jerome Willis**
Det. Sgt Grant **Ronald Wilson**
Supt Hartley **William Dextor**
Mrs Chalmers **Yvette Rees**
Dr Howard **Barrie Cookson**
Asst. Comm. Lucas **Keith Pyott**
Police Sgt. **Charles Bird**
Dr Kendal **John Moore**

Director: **Peter Hammond**
Designer: **Philip Harrison**

(1 September 1962)

Immigrant

adapted by **Terry Nation,** *from a story by* **Clifford Simak**
What is the secret of Kimon – the strange El Dorado planet, rich in mineral wealth, which only allows the very brightest minds to become immigrants, and from where no one has ever returned to spend the vast fortunes they have sent back to relatives on Earth? A baffled World Government asks the latest 'immigrant', Seldon Bishop, to solve the mystery.

Seldon Bishop **Gary Raymond**
Pat **Penelope Lee**
Maggie **Christine Shaw**
Johnston **Walter Glennie**
Roberts **Gary Hope**
Kate Bishop **Ann Saker**
Morley **John Horsley**
Kimonian man **Ian Shand**
Monty Archer **Bruce Boa**
Maxine **Vivienne Drummond**
For **Frank Singuineau**
Kimonian employment officer **Jill Melford**
David **Peter Layton**
Elaine **Jo Rowbottom**
Father **Donald Eccles**

Director: **Jonathan Alwyn**
Settings: **Voytek**

(8 September 1962)

Target Generation

adapted by **Clive Exton,** *from a short story by* **Clifford Simak**
A belief handed down through the centuries that when the Tremor comes it signifies the beginning of the End; a community where reading is heresy; and a letter marked 'to be opened only in an emergency'. These elements come together for Jon Hoff who *can* read and must decide whether the beginning of the End is emergency enough! (Remade for *Out of the Unknown*.)

Jon's father **Michael Golden**
Jon (as a boy) **Hugh Janes**
Jon Hoff **Dinsdale Landen**
Joe Manx **Paul Eddington**
Mary Hoff **Susan Maryott**
Martin **Edwin Finn**

Mrs Kane Ann Tirard
George Mathias Philip Madoc
Joshua Bert Palmer

Director: Alan Cooke
Designer: Douglas James

(15 September 1962)

The Tycoons

adapted by Bruce Stewart *from a story by* Arthur Sellings

When zealous taxman Oscar Raebone calls unexpectedly on the Project Research Company, a firm making novelty dolls, and encounters the Tycoons, mysterious strangers led by Abel Jones, he turns up a situation that can only be described as out of this world . . .

Abel Jones Charles Gray
Mary Jones Geraldine McEwan
Fred Smith John Cater
Miss Cook Patricia Mort
Oscar Raebone Ronald Fraser
Mr Starling Alastair Williamson
`Mr Crampsey* Edwin Apps
Bubbles Jill Curzon
Girl Sheree Winton

Director: Charles Jarrott
Designer: Patrick Downing

(22 September 1962)

THE OUTER LIMITS

'There is nothing wrong with your television set. Do not attempt to adjust the picture. We are controlling transmission . . . we will control the horizontal. We will control the vertical . . . For the next hour, sit quietly and we will control all you see and hear . . . You are about to participate in a great adventure. You are about to experience the awe and mystery which reaches from the inner mind to *The Outer Limits*.'

The Outer Limits was *the* bug-eyed monster show. Other series might explore the bizarre or the fantastic with the aim of exciting, amusing or merely arousing dormant grey cells, but this 1960s American anthology series was designed to scare the living daylights out of its audience.

Week after week, your television set was taken over by some of the creepiest aliens ever created for the small screen. These weren't cuddly ETs, these were full-blooded agents of terror, collectively dubbed 'the Bears' by producer Joseph Stefano.

Stefano, writer of the screenplay for Hitchcock's classic, *Psycho*, said of the grizzly creations: 'The Bear is that one splendid, staggering, shuddering effect that induces awe or wonder or tolerable terror . . .' And among his more memorable 'bears' were giant bugs with ugly humanoid faces for *The Zanti Misfits*, living rocks for *Corpus Earthling*, a shimmering mouthless Andromedan conjured up for *The Galaxy Being*, a flat-faced cyclops in *O.B.I.T.*, and *The Invisibles* – slug-like parasites that burrowed into their human hosts, attaching themselves to the spinal cord and dominating the subject's will.

But there was more to *The Outer Limits* than its monsters. Its brief was also to explore people and the nature of humanity through advancing and expanding diverse aspects of science such as time and space travel, other dimensions, strange experiments and alien psychologies.

The Outer Limits was created by television producer and playwright Leslie Stevens but it was Stefano who gave the show its discipline and its 'bears'. He encouraged the imaginative cinematography that won the series critical praise for its visual style – lots of low, wide-angled shots, deep shadows and dim lighting to heighten the tension and produce a 'film noir' look and feel.

The only 'regular' star apart from the disembodied voice of narrator Vic Perrin, was William O. Douglas Jr, who donned many of the outlandish monster costumes. But the show also gave big breaks to such 'promising' young actors as David McCallum, Robert Culp and Martin Landau.

The Outer Limits played in America between 1963 and 1965. Over here, the series was seen first on ITV in 1964, when Granada Television screened 34 episodes. Although it was picked up by some other ITV regions, this vintage series received its one-and-only, belated-but-welcome network showing when BBC2 transmitted *all* 49 episodes in 1980–1.

REGULAR CAST
Narrator **Vic Perrin**

Creator/executive producer: **Leslie Stevens**
Producers: **Joseph Stefano** *(Season One)* **Ben Brady** *(Season Two)*
Director of photography: **Conrad Hall**
Special effects: **Projects Unlimited, John Nickolaus, Kenneth Peach, M.B. Paul, Larry Butler, Frank Van Der Veer**
Music: **Dominic Frontiere, Harry Lubin** *(Season Two)*

A Daystar-Villa di Stefano Production for United Artists Television

49 60-minute episodes, black and white
UK premiere: 16 April 1964
(Granada)

(Author's note: as with many American series, the UK running order of *The Outer Limits* differed considerably from the original US seasons – and even varied around those ITV regions that took it. For ease of reference, the episodes are listed in the original American sequence, and are followed by title guides to the UK premiere run and the complete network showing on BBC2.)

Season One
32 episodes

The Galaxy Being

w **Leslie Stevens**
A radio station engineer experimenting with a 3-D TV receiver accidentally establishes contact with a friendly being from the galaxy Andromeda – and a surge of electrical power brings it to Earth where it causes unintentional terror.
Cast: **Cliff Robertson, Jacqueline Scott, Lee Philips, William O. Douglas, Mavis Neal, Allyson Ames**

Director: **Leslie Stevens**

The Hundred Days of the Dragon

w Allan Balter, Robert Mintz
The new US president is substituted with the agent of an Oriental despot who can alter skin structure and change his appearance.
Cast: Sidney Blackmer, Phil Pine, Mark Roberts, Nancy Rennick, Joan Camden, Clarence Lung, Richard Loo

Director: Byron Haskin

The Architects of Fear

w Meyer Dolinsky
A group of scientists create a fake alien to try to shock mankind from its course of self-destruction, but find that fear is not the answer . . .
Cast: Robert Culp, Geraldine Brooks, Leonard Stone, Martin Wolfson

Director: Byron Haskin

The Man with the Power

w Jerome Ross
A meek college professor acquires awesome and uncontrollable powers after a brain operation – powers to control interplanetary electro-magnetic forces.
Cast: Donald Pleasence, Priscilla Morrill, Edward C. Platt, Fred Beir

Director: Laslo Benedek

The Sixth Finger

w Ellis St Joseph *(additional material by Joseph Stefano)*
A scientist invents a machine that can speed up the process of evolution and tests it on a young, uneducated miner with immediate effect – the subject's forehead becomes higher, his fingers develop a third joint and the stub of a sixth finger begins to grow.
Cast: David McCallum, Edward Mulhare, Jill Haworth, Constance Cavendish, Nora Marlowe, Robert Doyle

Director: James Goldstone

The Man Who Was Never Born

w Anthony Lawrence
A spaceman passes through the time barrier into the future and finds Earth a barren desert – the result of Man's greed and selfishness. He brings back with him a battered, disfigured survivor from the 21st century – a man who can change the fatal course of history.
Cast: Martin Landau, Shirley Knight, John Considine, Karl Held, Maxine Stuart

Director: Leonard Horn

O.B.I.T.

w Meyer Dolinksy
A murder investigation reveals the existence of an alien via an electronic surveillance device.
Cast: Peter Breck, Jeff Corey, Harry Townes, Alan Baxter, Joanne Gilbert

Director: Gerd Oswald

The Human Factor

w David Duncan
The brains of two men are inadvertently switched during a secret experiment at a Greenland military base.
Cast: Gary Merrill, Harry Guardino, Sally Kellerman, Joe de Santis, Ivan Dixon

Director: Abe Biberman

Corpus Earthling

w Orin Borstein *(additional material by Lou Morheim and Joseph Stefano)*
A doctor overhears a sinister conversation between two 'rocks' planning to take over the Earth by possessing the bodies of humans. But is the plot real or all in his mind?
Cast: Robert Culp, Salome Jens, Barry Atwater

Director: Gerd Oswald

Nightmare

w Joseph Stefano
Creatures from the planet Ebon abduct some humans and subject their prisoners to an intensive interrogation.
Cast: Ed Nelson, James Shigeta, John Anderson, Martin Sheen, David Frankham, Bill Gunn

Director: John Erman

It Crawled Out of the Woodwork

w Joseph Stefano
A ball of dust sucked into a vacuum cleaner at the Energy Research Commission feeds on the motor's power and grows to an uncontrollable size.
Cast: Scott Marlowe, Kent Smith, Barbara Luna, Edward Asner, Michael Forrest, Joan Camden

Director: Gerd Oswald

The Borderland

w Leslie Stevens
Scientists and spiritualists open a door into the fourth dimension where they find everything is a mirror image of itself.
Cast: Nina Foch, Mark Richman, Gladys Cooper, Philip Abbott, Barry Jones, Gene Raymond, Alfred Ryder

Director: Leslie Stevens

Tourist Attraction

w Dean Riesner
A tycoon captures an enormous and supposedly extinct prehistoric fish while on a fishing cruise in South America.
Cast: Ralph Meeker, Henry Silva, Janet Blair, Jerry Douglas, Jay Novello

Director: Laslo Benedek

The Zanti Misfits

w Joseph Stefano
The dusty saloon of a Western ghost town – and a military garrison awaits the arrival of criminal exiles from the planet Zanti.
Cast: Bruce Dern, Michael Tolan, Robert F. Simon, Olive Deering, Claude Woolman

Director: Leonard Horn

The Mice

w Joseph Stefano, Bill S. Ballinger
(from an idea by Lou Morheim*)*
A cultural and scientific exchange has been arranged with the planet Chromo, and Earth awaits the arrival of the first Chromite.
Cast: Henry Silva, Diana Sands, Michael Higgins, Dabney Coleman, Ronald Foster, Hugh Langtry

Director: Alan Crosland Jr

Controlled Experiment

w Leslie Stevens
Two Martians decide to make a thorough investigation of an Earth murder, so they record, playback and analyse the actual killing.
Cast: Barry Morse, Carroll O'Connor, Robert Fortier, Grace Lee Whitney

Director: Leslie Stevens

Don't Open Till Doomsday

w Joseph Stefano
Eloping teenagers spend their wedding night in a room that has been unoccupied since 1929. In it is a box containing a particularly malevolent alien.
Cast: Miriam Hopkins, Russell Collins, Buck Taylor, Nellie Burt, Melinda Plowman, David Frankham

Director: Gerd Oswald

Z-Z-Z-Z-Z

w Meyer Dolinksy *(additional material by* Joseph Stefano)
An entomologist's new assistant is really a

queen bee in human form out to lure him into her world as a human drone.

Cast: Philip Abbott, Joanna Frank, Marsha Hunt, Booth Coleman

Director: John Brahm

The Invisibles

w Joseph Stefano

An undercover agent joins a secret society whose members have deliberately allowed their minds to be perverted by parasitic alien creatures.

Cast: Don Gordon, George Macready, Dee Hartford, Walter Burke, Tony Mordente, Neil Hamilton, Richard Dawson

Director: Gerd Oswald

The Bellero Shield

w Joseph Stefano, Lou Morheim

Experimenting with lasers, a scientist accidentally traps a space traveller from a remote light world. He is eager to learn the mysteries of the universe, but his wife tries to use the knowledge to her advantage.

Cast: Martin Landau, Sally Kellerman, Chita Rivera, Neil Hamilton, John Hoyt

Director: John Brahm

The Children of Spider County

w Anthony Lawrence

Five young geniuses vanish on the same day – and their father, an alien from a distant planet, arrives on Earth to claim his children.

Cast: Lee Kinsolving, Kent Smith, John Milford, Crahan Denton

Director: Leonard Horn

Specimen: Unknown

w Stephen Lord *(additional material by* Joseph Stefano)

An officer in an experimental spacecraft finds a strange limpet-like growth on the outside of the ship.

Cast: Stephen McNally, Richard Jaeckel, Arthur Batanides, Gail Kobe, Russell Johnson

Directors: Gerd Oswald *(and* Robert H. Justman*)*

Second Chance

w Lou Morheim *and* Lin Dane *(alias* Sonya Roberts*)*

A group of people board a space ride at a funfair – only to find it's the real thing.

Cast: Simon Oakland, Janet DeGore, Don Gordon, John McLiam

Director: Paul Stanley

Moonstone

w William Bast

Lunar Expedition 1 have established a base on the moon, and find a strange object that involves them in civil war on a distant planet.

Cast: Ruth Roman, Alex Nicol, Tim O'Connor, Curt Conway, Harri Rhodes

Director: Robert Flory

The Mutant

w Allan Balter *and* Robert Mintz*, from a story by* Joseph Stefano *and* Jerome Thomas

Earth's overflowing population has inhabited Annex One, a remote world with a climate similar to that of Earth. All goes well for the colonists until they meet . . . the 'thing'.

Cast: Larry Pennell, Warren Oates, Walter Burke, Betsy Jones-Moreland

Director: Alan Crosland Jr

The Guests

w Donald S. Sanford*, based on a tele-play by* Charles Beaumont

A drifter arrives at a house where time

stands still and where the residents are captives of a strange alien.

Cast: Geoffrey Horne, Nellie Burt, Vaughn Taylor, Gloria Grahame, Luana Anders

Director: Paul Stanley

Fun and Games

w Robert Specht, Joseph Stefano, *from a story by* Robert Specht
A man and a woman are mysteriously transported to a distant planet where they have been selected to fight beings from another world in a gladiatorial contest to the death, with the losers forfeiting the lives of their entire planet.

Cast: Nick Adams, Nancy Malone, Ray Kellogg, Bill Hart

Director: Gerd Oswald

The Special One

w Oliver Crawford *(additional material by* Joseph Stefano)
A private tutor engaged to give scientific training to a young boy is an alien from the planet Xenon – and his lessons are in conquest.

Cast: Richard Ney, Macdonald Carey, Flip Mark, Marion Ross

Director: Gerd Oswald

A Feasibilty Study

w Joseph Stefano
The Luminoids, grotesque inhabitants of a distant planet, select human beings for their slave labour.

Cast: Sam Wanamaker, Phyllis Love, Joyce Van Patten, David Opatoshu

Director: Byron Haskin

The Production and Decay of Strange Particles

w Leslie Stevens
A nuclear holocaust becomes imminent as a cluster of strange particles from another galaxy starts multiplying, unleashing incredible powers.

Cast: George Macready, Leonard Nimoy, Rudy Solari, Joseph Ruskin, Allyson Ames, John Duke, Signe Hasso

Director: Leslie Stevens

The Chameleon

w Robert Towne, *from a story by* Robert Towne, Lou Morheim *and* Joseph Stefano
An intelligence agent disguises himself as an alien to infiltrate a group of space creatures who have landed on Earth.

Cast: Robert Duvall, Henry Brandon, Howard Caine, Douglas Henderson

Director: Gerd Oswald

The Forms of Things Unknown

w Joseph Stefano
A group of women with murder on their mind encounter a man from the past, a corpse that won't lie down and an eerie house containing a thousand clocks. (Unused pilot for an unsold series *The Unknown.*)

Cast: David McCallum, Vera Miles, Sir Cedric Hardwicke, Barbara Rush, Scott Marlowe

Director: Gerd Oswald

Season Two
17 episodes

Soldier

w Harlan Ellison *(additional material by* Seeleg Lester*)*
A twist in time lands a soldier of the future in the present. He is the 'ultimate soldier', trained to utterly destroy his enemy. But who is his enemy? (Hugo award winner.)

Cast: Lloyd Nolan, Michael Ansara, Alan Jaffe, Tim O'Connor, Catherine McLeod, Jill Hill, Ralph Hart, Ted Stanhope

Director: Gerd Oswald

Cold Hands, Warm Heart

w Milton Krims, *from a story by* Dan Ullman

An astronaut returns in triumh from the first orbit of Venus. But his success is marred by strange dreams and inexplicable body temperature changes.

Cast: William Shatner, Geraldine Brooks, Malachi Throne, Lloyd Gough

Director: Charles Haas

Behold, Eck!

w John Mantley, *from a story by* William R Cox, *based on a novel by* Edwin Abbott

An eye specialist finds his lab wrecked, patients dead or in shock and babbling of strange beings. The doctor puts on a pair of his own glasses and sees . . . the Invisible.

Cast: Peter Lind Hayes, Joan Freeman, Parley Baer, Jack Wilson

Director: Byron Haskin

Expanding Human

w Francis Cockrell

A university professor experiments with a drug that expands human consciousness – which not only increases his sensitivity, but also his appearance.

Cast: Skip Homeier, Keith Andes, James Doohan, Vaughn Taylor, Aki Aleong, Mary Gregory, Barbara Wayne, Robet Doyle

Director: Gerd Oswald

Demon with a Glass Hand

w Harlan Ellison

Alien soldiers from the distant future invade Earth. Their mission: to try to stop a war that is to happen in the future between Earth and themselves. They capture what seems to be the last survivor – a man with a strange hand. (Hugo award winner.)

Cast: Robert Culp, Arline Martel, Steve Harris, Abraham Sofaer, Rex Holman, Robert Fortier

Director: Byron Haskin

Cry of Silence

w Robert C. Dennis, *based on a story by* Louis Charbonneau

Driving through a remote canyon, a couple are menaced by moving tumbleweeds.

Cast: Eddie Albert, June Havoc, Arthur Hunnicutt

Director: Charles Haas

The Invisible Enemy

w Jerry Sohl *(additional material:* Byron Haskin, Seeleg Lester, Ben Brady)

Holy sand sharks! The noble-minded, steel-nerved leader of an expedition to Mars is menaced by a strange monster that 'swims' in a sea of sand.

Cast: Adam West, Rudy Solari, Joe Maross, Chris Alcaide, Ted Knight, Bob Doqui, Peter Marko, Mike Mikler, Anthony Costello, James Tartan

Director: Byron Haskin

Wolf 359

w Seeleg Lester, *based on a story by* Richard Landau

A scientist solves the secrets of creation by reproducing a miniature planet. But its development is so accelerated that it soon surpasses Earth and a potential nightmare is unleashed.

Cast: Patrick O'Neal, Sara Shane, Ben Wright, Peter Haskell

Director: Laslo Benedek

I, Robot

w Robert C. Dennis, *based on stories by* Otto Binder

A robot is accused of murder. The authorities insist on its destruction but its owner insists on the due process of law and hires an attorney to defend it.

Cast: Howard da Silva, Ford Rainey, Leonard Nimoy, Marianna Hill, John Hoyt, Hugh Sanders, Read Morgan

Director: Leon Benson

The Inheritors

w Sam Newman, Seeleg Lester, *from an idea by* Ed Adamson *(A 2-part story)*
Four soldiers, struck by bullets handmade from the ore of a meteorite, develop a powerful alien intelligence that turns them into geniuses. They embark on a mysterious project involving a number of handicapped children.
Cast: Robert Duvall, Steve Ihnat, Ivan Dixon, Dee Pollack, James Frawley, Ted De Corsia

Director: James Goldstone

Keeper of the Purple Twilight

w Milton Krims, *based on a teleplay by* Stephen Lord
A sinister creature from outer space exchanges its advanced knowledge with a scientist's human emotions – but finds itself unable to understand such things as love and beauty.
Cast: Warren Stevens, Robert Webber, Gail Kobe, Curt Conway, Edward C. Platt

Director: Charles Haas

The Duplicate Man

w Robert C. Dennis, *from a story by* Clifford Simak
A 21st-century space anthropologist creates a duplicate of himself to recapture an escaped alien creature obsessed with a single emotion – hate.
Cast: Ron Randell, Sean McClory, Constance Towers, Mike Lane, Alan Gifford

Director: Gerd Oswald

Counterweight

w Milton Krims, *based on a short story by* Jerry Sohl
Six carefully chosen passengers board a spaceship for a flight to a distant planet. But an alien force, fearing for its own security, creates terror and panic aboard the vessel.

Cast: Michael Constantine, Jacqueline Scott, Larry Ward, Charles Hradilac, Shary Marshall, Crahan Denton

Director: Paul Stanley

The Brain of Colonel Barham

w Robert C. Dennis, *from a story by* Sidney Ellis
Space explorer Alec Barham, suffering from an incurable disease, consents to have his brain transplated into a robot man.
Cast: Grant Williams, Elizabeth Perry, Anthony Eisley *(Barham)*, Douglas Kennedy, Martin Kosleck, Peter Hansen, Wesley Addy, Paul Lukather, Robert Chadwick

Director: Charles Haas

The Premonition

w Sam Roeca, Ib Melchoir, *from a story by* Sam Roeca
A test pilot is about to crash when suddenly time stands still and the world around him freezes. As he struggles to return to the animate present, great danger threatens his family.
Cast: Dewey Martin, Mary Murphy, William Bramley, Emma Tyson, Dorothy Green, Kay Kuter

Director: Gerd Oswald

The Probe

w Seeleg Lester, *from a story by* Sam Neuman
A cargo plane flies into a hurricane and ditches into the sea. The crew scramble into a liferaft and run aground on a strange solid surface.
Cast: Mark Richman, Peggy Ann Garner, Ron Hayes, Janos Prohaska

Director: Felix Feist

For title guide to UK runs see page 306.

UK premiere run:
25 episodes
16 April–8 October 1964
(Granada Television)

The Hundred Days of the Dragon
It Crawled Out of the Woodwork
The Man Who Was Never Born
O.B.I.T.
The Sixth Finger
The Galaxy Being
The Zanti Misfits
Borderland
Controlled Experiment
Don't Open Till Doomsday
The Bellero Shield
The Man with the Power
Z-Z-Z-Z-Z
The Children of Spider County
Corpus Earthling
The Mutant
Specimen: Unknown
The Architects of Fear
The Special One
The Forms of Things Unknown
The Chameleon
A Feasibility Study
Moonstone
The Invisibles
Second Chance

followed by . . .
nine episodes
9 July–23 December 1966

The Inheritors (double-length episode)
Soldier
The Invisible Enemy
Expanding Human
Cry of Silence
The Brain of Colonel Barham
Counterweight
Demon with a Glass Hand

UK network run
49 episodes
(BBC2)

28 March–18 July 1980
Demon with a Glass Hand
Keeper of the Purple Twilight
Moonstone
Soldier

The Premonition
The Hundred Days of the Dragon
The Invisibles
Counterweight
The Man with the Power
The Sixth Finger
The Galaxy Being
The Man Who Was Never Born
I, Robot
It Crawled Out of the Woodwork
O.B.I.T.
The Human Fcator
Nightmare

15 August–19 September 1980
The Zanti Misfits
Borderland
Controlled Experiment
The Mice
Don't Open Till Doomsday
Z-Z-Z-Z-Z

22 November–13 December 1980
Second Chance
Children of Spider County
Behold Eck!
The Architects of Fear

10 January–7 March 1981
The Bellero Shield
The Mutant
Fun and Games
Production and Decay of Strange
   Particles
The Special One
The Chameleon
A Feasibility Study
The Forms of Things Unknown
Cold Hands, Warm Heart

3 April–17 July 1981
Corpus Earthling
Expanding Human
Cry of Silence
The Invisible Enemy
Wolf 359
Tourist Attraction
The Probe
The Guests
Specimen: Unknown
The Inheritors (2-parts)
The Duplicate Man
The Brain of Colonel Barham

PATHFINDERS . . .

A generation of sci-fi fans cut their teeth on adventures such as this trilogy of children's space serials, packaged as part of ITV's Sunday 'Family Hour' in 1960–1.

The three stories, *Pathfinders in Space*, *Pathfinders to Mars* and *Pathfinders to Venus*, continued the interplanetary adventures of the space family Wedgwood, launched in the spring of 1960 with *Target Luna* (see separate entry).

Initially, the formula was much the same as *Target Luna*, with Prof. Wedgwood's daring young son Jimmy and his pet hamster Hamlet repeating their rocket ride to the Moon (though this time his brother, sister and dad made the trip, too, and they actually landed there.) The later serials widened the field, introducing new characters, new destinations – and even new sets. Designer David Gillespie filled the Teddington studios with foam plastic to create a Martian landscape of lichen and quicksand; while on *Pathfinders in Space*, Canadian designer Tom Spaulding devised an alien space-ship made entirely of triangles – even down to the light fittings and seats.

Among the new faces were Gerald Flood as science reporter and all-round good guy Conway Henderson, Pamela Barney as Moon Buff Prof. Mary Meadows, George Coulouris as Harcourt Brown, a fanatic convinced that life exists on other worlds, and Graydon Gould (voice of Mike Mercury in *Supercar*) as an American astronaut Capt. Wilson.

All three sagas were scripted by Malcolm Hulke and Eric Paice with an eye to the possible, if not the probable . . . (Hulke later joined the ranks of the *Doctor Who* writers, contributing several stories between 1967 and 1974, notably *The War Games* which first introduced the Time Lords and explained the Doctor's origins, and both men wrote regularly for *The Avengers*).

(NB. These *Pathfinders* serials should not be confused with an ITV drama series of the Seventies, called *Pathfinders*, which was about the exploits of a wartime RAF bomber squadron.)

REGULAR CAST

Prof. Wedgwood **Peter Williams** *(Story One regular only)*
Geoffrey Wedgwood **Stewart Guidotti**   *Conway Henderson* **Gerald Flood**
Prof. Mary Meadows **Pamela Barney**   *John Field* **Astor Sklair**
Harcourt Brown **George Coulouris** *(Stories 2,3)*
Margaret Henderson **Hester Cameron** *(Stories 2, 3)*
Ian Murray **Hugh Evans**   *Jimmy Wedgwood* **Richard Dean** *(Story One only)*
Valerie Wedgwood **Gillian Ferguson** *(Story One only)*

Producer: **Sydney Newman**   *ABC Television Network Productions*
Programme advisor: **Mary Field**

Story One:

Pathfinders in Space

w Malcolm Hulke *and* Eric Paice
A sequel to *Target Luna*. Rocket man Prof. Wedgwood heads the first team of Moon explorers, successfully blasting off from his Scottish rocket station, Buchan Island, in MR1 (Moon Rocket One). When his back-up supply rocket fails due to the automatic pilot cracking up, science reporter Conway Henderson and the Wedgwood brood decide to pilot the ship manually, determined to save the mission. As both rockets fly on towards the Moon, a third craft appears from nowhere. The Wedgwood rockets duly land on the Moon – but they are 150 miles apart. While Prof. Wedgwood treks across the lunar desert, the others explore some caverns, discovering a calcified figure and an ancient alien spaceship – evidence that a previous civilisation had been there before them. As the reunited explorers prepare to return to Earth, one of their rockets is destroyed by meteorites. It takes a daring scheme by Prof. Wedgwood to get them *all* home safely, using the alien craft.
Dr O'Connell Harold Goldblatt
Jean Cary Irene Sutcliffe
Michael Kennedy Michael Guest

Director: Guy Verney
Designers: Tom Spaulding *(Eps 1, 3–7),* David Gillespie (Eps 1–2)

Seven 30-minute episodes, made in black and white

Convoy to the Moon
Spaceship from Nowhere
Luna Bridgehead
The Man in the Moon
The World of Lost Toys
Disaster on the Moon
Rescue in Space

11 September–23 October 1960

Story Two

Pathfinders to Mars

w Malcolm Hulke *and* Eric Paice
Hard on the heels of his last lunar expedi-
tion, Prof. Wedgwood plans another mission to the Moon. Unable to pilot his new rocket, MR4, due to a broken arm, Wedgwood entrusts the task to his friend Conway Henderson. With Wedgwood's eldest son Geoffrey, Henderson's young niece Margaret, Prof. Meadows (and, of course, Hamlet the pet hamster) the party await the arrival of the last crew member, Australian scientist Prof. Hawkins. However, unknown to them, they are joined instead by an impostor, Harcourt Brown, a fanatical sci-fi writer determined to prove that life exists on Mars – whatever the cost. Brown hijacks the rocket, holding Margaret hostage, and after six weeks enforced journey the MR4 reaches the red planet only to find airless deserts and dust. Searching for precious water for the journey back to Earth, the crew encounter terrifying quick-growing lichens and dangerous quicksands. But with Earth moving away from Mars at 20 miles a second, the explorers must leave soon or face 16 months in the lifeless Martian desert. With not enough fuel to get home, Henderson risks using the Sun's pull to aid their efforts
(Prof. Wedgwood Peter Williams *(Ep. 1 only)*
Prof. Hawkins Bernard Horsfall *(Eps 1–2 only)*

Director: Guy Verney
Designer: David Gillespie

Six 30-minute episodes, made in black and white

The Imposter
Sabotage in Space
The Hostage
Lichens!
Zero Hour on the Red Planet
Falling Into the Sun

11 December 1960–15 January 1961

Story Three

Pathfinders to Venus

w Malcolm Hulke *and* Eric Paice
While returning to Earth from their perilous journey to Mars, the MR4 inter-

By the power of the Adamcos! Geoffrey Bayldon leapt through time as the eccentric wizard 'Catweazle'

Davros (Michael Wisher), creator of the Daleks, in the 'Doctor Who' story Genesis of the Daleks

The third regeneration of 'Doctor Who', Jon Pertwee, with Elisabeth Sladen as Sarah Jane Smith aboard one of the series' lesser-known craft, the Whomobile, in the 1974 story 'The Planet of the Spiders'

Heroic astronaut Steve Zodiac, glamorous medic Venus and pet Zoonie joined the supermarioned crew of Gerry Anderson's first space fantasy 'Fireball XL5' in 1962's giant leap for puppetkind

'Gigantor' and his gang – Inspector Blooper, Dick Strong, Jimmy Sparks and Dr Bob Brilliant

The classic shot: David Vincent (Roy Thinnes) was forever on the run from 'The Invaders'

Above left: 'The invisible Man' Peter Brady and his niece Sally (Deborah Watling) go on a 1958 publicity walkabout at the Tower of London

Above right: lost in the 'land of the Giants' the hapless crew of the *Sprindrift* find life is a lot larger than the one they left behind

Left: Ray Walston (top) and Bill Bixby teamed up as 'Uncle' Martin and Tim O'Hara in the hugely popular 1960s sitcom 'My Favourite Martian'

'Out of This World' host Boris Karloff (Centre) on the set of the series' fourth play 'Imposter' with cast members (from left) Angela Browne, Patrick Allen, John Carson, June Shaw and Glyn Owen

Above: it may look like Del Boy's three-wheeler, but this mean machine was part of the elite Earth Space Control Fleet in 'Phoenix Five'

Left: this well-dressed monster was one of the parents of Spider County, come to reclaim his children in an episode of 'The Outer Limits'

Queen's Pawn Number Six (Patrick McGoohan) plays human chess in 'The Prisoner' episode Checkmate

John Mills was the last of the fabled quartet of TV professors in Nigel Kneale's 'Quatermass'

Glamour and grit: ex-New Avenger Joanna Lumley and retired man from UNCLE, David McCallum (above) as time detectives 'Sapphire & Steel'

Richard Coleman plunged uncharted depths of villainy as underwater scientist Dr Deraad in ITV's 1963 serial 'Secret Beneath the Sea'

Season Two of Gerry Anderson's galactic fantasy 'Space: 1999' saw the arrival of Catherine Schell as Maya, the series' glamorous resident alien, who had the power to transform herself into any animal

The forgotten heroes of TV puppet fantasy – Husky the Martian, the Gabblerdictum bird, Slim the Venusian and Captain Larry Dart – together they cruised the solar system in 'Space Patrol'

'Star Maidens' Fulvia (Judy Geeson) and Andrea (Uschi Mellin) in pursuit of their runaway men

Dressed for the moon: little Jimmy Wedgwood (Michael Hammond) in 1960's 'Target Luna'

Hard-pressed scientists Tony Newman (James Darran) and Doug Phillips (Robert Colbert) found no light relief at the end of 'The Time Tunnel' — they invariably emerged into an epic war or disaster

Simon (Spencer Banks) and Liz (Cheryl Burfield) in the 'Timeslip' story, The Year of the Burn-Up

A youthful William Shatner with Patricia Breslin in 'The Twilight Zone' tale, Nick of Time

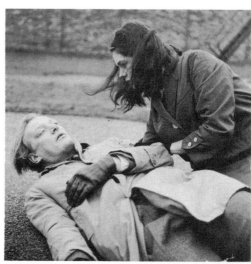

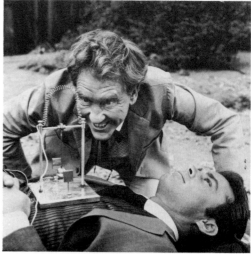

Above: reflections in the water face Straker (Ed Bishop) and Foster (Michael Billington): 'U.F.O.'

Top right: Jeremy Kemp and Rosemary Nicol in 'Undermind'. Right: Burgess Meredith plots the demise of Robert Conrad in 'The Wild, West West'

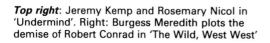

cepts a distress call being beamed from Venus by an American astronaut, Capt. Wilson. Responding to the SOS, they divert to Venus but all they find is the astronaut's ransacked spaceship – and evidence of alien life. Harcourt Brown wanders off, finds Capt. Wilson and persuades him to go with him in search of the Venusians. Pursuing them, the rest of the crew are threatened by carnivorous plants, cornered by primitive ape-men, trapped by roof-falls, menaced by molten lava and attacked by pterodactyls. Escaping all that, they head back to the MR4, only to find that the volcanic ash has turned the area into a raging inferno. Escape seems impossible but a little détente goes a long way, as a Russian ship is on the way with vital fuel supplies. Harcourt Brown, however, elects to remain on Venus to continue his quest for a higher intelligence.

Capt. Wilson **Graydon Gould**
Venusian **Bob Bryan** *(Eps 4–5, 8)*

Venusian child **Brigid Skemp** *(Eps 5–8)*
Col. Korolyov **Robert James** *(Ep. 8)*

Directors: **Guy Verney** *(Eps 1–5, 7)*
  Reginald Collin *(Eps 6, 8)*
Script associate: **Ivan Roe**
Designers: **David Gillespie** *(Eps 1–8)*
  Douglas James *(Eps 6–8)*
Special effects: **Derek Freeborn**

Eight 30-minute episodes, made in black and white

SOS From Venus
Into the Poison Cloud
The Living Planet
The Creature
The Venus People
The City
The Valley of the Monsters
Planet on Fire

5 March–23 April 1961

PHOENIX FIVE

Low-budget Australian space series that cheaply went where Star Trek had boldly gone before.

It followed the adventures of the crew of the galactic patrol ship *Phoenix Five*, 'the most sophisticated craft in the Earth Space Control Fleet'.

This handpicked team – Captain Roke, a typical Kirk clone with a solution to every problem; Ensign Adam Hargraves, a young space cadet always ready to shoot first and skip the questions; compassionate Cadet Tina Culbrick; and their computeroid Carl – roamed the planets protecting galactic citizens and warding off the repeated plots and attacks of the evil humanoid Zodian and a rebel scientist Platonus. The latter, a chip off the Ming block, dreamt of ruling the galaxies. By means of his computer, he subverted an innocent victim whom he used in an attempt to capture or destroy the Phoenix and its crew.

The series' limitations were apparent in the lack of supporting players, few sets (Platonus was invariably seen threatening all and sundry from the same set each time), the standard quarries and scrubland doubling as alien worlds, and very little model work – mostly just the Phoenix craft flying through space.

Each tale had a happy ending and a strong moral message.

About a third of the ITV network took the series – or some of it – in 1970, with STV leading the way. Some other regions, including London Weekend and Anglia, gave it a belated run in 1976.

REGULAR CAST

Captain Roke **Mike Dorsey**   Ensign Adam Hargraves **Damien Parker**
Cadet Tina Culbrick **Patsy Trench**   Carl **Stuart Leslie**
Earth Space Controller **Peter Collingwood**
Zodian **Redmond Phillips**   Platonus **Owen Weincott**

Writer/script editor: **John Warwick**
Director: **David Cahill**
Producers: **Peter Summerton** (Eps 1–10), **John Walters** (Eps 11–26)*

An Artransa Park Production in association with the Australian Broadcasting Commission
26 colour 25-minute episodes
10 January–3 July 1960
(STV)

* Took over following death of Peter Summerton.

Zone of Danger

Introducing the handpicked crew of *Phoenix Five*, assigned to patrol space and thwart the megalomaniacal designs of their arch-enemy Zodian.

Two Heads Are Better Than One

An emissary from the planet Tylantia begs for an audience with the controller. A large force field is closing in and threatens to destroy his planet. Roke and his crew are sent to investigate.

Human Relics

Aboard the *Phoenix Five*, the crew receive a strange signal from the asteroid Arcticus. Responding, they find a 20th-century space capsule and an astronaut in a coma.

The Stowaway

On rest leave, the crew are indulging in a 20th-century game of baseball when Adam is overcome by a strange chameleon.

The End Is to Begin

On a routine galactic patrol, Roke's crew see the planet Lionicus explode and sight a cargo ship off-course. Roke and Adam investigate and find the crew all missing.

Six Guns of Space

On a routine patrol, the *Phoenix Five* runs into an old-fashioned naval-style bombardment coming from one of the moons of Corallus.

The Pirate Queen

The Phoenix is escorting a cargo ship carrying vital medical supplies to an Earth space colony when the vessels are attacked by an old space frigate.

Two Into One Won't Go

Zodian devises a new plan to destroy Earth Control and rule the Federated Galaxies of Space. He bribes the pompous governor of Planetoid 93 into injecting a micro transistor into Capt. Roke's bloodstream.

Back to Childhood

Cadet Tina finds a rare Cannibalis plant which Capt. Roke decides to take back to Earth Control for examination.

A Sound in Space

Ensign Adam Hargraves 'materialises' a copy of the Pipes of Pan. He and Tina are hit by an unseen force when he blows a 'dead' note on the pipes. Carl the Computeroid absorbs the ultrasonic sound and sets out to discover the source.

A Gesture from Kronos

Capt. Roke is 'reversed' when he falls victim to a Zodian time warp. He talks backward, his uniform colours are reversed. His reaction powers are severely tested as he flies the Astro Scout Ship to the one person who can help him – Kronos, the guardian of time in space.

The Cat

Investigating the mysterious disappearance of the colonists of the planet Lynxonia, the Phoenix crew find just one clue – a tiny black kitten. Surely it could not be responsible for strange growling noises heard in the planet's dark rocky areas.

The Baiter is Bitten

The *Phoenix Five* flies into a strange phenomenon – fog, followed by rain and then deep water, causing the reactors to seize up, trapping the crew.

The Hunter

Platonus bribes the hunter king of a deserted planet to track down and kill the crew of the *Phoenix Five*.

Slave Queen

Roke is ordered to find the missing successor to the throne of Celex – a girl called Estella who was captured as a child by a warlike and backward race from another world.

Space Quake

A doctor on a dying planet injects Adam with an ageing serum but will only supply the antidote in return for safe passage to another planet.

The Planet of Fear

Exploring a strange planet, Roke and Adam meet an astronaut who was lost ten years earlier, and has acquired mysterious powers from the evil Platonus, turning him into a human booby trap.

Something Fishy

Phoenix Five is sent to find out why contact has been lost with the prison colony on the planet Zedden.

Toy Soldier

Tina shows Adam a tiny antique toy soldier she has bought while on leave.

The Bigger They Are

Platonus programmes a young gentle giant to destroy the *Phoenix Five* and her crew.

Shadow Ship

Returning to Earth for a routine check, Tina is struck down by an agonising virus.

Efficiency Minus

The crew are shocked when told they have failed their annual check-ups and will have to be separated.

Spark From a Dying Fire

Adam and Tina fall victim to the hypnotic powers of the strange sparks erupting from a fiercely destructive asteroid, and are set to fight a duel.

A Little Difficulty

Phoenix Five, pride of Earth Space Control's Galactic Fleet, disappears!

Dream City

Computeroid Carl picks a flower for Tina, unaware that Platonus has programmed him to pick a very special flower . . .

General Alarm

Roke and his crew are assigned to collect a reformed tyrant from a prison planet and return him to Earth.

PLANET OF THE APES

1974 adventure series based on the hugely successful film of the same name, with Ape star Roddy McDowall recreating his sympathetic role as the young chimp Galen.

Thrust a thousand years into the future when their spacecraft passes through a time warp, astronauts Alan Virdon and Pete Burke find the world has been turned upside down – the apes are the rulers, men little more than menials, technology virtually non-existent.

The main narrative thrust of the series is of the apes pursuing the astronauts whose superior knowledge could destabilise the simian society and threaten the ascendancy of the apes. Virdon and Burke, meanwhile, cling to the hope of finding a way of getting back to their own time.

But though essentially aimed at providing action entertainment for a family audience, the series did retain some of the flavour of Pierre Boulle's original allegorical novel, making a few trenchant observations on man's morality, prejudices and fears through the creation of the ape society in which orang-utans were the ruling class, gorillas the muscle-headed enforcers and chimpanzees the intellectuals. This aspect of the series was not lost on the British critics who gave it their blessing.

It is the thoughtful chimp Galen who befriends the astronauts and becomes their ally in the flight from the gorilla leader Urko. The other leading ape is the orang-utan councillor Zaius who spends much of his time trying to moderate the excesses of Urko. Roddy McDowall and the other 'ape' actors endured gruelling three-and-a-half hour make-up sessions to achieve the distinctive simian look.

Planet of the Apes premiered in Britain in October 1974 for a run that included most of the ITV network, and the series was a great success, regularly pulling in audiences of up to 12 million. But in

America it achieved a modest 27 per cent rating – three below the required maximum – and paymasters CBS abruptly halted production after just 14 of the scheduled 24 episodes, leaving the story hanging (literally) in mid-air.

REGULAR CAST

Galen Roddy McDowall   *Virdon* Ron Harper   *Burke* James Naughton
Urko Mark Lenard   *Zaius* Booth Colman

Producer: Stan Hough
Executive Producer: Herbert Hirschman
Make-up: Dan Striepeke

A 20th Century Fox Television Production for CBS
14 colour, 60-minute episodes
13 October 1974–19 January 1975
(London Weekend Television)

Escape from Tomorrow

w Art Wallace
Passing through a time warp, astronauts Virdon and Burke land back on Earth in an unimaginable future. Captured by gorillas, they find an ally in Galen who is fascinated by their origin. He helps them escape back to their spaceship where Virdon retrieves a magnetic memory disc that might help them return to the past, and the three become fugitives.
Farrow Royal Dano
Turvo Ron Stein
Veska Woodrow Parfrey
Ullman Biff Elliot
Proto Jerome Thor
Grundig William Beckley
Arno Bobby Porter

Director: Don Weiss

The Gladiators

w Art Wallace
The loss of the precious magnetic disc causes Burke and Virdon to become involved with gladiators, the burly Tolar and his reluctant son Dalton.
Jason Pat Renella
Tolar William Smith
Dalton Marc Singer
Barlow John Hoyt
Gorilla sergeant Eddie Fontaine

Director: Don McDougall

The Trap

w Edward J. Lasko
When Burke and Urko are trapped by an earthquake in an old San Francisco subway tunnel, Virdon and Galen get ape soldiers to cooperate in a rescue. Meanwhile, in the tunnel, Urko is enraged when he sees an old zoo poster showing caged apes being fed peanuts.
Zako Norm Alden
Mema Ron Stein
Olam Eldon Burke
Miller John Milford
Jick Mickey Leclair
Lisa Cindy Eilbacher

Director: Arnold Laven

The Good Seeds

w Robert W. Lenski
When Galen is wounded, the fugitives take refuge at a gorilla farm where they win over their hosts by teaching them some valuable lessons about farming and saving the hostile son's valuable cow which goes into a difficult labour to give birth to twins.
Anto Geoffrey Deuel
Polar Lonny Chapman
Zantes Jacqueline Scott
Remus Bobby Porter
Jillia Eileen Ditz Elber
Gorilla officer Dennis Cross

Director: Don Weiss

The Legacy

w Robert Hamner

In the ruins of a one-time city Virdon and Burke hope to find a key that could unlock their past. Instead, they barely escape the pursuing gorillas – aided in part by a young woman, Arn, and an opportunist street urchin, Kraik.

Scientist Jon Lormer
Gorilla captain Robert Phillips
Gorilla sergeant Wayne Foster
Kraik Jackie Earle Haley
Arn Zina Bethune

Director: Bernard McEveety

Tomorrow's Tide

w Robert W. Lenski

Virdon and Burke are captured by the chimp head of a fishing colony and nearly find themselves enslaved.

Hurton Roscoe Lee Browne
Romar Jim Storm
Soma Kathleen Bracken
Gahto John McLiam
Bandor Jay Robinson

Director: Don McDougall

The Surgeon

w Barry Oringer

When Virdon is shot and seriously wounded, Galen and Burke work out an elaborate scheme to enlist the aid of Kira, a female ape who is a surgeon.

Kira Jacqueline Scott
Leander Martin Brooks
Haman Ron Stein
Travin Michael Strong
Girl Janie Smith Jackson
Jordan Phil Montgomery

Director: Arnold Laven

The Deception

w Anthony Lawrence

Burke becomes the object of the affections of a blind female ape, Fauna.

Sestus John Milford

Fauna Jane Actman
Perdix Baynes Barron
Zon Pat Renella
Chilot Eldon Burke

Director: Don McDougall

The Horse Race

w David P. Lewis, Booker Bradshaw

Under Urko's very nose, Virdon manages to run a horse race, winning, as part of the stakes, the life of a blacksmith's young son.

Barlow John Hoyt
Prefect Henry Levin
Kagan Wesley Fuller
Zandar Richard Devon
Martin Morgan Woodward
Gregar Meegan King
Zilo Josepth Tornatore

Director: Jack Starrett

The Interrogation

w Richard Collins

Burke is captured and cruelly questioned, while Galen and Virdon work out a rescue plan with the help of Galen's parents, Ann and Yalu.

Wanda Beverly Garland
Ann Anne Seymour
Yalu Normann Burton
Nora Lynn Benesch
Dr Malthus Harry Townes
Peasant gorilla Eldon Burke
Gorilla leader Ron Stein

Director: Alf Kjellin

The Tyrant

w Walter Black

The fugitive trio help remove Aboro, a corrupt tyrant, from office, even though they have to risk an encounter with Urko to do it.

Aboro Percy Rodrigues
Daku Joseph Ruskin
Augustus Tom Troupe
Janor Michael Conrad
Mikal James Daughton

Director: Ralph Senensky

The Cure

w Edward J. Lasko

The astronauts come across a village devastated by malaria and manage to help the local medical officer, Zoran, to discover quinine.

Zoran David Sheiner
Amy Sondra Locke
Talbert George Wallace
Mason Albert Cole
Kava Ron Soble
Inta Eldon Burke
Neesa Ron Stein

Director: Bernard McEveety

The Liberator

w Howard Dimsdale

Galen and the astronauts are captured by a tribe of humans who prey on other humans and turn them over to gorillas as slaves.

Brun John Ireland
Miro Ben Andrews
Clim Peter G. Skinner
Talia Jennifer Ashley
Gorilla guard Ron Stein
Villager Mark Bailey

Director: Arnold Laven

Up Above the World So High

w S. Bar-David *(alias* Shimon Wincelberg*)*, Arthur Browne Jr

The astronauts help a human, Leuric, to make a workable hang glider, arousing the unwelcome interest of a lady chimp scientist, Carsia.

Leuric Frank Aletter
Konag Martin Brooks
Carsia Joanna Barnes
Gorilla guard Ron Stein
Trooper Eldon Burke

Director: John Meredyth Lucas

PLATEAU OF FEAR

Encouraged by the success of the *Pathfinders* trilogy in 1960–1, ABC's drama supervisor Sydney Newman came up with a new children's adventure set in a nuclear power station high in the Andes – and back came two of the Pathfinders to star in it.

Gerald Flood again played a reporter, this time science journalist Mark Bannerman, while Stewart Guidotti was cast as his young sidekick Peter Blake. Investigating a series of mysterious attacks at the Potencia One power plant in the Andean state of Santa Montana, they find victims telling tales of a 'night devil' and hear reports that a strange giant beast is responsible. Digging deeper, they uncover a campaign by villainous general Villagran to sabotage the work of power station chief Dr Miguel Aranda so that he can convert the reactor for military purposes.

A strong cast also included Ferdy Mayne, John Barron and Jan Miller as doctor heroine Susan Fraser, head of the plateau's research hospital which relies on Potencia One for a regular supply of isotopes.

Pathfinders director Guy Verney produced, with directing duties handled by 'newcomer' Kim Mills.

CAST

Dr Miguel Aranda **John Barron**   Dr Susan Fraser **Jan Miller**
Mark Bannerman **Gerald Flood**   Peter Blake **Stewart Guidotti**
Lorca **Peter Allenby**   Julietta Aranda **Maureen Lindholm**
General Villagran **Ferdy Mayne**   Ralph Morton **Richard Coleman**
General Perera (Ep. 6 only) **Roger Deglado**
and . . . **Cognac** the dog

Writers: **Malcolm Stuart Fellows** and
  Sutherland Ross
Producer: **Guy Verney**
Director: **Kim Mills**
Designers: **Roger King, James Douglas**
Programme advisor: **Mary Field**
Music: **Clive Rogers**

An ABC Television Network Production
Six 30-minute episodes, black and white

Terror at Potencia One
Menace in the Night
Cavern of Death
The Growing Peril
The Invisible Shield
Slam-Down

24 September–29 October 1961

PLAY FOR TOMORROW

Anthology series of six specially commissioned plays about the near future – providing six chastening visions of almost unrelieved gloom.

The six invited writers had been issued with tapes of a BBC seminar in which the future was discussed by a psychiatrist/geneticist, an economist, an ecologist, a computer scientist, a nuclear physicist, a teacher, a journalist and a novelist.

What emerged in the six prophetic plays was an overall portrait of a society going downhill all the way, with a large superfluous population, controlled by the state through dreams, drugs and technology.

Crimes concentrated on the way early 21st-century society might deal with its misfits, outcasts and criminal types – from a lobotomised murderer to a man locked away for refusing to confine himself to designated leisure areas. *Bright Eyes* was a hard-eyed study of turn of the century attitudes to dissent and political ideals; *The Nuclear Family* was a bleak exploration of empty lives; *Shades* showed a teenage population paid to live in idleness and live out computer-projected fantasies; and *Easter 2016* was an unoptimistic look at continuing sectarianism in Northern Ireland.

Only one play, *Cricket*, purported to be a comedy – about a cricket team plotting the downfall of their rivals with the aid of a computerised Wisden (voiced by Brian Johnston!), but it, too, had sinister undertones, with the cricket club a front for a guerilla army to fight the Forestry Commission which was gobbling up hill farms to feed the insatiable appetite for timber.

The 1982 series was produced by Neil Zeiger whose apparent affinity for futuristic suffering popped up again two years later in the play *Z for Zachariah*.

Producer: Neil Zeiger
Script editor: Chris Parr

A BBC Production
Six colour 60-minute plays
13 April–18 May 1982
(BBC1)

Crimes

w Caryl Churchill
The year: 2002. A time of controlled and restricted activity, over-populated prisons and the ever-increasing threat of nuclear war. In a group therapy session psychiatrist Melvyn encourages four convicted prisoners to tell of their preoccupations. In the psychiatrist's home, his wife Veronica watches a DIY programme called 'Select & Survive' about how to build, equip and arm your own nuclear shelter . . .
Jane Sylvestra Le Touzel
Ron Peter Whitbread
Elliot Rufus Collins
Bill Stephen Sweeney
Melvyn T.P. McKenna
Veronica Julia Foster
Smith Dave Hill
Larry Donald Gee

Director: Stuart Burge
Designer: Ian Rawnsley

Bright Eyes

w Peter Prince
New Year's Eve, 1999. Great Britain is entrenched in a European community in the midst of a Euro-war. In a brilliantly lit, electronically controlled French prison, Cathy, a revolutionary activist, is facing death for her part in the assassination of a right-wing politician. Her father, Sam, a successful man, urges her to renounce her beliefs and so save her life. But, as ironic flashbacks show, as a girl she had laughed at political committment, and it was *he* who had espoused radicalism.
Sam Howard Robin Ellis

Cathy Sarah Berger
Cathy (as a child) Corinna Reardon
Rachel Howard Kate Harper
John Constantine de Goguel
Charvier Julian Curry
Shapiro Stephen Grief
Michel Gilbert Gavin Campbell
with: Della Finch, Charles Baillie, John Hug, Ian Flintoff, Julian Wadham, Julia Gale, Adam Blackwood

Director: Peter Duffell
Designer: Nigel Curzon

Cricket

w Michael Wilcox
The year: 1997. In a small Northumbrian farming community, Coanwood CC meets to pick the team for a vital match against Blenkinsop CC. The selection committee consults the Wisden Computer Service which provides video recordings of past performances, advises on strategy and even predicts results. But when everything can be so easily filmed and recorded, is there not a danger that someone might be bugging their meeting?
John Ridley Malcolm Terris
Morna Ridley Anne Rait
Willie Ridley Paul Antony-Barber
Lord Slaggyford Jeremy Child
Colin Bayliss Simon Rouse
Tommy Coulthard Terence Halliday

Director: Michael Darlow
Designer: Philip Lindley

('The play accumulated half-smiles in the same niggardly way that Geoff Boycott accumulates runs' – Joe Steeples, *Daily Mail*.)

The Nuclear Family

w Tom McGrath

The year: 1999. Joe is the father of a family which lives a claustrophobic, flat-bound life with a computer terminal as its link with the outside world. Joe has been unemployed for 15 years and the two teenage children are the breadwinners. He decides to introduce them to the outmoded delights of a working holiday and the family sets off to sample the novelty of physical labour – polishing warheads and scrubbing floors at an underwater nuclear base, Sea Bed 6. The work proves a tonic for the family.

Joe Brown Jimmy Logan
Agnes Brown Ann Scott-Jones
Gary Brown Gerard Kelly
Ann Brown Lizzy Radford
Sgt Smellie Russell Hunter
Able-bodied Andrews Sarah Thurstan
Newcaster Gavin Campbell
Scientist Barbara Coles

Director: John Glenister
Designer: Tim Harvey

Shades

w Stephen Lowe

The year: 1999. Microchip technology has produced vast unemployment, but also vast wealth, so the government has paid off many teenagers and sent them to live in converted office blocks called Youth Units, where they amuse themselves by donning dark glasses through which their fantasies, from football to nude ballet, motor racing to pornography, can be projected. As they research the 1980s for a period party, one girl, Sheena, identifies too closely with a girl peace demonstrator in an old newsreel film and tries to jolt the others into accepting her beliefs.

Sheena/Angie Tracey Childs
Joe/Malcolm Stuart Mackenzie
Kate/Mary Emily Moore
Adam/Peter Neil Pearson
Diana/Paula Shelagh McLeod
Julie/Sue Francesca Gonshaw
Tony Michael Feldman

Director: Bill Hays
Designer: Don Taylor

Easter 2016

w Graham Reid

The year: 2016. The setting: Northern Ireland's only integrated teacher-training college. Some students and lecturers wish to commemorate the Dublin Easter Rising of 1916, but their desire precipitates a struggle between the liberal college principal, Cyril Brown, and the sadistic, repressive security director, Lennie North.

Cyril Brown Denys Hawthorne
Lennie North Derrick O'Connor
Connor Mullan Bill Nighy
Clare Williams Eileen Pollock
John Bingham Gerard McSorley
June Crawford Lise-Ann McLaughlin
Kevin Murphy Colm Meaney
Colette Brogan Susie Kelly
Student Kenneth Branagh

Director: Ben Bolt
Designer: Tony Snoaden

THE PRISONER

'The series was posing the question, "has one the right to tell a man what to think, how to behave, to coerce others? Has one the right to be an individual?" '

(Patrick McGoohan)

One of the most enigmatic and talked-about series ever, *The Prisoner* overturned the conventions of television drama by challenging its unsuspecting audience to think on more than one simple level.

It was devised by Patrick McGoohan who was its star and its executive producer. He also shared in the writing and direction. It was his series. Before it began he said: 'If people don't like it, there's only one person to blame – me!'

Faced with something that was part spy thriller, part fantasy, part allegory, many people found the effort too much and remained angry, frustrated and confused by the absence of quick, easy answers. But for daring to be different, *The Prisoner* won a passionate cult status that has remained unshakeable for more than 20 years.

It began innocently enough. A government employee abruptly resigns from his top-secret job. He goes home and is seen packing, apparently for a holiday. Suddenly gas hisses through the keyhole and he loses consciousness. He awakes apparently in the same room, but when he looks out of the window he sees the strange, beautiful landscape of The Village. Abducted by persons unknown, he has become *The Prisoner*.

Immediately the questions are thrown up. Where is this Village? Who runs it and why? It's a self-contained community with its own shops, a cafe, a labour exchange, and an old folks' home. It has its own radio and television service and its own newspaper, *The Tally Ho*. But its telephones only allow local calls and its taxis won't leave the village limits.

The village is full of people who used to work for various governments and who had access to classified information. Some help run the place, others are prisoners like himself. But everyone has a number. *The Prisoner* is told *he* is Number Six. At the head of the visible hierarchy is Number Two, served by an ever-present mute dwarf butler. But Number Two is answerable to the unseen authority of Number One.

As to *why* he is there, that becomes chillingly clear from the outset. The authorities want 'information', in particular, they want to know why he resigned. Successive Number Twos try every technique available, from drugs, brainwashing, torture, psychological warfare, even dream manipulation, to find out. Meanwhile, *The Prisoner* is seeking answers of his own – including the identity of Number One.

Above all, though, he wants to escape – a task made hard by constant electronic surveillance, and harder still by 'Rover', a bizarre large white balloon that hunts down and retrieves errant inmates.

The series becomes a cat-and-mouse battle with *The Prisoner* initially thwarted at each turn but refusing to submit and gradually gaining the upper hand until, in a riot of surreal chaos, he finally escapes . . . from his physical prison, at least.

What did it all mean? Certainly, the series could be viewed, on a limited level, as a story of an imprisoned secret agent, but it's the deeper issues raised and the wider meanings sought that have given it its enduring appeal. The series was a persuasive defence of a man's right to assert his individuality in the face of an increasingly conformist society, and the declaration 'I am not a number, I am a free man!' its most passionate slogan. The series also explored themes of education, democracy, misuse of power, psychiatry, drugs and violence. And ultimately it posed the premise that everyone is a prisoner of his or her self, hemmed in by our own weaknesses. In the final episode, The Prisoner 'unmasks' Number One who stands, fleetingly, revealed as himself, the enemy within.

The Prisoner was McGoohan's followup to the long-running *Danger Man*, and much speculation centred on whether Number Six was the same character, John Drake. Prisoner script editor George Markstein said it was, McGoohan said it wasn't. Others have suggested that *The Prisoner* was McGoohan's way of 'resigning' from *his* previous job . . .

REGULAR CAST

Number Six **Patrick McGoohan**   *Butler* **Angelo Muscat**
Supervisor (8 out of 17) **Peter Swanwick**
Voice of village announcer **Fenella Fielding**

Devised by: **Patrick McGoohan**
Executive producer: **Patrick McGoohan**
 (Except Eps 14–15, 17)
Producer: **David Tomblin**
Script editor: **George Markstein**
 (Eps 1–12, 16)
Director of photography: **Brendan J. Stafford**
Theme music: **Ron Grainer**

Filmed at MGM Studios, Borehamwood and on location at Portmeirion, North Wales

An Everyman Films Production for ATV
17 colour, 60-minute episodes
29 September 1967–2 February 1968
(ATV Midlands)
(and *many* repeats, the last being on Channel Four . . . in 1983–4)

For further information on *The Prisoner*, write to:
Six of One
The Prisoner Appreciation Society
PO Box 60, Harrogate HG1 2TP

Arrival

w **George Markstein, David Tomblin**
After abruptly resigning from his top secret job, a government employee is abducted to an idyllic-looking prison-camp called 'The Village'. Stripped of all identity, he is known as Number Six and so begins his titanic struggle to defy his jailers who want to pick his brain and find out why he resigned.

The woman **Virginia Maskell**
Number Two **Guy Doleman**
Cobb **Paul Eddington**
The New Number Two **George Baker**
Taxi driver **Barbara Yu Ling**
Maid **Stephanie Randall**
Doctor **Jack Allen**
Welfare worker **Fabia Drake**
Shopkeeper **Denis Shaw**
Gardener/Electrician **Oliver MacGreevy**
Ex-Admiral **Frederick Piper**

Waitress Patsy Smart
Labour exchange manager Christopher Benjamin
Supervisor Peter Swanwick
Hospital attendant David Garfield
Croquet players Peter Brace, Keith Peacock

Director: Don Chaffey

The Chimes of Big Ben

w Vincent Tilsley
With the aid of an apparent ally, Nadia, Number Six effects an escape by sea, air and land, ending up in what appears to be his London office. He is about to reveal why he resigned when the chiming of Big Ben tips him off that he has been tricked.
Number Two Leo McKern
Nadia Nadia Gray
General Finlay Currie
Fotheringay Richard Wattis
Colonel J Kevin Stoney
Number Two's assistant Christopher Benjamin
Karel David Arlen
Supervisor Peter Swanwick
Number 38 Hilda Barry
Judges Jack Le-White, John Maxim, Lucy Griffiths

Director: Don Chaffey

A, B & C

w Anthony Skene
Number Two subjects Number Six to an experimental process by which dreams can be penetrated and manipulated, using a wonder drug which turns subconscious thoughts into pictures on a TV screen.
Engadine Katherine Kath
Number Fourteen Sheila Allen
Number Two Colin Gordon
'A' Peter Bowles
Blonde lady Georgina Cookson
'B' Annette Carol
Flower girl Lucille Soong
Maid at party Bettine Le Beau
Thugs Terry Yorke, Peter Brayham
Henchman Bill Cummings

Director: Pat Jackson

Free for All

w Patrick McGoohan
Number Six views the impending election of a new Number Two as just another trick but runs for office all the same – only to find, as anticipated, that his victory is a hollow one.
Number Two Eric Portman
Number 58 Rachel Herbert
Labour exchange manager George Benson
Reporter Harold Berens
Man in cave John Cazabon
Photographer Dene Cooper
Supervisor Kenneth Benda
Waitress Holly Doone
Mechanics Peter Brace, Alf Joint

Director: Patrick McGoohan

The Schizoid Man

w Terence Feely
The Prisoner's double is brought into the village to try to break Number Six by convincing him that he is someone else . . . Number Twelve.
Alison Jane Merrows
Number Two Anton Rodgers
Supervisor Earl Cameron
Number 36 Gay Cameron
Doctor David Nettheim
Nurse Pat Keen
Guardians Gerry Crampton, Dinny Powell

Director: Pat Jackson

The General

w Lewis Greifer
Everyone in the Village is ordered to attend the sensational 'Speedlearn' classes promising a university degree in three minutes. Number Six thwarts the scheme with his computer-blowing question: Why?
Number Two Colin Gordon
Number Twelve John Castle
Professor Peter Howell
Announcer Al Mancini
Professor's wife Betty McDowall
Supervisor Peter Swanwick
Doctor Conrad Phillips

Man in buggy Michael Miller
Waiter Keith Pyott
Man in cafe Ian Fleming
Mechanic Norman Mitchell
Projection operator Peter Bourne
Corridor guards George Leech, Jackie Cooper

Director: Peter Graham Scott

Many Happy Returns

w Anthony Skene
Number Six awakes in a deserted village. There is no one to stop him as he escapes back to London by raft – a journey of 25 days. From calculations of times and tides, the Village is deemed to be off the coast of Morocco. Number Six flies off to locate it – only to be ejected from his plane to land back where he started.
The Colonel Donald Sinden
Thorpe Patrick Cargill
Mrs Butterworth Georgina Cookson
Group captain Brian Worth
Commander Richard Caldicott
Gunther Dennis Chinnery
Ernst Jon Laurimore
Gypsy girl Mike Arrighi
Maid Grace Arnold
Gypsy man Larry Taylor

Director: Patrick McGoohan

Dance of the Dead

w Anthony Skene
Death strikes amid the gaiety of a village carnival and Number Six is put on trial when he makes an audacious bid to smuggle out an SOS on the corpse.
Number Two Mary Morris
Doctor Duncan Macrae
Girl Bo-Peep Norma West
Town crier Aubrey Morris
Psychiatrist Bee Duffell
Day supervisor Camilla Hasse
Dutton Alan White
Night supervisor Michael Nightingale
Night maid Patsy Smart
Maid Denise Huckley
Postman George Merritt
Flowerman John Frawley

Lady in corridor Lucy Griffiths
Second doctor William Lyon Brown

Director: Don Chaffey

Checkmate

w Gerald Kelsey
Number Six participates in a bizarre game of chess in which the pieces are human beings. He is trying to discover who are the prisoners and who are the warders.
Rook Ronald Radd
First psychiatrist Patricia Jessel
Number Two Peter Wyngarde
Queen Rosalie Crutchley
Man with the Stick George Coulouris
Second psychiatrist Bee Duffell
Supervisor Basil Dignam
Painter Danvers Walker
Shopkeeper Denis Shaw
Assistant supervisor Victor Platt
Nurse Shivaun O'Casey
Skipper Geoffrey Reed
Sailor Terence Donovan
Tower guards Joe Dunne, Romor Gorrara

Director: Don Chaffey

Hammer Into Anvil

w Roger Woddis
Seeking to avenge the death of a persecuted girl, Number Six plays cat-and-mouse with Number Two, making him think that *he* is the one being spied on.
Number Two Patrick Cargill
Bandmaster Victor Maddern
Number 14 Basil Hoskins
Psychiatric director Norman Scace
New supervisor Derek Aylward
Number 73 Hilary Dwyer
Control room operator Arthur Gross
Supervisor Peter Swanwick
Shop assistant Victor Woolf
Lab technician Michael Segal
Shop kiosk girl Margo Andrew
Female code expert Susan Sheers
Guardians Jackie Cooper, Fred Haggerty, Eddie Powell, George Leach

Director: Pat Jackson

It's Your Funeral

w Michael Cramoy
Number Six averts a planned assassination – despite being subjected to a ruthless campaign to discredit him so that even the intended victim will not believe his warnings.
New Number Two Derren Nesbitt
Watchmaker's daughter Annette Andre
Number 100 Mark Eden
Retiring Number Two Andre Van Gyseghem
Watchmaker Martin Miller
Computer attendant Wanda Ventham
Number Two's assistant Mark Burns
Supervisor Peter Swanwick
Artist Charles Lloyd Pack
Number 36 Grace Arnold
Stallholder Arthur White
MC councillor Michael Bilton
Koshu opponent Gerry Crampton

Director: Robert Asher

A Change of Mind

w Roger Parkes
Number Six is the subject of a sinister plan to transform his mental processes by sound waves and drugs, but turns the tables by getting Number Two declared 'unmutual'.
Number 86 Angela Browne
Number Two John Sharpe
Doctor George Pravda
Number 42 Kathleen Breck
Supervisor Peter Swanwick
Lobo man Thomas Heathcote
Committee chairman Bartlett Mullins
Number 93 Michael Miller
Social group members Joseph Cuby, Michael Chow
Number 48 June Ellis
Woodland men John Hamblin, Michael Billington

Director: Patrick McGoohan

Do Not Forsake Me Oh My Darling

w Vincent Tilsley
Number Six's mind is imprisoned in the body of an army colonel via Professor Seltzman's 'mind-swopping' machine.
Janet Zena Walker
Number Two Clifford Evans
The Colonel Nigel Stock
Seltzman Hugo Schuster
Sir Charles John Wentworth
Villiers James Bree
Minister Kynaston Reeves
Stapleton Lloyd Lamble
Danvers Patrick Jorgan
Camera shop manager Lockwood West
Potter Fredric Abbott
Cafe waiter Gertan Klauber
Old guest Henry Longhurst
First new man Danvers Walker
Young guest John Nolan

Director: Pat Jackson

Living in Harmony

w David Tomblin, *from a story by* David Tomblin *and* Ian L. Rakoff
The Prisoner finds himself in a Wild West township, tricked into becoming a sheriff. It's really just a drug-induced trip – but can he be forced to carry a gun and kill?
The Kid (Number Eight) Alexis Kanner
The Judge (Number Two) David Bauer
Kathy Valerie French
Town elder Gordon Tanner
Bystander Gordon Sterne
Will Michael Balfour
Mexican Sam Larry Taylor
Town dignitary Monti De Lyle
Horse dealer Douglas Jones
Gunmen Bill Nick, Les Crawford, Frank Maher
Horsemen Max Faulkner, Bill Cummings, Eddie Eddon

Director: David Tomblin

The Girl Who Was Death

w Terence Feely, *from an idea by* David Tomblin
The Prisoner's 'bedtime story' for village children. Number Six meets a girl who believes they are made for each other; he is a born survivor, she is a born killer. (Note the name of the actor playing the bowler!)
Schnipps (Number Two) Kenneth Griffith
Sonja Justine Lord
Potter Christopher Benjamin

Killer Karminski Michael Brennan
Boxing MC Harold Berens
Barmaid Sheena Marsh
Scots Napoleon Max Faulkner
Welsh Napoleon John Rees
Yorkshire Napoleon Joe Gladwin
Bowler John Drake
Little girl Gaynor Steward
Little boys Graham Steward, Stephen
  Howe

Director: David Tomblin

Once Upon a Time

---

w Patrick McGoohan
It's make or break time as the Prisoner
faces ruthless interrogation from Number
Two in a process called 'Degree Absolute',
from which only one man will emerge the
winner.
Number Two Leo McKern
Supervisor Peter Swanwick
Umbrella man John Cazabon

Number 86 John Maxim

Director: Patrick McGoohan

Fall Out

---

w Patrick McGoohan
Controversial final episode which infuriated those looking for pat answers. Having
survived 'Degree Absolute', the Prisoner
finally wins the right to be an individual,
and discovers the identity of Number One
– himself. He escapes the Village – with
the former Number Two and Number 48
(the 'symbol' of youth revolt) plus the
omnipresent Butler – but remains a
prisoner of his own self.
Former Number Two Leo McKern
The President Kenneth Griffith
Number 48 Alexis Kanner
Supervisor Peter Swanwick
Delegate Michael Miller

Director: Patrick McGoohan

PROJECT UFO

In the United States, this was the only science fiction show ever to
figure in a year's national Top 20 (equal 19th in 1977!). Not even
Star Trek achieved that. In the UK, *Project UFO* has never reached
such elevated heights, with only four ITV regions taking all 26
episodes.

The series, described by US critics as 'National Enquirer
television' and allegedly based on real events, followed the
investigations of the American Air Force's Project Blue Book.
Major Jake Gatlin and his sidekick Sgt Harry Fitz were assigned to
look into reported UFO sightings of 'high strangeness' and 'high
credibility' across America.

Each episode was listed as an 'incident' and ranged from a
rancher and his family being assaulted by alien creatures (*The
Howard Crossing Incident*), an airliner chased by a boomerang-
shaped craft (*The Medicine Bow Incident*) and a whole rash of high-
flying careers jeopardised because sightings aroused disbelief. In
one episode (*The Rock and Hard Place Incident*) Gatlin and Fitz
even have a sighting of their own.

In Season Two, a new investigator, Capt. Ben Ryan joined the
team, but the formula was the same, with the subjects telling their
tales to the Blue Book team.

Executive producer for the series was Jack Webb, laconic star of the vintage crime series *Dragnet*.

The series first played in Britain in May 1979 in the Southern region. London, Anglia and TSW were the other areas to see both seasons. Yorkshire, Tyne Tees, Scottish and Ulster opted out altogether.

REGULAR CAST
Major Jake Gatlin **William Jordan**
Sgt Harry Fitz **Caskey Swaim**   *Libby Virdon* **Aldine King**
Capt. Ben Ryan (Season Two) **Edward Winter**

Executive producer: **Jack Webb**
Producer: **Col. William T. Coleman**

A Mark VIII Ltd Production in association with NBC TV
26 colour 60-minute episodes

Season One:
17 May–9 August 1979
Season Two:
3 January–10 April 1980
(Southern)

Season One:

The Washington DC Incident

A US Air Force pilot sights a UFO and gives chase until, over Washington DC, he plummets to his death.
with: **Anne Schebeen, Frances Reid**

The Joshua Flats Incident

Several prominent citizens see a UFO and the air force is called in.
with: **David Yanez, Barbara Luna, Jim Davis**

The Fremont Incident

A police officer sees an alien craft land and strange figures emerging from it, but when he reports the incident he is ridiculed.
with: **Rod Perry, Frank Aletter**

The Howard Crossing Incident

A rancher and his family are assaulted by alien creatures after a glowing white ball crashes to Earth on their land.
with: **Leif Erickson**

The Medicine Bow Incident

A boomerang-shaped craft chases a commercial airliner and a would-be politicain says he has been attacked by a UFO.
with: **Kenneth Mars, Paul Picerni**

The Nevada Desert Incident

An air force lieutenant sees four metallic flying objects and a huge mother ship. He reports it and endangers his career and marriage.
with: **Scott Hylands, Adrienne La Russa, Andrew Duggan, Donna Douglas**

The Forest City Incident

Two schoolboys spot a UFO but their headmaster fears bad publicity will arise from an official investigation.
with: **Stacy Keach Sr, Skip Homeier**

The Desert Springs Incident

An immense UFO pursues two men as they ride a cable car from the top of a mountain.
with: **Peggy Webber, Buckley Norris**

The French Incident

The son of a presidential envoy is abducted by a flying saucer in the village of Brebeuf – and the White House orders Gatlin and Fitz to investigate.
with: Eric Braeden, Kip Niven, Maria Grimm, Morgan Woodward

The Waterford Incident

The boys at a military academy claim a saucer flew over the school, discharging a strand-like substance.
with: Craig Stevens, Dr Joyce Brothers

The Doll House Incident

An elderly caretaker is confronted by two aliens who offer him a strange lotus-shaped loaf of bread in return for a jug of water.
with: Alf Kjellin, Marta Kristen

The Rock and Hard Place Incident

Gatlin and Fitz have their own UFO sighting as a flying saucer leaves a trail of exploding colour over the restaurant where they are dining.
with Elaine Joyce, Paul Brinegar, Robert Ginty

The St Hilary Incident

Two nuns see a UFO and after reporting the incident, are pressured by the church authorities to deny their claim.
with: Pamela Franklin

Season Two:

The Underwater Incident

(details unavailable)

The Devilish Davidson Lights

Ryan and Fitz investigate reported sightings in Davidson, California.
with: Kim Hunter, Jared Martin, Jenny Sullivan, Isaac Ruiz

The Pipeline Incident

The three-man crew of an Alaskan cargo plane is crossing the Yukon border when they see a target closing in on them at incredible speed. The object performs bizarre manoeuvres and gives chase.
with: Randolph Mantooth, Cameron Mitchell, Donald May

The Island Incident

A doctor and his party in the South Pacific see a small UFO fly out of a huge mother ship but the islanders later deny the sighting.
with: James Olson, Marlyn Mason

The Incident of the Cliffs

A woman with a history of mental illness sees four UFOs, but despite filmed evidence, her claims are refuted by her husband and psychiatrist.
with: Trish Stewart, William Reynolds

The Wild Blue Yonder Incident

A student pilot faces expulsion after sighting a supposed flying saucer during an air exercise and recklessly diving to chase it.
with: Rebecca York, W.K. Stratton

The Believe It or Not Incident

A student claims he has been warned by aliens that unless the world's pollution is cleared up they will take the Earth by force.
with: Mark Slade, Anne Lockhart

The Camouflage Incident

Three businessmen are attacked by a UFO. One of them manages to film the craft but refuses to reveal the results.
with: Gary Crosby

The I-Man Incident

A large, but very delicate UFO hovers over a 10-year-old girl on a beach and plays her a startling message, echoing a signal sent from Earth 15 years before.

The Superstition Mountain Incident

A student finds two pieces of pure magnesium left behind by a UFO and is warned by a gipsy to be careful in telling anyone about the Overlords' visit.

with: **Josh Albee, Leslie Ackerman, Anna Karen**

The Scoutmaster Incident

A scoutleader sees a strange light followed by a crash. He receives mysterious burns but then becomes reluctant to discuss the incident.

with: **Russell Wiggins, Steve Patrick**

The Whitman Tower Incident

A mysterious blip appears on the radar screen at Los Angeles Airport. Then residents of a nearby apartment building are startled by a UFO outside their windows.

with: **Fred Holliday, Linda Foster, Christopher Woods, Vic Perrin**

The Atlantic Queen Incident

A ship's officer sights a UFO on a return crossing but his captain believes he has invented the story.

with: **Peter Brown, John Anderson, Morey Amsterdam, Jayne Meadows**

QUATERMASS

The grand-daddy of TV science fiction, the Quatermass sagas still stand as landmarks of British television drama. Few creations have been as evocative or influential, and few characters as enduring as Professor Bernard Quatermass – a dedicated and well-intentioned rocket scientist, but a humanistic and fallible man.

There have been four Quatermass serials, all of them self-contained – three for the BBC in the 1950s and a belated fourth for Thames Television in 1979. The BBC trio were also memorably filmed by Hammer but, more significantly, the third – and best – story, *Quatermass and the Pit* (1959), was released on video in 1988, setting its eerie tale before a new generation to whom the early serials were only legendary heirlooms.

The only logical order in which to take the Quatermass legacy is the chronological one, and the story begins in 1953 . . .

THE QUATERMASS EXPERIMENT (1953)

In the summer of 1953, the BBC's new head of drama Michael Barry spent his entire first year's budget for commissioning new scripts – some £250 – on one author, youthful staff writer Nigel Kneale.

Kneale responded with an adventurous six-part thriller far removed from the theatrically oriented productions that were the staple of television drama. His story: an experimental spaceship with its three-man crew is knocked hundreds of thousands of miles off-course before finally returning to Earth. The sole survivor has been contaminated with an alien life-form that causes him to metamorphose into a hundred-foot tall vegetable monster capable of infinite reproduction, that wreaks havoc on London before it is finally destroyed in time to save the world. The scientist who tracks him down is the scientist who sent him up – British rocket group chief, Bernard Quatermass (a name plucked at random from a telephone book).

The Quatermass Experiment was the first of several collaborations between Kneale and producer/director Rudolph Cartier, and it took great faith and ingenuity to bring script to screen. TV drama at that time was played live and special effects were virtually unknown. Such horrific elements as were required had to be created within a series budget of just over £3500 and created on the night. Kneale himself 'played' the monster in the climax, using his gloved hands, covered with bits of vegetation and leather, stuck through a blown-up still of Westminster Abbey.

Aware of the technical limitations, Kneale relied on timeless dramatic strengths – a coherent plot and well-drawn characters – to tell his story. Its impact was tremendous, particularly as it was the first serial of its kind. Moreover, it was aimed at an adult audience and it *was* adults who climbed the walls in horrified excitement.

Hammer released a film version in 1956 which starred Brian Donlevy as Quatermass and was known in America as *The Creeping Unknown*.

MAIN CAST

Professor Bernard Quatermass **Reginald Tate**
Judith Carroon (chief assistant) **Isabel Dean**   *John Paterson* **Hugh Kelly**
James Fullalove **Paul Whitsun-Jones**   *Victor Carroon* **Duncan Lamont**
Dr Gordon Briscoe **John Glen** (from Ep. 2)
Chief Insp. Lomax **Ian Colin** *(from Ep. 2)*
Det. Sgt Best **Frank Hawkins** *(from Ep. 2)*

Writer: **Nigel Kneale**
Producer/director: **Rudolph Cartier**
Settings: **Richard R. Greenhough, Stewart Marshall**

A BBC Production ·
Six 30-minute episodes, black and white
18 July–22 August 1953

Contact Has Been Established

A British experimental rocket orbits the planet and crashes back to Earth in Wimbledon. When the ship is opened, only one member of the three-man crew emerges, Victor Carroon.
Peter Marsh **Moray Watson** *(plus Ep. 2)*
Blaker **W. Thorp Devereux**
Len Matthews **Van Boolen**

Mrs Matthews **Iris Ballard**
Policeman **Neil Wilson** *(plus Ep. 2)*
Miss Wilde **Katie Johnson** *(plus Eps 3–4)*
News Editor of Daily Gazette **Oliver Johnston** *(plus Eps 2, 4)*
Fireman **Colyn Davies**
Journalists **Patrick Westwood, Dominic Le Foe** *(plus Ep. 2)*
Police Inspector **Eugene Leahy** *(plus Ep. 2)*

Reveller Denis Wyndham
BBC Newsreader Nicholas Bruce
BBC reporter Pat McGrath
Sandwichman Macgregor Urquhart

Persons Reported Missing

Victor Carroon is subjected to various tests which indicate that he has taken on the identities of the other two men. Quatermass and Paterson find a gelatinous substance spread around the capsule's interior.
Dr Ludwig Rechenheim Christopher Rhodes *(plus Ep. 3)*
Charles Greene Peter Bathurst *(plus Ep. 3)*
Louisa Greene Enid Lindsay
Hospital sister Stella Richman
Policeman (Scotland Yard) Maurice Durant

Very Special Knowledge

Carroon is taken back to the crash site and a recording of what happened during the orbit is played back to him, with disturbing results. A group of journalists try to kidnap him, but he, in turn, attacks one of them as he begins to change . . .
American reporter Philip Vickers
Indian reporter Edward David

Believed to be Suffering

Carroon takes refuge inside a cinema (where a spoof film, 'Planet of the Dragons', is on screen). He then goes to a chemist where he appears to be in pain

and his hand is seen to be badly mutated.
Photographer Darrell Runey
Ramsay Jack Rodney
Boy Anthony Green *(plus Ep. 5)*
Chemist Richard Cuthbert (plus Ep. 5)
Cinema manager Lee Fox
Cinemagoer Janet Joyce
Usherette Bernadette Milnes *(plus Ep. 5)*
'Space lieutenant' Keith Herrington
'Space girl' Pauline Johnson

An Unidentified Species

Quatermass picks up Carroon's trail and believes that the mixture of chemicals he has taken will accelerate his metamorphosis. Meanwhile, the killing starts – and at Westminster Abbey a pulsating mass is revealed clinging to the building.
Janet Christie Humphrey
Ted John Stone
Park keeper Frank Atkinson
Police inspector Reginald Hearne
A drunk Wilfred Brambell
Sir Vernon Dodds John Kidd *(plus Ep. 6)*
OB producer Tony Van Bridge *(plus Ep. 6)*
OB commentator Neil Arden *(plus Ep. 6)*
Secretary Joseph Crombie

State of Emergency

A state of emergency is declared and the army is brought in. Quatermass plays the creature the rocket tape and appeals to the last vestiges of humanity left in Carroon to fight what he has become. The creature finally dies, just before it is due to spore . . .
Cabinet minister Keith Pyott

QUATERMASS II (1955)

Set some years after the first fateful mission, this second story was not a sequel, and only the central character of Quatermass himself was carried over from the first serial.

In the two years since *The Quatermass Experiment* space exploration had become an imminent fact, though the way ahead was dogged by frustration and failure. Such technical 'doldrums' provided the background for Kneale's second tale, with Quatermass's own work on his ambitious new Mark II Moon rocket at a standstill.

With a track record behind them, a bigger budget (some £7500) before them and the BBC's new 'Visual Effects Department' (run by Bernard Wilkie and John Kine) beside them, Kneale and Cartier were able to create a very different story, reversing the man into monster idea, in favour of a covert Martian invasion by infiltrating human minds and bodies.

The role of Quatermass was taken by a new actor, John Robinson, following the death of Reginald Tate just a few weeks earlier. Among now-familiar names lower down the cast were Rupert Davies, Roger Delgado and Wilfred Brambell, the latter already cornering the market in low-life roles following his 'old drunk' in the first Quatermass serial and 'old man' in *Nineteen Eighty-Four*.

The six 30-minute episodes (which inevitably overran slightly) were transmitted live on Saturday nights, and telerecorded for a repeat the following Monday. The serial polarised its audience – viewers either loved its 'thrilling story and effects', or loathed its 'horror comics' plot. A film version (aka *Enemy From Space*) was released by Hammer in 1957, again with Brian Donlevy in the star role.

MAIN CAST

Prof. Bernard Quatermass **John Robinson**
Paula Quatermass (his daughter) **Monica Grey**
Dr Leo Pugh (his assistant) **Hugh Griffiths**
Capt. John Dillon **John Stone** *(Eps 1–2, 5–6)*
Vincent Broadhead **Rupert Davies** *(Eps 2–3 only)*

Writer: **Nigel Kneale**
Producer: **Rudolph Cartier**
Designer: **Stephen Taylor**
Film cameraman: **Charles de Jaeger**
Special effects: **Bernard Wilkie, Jack Kine**

(location filming at the Shellhaven refinery, Essex)
A BBC Production
Six 30-minute episodes, made in black and white
22 October–26 November 1955

The Bolts

Army captain John Dillon defies a clampdown to take the remains of a crashed object to Quatermass's British Rocket Group. Quatermass returns with him to the crash site – a huge domed chemical plant. While they are there, another small object crashes, a gas seeps out and a small bubble appears on Dillon's cheek.
Sgt Grice **Brian Hayes**
Private **Tony Lyons**
Fred Large **Eric Lugg**
Mrs Large **Hilda Barry**
Robert **Herbert Lomas**

Landlord **Richard Cuthbert**
Technicians **Kim Grant, Peter Macarté**
Australian commentator **Peter Carver**

The Mark

Dillon has been affected and now has a scar on his cheek. He is taken away to the plant by some zombie-like guards and Quatermass is unable to find out what has happened to him. He later visits Vincent Broadhead, an MP who has been probing the plant's activities, and joins him at an official inquiry. But several of the commission also bears scars . . .

Fowler **Austin Trevor** *(plus Eps 3–4)*
Stenning **John Miller** *(plus Ep. 3)*
Tramp **Wilfred Brambell**
Insp. Clifford **Peter Carver**
Dawson **Michael Brennan**
Child **Sheila Martin**
Mother **Hilda Fenemore**
Thompson **Michael Collins**
Secretary **Diana Chesney**
Head of Commission **O'Donovan Sheill** *(plus Ep. 3)*

The Food

Broadhead becomes the latest victim of the gas. Quatermass tricks his way inside the plant with Ward and Fowler. Ward gets separated and strays into one of the food domes – then emerges covered in a burning synthetic food, and dies. Back at the rocket base, Pugh has discovered the origin of the objects – an asteroid on the dark side of the Earth.

Ward **Derek Aylward**
Doctor **John Cazabon**
Waitress **Margaret Flint**
Mother **Ilona Ference**
Father **Sydney Bromley**
Frankie **Melvyn Hayes**
Analyst **Trevor Reid**
Supervisor **Philip Levene***
Guard **Stephen Scott**

* Later a writer on *The Avengers*.

The Coming

Quatermass visits the community near the plant but encounters suspicion as he tries to stir up the workers – until a new falling of objects convinces them. They march on the plant and, inside, Quatermass sees a huge alien creature growing inside one of the food domes.

Conrad **Roger Delgado**
Paddy **Michael Golden** *(plus Ep. 5)*
McLeod **John Rae** *(plus Ep. 5)*
Mrs McLeod **Elsie Arnold**
Ernie **Ian Wilson** *(plus Ep. 5)*
Young workman **Desmond Jordan** *(plus Ep. 5)*
Technician **Martin Lane**
Guard **Tom Clegg**

The Frenzy

The workers take over the plant and it is destroyed by an explosion. Quatermass gets back to the Rocket Group and prepares to launch his *Quatermass II* rocket – destination: the asteroid.

Technicians **Denton de Gray** *(plus Ep. 6)*
   Martin Lane

The Destroyers

Quatermass succeeds in launching his rocket and he and Pugh head for the asteroid. But Pugh has been taken over and Quatermass must overcome his attack before he can defeat the evil force on the asteroid.

Doctor: **Denis McCarthy**
Control assistant **Cyril Shaps**

QUATERMASS AND THE PIT (1958/59)

By the time *Quatermass and the Pit* came along, the world had embraced a real space age, and audience expectations had undoubtedly moved on from the pioneering rocket project of the first 'experiment'.

But the character of Professor Quatermass, with his pangs of conscience and loathing of bureaucracy, was far from obsolete and the timing of the first episode – just before Christmas 1958 – was clear evidence that the BBC knew it had a ratings winner on its hands.

The Pit of the title sets the story firmly in its time, when the last of London's blitzed areas were being rebuilt. Real excavations had unearthed Roman or medieval remains, but Nigel Kneale's teasing premise had something far stranger being stirred up in the mud – evidence that Earth had been visited aeons ago by Martians who had imbued man's simian ancestors with their own faculties.

Drawing on elements of demonology and the occult, Kneale's idea thus explained all manner of unexplained superstitions and phenomena, from poltergeists to second sight and race memories. Everything is drawn together in a chilling climax as the dormant Martian influence reasserts itself.

Though much of the drama is again told – live – through the characters and actions, *Quatermass and the Pit* made the greatest use yet of filmed inserts and refined special effects: the workman, Sladden, attempting to flee the demonic forces that have gripped him, the ground rippling beneath his hand; the animated 'wild hunt' sequence; and the climactic appearance of the energy force rising up over London.

This was also the first major contribution by the BBC's newly formed Radiophonic Workshop producing an array of bizarre sound effects.

André Morell, who had been a chilling O'Brien in the Kneale/Cartier adaptation of *Nineteen Eighty-Four*, became the third (and definitive) TV incarnation of Quatermass, and Canadian Cec Linder played the palaeontologist Matthew Roney. Hammer filmed this story in 1967, in terrifying technicolour, with Andrew Keir as the good professor, though in America it laboured under the title *Five Million Years to Earth*.

MAIN CAST

Professor Quatermass André Morell   *Barbara Judd* Christine Finn
Dr Matthew Roney Cec Linder   *Col. Breen* Anthony Bushell
Capt. Potter John Stratton   *Sergeant* Michael Ripper
Corp. Gibson Harold Goodwin   *Pte West* John Walker
Soldiers Clifford Cox, Brian Gilmar
James Fullalove Brian Worth   *Sladden* Richard Shaw
Minister Robert Perceval   *Private secretary* Richard Dare

Writer: Nigel Kneale
Producer: Rudolph Cartier
Film cameraman: A.A. Englander
Film editor: Ian Callaway
Designer: Clifford Hatts
Special effects: Jack Kine *and* Bernard Wilkie
Music: Trevor Duncan

A BBC Production
Six 35-minute* episodes, black and white
22 December 1958–26 January 1959
Omnibus repeat: Two 90-minute episodes
2, 9 January 1960

* approx.

The Halfmen

Prof. Quatermass is resisting the planners of a grisly rocket project known as the Dead Man's Deterrent. But then comes an interruption . . . Excavation work at a building site in Hobbs Lane, London, unearths a human skull which Dr Roney estimates to be five million years old. Then a strange projectile is dug up . . .
Truck driver Van Boolen
Old workman George Dudley
Foreman John Rae
Museum official Malcolm Watson
Baines Arthur Hewlett
Armitage Michael Bird
Interviewer Janet Burnell
Teddy boy Tony Lyon
Police inspector Ian Ainsley *(plus Eps 4, 6)*
Stoutwoman Janet Joyce

The Ghosts

Col. Breen believes the projectile is a bomb – it is cold to the touch, slightly radioactive and made of an unknown substance. Roney's assistant Barbara Judd finds the area has a history of supernatural events, and a terrified Pte West claims to have seen an imp-like ghost: 'It went through the wall!'
Mrs Chilcot Hilda Barry *(plus Ep. 1)*
Mr Chilcot Howell Davies *(plus Ep. 1)*
Young PC Kenneth Warren *(plus Ep. 1)*
PC Ellis Victor Platt *(plus Ep. 1)*
Miss Groome Madge Brindley

Imps and Demons

Journalist James Fullalove helps Quatermass research the history of Hobbs Lane, finding its name derives from Hob – the devil. A technician, Sladden, succeeds in opening a sealed compartment in the capsule, revealing three petrified alien insects.
News editor Tony Quinn *(plus Eps 4, 6)*
Nuttall Keith Banks

George Frank Crane
Policeman Patrick Connor *(plus Ep. 4)*
Elderly librarian Donald McCollum
Abbey librarian Fletcher Lightfoot

The Enchanted

Roney and Quatermass develop their theory about the Martians' visit to Earth, instilling their essence into man's ancestors. Sladden, alone in the pit, flees in terror as strange forces are conjured up.
Dr Klein Kenneth Seeger
News vendor Bernard Spear
Journalists Allan McClelland *(plus Ep. 6)*
    Bill Shine *(plus E. 6)* Ian Wilson
Vicar Noel Howlett *(plus Ep. 5)*

The Wild Hunt

A brain scanner reveals alien pictures in Barbara Judd's mind of 'the Wild Hunt' – the frenetic purging of the Martian hives. A sceptical Breen dismisses it as a hoax. In the pit, a technician is killed as the capsule starts to glow . . .
Electrician Harold Siddons *(plus Ep. 6)*
Official Edward Burnham *(plus Ep. 6)*
Technician John Scott Martin
Woman journalist Anne Blake

Hob

Chaos reigns in the pit and the long-dormant Martian inheritance begins to assert itself in many people in the area – including Quatermass himself – driving them to a new racial purge. The capsule breaks open and an energy form rises up over London. Roney finds he is immune and strives to defeat it.
TV interviewer Anthony Pendrell
Newsvendor John Hamblin
Customer Bernard Spear
Blonde Louise Gainsborough
Man in blazer Arthur Brander
Tattered man Sydney Bromley
Newscaster Stuart Nichol
American pilot Budd Knapp

QUATERMASS (1979)

Twenty years on, Quatermass's last case is as much rooted in the anxieties of its age as the previous three had been. Kneale this time creates a fearful vision of a near-future in which civilisation is tottering on its last legs. Petrol is running out, law and order has surrendered to lawlessness, with violent street gangs, the Badders, battling it out behind the barricades, while the superpowers squander resources on a useless space project.

An older, world-weary Quatermass has been living as a recluse in Scotland. Now, as he comes south to search for his missing granddaughter, Hettie, he teams up with a young Jewish astronomer, Joe Kapp, to defeat an alien force which is 'harvesting' the young of the planet, sweeping them up in beams of light at ancient ritual sites, such as stone circles.

Like its predecessors, the series was intended to be 'science fiction with a human face', but its vastly increased budget of £1,250,000 and the greater expectations of its audience in terms of effects and locations, meant a more lavish production, lacking the intimacy of the old live serials. Its makers, Euston Films, took the show on the road, using Wembley Stadium for one key scene where the Planet People – young, anarchistic hippies – mass to await the beam they believe will take them to another galaxy.

Highly respected actor Sir John Mills, whose only previous TV series had been *The Zoo Gang*, five years earlier, was a credible Quatermass, but after a promising start the series was a comparative disappointment. Expectations were perhaps inflated, as the first episode was the main offering of ITV's first night back on the air after a 75-day strike.

The final chapter in this Quatermass saga was produced in two versions – the four-part, four-hour story for home TV (repeated in May 1984 as two two-hour instalments), and a shorter 105-minute TV movie, *The Quatermass Conclusion*, for the foreign market. Kneale also turned the tale into a novel which included slightly different material.

MAIN CAST

Prof. Quatermass **John Mills**   *Joe Kapp* **Simon MacCorkindale**
Clare Kapp **Barbara Kellerman** *(Eps 1–2 only)*   *Kickalong* **Ralph Arliss**
Caraway **Paul Rosebury**   *Bee* **Jane Bertish**   *Hettie* **Rebecca Saire** *(Eps 1–2, 4)*
Marshall **Tony Sibbald** *(Eps 1–3)*   *Annie Morgan* **Margaret Tyzack** *(Eps 2–3)*
Sal **Toyah Willcox** *(Eps 2–4)*   *Chisholm* **Donald Eccles** *(Eps 3–4)*
Gurov **Brewster Mason** *(Eps 2–4, plus voice-over Ep. 1)*

Writer: **Nigel Kneale**
Script executive: **Linda Agran**
Executive in charge of production:
 Johnny Goodman
Executive producer: **Verity Lambert**
Producer: **Ted Childs**
Director: **Piers Haggard**
Designer: **Arnold Chapkin**
Music: **Marc Wilkinson, Nic Rowley**

A Euston Films Production
Four colour 60-minute episodes
24 October–14 November 1979
Repeat: 9–16 May 1984
(ITV)

Ringstone Round

Professor Quatermass comes out of retirement to search for his missing granddaughter and finds a world on the verge of anarchy, and an American-Russian space station destroyed by unknown forces. He is befriended by astronomer Joe Kapp and they witness the obliteration of thousands of Planet People by a beam of light at the stone circle, Ringstone Round.
Roach Bruce Purchase *(plus Ep. 2)*
Chen David Yip *(plus Ep. 2)*
Alison Brenda Fricker *(plus Ep. 2)*
Toby Gough Neil Stacy *(plus Ep. 3)*
TV producer Joy Harrington
Make-up lady Barbara Keogh
First pay cop James Leith
Pay police captain Luke Hanson
Muggers Charles Bolton, Chris Driscoll
Taxi driver Stewart Harwood
Charm seller Rita Webb
Catskin man Trevor Lawrence
Medicine man Frederick Radley
Kapp children Joanna Joseph *(plus Ep. 2)* Sophie Kind *(plus Ep. 2)*

Lovely Lightning

Following the devastation at Ringstone Round, Quatermass hears of similar incidents worldwide and returns to London with district commissioner Annie Morgan and a Ringstone 'survivor' Isabel. En route they become separated in a shootout between rival gangs. Meanwhile, the beam of light descends again – near to Joe Kapp's home.
Isabel Annabelle Lanyon *(plus Ep. 3)*

What Lies Beneath

Joe Kapp returns home to find no signs of life. Hiding out below the London streets, Quatermass meets an elderly scientist, Chisholm, who he believes could help solve the growing mystery. Then the beam strikes again – on a vast gathering of 70,000 young people at Wembley Stadium.
TV director Tudor Davies
Prime minister Kevin Stoney
Hatherley David Ashford
Russian astronaut Jan Murzynowski
Woman minister Elsie Randolph *(plus Ep. 4)*
Jack Larry Noble *(plus Ep. 4)*
Edna Gretchen Franklin *(plus Ep. 4)*
Arthur James Ottaway *(plus Ep. 4)*
Jane Clare Ruane *(plus Ep. 4)*
Winnie Kathleen St John
Susie Beatrice Shaw
Security guard Declan Mulholland
Torrance Ian Price
Soldier Chris Quinten

An Endangered Species

The sky has turned green from the 'undigested particles' in the atmosphere. Quatermass, joined by the Russian, Gurov, recruits a team of old people to lay a trap for the alien force, using an artificial composite of the sound, smell and heat of a huge human crowd to bait a poison – a nuclear bomb. As the light descends, there is a final clash with the Planet People and Kapp is shot dead. But Quatermass's granddaughter suddenly appears and together they detonate the device.
Misru Ishaq Bux
Woman researcher Lennox Milne
Electronics expert John Dunbar
Lt General John Richmond
Orderly Charles Lamb
Pay Police Lt Brian Croucher

R3

R3 was about scientists and it was fiction, ergo . . .
   In fact, *R3* can be considered science fiction more by association than by design. A BBC drama series of the 1960s, its stated intent

was 'to go beyond the laboratory door and into the daily background of a scientist's life'. Series creator N.J. Crisp wanted to 'humanise' scientists, to show them both as professionals at work and people with home lives and problems like anyone else.

As a format, it could probably just as easily have been applied to doctors, airline pilots or civil servants. As a series, it inevitably covered a range of scientific ideas and issues, even if these were less for their own sake than as plot devices to show the characters reacting with each other and in themselves. Topics included drug safety, scientific secrecy, human guinea-pigs, space research, post-holocaust survival and even a possible space virus, making it something of a forgotten forerunner to the 1970s *Doomwatch*.

The series was set in Research Centre Number Three (R3), part of the Ministry of Research, and the first 13-part season established a scientific community headed by a director, Sir Michael Gerrard (familiar territory for a former Prof. Quatermass, John Robinson), and his deputy, Dr George Fratton. Season Two, also 13 episodes, switched attention to R3's trouble-shooting department, Consultancy Service, which solved problems beyond ordinary expertise. This was run by Phillip Boult and his good-natured right-hand man Dr Richard Franklin (a rare 'happy' role for hellraiser Oliver Reed).

REGULAR CAST

Sir Michael Gerrard **John Robinson**   *Miss Brooks* **Brenda Saunders**

SEASON ONE ONLY:

Dr May Howard **Elizabeth Sellars**   *Dr Peter Travers* **Richard Wordsworth**
Dr George Fratton **Moultrie Kelsall**   *Dr Jack Morton* **Simon Lack**
Pomeroy **Edwin Richfield**   *Betty Mason* **Janet Kelly**
Tom Collis **Derek Benfield**   *Porter* **Maxwell Foster**

SEASON TWO ONLY:

Phillip Boult **Michael Hawkins**   *Dr Richard Franklin* **Oliver Reed**

Script editor/story consultant (Season One): **N.J. Crisp**
Story editor (Season Two): **Ken Levison**
Producers: **Andrew Osborn** *(Season One)*, **John Robins** *(Season Two)*
Theme: **Ken Thorne**

A BBC Production
26 50-minute episodes, black and white

Season One:
20 November 1964–13 February 1965
Season Two:
1 July–28 September 1965

(Due to the scarcity of published material the episode guide to R3 does contain several gaps. If any reader has information that might help fill them, I'd be glad to see it!)

Season One
(13 episodes)

A State of Anxiety

w N.J. Crisp

Dr Travers sets out to investigate the effects of stress but must find the right person as a subject for a complicated – and potentially dangerous – experiment.
Hospital sister Jacqueline Blackmore
Saunders Barry Stanton
Dr Horrabin Kenneth Edwards
Jill Travers Patricia Healey
Nora Gerrard Betty Cooper
Committee chairman Gerald Young
Prof. Standish Ernest Hare
Humby Norman Wynne
Sharp Edmund Warwick

Director: Moira Armstrong
Designer: John Cooper

Against the Stream

w N.J. Crisp

Research by Dr Ralph Cox has cast doubts on the safety of a well-known drug. But with vast commercial interests at stake, he finds it hard to get his results published.
Dr Cox George Roubicek
Jenny Rosemary Nicols
Dr Rose Leonard Sachs
Miss Pearce Rosamond Burne
Dr Sibley Griffith Jones
Prof. Poole Ian Cunningham
Meredith Tom Macauley

Director: Bill Hays
Designer: John Cooper

On the Spike

w Bill Strutton

A sequence of alarming events at R3 causes Fratton to regret his earlier curt dismissal of a local reporter's questions.
Willis Richard Carpenter
Haley Eric Thompson
Doris Haley Stephanie Bidmead
Sheila Carson Carol Austin
Chris Marks Bryan Marshall

Dr Tayfield John Maxim
Dr Brinkman Frederick Schiller

Director: Terence Williams
Designer: Peter Sedden

The Patriot

w E.Y. Bannard

Questions are asked when Dr Frank Hillman wants to give up his post and join R3 – but as a scientist, why shouldn't he?
Dr Frank Hillman Albert Lieven
Dr Max Rankl Alex Scott
Col. Cunliffe Peter Bathurst
Nora Gerrard Betty Cooper
Minister David Langton
Miss Fisher Rosalie Westwater

Director: Eric Tayler
Designer: Donald Brewer

Thunderbolt

w Elaine Morgan
(no story details available)
Iris Preston Wendy Craig
Dr John Calvos Norman Bowler
Dr Hugh Willard Joseph O'Connor
Bill Smith Stanley Walsh
Studs Maguire Patrick Durkin
Reporter Thomas Hale

Director: Terence Williams
Designer: Donald Brewer

The Short Cut

w Bill MacIlwraith

Young scientist Dr Wilmer tests a newly discovered substance on himself and suffers bizarre hallucinations.
Dr Wilmer William Gaunt
Hugh Cassell Ronald Lacey
Mrs Fields Hilda Fenemore

Director: Moira Armstrong
Designer: John Cooper

The Forum

w Bill MacIlwraith

R3 staff join an international scientific conference.

Dr Henri Lefevre **Peter Wyngarde**
Dr Anna Shastikani **Moira Redmond**
Prof. Vergas **George Coulouris**
Mr Matuka **Thomas Baptiste**
Dr Stephens **David Blake Kelly**
Prof. Chernev **James Bree**
Mr Kramer **Warren Stanhope**
Mr Sarevsky **John Ringham**
Dr Stroud **John Tate**

Director: **Bill Hays**
Designer: **Peter Seddon**

Patterns of Behaviour

w **N.J. Crisp**
A birthday celebration teaches May Howard, Morton and Travers a lot about themselves and each other.
Dr John Malcolm **John Scott**
Dr Alec Foster **Richard Armour**
Jill Travers **Patricia Healey**
Janice **Janet Rossini**

Director: **Eric Tayler**
Designer: **John Cooper**

The Fratton Experiment

w **N.J. Crisp**
A crucial time for R3's deputy director, Dr George Fratton.
Pointer **Peter Tory**
Stubbs **Maxwell Foster**
Mrs Fratton **Nancie Jackson**
Matthews **Barry Wilsher**
Dr Crawley **John Law**
Sister Parker **Margery Withers**
Mrs Shaw **Joan Geary**

Director: **Peter Dews**
Designer: **Donald Brewer**

The Critical Moment

w **Bill MacIlwraith**
Helicopters have been crashing – but no fault can be found with either men or machines.
Lt Cmdr Johnson **Jerome Willis**
Capt. Richards **Glyn Owen**
Col. Gold **Philip Latham**
Lt Lewis **Michael Culver**

Petty officer **Michael Wilsher**
Brig. Waters **Maurice Hedley**

Director: **Bill Hays**
Designer: **John Cooper**

The Angel

w **Bill Macilwraith** and **Donald Bull**
(storyline and cast details unavailable)

Director: **Moira Armstrong**

The Astronaut

w **N.J. Crisp**
A man returns from outer space. Is there something wrong with him? And if so – what?
Jim Bartley **Richard Pasco**
Mark Bartley **Roy Hills**
Paul Bartley **Michael Sarson**
Ruth Bartley **Ann Morrish**
Jock Harris **Eric McCaine**
Group Capt. Trent **Tom Bowman**
Dr Max Rankl **Alex Scott**

Director: **Terence Williams**
Designer: **Peter Seddon**

A Whole Lot of Reasons

w **Donald Bull**
Dogged by cash problems at home and at work, Travers is offered a means of solving both.
Jill Travers **Patricia Healey**
Jan Wolkowski **Vladek Sheybal**
Joe Tilyard **James Ottaway**
Commentator **Donald Douglas**
Dr Brant **James Dyrenforth**

Director: **Peter Dews**
Designer: **Donald Brewer**

Season Two
13 episodes

The Big Balloon

w **David Chantler**
Gerrard, Boult and Franklin are all behind the effort to get a big balloon

launched on a journey to the edge of space. Balloon veteran Cmdr Murray has called off the launch six times on the grounds of danger. His true motives can only be revealed by a seventh attempt.
Murray Ralph Michael
Buzz Don Borisenko
Radio man Elric Hooper
Weather man Roy Spencer
Winnington Mark Singleton
Diana Isobel Black
Science correspondent Donald Bisset

Director: Douglas Hurn
Designer: Donald Brewer

Unwelcome Visitor

w John Maynard
A rare radioactive isotope goes missing and may be in the hands of a child unaware of its danger.
Mr Cargill Hugh Burden
Mr Scott Peter Stenson
Mrs Holmes Rhoda Lewis
Baxter Denis Cleary
Peter Armstrong Michael Newport
Armstrong David Morrell
Mrs Armstrong Anne Godfrey
Terry Phil Collins

Director: Paul Bernard
Designer: John Cooper

One Free Man

w William Emms
Space research and freedom make uneasy bedfellows.
Dr Randall Lyndon Brock
American scientist Warren Stanhope
Watkins Donald Pickering
Valentina Kubishev Nicolette Bernard
Sarah Randall Muriel Pavlow
Secretary Brigit Forsyth

Director: Bill Hays
Designer: Donald Brewer

Experiment in Depth

w N.J. Crisp
Undersea exploration becomes an experiment in survival.

Wilson Jeremy Young
Capt. Rogers David Blake Kelly
Peters Edward Judd
Turner Donald Hoath
Meteorologist Stephen John
First officer Peter Noel Cook
Price Philip Anthony

Director: Paul Bernard
Designer: Barry Newbery

Black Warning

w Arden Winch
R3 is involved in an experiment in survival after a nuclear attack.
Frank Bradley Alan Browning
George Barratt Kenneth Colley
Beryl Barratt Heather Stoney
TV interviewer Alex Macintosh
Robert Foster Patrick O'Connell
Harry Purkiss Robin Parkinson
BBC announcer Michael de Morgan

Director: Bill Hays
Designer: John Cooper

In Your Own Back Yard

w Diana Deacon
A local shopkeeper decides to take action against R3.
Dr Martin John Line
Christine Goddard Frances Cuka
Tony Bond John Woodvine
Capt. Fowler Keith Anderson
Mr Whiting John Kidd
Capt. Bland Jonathan Drew
Robert Keegan Gordon Gostelow

Director: Michael Leeston-Smith
Designer: Moira Tait

Witch Doctor

w Julian Bond
R3's faith in itself is put to the test.
Ann Thompson Hilary Bamford
Peter Thompson Jack May
Abel Simmonds John Abineri
TV interviewer Kevin McHugh
Bellows Emrys Leyshon
Landon Michael Beint
PC Frank Sieman

Director: Douglas Hurn
Designer: John Cooper

And No Birds Sing

w Donald Young
A virulent new pesticide has an immediate and dramatic effect – the mass extermination of wildlife.
Girl Frances Machin
Boy Garry Mason
Eric Ken Jones
Mr Scott Maurice Hedley
Vernon Garfield Morgan
Diana McHale Suzy Kendall

Director: Bill Hays
Designer: Ridley Scott

A Sudden Change of Programme

w Neil Shand
Can industrial man ever be satisfactorily replaced by machinery?
Peterson Terence Langdon
Ennals Keith Pyott
Dr Simon Bartram Andrew Crawford
Alison Bartram Jeanne Moody
Sarah Burden Rosemarie Reede
Owen David Garfield
Setter Alec Wallis

Director: Paul Bernard

It's Better To Know

w Kenneth Cavender
Boult, a man used to dealing with things and ideas, not with people, finds himself facing a military interrogator.
Major Green Bernard Archard
Louise Bolt Clare Austin
John Rawlins Tom Adams
Sarbutt Michael Brennan
Cobham Philip Madoc
Leftman John Castle
Croxley Mike Pratt
Bloom Talfryn Thomas

Director: Michael Leeston-Smith
Designer: John Cooper

A Source of Contamination

w Donald Bull
After a lifetime of fruitless research, Andrew Furness is facing tragedy.
Furness Cyril Luckham
Fred John Junkin
Hedi Iza Teller
Dr Gregory Leslie Glazer
Prof. Morse Richard Gatehouse
Lord Green Bruno Barnabe
Dr Rowan Walter Horsbrugh

Director: Douglas Hurn
Designer: Jean Peyre

Good Clean Fun

w William Emms
(no story details available)
Plowden Glynn Edwards
Winthrop Kevin Stoney
Health officer Richard Mathews
Miss Flint Margery Withers
Mrs Tennant Mary Holder
John Terry Palmer
Julie Vivienne Dodds
Mollie Annest Williams

Director: Paul Bernard

Personal Appearance

w Edwin Ranch
When Richard Franklin gets mixed up with TV, it exposes an unexpected side of his personality.
Martin Smith Tom Criddle
Sue Susan Jameson
Laura Croft Alexandra Bastedo
Interviewer Bernard Ganley
Mark Parrit Barry Letts
Jim Talbot Roy Purcell
Lord Hollington Clive Morton

Director: John Robins
Designer: Roy Stannard

THE RAY BRADBURY
THEATER

'I never know where the next story will take me.
The trip – exactly one half exhilaration, exactly
one half terror.'

(Ray Bradbury)

Respected cosmopolitan anthology series which has yet to find a
proper welcome here.

In a medium devoted to hooking the 'mass audience' series of
this nature have generally been considered too downbeat to pull
enough votes in the ratings campaign. ITV picked up the first trio
listed here in 1985, as a package called *The Bradbury Trilogy*, but
only one region, Grampian, played them the same year. *The
Playground* got a peak-time network screening in January 1986,
but it's taken until 1989 for *Marionettes Inc* and *The Crowd* to filter
round other regions – with some still holding back.

The second trio have played here in disguise – as *Mystery
Theatre*, with Thames screening them in May/June 1989 at the
ridiculous time of 4.00 am on a Friday morning!

As for the third batch . . . see accompanying author's note.

REGULAR CAST

Introduced by: **Ray Bradbury**

THE BRADBURY TRILOGY
Three colour 30-minute episodes

6–20 October 1985
(Grampian)

Marionettes Inc

w **Ray Bradbury**
Computer salesman John Braling has a
good job, an affectionate wife and a nice
suburban home, but is desperately seeking
his freedom. One day, a cryptic message
'Marionettes Inc: We Shadow Forth'
appears on his computer screen and continues to do so until Braling seeks out the
sender. The company's rep Fantocinni
explains his motive – to help an unhappy
man. He reveals a life-size robot of Braling
and explains that he can be off enjoying
himself while the robot is at home with his

wife. The idea works well – until the robot
makes a better job of being John Braling
than the real one does.
Braling **James Coco**
Fantocinni **Leslie Nielsen**

Director: **Paul Lynch**

The Playground

w **Ray Badbury**
Charles Underhill is a man haunted by
memories of childhood bullying and vows
that he will always protect his own son

from such cruelty. But while watching his son and some friends in a playground, Charles is suddenly, strangely summoned to fight the last battle of his childhood against some very bestial children.
Charles Underhill William Shatner
Steve Keith Dutson
Carol Kate Trotter
Ralph Mirko Malish
Charlie Steven Andrade
Peerless Barry Flatman

Director: William Fruet

The Crowd

w Ray Bradbury
One Christmas, Joe Spallner is returning home from a party when his car spins out of control and throws him onto the pavement. In great pain, Spallner looks up to find a menacing crowd gathering around him, the threat growing until he is taken to hospital. A few days later, Spallner is visited by his friend Morgan. As the two talk, Spallner hears a crash outside. He rushes out to find a crash victim surrounded by the same crowd and sets out to find out more about this mysterious group.
Spallner Nick Mancuso
Morgan R.H. Thomson

Director: Ralph Thomas

Other episodes:

The Screaming Woman

w Ray Bradbury
Heather Leary has a highly active imagination and spends much of her time reading stories about evil spirits. One afternoon she hears a faint moan from nearby woods. Investigating, she realises it is coming from underground. But when she tells her parents there is a woman buried alive they dismiss it as just another of her outlandish tales. So with her friend Dippy, Heather sets out to discover who is buried – and who buried her!
Heather Leary Drew Barrymore
Mrs Leary Janet-Laine Green
Mr Leary Roger Dunn
Dippy Ian Heath
Mr Kelly Ken James

Mrs Kelly Jacqueline McLeod
Mr Nesbitt Alan Scarfe
Screaming woman Mary Anne Cotes

Director: Bruce Pittman

(11 May 1989, Thames)

The Town Where No One Got Off

w Ray Bradbury
On a boring train ride across midwest America, a cynical salesman challenges Sam Cogswell to back up his belief that every town they pass is special. Sam accepts and disembarks at the next small hamlet, called Erehwon. There he is drawn into a cat-and-mouse game with an old man who has been waiting 20 years for a stranger to arrive – so he could kill him.
Sam Cogswell Jeff Goldblum
with Ed McNamara *and* Cec Linder

Director: Don McBrearty

(18 May 1979, Thames)

Banshee

w Ray Bradbury
Hollywood screenwriter Douglas Rogers visits movie director John Hampton at his stately manor in Ireland. Hampton, a lady-killer and devilish scoundrel, is an incurable practical joker and when a mournful cry emanates from the mist outside Hampton tells Rogers that the noise occurs one hour before someone dies. Rogers ventures forth and meets a beautiful woman who tells him she is seeking a notorious womaniser – who once lived at the mansion.
Douglas Rogers Charles Martin Smith
John Hampton Peter O'Toole
The Banshee Jennifer Dale

Director: Doug Jackson

(25 May 1989, Thames)

Producer: Seaton McLean

Produced by Atlantis Films Ltd in association with John Wilcox Productions Inc.

(Author's note: the following stories were made in Britain by Granada Television as part of an international package of *Ray Bradbury Theater*, but over-cautiously aired here in August 1988 under the heading *Twist in the Tale* [no relation to the 1978 American anthology series].

Of the 12 shows, Granada produced four, with the others being made in France and Canada. But though they played successfully there, and in America, the macabre mood of the tales didn't sit comfortably with ITV's light entertainment schedules.

The first two of the Granada quartet – *The Coffin* and *Punishment Without Crime* – were seen in August 1988. The second duo, *Small Assassin* and *There Was an Old Lady*, were shown a year later.)

Producer: **Tom Cotter**
Music **Bill Connor**

Granada Television Production
Four colour 30-minute episodes

The Coffin

w **Ray Bradbury**
Wealthy inventor Charles Brayling creates a coffin that literally walks to its own funeral and digs its own grave – with his avaricious ne'er-do-well brother trapped helplessly inside.
Charles Brayling **Dan O'Herlihy**
Richard Brayling **Denholm Elliott**
St John Court **Clive Swift**

Director: **Tom Cotter**
Designer: **Margaret Coombes**

(7 August 1988)

Punishment Without Crime

w **Ray Bradbury**
George Hill's wife takes a lover and George has murder in his heart. 'Facsimiles Ltd' offers him a way to commit the ultimate crime in such a way as to avoid the penalty.

Governor **Bill Croasdale**
Priest **Will Tacey**
George Hill **Donald Pleasence**
Katherine **Lynsey Baxter**
Facsimile interviewer **John McGlynn**
Lover **George Anton**
Policeman **William Ivory**
Judge **Peggy Mount**
Prosecuting counsel **Iain Cuthbertson**
Defence counsel **Frank Williams**

Director: **Bruce Macdonald**
Designer: **Alan Price**

(28 August 1988)

Small Assassin

w **Ray Bradbury**
Alice Leiber gives birth to a baby and is strangely frightened of it – not without reason, for the child has a peculiarly advanced sense of awareness and is out to kill both its parents.
Alice Leiber **Susan Wooldridge**
David Leiber **Leigh Lawson**
Dr Jeffers **Cyril Cusack**

Director: **Tom Cotter**
Designer: **Margaret Coombes**

Producer: **Tom Cotter**

(13 August 1989)

There Was an Old Woman

w **Ray Bradbury**
Aunt Tildy receives a visit from a mysterious stranger – Death, who has come to claim her. But Aunt Tildy is a strong-willed old lady who doesn't want to go, and her spirit proceeds to reclaim her body.
Aunt Tildy **Mary Morris**
Mr Death **Ronald Lacey**
Emily **Sylvestra Le Touzel**
Mortician **Roy Kinnear**

Director: **Bruce Macdonald**
Designer: **Alan Price**

(20 August 1989)

REALLY WEIRD TALES

Trio of fantasy stories from Canada unimaginatively screened in the UK as *Mystery Theatre*.

Really Weird Tales is a stablemate of Atlantis Films' *The Ray Bradbury Theater* – which has also been buried in the ITV schedules – and the three stories so far seen in Britain present an amiable balance of humour and fantasy with comic actors John Candy (*Planes, Trains and Automobiles*) and Martin Short (*The Three Amigos*) among the stars.

They certainly deserve better than 4.00 on a Friday morning which is where Thames Television played them in the London area.

REGULAR CAST
None

Executive producers: Michael MacMillan, Joe Flaherty
Producers: Seaton McLean, Pat Whitley
Theme: Fred Mollin

An Atlantis Films Ltd Production for Home Box Office
Three colour 30-minute episodes

All's Well That Ends Strange

w Joe *and* David Flaherty
Life for girlie magazine publisher Wade Jeffries is an unending party. One of his amusements is Shucky Forme, a second-rate lounge act with third-rate patter. While in Wade's Jacuzzi, Shucky falls for one of his mentor's buxom playmates. But before he can propose, he's confronted with a dead damsel and a workroom full of robots programmed to act like humans. What's going on in Wade's House of Ecstasy?
Wade Jeffries Don Harron
Shucky Forme Martin Short
Tippy Olivia d'Abo

Director: Paul Lynch

Cursed With Charisma

w Joe *and* David Flaherty, John McAndrew
Fitchville's inhabitants have seen better days – they can't even repair the community's sole statue. At a town meeting, depression is rife until Howard Jensen, a huge, well-coiffed albino, appears. This stranger spouts the power of positive thinking and soon everyone in Fitchville is a real estate tycoon. But who – or what – *is* Howard Jensen?
Howard Jensen John Candy

Director: Don McBrearty

I'll Die Loving

w Joe *and* David Flaherty, Catherine O'Hara
Raised in a convent, Theresa Sharpe always thought she was an orphan. Then she learns her father had left her with nuns because she was cursed with a love that kills: she has awesome powers of destruction, and her affection literally blew up her mother. Resigned to go through life hating the world, she gets a job in a complaints department. Then her boss falls in love with her . . .
Theresa Sharpe Catherine O'Hara
Todd Lamont David McIlwraith

Director: John Blanchard

RED DWARF

Cult sci-fi comedy series that breathed new life into the stale old sitcom.

It's set aboard the mining ship *Red Dwarf*, a five-mile long, three-mile wide claustrophobic hybrid of *Dark Star* and the *Nostromo*. All but one of the 169-strong crew perish in a radiation leak in the first episode. The survivor is Dave Lister – technician third class – the lowest of lowly crew members, who was quarantined in suspended animation for keeping a pet cat. Revived after three million years, Lister's only companions are a life-form that has evolved from his cat and a hologram of his obnoxious supervisor Arnold Rimmer. The other regular 'character' is Holly, the ship's lugubrious computer, and occasional contributions come from various talking appliances and a couple of silent robots called scutters.

Though the situation was novel, the comedy was rooted in tradition. The two main characters, Lister and Rimmer, are as compatible as *Steptoe and Son*, and the sparks that fly from their mutually disrespectful banter gives the humour a sharp cutting edge.

Lister is a 'megaslob' whose dream is to open a doughnut parlour on Fiji. Rimmer is astoundingly zealous, desperate for promotion and keeps his underpants on coathangers. It was his mistake that caused the fatal radiation leak.

However, the series' most original creation was the Cat. Played as a hopelessly narcissistic black dude in sharp suits, he got some of the best lines plus some terrific sight gags, including spraying perfume to mark his territory and 'licking' his laundry clean.

Red Dwarf was the latest in a string of original comedy successes steered to the screen by the show's executive producer Paul Jackson, whose roll call includes *The Young Ones* (1984), *Happy Families* (1984) *Filthy, Rich and Catflap* (1986) and *Saturday Live* (1985). Its writers, Rob Grant and Doug Naylor, were one-time head writers for *Spitting Image*, and it was excellently cast with first major TV roles for Liverpudlian poet/comedian Craig Charles and song and dance man Danny John-Jules. Chris Barrie was the voice behind many *Spitting Image* puppets, notably Ronald Reagan.

The series first appeared in February 1988, with a second season following that autumn and a third in November 1989.

MAIN CAST

Arnold Rimmer, BSC, SSC **Chris Barrie**   *Dave Lister* **Craig Charles**
Cat **Danny John-Jules**   *Holly* **Norman Lovett**
Kryten **Robert Llewellyn**   *Holly* **Hattie Hayridge** *(both Season 3)*

Writers: **Rob Grant** *and* **Doug Naylor**
Lighting: **John Pomphrey**
Designer: **Paul Montague**
Visual effects designer: **Peter Wragg**
Music: **Howard Goodall**
Executive producer: **Paul Jackson**
Producer/director: **Ed Bye**

*A Paul Jackson Production for BBC
North West*
18 colour 30-minute episodes
Season One: 15 February–21 March 1988
Season Two: 6 Sept–11 October 1988
Season Three: 14 November–19
December 1989

The End

Lister is put in suspended animation for 18 months for having a pet cat; Rimmer's radiation leak kills the crew. Three million years later, the stage is set . . .
Todhunter **Robert Bathurst**
Chen **Paul Bradley**
Selby **David Gillespie**
Captain Hollister **Mac McDonald**
McIntyre **Robert McCulley**
Peterson **Mark Williams**
Kochanski **C.P. Grogan**

Future Echoes

Having accelerated constantly for three million years, *Red Dwarf* breaks the light barrier. Rimmer and Lister overtake themselves in time and witness images of the future.
Toaster **John Lenahan**
Dispensing machine **Tony Hawks**

Balance of Power

A bored Lister wants a date with dead console officer Christine Kochanski – but first he must persuade Rimmer to turn himself off so she can take his place for a few hours.
Kochanski **C.P. Grogan**
Chef/Trout à la Creme **Rupert Bates**
Chen **Paul Bradley**
Selby **David Gillespie**
Peterson **Mark Williams**

Waiting for God

Cat's holy book of smells reveals Lister in a divine light as the cat-god Cloister and leads to an encounter with a cat-priest.
Cat priest **Noel Coleman**
Toaster **John Lenahan**

Confidence and Paranoia

Lister develops a mutated form of pneumonia that causes his hallucinations to become solid. These include the two sides of his personality, the overbearing Confidence and the insecure Paranoia. Egged on by Confidence, Lister tries to revive Kochanski as a hologram but duplicates Rimmer instead.
Paranoia **Lee Cornes**
Confidence **Craig Ferguson**
Dispensing machine **Tony Hawks**

Me²

The two Rimmer holograms move in together and all is tickety-boo until they begin to get on each other's nerves – and Lister's. One Rimmer will have to go.
Arnold Rimmer 2 **Chris Barrie**
Capt. Hollister **Mac McDonald**

Season Two

Kryten

A distress call from a marooned spaceship with 'three woman survivors' has *all* the Red Dwarfers preparing for their first date in three million years. But all they find are skeletons, tended by a servile android, the very admirable Kryten.
Kryten **David Ross**
Esperanto woman **Johanna Hargreaves**
Android actor **Tony Slattery**

Better Than Life

A post pod brings a batch of computer games including the latest 'total immersion video' Better Than Life which enables the players to experience their wildest dreams.
Rimmer's dad **John Abineri**

Marilyn Monroe Debbie Ash
Rathbone Jeremy Austin
The Captain Nigel Carrivick
The guide Tony Hawks
McGruder Judy Hawkins
Newsreader Tina Jenkins
Taxman Ron Pember
Gordon Gordon Salkilld

Thanks for the Memory

The crew of the *Red Dwarf* awake one morning to discover that someone has erased their memory of the last four days, broken Lister and the Cat's legs and done Lister's jigsaw. Finding out why brings even more pain . . . for Rimmer.
Lise Yates Sabra Williams

Stasis Leak

A leak creates a doorway to the past. Lister tries his luck with Kochanski; Rimmer tries to warn himself about the future.
Lift hostess Morwenna Banks
Kochanski C.P. Grogan
Room mate Sophie Doherty
Orderly Richard Hainsworth
Suitcase Tony Hawks
Capt. Hollister Mac McDonald
Petersen Mark Williams

Queeg

Holly's increasingly erratic behaviour prompts a takeover by the *Red Dwarf*'s back-up computer, a 'black drill-sergeant' type called Queeg 500. The crew are driven to despair until Holly reveals it was him all along – his 'wheeze of the week'.
Queeg Charles Augins

Parallel Universe

Holly devises a faster-than-light drive which immediately goes wrong and propels *Red Dwarf* into a parallel universe, where Holly, Lister and Rimmer meet their female counterparts and the Cat is paired off with a dog.
Arlene Suzanne Bertish
Deb Angela Bruce
Pooch Matthew Devitt
Hilly Hattie Hayridge

Season Three

(Late entry: episode titles only)
Backwards
Marooned
Polymorph
Body Swap
Timeslides
The Last Day

THE RETURN OF CAPTAIN NEMO

Three-part American mini-series updating the adventures of Jules Verne's classic character to the 1980s.

Two US Navy divers discover Captain Nemo and his strange craft, *Nautilus*, wedged deep in the Pacific. They free him from a state of suspended animation and enlist his help in overcoming Prof. Waldo Cunningham, an evil genius who is threatening to destroy Washington unless he is paid one billion dollars in gold. The Captain also has to repair a leak of radioactive waste buried 36,000 ft down in the Mindinao Trench, before finally confronting his adversary in the fabled lost city of Atlantis.

Two Hollywood stalwarts, José Ferrer and Burgess Meredith, starred as the undersea rivals, and the whole affair was produced with his customary gusto by Irwin Allen, veteran of many a *Voyage to the Bottom of the Sea*.

MAIN CAST

Captain Nemo **José Ferrer**   *Cmdr Tom Franklin* **Tom Hallick**
Lt Jim Porter **Burr DeBenning**   *Prof. Cunningham* **Burgess Meredith**
Kate **Lynda Day George**   *Dr Cook* **Mel Ferrer**
Mr Miller **Warren Stevens**   *King Tibor* **Horst Buchholz**
Tor **Med Flory**   *Helmsman* **Randolph Roberts**
Lloyd **Stephen Powers**   *Sirak* **Yale Summers**
Bork **Anthony Geary**

Writers: **Norman Katkov, Preston Wood, Robert Dennis, William Keys, Mann Rubin, Robert Bloch, Larry Alexander**
Director: **Alex March**
Producer: **Irwin Allen**

An Irwin Allen Production
Three colour 45-minute episodes
13–15 April 1981
(BBC1)

RETURN TO THE LOST PLANET

Second of Angus MacVicar's TV adaptations of *her* radio space sagas, this six-part sequel to *The Lost Planet* (see separate entry) landed in the BBC's teatime slot exactly one year later, with its hero, Lachlan McKinnon, marooned on the surface of Hesikos, facing almost certain death in the lost planet's icy winter.

Radio Times readers were told that Hesikos was not a name just plucked out of nowhere, that it was a minor planet mentioned by Plato which supposedly swung close to Earth some 10,000 years ago. Pythagoras even predicted its reapparance – in the 20th century.

This second series introduced the Hesikosians – a gentle race ruled by the beneficent Solveg and his daughter Asa, who kept in touch with their new Earth friends via the electronome, a device which could direct thought-beams around the universe.

Just a month earlier, actor Van Boolen had appeared in the controversial *Nineteen Eighty-Four*. Now he was once again snarling as the dastardly Hermanoff. Other survivors from the first series were Peter Kerr as Jeremy Grant, Joan Allen as Madge Smith, and John Stuart as the heroic McKinnon.

CAST

Jeremy Grant **Peter Kerr**   Dr Lachlan McKinnon **John Stuart**
Madge Smith **Joan Allen**   Andrieff **Wolfe Morris**
Janet Campbell **Greta Watson**   Prof. Bergman **Derek Benfield**
Prof. Hermanoff **Van Boolen**   Spike Stranahan **Michael Alexander**
Solveg **Peter Alexander**   Asa **Julie Webb**   Dorman **Michael Segal**
with: **Donald Masters, C.B. Poultney, Christopher Hodge, Ronald Marriott,
Eugene Leahy**

Writer: **Angus MacVicar** (alias **André
Norton**)
Producer: **Kevin Sheldon**
Designer: **John Cooper**

A BBC Production
Six 30-minute episodes, black and white

A Message from Space
The Crystal Sand
The Underground Cavern
The Secret City
The Electronome
The Roaring Torrent

8 January–19 March 1955

SALVAGE-1

'A one-hour adventure series that proves one
man's trash is another man's treasure.'

(series publicity)

The exploits of scrap dealer Harry Broderick and his 'junkyard spaceship' resulted in an oddball series that at times came to resemble an live version of *Thunderbirds*!

Salvage expert Harry builds his rocket to fly to the Moon to pick up the multi-million dollar pieces left behind there by the *Apollo* missions. He hires two ex-NASA engineers, Fred and Mack, recruits maverick astronaut Skip Carmichael and shapely rocket fuel expert Melanie Slozar and begins procuring vast amounts of NASA surplus stock – all of which arouses the suspicions of the FBI.

Salvage-1 takes off minutes before FBI agents storm the junkyard and, after navigating various dangers, the mission is a success, turning Harry and his cohorts into national heroes.

Thereafter, Salvage-1 (also known as the *Vulture*) becomes their own unique mode of transport enabling them to travel to the furthest corners of the world at a moment's notice. In future episodes they help an amnesiac robot (*Mermadon*), tow an iceberg to a drought-stricken island (*Hard Water*), stage a space rescue (*Golden Orbit*), depressurise a volcano (*Diamond Volcano*), help a stranded Andromedan visitor (*The Haunting of Manderly*

Mansion), rescue a little girl trapped by an earthquake (*Shelter Five*) and, in the series' opener, encounter a Robinson Crusoe scientist and a giant King-Kong like apeman (*Dark Island*). All invariably under the glowering eye of FBI agent Jack Klinger.

The series, produced by Harve '*Six Million Dollar Man*' Bennett and Harris Katleman, was actually cancelled in America after the opening two-parter of the second season, but *all* the episodes were shown in the UK, between 1979 and 1981.

REGULAR CAST

Harry Broderick **Andy Griffith**　*Melanie Slozar* **Trish Stewart**
Skip Carmichael **Joel Higgins**　*Mack* **J. Jay Saunders**
Jack Klinger **Richard Jaeckel**

Creator/supervising producer: **Mike Lloyd Ross**
Executive producers: **Harve Bennett, Harris Katleman**
Producer: **Ralph Sariego**
Writers: Various, including **Mike Lloyd Ross, Robert Swanson, Ruel Fischmann**
Directors: Various, including **Ray Austin, Ron Satlof**

A Bennett/Katleman Production in association with Columbia Pictures Television
18 colour 60-minute episodes (plus 100-minute pilot)
UK premiere:
15 May 1979
(Thames)

US Season One:

Salvage-1 (pilot movie)
Dark Island
Shangri-La Lil
Shelter Five
The Haunting of Manderly Mansion (aka Ghost Trap)
Bugatti Treasure (aka The Bugatti Map)
Golden Orbit (A 2-part story)
Operation Breakout
Mermadon
Up, Up and Away
Energy Solution
Confederate Gold

Season Two

Hard Water (A 2-part story)
Round Up
Harry's Doll
Dry Spell
Diamond Volcano

SAPPHIRE & STEEL

'All irregularities will be handled by the forces controlling each dimension. Transuranic heavy elements may not be used where there is life. Medium atomic weights are available: Gold, Mercury, Copper, Jet, Diamond, Radium, Sapphire, Silver and Steel. Sapphire and Steel have been assigned!'

Thus spake . . . someone (it was never clear who), announcing the imminent arrival of two time detectives, elemental beings who assumed human form to deal with the aforementioned irregularities – threats to or from time.

Their twice-weekly series of adventures was created by P.J. Hammond, better known for scripting more routine police shows such as *Z-Cars* or *Hunter's Walk*. His premise was that instead of having people going from everyday life into time, he would have time breaking into everyday life.

Thus, Sapphire tells us, in the first episode, that 'time is a corridor . . . Once in a while Time itself can try to enter into the Present – break in – burst through, to take things . . . to take people'.

It was the job of the 'timebusters' to confront whatever malevolent force had broken through and seal up the holes in the time corridor. As a drama, it relied almost wholly on the careful build-up of suspense rather than gadget-filled action. Intensely claustrophobic and theatrical in its settings, the atmosphere of menace or unease was often conveyed by sound-effects, lighting and moody music.

The principals in this paranormal crime squad were ex-*New Avenger* Joanna Lumley, dressed in blue as the psychic Sapphire (described by one critic as 'the head girl of the universe'), and David McCallum as the grey-suited, broody Steel, a cool and logical character with enormous strength and the power to withstand the flow of time. A couple of other elements appeared from time to time – Silver, a slightly wimpish technical genius, and Lead, a huge, powerful character.

Sapphire & Steel polarised the viewing public and the critics – you were either baffled and bored or baffled and absorbed.

(The first series was interrupted by the 1979 ITV technicians' strike, when most regions had only just begun the second story. When the strike ended, rather than pick up where it had left off, ITV backtracked and began again at episode 7, the start of the second adventure. None of the stories had titles and became known simply as Adventure One, Adventure Two etc).

REGULAR CAST

Sapphire Joanna Lumley   *Steel* David McCallum
Silver David Collings

Creator/writer: P.J. Hammond
Producer: Shaun O'Riordan
Executive producer: David Reid
Designer: Stanley Mills *(except Adventure Five:* Sue Chases)
Music: Cyril Ornadel

An ATV Network Production
34 colour 30-minute episodes
Season One:
10 July–22 November 1979
Season Two:
6 January–5 February 1981
Season Three:
11–26 August 1981
Season Four:
19–31 August 1982

Season One
(14 episodes)

Adventure One

(A 6-part story)
In an isolated country house, young Robert is bent over his homework. Clocks tick and the muffled sounds of his parents reading to his younger sister Helen drift downstairs. Suddenly, a great rushing wind sweeps the house then dies away, leaving an absolute silence in its wake – all the clocks in the house have stopped ticking. Robert dashes upstairs to find his sister alone – their parents have vanished. Minutes later, Sapphire and Steel arrive to challenge the 'invader' who has spirited away the children's parents. It's a battle in which only the ground floor is safe and in which Sapphire enters a painting and is menaced by Roundhead soldiers. Steel calls on Lead's assistance and between them they finally defeat the enemy – depicted as three patches of light – and reunite the children with their parents.
Rob Steven O'Shea
Helen Tamasin Bridge
Mother Felicity Harrison
Father John Golightly
Countryman Ronald Goodale
Lead Val Pringle

Director: Shaun O'Riordan

Adventure Two

(An 8-part story)
Psychic expert George Tully is convinced his railway station is haunted. His ghost-hunting involves Sapphire and Steel in a clash with a sinister outside force which is feeding on the resentment of the dead and creating havoc with the balance of time. The spectre appears as a figure dressed in the uniform of a World War One soldier. Tully succeeds in contacting the 'dead man' only to unleash a frightening force which becomes a duplicate of Sapphire.
Tully Gerald James
Soldier (Pearce) Tom Kelly
Pilot David Cann
Submariner David Woodcock

Directors: Shaun O'Riordan, David Foster

Season Two
(10 episodes)

Adventure Three

(A 6-part story)
Sapphire and Steel investigate an invisible penthouse atop a modern-day block of flats which is occupied by Eldred and Rothwyn, two time-travellers from the future. But the couple, who are heard but not seen, have brought something with them – a strange 'changeling' that seizes Sapphire. Joined by Silver, Steel tracks down the time source which is endangering Earth and must be closed.
Silver David Collings
Eldred David Gant
Rothwyn Catherine Hall
Changeling Russell Wootton

Director: Shaun O'Riordan

Adventure Four

(A 4-part story)
Sapphire and Steel find the 'in between' children who have been released from old photographs, and encounter the Shape, a being which can pass in and out of photographs, escaping to their time zones. To defeat it, and repair the break in the time corridor, Sapphire and Steel must also enter a photograph.
Liz Alyson Spiro
Shapes Philip Bird, Bob Hornery
Ruth Shelagh Stephenson
Parasol girl Natalie Hedges

Director: David Foster

Season Three
(6 episodes)

Adventure Five

(A 6-part story)
w Don Houghton, Anthony Read
A murder is rerun in a time warp at a party given by businessman Lord Mullrine, and Sapphire and Steel find themselves watching the events turn towards an inevitable conclusion.
Emma Mullrine Patience Collier
Lord Mullrine Davy Kaye
Felicity McDee Nan Munro

Felix Harborough **Jeffry Wickham**
Howard McDee **Jeremy Child**
Annabelle Harborough **Jennie Stoller**
Greville **Peter Laird**
George McDee **Stephen Macdonald**
Tony Purnell **Christopher Bramwell**
Anne Shaw **Patricia Shakesby**
Veronica Blamey **Debbie Farrington**

Director: **Shaun O'Riordan**

Season Four
(4 episodes)

Adventure Six

(A 4-part story)
On what starts as a normal patrol,

Sapphire & Steel discover a service station where the only travellers are from the past. A man is heard approaching, but only a shadow arrives. Silver joins them and suggests there must be a plan behind such trickery, and the time detectives duly discover that they are the central figures in a drama that ends with them being cast adrift in time and space in a window in the sky.

Silver **David Collings**
Man **Edward de Souza**
Woman **Johanna Kirby**
Old man **John Boswall**
Johnny Jack **Chris Fairbank**

Director: **David Foster**

SCIENCE FICTION THEATRE

This American anthology of 30-minute dramas was the second science fiction series to be picked up by the fledgling ITV service (starting the day after *Superman*), with ATV in the Midlands giving it a prolonged run in 1956. Based on flights of fact rather than fancy, *Science Fiction Theatre* was hosted and narrated by newsman Truman Bradley who opened each show with a demonstration of the scientific concept at the heart of that week's story. These included suspended animation, telepathy, transplants, time and space travel, and medical advancements. A series aimed at adults, it generally took a positive view of science and avoided twist-in-the-tail endings.

One episode singled out for critical praise was *Strange People at Pecos* in which the words 'Martians Go Home!' are scrawled in childish letters on a pavement as a town – adults and children alike – turns against a family who appear to be alien. The story offered no definitive conclusion, but that week's 'concept' was teleportation . . .

Several familiar names, including Vincent Price and Vera Miles, appeared in the series. In one story, *The Strange Dr Lorenz*, veteran actor Edmund Gwenn (Kirs Kringle in *Miracle on 34th Street*) played a beekeeper whose honey had remarkable healing properties. In another, William Lundigan, moonbound star of the 1959 series *Men Into Space*, played a test pilot driven franatic by high-level refusal to believe his story of *something* flying at three times the speed of sound that nearly collided with his plane. And 'Bones' himself, DeForest Kelley, appeared in an episode,

Y.O.R.D., about strange signals from space picked up by a weather station.

In America, the series ran for 78 episodes between 1955 and 1957, in both black and white and colour. Over here, ATV screened 28 of them, all monochrome, on Friday evenings between February and September 1956. (Incidentally, when the run finished the slot was taken over by *Sailor of Fortune*, an early outing for that well-known space cowboy, Lorne Greene.)

Host/narrator: **Truman Bradley**
Producer: **Ivan Tors**

First UK transmission: 24 February–14 September 1956 (ATV Midlands)

SECRET BENEATH THE SEA

Six-part sequel to *City Beneath the Sea* which brought scientific journalist Mark Bannerman and his youthful assistant Peter Blake face to face with an old adversary and a new friend before encountering fresh dangers in the subterranean city of Aegira.

The plot concerned the duo's efforts to obtain samples, from the sea bed, of Phenicium, a rare metal vital for space research because of its resistance to the most intense heat. The old foe was former wartime U-boat ace Kurt Swendler who seeks their help when the unscrupulous head of an international metal combine tries to corner the world market in Phenicium. The new friend who shared the underwater adventure was teenager Janet Slayton whose prizewinning entry in an essay competition earns her a trip to Aegira. Naturally, she gets caught up in the events that follow, including a spate of life-threatening sabotage, before the heroes can fulfil their mission.

MAIN CAST

Mark Bannerman **Gerald Flood**   *Peter Blake* **Stewart Guidotti**
Capt. Payne **Peter Williams**   *Dr Deraad* **Richard Coleman**
Janet Slayton **Ingrid Sylvester**   *Dr Ellen Carey* **Delena Kidd**
Prof. Gordon **Robert James**   *Prof. Soobiah* **David Spenser**
with: Helmsman **Michael Darlow**   *Engineer* **Derek Smee**
Sanders **Murray Hayne**   *Sir George* **Reginald Smith**
Insp. Lovatt **Anthony Woodruff**   *Kurt Swendler* **Denis Goacher**
Seaman **Christopher Sandford**   *Tug master* **Harry Webster**
Doctor **Brian Hawksley**   *Sentry* **Peter Jesson**

Writer: **John Lucarotti**
Director: **Kim Mills**
Producer: **Guy Verney**

Settings: **James Goddard** *and* **Stanley Woodward**
Programme adviser: **Mary Field**

An ABC Television Network Production
Six 30-minute episodes, black and white

The Mysterious Metal
Voyage Into Danger
Sabotage

The X-Layer
Take-over
The Death Trap

16 February–23 March 1963

THE SECRET SERVICE

'Parochial guile and crafty for the deep joy of the
Secret Serve.'

This curious blend of live action and puppetry has become
something of an enigmatic detour in the upwardly mobile career of
Gerry Anderson.

As far as most of the country is concerned, it might as well not
have existed at all, as only three ITV regions actually screened the
13-part series – ATV Midlands, Granada and Southern.

The Andersons had already branched out into live action via the
movie feature *Doppelganger* (1969) but, in television terms, *The
Secret Service* appears as a partially submerged stepping stone
between the last of the pure Supermarionation puppet shows, *Joe
90*, and the first of Century 21's live action series *U.F.O.*

Released in the autumn of 1969, *The Secret Service* blends the
two forms of production by using a human star and his puppet
double (or vice versa!) – appropriate casting for double-talk
comedy actor Stanley Unwin whose gobbledygook was a feature of
the shows. Essentially, puppets were used for close-ups and studio
work, while actors stood in on long shots and location. In particular
this enabled the characters to be seen walking and standing
properly, overcoming a perennial puppet problem.

It's a series bereft of the futuristic hardware of *Thunderbirds* or
Captain Scarlet, set instead in an England of the then present day (à
la *Avengers*), and centring on the exploits of Father Stanley Unwin,
an amiable 57-year-old country vicar who unexpectedly finds
himself working for the Bishop – British Intelligence Service
Headquarters Operation Priest. Father Unwin uses a device called
a minimiser – a bequest from a late parishioner – concealed inside a
book, to miniaturise his gardener Matthew Harding (a highly
trained agent posing as a slow-witted country bumpkin) and carry
him around in a briefcase equipped with a chair, periscope and
miniature tool kit.

Totally unaware of their covert activities is kindly housekeeper
Mrs Appleby, voiced by Sylvia Anderson.

The series' other 'star' was Gabriel – Father Unwin's vintage Model T Ford. The genuine article was used on location, with a radio-controlled replica used for the puppet Unwin.

Gerry Anderson has described *The Secret Service* as 'one of the most charming series I've ever made'. But the charm didn't work on ATV chief Lew Grade who had reservations about its commercial potential – and its cost. At £20,000 an episode, it was proving extremely expensive and with just six episodes filmed, Grade called time, setting a limit of unlucky 13 for Anderson.

REGULAR CAST

Father Unwin **Stanley Unwin**

WITH THE VOICES OF:

Stanley Unwin *(Fr Unwin)*, **Keith Alexander** *(yokel Matthew)*
Gary Files *(agent Matthew)*, **Sylvia Anderson** *(Mrs Appleby)*,
Jeremy Wilkin *(The Bishop)*, **David Healy**

Creators: **Gerry** *and* **Sylvia Anderson**
Producer: **David Lane**
Executive Producer: **Reg Hill**
Production supervisor: **Desmond Saunders**
Script editor: **Tony Barwick**
Visual effects supervisor: **Derek Meddings**

Music: **Barry Gray**
Theme song: **The Mike Sammes Singers**

Century 21/ITC Production for ATV
13 colour 30-minute episodes.
21 September–14 December 1969 (ATV Midlands)

A Case for the Bishop

w **Gerry** *and* **Sylvia Anderson**
The Bishop discovers that a stolen computer – vital for future exports – is to be smuggled out of the country in a foreign ambassador's diplomatic bag. He calls in Father Unwin who sneaks a miniaturised Matthew on board the ambassador's plane to commit sabotage.

Director: **Alan Perry**

A Question of Miracles

w **Donald James**
Father Unwin and Matthew race against time as they probe the possibility of sabotage at a series of water-purifying plants which have exploded after 250 hours of service.

Director: **Leo Eaton**

To Catch a Spy

w **Pat Dunlop**
When a top spy is sprung from jail in a daring night-time helicopter raid, a homing device in his uniform leads the security services to the home of influential Sir Humphrey Burton. A minimised Matthew infiltrates his house and discovers that the spy is to be smuggled away by submarine.

Director: **Brian Heard**

The Feathered Spies

w **Tony Barwick**
Father Unwin discovers that pigeons are being used to take aerial photos of a new fighter plane at an isolated airfield . . . but the next one will be carrying a bomb.

Director: **Ian Spurrier**

Last Train to Bufflers Halt

w Tony Barwick

After one unsuccessful robbery attempt, Father Unwin and Matthew are assigned to guard a trainload of gold and when the train is hijacked and the crew captured, it's up to mini-Matthew to beat the crooks.

Director: Alan Perry

Hole in One

w Shane Rimmer

General Brompton is suspected of passing on information being used to tamper with a vital satellite's orbit. Fr Unwin believes the general is unwittingly involved and finds the answer lies on the golf course – at the 15th hole.

Director: Brian Heard

Recall to Service

w Pat Dunlop

Father Unwin gets miniaturised Matthew hidden inside a new tank which has suffered a computer fault and finds it heading straight for a building containing top NATO officials.

Director: Peter Anderson

Errand of Mercy

w Tony Barwick

Confined to bed by illness, Father Unwin dreams that he and Matthew are flying to Africa in his Model T Ford, Gabriel, to deliver vital medical supplies and are forced to fight off a rocket attack.

Director: Leo Eaton

The Deadly Whisper

w Donald James

Matthew discovers that Father Unwin's friend Prof. Soames and his daughter are being held hostage by saboteurs who want to use the scientist's latest sonic invention to wreck a new aircraft.

Director: Leo Eaton

The Cure

w Pat Dunlop

Father Unwin trails an infamous agent, Sakov, to a health centre and discovers that the man is planning to sabotage a car testing a revolutionary new fuel. But he is unable to warn Matthew, who is hidden inside the car.

Director: Leo Eaton

School for Spies

w Donald James

Father Unwin infiltrates a group of mercenaries who are posing as priests for a series of sabotage missions. His role: explosive expert.

Director: Ken Turner

May-day, May-day!

w Bob Keston

Having survived four assassination bids, an Arab king arrives in London to sign an oil treaty. Father Unwin and Matthew are assigned to protect him and find themselves on a plane with a bomb on board. What's more: the crew have all been gassed!

Director: Alan Perry

More Haste – Less Speed

w Tony Barwick

Father Unwin miniaturises himself, Matthew and Gabriel to thwart an eccentric bunch of crooks all trying to get their hands on a counterfeiter's printing plates.

Director: Ken Turner

THE SECRET WORLD OF POLLY FLINT

Enchanting six-part children's fantasy about a girl who encounters the strange world of a village lost in time.

Polly Flint is devastated when she is sent to live with her aunt while her father struggles to recover from a tragic mining accident that has left him paralysed. Heartbroken at being separated from her parents, Polly is even more unhappy when she discovers the strict regime of her starchy Aunt Em.

But the heartache erases when Polly hears a local legend about the lost village of Grimstone. She meets an odd character called Old Mazy who tells her that Grimstone vanished one May Day 400 years ago. It 'slipped the nets of time', he says. Enchanted by the notion, Polly begins to appreciate her lifestyle and a whole magical world opens up when she meets and befriends the strange folk from the lost village, the 'Time Gypsies', and helps them get back to their own time.

The Secret World of Polly Flint was filmed entirely on location in the Dukeries area of north Nottinghamshire, with the National Trust's Clumber Park providing the setting for the medieval village of Grimstone.

CAST

Narrator **Michael Hordern**	*Polly Flint* **Katie Reynolds**
Alice Flint **Emily Richard**	*Tom Flint* **Malcolm Storry**
Aunt Em **Susan Jameson**	*Old Mazy* **Don Henderson**
Davey Cole **Dylan Champion**	*Sam Porter* **Daniel Pope**
Granny Porter **Brenda Bruce**	*Gil Porter* **Jeremy Coote**
Doris **Daphne Neville**	*Miner* **Stacy Davies**

Writer: **Helen Cresswell**
Producer/director: **David Cobham**
Designer: **Giovanni Guarino**
Music: **Paul Lewis**

A Central Production in association with Revcom Television
Six colour 30-minute episodes
16 February–23 March 1987

SIERRA NINE

Children's adventure series about a trio of scientific trouble-shooters who were a sort of junior-league cross between *The Avengers* and *The Professionals*.

Sierra Nine was a watchdog organisation set up to keep tabs on anything – or anyone – that threatened the scientific equilibrium of the age, be it a stolen missile, secret formula or deadly new weapon. S9 was led by Sir Willoughby Dodd, an eccentric ageing scientist described by his creator, scriptwriter Peter Hayes, as 'a nut case at first sight, but a genius underneath'. Sir Willoughby directed two young assistants, Peter Chance and Anna Parsons, from an exotic office off Trafalgar Square.

The 1963 series was devised when John Rhodes, then ITV's head of Children's Television, asked Hayes and director Marc Miller to come up with a new slant on science fiction. The result was four assorted stories, spread over 13 weeks.

REGULAR CAST

Sir Willoughby Dodd **Max Kirby**   *Dr Peter Chance* **David Sumner**
Anna Parsons **Deborah Stanford**   *The Baron* **Harold Kasket** *(Stories 1 and 4)*

Writer: **Peter Hayes**
Director: **Marc Miller**

Associated Rediffusion Network Production
13 30-minute episodes, black and white
7 May–30 July 1963

Story One

The Brain Machine

(A 4-part story)
Peter and Anna are rushed to the oil kingdom of Mirzan in the Middle East to locate and destroy a device operated by a renegade scientist known as 'The Baron'. Using microwave radio, he is warping the minds of research wrokers all over the world by telepathic hypnosis.
Prof. Portman **Ronald Ibbs**
Jane Brightside **Ann Rye**
Beamish **Robert Mill**
Arab spy **Robert Chapman**
King Sharifa **Henry Soskin**
Col. Selim **Julian Sherrier**
Bernard Portman **Raymond Mason**
Arab guard **Oswald Laurence**
Paratroop major **John Trenaman**

Settings: **Bernard Goodwin**

Story Two

The Man Who Shook the World

(A 3-part story)
A minute atomic warhead, designed by

eminent nuclear physicist Sir Hugo Petersham, is stolen on its way to be tested in America. When the detonator circuit is activated, Anna and Peter must track down the thieves before the device explodes.
Sir Hugo Petersham **David Garth**
Graham Lambert **George Roubicek**
Security guard **Norman Mitchell**
Ernie **Timothy Bateson**
Scowse **Peter Thomas**
US Army colonel **Gordon Tanner**
Miguel Alvarez **George Little**

Settings: **Duncan Cameron**

Story Three

The Elixir of Life

(A 2-part story)
Chance and Anna go to a French monastery where monks claim to have a potion enabling people to live forever, to find out who is out to steal the secret.
Father Gabriel **Jack May**
Brother Theodore **Brian Poiser**
Brother Victor **Blake Butler**

Settings: **Andrew Drummond**

Story Four

The Q-Radiation

(A 4-part story)
The theft of a terrifying new weapon leads to another encounter with 'The Baron' for Chance and Anna who find themselves facing annihilation by death ray.

Dr John Quendon **Peter Halliday**
Tom Batley **Rodney Bewes**
Lord Cardington **John Gabriel**
Prof. Tudor Owen **Ivor Salter**
Foley **Alan White**
Galliver **Robert Brown**

Settings: **Ken Jones**

THE SIX MILLION DOLLAR MAN

Based on the novel *Cyborg* by Martin Caiden, *The Six Million Dollar Man* began with a strong science fiction premise that became less significant as the series wore on.

The bionic man, played by former *Big Valley* star Lee Majors, was introduced in a 1974 TV movie which told how astronaut and NASA test pilot Col. Steve Austin – 'a man barely alive' – was literally rebuilt after a catastrophobic plane crash which robbed him of both legs, an arm and an eye. At a cost of six million dollars, medical scientists, led by Dr Rudy Wells, equipped him with nuclear-powered limbs and a bionic eye (vividly depicted in the series' opening graphics), enabling him to run and swim at 60 mph, bend metal, smash down walls, leap fences (and small buildings) at a single bound, and see vast distances.

Initially, Austin finds it hard to reconcile himself with being a 'freak' and tries to commit suicide – a touching display of human emotion that went down well with critics and public. Once he came to terms with his lot, however, there was no stopping him. The man, like the series, ran and ran.

Austin starts work for a CIA-like government agency, the Office of Strategic Investigations (OSI), headed by the intransigent Oscar Goldman who assigns his high-priced agent all the high-risk missions. These ran the gamut of story possibilities, from political, crime or scientific thrillers and personal dramas, to a few more overtly sf adventures involving space and aliens.

In *Burning Bright*, William Shatner guest-starred as an astronaut friend of Austin who is affected in space by an electrical field that gives him the power to communicate with dolphins and control people's minds. In *Straight on 'Til Morning* Austin befriends a radioactive extraterrestrial (Meg Foster) and helps her return to her mother spacecraft before the authorities get to her.

The Pioneers featured *M*A*S*H* star Mike Farrell as one half of a cryogenically frozen pair of astronauts who gains superhuman strength; and *Just a Matter of Time* had Steve Austin returning from an orbital flight to learn six years had elapsed.

Lee Majors' wife Farrah Fawcett-Majors guest-starred in three stories – twice as Major Kelly Wood, stranded in space in *The Rescue of Athena One* and accused of espionage in *Nightmare in the Sky*, and once as a gambler, Trish Hollander, in *The Golden Pharoah*.

Then, of course, there was *The Bionic Woman*, Jaime Sommers (Lindsay Wagner) – see separate entry – whose successful introduction in a couple of SMDM stories earned her a series of her own, and *The Bionic Boy* (Vince Van Patten). One episode, *The Seven Million Dollar Man*, featured a new 'state of the art' bionic man, but he cracked up under the strain.

Another of the series' more memorable characters was Bigfoot, (played first by André the Giant, and, later, by *Addams Family* star Ted Cassidy). Sasquatch was first revealed in *The Secret of Bigfoot* as a creature created by aliens in their underground laboratory.

The Six Million Dollar Man premiered in Britain in September 1974 and, with *The Bionic Woman*, became one of the most successful American imports of the mid-1970s before the law of diminishing re-runs finally caught up with the 60 mph man in the early 1980s. (The series has now been acquired by the BBC.)

Most areas have seen most of the 102 episodes (plus pilot) but one tale, *Outrage in Balinderry*, about an Irish terrorist group called the IBA (!), was only seen on Southern before being banned.

REGULAR CAST

Steve Austin **Lee Majors**   *Oscar Goldman* **Richard Anderson**
Dr Rudy Wells **Alan Oppenheimer** *(later* **Martin E. Brooks***)*

Executive producers: Glen A. Larson, Harve Bennett, Allan Balter
Producers: Michael Gleason, Lee Sigel, Joe L. Cramer, Fred Freiberger
Writers: Numerous
Directors: Various
Music: Oliver Nelson

A Universal Television Production
102 colour episodes (60 mins unless stated), plus pilot movie
UK premiere: 5 September 1974

(Author's note: ITV regionalisation meant that the length and composition of the various UK runs varied considerably around the country. So, for ease of reference, I've listed the episodes in their original American seasons.)

Pilot film

The Six Million Dollar Man (85 mins)

Season One

Wine, Women and War (90 mins)
The Solid Gold Kidnapping (90 mins)
Population Zero
Survival of the Fittest
Operation Firefly
Day of the Robot
Little Orphan Airplane
Doomsday and Counting
Eyewitness to Murder
The Rescue of Athena One
Dr Wells is Missing
The Last of the Fourth of Julys

Burning Bright
The Coward
Run, Steve, Run

The Golden Pharaohs
Love Song for Tanya
The Bionic Badge
Big Brother

Season Two

Nuclear Alert
The Pioneers
Pilot Error
The Pal-Mir Escort
The Seven Million Dollar Man
Straight on 'Til Morning
The Midas Touch
The Deadly Replay
Act of Piracy
The Peeping Blonde
Cross Country Kidnap
Lost Love
Return of the Robot Maker
Taneha
Last Kamikaze
Look Alike
The E.S.P. Spy
The Bionic Woman (a 2-part story)
Stranger in Broken Fork
Outrage in Balinderry
Steve Austin, Fugitive

Season Four

The Return of Bigfoot (Part 1)**
Nightmare in the Sky
Double Trouble
The Most Dangerous Enemy
H+2+O = Death
Kill Oscar (Part 2)†
The Bionic Boy (2 hours in US, shown as
a 2-part story in UK)
Vulture of the Andes
The Thunderbird Connection (2 hours in
US, shown as a 2-part story in UK)
A Bionic Christmas Carol
Task Force
The Ultimate Impostor (unsold pilot)
Death Probe (a 2-part story)
Danny's Inferno
The Fires of Hell
The Infiltrators
Carnival of Spies
U-509
Privacy of the Mind
To Catch the Eagle
The Ghostly Teletype

Season Three

The Return of the Bionic Woman (a 2-part story)
The Price of Liberty
The Song and Dance Spy
The Wolf Boy
The Deadly Test
Target in the Sky
One of Our Running Backs Is Missing
The Bionic Criminal
The Blue Flash
The White Lightning War
Divided Loyalty
Clark Templeton O'Flaherty
The Winning Smile
Welcome Home, Jaime (Part 1)*
Hocus-Pocus
The Secret of Bigfoot (a 2-part story)

Season Five

Sharks (a 2-part story)
Deadly Countdown (a 2-part story)
Bigfoot V
Killer Wind
Rollback
Dark Side of the Moon (a 2-part story)
Target: Steve Austin
The Cheshire Project
Walk a Deadly Wing
Just a Matter of Time
Return of Death Probe (a 2-part story)
The Lost Island (2 hours)
The Madonna Caper
Deadly Ringer
Date With Danger (a 2-part story)
The Moving Mountain

* 'Part 2' was the premiere episode of *The Bionic Woman* series. In the UK, *both* parts were shown as *The Bionic Woman*.
** Again, 'Part 2' was originally shown in America as an episode of *The Bionic Woman*, but in the UK, *both* parts went out as *The Six Million Dollar Man*.
† Second of a three-part story, the other two being episodes of *The Bionic Woman*. Over here, they *all* went out as *The Bionic Woman*.

SKY

Back in the 1970s, when nearly every science fiction series ITV mounted was touted as a rival to *Doctor Who*, all the best ideas emerged in the children's slots (*Timeslip*, *Ace of Wands*, *The Tomorrow People*).

Sky was another such contender. Written by one-time *Doctor Who* writers Bob Baker and Dave Martin, it told the story of a young time-travelling deity from another dimension who gets knocked off course by a black hole and becomes stranded on Earth. Though immature, Sky has the power to compel humans to do what he wants. Enter a trio of West Country teenagers, Arby and Jane Vennor and Roy Briggs, who become caught up in helping the blond, blue-eyed stranger to return to his own dimension, via the 'Juganet'. Neither outright hero nor villain, Sky is opposed on Earth by Goodchild, a sinister character who can materialise and dematerialise at will, representing 'the natural opposition of Earth to anything out of place'. Sky's presence has evoked a disturbing reaction from nature – one scene has tree roots trying to throttle him when he shelters below ground. Sky must find the 'Juganet' before the opposing forces grow too strong.

Much of the series was filmed around Stonehenge, Glastonbury and Avebury, giving it an added mystical twist. Of the cast, Richard Speight, who played Roy, had done his own travelling through space and time as the young Time Guardian, Peter, in *The Tomorrow People*.

Sky, which appeared in 1976, was one of several strong fantasy and adventure series produced by HTV, whose output also included *Children of the Stones* (1977) and *King of the Castle* (1978), the latter also scripted by Baker and Martin.

CAST

Sky **Mark Harrison**   *Roy Briggs* **Richard Speight**   *Arby Vennor* **Stuart Lock**
Jane Vennor **Cherrald Butterfield**   *Goodchild* **Robert Eddison**
Major Briggs **Jack Watson**   *Mr Vennor* **Thomas Heathcote**
Mrs Vennor **Frances Cuka**
with: *Sgt Simmons* **David Jackson**   *Dr Marshall* **Rex Holdsworth**
Nurses **Ursula Barclay, Monica Lavers**   *Orderly* **Geoff Serle**
Dr Saul **Gerard Hely**   *Tom* **Meredith Edwards**   *Receptionist* **Barbara Baber**
Michael **Sean Lynch**   *Susannah* **Prunella Ransome**   *Rex* **Trevor Ray**
Policeman **John Curry**   *Haril* **Bernard Archard**   *Revil* **Peter Copley**

Writers: **Bob Baker, Dave Martin**
Director: **Derek Clark**
Producer: **Leonard White**
Executive producer: **Patrick Dromgoole**
Designer: **John Biggs**

An HTV Production
Seven colour 30-minute episodes

Burning Bright
Juganet
Goodchild
What Dread Hand

Evalake
Life Force
Chariot of Fire

7 April–19 May 1976

SMALL WONDER

Amiable US sitcom about a precocious 10-year-old girl called Vicki who's really a robot. Adopted by her inventor's family, the Lawsons, Vicky is actually VICI – Voice Input Child Indenticat – and gets up to the usual domestic hi-jinks, especially with the Lawsons' son Jamie. Routine comedy with a dutiful moral tagged on to the end of each episode. Picked up by most ITV regions in 1985.

REGULAR CAST

Ted Dick Christie   *Joan* Marla Pennington
Jamie Jerry Supiran   *Vicki* Tiffany Brissette
Harriet Emily Schulman

Executive producer: Howard Leeds, *for*

Metromedia Producers Corporation
UK: 18 colour 30-minute episodes

UK premiere:
5 October 1985
(Anglia, and other ITV regions – not fully networked)

SPACE

Exhausting £35 million, 14½-hour marathon 'mini-series' for America, based on James Michener's epic account of the US space effort through the lives of a group of fictional characters whose lives become entwined in the country's space programme.

Space expensively chronicles the years from the end of World War Two, when the American government secretly sought to round up Nazi Germany's top rocket scientists, through the first stirrings of the space programme and man's exploration of the Moon in the early 1970s, to the decline of NASA in the early 1980s.

As well as the headline-making public events of space walks, test pilot flights, lunar landings and horrific crashes, the series focusses on the private battles of its central characters. Top of the tree is Norman Grant, a naval hero who finds himself a natural for the Senate where he latches on to the fledgling space effort as his route to the top.

Other main characters are Grant's emotionally fragile wife, Elinor, 'good ol' boy' astronaut Randy Claggett, dedicated engineer Stanley Mott, Navy flier turned top test pilot and astronaut John Pope, his wife Penny, rocket genius Dieter Kolff, muck-raking journalist Cindy Rhee and TV evangelist Leopold Strabismus.

James Garner headed the proverbial all-star cast, which featured Bruce Dern, Michael York, Beau Bridges and Harry Hamlin.

Space was stripped across seven nights in the space of a month by ITV but never took off in the ratings.

MAIN CAST

Norman Grant **James Garner**   *Elinor Grant* **Susan Anspach**
Stanley Mott **Bruce Dern**   *Rachel Mott* **Melinda Dillon**
Randy Claggett **Beau Bridges**   *John Pope* **Harry Hamlin**
Penny Pope **Blair Brown**   *Dieter Kolff* **Michael York**
Leopold Strabismus **David Dukes**   *Senator Glancey* **Martin Balsam**
Marcia Grant **Jennifer Runyon**   *Cindy Rhee* **Maggie Han**
Paul Stidham **Ralph Bellamy**   *Leisl Kolff* **Barbara Sukowa**

Writers: **Dick Berg, Stirling Silliphant,**
  from the novel by **James Michener**
Directors: **Lee Philips, Joseph Sargent**
Producer: **Martin Manulis**
Executive Producer: **Dick Berg**

A Dick Berg/Stonehenge Production in association with Paramount Network Television Productions
Seven colour episodes (60 mins – 180 mins)
13 July–17 August 1987

SPACE ACADEMY

American adventure series about a new generation of space explorers being trained to push mankind's frontiers into deepest space. Showed briefly on ITV in 1980 as a Saturday morning kids show.

15 colour 25-minute episodes
(7-episode run on LWT)

A Filmation Production

SPACE: 1999

Space: 1999 was the series which began with a bang and went out with a whimper.

Stylishly and extravagantly filmed, it devoured a fortune in special effects, took two years to plan, 15 months to make and should have been television's most exhilarating adult space odyssey.

But though it spent two more years and 48 episodes roaming the outer reaches of the universe, *Space: 1999* never found the audience it was looking for. Its creator, Gerry Anderson, was the proverbial prince without honour in his own land. While the series was a worldwide success, with particularly big followings in America, Japan, France and Italy, Britain dithered, dallied and, by the end, virtually ignored it.

The format was simple enough: in the opening episode the Moon is ripped apart by a massive atomic explosion – the result of a 20-year build-up of nuclear waste from Earth. The surviving half, with the 300-strong colony of Moonbase Alpha aboard, is hurled out of Earth orbit and off on an endless journey through space. Thereafter, as the Alphans search in vain for a new home, they have a string of bizarre encounters with invariably hostile aliens, cosmic phenomena and strange worlds.

American husband-and-wife stars Martin Landau and Barbara Bain teamed up for the first time since *Mission Impossible*, as Moonbase commander John Koenig and chief medical officer Dr Helena Russell. And *Fugitive*-chasing Barry Morse played the intellectual scientist father-figure of Victor Bergman.

Visually, *Space: 1999* was a treat – its spectacular sets and effects masterminded by Brian Johnson who brought much of the grace of his work on *2001: A Space Odyssey* to the aerial sequences with the insect-like spacecraft, the Eagles. But the show was marred by po-faced acting, wildly implausible plots, one-dimensional characters and an almost total lack of warmth or humour.

For the second season, American producer Fred Freiberger (of *Star Trek* fame) was brought in to try to 'humanise' the series, beefing up the romantic bond between Koenig and Dr Russell and adding a few new regulars, notably Maya, an exotic alien with the power to transform herself into any living thing. But the stories became increasingly silly and the Alphans reached the end of the road without ever getting anywhere.

Space 1999: premiered here in September 1973, but ITV's network committee denied the show a network run, leaving the Alphans to fight a fragmented battle for ratings around the regions – a battle they largely lost. The second series fared even worse, with even the 'home team' ATV, contriving to lose one episode altogether (*The Dorcons*). In London Season Two was eventually consigned to the Saturday morning children's schedules, but some areas gave it a miss altogether.

MAIN CAST

Cmdr John Koenig **Martin Landau**   *Dr Helena Russell* **Barbara Bain**
Prof. Victor Bergman **Barry Morse***   *Alan Carter* **Nick Tate**
Sandra Benes/Sahn **Zienia Merton**   *Paul Morrow* **Prentis Hancock***
Dr Mathias **Anton Phillips**   *David Kano* **Clifton Jones***
Maya **Catherine Schell†**   *Tony Verdeschi* **Tony Anholt†**
Yasko **Yasuko Nagazumi†**   *Voice of Moonbase computer* **Barbara Kelly**

Creators: **Gerry** *and* **Sylvia Anderson**
Executive producer: **Gerry Anderson**
Producers: **Sylvia Anderson** *(Season One),*
  Fred Freiberger *(Season Two)*
Special effects: **Brian Johnson**
Music: **Barry Gray** *(Season One),* **Derek**
  Wadsworth *(Season Two)*
Costumes: **Rudi Gernreich**

An ITC Production
48 colour 60-minute episodes
Season One:
4 September 1975–19 February 1976
Season Two:
4 September–23 December 1976
4 August–1 September 1977
plus 1 May 1978
(ATV Midlands)

* Season One only
† Season Two only

Season One
(24 episodes)

Breakaway

w **George Bellak**
John Koenig arrives at Moonbase Alpha to oversee final plans for a deep space probe, and finds his crew stricken by a mystery illness linked to the nuclear waste dumps on the dark side of the Moon. Within hours a massive nuclear explosion rips the heart out of the Moon, hurling the Moonbase half out of Earth orbit and into the depths of space.
Commissioner Simmonds **Roy Dotrice**
Commander Gorski **Philip Madoc**
Ouma **Lon Satton**
Collins **Eric Carte**

Director: **Lee Katzin**

Force of Life

w **Johnny Byrne**
Technician Anton Zoref is possessed by an alien force with an all-consuming craving for heat. Everything he touches – including people – freezes instantly. To destroy him, Koenig must deny him any source of light and warmth.
Anton Zoref **Ian McShane**
Eva Zoref **Gay Hamilton**

Mark Dominix **John Hamill**
Jane **Eva Rueber-Staier**

Director: **David Tomblin**

Collision Course

w **Anthony Terpiloff**
The Moon is on a collision course with the giant planet Astheria. Bergman suggests diverting their path with a series of mines in space, but Koenig meets the planet's aged queen Arra who says the 'collision' is their destiny: 'Our separate planets have met in the body of Time for the great purpose of mutation.'
Arra **Margaret Leighton**

Director: **Ray Austin**

War Games

w **Christopher Penfold**
Moonbase Alpha finds itself seemingly under attack from an unnamed planet. With 129 dead and Moonbase no longer habitable, Koenig and Dr Russell journey to the enemy planet to seek terms and a new life – but they are told the Alphans carry a 'plague of fear' that would destroy the perfect world, and that they have nothing to fear but fear itself . . .

Alien man **Anthony Valentine**
Alien woman **Isla Blair**

Director: **Charles Crichton**

Death's Other Dominion

w **Anthony Terpiloff** *and* **Elizabeth Burrows**
The Alphans discover an ice planet, 'Ultima Thule', where they are invited to share an immortal life on 'this paradise' with former inhabitants of Earth.
Rowland **Brian Blessed**
Jack Turner **John Shrapnel**
Freda **Mary Miller**

Director: **Charles Crichton**

Voyager's Return

w **Johnny Byrne**
Moonbase encounters an old Voyager probe that has been polluting space with deadly 'fast neutrons' from its Queller drive. Koenig wants to destroy the probe, but Bergman wishes to salvage its information and enlists the help of scientist Ernst Linden – unaware that he is really Queller, inventor of the deadly drive.
Linden **Jeremy Kemp**
Jim Haines **Barry Stokes**
Aachon **Alex Scott**
Abrams **Lawrence Trimble**

Director: **Bob Kellett**

Alpha Child

w **Christopher Penfold**
The first birth on Alpha – and the astonishingly quick growth of the child – draws Moonbase into an alien attempt to save its own race from its pursuing enemies by inhabiting the bodies of others.
Cynthia/Rena **Cyd Hayman**
Jarak **Julian Glover**
Jackie **Wayne Brooks**

Director: **Ray Austin**

Dragon's Domain

w **Christopher Penfold**
Astonaut Tony Cellini – lone survivor of a deep space probe – has endured years of mental torment; his story of a spaceship graveyard and a terrifying, tentacled monster has never been believed. Now Moonbase has drifted into the same area, involving Koenig in a crescendo of horror.
Cellini **Gianni Garko**
Commissioner Dixon **Douglas Wilmer**
Dr Monique Fauchere **Barbara Kellermann**
Dr King **Michael Sheard**
Dr Mackie **Susan Jameson**

Director: **Charles Crichton**

Mission of the Darians

w **Johnny Byrne**
Moonbase responds to a distress call and finds a whole world that has been flying through space for 900 years. But its survivors have kept alive through a form of cannibalism and the Alphans look like becoming human fodder.
Kara **Joan Collins**
High priest **Aubrey Morris**
Neman **Dennis Burgess**
Hadin **Robert Russell**
Lowry **Paul Antrim**

Director: **Ray Austin**

The Black Sun

w **David Weir**
When Moonbase gets drawn into a 'black sun', Koenig pins hopes of survival on Prof. Bergman's new forcefield. But they are in for a strange, bewildering experience . . .
Ryan **Paul Jones**
Smitty **Jon Laurimore**

Director: **Lee Katzin**

Guardian of Piri

w **Christopher Penfold**
A beautiful woman offers the Alphans a blissful existence on the paradise planet Piri. Only Koenig has the will to resist and he fights to save his people from the 'living death'.
Guardian **Catherine Schell**

Irving Michael Culver
Davis John Lee-Barber
Johnson James Fagan

Director: Charles Crichton

End of Eternity

w Johnny Byrne
Koenig inadvertently frees a psychopathic killer with the power of immortality, and must put his own life on the line to defeat him.
Balor Peter Bowles
Baxter Jim Smilie

Director: Ray Austin

Matter of Life and Death

w Art Wallace, Johnny Byrne
Helen's husband Lee, believed killed on a space mission years before, reappears with a grim warning for the Alphans – that Terra Nova, the planet they are preparing to land on, is anti-matter and will destroy them.
Lee Richard Johnson
Parks Stuart Damon

Director: Charles Crichton

Earthbound

w Anthony Terpiloff
An alien spaceship lands on the Moon and its captain, Zandor, reveals that they are heading for Earth. Commissioner Simmonds, trapped on the Moon since it broke out of orbit, is determined to take this chance to return to Earth.
Simmonds Roy Dotrice
Zandor Christopher Lee

Director: Charles Crichton

The Full Circle

w Jesse Lasky Jnr *and* Pat Silver
The crews of two Eagle cruisers find themselves hunting each other after flying through a time warp into the Stone Age.
Spearman Oliver Cotton

Director: Bob Kellett

Another Time Another Place

w Johnny Byrne
A strange phenomenon creates duplicates of the Moon and Moonbase personnel who are surprised to find themselves in Earth's orbit again. But it is a duplicate Earth and the Alphans find themselves face to face with other, future selves.
Regina Kesslann Judy Geeson

Director: David Tomblin

The Last Sunset

w Christopher Penfold
A new planet, Ariel, is discovered and seems to hold out the prospect of a normal life in Operation Exodus – but the dream fades with the emergence of a new alien force.

Director: Charles Crichton

The Infernal Machine

w Anthony Terpiloff *and* Elizabeth Burrows
A living machine and its aged, sick 'companion' arrive on Moonbase. When the companion dies, the machine demands that Koenig and Helena take his place – for the rest of their lives.
Companion Leo McKern
Winters Gary Waldhorn

Director: David Tomblin

Ring Around the Moon

w Edward Di Lorenzo
Moonbase becomes a prisoner of a probe from the long-dead alien planet Triton – and Dr Russell is turned into an involuntary informer. To save her – and Moonbase – Koenig must convince the Tritonians that their home planet no longer exists.
Ted Clifford Max Faulkner

Director: Ray Austin

Missing Link

w Edward Di Lorenzo
Critically injured in an Eagle crash,
Koenig finds himself 'transported' in time
and space to the planet Zenno where an
anthropologist wants to study him. His
daughter Vana falls in love with Koenig
who is torn between staying with her or
'returning' to his real life.
Raan Peter Cushing
Vana Joanna Dunham

Director: Ray Austin

Space Brain

w Christopher Penfold
Moonbase is heading for a strange
gossamer-like space organism which
destroys one investigating Eagle and takes
over the mind of another crewman. The
Alphans hope to destroy it by aiming an
explosive-packed Eagle straight at it – but
the plan threatens to backfire.
Kelly Shane Rimmer
Wayland Derek Anders
Melita Carla Romanelli

Director: Charles Crichton

The Troubled Spirit

w Johnny Byrne
Botanist Mateo, forbidden to continue his
experiments in communicating with plants,
is haunted by his own murderous ghost
seeking to avenge a death that has not yet
happened.
Dan Mateo Giancarlo Prette
Dr James Warren Anthony Nicholls
Laura Adams Hilary Dwyer

Director: Ray Austin

The Testament of Arkadia

w Johnny Byrne
The Moon comes to an inexplicable halt –
held by some strange influence from a
nearby planet. Investigating the barren
world, called Arkadia, Koenig's team find
evidence that life on Earth originated

here, its seeds carried there by Arkadians
fleeing their dying world.
Luke Ferro Orso Maria Guerrini
Anna Davis Lisa Harrow

Director: David Tomblin

The Last Enemy

w Bob Kellett
The Moon drifts into the middle of an
inteplanetary war and Koenig must
negotiate a ceasefire between the two
planets before Moonbase is destroyed in
the 'crossfire'.
Dione Caroline Mortimer
Talos Kevin Stoney
Theia Maxine Audley

Director: Bob Kellett

Season Two
(24 episodes)

The Metamorph

w Johnny Byrne
The Alphans are threatened by an evil-
minded alien, Mentor, who wants to drain
their minds to repair his planet's biological
computer and restore its civilisation. But
Mentor's daughter Maya – who can trans-
form herself into any living creature –
discovers his plan and helps the Alphans
to escape.
Maya Catherine Schell (into)
Mentor Brian Blessed
Annette Fraser Anouska Hempel
Bill Fraser John Hug
Ray Torens Nick Brimble
Petrov Peter Porteous

Director: Charles Crichton

The Exiles

w Donald James
The Alphans revive two apparently harmless young aliens found inside mysterious
cylinders circling the Moon. But the pair
turn out to be rebel leaders and abduct
Helena and Tony, transporting them to
their home planet.

Cantar **Peter Duncan**
Zova **Stacy Dorning**
Mirella **Margaret Inglis**

Director: **Ray Austin**

Journey to Where

w **Donald James**
Moonbase receives a message from 22nd-century Earth offspring to bring the Alphans home via a transference device. But instead, Koenig, Helena and Alan Carter are transported back in time to Scotland in the year 1339 where they face execution as plague carriers.
Dr Logan **Freddie Jones**
Carla **Isla Blair**
Macdonald **Roger Bizley**
Dr Ben Vincent **Jeffrey Kissoon**
Jackson **Laurence Harrington**

Director: **Tom Clegg**

One Moment of Humanity

w **Tony Barwick**
Helena and Tony are abducted by Zamara who wants to use them as emotional blueprints for her race of androids and so teach them how to kill.
Zamara **Billie Whitelaw**
Zarl **Leigh Lawson**
Number Eight **Geoffrey Bayldon**
Choreographer **Lionel Blair**

Director: **Charles Crichton**

Brian the Brain

w **Jack Ronder**
A super-robot, built by an early Earth space mission, kidnaps Koenig and Helena, taking them to a small planet. Tony and Maya mount a rescue bid and, with Maya's powers of transformation, manage to trick Brian into defeat.
Capt. Michaels **Bernard Cribbins**
Brian/robot **Michael Sharvill-Martin**
Pilot **John Hug**
Operative **Annie Lambert**

Director: **Kevin Connor**

New Adam, New Eve

w **Terence Feely**
Magus, a saintly, impressive figure, appears before the Alphans, declaring himself to be 'your creator' and offering them a new Eden – with Koenig and Maya, Helena and Tony as his chosen Adams and Eves.
Magus **Guy Rolfe**
Humanoid **Bernard Kay**
Beautiful girl **Barbara Wise**

Director: **Charles Crichton**

The Mark of Archanon

w **Lew Schwartz**
Two aliens, Pasc and his son Etrec, are discovered in suspended animation in a metal cabinet below the Moon's surface. But Pasc is affected by a strange virus and all Moonbase is at risk.
Pasc **John Standing**
Etrec **Michael Gallagher**
Maruna **Veronica Lang**
Dr Nunez **Raul Newney**
Carson **Anthony Forrest**
Johnson **John Alkin**

Director: **Charles Crichton**

The Rules of Luton

w **Charles Woodgrove** *(alias* **Fred Freiberger***)*
After picking a flower and some berries on a planet rich in vegetation, Koenig and Maya are abruptly accused of murder by the 'Judges of Luton' (trees!) and forced to fight for their lives against three terrifyingly powerful aliens.
'Strong' **David Jackson**
'Transporter' **Godfrey James**
'Invisible' **Roy Marsden**

Director: **Val Guest**

All That Glisters

w **Keith Miles**
The Alphans are lured to an arid planet by a strange life form – living rocks that can communicate, move and kill. The rocks

need water . . . and the human body is mostly water.
Dave O'Reilly **Patrick Mower**

Director: **Ray Austin**

The Taybor

w **Thom Keyes**
A flamboyant, nautical-sounding space trader arrives on Alpha and offers to trade a jump-drive device that could take them back to Earth – but he wants Maya in exchange!
Taybor **Willoughby Goddard**
Arkaren **Laraine Humphreys**
Slatternly woman **Rita Webb**
Andrews **Mel Taylor**

Director: **Bob Brooks**

Seed of Destruction

w **John Goldsmith**
A jewel-like asteroid is draining power from Alpha. Koenig investigates and encounters a replica of himself which returns to Moonbase in his place, carrying a crystal seed which will use the Moon's store of energy to restore life to the asteroid.
Dr Vincent **Jeffrey Kissoon**

Director: **Kevin Connor**

The A-B Chrysalis

w **Tony Barwick**
Alpha is rocked by powerful energy beams from an unidentified planet. One more could spell destruction. Koenig's team investigate and find that the planet's humanoid population are in a chrysalid stage of evolution, protected by a computer which automatically destroys any threat – and that includes Alpha.
A **Ina Skriver**
B **Sarah Douglas**
Sphere voice **Robert Rietty**

Director: **Val Guest**

The Catacombs of the Moon

w **Anthony Terpiloff**
Dr Russell fights to save the life of an Alphan woman whose engineer husband had visions of Moonbase being destroyed by fire – visions made more ominous when a fire storm heads towards them.
Osgood **James Laurenson**
Michelle **Pamela Stephenson**
Engineers **Lloyd McGuire, Saul Reichlin**
Nurse **Karen Ford**

Director: **Robert Lynn**

Space Warp

w **Charles Woodgrove** *(alias* **Fred Freiberger***)*
Moonbase Alpha disappears into a space warp, instantly moving five light years away. Left behind in Eagle One, Koenig and Tony search desperately for the space 'window', while on Moonbase Maya is afflicted by a mysterious fever and her transformation powers run wild.
Security guard **Tony Osoba**
Petrov **Peter Porteous**

Director: **Peter Medak**

A Matter of Balance

w **Pip** *and* **Jane Baker**
While exploring an apparently lifeless planet, Alphan botanist Shermeen comes under the influence of Vindrus, an anti-matter being who wants to replace all the Moonbase personnel with members of his own race.
Shermeen **Lynne Frederick**
Vindrus **Stuart Wilson**
Eddie Collins **Nicholas Campbell**

Director: **Charles Crichton**

The Beta Cloud

w **Charles Woodgrove** *(alias* **Fred Freiberger***)*
A mystery illness strikes the Alphans and a terrifying space creature runs amoke in Moonbase, impervious to laser gun fire.

All efforts to stop it fail until Maya realises that it is a robot and finds a way to reach its control centre.

Creature **Dave Prowse**
Space animals **Albin Pahernik**

Director: **Robert Lynn**

The Lambda Factor

w **Terrance Dicks**
The Moon passes through a cosmic gas cloud which gives one of the Alphan women fearsome paranormal powers which she uses to take control of Moonbase.

Carolyn Powell **Deborah Fallender**
Mark Sanders **Jess Conrad**
George Crato **Anthony Stamboulieh**
Carl Renton **Michael Walker**
Peter Garforth **Gregory de Polnay**
Sally Martin **Lydia Lisle**

Director: **Charles Crichton**

(Season break)

The Bringers of Wonder

w **Terence Feely** *(A 2-part story)*
Everyone on Moonbase Alpha is celebrating the arrival of a spaceship from Earth whose crew promise to take the Alphans home. Everyone, that is, except Koenig. Where the others see old friends or relatives, he sees hideous aliens.

Guido **Stuart Damon**
Jack Bartlett **Jeremy Young**
Joe Ehrlich **Drewe Henley**
Louisa **Cher Cameron**
Sandstrom **Earl Robinson**
Dr Shaw **Patrick Westwood**
Peter Rockwell **Nicholas Young**
Lizard animal **Albin Pahernik**

Director: **Tom Clegg**

The Seance Spectre

w **Donald James**
A group of Alphans hold a seance which convinces them that a newly sighted planet is habitable. Koenig goes to investigate and finds nothing but a dust bowl.

Worse, the planet is on a collision course with the moon.

Sanderson **Ken Hutchinson**
Eva **Carolyn Seymour**
Cernik **Nigel Pegram**
Stevens **James Snell**

Director: **Peter Medak**

Dorzak

w **Christopher Penfold**
A spaceship arrives on Moonbase carrying a prisoner, Dorzak, a surivivor from Maya's home planet, Psychon. His ability to control minds threatens all on Alpha.

Dorzak: **Lee Montague**
Sahala **Jill Townsend**
Yesta **Kathryn Leigh Scott**

Director: **Val Guest**

Devil's Planet

w **Michael Winder**
Answering a distress signal, Koenig is forced to crash-land his Eagle on a planet's penal colony where he is taken prisoner by the beautiful Elizia and her cat-suited prison guards.

Elizia **Hildegard Neil**
Crael **Roy Marsden**
Blake Maine **Michael Dickinson**
Sares **Cassandra Harris**
Interrogator **Dora Reisser**

Director: **Tom Clegg**

The Immunity Syndrome

w **Johnny Byrne**
Exploring an Earth-type planet, Koenig's reconnaissance team come across a 'being' composed of blinding light and sound whose efforts to communicate drive unprotected people insane.

Zoran **Nadim Sawalha**
Joe Lustig **Roy Boyd**
Travis **Karl Held**
Voice **Hal Galili**

Director: **Bob Brooks**

(1 May 1978)

The Dorcons

w Johnny Byrne

A huge Dorcon spaceship appears on the Moonbase screens and their leader Varda demands that the Alphans hand over Maya, who the Dorcons believe can give them immortality. Koenig refuses but Moonbase is attacked and invaded. Forced to hand over Maya, Koenig makes a desperate bid to save her.

Archon Patrick Troughton
Varda Ann Firbank
Malic Gerry Sundquist
Alibe Alibe Parsons
Medical officer Hazel McBride

Director: Tom Clegg

(12 November 1977: LWT)

SPACE PATROL

'Gamma rays on . . . Yabba rays on!'

Space Patrol is one of the 'lost' brigade of television fantasy, overshadowed by the federation of TV puppet shows created by Gerry Anderson.

It debuted in 1963, a few months after Anderson's *Fireball XL5* and in some ITV regions the two overlapped. Invariably linked with and often confused with its more illustrious contemporary, *Space Patrol* did succeed, however, in its own right. In America it became the top-rated children's show within one month of its launch.

Its creator was Roberta Leigh, a former romantic novelist who had previously written the stories for Gerry Anderson's earliest series, *The Adventures of Twizzle* and *Torchy the Battery Boy*, (who himself took off for the stars in a rocket fired by sparklers). Like *Fireball XL5*, *Space Patrol* charted the interplanetary adventures of one crew and one craft among a fleet of many. Set in the year 2100, its heroes were Earthman Captain Larry Dart, Slim the Venusian and Husky the Martian who patrolled the solar system in their melodious Galasphere 347, as part of the United Galactic Organisation – a peace-keeping force set up by Earth, Mars and Venus.

Other main characters were the base commander Colonel Raeburn, his blonde Venusian secretary Marla, a wacky genius inventor Professor Aloysius O'Rourke O'Brien Haggerty and his daughter Cassiopea, and a loquacious Martian parrot called the Gabblerdictum (a tour de force vocal performance from comedienne Libby Morris).

As with so many shows of the time, *Space Patrol* steered an erratic course around the country, with running order and transmission dates varying throughout. For example, ABC was first off the mark, in April 1963, but took three takes to show the 26 first-season episodes (ending in February 1964). Associated-Rediffusion in London began in July '63 and finished the first season in January '64. London then moved on to Season Two six weeks later, while ABC viewers had to wait *two years* for their first Season Two episode and more than *four years* for their last! And so it went on . . .

VOICE CAST

Capt. Larry Dart **Dick Vosburgh** *Husky/Slim/Prof Haggerty* **Ronnie Stevens**
Col. Raeburn **Murray Kash** *Marla/Cassiopea/Gabblerdictum* **Libby Morris**

Created and written by: **Roberta Leigh**
Producers: **Roberta Leigh** *and* **Arthur Provis**
Director: **Frank Goulding**
Models: **Derek Freeborn**
Special effects/animation: **Bill Palmer, Brian Stevens, Bert Walker**

A National Interest Picture Production/Wonderama Productions Ltd
39 30-minute episodes, black and white

Season One: 5 July 1963–30 January 1964
Season Two: 19 March–11 June 1964
(Dates as Associated Rediffusion, London)

(Author's note: Although ABC began transmission of the series first, on 7 April 1963, Rediffusion actually caught up and overtook their Northern colleagues. The running order is taken from *TVTimes'* London edition.)

Season One (26 episodes):

The Wandering Asteroid

Larry Dart and his crew are assigned to destroy an asteroid that has been deflected from its orbit and is heading straight for the Martian capital.

The Dark Planet

Prof. Haggerty discovers that a new breed of plant brought from Uranus can walk and talk.

The Slaves of Neptune

Dart's crew investigate the strange disappearance of three spaceships and find themselves in the grip of mysterious forces. (Introducing the Gabblerdictum.)

Fires of Mercury

Haggerty develops a machine that can translate the language of ants and turn infra-red rays into radio waves. Col. Raeburn grows concerned that Pluto is becoming too cold to sustain life.

The Shrinking Spaceman

When a sonar beam transmitter on the asteroid Pallas stops working, Galasphere 347 is sent to check it out. Husky cuts his hand on a contaminated meteorite fragment and later begins to shrink.

The Robot Revolution

Slim goes home to Venus on leave, while Larry and Husky visit an Atlantic undersea farm where an explosion makes the 5000 robot workers run amok.

The Cloud of Death

The sky goes dark above Space Control due to a cloud created by alien invaders to cut the Earth off from the sun's rays and freeze the planet to death. Galasphere finds itself playing a deadly game of cat and mouse.

The Rings of Saturn

Dart encounters a Saturnian ship in space and is taken down to the planet where he is able to persuade its reptilian leader to join the United Galactic Organisation.

Volcanoes of Venus

Col. Raeburn's secretary Marla is concerned about a mysterious virus that is paralysing her home planet. Slim goes to investigate.

Mystery on the Moon

A powerful beam from the Moon is destroying buildings at Space Headquarters. The Space Patrol are sent to investigate and clash with a dangerous criminal who threatens to destroy the world.

The Miracle Tree of Saturn

A mystery fungus is wiping out food crops on Earth. Haggerty discovers that leaves from the Miracle Tree of Saturn can counteract it, but Dart's mission to collect some is jeopardised by a stowaway.

The Forgers

A glut of forged banknotes is flooding world currencies. Dart and Husky set off for the Dictum Forest to track down the forgers and encounter some strange insects called glooks.

The Swamps of Jupiter

Larry Dart and his crew are sent to investigate the unexplained fate of a team of scientists exploring Jupiter and discover they've been killed by two wicked Martians who are now skinning the Loomis birds. (This episode features a different Galasphere and was used as a pilot episodes in some other regions.)

The Planet of Thought

Tyro, leader of the Neptunians, persuades Col. Raeburn's secretary Marla to go to Neptune with him, but Raeburn does not believe she has gone willingly and sends Dart to bring her back.

The Glowing Eggs of Titan

When Dart and Co make an emergency landing on Titan to repair their Galasphere, they make a curious discovery that could prove the answer to Mars' electricity crisis.

Planet of Light

Dart and Slim visit Lumen, a planet with no oxygen in its atmosphere, as the gas means death to its inhabitants.

The Time Watch (aka Time Stands Still)

Haggerty's new invention, a time watch, enables Dart to defeat a renegade Martian, Zota, by speeding up his reactions 60 times, thus rendering himself invisible.

The Invisible Martian (aka Husky Becomes Invisible)

Prof. Zeffer of the Martian observatory invents a machine for measuring the distance between stars – but Husky finds it has *other* properties when he accidentally gets caught in its rays.

The Walking Lake of Jupiter

A strange moving lake is discovered on Jupiter that brings peril to the planet.

The New Planet

Galasphere 347 hurtles off course into deep space where the crew discover a new planet out beyond Pluto, populated by giants.

The Human Fish

Larry, Slim and Husky investigate reports that a breed of fish on Venus is developing human form and starting to attack fishermen.

The Invisible Invasion

Strange beings from Uranus plan to take over Earth by becoming invisible and entering the minds of other people.

The Talking Bell

On a hunting trip Col. Raeburn and Prof. Haggerty trap a strange bell-like creature which at first seems like a nuisance, but finally helps save Dart when he is buried in a cave without food or water.

The Buried Space Ship

The Galasphere 347 crew are assigned to take part in Operation Ice Cube – transporting ice blocks from the frozen planet Pluto to help alleviate a desperate drought on Mars – but their ship becomes trapped in an icy crevasse.

Message from a Star

Signals from Alpha Centauri herald a visit by a creature from another galaxy seeking Space Patrol's help.

Explosion on the Sun

Col. Raeburn is faced with a dangerous situation when a would-be dictator sets himself up on the satellite Ganymede and starts interfering with the Sun – causing a tremendous heatwave.

Season Two (13 episodes):

The Unknown Asteroid

Col. Raeburn sends Larry Dart and his crew to track down some space pirates who have been plundering cargo ships.

The Evil Eye of Venus

Venusian scientist Borra invents a mechanical eye that will repel any alien metal that comes within three miles. But when Borra is accidentally killed, the Eye goes out of control threatening *all* metal. Dart's crew set out to destroy the Eye using ultrasonic beams. It's a mission which calls for precise manoeuvring . . .

Secret Formula

Husky gets trapped in a Martian spider's web and looks like being there for good until Prof. Haggerty and Gabbler come up with a solution.

The Telepathic Robot

Prof. Haggerty's latest invention, a robot servant, is supposed to respond to the brain impulses of its controller. But it soon develops a will of its own.

The Deadly Whirlwind

The Galasphere 347 crew are ordered to spray a chemical poison over every inch of Martian vegetation to halt a dust virus.

The Jitter Waves

The Earth's surface is shaken by a strange force and Space Patrol is given the task of finding out who – or what – is behind it.

Sands of Death

The Martian president calls on Col. Raeburn for help in thwarting an opposition plot to seize power using a nerve gas.

The Hairy Men of Mars

Forced to land in unexplored jungle terrain, Captain Dart and his crew encounter the Martian equivalent of the missing link.

The Grass of Saturn

A new anti-UGO leader assumes power on Saturn and plots to conquer Earth by planting a Saturnian species of grass there, which absorbs oxygen and gives off CO_2, thus making the population drowsy and listless.

Force Field X

The Neptunians evolve a diabolical plan to enslave Earth by inflicting extreme heat on the planet. When Dart returns from an unsuccessful effort to counter the plan, things look grim . . .

The Water Bomb

Taking an urgent cargo of oxygen and hydrogen for an irrigation project on Mars, Dart and his Galasphere are captured by a sinister Martian renegade.

Destruction by Sound

Haggerty uses his daughter Cassiopea for a strange travel experiment that affects events in another galaxy.

The Shrinking Gas of Jupiter

Slim starts to shrink after an encounter with a strange gas in a Jupiter swamp.

SPACE SCHOOL

Children's drama of the old school. This four-part BBC serial, produced for Children's Television in 1956, followed the adventures of the Winter kids – Wallace, Winifred and Wilfred – who lived with their mum in a small house on the inside rim of Earth Satellite One, while their father was away surveying possible landing sites on the moons of Mars.

Its cast of characters included a dedicated Space Commodore (played by children's favourite John Stuart – Lachlan McKinnon of the *Lost Planet* serials), a hot-headed Irish daredevil, a cockney and an ace newshound for the Interplanetary Television Commission.

The series was notable as much as anything for the efforts taken to improve the quality of hardware and sets, including an artificial satellite turning slowly in space, and space tankers darting from planet to planet.

CAST

Space Commodore Hugh Sterling John Stuart
Space Captain Michael O'Rorke Matthew Lane
Space Engineer 'Tubby' Thompson Donald McCorkindale
Sam Scroop, cook Neil McCallum   *Miss Osborne* Julie Webb
Wallace Michael Maguire   *Wilfred* Meurig Jones
Winifred Ann Cooke   *Humphrey Soames* David Drummond
Captain of the School Anthony Toller
Mrs Winter Maud Long   *Pupil* Alanna Boyce
The Stranger Shay Gorman   *Announcer* Edmund Warwick

Writer: Gordon Ford
Producer: Kevin Sheldon
Designer: Gordon Roland
Film cameraman: David Prosser
Spaceships/satellites built by: John Ryan

A BBC Production
Four 30-minute episodes, black and white
8–29 January 1956

STAR COPS

When Nathan Spring and his posse of space deputies rode into the BBC schedules in 1987, they evoked echoes of the lawmen of the old West.

Space was (as someone once said) the final frontier, and this nine-part series set in 2027 depicted an international frontier community of around 3000 strung out over five permanently manned space stations, a Moonbase and a colony on Mars – but with *no* aliens.

The International Space Police Force (nicknamed the Star Cops) were initially a handful of part-timers, volunteers who got the badge and had to keep law and order while holding down other jobs.

Nathan Spring is a dedicated, irascible, professional detective appointed to whip them into shape. An outsider, he is immensely suspicious of the computerised world in which he lives, believing that it discourages people from thinking for themselves. He starts to build an international team around himself, beginning with Theroux, a young black American flight engineer, Australian Pal Kenzy and chauvinistic womaniser, chubby Colin Devis, and later to include young Japanese scientist Anna Shoun.

The Star Cops investigate everything from murder, sabotage, theft and hijacking, with Spring frequently clashing – somewhat half-heartedly – with Krivenko, the Russian coordinator of Moonbase where they establish their headquarters.

The series was devised by Chris Boucher, a veteran of *Doctor Who* and *Blake's 7*, who was keen to get away from space opera and back to what he considered the nuts and bolts of an intelligent, realistic detective series set in space. A contributor to such earthbound crime series as *Bergerac*, *Juliet Bravo* and *Shoestring*, Boucher intended the drama to come, not from the realms of the fantastic, but from the developing characters and the strength of the plots.

Only a modest success in its BBC2 Monday evening slot, the series has never been given the 'seal of approval' of a repeat run on BBC1.

REGULAR CAST

Nathan Spring **David Calder**   *David Theroux* **Erick Ray Evans**
Pal Kenzy **Linda Newton**   *Colin Devis* **Trevor Cooper** *(from Ep. 2)*
Alexander Krivenko **Jonathan Adams** *(from Ep. 4)*
Anna Shoun **Sayo Inaba** *(from Ep. 6)*

Devised by: **Chris Boucher**	*A BBC Production*
Producer: **Evgeny Gridneff**	Nine colour 55-minute episodes
Script editor: **Joanna Willett**	6 July–31 August 1987
Video effects: **Robin Lobb**	(BBC2)
Theme music: **Justin Haywood**	

An Instinct for Murder

w Chris Boucher
The year: 2027. At the Charles de Gaulle space station, crew members die when their spacesuit backpacks malfunction. On Earth, Nathan Spring, an old-fashioned, instinctive policeman, proves a drowned man was murdered, but is far from pleased when he is told he has been short-listed for the post of Head of the International Space Force – whose inefficiency has branded them with the nickname 'Star Cops'.
Commander **Moray Watson**
Controller **Keith Varnier**
Lee Jones **Gennie Nevinson**
Brian Lincoln **Andrew Secombe**
Hans Diter **Frederik de Groot**
Lars Hendvorrsen **Luke Hanson**
Marie Mueller **Katja Kersten**

Director: **Christopher Baker**
Designer: **Dick Coles**

Conversations with the Dead

w Chris Boucher
A freight ship on its way to the Martian colony suddenly develops computer failure and goes off course. The crew is still alive but, as any recovery mission might take years, technically the two men are dead. In Britain, Nathan's girlfriend Lee Jones is murdered in his flat.
Lee Jones **Gennie Nevinson**
Corman **Siân Webber**
Paton **Alan Downer**
Fox **Sean Scanlan**
Gina **Carmen Gomez**
John Smith **Benny Young**

Traffic controller **Deborah Manship**
Mike **Richard Ireson**
Lara **Rosie Kerslake**

Director: **Christopher Baker**
Designer: **Dick Coles**

Intelligence Listening for Beginners

w Chris Boucher
Nathan and Theroux visit an outpost on the Moon owned by millionaire Michael Chandri who appears to be involved in listening systems and bugging devices. He tells them that he has heard of a plot to hijack an Earth-Moon shuttle.
Michael Chandri **David John Pope**
Leo **Trevor Butler**
Ben **Thomas Coulthard**
Shuttle hostess **Tara Ward**
Shift foreman **Peter Quince**
Process operator **Peter Glancy**

Director: **Christopher Baker**
Designer: **Dick Coles**

Trivial Games and Paranoid Pursuits

w Chris Boucher
Dilly Goodman tries to contact her brother who has been working as a research scientist on the American space station, the *Ronald Reagan*. But they have no record of him. He does not seem to exist. Meanwhile, Moonbase gets a new Russian commander.
Cmdr Griffin **Daniel Benzali**
Dilly Goodman **Marlena Mackey**

Peter Lennox **Robert Jezek**
Marty **Russell Wootton**
Lauter **Angela Crow**
Harvey Goodman **Morgan Deare**
Receptionist **Shope Shodeinde**

Director: **Graeme Harper**
Designer: **Malcolm Thornton**

This Case to be Opened in a Million Years

w **Philip Martin**
A shuttle, used for dumping nuclear waste in space, crashes on launch, causing a nuclear alert on Moonbase. Nathan has to return to Earth where a killer is lying in wait for him in the catacombs of northern Italy. (Stewart Guidotti, who appears in this episode, was one of television's earliest men in space as young Geoffrey Wedgwood in ITV's pioneering *Pathfinders* series in 1960–1.)
Carlo Santanini **Michael Chesden**
Marla Condarini **Susan Curnow**
Insp. Canova **Stewart Guidotti**
Lina Margello **Vikki Chambers**
Personnel officer **Flip Webster**
Pordenne **André Winterton**
Tour guide **Carl Forgione**

Director: **Graeme Harper**
Designer: **Malcolm Thornton**

In Warm Blood

w **John Collee**
When the geological survey ship, *Pluto 5*, returns from an exploratory mission, the Star Cops are presented with a complicated problem – the whole crew has been dead for at least a year – and they all died at the same moment.
Anna Shoun **Sayo Inaba** (intro)
Richard Ho **Richard Rees**
Christina Janssen **Dawn Keeler**
Receptionist **Susan Tan**

Director: **Graeme Harper**
Designer: **Malcolm Thornton**

A Double Life

w **John Collee**
Three embryos are mysteriously stolen from the Moonbase hospital, and their mother, Chamsya Assadi, threatens to withdraw financial support. Anna identifies the kidnapper as concert pianist James Bannerman – but he was giving a concert on Earth at the time . . .
Bannerman/Albi **Brian Gwaspari**
Chamsya Assadi **Nitza Saul**

Director: **Christopher Baker**
Designer: **Dick Coles**

Other People's Secrets

w **John Collee**
Psychiatrist Dr Angela Parr visits Moonbase to conduct a study into the effects of living in space. And a series of small technical faults occur while Safety Controller Ernest Wolffhart is on Moonbase. Overworked maintenance engineer Hooper claims it's sabotage.
Wolffhart **Geoffrey Bayldon**
Angela Parr **Maggie Ollerenshaw**
Hooper **Barrie Rutter**
Anderson **Leigh Funnell**

Director: **Christopher Baker**
Designer: **Dick Coles**

Little Green Men and Other Martians

w **Chris Boucher**
The news that something outstanding has been discovered on Mars and is now on its way to the Moon results in Moonbase being invaded by nosy journalists. Meanwhile, Nathan also has to cope with a case of drugs smuggling.
Daniel Larwood **Roy Holder**
Philpot **Nigel Hughes**
Susan Caxton **Lachelle Carl**
Operations manager **Wendy MacAdam**
Co-pilot **Bridget Lynch-Rose**
Pilot **Kenneth Lodge**
Customs officer **Peter Neathey**
Outpost controller **Phillip Rowlands**
Surveyor **David Janes**

Director: **Graeme Harper**
Designer: **Malcolm Thornton**

STAR FLEET

Animated puppet series from Japan, set in the year 2999. Space War Three has ended and the solar system is being rebuilt, led by planet Earth. But hostile powers and aliens are out to sabotage their efforts.

At the heart of the story is Lamia, a young princess-like character whose destiny is bound up with the advent of the third millennium when she will emerge as the mysterious F-01, a benign force with the power to bring peace and order to the whole solar system.

year 3000, otherwise his evil power cannot rule the galaxy. He sends his forces, led by Commander Makara, a bizarre male/female Fu Manchu-type character, on a seek and destroy mission. Standing in their way are Earth's *Star Fleet*, under General Kyle. The fleet's principal craft is the X-bomber, designed by Prof. Hagen and crewed by his son Shiro, Barry Hercules, John Lee, Doctor Benn and Lamia. Lurking protectively in the background is another mystery man, Capt. Halley, commander of a space galleon called The Skull.

The tide of battle ebbs and flows until Lamia and the Star Fleet win a final victory.

Writer: **Michael Sloan**
Producer/director: **Louis Elman**
Executive producer: **Kevin Morrison**
Music: **Paul Bliss**

A Leah International Jin Production
24 colour 30-minute episodes
23 October 1982–4 September 1983
(LWT)

STAR MAIDENS

Question: in what TV series did Gareth Thomas play a rebel on the run, pursued by a powerful, dominant female? Yes, yes, *Blake's 7*, of course. But two years earlier he was fleeing a regiment of women in a quite different science fiction series, *Star Maidens*.

Touted as a tongue-in-cheek fantasy, this 13-part Anglo-German production depicted a role-reversed planet Mendusa, where women rule and men are the domestic drudges. Two male servants, Adam and Shem, escape to Earth in a stolen spacecraft in search of a better life. But they are pursued by Supreme Councillor Fulvia who wants to rechain them to the kitchen sink. When they are unable to recapture the runaways, Fulvia and her crew return with two Earth hostages. Thus the scene is set for a two-centre culture clash.

The series, based on an original idea by a pair of German film-makers, Graf and Graefin Von Hardenberg, was made by a British independent company, Portman Productions, at Bray Studios. Its quartet of writers included three renowned exponents of British telefantasy – Eric Paice, Ian Stuart Black and John Lucarotti – and it boasted a starry international cast, including Judy Geeson, Dawn Addams and Lisa Harrow. Ronald Hines appeared as a dour police inspector bewildered by his encounter with the liberated ladies of Mendusa, and Alfie Bass chipped in a cameo role as a castle gatekeeper captured by the Mendusan runaways. The foreign stars included Christiane Kruger (daughter of Hardy) and Christian Quadflieg, from Germany, plus French-born Pierre Brice.

Series producer was James Gatward (lately Chief Executive of TVS). He was also one of the four directors, along with veteran cinematographer Freddie Francis.

Produced at a cost of around £50,000 per episode, *Star Maidens* was sold to more than 40 countries as diverse – given the 'liberated' theme – as America, Hungary, South Africa and the Arab states of the Middle East. Over here, it premiered on Scottish Television in September 1976, with most ITV regions following in 1977.

But the maidens won few admirers, something Portman executive Ian Warren attributed to the difficulty of doing comedy with the Germans. 'It was meant to be fantasy but the Germans kept trying to make it more realistic.'

Plans were laid to make a second series in Canada but they proved too expensive and were quietly shelved.

MAIN CAST

Fulvia **Judy Geeson** *The President* **Dawn Addams** *Adam* **Pierre Brice**
Shem **Gareth Thomas** *Octavia* **Christiane Kruger**
Liz **Lisa Harrow** *Rudi* **Christian Quadflieg** *Prof. Evans* **Derek Farr**

Producer: **James Gatward**

A Portman Production (for Scottish and Global Television Enterprises in co-production with Jost Graf von Hardenberg & Co and Werbung-in-Rundfunk, Frankfurt/Main)

13 colour 30-minute episodes
UK premiere:
1 September–1 December 1976
(STV)

Escape to Paradise

w **Eric Paice**
Mendusan servants Adam and Shem steal a space yacht belonging to Adam's mistress, Supreme Councillor Fulvia, and head for Earth. A distraught Fulvia decides to lead the pursuit herself.
Insp. Stanley **Ronald Hines** *(plus Ep. 2)*
Announcer **Penelope Hunter**

Director: **James Gatward**

Nemesis

w Eric Paice

Earth scientist Prof. Evans has monitored the arrival of the spacecraft. Adam and Shem, recoiling in horror from all contact with the female sex, seek police protection. Meanwhile, Fulvia and Octavia step up their pursuit.
Katy Moss Jenny Morgan
Sgt Innes Wilfred Grove
Mrs Moss Kristine Howarth
Desk Sgt Norman Warwick *(plus Ep. 3)*

Director: Wolfgang Storch

The Nightmare Cannon

w Eric Paice

Adam and Shem capture a castle. Octavia and Fulvia, treating the Earth men as servants, demand the return of the runaways. Thwarted, they take Prof. Evans's assistants Rudi and Liz as hostages.
Gatekeeper Alfie Bass
Minister Graham Crowden *(plus Ep. 11)*

Director: Wolfgang Storch

The Proton Storm

w John Lucarotti

Fulvia returns to Earth and offers an exchange with the hostages, but the two Mendusans refuse – unless they can return as equals. On Mendusa the Earth pair are separated – Rudi to the men's menial quarters, Liz to a life of luxury.
Andrea Uschi Mellin *(plus Ep. 5)*

Director: Wolfgang Storch

Kidnap

w John Lucarotti

Two foreign scientists get Fulvia drunk on champagne then take her to a villa to link her with a computer brain to store her advanced scientific knowledge. Adam, experiencing the novel emotion of jealousy, stages a rescue.
Sforza Philip Stone
Gregori Terence Alexander

Carlo Stanley Lebor
Hotel manager Hedger Wallis

Director: Freddie Francis

The Trial

w Ian Stuart Black

On Mendusa, the men stage a revolt against the 'Petticoat Government'. Liz is forced to treat Rudi as an inferior in order to obtain a spacecraft in which they can escape. Rudi is caught trying to learn the planet's security secrets and is sent for trial by computers.
Troy Roland Astor
Guard Susie Baker
Octavia's assistant Ann Maj-Britt *(plus Eps 9–10)*
Clara's assistants Annette Lynton *(plus Eps 7–8)* Clare Russell *(plus Ep. 7)*

Director: Wolfgang Storch

Test for Love

w Ian Stuart Black

Liz keeps up the pretence of treating Rudi as an inferior while secretly plotting with him to escape. To discredit her, Octavia puts Liz on a 'sexometer' – but she causes it to blow up!
Nola Veronica Lang
Ercule John Wyman
Zita Belinda Mayne
Guard Diana Weston

Director: Freddie Francis

The Perfect Couple

w Ian Stuart Black

Two women's libbers try to use Fulvia as a propagandist for their cause, but Adam is succeeding in winning her over to domestic life on Earth. They decide to become a suburban couple – though reversing the normal roles – but Fulvia becomes jealous of Adam's tea-parties with the local housewives!
Col. Kipple Ronald Fraser
Garcia Dorothea Kaiser
Freda Marianne Nebel
Wife Jenny Till

Director: Hans Heinrich

What Have They Done To the Rain?

w Ian Stuart Black

Rudi discovers that there has been a chemical change on Mendusa which is causing the planet's surface to dissolve – but only Liz will heed his warnings.
Announcer Anna Carteret
Guard Kirstie Pooley

Director: Freddie Francis

The End of Time

w Eric Paice

Octavia returns to Mendusa with Prof. Evans to arrange an exchange of hostages. The streets are deserted, all the women have disappeared and the men look like zombies. They find the President, Clara, who appears to be dead.
Fidelia Ciaren Madden
Theda Barbara Trentham
Doctor Imogen Clare

Director: Wolfgang Storch

Hideout

w Otto Strang

Adam and Shem are on the run again – the Minister assures Fulvia that they will be recaptured. Shem is sheltered by a woman, Rose, and the two fall in love. But capture comes eventually.
Rose Corny Collins
Police Sgt Don McKillop
Desk Sgt George Hilsdon
Youth Adrian Shergold
Policeman David Ellison
TV announcer John Pennington

Director: Freddie Francis

Creatures of the Mind

w Ian Stuart Black

Asked to help search out old records of experiments in physical, biological and mental energy, Liz is terrified when she is trapped in a vault, sees strange shapes and hears voices.

Director: James Gatward

The Enemy

w Otto Strang

Arrangements are made for the exchange of hostages. Two space ships, one taking Liz and Rudi back to Earth, the other taking Adam and Shem to Mendusa, will pass each other midway. But as they cross, an enemy craft intercepts – and the Mendusan code forbids them to fight.

Director: Freddie Francis

STAR TREK

'I realised that by creating a separate world, a new world with new rules, I could make statements about sex, religion, Vietnam, unions, politics and intercontinental missiles. Indeed, we did make them on *Star Trek*; we were sending messages, and fortunately they all got by the network.'

(Gene Roddenberry, creator/producer)

Britain came late to *Star Trek*. By the time we joined the Starship *Enterprise* for its five-year mission to boldly go where no man had gone before, that mission was already over.

Back in America, the series had been axed by NBC after a three-year run. The battles – to keep a pointy-eared alien in the crew, to keep a negro on the bridge, even just to keep the show alive – had been fought and won . . . and finally lost.

Or so it seemed. In the end this is one show that has run and rerun, its stamina virtually unsurpassed. Today, boosted by a cartoon series and the five feature films, and kept alive by the devotion of its fans, *Star Trek* remains a multi-million dollar industry. And the series, with its unforgettable characters and catchphrases, has become an indelible part of Western culture. They even named a space shuttle in its honour.

Star Trek was created by Gene Roddenberry, a former World War Two aviator and Los Angeles cop, who conceived it as an adult science fiction series.

Its premise: in the 23rd century, Earth is part of the United Federation of Planets, a peaceful alliance of democratic worlds which runs a 'Starfleet' of space vessels to patrol the 'final frontier' of space.

These, then, were the voyages of the Starship *Enterprise*. Its mission, restated at the start of each episode; 'to explore strange new worlds, to seek out life and new civilisations, to boldly go where no man has gone before'.

Its heroes: Captain James T. Kirk (the 'T' stood for Tiberius), a courageous and unflinchingly noble commander; his first officer Mr Spock, a half-human, half-Vulcan with pointed ears and arched eyebrows who lived by logic; Chief Medical Officer Leonard 'Bones' McCoy, an intemperate Southerner who insisted he was 'just a simple country doctor at heart'; and Chief Engineer Montgomery 'Scottie' Scott, an old-fashioned nuts 'n' bolts man devoted to his engines.

The characters may have been corny (with the exception of Spock), but the chemistry was special, creating a unique sense of family – especially between Kirk, Spock and McCoy. You just knew that beneath that grumpy exterior, McCoy really cared for Spock. And the Vulcan's own inner turmoil as he strove to reconcile his logical self with the human side of his nature made him the most interesting character.

Yet Roddenberry had had to fight to keep Spock in the show in the face of a network initially unwilling to welcome him aboard, in the belief that nobody would relate to him.

Leonard Nimoy, too, was reluctant about the part. He believed the ears would wipe him out as an actor. Roddenberry promised him an 'ear job' after the 13th episode if he was still unhappy. He wasn't.

Star Trek's special effects weren't elaborate, but they were memorable. The *Enterprise* itself consisted of several different models, ranging in size from three inches to 14 feet. The warp drive, phasers, photon torpedoes and communicators became an integral part of the show but the most famous trick was the transporter, the device used to 'beam' the crew down to nearby planets, with aluminium dust thrown into a beam of light to enhance the dematerialisation effect.

But every assessment of *Star Trek*'s enduring appeal has always come down to two things – its humanity and its optimism. The crew's line-up reflected a united mankind, a society free of racial and sexual discrimination. Aside from the half-caste science officer, it had a black woman, Lt Uhura, as head of communications, and the navigators were Japanese (Mr Sulu) and Russian (Chekov was reputedly added to the crew when a *Pravda* critic acidly noted that the first nation into space was unrepresented on the *Enterprise*).

Each episode was a morality tale and the series constantly maintained an indomitable faith in man as an essentially noble animal. Flawed maybe, a little impulsive at times, but with his heart in the right place.

And so it was with *Star Trek*. For all its faults – and critics have always loved to pick holes – *its* heart was in the right place. As Roddenberry remarked: 'We were probably the only show on American television that said there is a tomorrow, that all the excitement and adventures and discoveries were not behind us.'

REGULAR CAST

Captain James T. Kirk **William Shatner**   *Mr Spock* **Leonard Nimoy**
'Bones' McCoy **DeForest Kelley**   *Scottie* **James Doohan**
Mr Sulu **George Takei**   *Ensign Chekov* **Walter Koenig** *(from Season Two)*
Lt Uhura **Michelle Nichols**   *Nurse Christine Chapel* **Majel Barret**
Yeoman Janice Rand **Grace Lee Whitney** *(Season One only)*

Creator/Executive producer: **Gene Roddenberry**
Producers: **Gene Roddenberry, Gene L. Coon, John Meredyth Lucas, Fred Freiberger** *(US Season Three Only)*
Story consultants: **Steven Carabatsos, D.C. Fontana**
Music: **Alexander Courage, Gerald Fried**

A Norway Production for Paramount Television
79 colour 50-minute episodes
UK Premiere: 12 July 1969*
BBC1 – colour from 15 November 1969

(Author's note: The BBC running order for *Star Trek* differed considerably from the US original, with a fair amount of season crossovers – plus the infamous trio of unscreened episodes: *Plato's Stepchildren*, *The Empath* and *Whom Gods Destroy*. And while the series has enjoyed regular repeat runs, one episode, *Miri*, has only been screened once in the UK. For ease of reference, the episodes are grouped in their original American seasons and running order, followed by a listing of the UK premiere runs.)

---

* First broadcast in America in 1966, *Star Trek*'s 79 episodes have been shown and reshown throughout the world. In the UK there have been *Star Treks* every year from 1969 to 1981, and 1984–6 with the series clocking up five screenings.

Season One
(29 episodes)

The Man Trap

w George Clayton Johnson
On a routine visit to the planet M113, McCoy meets an old flame, Nancy Crater, and refuses to believe that she is really a salt vampire capable of assuming human form.
Nancy Jeanne Bal/Francine Pyne
Prof. Crater Alfred Ryder
Green Bruce Watson
Darnell Michael Zaslow

Director: Marc Daniels

Charlie X

w D.C. Fontana, *story by* Gene Roddenberry
The petulance of a young passenger struggling to cope with human emotions develops into a trial of wills with Kirk which threatens the safety of the *Enterprise*.
Charlie Evans Robert Walker Jr
Thasian Abraham Sofaer

Director: Lawrence Dodkin

Where No Man Has Gone Before

w Sam Peebles
The *Enterprise* is ordered beyond the limits of explored space and after penetrating a strange force-field, two crew members become god-like beings.
Lt Cmdr Gary Mitchell Gary Lockwood
Dr Elizabeth Dehner Sally Kellerman
Dr Piper Paul Fix
Lt Alden Lloyd Haynes
Lt Lee Kelso Paul Carr
Yeoman Smith Andrea Dromm

Director: James Goldstone

The Naked Time

w John D.F. Black
The *Enterprise* is charged with observing the disintegration of a doomed planet. But a mystery virus robs the crew of their emotional control and the ship hurtles towards the planet – and certain destruction.
Riley Bruce Hyde
Tormolen Stewart Moss
Dr Harrison John Bellah
Lt Brent Frank da Vinci
Singing crewman William Knight

Director: Marc Daniels

The Enemy Within

w Richard Matheson
The roles of good and evil are thrown into stark relief when a transporter malfunction splits Kirk into two people – one heroic and good, the other agressive and negative.
Lt John Farrell Jim Goodwin
Technician Fisher Edward Madden
Technician Wilson Garland Thompson

Director: Leo Penn

Mudd's Women

w Steven Kandel, *story by* Gene Roddenberry
Kirk and his crew have to make room for Harry Mudd and his illicit human cargo of three gorgeous girls.
Mudd Roger C. Carmel
Magda Susan Denberg
Ruth Maggie Thrett
Eve Karen Steele
Ben Childress Gene Dynarski

Director: Harvey Hart

What Are Little Girls Made Of?

w Robert Bloch
Crazed Dr Korby dreams of conquest with his race of androids, including a duplicate of Kirk.
Dr Roger Korby Michael Strong
Andrea Sherry Jackson
Ruk Ted Cassidy
Dr Brown Harry Basch

Director: James Goldstone

Miri

w Adrian Spies
The *Enterprise* crew beam down to a planet inhabited by a Peter Pan race who look like children but are 300 years old. (Screened in an 'abridged' form in the UK.)
Miri Kim Darby
Jahn Michael J. Pollard
Lt Farrell Jim Goodwin
'Creatures' Ed McCready

Director: Vincent McEveety

Dagger of the Mind

w Shimon Wincelberg
Pressed by nagging doubts over a crate received from the penal colony, Tantalus, Kirk probes further and uncovers a cruel and dangerous conspiracy.
Dr Helen Noel Marianna Hill
Dr Simon Van Gelder Morgan Woodward
Dr Tristan Adams James Gregory
Lethe Suzanne Wasson

Director: Vincent McEveety

The Corbomite Maneuver

w Jerry Sohl
Threatened by a horrifying alien's all-powerful space craft, Kirk plays a tactical bluff to save his ship from destruction – and then discovers his adversary is not what he seems . . .
Lt Bailey Anthony Call
Balok Clint Howard

Director: Joseph Sargent

The Menagerie

w Gene Roddenberry *(A 2-part story)*
A mutinous Spock kidnaps his former commanding officer Capt. Pike and sets the *Enterprise* on a course for the forbidden planet Talos IV. In Part Two, Spock submits to a court martial and tells the bizarre story of Captain Pike's journey to Talos IV 13 years before. (This Hugo Award-winning story used footage from *Star Trek*'s original pilot, *The Cage*.)

Capt. Pike Jeffrey Hunter/Sean Kenney
Commodore Mendez Malachi Throne
Vina Susan Oliver
The Keeper Meg Wyllie
Miss Piper Julie Parrish
Dr Phillip Boyce John Hoyt
Number One M. Leigh Hudec *(Majel Barrett)*
Yeoman Colt Laurel Goodwin

Directors: Marc Daniels, Robert Butler

The Conscience of the King

w Barry Trivers
The arrival of a troupe of actors raises the curtain on the last scene of a drama which began 20 years before with the slaughter of innocents, by Kodos the Executioner.
Dr Leighton William Sargent
Anton Karidian (Kodos) Arnold Moss
Lenore Barbara Anderson
Lt Kevin Riley Bruce Hyde

Director: Gerd Oswald

Balance of Terror

w Paul Schneider
Kirk wages a battle of wits and courage with a Romulan ship's commander.
Lt Andrew Stiles Paul Comi
Romulan Commander Mark Lenard
Centurion John Warburton
Decius Lawrence Montaigne
Angela Martine Barbara Baldavin

Director: Vincent McEveety

Shore Leave

w Theodore Sturgeon
The crew look forward to a well-earned rest on a beautiful planet but their pleasure turns to terror as they encounter people and images from their past – including a ferocious Samurai warrior and a large white rabbit!
Finnigan Bruce Mars
Lt Rodriguez Perry Lopez
Tonia Barrows Emily Banks
Ruth Shirley Bonnie
Caretaker Oliver McGowan

Director: Robert Sparr

The Galileo Seven

w Oliver Crawford and S. Bar David
  (alias Shimon Wincelberg)
Mr Spock's first independent command looks like being his last when his shuttle becomes marooned on Taurus II where the crew come under attack from its ape-like inhabitants.
High Commissioner Ferris John Crawford
Gaetano Peter Marko
Latimer Rees Vaughn
Lt. Boma Don Marshall
Lt. Commander Kelowitz Grant Woods

Director: Robert Gist

The Squire of Gothos

w Paul Schneider
Kirk is forced to play a deadly game with an urbane alien maniac with the fate of the Enterprise at stake.
Yeoman Teresa Ross Venita Wolf
General Trelane William Campbell
Lt. DeSalle Michael Barrier
Lt. Jaeger Richard Carlyle
Mother's voice Barbara Babcock
Father's voice James Doohan

Director: Donald McDougall

Arena

w Gene L. Coon, story Frederick Brown
After the relentless pursuit of a treacherous alien vessel, Kirk must fight the rival commander – a Godzilla-like creature called Gorn – in single combat.
Lt. O'Herlihy Jerry Ayres
Metron Carole Shelyne

Director: Joseph Pevney

Tomorrow is Yesterday

w D.C. Fontana
A freak of gravity propels the Enterprise back into the past where it becomes a UFO of the 1960s, and beams aboard a fighter pilot.
Capt. Christopher Roger Perry
Col. Fellini Ed Peck

Crewman Sherri Townsend
Air Police Jim Spencer

Director: Michael O'Herlihy

Court Martial

w Don Mankiewicz, Steven Carabatsos
Charged with causing the death of a missing officer, Kirk is put on trial, but finds his version of the events is at odds with the computer record – and the computer doesn't lie.
Commodore Stone Percy Rodriguez
Lt. Areel Shaw Joan Marshall
Samuel T. Cogley Elisha Cook
Lt. Cmdr Finney Richard Webb
Jamie Finney Alice Rawlings

Director: Marc Daniels

Return of the Archons

w Boris Sobelman, story Gene Roddenberry
On the planet Beta 3000, Kirk encounters a peculiarly placid community ruled by Landru – a baleful computer deity.
Landru Charles Macaulay
Reger Harry Townes
Tula Brioni Farrell
Marplon Torin Thatcher
Tamar Jon Lormer
Hacom Morgan Farley

Director: Joseph Pevney

Space Speed

w Carey Wilbur, Gene L. Coon
The Enterprise encounters a derelict spaceship carrying the survivors of a past civilisation – a race of supermen, lead by the wrathful Kahn. (The character was revived again in the second Star Trek feature film The Wrath of Kahn.)
Kahn Ricardo Montalban
Lt. Marla McGivers Madlyn Rhue
Lt. Spinelli Blaisdell Makee
Joaquin Mark Tobin
Elite crewmen Kathy Ahart

Director: Marc Daniels

A Taste of Armageddon

w Robert Hamner, Gene L. Coon
Kirk and Spock take an Earth ambassador to a distant planet which has been engaged in a 500-year-long war, waged at long distance by computer.
Ambassador Fox Gene Lyons
Anan 7 David Opatoshu
Mea 3 Barbara Babcock
Sar 6 Robert Sampson
Lt. DePaul Sean Kenney
Lt. Galloway David L. Ross

Director: Joseph Pevney

This Side of Paradise

w D.C. Fontana, story by Nathan Butler (alias Jerry Sohl) and D.C. Fontana
Seeking survivors on a planet exposed to deadly rays, Kirk is astounded to find the colonists alive and content, but he is enraged at the insidious effect their behaviour has on his crew – even Spock.
Elias Sandaval Frank Overton
Leila Jill Ireland
Lt. Cmdr Kelowitz Grant Woods
Lt. DeSalle Michael Barrier

Director: Ralph Senensky

The Devil in the Dark

w Gene L. Coon
Kirk confronts an unknown monster which has been hideously destroying workers on the mining colony of Janus.
Chief Engineer Vanderberg Ken Lynch
Lt. Cmdr Giotto Barry Russo
Horta Janos Prohaska
Ed Appel Brad Weston

Director: Joseph Pevney

Errand of Mercy

w Gene L. Coon
Kirk tries to warn the rulers of the planet Organia of the threat of Klingon invasion, but finds them curiously indifferent to his efforts.
Ayelborne Jon Abbott
Trefayne David Hillary Hughes

Claymore Peter Brocco
Cmdr. Kor John Colicos

Director: John Newland

The Alternative Factor

w Don Ingalls
An immense magnetic phenomenon fractures space from end to end and Kirk and crew are bound up in the struggle of a crazed time traveller.
Lazarus Robert Brown
Lt. Charlene Masters Janet MacLachlen
Commodore Barstow Richard Derr
Lt. Leslie Eddie Paskey
Engineering assistant Arch Whiting

Director: Gerd Oswald

The City on the Edge of Forever

w Harlan Ellison
When a time vortex sweeps a deranged McCoy back to New York in the 1920s, Kirk and Spock follow him and Kirk finds himself faced with the agonising choice of preserving something fine in the past or letting events take their natural course. (Hugo Award winner.)
Edith Keller Joan Collins
Lt. Galloway David L. Ross
Rodent John Harmon

Director: Joseph Pevney

Operation Annihilate!

w Steven Carabatsos
A spaceship hurtling to the sun, her crew preferring the holocaust to the horror which befell them, warns Kirk of danger on the planet Deneva – a parasitic invader which drives its hosts insane, and which attacks Spock.
Aurelan Kirk Joan Swift
Peter Kirk Craig Hundley
Kartan Dave Armstrong
Yeoman Zahra Jamal Maurishka Taliferro
Denevans Fred Carson, Jerry Catron

Director: Herschel Daugherty

Season Two
(26 episodes)

Amok Time

w Theodore Sturgeon
When Spock is gripped by the mind-bending Vulcan mating drive, Kirk accompanies him to his home planet where he finds he must fight his friend in a contest to the death.
T'Pring Arlene Martel
T'Pau Celia Lovsky
Stonn Lawrence Montaigne
Komack Byron Morrow

Director: Joseph Pevney

Who Mourns for Adonais?

w Gene L. Coon, Gilbert Ralston
A huge hand reaches out from the heavens and seizes the *Enterprise*. Kirk reaches Olympian heights in his defiance of the god-like being who demands his homage.
Apollo Michael Forest
Carolyn Leslie Parrish
Lt. Kyle John Winston

Director: Marc Daniels

The Changeling

w John Meredyth Lucas
Nomad, an ancient man-made exterminator of imperfect life forms, comes aboard the *Enterprise* and the ship is threatened with destruction until Kirk succeeds in outwitting the robot probe.
Voice of Nomad Vic Perrin
Mr Singh Blaisdell Makee
Astrochemist Barbara Gates
Lt. Carlisle Arnold Lessing

Director: Marc Daniels

Mirror, Mirror

w Jerome Bixby
An ion storm during transporation hurls Kirk and three officers into a parallel universe, while their counterparts materialise aboard the *Enterprise*.

Marlena Barbara Luna
Tharn Vic Perrin
Lt. Kyle John Winston
Farrell Peter Kellett

Director: Marc Daniels

The Apple

w Max Erlich, Gene L. Coon
Kirk discovers a Garden of Eden where life could not be more perfect – or less like living. Someone must play the snake to free the people of Paradise from innocence and their ruler Vaal.
Martha Landon Celeste Yarnall
Akuta Keith Andes
Makora David Soul
Sayana Shari Nims

Director: Joseph Pevney

The Doomsday Machine

w Norman Spinrad
The *Enterprise* is nearly destroyed by a rampaging 'doomsday machine' after rescuing Commodore Decker from the disabled starship, *Constellation*.
Commodore Decker William Windom
Elliot John Copage
Lt. Palmer Elizabeth Rogers
Washburn Richard Compton

Director: Marc Daniels

Catspaw

w Robert Bloch, D.C. Fontana
The *Enterprise* is trapped in a cosmic cauldron and the landing party of Pirus VI become the 'guests' of Korob and Sylvia, weavers of sinister spells.
Korob Theo Marcuse
Sylvia Antoinette Bower
Lt. DeSalle Michael Barrier

Director: Joseph Pevney

I, Mudd

w Stephen Kandel *and* David Gerrold
Kirk and his crew are abducted to a planet where space scoundrel Harry Mudd seems

to be living a life of ease with beautiful androids programmed to satisfy his every desire. But Harry wants his freedom . . .
Mudd Roger C. Carmel
Norman Richard Tatro
Stella Mudd Kay Elliot

Director: Marc Daniels

Metamorphosis

w Gene L. Coon
A shuttlecraft carrying Kirk, Spock and a critically ill Federation Commissioner is held by a mysterious force.
Cochrane Glenn Corbett
Commissioner Nancy Hedford Elinor Donahue
Voice of companion Majel Barrett

Director: Ralph Senensky

Journey to Babel

w D.C. Fontana
The *Enterprise* takes charge of a group of feuding Federation members and Spock meets again the father from whom he parted in bitterness 18 years before.
Sarek Mark Lenard
Amanda Janet Wyatt
Thelev William O'Connell
Shras Reggie Nalder

Director: Joseph Pevney

Friday's Child

w D.C. Fontana
Kirk inadvertently breaks a tribal taboo on the planet Capella and the crew have to flee – along with the chief's wife.
Eleen Julie Newmar
Kras Tige Andrews
Maab Michael Dante
Keel Cal Bolder

Director: Joseph Pevney

The Deadly Years

w David P. Harmon
On a visit to the planet Gamma Hydra IV,

Kirk, Spock, Scott and McCoy pick up a strange infection which causes them to age rapidly.
Capt. Stocker Charles Drake
Janet Wallace Sarah Marshall
Lt. Arlene Galway Beverly Washburn
Robert Johnson Felix Locher

Director: Joseph Pevney

Obsession

w Art Wallace
For the second time in his career, Kirk encounters a deadly gaseous creature which kills two of his crew, and he disregards vital orders in a fanatical bid to destroy it and ease his conscience.
Ensign Rizzo Jeffrey Ayres
Ensign Garrovick Stephen Brooks

Director: Ralph Senensky

Wolf in the Fold

w Robert Bloch
All the evidence points to Scottie as having savagely slain three women, until Kirk isolates the real culprit – the evil spirit of Jack the Ripper.
Hengis John Fiedler
Jaris Charles Macaulay
Sybo Pilar Seurat
Tark Joseph Bernard
Morla Charles Dierkop

Director: Joseph Pevney

The Trouble with Tribbles

w David Gerrold
The *Enterprise* crew find their troubles multiplying – in the cuddly, purring form of Cyrano Jones's tiny creatures, the tribbles.
Cyrano Jones Stanley Adams
Nilz Barris William Schallert
Koloth William Campbell
Mr Lurry Whit Bissell

Director: Joseph Pevney

The Gamesters of Triskelion

w Margaret Armen
Kirk, Uhura and Chekov are spirited to a planet where they are trained to fight for the amusement of the planet's rulers.
Galt Joseph Ruskin
Shahna Angelique Pettyjohn
Lars Steve Sandor
Ensign Jana Haines Victoria George

Director: Gene Nelson

A Piece of the Action

w David Harmon, Gene L. Coon
Investigating the disappearance of a federation starship 100 years earlier, the crew land on a remote planet resembling prohibition-era Chicago.
Bela Anthony Caruso
Krako Vic Tayback
Kalo Lee Delano
Zabo Steve Marlo
Tepo John Harmon

Director: James Komack

The Immunity Syndrome

w Robert Sabaroff
The *Enterprise* is confronted by a 1000-mile-wide amoeba-like creature and Spock embarks on a suicide mission.
Lt. Kyle John Winston

Director: Joseph Pevney

A Private Little War

w Gene Roddenberry
Starfleet orders specifically forbid intervention in the evolution of other races, but when the Klingons arm natives on a primitive planet, Kirk takes the grave risk of running guns to rival tribes to maintain the balance of power.
Nona Nancy Kovak
Tyree Michael Whitney
Krell Ned Romero
Mugato Janos Prohaska

Director: Marc Daniels

Return to Tomorrow

w John Kingsbridge *(alias* Gene Roddenberry*)*
The *Enterprise* is lured a thousand light years beyond explored space by a strange distress call from a seemingly lifeless world and Kirk and Spock find themselves playing hosts to the minds of an advanced civilisation.
Ann Mulhall Diana Muldaur

Director: Ralph Senensky

Patterns of Force

w John Meredyth Lucas
Kirk and Spock land on a backwood planet with a Nazi-type military regime.
Melakon Skip Homeier
Isak Richard Evans
Daras Valora Norand
Gill David Brian
Abrom William Wintersole
SS Major Gilbert Green

Director: Vincent McEveety

By Any Other Name

w Jerome Bixby, D.C. Fontana
Kirk and his crew are hijacked by Andromedan monsters intent on destroying all human existence. Masters of metabolism, the many-limbed monsters fortunately assume the frailty of human form to achieve their aims.
Rojan Warren Stevens
Kelinda Barbara Bouchet
Hanar Stewart Moss
Yeoman Leslie Thompson Julie Cobb
Lt. Shea Carl Byrd

Director: Marc Daniels

The Omega Glory

w Gene Roddenberry
'If you've come aboard, you're dead men – don't go back to your starship.' After finding a sinister warning in a deserted, aimlessly orbiting starship, the USS *Exeter*, Kirk and his boarding party beam down to the planet Omega where they

meet a man who believes he has found the secret of immortality.

Capt. Tracy **Morgan Woodward**
Cloud William **Roy Jensen**
Lt. Galloway **David L. Ross**
Dr Carter **Ed McCready**
Sirah **Irene Kelly**

Director: **Vincent McEveety**

The Ultimate Computer

w **D.C. Fontana,** *story* **Lawrence N. Wolfe**
M5, a huge computer, is installed in the *Enterprise* in place of the human crew. But it goes beserk and Starfleet Command orders its other starships to 'Destroy the *Enterprise!*'

Dr Richard Daystrom **William Marshall**
Commodore Wesley **Barry Russo**
Voice of M5 **James Doohan**

Director: **John Meredyth Lucas**

Bread and Circuses

w **Gene L. Coon** *and* **Gene Roddenberry**
Kirk is forced into furious combat to save his crew from being butchered on a planet whose society is just like that of ancient Rome with its gladiators and arena.

Merik **William Smithers**
Claudius **Logan Ramsey**
Septimus **Ian Wolfe**
Drusilla **Lois Jewell**
Flavius **Rhodes Reason**

Director: **Ralph Senensky**

Assignment: Earth

w **Art Wallace, Gene Roddenberry**
Cosmic records say that the old world narrowly escaped disaster in 1968 and the *Enterprise* is assigned to discover what happened. But the mission assumes more than academic interest when the mysterious Gary Seven is beamed aboard.

Gary Seven **Robert Lansing**
Roberta London **Terri Garr**

Director: **Marc Daniels**

Season Three
(24 episodes)

Spock's Brain

w **Lee Cronin** *(alias* **Gene L. Coon***)*
A beautiful and mysterious woman renders Spock the victim of a critical brain-drain. Kirk and McCoy have just 24 hours to restore his brain to his body.

Kara **Marj Dusay**

Director: **Marc Daniels**

The Enterprise Incident

w **D.C. Fontana**
To the astonishment of his own crew – including Spock – Kirk orders his ship to invade the Romulan neutral zone where it is captured and threatened with confiscation.

Romulan commander **Joanne Linville**

Director: **John Meredyth Lucas**

The Paradise Syndrome

w **Margaret Armen**
Oblivious to his duties, Kirk takes a wife and idles time away while Spock tries to divert a huge asteroid hurtling on a collision course.

Miramanee **Sabrina Scharf**
Salish **Rudy Solari**

Director: **Jud Taylor**

And the Children Shall Lead

w **Edward J. Lasko**
Investigating a disaster call from the planet Triacus, Kirk is puzzled to find children playing beside the sprawled bodies of their dead parents. Under the influence of the alien Gorgan, the children play on the hidden fears of the crew.

Gorgan **Melvin Belli**
Tommy Starnes **Craig Hundley**
Professor Starnes **James Wellman**

Director: **Marvin Chomsky**

Is There In Truth No Beauty?

w Jean Lisette Aroeste
Special visors are issued to the *Enterprise* officers for the arrival of the Medusan ambassador, emissary of a gentle race but so hideous in appearance that one look can drive a man mad. Spock gazes on the Medusan – and only a Vulcan mind-link can save him.
Dr Miranda Jones **Diana Muldaur**
Lawrence Marvick **David Frankham**

Director: **Ralph Senensky**

Spectre of the Gun

w Lee Cronin *(alias* Gene L. Coon*)*
As a result of Kirk's persistence in exploring a forbidden planet, he, Chekov, Spock and McCoy are trapped in a reconstruction of the Gunfight at the OK Corral.
Sylvia **Bonnie Beecher**
Wyatt Earp **Ron Soble**
Morgan Earp **Rex Holman**
Doc Holliday **Sam Gilman**
Johnny Behan **Bill Zuckert**
Melkot voice **Abraham Sofaer**

Director: **Vincent McEveety**

Day of the Dove

w Jerome Bixby
An intangible monster that feeds upon hatred insidiously invades the *Enterprise*, bringing the ship to the brink of destruction as crew and Klingons clash in blind fury, until Kirk finds a 'peaceful' solution.
Kang **Michael Ansara**
Mara **Susan Howard**
Lt. Johnson **David L. Rose**

Director: **Marvin Chomsky**

For the World Is Hollow and I Have Touched the Sky

w Rik Vollaerts
A stricken McCoy, who learns he has only one year to live, submits to electronic enslavement by the alien queen of a mysterious asteroid speeding towards a populated planet and certain doom.
Natira **Kate Woodville**

Director: **Tony Leader**

The Tholian Web

w Judy Burns, Chet Richards
While Kirk finds himself a lonely passenger aboard the devastated hulk of the Starship *Defiant*, his own vessel lies floundering in another universe, slowly being strangled by a web of pure energy.

Director: **Ralph Senensky**

Plato's Stepchildren

w Meyer Dolinsky
Responding to a distress call from the planet Platonius, *Enterprise* officers are enslaved by a creature with advanced telepathic powers.
Alexander **Michael Dunn**
Parmen **Liam Sullivan**
Philana **Barbara Babcock**

Director: **David Alexander**

Wink of an Eye

w Arthur Heinemann, *story by* Lee Cronin *(alias* Gene L. Coon*)*
A strange high-pitched hum, noticed on the planet Scalos, pervades the *Enterprise*, intangible evidence of a takeover by the rapid-moving Scalosian Queen Deela – to whom every second is like an hour.
Deela **Kathie Brown**
Rael **Jason Evers**
Compton **Geoffrey Binney**
Ekor **Eric Holland**

Director: **Jud Taylor**

The Empath

w Joyce Muscat
On a doomed planet, Kirk, Spock and McCoy are tortured by powerful aliens who are testing the capacity for self-sacrifice and compassion of a frail, mute

girl called Gem, to determine whether her empathic species should be saved. (This episode was scheduled in the UK, even being billed in *Radio Times*, but was withdrawn and replaced with *The Paradise Syndrome*. However it *might* have gone out in BBC Wales).
Gem Kathryn Hays
Lal Alan Bergman
Thann Willard Sage

Director: John Erman

Elaan of Troyius

w John Meredyth Lucas
A clash with the Klingons is the least of Kirk's worries as he tries to cope with the peculiar potency of an alien woman's tears.
Elaan France Nuyen
Lord Petri Jay Robertson
Kryton Tony Young
Watson Victor Brandt
Evans Lee Duncan

Director: John Meredyth Lucas

Whom Gods Destroy

w Lee Erwin, *story by* Jerry Sohl *and* Lee Erwin
Journeying to an asylum planet with a new cure for mental illness, Kirk and Spock are threatened by Garth, a madman with the ability to change his form, who wants to conquer the universe, using an 'ultimate' explosive.
Garth of Izar Steve Ihnat
Marta Yvonne Craig
Donald Cory Keye Luke
Andorian Richard Geary
Tellarite Gary Downey

Director: Herb Wallerstein

Let That Be Your Last Battlefield

w Oliver Crawford, *story by* Lee Cronin *(alias* Gene L. Coon*)*
Two warring aliens carry a 50,000-year conflict onto the *Enterprise* and Kirk orders the destruction of his own ship in an extreme bid to end it.

Lokai Lou Antonio
Bele Frank Gorshin

Director: Jud Taylor

Mark of Gideon

w George F. Slavin, Stanley Adams
Kirk is lured onto a fake – and deserted – *Enterprise* where he feels the shattering experience of the tormented inhabitants of the planet Gideon.
Odona Sharon Acker
Hodin David Hurst
Krodak Gene Dynarski
Admiral Fitzgerald Richard Derr

Director: Jud Taylor

That Which Survives

w John Meredyth Lucas, D.C. Fontana
Stranded on a hostile planet after the *Enterprise* is flung a thousand light years away, Kirk and McCoy face starvation and a deadly enemy. It hardly seems the time for childish games . . .
Lt. D'Amato Arthur Batanides
Lt. Rahda Naomi Pollack
Losira Lee Meriwether

Director: Herb Wallerstein

Lights of Zetar

w Jeremy Tarcher, Shari Lewis
In the vicinity of Memory Alpha, Lt. Mira Romaine proves exceedingly attractive to Scottie – and to some very colourful bodysnatchers.
Lt. Mira Romaine Jan Shutan
Lt. Kyle John Winston
Technician Libby Erwin

Director: Herb Kenwith

Requiem for Methuselah

w Jerome Bixby
The *Enterprise* crew meet a powerful alien who claims to be immortal and to have lived his life as a series of famous Earth figures.

Flint James Daly
Reena Louise Sorel

Director: Murray Golden

The Way to Eden

w Michael Richards *(alias* D.C. Fontana*)*,
Arthur Heinemann
A band of space hippies boards the *Enterprise* en route to the mythical planet of
Eden. The normally 'square' Spock finds a
rapport with them, but Kirk is short on
peace, love or understanding.
Dr Sevrin Skip Homeier
Adam Charles Napier
Irina Mary Linda Rapelye
Tongo Rad Victor Brandt
Lt. Palmer Elizabeth Rogers
Mavig Deborah Downey

Director: David Alexander

The Cloud Minders

w Margaret Armen, *story by* David
Gerrold *and* Oliver Crawford
A mercy mission to Stratos City leads to
Kirk's involvement in a slave rebellion, as
he tries to make both sides see reason.
Plasus Jeff Corey
Vanna Charlene Polite
Droxine Diana Ewing

Director: Jud Taylor

The Savage Curtain

w Gene Roddenberry, Arthur
Heinemann
Kirk and Spock are teamed with their
historical heroes against the most wicked
men in history in a bizarre test of good
versus evil.
Abraham Lincoln Lee Bergere
Surak Barry Atwater
Col. Green Phil Pine
Ghenghis Khan Nathan Young
Zora Carol Daniels Dement
Kahless Robert Herron

Director: Herschel Daughtery

All Our Yesterdays

w Jean Lisette Aroeste
An extraordinary device in the library of a
doomed planet sends Kirk, McCoy and
Spock into different eras of Earth's past.
Atoz Ian Wolfe
Zarabeth Mariette Hartley
Woman Anna Karen

Director: Marvin Chomsky

Turnabout Intruder

w Arthur Singer, *story by* Gene
Roddenberry
Kirk's mind is transferred to the body of
Dr Janice Lester – while she takes over
the *Enterprise* as the Captain.
Dr Janice Lester Sandra Smith
Dr Coleman Harry Landers
Angela Barbara Baldavin

Director: Herb Wallerstein

The BBC first screened Star Trek in four
seasons, (interspersed with repeats) which
were as follows:

UK Series One
(12 July–27 December 1969)

Where No Man Has Gone Before
The Naked Time
The City on the Edge of Forever
A Taste of Armageddon
Mudd's Women
Tomorrow Is Yesterday
The Menagerie (a 2-part story)
The Devil in the Dark
Charlie X
Shore Leave
Space Seed
Man Trap
Dagger of the Mind
The Corbomite Maneuver
Balance of Terror
The Squire of Gothos
What Are Little Girls Made Of?
Arena
Return of the Archons
This Side of Paradise
The Doomsday Machine
Errand of Mercy
The Conscience of the King
The Galileo Seven

UK Series Two
(6 April–7 September 1970)

Court Martial
The Enemy Within
Catspaw
Who Mourns for Adonais?
The Apple
Metamorphosis
Wolf in the Fold
The Changeling
The Trouble with Tribbles
Bread and Circuses
Journey to Babel
The Deadly Years
A Private Little War
Obsession
By Any Other Name
I, Mudd
Patterns of Force
The Immunity Syndrome
Return to Tomorrow
The Omega Glory
A Piece of the Action

UK Series Three
7 October 1970–10 February 1971)

The Ultimate Computer
Friday's Child
Assignment Earth

Mirror, Mirror
The Gamesters of Triskelion
Amok Time
Miri
Operation Annihilate
The Paradise Syndrome
Requiem for Methuselah
All Our Yesterdays
Day of the Dove
The Way to Eden
Let That Be Your Last Battlefield
Wink of an Eye
The Cloud Minders

UK Series Four
(15 September–15 December 1971)

Spectre of the Gun
Elaan of Troyius
The Enterprise Incident
And the Children Shall Lead
Spock's Brain
Is There in Truth No Beauty?
For the World Is Hollow and I Have
   Touched the Sky
That Which Survives
Mark of Gideon
Lights of Zetar
The Savage Curtain
The Tholian Web
The Alternative Factor
Turnabout Intruder

STINGRAY

Gerry and Sylvia Anderson's third venture in the supermarionation series, after *Supercar* (1961) and *Fireball XL5* (1962). Though
outstripped later, this was their costliest yet, running up a £1
million bill for the 39 half-hour adventures. It introduced the men
and women of WASP – the World Aquanaut Security Patrol –
dedicated to making the undersea world of the year 2000 a safer
place.

   Stingray, an atomic-powered sub equipped with 16 Sting missiles
and possessing dolphin-like agility, was captained by Troy Tempest,
a handsome, fearless 22-inch chip off the Mike Mercury/Steve
Zodiac block. Alongside him were loyal hydrophones operator Lt.
George 'Phones' Sheridan, and the enchanting, green-haired
Marina, mute daughter of Aphony, emperor of the peaceful
undersea kingdom of Pacifica. Pulling their strings at WASP

headquarters, Marineville, was the organisation's founder, Commander Sam Shore, a crippled sub veteran who controlled operations from his hover-chair.

The series' bad guys were the tyrannical Titan, ruler of Titanica, and his aquaphibians, a monstrous underwater race who waged war in their mechanical Terror Fish which fired missiles from their gaping mouths. Other regular characters were Commander Shore's daughter Atlanta, sub-lieutenant Fisher and agent X20, a hapless Titan spy whose subversive efforts invariably ended in failure and a ticking off from his boss.

A running subplot, highlighted by the closing credit sequence, was the unrequited eternal triangle – Atlanta doted on Troy who mooned over Marina.

Though produced for the traditional children's teatime slot, *Stingray* has enjoyed enduring success with a wider audience. Its visual invention, imaginative flair, characterisation and continuity of detail endeared it to the discerning supermarionation fans. The first Gerry Anderson series to be shot in colour, it was originally screened here in black and white, but has been seen in colour since 1969.

VOICE CAST:

Troy Tempest **Don Mason**   *Phones/Agent X20* **Robert Easton**
Commander Shore/Titan/Sub-Lt. Fisher **Ray Barrett**
Atlanta **Lois Maxwell**

Created by: **Gerry** and **Sylvia Anderson**
Producer: **Gerry Anderson**
Associate producer: **Reg Hill**
Special effects: **Derek Meddings**
Music: **Barry Gray**
Title song sung by: **Gary Miller**

An AP Films Production in association with ATV for ITC Worldwide Distribution
39 colour 30-minute episodes
4 October 1964–27 June 1965
(Dates as ATV, London region)

Stingray (the pilot)

w **Gerry** *and* **Sylvia Anderson**
Investigating strange explosions at sea, Troy and Phones are captured by Titan and condemned to die. They are saved by Titan's slave girl Marina who helps them to escape and joins the WASP crew.

Director: **Alan Pattillo**

Emergency Marineville

w **Alan Fennell**
While investigating a missile threat to Marineville, the *Stingray* crew are captured. Troy is forced to give the correct course for the missile but manages to remove the explosive warhead so that it lands with a harmless thud – and a message that brings rescue.

Director: **John Kelly**

The Ghost Ship

w **Alan Fennell**
Checking out a mysterious fog-shrouded galleon, Commander Shore and Phones find themselves in the clutches of a strange creature called Idotee who orders Troy to join them. But wily Troy fills his air

cylinders with laughing gas and when he releases it Idotee collapses with laughter.

Director: Desmond Saunders

Subterranean Sea

w Alan Fennell

The *Stingray* crew's holiday in the sun is interrupted by a mission to investigate the depth of the Subterrain – but they end up discovering a beautiful tropical island in a subterranean sea. It's the perfect place for a holiday.

Director: Desmond Saunders

Loch Ness Monster

w Dennis Spooner

Stingray is sent to Scotland to investigate the legend of the Loch Ness monster. But the ferocious-looking dragon that 'attacks' them turns out to be a fake, rigged up by two brothers to attract the tourist trade.

Director: Alan Pattillo

Set Sail for Adventure

w Dennis Spooner

Phones and Lt. Fisher find themselves before the mast on an ancient sailing ship when Commander Shore takes up an old friend's challenge to test the mettle of his men. But when a storm blows up and mishaps mount, it's a good job *Stingray* is close behind.

Director: David Elliott

The Man from the Navy

w Alan Fennell

A feud flares between Troy and a boastful naval captain. When the navy man becomes the innocent pawn in another of X20's plots to destroy *Stingray*, it is Troy who clears his adversary's name, though he gets little thanks!

Director: John Kelly

An Echo of Danger

w Dennis Spooner

Agent X20's decoy signal and psychiatrist disguise succeed in discrediting Phones. X20 turns his attention to Troy, but Lt. Fisher helps thwart his plot and Phones is cleared.

Director: Alan Pattillo

Raptures of the Deep

w Alan Fennell

Going to the rescue of two illicit treasure-hunters, Troy runs short of air and deliriously dreams that he is in a fabulous palace with Marina, Atlanta and Phones at his beck and call. But he is glad to reawaken when the dream turns nasty.

Director: Desmond Saunders

Titan Goes Pop

w Alan Fennell

Titan is totally baffled by the strange VIP that Agent X20 has kidnapped from Marineville. It turns out to be pop star Duke Dexter, but such is Duke's power to throw the terrans into a tizzy, that Titan is convinced the singer is on their side!

Director: Alan Pattillo

In Search of the Tajmanon

w Dennis Spooner

How can a submerged palace just disappear? That's the riddle facing the *Stingray* crew who are joined by Atlanta on a perilous quest to Africa where the mystery is finally solved.

Director: Desmond Saunders

A Christmas to Remember

w Dennis Spooner

It's definitely a memorable experience for the young orphaned son of an ex-WASP aquanaut who comes to stay at Marineville when he joins Troy on a *Stingray* patrol with unexpectedly dangerous results.

Director: Alan Pattillo

Tune of Danger

w Alan Fennell
Troy discovers that a bomb has been planted inside one of the instruments of a jazz group that is due to perform for Marina's father Aphony in his underwater city. Troy starts a desperate race against time to avert disaster.

Director: John Kelly

The Ghost of the Sea

w Alan Fennell
The story behind Commander Shore's injury which has left him a cripple is revealed in a series of nightmare 'flash-backs'. But the mysterious stranger who once saved his life is now suspected of destroying an oil rig. Troy and the Commander investigate and Troy saves the stranger's life, so repaying Commander Shore's debt – and bringing peace.

Director: David Elliott

Rescue from the Skies

w Dennis Spooner
Lt. Fisher's training exercise in Stingray runs into danger when X20 cripples the vessel and places a sticker bomb on the hull to finish it off. Troy must jet to the scene in time to remove the bomb and save his friends.

Director: Desmond Saunders

The Lighthouse Dwellers

w Alan Fennell
When a pilot crashes after mistaking the flashing beacon of a supposedly disused lighthouse for his airstrip, *Stingray* is sent to investigate. Troy and Phones discover that a race of underwater people have been harnessing the lighthouse's power for their own city.

Director: David Elliott

The Big Gun

w Alan Fennell
Troy and his crew investigate the mysterious destruction of three Pacific islands and must face enemies from an ocean *below* the Pacific itself. Only Marina can withstand the intense water pressure and destroy the underwater city.

Director: David Elliott

The Cool Caveman

w Alan Fennell
Troy is stuck for a costume for Atlanta's fancy dress party, until a dream that he and Phones clash with a band of underwater cavemen gives him a novel idea – or so he thinks . . .

Director: Alan Pattillo

Deep Heat

w Alan Fennell
Two underwater beings lure *Stingray* to their stronghold beneath the Earth's crust and beg to be rescued from destruction by a volcanic eruption. But the crew's kindness is repaid by treachery!

Director: John Kelly

Star of the East

w Alan Fennell
Would-be WASP member El Hudat is enraged when a revolution in his home state robs him of WASP eligibility. He kidnaps Marina, and Troy needs all his aquanaut's skills to bring the renegade to book.

Director: Desmond Saunders

Invisible Enemy

w Alan Fennell
Troy and his crew rescue a mysterious stranger and resume patrol, unaware that the man has been hypnotised by an alien underwater race to put the whole of

Marineville into a trance, leaving the city vulnerable to attack. Luckily they return in time to revive everyone!

Director: **David Elliott**

Tom Thumb Tempest

w Alan Fennell
Danger and adventure as *Stingray* shrinks to miniature size and the crew find themselves midgets in a bewildering giant world, threatened by Titan's forces and trapped in a fish tank. All seems lost . . . until Troy awakens from his vivid dream.

Director: **Alan Pattillo**

Eastern Eclipse

w Alan Fennell
Which brother is which? That's the poser for Commander Shore after Agent X20 frees Eastern dictator El Hudat from Marineville by substituting his deposed twin brother Ali Khali. The only answer is to lock them both up!

Director: **Desmond Saunders**

Treasure Down Below

w Dennis Spooner
An old treasure map leads *Stingray* into a rocky cavern where the crew are taken prisoner by two fish-people who have lived comfortably for 300 years on the proceeds of underwater piracy. Troy's bravery saves his friends and foils the fishy felons.

Director: **Alan Pattillo**

Stand By for Action

w Dennis Spooner
Troy is put out when a film unit makes a movie at Marineville – with a handsome screen star playing his part! But it's really just another of Agent X20's fiendish schemes to dispose of the superhero, and when the plot thickens it's the real Troy who saves the day – and gets the girl!

Director: **Alan Pattillo**

Pink Ice

w Alan Fennell
Investigating a strange pink liquid that is freezing over the world's oceans, *Stingray* becomes trapped as the water around it turns to pink ice. Only a missile bombardment from Marineville can free them – but one stray shot could scupper them!

Director: **David Elliott**

The Disappearing Ships

w Alan Fennell
Probing the disappearance of three disused freighters which were due to be blown up, Troy and Phones discover them in a Shipwreck City inhabited by a Nomad tribe who are unaware that their new homes are time-bombs – until, one by one, the ships explode.

Director: **David Elliott**

Secret of the Giant Oyster

w Alan Fennell
Marina is worried when Troy is sent to help two conniving divers retrieve a huge, priceless pearl from a giant oyster, protected by thousands of satellite oysters; bad luck is said to befall whoever removes it. Troy does indeed run into danger but both he and the giant oyster are saved by the protective satellites.

Director: **John Kelly**

The Invaders

w Dennis Spooner
Captured by an underwater race, Troy, Phones and Marina little realise their thoughts have been read – and vital secrets revealed. The invaders burrow into Marineville but Troy is able to sound the alarm and foil the takeover bid.

Director: **David Elliott**

A Nut for Marineville

w Gerry *and* Sylvia Anderson
Egghead boffin Professor Burgoyne is
called in to design a new super missile
after *Stingray*'s old ones fail to destroy a
powerful alien craft heading for Marineville.

Director: David Elliott

Trapped in the Depths

w Alan Fennell
Atlanta is staying on a remote fish farm
when she stumbles on a crazy professor's
plan to hijack *Stingray* by luring Troy and
Phones into a mock-up, while his forces
use the real one to attack Marineville.

Director: John Kelly

Count Down

w Dennis Spooner
Claiming to be able to teach dumb people
to speak, Agent X20 lures Marina into his
underwater craft and leaves her trapped
aboard it in Marineville's launch tunnel
with a bomb primed to explode. Troy and
Phones thwart his master-plan with just
seconds to spare.

Director: Alan Pattillo

Sea of Oil

w Dennis Spooner
Atlanta is captured by an undersea race
who believe Troy is trying to destroy their
city. She is told a bomb has been placed
on *Stingray* which will explode when the
craft submerges . . .

Director: John Kelly

Plant of Doom

w Alan Fennell
Marina is used by Agent X20 as the
unsuspecting dupe in a deadly scheme that
has her suspected of trying to kill Atlanta
– until Troy proves her innocence.

Director: David Elliott

The Master Plan

w Alan Fennell
Poisoned in an aquaphibian attack, Troy
lies dying. Only Titan has the antidote but
he wants his ex-slave girl Marina in exchange.

Director: John Kelly

The Golden Sea

w Dennis Spooner
Titan tries to use a giant swordfish's
electrical energy to destroy *Stingray*,
which has been assigned to assist scientists
who have found a way to mine gold from
the sea – but Troy turns the tables on the
old tyrant.

Director: John Kelly

Hostages of the Deep

w Alan Fennell
Stingray responds to a distress call which
includes a coded warning of a trap, and
the crew encounters Gadus, a dastardly
underwater inhabitant. Marina is captured
and looks set to meet a nasty end at the
point of a swordfish's razor-sharp sword
until Troy and Phones effect a last-minute
rescue.

Director: Desmond Saunders

Marineville Traitor

w Alan Fennell
Commander Shore a traitor? Surely not!
But when a vital piece of equipment is
stolen, it certainly looks that way. However, it's all a trap to lure the *real* traitor
into the open and the Commander finds
himself in deadly danger.

Director: Desmond Saunders

Aquanaut of the Year

w Gerry *and* Sylvia Anderson
After a party to celebrate his Aquanaut of
the Year award, Troy finds himself the

subject of *This is Your Life* and relives moments from his most exciting adventures. But just as the host is asking whether he and Atlanta are more than just good friends, the alert is sounded, leaving Atlanta to remark that 'there just isn't time for romance in the World Aquanaut Security Patrol'.

Director: Alan Pattillo

THE STRANGE WORLD OF PLANET X

'. . . . we must go on, they cry, and hurtle to destruction, and they don't care who they take with them.'

Its producer, Arthur Lane, called it 'adult science fiction' and paralleled it with *Gun Law*, 'the adult Western'.

The Observer TV critic Maurice Richardson voted it ITV's 'worst serial of the year', and called it 'a poor man's *Quatermass*'.

Those viewers who opted to make the trip were transported to *The Strange World of Planet X* over the space of seven autumn weeks in 1956. The story, penned by actress, novelist and scriptwriter Rene Ray, followed the experiences of two scientists, David Graham and Gavin Laird, whose discovery of the 'devastating' Formula MFX – Magnetic Field X (where X equals the unknown!) – gave them the freedom of Time – the Fourth Dimension. Two others who came under the influence of Formula MFX were Laird's wife Fenella (played by Trevor Howard's actress wife Helen Cherry), and another woman, Pollie Boulter (played by comedienne Maudie Edwards). As the episodes unfolded, the characters were transported to the strange, eerie world of Planet X – depicted as an abstract, moon-like landscape.

The serial was directed by Quentin Lawrence who, just a couple of months later, unleashed *The Trollenberg Terror* on ITV.

(The quote at the beginning is from the *TVTimes* billing for episode four. The previous week's asked: 'Was it just a dream? Or have you been to *The Strange World of Planet X*?' Well, have you?)

CAST

Fenella Laird Helen Cherry   *David Graham* William Lucas
Gavin Laird David Garth   *Prof. Kollheim* Paul Hardtmuth
Pollie Boulter Maudie Edwards

Writer: Rene Ray
Producer: Arthur Lane
Director: Quentin Lawrence

An ATV Network Production
Seven 30-minute episodes, black and white
15 September–27 October 1956

THE STRANGER

Science fiction tale from Australia about three teenagers who become involved in an alien's mission to Earth to find a new home for his people.

The story was told in two six-part serials, screened by the BBC in 1965 and 1966. In the first series, the stranger, Adam Suisse, arrives in Australia to seek help for the people of his planet, Soshuniss, who want to migrate to Earth. He is befriended by Bernie and Jean Walsh, whose father is the headmaster of the local school, and their pal Peter. Intrigued by the stranger's lengthy expeditions to the Blue Mountains, the trio follow him, learning his real identity and meeting a co-emissary Varossa, as well as taking a trip of their own to Soshuniss.

As the sequel opens, the people of Soshuniss are no nearer a solution, and are unhappy about the way the world – and particularly the Press – have reacted to the visit of their emissaries. As a result they hold Peter hostage on Soshuniss.

Happily, a peaceful solution is eventually found – thanks in large part to the Australian Prime Minister.

REGULAR CAST

Mr Walsh **John Fraser**   Mrs Walsh **Jessica Noad**
Bernard Walsh **Bill Levis**   Jean Walsh **Janice Dinnen**
Peter Cannon **Michael Thomas**
Adam Suisse (The Stranger) **Ron Haddrich**
Varossa **Reginald Livermore**   Prof. Mayer **Owen Weingott**

Writer: G.K. Saunders

An Australian Broadcasting Corporation Production

12 30-minute episodes, black and white
25 February–1 April 1965
11 January–15 February 1966
(BBC1)

STRANGER FROM SPACE

Britain's very first science fiction cliffhanger serial was a fortnightly offering broadcast as part of *Whirligig* – the children's corner of the box back in the innocent early 1950s.

First shown in 1951, with viewers encouraged to write in with their suggestions for what should happen next, the tale of young Ian Spencer and his adventures with a Martian boy, Bilaphodorus whose 'Space Boat' crashes on Earth, gained enough response to justify a second serial the following autumn. That one also featured

Valentine Dyall (the Black Guardian in *Doctor Who*) as a Martian, Gorgol.

Stranger From Space was a departure for the BBC whose previous ventures into science fiction had been one-off plays – Karel Capek's *R.U.R.* (1937) and H.G. Wells' *The Time Machine* (1949). In its modest way it opened the door for a succession of interplanetary adventures for the corporation's various Children's Television slots. (See *The Lost Planet, Return to the Lost Planet, Space School.*)

CAST

Ian Spencer **Brian Smith**   *Bilaphodorous* **Michael Newell**
John Armitage **John Gabriel**   *Mrs Spencer* **Betty Woolfe***
Professor Watkins **Richard Pearson***
Pamela Vernon **Isabel Georget**   *Delpho* **Bruce Beeby†**
Gorgol **Valentine Dyall†**   *Petrio* **Peter Hawkins†**

Writers: **Hazel Adair** *and* **Ronald Marriott**
Whirligig *devised and produced by* **Michael Westmore**
Introduced by **Humphrey Lestocq**

A BBC Production
17 (short) episodes, black and white

Series One:
Crash Landing
On the Run
Come to the Fair
The Trap
The House on Reigate Downs
The Intruders

Lost Energy
The New Power
Journey Through Space
Journey Through Space (cont.)
The Prisoner

20 October 1951–22 March 1952

Series Two:
Message From Mars
Return Journey
The Cage
Trouble in the Air
Total Eclipse
The Battle of Power

11 October–20 December 1952

* Series One only
† Series Two only

SUPERBOY

From the team that brought the *Superman* legend to the big screen in 1978, comes . . . *Superboy – the Series*.

Superboy focuses on a hitherto neglected chapter in the life of the Man of Steel – his college years, twixt Smallville High and Metropolis. Clark Kent is a journalism student at Shuster University where his best friends are Lana Lang and T.J. White, aspiring photographer son of *Daily Planet* editor. Occasional glimpses of villainy are provided by another Shuster student – Lex Luthor.

The series set out to portray a time of transition – both psychological and physical – for Clark who, for the first time, unveils the famous costume to an incredulous world while reciting the immortal creed of 'truth, justice and the American way'.

And it is set firmly in the 1980s/90s – allowing the boy of steel to tackle contemporary ills such as drug abuse, environmental issues, big-city gangs and the homeless.

There was no problem about making a TV audience believe a boy could fly. Besides the involvement of Alexander and Ilya Salkind, other *Superman* 'old boys' made the transition to the small screen, including producer Bob Simmonds, directors Colin Chilvers and Jackie Cooper (who played the movies' Perry White) and Bob Harmon who supervised the flying effects. A wry twist in the first episode had Superboy catch Lana Lang in a fall from a helicopter – as Christopher Reeve had done with Lois Lane in his first *Superman* film.

Clark/Superboy was played by an unknown actor, John Haymes Newton, a 22-year-old former bodyguard.

On the evidence of the first episodes screened in Britain in 1989, *Superboy* is hardly compulsive viewing – the constraints of the half-hour format with its need to establish and thwart a menace in less than 30 minutes allowed little time to explore the characters. It actually bombed in the ratings and was ditched by ITV before the scheduled 13-episode run was completed.

MAIN CAST

Superboy/Clark Kent **John Haymes Newton**   *Lana Lang* **Stacy Haiduk**
T.J. White **Jim Calvert**   *Lex Luthor* **Scott Wells**

Series created by: **Alexander** *and* **Ilya Salkind**
Executive producer: **Ilya Salkind**
Producer: **Bob Simmonds**
Executive story consultant: **Fred Freiberger**
Director of photography: **Orson Ochoa**
Theme: **Kevin Kiner**

An Alexander and Ilya Salkind Production
UK: 11 colour 30-minute episodes to date (series still in production at time of going to print)
7 January–18 March 1989

Season One

Countdown to Nowhere

w Fred Freiberger
Superboy makes his presence known for the very first time when Lana unwittingly gets caught up in a plot to steal an experimental laser gun.
Roscoe Williams Doug Barr

Director: Colin Chilvers

Bringing Down the House

w Michael Morris
Superboy probes a strange and deadly link between bizarre threats at a baseball game and amusement park and the return of rock star Judd Faust.
Judd Faust Leif Garrett

Director: Colin Chilvers

The Beast and Beauty

w Bernard M. Kahn
Superboy confronts a crazed impostor who wants to steal a million dollars to 'buy' the hand of a beauty queen.
Hugo Stone David Marciano
Jennifer Jenkins Lonnie Shaw

Director: Jackie Cooper

The Fixer

w Aiden Schwimmer
The boy of steel foils a plot to fix a university basketball game masterminded by . . . Lex Luther.
Lex Luthor Scott Wells
Stretch Michael Landon Jr

Director: Colin Chilvers

Return to Oblivion (aka The Hiding Place)

w Fred Freiberger
Superboy must overcome some maniacal machines built out of scrap metal to rescue Lana from the clutches of an old man who has mistaken her for his daughter, killed by the Nazis in World War Two.
Wagner Abe Vigoda

Director: Colin Chilvers

A Kind of Princess

w Michael Morris, Howard Dimsdale
Superboy fights organised crime as he rescues Sarah Danner, one of 'Clark's' classmates and the daughter of mob boss Matt Danner, from the hands of a rival mobster.
Sarah Julie McCullough
Matt Danner Ed Winter
Casey Harry Cup

Director: Reza Badiyi

The Russian Exchange Student

w Sarah V. Finney *and* Vida Spears
T.J. falls in love with a Russian exchange student who is suspected of sabotaging secret energy experiments at Shuster University. (Guest star Ray Walston played Uncle Martin in the 1960s series *My Favourite Martian*.)
Natasha Pokrovsky Heather Haase
Prof. Abel Gordon Ray Walston
Jeff Hilford Courtney Gaines

Director: Reza Badiyi

The Jewel of Techacal

w Fred Freiberger
Prof. Lang visits his daughter, Lana, at the university with his latest archaeological find; the Jewel of Techacal.
Prof. Thomas Lang Peter White

Director: Reza Badiyi

Birdwoman of the Swamps

w (not available)
The construction of new housing for the poor is endangering the local wildlife, and a mysterious old woman, claiming to use ancient Indian magic, is sabotaging it for the sake of the environment.

Director: (not available)

The Invisible People

w (not available)
Superboy goes to the assistance of some homeless people whose 'tent city' has been savagely firebombed.
Gerold Manfred Sonny Shroyer
Damon Greg Morris

Director: (not available)

Troubled Waters

w Dick Robbins
Superboy returns to his parents' home in Smallville and uncovers a sinister plot to sell all the water from an underground river in the town.
Jonathan Kent Stuart Whitman
Martha Kent Salome Jens
Ellen Jensen Juli Donald
Carl Kenderson Peter Palmer

Director: Reza Badiyi

SUPERCAR

Supercar started the run of Supermarionation sci-fi series in 1961, but the Gerry Anderson puppet story was already five years old by then.

It all began, as they say, in 1956, in a converted mansion in Maidenhead, Berkshire, where the 27-year-old, near-penniless former film cutting-room assistant launched his own company AP Films into its maiden venture, a low-budget puppet project about a character who could stretch his limbs. *The Adventures of Twizzle* ran for 52 15-minute episodes, closely followed by 52 tales of *Torchy the Battery Boy*, dazzling the first generation of ITV toddlers. (Both these were scripted by Roberta Leigh who later created *Space Patrol*.) Then came a full-scale puppet production, the Western series *Four Feather Falls*, with Nicholas Parsons and Kenneth Connor among the actors voicing the characters.

Anderson's technique was improving – incorporating moving eyes and electronically controlled mouth movements – and he and his associates, Reg Hill, John Read, and wife Sylvia, were realising the potential of this type of film-making. A new word was coined to set the puppets as a race apart – Supermarionation – and *Supercar* swept it across the screens.

A wonderfully versatile craft, Supercar could travel over land, in the sea and through the air – anywhere in the world. It had folding wings for flights and a periscope for submarine work. The regular cast included Supercar's fatherly inventor, Professor Popkiss, a sort of mid-European scientist; his assistant Dr Beaker, a British boffin with a balding head and a stammer; fearless test pilot Mike Mercury; 10-year-old Jimmy Gibson who was the first person to be rescued by Supercar, after a plane crash; and his pal Mitch, a mischievous talking monkey. They were the good guys. Out to steal Supercar were Masterspy, a devious deep-voiced mercenary, and his weedy, worm-like accomplice Zarin; and their British counterparts Judd and Harper.

Supercar itself, a seven-foot craft made mostly of lightweight balsa wood, was designed by Reg Hill and cost £1000 to build – a small fortune for a company so short of cash that it used 1500 empty egg cartons stuck on the walls to soundproof its new studio in a disused factory in Slough.

Supercar was dreamt up in 1959, but with Anderson's previous backers, Granada Television, shying away from the new project, production was saved when Lew Grade's ITC put up the money.

The series was a soaraway success. Its 39 episodes turned the tide for Anderson, selling into more than 100 US markets and more than 40 countries. Indeed, Lew Grade liked the results so much he subsequently bought the company!

VOICE CAST

Mike Mercury Graydon Gould   *Jimmy Gibson* Sylvia Anderson (Sylvia Thamm)
Prof. Popkiss/Masterspy George Murcell *(Season One)*, Cyril Shaps *(Season Two)*
Mitch/Zarin/Dr Beaker David Graham

From an idea by Gerry Anderson *and* Reg Hill
Producer: Gerry Anderson
Music: Barry Gray
Special effects: Derek Meddings

An AP Films Production for ATV/ITC
39 30-minute episodes, black and white
Season One:
28 January–6 August 1961
Season Two:
4 February–29 April 1962
(Dates as London, ATV)

Season One
(26 episodes)

Rescue

w Martin *and* Hugh Woodhouse
On his maiden rescue flight Mike Mercury uses Supercar's Clearvu device to navigate through dense fog to save brothers Bill and Jimmy Gibson who are drifting on a life-raft after their plane crashed into the sea.

Director: David Elliott

False Alarm

w Martin *and* Hugh Woodhouse
Masterspy and Zarin send out a phoney SOS so they can steal Supercar when it comes to the rescue. Their plan nearly works until Prof. Popkiss switches Supercar to remote and hands the controls over to Mitch who gives the dastardly duo a hair-raising ride.

Director: Alan Pattillo

Talisman of Sargon

w Martin *and* Hugh Woodhouse
Masterspy, disguised as a geologist, tricks Dr Beaker into deciphering the secret of the Tomb of Sargon which contains a priceless jewel said to bestow magic powers on its owner. Mike and his team race to stop him using it.

Director: David Elliott

What Goes Up

w Martin *and* Hugh Woodhouse
When a test balloon carrying a new USAF rocket fuel drifts out of control, Mike risks his life to take Supercar close enough to detonate it before it can fall back to Earth and returns with only scorched paintwork to show for his adventure.

Director: David Elliott

Amazonian Adventure

w Martin *and* Hugh Woodhouse
Mitch goes down with sleeping sickness and Mike and Dr Beaker take off to the Amazon jungle to find a cure – the rare t'logi plant. Captured by headhunters, Mike uses Supercar to impress the natives while Beaker conjures up some magic of his own.

Director: Alan Pattillo

Grounded

w Martin *and* Hugh Woodhouse
Crooks Harper and Judd steal some printed circuits designed by Beaker and sabotage Supercar, causing it to crash as it takes off in pursuit. Down but not out, Supercar takes its first journey by road to intercept the unsuspecting thieves before they can leave the country.

Director: David Elliott

Keep It Cool

w Martin and Hugh Woodhouse
Masterspy and Zarin ambush Bill Gibson and Dr Beaker in the desert, stealing the highly volatile new fuel they are carrying. Knowing the fuel will explode when the temperature rises above freezing point, Mike sets out in Supercar to find them.

Director: Alan Pattillo

Jungle Hazard

w Martin and Hugh Woodhouse
Masterspy and Zarin plot to take over a dilapidated Malayan plantation from its new owner, Felicity Farnsworth. Unknown to them, however, Felicity is Beaker's cousin and the Supercar team are quickly on the scene.

Director: David Elliott

High Tension

w Martin and Hugh Woodhouse
Masterspy kidnaps Dr Beaker and demands Supercar in exchange for his release. But when Masterspy and Zarin try to take possession they get a nasty shock – the hull has been secretly charged with electricity 'to scare away inquisitive creatures'.

Director: David Elliott

Island Incident

w Martin and Hugh Woodhouse
The deposed president of the island of Pelota seeks Supercar's help in exposing his brother who has usurped his rule. Mike takes Supercar underwater to breach the island's defences.

Director: David Elliott

Ice-Fall

w Martin and Hugh Woodhouse
Exploring an ice-fall in an underground cavern, Beaker becomes trapped when more ice collapses around him. Mike fires Supercar's jets at the wall of ice to free his friend.

Director: Desmond Saunders

The Phantom Piper

w Martin and Hugh Woodhouse
Mike and the Supercar team fly to Scotland to help Beaker's cousin Felicity and their Great Uncle Angus solve the mystery of the phantom piper. They uncover a cunning scheme to steal a priceless topaz.

Director: Alan Pattillo

Pirate Plunder

w Martin and Hugh Woodhouse
The Supercar team decide to rid the seas of the pirate Black Morgan, using a millionaire's yacht as bait. But their plan nearly ends in disaster when Morgan fires a torpedo at them. Luckily Beaker is able to jam the missile and Mike finally sinks the pirate ship.

Director: David Elliott

A Little Art

w Martin and Hugh Woodhouse
Beaker buys a painting from a shady art dealer who later discovers it contains a clue to the location of a forger's counterfeit plates and steals it back. But Beaker has photographed it and Supercar joins the hunt.

Director: Alan Pattillo

Flight of Fancy

w Gerry and Sylvia Anderson
Jimmy dreams that he and Mitch fly off in Supercar to rescue a princess from the clutches of the wicked politicians Hertz and Marzak – who look more than a little like Masterspy and Zarin.

Director: Alan Pattillo

Deep Seven

w Martin and Hugh Woodhouse
Supercar undergoes a rigorous under-water test, diving 400 ft to the sea bed. Then the cockpit starts leaking and the craft becomes entangled in a mine cable. Bill Gibson dons his diving gear and swims to the rescue.

Director: Desmond Saunders

Hostage

w Martin and Hugh Woodhouse
On holiday in Ireland, Dr Beaker calls up Mike and Supercar to help foil a kidnap plot staged by crooked duo Judd and Harper. The villains nearly succeed in blowing up Supercar but the tables are turned on them by an irate Mitch armed with a baseball bat.

Director: Desmond Saunders

The Sunken Temple

w Martin and Hugh Woodhouse
A harmless underwater expedition in the Med turns into a dangerous encounter with the ruthless bandit Spyros when Mike and Dr Beaker discover his stolen loot in a safe on the sea bed.

Director: David Elliott

The Lost City

w Gerry and Sylvia Anderson
Mike and Dr Beaker stumble on the secret hideout of a mad English scientist, Professor Watson, who plans to launch a missile upon Washington. It takes all their courage and ingenuity to foil this plot.

Director: Alan Pattillo

Trapped in the Depths

w Martin and Hugh Woodhouse
When contact is lost with the crew of a new bathyscape in the Pacific, Supercar dives to the rescue and finds it has been attacked by a giant fish. Using Supercar's ultrasonic gun to drive away the monster, Mike succeeds in saving the trapped divers.

Director: Alan Pattillo

Dragon of Ho Meng

w Martin and Hugh Woodhouse
Grounded by a typhoon near China, Mike, Jimmy and Mitch meet Ho Meng and his daughter Lotus Blossom, guardians of an ancient temple. Ho Meng regards Supercar as a dragon, a harbinger of disaster, but is soon glad it's around when he is seized by the villainous Mr Fang who wants to blow up the temple.

Director: David Elliott

Magic Carpet

w Martin and Hugh Woodhouse
On a mercy mission to deliver medicines to Prince Hassan, the Supercar team are thrown into jail by the dastardly Alif Bey who wants the prince to die so that he can assume power. But with the aid of a pocket remote control Mike and Co. manage to save the day.

Director: Desmond Saunders

Supercar Take One

w Gerry and Sylvia Anderson
Dr Beaker makes a movie of Supercar with his new cine camera but when his processed film gets mixed up with one taken by some spies, Mike and the team fly to New York to challenge the foreign agents.

Director: Desmond Saunders

Crash Landing

w Gerry and Sylvia Anderson
Engine trouble forces Supercar down in the jungle. Then Mitch goes missing and after an anxious search is found in the company of an adoring female monkey. Mitch is mortified to leave her – but

delighted when they find she has stowed away in Supercar!

Director: Desmond Saunders

The Tracking of Masterspy

w Martin *and* Hugh Woodhouse

Masterspy steals the plans to Supercar plus what he thinks is a new secret project. But it's really a tracking device, enabling Mike to trail him back to his lair.

Director: David Elliott

The White Line

w Martin *and* Hugh Woodhouse

The Supercar team are called in by Scotland Yard to solve a series of bank and armoured car raids by a pair of Chicago gangsters – the Hoyle Brothers. When Dr Beaker takes out the next armoured car, Supercar must move fast to stop him driving into the brothers' deadly detour trap.

Director: Alan Pattillo

Season Two:
(13 episodes)

The Runaway Train

w Gerry *and* Sylvia Anderson

Dr Beaker's latest invention, a magnet capable of lifting 100 tons, helps save the lives of Beaker and Prof. Popkiss when the atomic train they're travelling on is sabotaged by Masterspy and Zarin.

Director: David Elliott

Precious Cargo

w Gerry *and* Sylvia Anderson

Servant girl Zizi, badly treated by her wine merchant employer, hits upon an idea to escape when a special order arrives from the Supercar lab.

Director: Alan Pattillo

Operation Superstork

w Gerry *and* Sylvia Anderson

Beaker, Jimmy and Mike are cast adrift in a new air balloon when Mitch unties a guy rope, so Mike has to parachute to the ground before he can rescue the others in Supercar.

Director: Desmond Saunders

Hi-Jack

w Gerry *and* Sylvia Anderson

Jimmy's brother Bill takes Beaker and Jimmy with him on his first flight to train airline pilots. Unknown to him, his first pupil is an impostor – part of a plan by Masterspy and Zarin to hijack an airliner.

Director: Bill Harris

Calling Charlie Queen

w Gerry *and* Sylvia Anderson

Mike and Dr Beaker answer a 'ham' radio message for help and find themselves involved in a plot by Prof. Karloff to take over America by 'miniaturising' its citizens.

Director: Alan Pattillo

Space for Mitch

w Gerry *and* Sylvia Anderson

Supercar sets off to rescue Mitch after the mischievous monkey has shot himself into space in a rocket.

Director: Desmond Saunders

Atomic Witch Hunt

w Gerry *and* Sylvia Anderson

The Supercar team try to find out who planted atomic bombs all over America, set to explode simultaneously, and find themselves in the clutches of a villainous sheriff.

Director: Desmond Saunders

70-B-Low

w Gerry *and* Sylvia Anderson
Prof. Popkiss needs an urgent blood trans-
fusion. But his is a rare blood group and
the nearest donor is a scientist stranded in
the Arctic.

Director: Alan Pattillo

The Sky's the Limit

w Gerry *and* Sylvia Anderson
Masterspy and Zarin try to buy Supercar,
using counterfeit money. When this
doesn't work they hire two villains to steal
it – but all four get a surprise.

Director: Bill Harris

Jail Break

w Gerry *and* Sylvia Anderson
Dr Beaker's latest invention – an ejector
seat – helps to recapture an escaped
criminal, Joe Anna, who forces Mike to
fly him across the Mexican border in
Supercar.

Director: Bill Harris

The Day That Time Stood Still

w Gerry *and* Sylvia Anderson
Mike's birthday is interrupted when time
is frozen and a stranger from space
presents him with a flying belt . . . but
Mike awakes to find it was just another
flight of fancy . . .

Director: Alan Pattillo

Transatlantic Cable

w Gerry *and* Sylvia Anderson
Answering a call from the Tele-Cable
Corporation, the Supercar team find
Masterspy has been tapping into a trans-
atlantic cable from his undersea hideout.
So Mike decides to tap into Masterspy's
lair!

Director: Desmond Saunders

King Kool

w Gerry *and* Sylvia Anderson
Mitch resents Jimmy's interest in King
Kool, a gorilla jazz-drummer, but when
he visits the star he is tricked into a cage.

Director: Bill Harris

SURVIVORS

Survivors saw the end of civilisation as we knew it – the world
going down not with a nuclear bang but with a global whimper that
wiped out 95 per cent of the human race.

A virus accidentally released into the atmosphere (the credit
sequence showed an oriental scientist dropping a test-tube) spreads
rapidly around the world, killing all but the five per cent who either
don't catch it or recover.

The BBC series took up the story from there, following a central
group of characters as they struggle, initially to come to terms with
their situation, then to adapt and, finally, to try and rebuild
something of the world they've lost.

Survivors was created by Terry Nation who saw disaster round
the corner and worried about mankind's ability to cope. What if, he

queried, the rug was pulled from beneath our complex society based (as it still is) on mutual co-operation and increased dependence on technology. Could impractical modern man adapt to the rigours of survival?

As a notion it was ripe for the 1970s advocates of 'alternative lifestyles', and it was also something everyone could relate to – every viewer could wonder 'what would *I* do? How would *I* cope?'

But this wasn't a *Good Life* vision of self-sufficiency. *Survivors* depicted a grim, relentless struggle in which even mundane items such as soap or matches became precious.

Contemporary critics carped that the heroes were almost exclusively middle class, and took perverse delight in their discomfiture. Certainly, the lead roles of Abby Grant (suburban housewife), Greg Preston (engineer), Charles Vaughan (architect) and Jenny Richards (secretary/young mum) represented the acceptable face of survival, ranged against the bolshie regional and working classes. But the series was, nevertheless, an uncompromising portrait of civilisation in reverse.

Survivors ran for three seasons, each with a distinct theme. Initially there was the aftermath and the 'quest' – Abby's search for her son, Peter, the survivors' search for trust, friendship, order from chaos, the need to regroup on the smallest of scales.

Season Two saw more settled and established communities, forming in rural areas away from the towns which were depicted as plague-pits, rife with pollution and vermin. The challenge they now faced was to acquire – and acquire fast – the skills to replace their diminishing supplies of things they had once taken for granted.

Season Three again took to the road, as the survivors began to explore further afield, to establish links with other settlements and seek out people with the special skills to build a future, through trade, a railway and, ultimately, hydro-electricity. The series, which began on an overwhelmingly gloomy note, ended on an optimistic one.

REGULAR CAST

SEASON ONE

Abby Grant **Carolyn Seymour**   *Jenny Richards* **Lucy Fleming**
Greg Preston **Ian McCulloch**   *Tom Price* **Talfryn Thomas** *(Eps 1–3, 7–10)*
John **Stephen Dudley** *(from Ep. 5)*   *Lizzie* **Tanya Ronder** *(from Ep. 5)*
Vic Thatcher **Terry Scully** *(Eps 2, 8–11, 13)*
Paul Pitman **Christopher Tranchell** *(from Ep. 8)*
Mrs Emma Cohen **Hana-Maria Pravda** *(from Ep. 7)*
Charmian Wentworth **Eileen Helsby** *(from Ep. 8)*
Arthur Russell **Michael Gover** *(from Ep. 8)*

SEASON TWO

Ian McCulloch *(Eps 1–8, 10–13)*, **Lucy Fleming** *(Eps 1–3, 5, 7–8, 11–13)*,
Stephen Dudley *and* **Tanya Ronder** *(Eps 1–2, 5–8, 10–13)*,
Michael Gover *(Eps 1–2, 5, 7–8, 11)*, **Chris Tranchell** *(Eps 1–2 only)*

PLUS
Charles Vaughan **Denis Lill**   *Pet Simpson* **Lorna Lewis** *(Eps 1–2, 5–13)*
Ruth Anderson **Celia Gregory** *(Eps 1–6, 8, 10–13)*
Hubert **John Abineri** *(Eps 1, 5–8, 11–13)*
Jack **Gordon Salkilld** *(Eps 2, 5–6, 8, 11, 13)*

SEASON THREE
Denis Lill *(eps 1, 3–9, 11–12)*, **Lucy Fleming** *(Eps 1–3, 5–9, 11–12)*,
John Abineri *(Eps 1, 3, 5–9, 11–12)*, **Lorna Lewis** *(Eps 1, 6–7, 10)*,
Stephen Dudley *(Eps 1, 6, 10)*, **Ian McCulloch** *(Eps 2, 10)*,
Gordon Salkild *(Eps 1, 6, 10)*

PLUS
Lizzie **Angie Stevens** *(Eps 1, 6, 10)*   *Agnes* **Anna Pitt** *(Eps 2–3, 5, 10–11)*

Series created by: **Terry Nation**
Producer: **Terence Dudley**
Music: **Anthony Isaac**

A BBC Production
38 colour 50-minute episodes

Season One:
16 April–16 July 1975
Season Two:
31 March–23 June 1976
Season Three:
16 March–8 June 1977

Season One
(13 episodes)

The Fourth Horseman

w **Terry Nation**
A deadly virus is accidentally released and spreads rapidly around the world. A decimated civilisation begins to break down: the trains stop running, traffic piles up, a radio station goes off the air, hospitals can't cope. In a Home Counties stockbroker belt, Abby Grant goes into a coma. When she recovers she finds her husband dead and the village strewn with corpses. Meanwhile, in London, secretary Jenny Richards has set out on foot to find other survivors.
Mrs Transon **Margaret Anderson**
Dr Gordon **Callum Mill**
Mr Pollard **Blake Butler**
Patricia **Elizabeth Sinclair**
David Grant **Peter Bowles**
Andrew Tyler **Christopher Reich**
First youth **Len Jones**
Tom Price **Talfryn Thomas** *(intro)*
Kevin Lloyd **Giles Melville**
Dr Bronson **Peter Copley**

Director: **Pennant Roberts**
Designer: **Austin Ruddy**

Genesis

w **Terry Nation**
Engineer Greg Preston arrives back in England by helicopter. After discovering his wife is dead, he drives aimlessly across country, encountering 'spoilt bitch' Anne Tranter and Vic Thatcher. Vic is injured in a tractor accident, but Anne callously tells Greg he is dead. Abby encounters ex-union leader Arthur Wormley who is bent on imposing his own brand of martial law.
Greg Preston **Ian McCulloch** *(intro)*
Anne Tranter **Myra Frances**
Vic Thatcher **Terry Scully** *(intro)*
Arthur Wormley **George Baker**
Dave Long **Brian Peck**
First man **Peter Jolley**
Colonel **Edward Brooks**

Director: **Gerald Blake**
Designer: **Ray London**

Gone Away

w **Terry Nation**
Abby, Jenny and Greg's camp is broken into by Welsh labourer Tim Price. Needing to replenish their supplies, they visit a food warehouse. Inside is the

hanged body of a looter. Abby insists that they start to load their cars, but they are interrupted by the arrival of three of Wormley's men.

Boy Graham Fletcher
Phillipson Robert Fyfe
Dave Long Brian Peck
Reg Gunnel Barry Stanton
John Milner Robert Gillespie

Director: Terence Williams
Designer: Richard Morris

Corn Dolly

w Jack Ronder

'We must make sure there's a next generation . . . we're being helped . . . I've found that with the scarcity of people, the problems we face, everyone loves everyone.' Abby and her friends come across former architect Charles who has his own ideas about how to ensure the survival of the human race.

Charles Denis Lill *(intro)*
Isla Yvonne Bonnamy
Loraine Annie Hayes
Mick Keith Jayne
Tessa June Bolton
Woman Maureen Nelson

Director: Pennant Roberts
Designer: Austin Ruddy

Gone to the Angels

w Jack Ronder

'Abby, you're truthful and you're searching. Please don't be afraid.' Abby gets a clue that her son may have gone to a religious community in the Peak District. She sets off with Jenny and Greg, but circumstances force her to continue alone.

John Stephen Dudley *(intro)*
Lizzie Tanya Ronder *(intro)*
Lincoln Peter Miles
Jack Frederick Hall
Matthew Nickolas Grace
Robert Kenneth Caswell

Director: Gerald Blake
Designer: Ray London

Garland's War

w Terry Nation

Abby gets drawn into the struggle between young landowner Jimmy Garland and a group of men, led by the ruthless Knox, who have taken over his house to set up a self-appointed 'shotgun and pick-axe' Government.

Peter Steve Fletcher
Garland Richard Heffer
John Carroll Dennis Chinnery
Bates David G. Marsh
Knox Peter Jeffrey
Harris Robert Oates
Sentry Roger Elliott
Ken Michael Jamieson
Betty Susanna East

Director: Terence Williams
Designer: Richard Morris

Starvation

w Jack Ronder

Abby and her friends, still on their travels, encounter a teenage girl, Wendy, and an old Jewish lady, Mrs Cohen, who are living in an area ravaged by wild dogs, and rescue them from the clutches of Price.

Wendy Julie Neubert *(intro)*
Mrs Cohen Hana-Maria Pravda *(intro)*
Barney John Hallet *(intro)*

Director: Pennant Roberts
Designer: Robert Berk

Spoil of War

w M.K. Jeeves *(alias* Clive Exton*)*

'You left me! You left me to die like a pig in my own filth! You left me in agony . . . just took what you wanted and left me.' The community is swelled by agricultural student Paul Pitman, ex-financier Arthur Russell and his secretary Charmian. Returning to the quarry, Greg meets a man he thought was dead . . .

Paul Pitman Christopher Tranchell *(intro)*
Barney John Hallet
Wendy Julie Neubert
Charmian Wentworth Eileen Helsby *(intro)*

Arthur Russell **Michael Gover** *(intro)*
Vic Thatcher **Terry Scully** *(re-intro)*

Director: **Gerald Blake**
Designer: **Richard Morris**

Law and Order

w **M.K. Jeeves** *(alias* **Clive Exton***)*
To raise morale, Abby suggests holding a party. But during the festivities Wendy is killed and the finger of blame points at the simple-minded Barney. He is 'tried', convicted and executed, before Greg discovers Tom Price was the real murderer.
Barney **John Hallet** *(exit)*
Wendy **Julie Neubert** *(exit)*

Director: **Pennant Roberts**
Designer: **Richard Morris**

The Future Hour

w **Terry Nation**
A young pregnant widow seeks shelter with Abby's community because her own group has ruled that her child must be abandoned at birth.
Laura Foster **Caroline Burt**
Norman **Denis Lawson**
Bernard Huxley **Glyn Owen**
Phil **James Hayes**

Director: **Terence Williams**
Designer: **Richard Morris**

Revenge

w **Jack Ronder**
Vic Thatcher has now become accepted as the tutor of the two children, John and Lizzie. Confined to a wheelchair, he finds his incapacity irksome, but is comforted by the children's need for him. Then Anne Tranter, who had abandoned him badly injured in the quarry, wanders into the community.
Anhe Tranter **Myra Frances**
Donny **Robert Tayman**

Director: **Gerald Blake**
Designer: **Richard Morris**

Something of Value

w **Terry Nation**
A storm floods the cellar which houses the community's precious provisions. Everything is ruined and Greg starts out with the tanker to a neighbouring settlement where he hopes to trade petrol for supplies. While he is away, the community is raided.
Robert Lawson **Matthew Long**
Jim Buckmaster **Murray Hayne**
Thorpe **Paul Chapman**

Director: **Terence Williams**
Designer: **Richard Morris**

A Beginning

w **Terry Nation**
A sick girl, Ruth, is left at the community where the weight of leadership has taken its toll on Abby. At the end of her tether, she leaves and makes for Waterhouse, the home of Jimmy Garland, while Greg and Arthur try to get the communities in the area to join together.
Burton **Harry Markham**
Ruth **Annie Irving**
Jimmy Garland **Richard Heffer**

Director: **Pennant Roberts**
Designer: **Richard Morris**

Season Two
(13 episodes)

Birth of a Hope

w **Jack Ronder**
Decimated by a fire which kills several of their number, Greg's community joins the Whitecross settlement led by Charles Vaughan. Jenny's baby is due and Greg anxiously awaits the return of Ruth, their doctor.
Pet Simpson **Lorna Lewis** *(intro)*
Hubert **John Abineri** *(intro)*
Ruth Anderson **Celia Gregory** *(intro)*

Director: **Eric Hills**
Designer: **Ian Watson**

Greater Love

w Don Shaw

Jenny falls ill and Ruth needs to operate to save her life. But that means getting equipment from a hospital and it's courting death to enter the urban area. Paul volunteers to try . . .
Jack Gordon Salkild *(intro)*

Director: Pennant Roberts
Designer: Ian Watson

Lights of London (Part 1)

w Jack Ronder

Ruth is tricked into going to London by the leaders of the 500 survivors there. The Londoners, led by an exhausted former health officer and an ambitious ex-street trader, have gone to ground. Once there, Ruth cannot escape, for the metropolis is in the grip of disease and menaced by rats.
Doctor Patrick Holt
Nessie Lennox Milne
Stan David Troughton
Amul Nadim Sawalha
Penny Coral Atkins
Wally Roger Lloyd Pack
George Lloyd McGuire
Maisie Paula Williams
Manny Sydney Tafler
Barbara Wendy Williams

Director: Terence Williams
Designers: Ian Watson, Peter Kindred

Lights of London (Part 2)

w Jack Ronder

Greg and Charles finally reach Ruth, only to find she is unwilling to return with them. Reluctantly, they decide to stay on and help the Londoners in their big move.
Guest cast as Part 1, except David Troughton, Paula Williams

Director: Pennant Roberts
Designer: Paul Allen, Ian Watson

Face of the Tiger

w Don Shaw

Greg welcomes a stranger, Alistair McFadden, who says he has lived alone for a year. He seems a gentle man, but the community is chilled to discover the truth, in an old newspaper, that he is a child murderer.
Alistair McFadden John Line

Director: Terence Willams
Designer: Ian Watson

The Witch

w Jack Ronder

Mina, an eccentric who lives apart from the community with her baby son, spurns Hubert's amorous advances. He then stirs up the children, John and Lizzie, into believing that she is a witch. When their fear spreads to Peggy, a superstitious Irishwoman, the whole group is affected and Mina's life is threatened.
Mina Delia Paton
Peggy Catherine Finn

Director: Terence Williams
Designer: Ian Watson

A Friend in Need

w Ian McCulloch

The community hunt for a sniper who is killing attractive young women and are startled to discover the killer is also a woman.
Boult William Wilde
Mrs McGregor Vivienne Burgess
Roberts Emrys Leyshon
Morris Paul Grist
Daniella Gigi Gatti

Director: Eric Hills
Designer: Ian Watson

By Bread Alone

w Martin Worth

The community, which has forgotten spiritual needs in the struggle for survival, is unsettled by the revelation that Lewis Fearn was formerly a curate.
Judy Julie Peasgood
Lewis Fearn Roy Herrick
Alan Stephen Tate

Philip Martin Neil
Daniella Gigi Gatti

Director: Pennant Roberts
Designer: Ian Watson

The Chosen

w Roger Parkes

Charles and Pet, returning from a trip to the Cheshire brine pits, stumble upon a Spartan-like community run by Max Kershaw. Charles is curious about the settlement, but his interest is misinterpreted by Kershaw who decides to eliminate the 'intruders'.

Max Kershaw Philip Madoc
Kim David Sibley
Nancy Vanessa Millard
Lenny Carter James Cosmo
Joy Clare Kelly
Sammy Waters David Goodland
Mike David Neilson
Susan Elizabeth Cassidy

Director: Eric Hills
Designer: Ian Watson

Parasites

w Roger Marshall

A travelling man, John Millen, is in love with Mina, but ultimately falls foul of two ex-Dartmoor prisoners who menace the Whitecross community and hold John and Lizzie hostage.

John Millen Patrick Troughton
Mina Delia Paton
Lewis Roy Herrick
Kane Kevin McNally
Grice Brian Grellis

Director: Terence Williams
Designer: Ian Watson

New Arrivals

w Roger Parkes

Ruth brings to Whitecross the remaining members of a community ravaged by a flu epidemic. Among them is Mark Carter, who has a degree in agriculture but whose manner quickly alienates everyone in the settlement.

Carter Ian Hastings
Alan Stephen Tate
Melanie Heather Wright
Sally June Page
Dave Peter Duncan
Pete Roger Monk

Director: Pennant Roberts
Designer: Ian Watson

Over the Hills

w Martin Worth

The Whitecross women are in open revolt over Charles' latest attempt to spark a 'baby boom'. When it's learned that Sally is expecting Alan's child, Charles is delighted. But she will only have the baby if she can live with Alan as his wife – and he prefers Melanie . . .

Guest cast as previous episode, except
    Ian Hastings, *but plus:*
Daniella Gigi Gatti

Director: Eric Hills
Designer: Ian Watson

New World

w Martin Worth

The settlers sight a balloon passing over Whitecross and give chase. When they track it down they find the balloonists are a Norwegian engineer and his daughter Agnes, offering hope of contacts with mainland Europe. Greg is determined to make the most of this unexpected windfall . . .

Guest cast as previous episode, except
    Gigi Gatti, *but plus:*
Seth Dan Meaden
Agnes Sally Osborn

Director: Terence Williams
Designer: Ian Watson

Season Three
(12 episodes)

Manhunt

w Terence Dudley

Jack, who had ballooned off with Greg, is back with a sorry tale about Greg being in danger. Charles and Jenny ride off to find him. It's a search that will invariably see them one step behind the always felt but rarely seen Greg who is trying to make contact with as many settlements as possible in the quest for a unified federation.

Seth Dan Meaden
Susan June Brown
Roberts David Freedman
Summers John Rolfe
Clifford Michael Hawkins
Miedel Anthony Jacobs

Director: Peter Jefferies
Designer: Geoff Powell *(all Season Three)*

A Little Learning

w Ian McCulloch

Greg and Agnes meet an elderly woman, Mrs Butterworth, who asks them to protect her from 'raiding Indians'. The marauders turn out to be a gang of children who are found to be dying after eating contaminated rye.

Agnes Anna Pitt *(intro)*
Millar Sean Caffrey
McIntosh Prentis Hancock
Mrs Butterworth Sylvia Coleridge
Eagle Joseph McKenna
Mr Oliver John Harrard
Philip Christopher Huxtable
Libbie Johanna Sheffield
Cliff Richard Beaumont
Bernie Keith Collins
Annie Nicola Glickman

Director: George Spenton Foster

Law of the Jungle

w Martin Worth

Brod, an ex-butcher, believes that man must revert to hunting to survive. His community hunts with crossbows, on horseback, and lives in three abandoned railway carriages. When Charles and Jenny arrive in the area, Brod sees them as a threat.

Brod Brian Blessed
Edith Barbara Lott

Steve Eric Deacon
Owen Keith Varnier
Mavis Cheryl Hall

Director: Peter Jefferies

Mad Dog

w Don Shaw

Charles meets Fenton, a former lecturer, who reveals that he has rabies. Charles is later forced to run for his life from men who believe he is also infected.

Fenton Morris Perry
Sanders Bernard Kay
Jim Ralph Arliss
Phil Max Faulkner
Ron Stephen Bill
Ellen Heather Canning
Engine driver Eric Francis
Fireman Robert Pugh
Young girl Jane Shaw

Director: Tristan de Vere Cole

Bridgehead

w Martin Worth

Charles decides that the survivors need a market – not just for the exchange of goods, but as a place where people can meet and make contacts, and exchange ideas and skills.

Edith Barbara Lott
Steve Eric Deacon
Owen Keith Varnier
Mavis Cheryl Hall
Bill Sheridan John Ronane
Alice Hazel McBride
Elphick Harry Jones
Bagley John Ruddock
Susan Rosalind Elliot

Director: George Spenton Foster

Reunion

w Don Shaw

Jenny and Hubert, continuing their search for Greg, come across a young widow called Janet Milton. Going through a family album, Jenny realises Janet is young John's mother, and the two are reunited.

Walter **George Waring**
Philip Hurst **John Lee**
Janet Milton **Jean Gilpin**

Director: **Terence Dudley**

The Peacemaker

w **Roger Parkes**
Charles, Jenny and Hubert discover a community which survives by milling grain for other settlements. Frank Garner claims to be its leader, but Charles begins to suspect that he is really a prisoner.
Frank Garner **Edward Underdown** *(plus Eps 8–9)*
Bentley **Norman Robbins**
Michael **Brian Conly**
Henry **Alan Halley**
Grant **Paul Seed**
Blossom **Nicolette Roeg**
Rutna **Heather Emmanuel**
McLain **John Grieve**
Cyril **Derek Martin**

Director: **George Spenton Foster**

Sparks

w **Roger Parkes**
Alec Campbell, an electrical engineer, lives alone in squalor, refusing all invitations to join Charles's group. Campbell is racked with guilt for abandoning his wife and children when plague overtook them, but the community badly needs an electrician and resorts to shock treatment to bring him round.
Alec **William Dysart** *(plus Eps 9, 11–12)*
Letty **Gabrielle Hamilton**
Jim **John Bennett**
Vic **John White**
Bet **Linda Polan**

Director: **Tristan de Vere Cole**

The Enemy

w **Roger Parkes**
Leonard Woollen, the leader of a mining community, clashes with Sam Mead, a latter-day Luddite, who tries to persuade the survivors to abandon their quest for hydro-electricity.

Sam **Robert Gillespie** *(plus Eps 11–12)*
Grant **Martyn Whitby**
Leonard Woollen **Bryan Pringle**
Harper **Terence Davies**
Mrs Jay **Peggy Ann Wood**
Mary-Jean **Frances Tomelty**

Director: **Peter Jefferies**

The Last Laugh

w **Ian McCulloch**
Hunting for a doctor he believes is being held prisoner, Greg is attacked by an apocalyptic quartet of horsemen, and his list of settlements stolen. Recovering, he finds Dr Adams, only to discover he has smallpox. Greg also contracts the disease but, before his inevitable death, is able to use it to exact 'revenge' on his earlier attackers.
Mason **George Mallaby**
Chris **Richard Cornish**
Tilley **Roy Boyd**
Dave **Jon Glover**
Irvine **David Cook**
Powell **Paul Humpoletz**
Dr Adams **Clifton Jones**

Director: **Peter Jefferies**

Long Live the King

w **Martin Worth**
Heading north, Charles finds a message from Greg seeking a meeting at a disused army camp. There he learns about Greg's work in bringing people together from Agnes who is determined to see him 'live on' as the symbolic king of the new emerging nation. But a villainous character, the Captain, also wants to take over.
The Captain **Roy Marsden**
Mitch **Frank Vincent**
Mrs Hicks **Gabrielle Day**
Les Norton **John Comer**
Mike **Sean Mathias**
Joe Briggs **Ray Mort**
Tom Walter **Barry Stokes**
Albert Banks **Denis Holmes**

Director: **Tristan de Vere Cole**

Power

w Martin Worth

Charles and his companions arrive in the Scottish Highlands where they find Scottish nationalism alive and well in the form of McAlister, a local laird who resents their attempts to tap his hydroelectricity to revive English industry.

McAlister Iain Cuthbertson
Davey William Armour
Mrs Crombie Dorothy Dean
Hamish Brian Carey
Rob Ray Jefferies

Director: George Spenton Foster

TALES OF MYSTERY

Early sixties anthology series of uncanny and supernatural tales by renowned ghost storyteller Algernon Blackwood. These forays into an at times bizarre imagination were hosted by Scottish actor John Laurie (still best rememberd as Cpl. Fraser in *Dad's Army*) whose wide, staring eyes and quietly sinister delivery set the tone for an eerie series.

Though early tales stuck closely to the 'ghost story' theme, the second season saw the series' scope branch out to include some broader-based fantasies. *The Man Who Found Out* starred Charles Lloyd Pack as a man seeking for the secret of the universe. He discovers a set of engraved tablets buried in the Middle East, deciphers them and finds that they tell the story of the whole future of humanity. But the secret is too terrible to bear and he dies after reading the message. Another story, *Nephele*, concerns an archaeologist who finds the shoes of a slave dancer of ancient Rome and is possessed by their strange power which compels him to 'witness' a tragic drama played out 17 centuries before. *The Telephone* explored the teasing idea of inanimate objects apparently developing lives of their own. In *The Pikestaffe Case* an enigmatic lodger offers his landlady the chance to change the whole pattern of her life. And in a Season Three tale, *The Insanity of Jones*, a man who can see back through time avenges a 400-year-old crime.

Among familiar names appearing in the series were Dinsdale Landen, Harry H. Corbett, Peter Barkworth, Patrick Cargill, Francesca Annis, John Barron and Tenniel Evans.

REGULAR CAST
Narrator/Algernon Blackwood John Laurie

All stories by Algernon Blackwood
Adapted by: Giles Cooper, Owen Holder, Philip Broadley, Barbara S. Harper, John Richmond, Bill MacIlwraith, Kenneth Hyde, Denis Butler

Directors: John Frankau (stories 2, 4, 6, 8–13, 15–16, 18–22, 24, 28–29)

Geoffrey Hughes, Peter Graham Scott,
  Jonathan Alwyn, Peter Moffatt,
  Raymond Menmuir, Mark Lawton,
  Wilfred Eades, James Omerod
Producer: Peter Graham Scott

Executive producer: John Frankau
  (Season Three)

An Associated-Rediffusion Network
Production
29 30-minute stories, black and white

Season One

The Terror of the Twins
The Promise
The Man Who Was Milligan
The Tradition
The Empty Sleeve
Accessory Before the Fact
The Woman's Ghost Story
The Decoy

29 March–17 May 1961

Season Two

Confession
Chinese Magic
Max Hensig
The Man Who Found Out
Nephele
Ancient Sorceries

Deferred Appointment
The Pikestaffe Case
The Telephone
The Call
Wolves of God

4 July–12 September 1962

Season Three

Old Clothes
The Doll
Egyptian Sorcery
The Damned
The Second Generation
A Case of Eavesdropping
Petershin and Mr Snide
The Lodger
The Insanity of Jones
Dream Cottage

10 January–14 March 1963

TARGET LUNA

This 1960 comic-book-style saga sent one young boy to the Moon and launched a family into a trilogy of pioneering space adventures.

Despite its sf theme, Target Luna was an unashamedly old-fashioned 'boy's own' fantasy in which a youngster takes centre stage doing all the things grown-ups do (and doing them better). Acted with gusto, it was as wholesome as marmite soldiers and went down a treat in its Sunday teatime slot.

The scene is set on an island rocket station off Scotland (though the open-air sequences were filmed off the Essex coast). Professor Wedgwood, having successfully sent a man into space, has invited his three children to join him for Easter. There the youngsters, Valerie, Geoffrey and Jimmy (plus obligatory pet hamster, Hamlet) find an even more daring experiment in preparation – the first manned rocket round the Moon. At the last moment the pilot, Flight Lt. Williams, falls ill and the experiment looks set to fail. But little Jimmy (hitherto dressed, like every well brought-up astronaut, in school blazer and tie) secretly takes his place and is shot into space. As an electrical storm cuts radio contact with Earth, Jimmy must operate the rocket's heating system or risk freezing to death behind the Moon.

Naturally, the young hero successfully circles the Moon and heads back to Earth (though not fast enough to escape a bombardment of cosmic particles, and not too fast lest he overshoot). Finally, he is talked down to the requisite safe landing.

A happy ending, of course, but an even happier beginning for the writers Malcolm Hulke and Eric Paice who took the Wedgwood family further into space the following autumn (see *Pathfinders*).

The series (and its three successors) was produced by Sydney Newman, doyen of ABC's *Armchair Theatre*, and soon to spawn the longest-running science fiction series of all – *Doctor Who*.

MAIN CAST

Professor Wedgwood **David Markham**   *Jimmy Wedgwood* **Michael Hammond**
Valerie Wedgwood **Sylvia Davies**   *Geoffrey Wedgwood* **Michael Craze**
Mrs Wedgwood **Annette Kerr**   *Mr Henderson* **Frank Finlay**
Ian Murray **John Cairney**   *Jean Cary* **Deborah Stanford**
Dr Stevens **Robert Stuart**   *Mr Field* **Michael Verney**
Pat Maxwell **Phyllis Kenny**   *Fl. Lt. Williams* **William Ingram**

Writers: **Malcolm Hulke** *and* **Eric Paice**
Director: **Adrian Brown**
Designer: **David Gillespie**
Producer: **Sydney Newman**
Series adviser: **Mary Field**

An ABC Television Network Production
Six 30-minute episodes, made in black and white

The Rocket Station
Countdown
The Strange Illness
Storm in Space
Solar Flare
The Falling Star

24 April–29 May 1960
(ATV, London)

TERRAHAWKS

*T*errahawks was Gerry Anderson's return to puppetry after his forays into live-action TV. And, 14 years on from 1969's *The Secret Service*, Anderson coined a new word for a new sophisticated technique – Supermacromation.

These puppets had no strings attached. Deployed at a cost of £5m for the first 26 episodes, the Terrahawks were packed with advanced electronics and operated by hand – in some cases, more than one pair.

The format was familiar enough. In the year 2020, a crack fighting force, the Terrahawks, are dedicated to saving Earth from attack by an evil intergalactic adversary – in this case Zelda, the witch-queen of Guk. An android with a face like a pickled chestnut and a horrible harridan's cackle, Zelda was assisted by her equally ugly cronies, inept son Yung-Star and bitchy sister Cy-Star.

Heading the Terrahawks was Dr Tiger Ninestein, one of nine clones created from an American-Austrian professor called Gerhard Stein. On his team were daredevil pilot Mary Falconer, pop-singer/pilot Kate Kestrel, Japanese computer genius Lt. Hiro, and Lt. Hawkeye, an American athlete with computer-assisted eyesight. They were aided by a battalion of silver spherical robots called Zeroids, commanded by Sgt. Major Zero.

From their secret base, Hawknest, in South America, the Terrahawks foiled every dastardly plot and fiendish monster that Zelda could throw at them. And these being the 'sophisticated' 1980s, it was all done with plenty of tongue-in-cheek humour. Sgt Major Zero was played by Windsor Davies in his fruitiest *It Ain't Half Hot, Mum* voice and there was a nod to the pink star of *Thunderbirds* with Hudson, a posh-talking Rolls-Royce, which drove itself and changed colour with its moods.

Despite its impressive array of hardware and some imaginative baddies, *Terrahawks* relied too much on elements from series past, but without ever coming close to re-creating their charm.

It did run for three seasons on ITV, between 1983 and 1986, with repeats as recently as 1988.

VOICE CAST

Zelda/Mary Falconer **Denise Bryer**   *Sgt. Major Zero* **Windsor Davies**
Dr Ninestein/Hiro/Johnson **Jeremy Hitchin**
Kate Kestrel/Cy-Star **Anne Ridler**
Hudson/Space Sgt 101/Yung-Star **Ben Stevens**

Creator: **Gerry Anderson**
Producers: **Gerry Anderson, Christopher Burr**
Associate producer: **Bob Bell**
Writer: **Tony Barwick** *(except where stated)*
Music: **Richard Harvey**
Special effects: **Stephen Begg**

Produced by Anderson Burr Pictures in association with London Weekend Television
39 colour 30-minute episodes
Season One:
9 October–31 December 1983
Season Two:
23 September–30 December 1984
Season Three:
3 May–26 July 1986

Season One
(13 episodes)

Expect the Unexpected

w **Gerry Anderson** *(a 2-part story)*
The year is 2020. The evil android Zelda has invaded Mars from where she plans to strike against Earth. The Terrahawks mobilise to counter the attack, but using her incredible powers and aided by her robot Cubes, Zelda traps Ninestein and Mary in a force field. Will Zero come to the rescue in time?

Director: **Alan Pattillo**

Thunder Roar

Zelda releases a hideous ally, Sram, from suspended animation and unleashes him on Earth. Sram has a thunderous voice so powerful that it can destroy a mountain.

Director: Alan Pattillo

Happy Madeday

Moid, a faceless alien who is a master of disguise, assumes the form of Hiro and takes his place as Spacehawk's commander. With the Terrahawks' first line of defence neutralised, Zelda launches a massive attack.

Director: Tony Lenny

The Ugliest Monster of All

Zelda releases Yuri, a cuddly space bear from cyrogenic storage. It's picked up by the unsuspecting Terrahawks and Mary and Kate take it to their hearts – but the bear has strange and terrible powers.

Director: Tony Lenny

Close Call

In an effort to trace the secret location of Hawknest, Zelda places unscrupulous journalist Mark Darrol aboard the Overlander, a futuristic land train that takes vital supplies to the Terrahawks' base.

Director: Desmond Saunders

The Gun

An unmanned space transporter carrying a rare titanium ore returns to Earth but with a deadly surprise aboard – Zelda's robot cubes, ready to transform themselves into a giant space gun.

Director: Tony Bell

Gunfight at Oakey's Corral

After a gunfight between Zelda's cubes and Sgt Major Zero out in the Arizona desert, one of the cubes escapes. Ninestein leads the chase and finds himself in a final shoot-out at high noon.

Director: Tony Bell

Thunder Path

The Overlander is hijacked by the fearsome Lord Sram who drives it straight at an oil refinery. The Terrahawks race against time to stop him.

Director: Tony Lenny

From Here to Infinity

Spacehawk sights the battered remains of Space Probe Alpha, first launched in 1999. The Terrahawks set to work examining it, unaware that Zelda has placed one of her cube robots on it, with a gravity bomb.

Director: Alan Pattillo

Mind Monster

The Terrahawks discover a capsule which, when opened, is apparently empty. But they have released a mind monster and each find themselves facing a deadly foe.

Director: Tony Bell

A Christmas Miracle

As all at Hawknest prepare to celebrate Christmas, Zelda realises their guard will be down and decides to launch an all-out attack – on Christmas Day.

Director: Tony Lenny

To Catch a Tiger

Zelda takes the two-man crew of a space transporter hostage on Mars and demands Ninestein in exchange for their release.

Director: Tony Lenny

Season Two
(13 episodes)

Operation SAS

When Yung-Star seizes the chance to fly to Earth, Zelda makes him take Yuri the Space Bear with him. Then Kate is captured and only an SAS-style operation, led by Zero, can rescue her.

Director: Tony Lenny

Ten Top Pop

As determined as ever, Zelda takes control of Stew Dapples and uses him as a dupe in another assault.

Director: Tony Bell

Play It Again, Sram

After Kate Kestrel wins the World Song Contest, Zelda issues an unexpected challenge – and the mighty Sram lurks ready to destroy the Terrahawks.

Director: Tony Bell

The Ultimate Menace

The Terrahawks are baffled when Ninestein orders the whole team to fly to Mars – Zelda's base – but find themselves once again pitted against her robot cubes.

Director: Tony Lenny

Midnight Blue

Spacehawk fires at a Zeaf but it gets through. Now Hawkwing takes up the pursuit, until Ninestein realises the Zeaf has been miniaturised, Hawkwing has chased too far and is trapped in orbit.

Director: Tony Lenny

My Kingdom for a Zeaf

What is Richard III doing with Yung-Star in the 21st Century. The answer threatens death for one of the Terrahawks team.

Director: Tony Lenny

Zero's Finest Hour

Zelda delivers some flowers to the Terrahawks via the Overlander and the pollen puts Ninestein and the rest of his team into a coma. It's left to Zero to save the day.

Director: Tony Bell

Cold Finger

Zelda and her new ally Cold Finger plan to attack Earth by bombarding it with millions of tons of ice. Can the Terrahawks save the world?

Director: Tony Bell

Unseen Menace

Moid (Master of Infinite Disguise) perfects his most awesome impersonation to date, travelling to Earth as the Invisible Man to wreak havoc among the Terrahawks.

Director: Tony Bell

Space Giant

When two space miners capture a small Sporilla, they decide to smuggle it back to Earth. But it's just another fiendish plan devised by old Zelda and a terrifying monster is unleashed.

Director: Tony Lenny

Cry UFO

When Stew Dapples sees a UFO, no one will believe him. But the ship is part of Zelda's latest plan – and the Terrahawks must find and destroy it.

Director: Tony Bell

The Midas Touch

w Trevor Lansdown, Tony Barwick

The world's gold reserves are locked in a space Fort Knox. Zelda realises that to wipe it out would cause economic havoc on Earth and despatches the monstrous Krell to do the job.

Director: Alan Pattillo

Ma's Monsters

So far, the best efforts of Zelda's worst monsters have failed to defeat the Terrahawks. But she has a powerful surprise in store.

Director: Tony Bell

Season Three
(13 episodes)

Two For the Price of One

The Terrahawks plan an attack on Zelda's Martian base and find out that Cy-Star is about to produce a baby.

Director: Tony Lenny

First Strike

Against Ninestein's better judgement, the military send a giant space carrier on a first-strike raid against Zelda's base. The Terrahawks just manage to avert a major disaster.

Director: Tony Lenny

Terrabomb

A Zeaf crash-lands on Earth, and Battle Tank is sent out to investigate and destroy it. Then Zelda announces that there is a bomb in Hawknest. But how did it get there? And can the Terrahawks find it in time?

Director: Tony Bell

Space Cyclops

An alien meteorite crashes into the Moon and a terrifying Cyclops begins to form from the wreckage. The Zeroids attack, but the Cyclops can absorb metal.

Director: Tony Lenny

Doppelganger

The Terrahawks investigate the mysterious appearance of two statues in a museum – one of Yung-Star, and the other of Cy-Star. Then one of the statues begins to move . . .

Director: Tony Lenny

Child's Play

Birlgoy produces a super explosive and Zelda plants a giant bomb under the Trans-American pipeline. Mary has to try to defuse it – but it could be a trap.

Director: Tony Bell

Jolly Roger One

A space pirate joins forces with Zelda and her family to confront the Terrahawks, and the pirate spaceship and Spacehawk fight out a terrifying battle.

Director: Tony Lenny

Runaway

All looks hopeless for the Terrahawks when it seems that Zelda has at last discovered the location of Hawknest and sends her missiles to destroy it.

Director: Tony Bell

Space Samurai

Tamura, space samurai and the commander of a powerful space cruiser, insists that Zelda and Ninestein meet to work out their differences. Ninestein reluctantly agrees, but can Zelda be trusted?

Director: Desmond Saunders

Time Warp

Zelda, using Lord Tempo's powers, tries to introduce a time warp into Hawknest. Mary's mind is too strong and rejects the attempt, but Sgt Major Zero is more receptive.

Director: **Tony Bell**

The Sporilla

The Terrahawks travel to the distant moon Callisto, where an unarmed remote tracker station has gone off the air. When they arrive they are faced by one of Zelda's most terrifying monsters, the Sporilla.

Director: **Tony Bell**

Operation Zero

Sgt Major Zero is admitted to the Zeroid hospital for an operation. When he recovers, he finds to his horror that Zelda has infiltrated Hawknest and Ninestein speaks with Yung-Star's voice.

Director: **Tony Lenny**

Gold

When the Zeroids explore the crater of a meteorite they think they have found a nugget of gold. Secretly, they bring it back to Hawknest, but it is a golden bomb planted by Zelda.

Director: **Desmond Saunders**

THEY CAME FROM SOMEWHERE ELSE

Six-part science fiction comedy series written and performed by a Brighton theatre group who adapted it from their own stage show.

It wasn't quite a sitcom, neither was it sketch comedy. It plundered soap opera, sf adventure, gory low-budget horror and surreal comedy ranging from the gentle to the viciously black to produce an affectionate send-up.

The setting was the present-day new town of Middleford which was transformed into a living nightmare with the arrival of an American stranger. Innocent shoppers are sucked down drains, giant prawns stalk the sewers, goldfish attack their owners, sofas consume policewomen, it rains liver.

They Came From Somewhere Else came from TVS, but showed up on Channel 4.

REGULAR CAST

Wendy **Rebecca Stevens** *Colin* **Peter McCarthy**
Martin **Tony Haase** *Stranger* **Robin Driscoll**
The 'They're Coming' Man **Paddy Fletcher**
with: **Dave Gale, Ella Wilder, Tamsin Heatley, Patti Bee, Harry Ditson, Tyrone Huggins, Peter Leabourne**

Written by: **Cliffhanger,** *alias* **Robin Driscoll, Tony Haase, Peter McCarthy, Rebecca Stevens**
Director: **Jim Hill**
Producer: **John Dale**

A TVS Production for Channel 4
Six colour 30-minute episodes
14 July–18 August 1984

THUNDERBIRDS

One of the most popular TV series ever, *Thunderbirds* has become ingrained in the popular culture of more than one generation.

Gerry Anderson's seventh puppet series and the fourth in the Supermarionation saga, it was television's first one-hour puppet series, with the big wide world of family primetime as its prize. Anderson had originally intended it to continue the half-hour format established by *Supercar, Fireball XL5* and *Stingray*, but his ATV backer Lew Grade – who was paying the piper to the tune of some £38,000 an episode – insisted on hour-long stories. It meant reshooting several episodes but gave unprecedented scope for plot development, characterisation and technological invention.

Boasting an unusually large regular cast – both of characters and creations – the series centred on the exploits of a secret organisation called International Rescue, run from a hidden base on a remote Pacific island by former astronaut and multi-millionaire Jeff Tracy and his five sons, named after the first American astronauts. Using a remarkable range of five supercraft, they performed heroic feats of rescue against the odds anywhere in the world – and sometimes out of it, too.

The protagonists – mechanical and marionette – were:

Thunderbird 1 – a silver-grey scout craft whose 7000 mph top speed enabled it to be first on the scene of a crisis. Piloted by Scott Tracy, eldest son and decisive rescue organiser.

Thunderbird 2 – a giant green freighter designed to carry heavy rescue equipment to the danger zone in a range of integral pods. Piloted by Virgil, a reliable and steady character who worked closely with Scott.

Thunderbird 3 – an orange spaceship piloted by Alan, the impetuous brother, also an expert motor racing driver and 'romantic lead'.

Thunderbird 4 – a yellow, underwater craft, carried to rescues in one of Thunderbird 2's pods. Controlled by Gordon, the youngest son, enthusiastic and a bit of a joker.

These four craft were based at International Rescue's island HQ, but completing the quintet was the space satellite *Thunderbird 5*, the organisation's eyes and ears in outer space where it monitored every frequency on Earth, automatically translating any SOS into English and transmitting the alerts back to Earth. On duty in Thunderbird 5 was the patient and solitary figure of John Tracy.

The other 'star' of the show was a shocking pink, six-wheeled Rolls Royce, FAB 1, equipped with a formidable battery of gadgets including TV and radio transmitters, retro-rocket brakes, hydrofoils, oil slick ejector and a machine gun housed behind the radiator grille. It was owned by Lady Penelope, International Rescue's chic blonde London agent, and driven by Parker, Lady P's chauffeur/manservant, a droll Cockney ex-con with a talent for safe-blowing.

Other regular characters were Brains, the bespectacled, hesistantly spoken scientific genius; The Hood, principal villain and master of disguise, dedicated to getting his hands on the secrets of the Thunderbirds; Kyrano, the Hood's half-brother but loyal servant to the Tracys; Tin-Tin, Kyrano's daughter and romantically linked to Alan. Lastly, there was Grandma Tracy who looked after Jeff and the boys.

Although the Tracy 'airwalk' became the butt of countless affectionate jokes, *Thunderbirds* did continue AP Films' progressive ingenuity in the puppet world – each character had a variety of heads to reflect their different moods – and in 1966 the series won a Television Society Silver Medal as 'work of outstanding artistic merit'.

First screened on ITV from October 1965, the series enjoyed many repeat runs during the 1970s and 1980s, and has also emerged on video. Two feature films were made for United Artists – *Thunderbirds Are Go* (1966) and *Thunderbird 6* (1968) – and in 1986, a Japanese-made cartoon series, *Thunderbirds 2086*, cashed in on the name.

Thunderbirds continued to push up AP Films' production costs, swallowing around £1m. But it also made a fortune, notching up advance world sales of £350,000 even before it was screened here. The 32 episodes have been seen in 66 countries, and, indeed, are still being seen . . . somewhere.

VOICE CAST

The Hood/John Tracy Ray Barrett   *Jeff Tracey* Peter Dyneley
Brains/Kyrano/Parker/Gordon Tracy David Graham
Lady Penelope Sylvia Anderson   *Tin-Tin* Christine Finn
Virgil Tracy David Holliday   *Scott Tracy* Shane Rimmer
Alan Tracy Matt Zimmerman   *Virgil (Season Two)* Jeremy Wilkin
with: John Tate

Created by: Gerry and Sylvia Anderson
Producers: Gerry Anderson *(Season One)*, Reg Hill *(Season Two)*
Associate producer: Reg Hill

Director of photography: John Read
Special effects: Derek Meddings
Art director: Bob Bell
Music: Barry Gray

An *AP Films Production for ATV/ITC*
32 colour 60-minute episodes
Season One:
2 October 1965–2 April 1966

Season Two:
2–30 October 1966, plus 25 December 1966
(Dates as ATV, London)

Trapped in the Sky

w Gerry *and* Sylvia Anderson
Mysterious villain the Hood plants a bomb aboard atomic-powered new airliner, the *Fireflash*, thus drawing International Rescue into its first mission so that he can take photographs of the fabulous *Thunderbirds*. The organisation must help the stricken airliner to land safely, using three remote-controlled landing vehicles, while Lady Penelope goes after the snap-happy Hood in her remarkable Rolls.

Director: Alan Pattillo

Pit of Peril

w Alan Fennell
A revolutionary new army vehicle, the *Sidewinder*, runs into trouble on a jungle test-run, disappearing beneath the ground into a disued rubbish dump that has become a raging inferno. International Rescue faces one of its trickiest operations to reach the trapped men.

Director: Desmond Saunders

The Perils of Penelope

w Alan Pattillo
Taking strain train, Lady Penelope winds up tied to a railway track in the path of an oncoming express by the opportunistic Dr Godber who's trying to extort a secret fuel formula from her travelling companion, Sir Jeremy Hodge.

Directors: Alan Pattillo *and* Desmond Saunders

Terror in New York City

w Alan Fennell
While filming the moving of the Empire State Building to another part of New York, TV reporter Ned Cook and his cameraman are trapped in the icy waters of an underground river when the ground gives way and the building collapses above them. Only *Thunderbird 4* can get to them, but *Thunderbird 2* is out of action following an earlier run in with Cook!

Directors: David Lane *and* David Elliott

The Edge of Impact

w Donald Robertson
The Hood sabotages a Red Arrow aircraft, causing it to crash into a tall tele-relay station manned by two controllers. When a storm blows up, the weakened structure is in danger of imminent collapse. Conventional rescue is impossible and the Thunderbirds move in.

Director: Desmond Saunders

A Day of Disaster

w Dennis Spooner
A giant Martian Probe rocket is being transported across a bridge when the structure collapses beneath its weight, sending the rocket toppling into the water below. Two horrified technicians in the nose cone realise the fall has triggered the countdown. Working in *Thunderbird 4*, Gordon tries to clear the debris around the capsule. But it's a painfully slow job . . .

Director: David Elliott

30 Minutes After Noon

w Alan Fennell
A complex underworld plot to destroy a nuclear store misfires, trapping the gang in a vault with explosives that could cause the biggest blast the world has seen. In a delicate laser operation, Scott, Virgil and Alan must reach the men before the bombs go off.

Director: David Elliott

Desperate Intruder

w Donald Robertson
Brains and Tin-Tin go in search of treasure believed to be hidden in a submerged temple in Lake Anasta. But the Hood learns of their plans and overpowers them in an attempt to get to the treasure first. Worried when Brains fails to phone home, Jeff Tracy sends his Thunderbirds team to the scene where they clash with the Hood.

Director: David Lane

End of the Road

w Dennis Spooner
International Rescue face a dilemma when they are called in to save a man who knows them, construction boss Eddie Houseman whose bid to avert a mountain sliding into his new road has thrown him to a precarious perch on a high ledge. Pulling off the rescue without showing their faces proves a tricky test for the Tracys.

Director: David Lane

The Uninvited

w Alan Fennell
Scott flies to the Sahara to help two stranded archaeologists who had earlier helped *him* after unknown attackers had forced *Thunderbird 1* to crash-land in the desert. He arrives just as the two men stumble on the lost pyramid of Khamandides – secret base of a subterranean race, the Zombites, who capture them.

Director: Desmond Saunders

Sun Probe

w Alan Fennell
A super spaceship on a mission to collect particles of matter from the Sun loses control and is heading straight for the great ball of fire. Alan and Scott set off in *Thunderbird 3* and succeed in steering the

Sun Probe clear – only to find themselves on a collision course instead . . .

Director: Alan Pattillo

Operation Crash Dive

w Martin Clump
International Rescue agree to help solve a series of mysterious crashes that are plaguing the giant *Fireflash* airliners, and Gordon catches a saboteur in the act. But can he undo the damage in time to avert yet another crash?

Director: Desmond Saunders

Vault of Death

w Dennis Spooner
A Bank of England employee is trapped in an impregnable new vault which automatically pumps all the air out. As Virgil and Alan try to find a way in via the tunnels of the London Underground, Lady Penelope arrives with bank boss Lord Sefton. But he has forgotten the key and, with time running out, it's left to Parker – and a hairpin – to save the day.

Director: David Elliott

The Mighty Atom

w Dennis Spooner
The best-laid plans of mice and men go awry for the Hood when he steals a robot rodent equipped with a camera device to take secret snaps of the Thunderbirds. Setting an atomic plant ablaze to lure the craft to the scene, he is doubly thwarted when the IR boys' quick work averts disaster while his pet paparazzo returns with nothing more than shots of Lady Penelope screaming her lovely head off.

Director: David Lane

City of Fire

w Alan Fennell
Fire, set off when a woman driver crashes in an underground car park, is raging

through the basement of a vast new shopping complex. A family is trapped in a sealed-off corridor. To reach them, Scott and Virgil must use Brains's new cutting gas – gas which has already caused them to pass out during trials.

Director: **David Elliott**

The Impostors

w **Dennis Spooner**
Two mystery men posing as members of International Rescue steal some top secret papers – prompting a worldwide search for the organisation's base. Jeff Tracy dare not launch the Thunderbirds until their name is cleared, but a space laboratory needs their help . . .

Director: **Desmond Saunders**

The Man from MI5

w **Alan Fennell**
Lady Penelope is kidnapped in the South of France while trying to track down saboteurs who have stolen vital nuclear plans. Tied up aboard a boat with a bomb at her feet, she manages to summon International Rescue who must find the gang before they detonate the bomb.

Director: **David Lane**

Cry Wolf

w **Dennis Spooner**
Two young Australian boys playing International Rescue on their two-way radios inadvertently draw Thunderbird 1 to the scene. Accepting the boy's apology over the false alarm, the Tracys show them the IR base. Later, a second SOS is received from the boys, but this time it's for real.

Director: **David Elliott**

Danger at Ocean Deep

w **Donald Robertson**
John joins Virgil in Thunderbird 2 as the International Rescue team race to save the crew of a tanker, *Ocean Pioneer 2*, before the vessel is blasted sky high by a chemical reaction between its cargo of liquid fuel and a substance called OD 60 in the sea.

Director: **Desmond Saunders**

Move and You're Dead

w **Alan Pattillo**
Victims of a plot by a vanquished motor-racing rival, Alan and Grandma are trapped on a high bridge girder with a fiendish bomb that will explode if they move. Unable to get near in the Thunderbirds, Brains must disarm the bomb, using a long-distance neutraliser.

Director: **Alan Pattillo**

The Duchess Assignment

w **Martin Crump**
Lady Penelope's old friend the Duchess of Royston is kidnapped by art thieves and imprisoned in the basement of an old house. Rescue is hampered when, in trying to escape, the Duchess sets the house ablaze. With the building collapsing, Virgil brings on the Mole!

Director: **David Elliott**

Brink of Disaster

w **Alan Fennell**
Posing as an investor in a dubious monorail scheme, Jeff Tracy, Tin-Tin and Brains face deadly peril in a monotrain that's heading towards a broken section of track. Their only chance of survival lies with the resourceful Thunderbirds.

Director: **David Lane**

Attack of the Alligators

w **Alan Pattillo**
Scott and four other men are besieged in an isolated house up the Amazon by three giant alligators who have grown to four times their normal size after drinking

water polluted with a startling new growth drug. Armed with tranquillising guns, Virgil, Alan and Gordon try to lure the monsters away.

Director: David Lane

Martian Invasion

w Alan Fennell
International Rescue are called in to free two actors trapped in a cave while filming a sci-fi movie. Also on location is the Hood who uses one of the movie cameras to record the Thunderbirds in action. When his treachery is discovered, the chase is on to recover the film.

Director: David Elliott

The Cham-Cham

w Alan Pattillo
American rocket flights are mysteriously crashing and, astonishingly, the finger of suspicion points to chart-topping pop group, the Cass Carnaby Five. Each time the rockets crashed the crews had been listening to them play. Penelope and Tin-Tin go undercover in the music biz.

Director: Alan Pattillo

Security Hazard

w Alan Pattillo
A small boy stows away in *Thunderbird 2* during a rescue and reaches the Tracys' hideout. As Scott, Alan, Gordon and Virgil happily chatter to their young security hazard, Jeff wonders how to get him home without blowing their cover.

Director: Desmond Saunders

Season Two:

Atlantic Inferno

w Alan Fennell
A vacationing Jeff leaves Scott in charge, then chides him for getting involved after an underwater blast starts a fire near the

Seascape oil rig. When a second SOS comes from the rig, Scott delays until the situation becomes critical . . .

Director: Desmond Saunders

Path of Destruction

w Donald Robertson
An atomic-powered logging machine called the Crablogger goes out of control after its drivers pass out from heat and food poisoning, and rips through a town as it heads towards a huge dam. To avert certain catastrophe, Scott, Virgil and Brains must shut down the machine's reactor.

Director: David Elliott

Alias Mr Hackenbacker

w Alan Pattillo
Lady Penelope organises a charity fashion show aboard the maiden flight of a new plane, *Skythrust*, fitted with a revolutionary safety device invented by Hiram K. Hackenbacker, alias Brains. When the plane is hijacked, Brains's new invention is put to an early test.

Director: Desmond Saunders

Lord Parker's 'Oliday

w Tony Barwick
The Mediterranean resort of Monte Bianco is threatened when a storm dislodges a giant solar reflector, pointing it straight at the town. As *Thunderbird 2* struggles to right the reflector before the sun's rays strike, Parker avoids panic among hotel guests by getting them to play bingo.

Director: Brian Burgess

Ricochet

w Tony Barwick
The destruction of a space rocket damages pop pirate Rick O'Shea's orbiting TV station. Alan is launched in *Thunderbird 3*

to evacuate the two-man crew while Brains and Virgil wait to destroy the space station before it crashes back to Earth on a large oil refinery.

Director: **Brian Burgess**

Give or Take a Million

w **Alan Pattillo**
A robbery is foiled when two crooks take an unexpected ride in a rocket full of toys destined for a children's hospital, and one lucky child gets to spend a fairytale Christmas with International Rescue on Tracy Island.

Director: **Desmond Saunders**

TIME EXPRESS

Distinguished husband and wife duo Vincent Price and Coral Browne starred as the host and hostess aboard a mysterious train that transports its passengers back into the past. Thus, an assortment of travellers were able to relive crucial moments, alter previous decisions and create a new and, hopefully, better future.

The Time Express made just four journeys, all scheduled on BBC1 in 1979.

REGULAR CAST

Jason Winters **Vincent Price**   *Margaret Winters* **Coral Browne**
Ticket clerk **Woodrow Parfrey**   *R.J. Walker* **James Reynolds**
Engineer Callahan **William Edward Phipps**

Executive producers: **Ivan Goff, Ben Roberts**

Four colour 50-minute episodes
27 November–18 December 1979
(BBC1)

Journey One

w **Ivan Goff, Ben Roberts**
For two couples, a chance to travel back in time and change their lives together.
Michael Bennett **Steve Kanaly**
Tony Marcello **Paul Sylvan**
Elizabeth Stone **Jaime Lyn Bauer**
Lisa Marcello **Linda Scruggs Bogart**

Director: **Alan J. Levi**

Journey Two

w **Gerald Sanford**
A millionaire and a young doctor board

the Time Express. For one, a journey to ease his conscience, for the other a desperate search to save his wife.
Dr Mark Toland **James McArthur**
Edward Chernoff **Jerry Stiller**
Olivia **Pamela Toll**
Gloria **Anne Meara**

Director: **Arnold Laven**

Journey Three

w **A. Hayes**
The stories of two men – one a former detective running for public office, the other a daredevil rodeo rider.
Roy Culper **John Beck**

Sara Mason **Marcia Strassman**
John Slocum **Robert Hooks**
Charlie Enright **Vic Tayback**

Director: **Alan J. Levi**

Journey Four

---

w **Stephen Kandel, Richard Bluebell,
Pat Fielder**

Two bittersweet broken love affairs are given the opportunity to make fresh starts.
Sam Loring **Richard Masur**
David Blaine **Lyle Waggoner**
Michelle Flemming **Morgan Fairchild**
Vanessa **Lee Meriwether**
Jill **Terri Nunn**
Paul Venard **François-Marie Benard**

Director: **Michael Caffey**

TIME IS THE ENEMY

Seven-part adventure for children about a man who steps through an attic door in his new London home and finds himself in the year 1808 – 150 years in the past. Once there, the hero, Jim Barnaby, is accused of being a French spy. He escapes back into his own time where no one will believe his story and winds up accused of theft while trying to provide proof. The story reaches its climax when Barnaby goes back into the past one last time to face his enemy – despite having read an account of his own death in a history book!

CAST

Jim Barnaby **Clifford Elkin**   *Mr Porter* **Nigel Arkwright**
Mrs Deveril **Betty Huntley-Wright**
August Bellini **David Lander**   *Sir Adrian Mayne* **Edward Rhodes**
Patience Mee **Anne Reid**   *Mr Lancaster* **Derek Waring**
Rollings **Edward Higgins**   *Col. Deveril* **Ross Hutchinson**
Anne Deveril **Lilian Grasson**   *Hodge* **Laurence Taylor**

Writer: **Sheilah Ward**
Designer: **John Emery**
Director: **Daphne Shadwell**
Production company: not known

Seven 30-minute episodes, made in black and white
18 March–29 April 1958 (ITV)

THE TIME TUNNEL

For anyone growing up with television from the mid-1960s, Irwin Allen's contribution to that cultural shock has been virtually inescapable. For around a decade, hardly a week passed when one of his science fiction series wasn't playing . . . somewhere.

The Time Tunnel was his third offering (after *Voyage to the Bottom of the Sea* and *Lost in Space*) and followed the time-travelling adventures of two scientists, Doug Phillips and Tony Newman, into the past and, occasionally, the future, while back in the lab their colleagues watched on a viewing screen and waited to pull them back in the nick of time.

The series began with a scientific premise – the invention of a machine which can transport people back and forth through time. Pressed by fears of losing their Government grant and over-anxious to test it out, Newman steps into the tunnel and is thrown back into the past, landing on the deck of the *Titanic*. While he tries – unsuccessfully – to persuade the captain to change course (and history), his scientist colleagues send Phillips to help him while they figure out a way to bring both men back. A last-minute rescue is achieved.

Thereafter, the series became virtually a guide to the hot-spots of history, from the Alamo and Pearl Harbor to Krakatoa and the Little Big Horn.

The tunnel itself was the most impressive effect in the series, a striking two-tone vortex which seemed to stretch into the back of the TV set. But commercial success didn't come and only 30 trips were made.

The Time Tunnel first appeared in Britain in 1968, when the BBC screened just 13 episodes in an early evening slot. The series was then picked up by ITV who started showing it two years later.

REGULAR CAST

Dr Tony Newman **James Darren**   *Dr Doug Phillips* **Robert Colbert**
Dr Ann MacGregor **Lee Meriwether**   *Dr Raymond Swain* **John Zaremba**
Lt. Gen. Heywood Kirk **Whit Bissell**

Created by: **Irwin Allen**
Executive producer: **Irwin Allen**
Director of photography: **Winton Hoch**
Special effects: **L.B. Abbott**
Music: **Johnny Willams**

30 colour 50-minute episodes
UK premiere: 9 July 1968 (BBC)

(Author's note: the BBC's 13-week run was from 9 July–1 October 1968, and featured the first seven episodes as shown below, then *Devil's Island, Reign of Terror, Night of the Long Knives, Invasion, Kill Two By Two* and *Visitors From Beyond the Stars*.

The first ITV region to show episodes was London, with an 11-week Sunday afternoon run from 5 July 1970, but rather than start at the beginning, London Weekend Television kicked off with the episode *Massacre*. Successive runs in 1973 and 1974 redressed the balance and filled in the gaps, but it wasn't until 12 December 1974 that the last episode was transmitted.* The series had still not played in all ITV regions when, in 1989, ITV bought the rights once again. Regional runs began in April when TVS made it their Viewers' Choice for a late-night slot.

For ease of reference, I've listed the episodes in their original US running order.)

---

* I've been unable to pin down a transmission date for one episode *Idol of Death*, which may have been withdrawn from early runs and is *not* part of the current revival, along with *Raiders from Outer Space*.

Rendezvous with Yesterday

w Harold Jack Bloom, *from a story by*
  Irwin Allen
Dr Tony Newman takes his first trip in the
Time Tunnel and tries to change the
course of history when he lands on the
deck of the *Titanic*.
Capt. Malcolm Smith Michael Rennie
Althea Hall Susan Hampshire
Senator Clark Gary Merrill
Grainger Don Knight
Marcel Gerald Michenand

Director: Irwin Allen

One Way to the Moon

w William Welch
When the time travellers land in a Mars-
bound spaceship, their added weight en-
dangers the trip.
Sgt Jiggs Wesley Lau
Beard James T. Callahan
Harlow Warren Stevens
Kane Larry Ward
Admiral Killian Berry Kelley
Dr Brandon Ross Elliott

Director: Harry Harris

End of the World

w William Welch, Peter Germano
Tony and Doug land in a small American
town at the time of an appearance by
Halley's Comet and have to convince a
panicking population that the world is not
coming to an end.
Henderson Paul Fix
Blaine Paul Carr
Prof. Ainsley Gregory Morton
Preacher Nelson Leigh
Jerry Sam Groom

Director: Sobey Martin

The Day the Sky Fell Down

w Ellis St Joseph
The time tunnellers are trapped in Pearl
Harbor just before the Japanese attack –
and Tony meets both his own father and
himself as a child.

Jerry Sam Groom
Cmdr. Newman Linden Chiles
Lt. Anderson Lew Gallo
Tasaka Bob Okazaki
Louise Susan Flannery
Little Tony Sheldon Golomb
Okuno Jerry Fujikawa

Director: William Hale

The Last Patrol

w Bob *and* Wanda Duncan
The time travellers are nearly executed as
British spies when they land in the last
battle of the war of 1812.
General Southall/Col. Southall Carroll
  O'Connor
Capt. Hotchkiss Michael Pate
Lt. Reynerson David Watson
Capt. Jenkins John Napier

Director: Sobey Martin

The Crack of Doom

w William Welch
Doug and Tony choose the wrong day in
1883 to visit Krakatoa – it's the day the
island blew up.
Dr Holland Torin Thatcher
Karnosu Vic Lundin
Eve Holland Ellen McRae
Young native George Matsui

Director: William Hale

Revenge of the Gods

w William Read Woodfield *and* Allan
  Balter
Arriving in the Mediterranean in about
500 BC, Doug and Tony become involved
in the Greeks' war against the Trojans.
Sgt Jiggs Wesley Lau
Ulysses John Doucette
Helen of Troy Dee Hartford
Epeios Abraham Sofaer
Greek sword leader Kevin Hagen
Sardis Joseph Ruskin

Director: Sobey Martin

Massacre

w Carey Wilbur
Doug and Tony land on the site of Custer's last stand and try to save themselves from the massacre.
Crazy Horse Christopher Dark
Yellow Elk Lawrence Montaigne
Gen. Custer Joe Maross
Sitting Bull George Mitchell
Major Reno John Pickard
Tom Custer Bruce Mars
Tim Jim Halferty

Director: Murray Golden

Devil's Island

w Bob *and* Wanda Duncan
Tony and Doug are mistaken for escaped prisoners when they land on Devil's Island.
Boudaire Marcel Hillaire
Commandant Oscar Beregi
Lescoux Theo Marcuse
Perrault Steven Geray
Claude Alain Patrice
Capt. Dreyfus Ted Roter

Director: Jerry Hopper

Reign of Terror

w William Welch
Materialising at the time of the French Revolution, Doug and Tony plot to save the life of Marie Antoinette's son, the Dauphin.
Shopkeeper David Opatoshu
Simon Louis Mercier
Dauphin Patrick Michenau
Querque Whit Bissell
Bonaparte Joey Tata
Marie Antoinette Monique Lemaire

Director: Sobey Martin

Secret Weapon

w Theodore Apstein
When an enemy scientist, Dr Biraki, comes claiming to have defected to the West, Tony and Doug go back in time to check him out and discover a primitive version of the Time Tunnel.
Jerry Sam Groom
Dr Biraki Nehemiah Persoff
Hruda Michael Ansara
Alexis Gregory Gay
McDonnell Kevin Hagen
Gen. Parker Russell Conway

Director: Sobey Martin

The Death Trap

w Leonard Stadd
The famous detective, Pinkerton, thinks Tony and Doug are part of a plot to assassinate Lincoln when they arrive before the Civil War.
Jeremiah Scott Marlowe
Pinkerton R.G. Armstrong
Matthew Tom Skerritt
David Christopher Harris
Lincoln Ford Rainey

Director: William Hale

The Alamo

w Bob *and* Wanda Duncan
The untimely travellers arrive at the Alamo – just nine hours before it is due to fall to Santa Ana's Mexican army.
Dr Armandez Edward Colmans
Capt. Reynerson John Lupton
Mrs Reynerson Elizabeth Rogers
Col. Bowie Jim Davis
Col. Travis Rhodes Reason

Director: Sobey Martin

The Night of the Long Knives

w William Welch
Tony and Doug materialise in the Indian desert during a critical battle between British forces and a border chieftain.
Jerry Sam Groom
Kipling David Watson
Ali George Keymas
Gladstone Dayton Lummis
Cabinet minister Ben Wright
Singh Malachi Throne

Director: Paul Stanley

Invasion

w Bob *and* Wanda Duncan
The time travellers land in Cherbourg two days before D-Day and Doug falls into the hands of a German scientist experimenting with brainwashing.
Major Hoffman Lyle Bettger
Mirabeau Robert Carricart
Dr Kleinmann John Wengraf
Duchamps Michael St Clair
Verlaine Joey Tata

Director: Jerry Briskin

Robin Hood

w Leonard Stadd
The time travellers are dropped into the conflict between Robin Hood and King John.
Little John John Alderson
Baroness Brin O'Brien Moore
Dubois James Lanphier
Friar Tuck Ronald Long
Huntington Donald Herron
King John John Crawford

Director: William Hale

Kill Two by Two

w Bob *and* Wanda Duncan
Dropped onto a Pacific Island in 1945, Tony and Doug engage in a deadly game with a despairing Japanese flyer.
Lt. Nakamura Mako Iwamatsu
Sgt Itsugi Kam Tong
Dr Nakamura Phillip Ann

Director: Herschel Daugherty

Visitors from Beyond the Stars

w Bob *and* Wanda Duncan
The time travellers fall into the hands of silver-skinned aliens ruthlessly scouring the Universe for food.
Williams Byron Foulger
Crawford Tristram Coffin
Centauri Jan Merlin
Taureg Fred Beir
Alien leader John Hoyt

Director: Sobey Martin

The Ghost of Nero

w Leonard Stadd
Doug and Tony wrestle with the avenging ghost of Nero during an Italian-German battle in World War One.
Galba Eduardo Cianelli
Neistadt Gunnar Helstrom
Dr Steinholtz John Hoyt
Mussolini Nino Candido
Mueller Richard Jaeckel

Director: Sobey Martin

The Walls of Jericho

w Ellis St Joseph
Landing outside the Biblical city of Jericho, Tony and Doug become the spies who, according to the Bible, entered the city.
Captain Michael Pate
Father Abraham Sofaer
Malek Arnold Moss
Joshua Rhodes Reason
Rahab Myrna Fahey

Director: Jerry Juran

Idol of Death

w Bob *and* Wanda Duncan
Tony and Doug are once again mistaken for spies – this time in Mexico at the time of Cortez.
with: Rodolfo Hoyos, Lawrence Montaigne, Anthony Caruso, Peter Brocco

Director: Sobey Martin

Billy the Kid

w William Welch
Doug and Tony have a near-fatal run-in with Wild West outlaw William Bonney – alias Billy the Kid.
Billy Robert Walker
Pat Garrett Allen Case
Marshal Phil Chambers
Wilson Harry Lauter
McKinney Pitt Herbert

Director: Jerry Juran

Pirates of Deadman's Island

w Barney Slater
Doug and Tony fall into the hands of
Barbary Coast pirates in the year 1805.
Dr Berkhart Regis Toomey
Capt. Beal Victor Jory
Mr Hampton James Anderson
Stephen Decatur Charles Bateman

Director: Sobey Martin

Chase Through Time

w Carey Wilbur
When a technician turned spy plants a
bomb in the Time Tunnel complex and
then escapes into time, Tony and Doug
pursue him into the far future and to the
distant past.
Nimon Robert Duvall
Vokar Lew Gallo
Zee Vitina Marcus
Jiggs Wesley Lau
Magister Joe Ryan

Director: Sobey Martin

The Death Merchant

w Bob *and* Wanda Duncan
Tony and Doug land at Gettysburg and
find themselves on opposite sides of the
Civil War.
Major John Crawford
Sgt Maddox Kevin Hagen
Michaels Malachi Throne
Corporal Kevin O'Neal

Director: William Hale

Attack of the Barbarians

w Robert Hamner
Tony and Doug are caught between the
forces of Kubla Khan and the Mongol
hordes.
Marco Polo John Saxon
Ambahai Paul Mantee
Batu Arthur Batanides
Sarit Vitina Marcus

Director: Sobey Martin

Merlin the Magician

w William Welch
In 6th-century England, Merlin forces
Tony and Doug to help Arthur, the future
king, defeat the Vikings.
Merlin Christopher Cary
Guinevere Lisa Jack
King Arthur Jim McMullan
Wogan Vincent Beck

Director: Harry Harris

The Kidnappers

w William Welch
Tony and Doug are sent to rescue their
colleague, Ann MacGregor, who has been
kidnapped by an aluminium-coloured man
from the distant future.
Ott Del Monroe
Curator Michael Ansara
Hitler Bob May

Director: Sobey Martin

Raiders from Outer Space

w Bob *and* Wanda Duncan
At the battle of Khartoum, the time
travellers encounter an alien who has
come to destroy the world.
Henderson John Crawford
Planet leader Kevin Hagen

Director: Jerry Juran

Town of Terror

w Carey Wilbur
Landing in a New England town, in 1978,
Tony and Doug find it has been taken
over by aliens who want to drain the
oxygen from Earth's atmosphere.
Sarah Mabel Albertson
Alien Sarah Kelly Thordsen
Pete Gary Haynes
Joan Heather Young
Alien leader Vincent Beck

Director: Herschel Daugherty

TIMESLIP

Few series, let alone a children's drama, can claim to have started with a lesson in scientific theory. Yet that was how *Timeslip* began in 1970, with ITN's science correspondent Peter Fairley demonstrating the programme's concept of time travel.

Sitting in a transparent sphere intended to represent the Universe, Fairley bounced a balloon back and forth to convey the idea of a bubble of information moving around in time and in which someone could be carried into the past and the future.

It was a measure of how seriously this intelligent 26-part ATV series took both itself and its audience, though it was never po-faced about it. Devised by Ruth Boswell (later to produce another time-travel drama, *The Tomorrow People*) and her husband James, *Timeslip* took its two young heroes, Liz Skinner and Simon Randall, through four exciting adventures in time.

Also heavily involved were Liz's parents, Frank and Jean, and the sinister figure of Commander Traynor – seen in no fewer than five different incarnations, including a clone. Liz and Simon also met a younger version of Liz's father and an older version of her mother, plus older versions of themselves. And Liz's mother had a telepathic link with her daughter enabling her to 'see' Liz's experiences in the past.

The time travel itself was painless. Encountering an invisible barrier in a Midlands village, Liz and Simon simply fell through a 'hole' into another time and sometimes another location. It made for some imaginative paradoxes. At one point Liz and Simon, in 1940, can see, beyond the barrier, Frank and Traynor in 1970, while, in their time, Frank and Traynor *cannot* see the children. Later, Liz is shot but though she feels pain and sees blood, there is no wound as she does not really exist in that time.

The effect of the barrier itself was achieved using a split-screen process whereby the same film was used twice, each time with a different half masked, thus allowing a character apparently to vanish into thin air.

Among the regular cast, Spencer Banks, who played Simon, went on to star in two further ITV series – a spy drama, *Tightrope* (1972) and another time adventure, *The Georgian House* (1976). He also appeared in *Crossroads* . . .

Derek Benfield, who played Frank Skinner, became a familiar face to adult TV audiences in the BBC saga *The Brothers* while Iris Russell had been 'Father' in one episode of *The Avengers*.

Timeslip was fully networked (though with ATV running ahead of the other ITV regions by three days) and enjoyed a successful repeat run in 1973–4.

REGULAR CAST

Simon Randall **Spencer Banks**   Liz Skinner **Cheryl Burfield**
Frank Skinner **Derek Benfield**   Jean Skinner **Iris Russell**
Commander Traynor **Denis Quilley**

Script editor: **Ruth Boswell**
Producer: **John Cooper**
Scientific adviser: **Geoffrey Hoyle**

An ATV Network Production
26 half-hour episodes, colour (except eps
22 and 23 – made in black and white
28 September 1970–22 March 1971
(ATV, Midlands)

Story One:

The Wrong End of Time

w **Bruce Stewart** (Eps 1–6)
In the Midlands village of St Oswald, a young girl, Sarah, feels her way along an apparently invisible barrier near the site of a disused wartime naval base. Suddenly, she vanishes into thin air, her disappearance witnessed only by a local drunk.

Also in St Oswald are Simon Randall and Liz Skinner, on holiday with Liz's parents Jean and Frank, who was stationed at the base during the war. Out for a walk, they meet Commander Traynor, Frank's old CO, who has come to investigate the disappearance of the girl, Sarah. The children's walk takes them to the base and they, too, find the hole in the invisible barrier.

Liz and Simon emerge in 1940, where – or rather, when – they find the base fully operational and the scene of secret laser experiments. They encounter younger versions of Liz's father and Traynor, and Simon's belief that they have somehow travelled back in time is borne out by an invasion by a party of Germans, led by scientist Gottfried bent on learning the secrets of the base's work. They also meet the now distraught Sarah, and Liz manages to escape with her back through the barrier to 1970 where their story confirms Traynor's theory of an energy bubble by which certain sensitive people can move back and forwards in time.

Liz learns that her father was supposed to have dismantled the laser equipment before the Nazis got to it, but due to an accident cannot remember if he succeeded. Liz returns to 1940 where she and Simon help the younger Frank to complete his

task. They leave the base as Gottfried also decides to make an 'honourable' withdrawal. But as one story ends, another begins. Crawling through the barrier, Liz and Simon emerge, not in familiar 1970, but in an icy wasteland where, overcome by the cold, they quickly collapse.

Frank (1940) **John Alkin**
Gottfried **Sandor Elès**
Graz **Paul Humpoletz**
Arthur Griffiths **John Garrie**
George Bradley **Royston Tickner**
Ferris **Peter Sproule**
Phipps **John Abbott**
Dr Fordyce **Kenneth Watson**
Alice Fortune **Virginia Balfour**
Sarah **Sally Templer**
Fritz **Hilary Minster**

Director: **John Cooper**
Designer: **Gerry Roberts**
Introduced by: **Peter Fairley** (Ep. 1)

Story Two:

The Time of the Ice Box

w **Bruce Stewart** (Eps 7–12)
After collapsing from the severe cold, Liz and Simon awake to find themselves in the Ice Box, an Antarctic research base, in the year 1990, where a series of experiments are being carried out on humans, including trials of a longevity drug HA57. Liz hates the place, particularly a rude woman called Beth. As they depart, Liz suddenly sees her mother there . . .

Arriving back in 1970, Simon is persuaded by Traynor to return to the future to try to learn more about the Ice Box and HA57. Liz follows, curious to find out why her mother should be there, and discovers that Beth is an elder version of herself!

The most horrific discovery though, is of the body of an Australian, Dr Edith Joynton, who took a faulty dose of HA57 and aged dramatically to 100 years old. Errors begin to mount, linked to the base director Morgan C. Devereaux who, Simon learns, is actually the world's first clone. Liz finds her father preserved in an ice block – result of an earlier failed experiment. Finally, unable to live with his own imperfection, Devereaux runs out onto the icecap and freezes to death. Appalled by the callous experiments, Liz and Simon return to the time barrier, determined to prevent what they know to be a projection of a possible future.

Devereaux John Barron
Beth Skinner Mary Preston
Dr Edith Joynton Peggy Thorpe-Bates
Dr Bukov John Barcroft
Larry Robert Oates

Director: Peter Jefferies
Designers: Gerry Roberts *(Ep. 7),* Michael Eve *(Eps 8–12)*
Introduced by: Peter Fairley *(Ep. 7)*

Story Three:

The Year of the Burn-Up

(Eps 13–20)
w Bruce Stewart *(Eps 13–19),* Victor Pemberton *(Ep. 20)*
Simon is manipulated by Traynor into going into the future once again. A reluctant Liz follows. This time the barrier opens out onto a jungle. In a small straw hut community, the children meet a different, friendly Beth and also Simon's future self, a man known only as 2957. He is leading a group of clones, ranked from high-grade Alphas to lower Deltas, on a project to change world climates (hence a tropical England in 1990). But Simon discovers that an ageing Traynor is sabotaging the project.

As things go disastrously wrong, the world's atmosphere thins, the heat level soars, the water level falls and wildlife withers. Saddened by the prospect of such a grim future, Liz and Simon manage to halt the project, before returning to the barrier, leaving at least some vestige of hope.

Beth Mary Preston
2957 David Graham
Miss Stebbins Teresa Scoble
Vera Merdel Jordine
Alpha 4 Ian Fairbairn
Alpha 16 Teresa Scoble
Alpha 17 Lesley Scoble
Paul Brian Pettifer
Delta 22 Patrick Durkin
Technician Stuart Henry

Directors: Ron Francis *(Eps 13, 20)* Peter Jeffries *(Eps 14–19)*
Designers: Gerry Roberts *(Eps 13, 20)* Michael Eve *(Eps 14–19)*

Story Four:

The Day of the Clone

w Victor Pemberton *(Eps 21–26)*
Simon sets out to rescue Liz who is being held by Traynor in a research station, R1, near St Oswald. Aided by Dr Frazer, he finds and frees her. Pursued by Traynor's men, the children head for the barrier, passing through it into Simon's living room in 1965. Heading back to St Oswald, and R1, they witness strange experiments and discover Devereaux is charge of a cloning project. Escaping *back* to 1971, they are recaptured by Traynor and taken again to R1.

Meanwhile, Liz's mother has had visions of her daughter's various plights and she and Frank follow the trail to R1, where Traynor has now discovered that *he himself* is a clone, created in the Sixties by Devereaux. The knowledge has unhinged him, but Dr Frazer is on hand to reunite them with the children. They then come across the *real* Traynor who has been imprisoned since 1965. As the story – and the series – ends they *all* pursue the Traynor clone to the barrier and the closing sequence has him/it being dragged screaming through the hole to . . . who knows where – or when.

Dr Frazer Ian Fairbairn
Pitman John Swindells
Stebbins Teresa Scoble
Maria Mary Larkin
Desk attendant Bruce Beeby
Commissionaire Harry Davis
Driver Dennis Balcombe
Devereaux John Barron

De Saram **Derek Sydney**
Mr Randall **John Cazabon**
Newsvendor **John Herrington**
Ward sister **Hilary Liddell**
Dr Ferguson **Keith Grenville**
George Pointer **Richard Thorp**

Director: **Dave Foster** *(Eps 21–24)*, **Ron Francis** *(Eps 25–26)*
Designer: **Gerry Roberts**

THE TOMORROW PEOPLE

This 1970s children's adventure series introduced a new breed of youngster – Homo Superior. Described by creator/writer/director Roger Price as the next stage in human evolution, *The Tomorrow People* were completely telepathic, possessed telekinetic powers and had the ability to teleport themselves instantaneously from place to place – a process catchily known as 'jaunting'.

From their secret base – called The Lab – off a disused tunnel of the London Underground, *The Tomorrow People* looked out for one another's emergence and dedicated their amazing powers to saving mankind and the world from diverse alien threats. In this they were aided by TIM, their talking biotronic computer, and various friends, including Ginge and Lefty, a pair of leather-jacketed motorcyclists.

As the opening story revealed, *The Tomorrow People* weren't always Homo Superior. They all began as plain Homo Sapiens (affectionately referred to as 'Saps') and the evolution into a Tomorrow Person was called 'breaking out'. You, too, the theory went, could be a latent Homo Superior.

Over the series' eight seasons, Tomorrow People came and went, with departing stars explained away as representing Earth on the Galactic Trig, a kind of huge space complex, staffed by super-intelligent beings from all over the Universe.

The group's leader, John, was the only member to last the series' distance, though Elizabeth (played by black actress Elizabeth Adare) joined in Season Two and stayed to the end. The other longest-serving recruits were Stephen (four seasons) and Mike (five seasons), the latter being played by actor/singer Mike Holoway of the Flintlock pop group.

Produced by Thames Television to fill the vacuum left by *Ace of Wands*, *The Tomorrow People* was touted in the popular press as ITV's answer to *Doctor Who*, and though the series spanned six years, its weekday teatime slot meant it never gathered the adult following of the Time Lord. Moreover, what had begun as an intelligent, innovative 'thinking kid's' series declined into increasingly humorous action. Strictly for the Saps!

REGULAR CAST

THE TOMORROW PEOPLE

John *(Seasons 1–8)* **Nicholas Young**   Stephen *(Seasons 1–4)* **Peter Vaughan-Clarke**
Carol *(Season 1)* **Sammie Winmill**   Kenny *(Season 1)* **Stephen Salmon**
Elizabeth *(Seasons 2–8)* **Elizabeth Adare**   Tyso *(Seasons 3–4)* **Dean Lawrence**
Mike Bell *(Seaons 4–8)* **Mike Holoway**   Hsui Tai *(Seasons 6–8)* **Misako Koba**
Andrew Forbes *(Seasons 7–8)* **Nigel Rhodes**

OTHERS:

Voice of TIM **Philip Gilbert**   Ginge *(Season 1)* **Michael Standing**
Lefty *(Season 1)* **Derek Crewe**   Prof. Sawston *(Seasons 2–3)* **Brian Stanion**
Chris *(Season 2)* **Christopher Chittell**

Created by: **Roger Price**
Producers: **Ruth Boswell** *(Seasons 1–3)*, **Roger Price** *(Seasons 1 and 4)*, **Vic Hughes** *(Seasons 5–8)*
Script editor (Season 4): **Ruth Boswell**
Music: **Dudley Simpson, Brian Hodson**

Thames Television Production
68 colour 30-minute episodes

Season One:
30 April–30 July 1973
Season Two:
4 February–6 May 1974
Season Three:
26 February–21 May 1975

Season Four:
28 January–10 March 1976
Season Five:
28 February–4 April 1977
Season Six:
15 May–26 June 1978
Season Seven:
9 October–13 November 1978
Season Eight:
29 January–19 January 1979

(Author's note: From Season Two onwards each episode has its own title, but the stories are known collectively by the titles given here.)

Season One

The Slaves of Jedikiah

w Brian Finch *and* Roger Price *(A 5-part story)*
Introductions all round . . . as Stephen, an ordinary 14-year-old schoolboy haunted by strange voices in his head, learns that he's not going mad, but is 'breaking out' – changing into a Tomorrow Person. He meets the other Tomorrow People, Carol, John and Kenny, and they face the threat of Jedikiah, a fierce, shape-changing alien robot.
Jedikiah **Francis de Wolff**
Cyclops **Robert Bridges**

Director: **Paul Bernard**
Designer: **Harry Clark**

The Medusa Strain

w Brian Finch *and* Roger Price *(A 4-part story)*
The Tomorrow People combat a revenge-seeking Jedikiah who has teamed up with a space pirate, Rabowski, to capture Peter, a young guardian of time, and succeeded in immobilising the world with the aim of stealing the Crown Jewels.
Jedikiah **Roger Bixley**
Rabowski **Roger Booth**
Peter **Richard Speight**
Android **David Prowse**
The Medusa **Norma McGlen**

Director: **Roger Price**
Designer: **Harry Clark**

The Vanishing Earth

w Brian Finch *and* Roger Price *(A 4-part story)*
The Tomorrow People face the awesome challenge of the Spidron, an alien with the power to inflict earthquakes and hurricanes and cause volcanoes to erupt. As the full force of his fury is unleashed, the jaunters stand by helplessly, unable to warn the Saps that the world may be coming to an end.
Steen Kevin Stoney
Smithers Kenneth Farrington
Joy Nora Llewellyn
Spidron John Woodnutt

Director: Paul Bernard
Designer: Harry Clark

Season Two

The Blue and the Green

w Roger Price *(A 5-part story)*
With Carol and Kenny departed (to represent Earth on the Galactic Federation Council), Stephen and John are joined by a new Tomorrow Person, a student teacher called Elizabeth. Together they solve the mystery surrounding a series of riots spreading through schools all over England, and the strange changing paintings that cast an evil spell on those around them.
Robert Jason Kemp
Johnson Ray Burdis
Grandfather Nigel Pegram
Police Inspector Simon Merrick

Director: Roger Price
Designer: Michael Minas

A Rift in Time

w Roger Price *(A 4-part story)*
Stephen and John share a dream in which Peter, the young Time Guardian (from 'The Medusa Strain'), calls for their help in stopping a time meddler who is tampering with the past by giving Roman technology the steam engine. Using a time disc, the Tomorrow People must correct the time warp to save civilisation as they know it.
Peter Richard Speight

Prof. Freda Garner Sylvia Coleridge
Prof. Cawston (intro) Bryan Stanion
Gaius Stanley Lebor
Zenon Stephen Jack
Guthrun Mike Lee Lane
Lothar Leonardo Pieroni
Cotus Peter Duncan
Trystan Leonard Gregory
Carol Sammie Winmill

Director: Roger Price
Designer: Michael Minas

The Doomsday Men

w Roger Price *(A 4-part story)*
The Tomorrow People clash with a secret society dedicated to preserving war who take over the space station *Damocles* and threaten to devastate the world with its nuclear power. Striving to halt the catastrophe, Stephen and his friends jaunt up to *Damocles* where they come face to face with General 'Iron Mac' McLelland, leader of the Doomsday Men.
Paul Simon Gipps-Kent
Douglas McLelland William Relton
Lt. Gen. McLelland Lindsay Campbell
Dr Laird Arnold Peters
Lee Wan Eric Young
Major Longford Derek Murcott
Traffic warden Nigel Pegram

Director: Roger Price
Designer: Michael Minas

Season Three

Secret Weapon

w Roger Price *(A 4-part story)*
John, Elizabeth and Stephen hear a new Tomorrow Person, Tyso, breaking out, asking for help. Their search for him leads them to Col. Masters and a secret Research Establishment where the colonel's assistant Miss Conway is trying to use her mind-reading ability to learn the secrets of Homo Superior.
Tyso (intro) Dean Lawrence
Col. Masters Trevor Bannister
Tricia Conway Ann Curthoys
Mrs Boswell Joanna Tope
Evergreen Denise Cook
Father O'Connor Frank Gatliff

Chris **Christopher Chittell**
Prime Minister **Hugh Morton**

Director: **Stan Woodward**
Designer: **Philip Blowers**

Worlds Away

w **Roger Price** *(A 3-part story)*
Timus Irnok Nosta, ambassador from the
Galactic Federation, begs the Tomorrow
People to try to free the enslaved inhabit-
ants of the planet Peerie, who are being
terrorised by a strange creature, the
dreaded Khultan. There, they find the
Vesh, the Tomorrow People of Peerie, are
being hunted and burned by the Vesh-
takers.
Timus/Tikno **Philip Gilbert**
Lenda **Lydia Lisle**
Veshtaker **Barry Linehan**
Arkron **Keith Chegwin**
Vanyon **Reg Lye**
Mrs Boswell **Joanna Tope**
Evergreen **Denise Cooke**

Directors: **Dennis Kirkland, Vic Hughes**
Designer: **Philip Blowers**

A Man for Emily

w **Roger Price** *(A 3-part story)*
John and Elizabeth jaunt into space to
investigate an alien spaceship and meet
The Momma, her spoilt daughter Emily
and Emily's servant/companion Elmer.
When Elmer escapes to Earth, where he
causes chaos, lands up in jail and refuses
to return to the ship, John finds himself on
the Momma's 'wanted' list as Elmer's
replacement.
The Momma **Margaret Burton**
Emily **Sandra Dickinson**
Elmer **Peter Davison**
Publican **Robin Parkinson**
Mr Greenhead **Bill Dean**

Director: **Stan Woodward**
Designer: **Philip Blowers**

The Revenge of Jedikiah

w **Roger Price** *(A 3-part story)*
A vengeful Jedikiah assumes Stephen's
form (appearing on *Opportunity Knocks!*)

to shoot Col. Masters at his research
establishment. Then, as Miss Conway, he
sets a deadly trap for John and Elizabeth.
A desperate TIM seeks the aid of Tikno.
Though this is against the galactic code,
Tikno agrees – but pays with his life. The
stage is set for a final confrontation in the
Lab.
Jedikiah **Francis de Wolff**
Miss Conway **Ann Curthoys**
Prof. Cawston **Bryan Stanion**
Mustaf **Ali Bongo**
Evergreen **Denise Cooke**
TIM/Timus/Tikno **Philip Gilbert**
Prof. Johnston **Anne Ridler**
Sgt Evans **John Lyons**

Director: **Vic Hughes**
Designer: **Philip Blowers**

Season Four

One Law

w **Roger Price** *(A 3-part story)*
Young Mike Bell has discovered that he
can open locks with his mind. Unaware
that he is really 'breaking out', he decides
to use his power to 'break in' and rob
banks, but falls into the unscrupulous
clutches of Lord Dunning who is out to
steal a fortune in gold. The Tomorrow
People must convince Mike that his true
destiny lies elsewhere.
O'Reilly **Patrick McAlinney**
Two Tone **John Hollis**
Slow **Norman Mitchell**
Insp. Burke **Tim Barrett**
Lord Dunning **Harold Kasket**
Thwaites **Arnold Diamond**

Director: **Leon Thau**
Designer: **Peter Elliot**

Into the Unknown

w **Jon Watkins** *(A 4-part story)*
Mike is composing a pop song in the Lab
when an SOS comes in from Outer Space,
taking the Tomorrow People on a journey
to the Pluto Five region of the solar
system to help a stricken spaceship which
is being slowly drawn into a black hole.
But treachery is afoot and they find
themselves helplessly trapped.

Kwaan Stephen Garlick
Tiraiyaan Geoffrey Bayldon
Vaktaan Brian Coburn
Ralaa Raymond Boyd

Director: Roger Price
Designer: Peter Elliott

Season Five

The Dirtiest Business

w Roger Price *(A 2-part story)*
Mike, John and Elizabeth race against time to free Pavla, a young girl agent, from the clutches of the SIS and the KGB. Can they rescue her from Major Turner's sinister brainwashing machine and prevent the Russians triggering off their mysterious X-delta device.
Pavla Anulka Dubinska
Major Ann Turner Vivien Heilbron
KGB man Jan Murzynowski
Radio producer Beth Ellis
SIS Sgt Steve Ismay
KGB chauffeur Freddie Clemson
Policeman Ian Barritt
Hippy Gaynor Ward
Doctor Royce Mills

Director: Vic Hughes
Designer: David Richens

A Much Needed Holiday

w Roger Price *(A 2-part story)*
A trip to the planet Gallia to carry out an archaeological survey involves the Tomorrow People in a daring attempt to rescue the Gallian boy slaves from the clutches of their tyrannical masters, the Kleptons.
Gremlon Anthony Garner
Trig Guy Humphries
Trop David Corti
Timus Philip Gilbert

Director: Richard Mervyn
Designer: David Richens

The Heart of Sogguth

w Roger Price *(A 2-part story)*
Jake, a university head of Ethnic Studies and leader of a religious sect, offers to manage Mike's pop group and the Tomorrow Person finds that playing an African tribal drum on television could raise the forces of hell to bring about the destruction of the Universe.
Jake Roddy Maude-Roxby
Mike Harding James Smilie
Susan Gill Rosalyn Elvin
Derek Derek Pascoe
Bill Bill Rice
Group members Jamie Stone, John Summerton

Director: Vic Hughes
Designer: David Richens

Season Six

The Lost Gods

w Roger Price *(A 2-part story)*
A telepathic message from an oriental 'goddess' takes the Tomorrow People to the Far East where they meet a new Homo Superior, Hsui Tai, and find themselves lined up to become sacrifices in a religious cult's ceremony of fire.
Matsu Tan Burt Kwouk
Sage Robert Lee

Director: Peter Webb
Designer: David Richens

Hitler's Last Secret

w Roger Price *(A 2-part story)*
Why do a group of young British soldiers turn against their commanding officer when they hear the sound of Hitler's voice? The answer brings the Tomorrow People face to face with the evils of the Third Reich.
Hitler Michael Sheard
Prof. Friedl Richard Warner
Major Hughes Leon Eagles
Karl Brandt Nicholas Lyndhurst
Willi Frisch Earl Rhodes
Blitz Ray Burdis
Wolfgang Grass Charles Skinner
Corporal Spencer Banks

Director: Leon Thau
Designer: Allan Cameron

The Thargon Menace

w Roger Price *(A 2-part story)*
A terrifying Ripper Ray weapon, powerful enough to destroy a planet, falls into the hands of a mad despot, General Papa Minn. From space he broadcasts his ultimatum to the governments of the world – surrender all power within one hour or perish. It's up to the Tomorrow People to save the world.

General Papa Minn Olu Jacobs
Major Marcos Eric Roberts
Sula Jackie Cowper
Flyn Michael Audreson
Captain Graham Lines
Puppet voices David Graham

Director: Peter Yolland
Designer: Martyn Hebert

Season Seven

Castle of Fear

w Roger Price *(A 2-part story)*
A fifth member joins the team – Scots lad Andrew Forbes – in an adventure in which the Tomorrow People dream of a headless highlander, go in search of the Loch Ness Monster and meet Frankenstein's creation.

Bruce Forbes Dominic Allan
Dr Gail Mayer Jennifer Watts
Angus Macduff Bill Gavin
Prof. Young Brian Jackson

Director: Vic Hughes
Designer: Gordon Toms

Achilles Heel

w Roger Price *(A 2-part story)*
With their special powers taken away from them by two mysterious alien visitors, the Tomorrow People have just ten minutes to prevent a disaster that will instantaneously affect every corner of the galaxy. (Makes *Beat the Clock* look generous.)

Bruce Dominic Allan
Yagon Hilary Minster

Cantor Christian Rodska
Glip Stanley Bates
Accompanist Ted Taylor

Director: Vic Hughes
Designer: Gordon Toms

The Living Skins

w Roger Price *(A 2-part story)*
The Tomorrow People investigate the link between sinister goings-on in the cellar of a fashionable boutique and disturbances in deep space. John gives a priceless gift to the world which costs him nothing, but saves all life on Earth from becoming extinct.

Wilton Ralph Lawford
Girl Judith Fielding
Guard David Carter

Director: Stan Woodward
Designer: Gordon Toms

Season Eight

War of the Empires

w Roger Price *(A 4-part story)*
When Earth becomes drawn into an intergalactic conflict between two warring races, the Thargons and the Sorsons, the Tomorrow People appeal in vain for help from the Galactic Federation. Then the Sorson leader makes a pact with the American president. Finally, the young heroes find themselves facing the might of the Thargon space fleet, armed only with their 'imagination'.

American president John F. Parker
American general Hal Galili
Morgan Evans David Baxt
Dave Ricardo Weston Gavin
Sorson general Richard Bartlett
Sorson captain Terence Woodfield
Thargon commander Percy Herbert
Thargon officer Anthony Stafford
American lady Mary Law
Chaircreature David Cann

Director: Vic Hughes
Designer: John Plant

A TRAVELLER IN TIME

Not a time machine in sight, just a doorway into the Elizabethan past for a five-part children's historical adventure.

A young girl, Penelope, goes to stay with her uncle and aunt in their Derbyshire farmhouse which was once the home of an Elizabethan family, and finds herself slipping back into the past where she becomes involved with the Babington family and an attempt to save Mary, Queen of Scots.

MAIN CAST

Penelope **Sophie Thompson**　*Uncle Barnabas* **Gerald James**
Aunt Tissie/Dame Cicely **Elizabeth Bradley**
Mistress Babington **Mary Maude**　*Tabitha* **Sarah Benfield**
Francis Babington **Simon Gipps-Kent**
Jude **Louis Hammond**　*Anthony Babington* **Charles Rogers**
Tom Snowball **Michael Greatorex**　*Arabella* **Michele Copsey**
Adam Deedick **Graham Rigby**　*Mary Queen of Scots* **Heather Chasen**

Writer: **Alison Uttley**
Dramatised by: **Diana De Vere Cole**
Executive producer: **Anna Home**
Director: **Dorothea Brooking**
Designer: **Walter Miller**

A BBC Production
Five colour 30-minute episodes
4 January–1 February 1978
(BBC1)

THE TRIPODS

It was supposed to be the adventure story to cap all adventure stories – a £1 million BBC family science fiction serial spread over three seasons, a saga to woo the Saturday teatime audience for years to come.

In the end, BBC1 controller Michael Grade pulled the plug two-thirds of the way through, as poor reviews and lousy ratings persuaded the corporation to cut and run. And unlike the 1985 axe Grade dangled over *Doctor Who*, there was no reprieve. The TV story of *The Tripods* remains unfinished.

Adapted by Alick Rowe from John Christopher's trilogy of the same name, *The Tripods* is set in the 21st century and follows the adventures of two teenage cousins, Will and Henry Parker and their friends, as they get caught up in a struggle to free Earth from Alien control. The Tripods themselves are towering three-legged alien machines which dominate mankind, stifling rebellion by a mind-control technique called 'capping'. Under their 100-year rule society has reverted to a medieval pattern.

The young protagonists, Will and Henry, are due to be capped in a special ceremony at their village in England, which will mark their transition to adulthood. But the pair wish to remain free and decide to head off in search of the 'Free Men' in the White Mountains of Switzerland.

The series was generally well-acted and its special effects scenes with the Tripods well-realised. Extensive location filming made appealing use of the settings (including Portmeirion). Its downfall lay in the relative brevity of the original work and an overall lack of incident, especially in the crucial first season, when the metal monsters themselves were seen all too infrequently, their presence felt more off-stage than on.

REGULAR CAST

William Parker **John Shackley**   *Beanpole* **Ceri Seel**
Henry Parker **Jim Baker** *(Season One, plus Season Two eps 1–2)*
Fritz **Robin Hayter** *(Season Two only)*

Adapted by: **Alick Rowe**, *from the trilogy by* **John Christopher**
Producer: **Richard Bates**
Music: **Ken Freeman**
Video effects designer: **Robin Lobb**
Visual effects designers: (Season One) **Steven Drewett, Kevin Molloy** *(Season Two)* **Steve Bowman, Simon Tayler, Michael Kelt**

A BBC Production
25 colour 30-minute episodes
Season One:
15 September–8 December 1984
Season Two:
7 September–23 November 1985
(BBC1)

Season One

(A 13-part story)
The year: 2089. The place: rural England. The Tripods have ruled for more than 100 years and, by 'capping' each child at 16, control men's minds and ensure total submission. But cousins Will and Henry Parker are determined to stay free and, encouraged by a vagrant, Ozymandias, run away.

Setting out to join the Free Men in the Swiss mountains, Will and Henry cross to France where they gain a new companion Jean-Paul (Beanpole), and visit the abandoned city of Paris. When Will gets a fever, the trio are given refuge at Château Ricordeau where Will falls in love with the beautiful Eloise. He is torn between her and his friends who go on without him. But the jealous Duc de Sarlat chooses the already capped Eloise to serve the Tripods and a broken-hearted Will leaves to rejoin his friends.

However, he is captured by a Tripod and freed with a homing device inserted in his armpit to lead it to the others. Though the device is found and cut away, Will loses much blood and needs help. The trio find brief sanctuary at the Vichot family's vineyard before pressing on towards the White mountains.

Tired and hungry, they are caught stealing a loaf of bread and again face the prospect of capping, but manage to escape – destroying a Tripod.

Then, with their goal in sight, they are caught by 'black guards'. Only after an interrogation do they find that they are really safe in the hands of the Free Men.
Ozymandias **Roderick Horn**
Mrs Parker **Lucinda Curtis**
Mr Parker **Michael Gilmour**
Schoolmaster **John Scott Martin**
Captain Curtis **Harry Meacher**
Duc de Sarlat **Robin Langford**
Count **Jeremy Young**
Countess **Pamela Salem**

Eloise Charlotte Long
Trouillon Terry Forrestal
Mme Vichot Anni Lee Taylor
Vichot Stephen Marlowe
Daniel Julian Jones
Chief Black guard Peter Halliday
Julius Richard Wordsworth

Directors: Graham Theakston *(Eps 1–8),*
   Christopher Barry *(Eps 9–13)*
Designers: Victor Meredith *(Eps 1–8),*
   Martin Collins *(Eps 9–13)*

Season Two

(A 12-part story)
At their hideout in the Swiss Alps the Free
Men must devise a plan to overthrow the
Tripods and free mankind. Will, Beanpole
and a German boy, Fritz, are among those
chosen to compete at the Tripods' Annual
Games in the hope that may provide a
means to get inside the Tripods' city and
learn some of their secrets.

During a hazardous journey they fall
foul of the villainous Kommandant Goetz,
but are helped by a couple of girls, Zerlina
and Papagena.

After success in the Games, Will and
Fritz are transported to the City of Gold,
leaving Beanpole to wait for their return.
Will is chosen to serve one of the 'Masters'
– the alien creatures who created the

Tripods – and Fritz winds up working with
the slave gangs in underground caverns,
but both learn much about the Masters'
plans for the future of Earth. Will also
finds Eloise – in suspended animation in a
hall of beauty – and dances with her in a
dream.

When their intentions are found out,
Fritz elects to stay in the city, while Will
escapes via an underground river. Meeting
up with Beanpole, they join Ali Pasha's
travelling circus disguised as clowns, in the
hope of getting their vital information
back to the White Mountains.

Julius Richard Wordsworth
Goetz Godfrey James
Zerlina Lisa Maxwell
Papagena Elizabeth Morton
Master 468 John Woodvine
Speyer Alfred Hoffman
Power Master Bernard Holley
Borman James Coyle
Boll Edward Highmore
Eloise Cindy Shelley
Coggy Christopher Guard
Dorfen Alex Leppard
Slave Master Garfield Morgan
Ali Pasha Bruce Purchase

Directors: Christopher Barr *(Eps 1–4,*
   11–12), Bob Blagden *(Eps 5–10)*
Designers: Martin Collins *(Eps 1–4,*
   11–12), Philip Lindley *Eps 5–10)*

THE TROLLENBERG TERROR

Suspense and horror combined in a 1956 six-part tale of malevolent alien influences at work around the Trollenberg mountain in
the Swiss Alps.

Much of the drama centred on a small Alpine hotel, nestling in
the ominous shadow of the peak, where a mind-reading act, the
Pilgrim Sisters, found themselves drawn in to help Prof. Crevet
ward off the advance of the Ixodes – tentacled, brain-like creatures
from another world.

Quentin Lawrence, who directed the series, repeated the trick for
a 1958 film version, also called *The Trollenberg Terror*, which
included rather more graphic horror sequences such as gruesome
close-ups of severed heads and melting flesh! Laurence Payne

starred in both versions – though in the movie Forrest Tucker played the hero, a UN scientific investigator called Alan Brooks – while Stuart Saunders reprised his role of Dr Dewhurst, an early victim of climber George Brett who is taken over by the alien powers.

Rosemary Miller, who played Ann Pilgrim in the series, found stardom just a few weeks later as Nurse Roberts in ATV's pioneering medical soap *Emergency Ward 10*.

CAST

Sarah Pilgrim **Sarah Lawson**   Ann Pilgrim **Rosemary Miller**
Petitjean **Michael Anthony**   Philip Truscott **Laurence Payne**
Albert **Roland O'Casey**   Dr Dewhurst **Stuart Saunders**
George Brett **Glyn Owen**   Dr Spielmann **Frederick Schrecker**
Prof. Crevet **Raf de la Torre**

Writer: **Peter Key**
Producer/director: **Quentin Lawrence**
Designer: **Tom Lingwood**

An ITV Network Production
Six 30-minute episodes, black and white

The Mind of Ann Pilgrim

First Blood
The Giggle of Madness
The Power of the Ixodes
The Trap
'Final Episode'

15 December 1956–19 January 1957
(ITV)

THE TWILIGHT ZONE (1959–64)

'There is a fifth dimension beyond those known to man. It is a dimension vast as space and timeless as infinity. It is the middle ground between light and shadow, between the pit of his fears and the summit of his knowledge. This is the dimension of imagination. It is an area we call . . . *The Twilight Zone*.'

One of the most revered fantasy series ever made, *The Twilight Zone* received its first network run in Britain in 1983 – some 23 years after its American debut.

Until that season of 39 episodes on BBC2, this country's exposure to *The Twilight Zone* had been confined to sporadic runs on a handful of ITV regions back in the 1960s.

Yet few series have bequeathed a more treasured legacy of ideas and style, and it still stands as the role model for the anthology genre. Its trenchant parables on humanity draw the viewer in by quietly tugging at the sleeve of his imagination and, through fantasy, explore human hopes and despairs, prides and prejudices, strengths and weaknesses, in ways conventional drama never can.

The Zone was created by Rod Serling, a butcher's son from Binghampton, New York, whose writing talent had flourished in the early days of TV drama, winning him three Emmy awards. A relentless, prolific writer, Serling himself wrote the majority of the show's 156 scripts. Said to have suffered from insomnia, he kept a tape recorder by his bed to dictate ideas that came to him as he tried to sleep.

The series' other major contributors were Richard Matheson and Charles Beaumont and each had his own distinctive style. Where Serling's tales tended to be more whimsical and sentimental, Beaumont's were darker and more disturbing, while Matheson rung every nuance of suspense out of his carefully structured stories. But *all* the episodes were topped and tailed by Serling's memorable, measured narration.

On the acting side, *The Twilight Zone* featured many young, now established stars, from *Star Trek*'s William Shatner, Leonard Nimoy and George Takei, to film giants such as Charles Bronson, Lee Marvin, James Coburn, Burt Reynolds, Telly Savalas, Roddy McDowall, Robert Redford, Burgess Meredith, Mickey Rooney and Dennis Hopper, plus Jack '*Quincy*' Klugman and Peter '*Columbo*' Falk.

The Twilight Zone premiered in America on 2 October 1959 and its original five-season run lasted until 1964. The UK debut was in the humble Border region, on 27 January 1963, but it was a year before episodes appeared in other regions. Seasons were scarce until BBC2 revived it in 1983 and since 1986 it has found a new home on Channel 4.

REGULAR CAST

Host/Narrator **Rod Serling**

Created by: **Rod Serling**
Executive producer: **Rod Serling**
Producers: **Buck Houghton, Herbert Hirschman, Bert Granet, William Froug**
Special Effects: **Virgil Beck, Bob Waugh**
Theme Music: **Bernard Herrmann, Marius Constant, Jerry Goldsmith**

A Cayuga Production (filmed at M-G-M)
156 episodes (138 half-hour, 18 one-hour)
black and white

UK premiere: 27 January 1963
(Border)

(Author's note: Once again, for ease of reference I've listed the 156 episodes in the original American running order, followed by title guides to some of the principal UK runs on ITV, BBC2 and C4. At the time of going to press, C4 were in the middle of a further batch of 25 episodes, some of which were being seen for the first time on British television.

Season One
36 30-minute episodes

Where Is Everybody?

w Rod Serling
Greeted by empty streets, a man searches a small town to find that he is completely alone – and inexplicably terrified.
Cast: Earl Holliman, James Gregory

Director: Robert Stevens

One for the Angels

w Rod Serling
Informed that his time on Earth is about up, a gentle-natured sidewalk salesman talks Mr Death into letting him make one really big pitch. When he tries to welsh on the deal, Mr Death picks a little girl to die in his place, forcing him to keep his side of the bargain.
Cast: Ed Wynn, Murray Hamilton, Dana Dillaway, Jay Overholts, Merritt Bohn, Mickey Maga

Director: Robert Parrish

Mr Denton on Doomsday

w Rod Serling
A broken-down gunslinger finds a magic potion that restores his shooting skill, but brings an end to his fast-draw career.
Cast: Dan Duryea, Malcolm Atterbury, Martin Landau, Ken Lynch, Doug McClure, Jeanne Cooper, Arthur Batanides, Robert Burton

Director: Allen Reisner

The Sixteen-Millimeter Shrine

w Rod Serling
A forgotten star of the Thirties uses films of her old movies to re-create the spirit of her heyday.
Cast: Ida Lupino, Martin Balsam, Alice Frost, Ted de Corsia, John Clarke, Jerome Cowan

Director: Mitch Leisen

Walking Distance

w Rod Serling
A man's need to escape the pressure of his work is so great that he slips back 30 years into his own childhood.
Cast: Gig Young, Michael Montgomery, Byron Foulger, Joseph Corey, Frank Overton, Irene Tedrow, Buzz Martin

Director: Robert Stevens

Escape Clause

w Rod Serling
A man makes a pact with the devil for immortality then finds he doesn't get a kick out of living anymore.
Cast: David Wayne, Wendell Holmes, Raymond Bailey, Dick Wilson, Paul E. Burns, Allan Lurie, Virginia Christine, Thomas Gomez, Nesdon Booth, Joe Flynn, George Baxter

Director: Mitch Leisen

The Lonely

w Rod Serling
Convicted of murder and sent to a deserted asteroid for 40 years, a man is given a robot woman for company.
Cast: Jack Warden, John Dehner, Jim Turley, Jean Marsh, Ted Knight

Director: Jack Smight

Time Enough at Last

w Rod Serling, *from a story by* Lynn Venable
Near-sighted, meek bank clerk Henry Bemis is the sole survivor of an H-bomb attack. At last he has the time to engulf himself in his passion for books.
Cast: Burgess Meredith, Vaughn Taylor, Jacqueline de Wit, Lela Bliss

Director: John Brahm

Perchance to Dream

w Charles Beaumont
A terrified man stumbles into a psychia-

trist's office, afraid that if he falls asleep a woman in his dream will murder him.
Cast: Richard Conte, John Larch, Suzanne Lloyd, Eddie Marr, Ted Stanhope, Russell Trent

Director: Robert Florey

Judgement Night

w Rod Serling
A passenger on board a wartime freighter has a premonition that the ship will be sunk by a Nazi submarine at 1.15 am – but no one believes him.
Cast: Nehemiah Persoff, Patrick Macnee, Leslie Bradley, Kendrick Huxhum, Ben Wright, Hugh Sanders, Deirdre Owen, James Franciscus

Director: John Brahm

And When the Sky Was Opened

w Rod Serling, *from a short story by* Richard Matheson
Three astronauts, returning from man's first space flight, cannot remember the events of their trip. Then each disappears without trace.
Cast: Rod Taylor, James Hutton, Charles Aidman, Sue Randall, Gloria Pall, Maxine Cooper, Paul Bryar

Director: Douglas Heyes

What You Need

w Rod Serling, *from a story by* Lewis Padgett *(alias* Henry Kuttner *and* C.L. Moore)
A down-and-outer tries to turn another man's ability to tell the future into a money-making scheme.
Cast: Steve Cochran, Read Morgan, Arline Sax, Frank Alloca, Ernest Truex, William Edmonson, Norman Sturgis, Mark Sunday

Director: Alvin Ganzer

The Four of Us Are Dying

w Rod Serling, *from a story by* George Clayton Johnson
Arch Hammer can change his face to look exactly like someone else, a talent which he depends on for a living – but which could prove fatal.
Cast: Harry Townes *(Arch),* Philip Pine, Don Gordon, Bernard Fein, Beverly Garland, Ross Martin, Peter Brocco, Milton Frome

Director: John Brahm

Third from the Sun

w Rod Serling, *from a short story by* Richard Matheson
Two families steal a rocket ship and flee to another world before atomic war devastates their own. Their destination . . . Earth.
Cast: Fritz Weaver, Edward Andrews, Lori March, Will J. White, Joe Maross, Denise Alexander, Jeanne Evans

Director: Richard Bare

I Shot An Arrow Into the Air

w Rod Serling, *from an idea by* Madelon Champion
A panicky space traveller, believing his ship has crashed on a deserted asteroid, kills his two companions to save water, then discovers a highway and the sign 'Las Vegas – 15 miles'.
Cast: Dewey Martin, Edward Binns, Ted Otis

Director: Stuart Rosenberg

The Hitch-Hiker

w Rod Serling, *from a radio play by* Lucille Fletcher
Driving cross-country, a girl keeps seeing the same hitch-hiker on the road ahead, beckoning her towards a fatal accident.
Cast: Inger Stevens, Leonard Strong, Adam Williams, Dwight Townsend,

Mitzi McCall, Eleanor Audley, Lew Gallo, Russ Bender, George Mitchell

Director: Alvin Ganzer

The Fever

w Rod Serling
A man fanatically opposed to gambling battles a Las Vegas one-armed bandit with a malevolent will of its own.
Cast: Everett Sloane, William Kendis, Art Lewis, Carole Kent, Vivi Janiss, Lee Millar

Director: Robert Florey

The Last Flight

w Richard Matheson
Fleeing from a World War One dogfight, a cowardly British pilot lands his 1917 biplane at a modern jet air base in France . . . in 1959. There he learns that a fellow pilot he had moments before left to the mercy of German planes is now a high-ranking officer.
Cast: Kenneth Haigh, Alexander Scourby, Simon Scott, Robert Warwick, Harry Raybould

Director: William Claxton

The Purple Testament

w Rod Serling
A soldier unexpectedly acquires the power to recognise death in the faces of men about to die in battle.
Cast: William Reynolds, Dick York, Barney Phillips, Warren Oates, Ron Masak, William Phipps, Marc Cavell, Paul Mazursky

Director: Richard Bare

Elegy

w Charles Beaumont
Earth-like scenes from many historical periods greet three space travellers who land on a strange planet.

Cast: Cecil Kellaway, Kevin Hagen, Jeff Morrow, Don Dubbins

Director: Douglas Heyes

Mirror Image

w Rod Serling
A young woman grows panicky when she is haunted by a strange double who keeps appearing in a bus depot.
Cast: Vera Miles, Martin Milner, Joe Hamilton

Director: John Brahm

The Monsters Are Due on Maple Street

w Rod Serling
A mysterious power failure causes paranoid suburban residents to suspect one another of being disguised creatures from outer space.
Cast: Claude Akins, Jack Weston, Barry Atwater, Jan Handzlik, Burt Metcalfe, Mary Gregory, Anne Barton, Lea Waggner, Ben Erway, Lyn Guild, Sheldon Allman, William Walsh

Director: Ron Winston

A World of Difference

w Richard Matheson
A businessman inexplicably finds his office has become a set for a movie in which he is a character.
Cast: Howard Duff, Gail Kobe, Peter Walker, Eileen Ryan, Frank Maxwell

Director: Ted Post

Long Live Walter Jameson

w Charles Beaumont
A college professor is startled to learn that his young colleague and prospective son-in-law was born 2000 years ago with the gift of eternal life.
Cast: Kevin McCarthy *(Walter),* Edgar Stehli, Dody Heath, Estelle Winwood

Director: Anton Leader

People Are Alike All Over

w Rod Serling, *from a short story by*
  Paul Fairman
Sam Conrad, the first earthman to visit
Mars is relieved to find that Martians
resemble humans and treat him kindly,
even building him a house like his home
on Earth, until he realises he is an exhibit
in a Martian zoo.
Cast: Roddy McDowall *(Conrad),* Paul
Comi, Vic Perrin, Susan Oliver, Byron
Morrow, Vernon Gray

Director: Mitchell Leisen

Execution

w Rod Serling, *from a story by* George
  Clayton Johnson
An outlaw in the Wild West of the 1880s is
snatched from the hangman's noose by a
modern scientist's time machine.
Cast: Albert Salmi, Russell Johnson,
Than Wyenn, George Mitchell, Jon
Lormer, Fay Roope, Richard Karlan,
Joe Howarth

Director: David Orrick McDearmon

The Big Tall Wish

w Rod Serling
A 10-year-old boy tells a prize fighter that
he will make a wish for him to win his
comeback fight.
Cast: Steven Perry, Ivan Dixon, Kim
Hamilton

Director: Ron Winston

A Nice Place to Visit

w Charles Beaumont
A small-time hoodlum gets killed by the
police during a robbery and finds an
afterlife where anything he wants he can
have.
Cast: Larry Blyden, Sebastian Cabot,
Sandra Warner

Director: John Brahm

Nightmare as a Child

w Rod Serling
A schoolteacher's encounter with herself
as a child unlocks her memory of witnessing
her mother's murder.
Cast: Janice Rule, Terry Burnham,
Shepperd Strudwick

Director: Alvin Ganzer

A Stop at Willoughby

w Rod Serling
A harrassed executive escapes into the
peaceful town of Willoughby – July 1880.
Cast: James Daly, Howard Smith,
Patricia Donahue, James Maloney

Director: Robert Parrish

The Chaser

w Robert Presnell Jr, *from a short story
by* John Collier
A lovesick man buys a potion from a
stranger to help woo the woman he desires
– with unexpected results.
Cast: George Grizzard, John McIntire,
Patricia Barry, J. Pat O'Malley

Director: Doug Heyes

A Passage for Trumpet

w Rod Serling
A down-on-his-luck trumpet player is
given a second crack at life – after being
struck down by a truck.
Cast: Jack Klugman, Mary Webster,
John Anderson, Frank Wolff

Director: Don Medford

Mr Bevis

w Rod Serling
A happy-go-lucky man loses his job, his
car and his home in one morning then
meets his 'guardian angel' who tells him
they will start the day anew.

Cast: Orson Bean, Henry Jones, Charles Lane, William Schallert, Horace McMahon

Director: William Asher

The After Hours

w Rod Serling
A woman buys a gold thimble on the 9th floor of a department store, then later discovers that the floor doesn't exist and that the sales girl was really a mannequin.
Cast: Anne Francis, Elizabeth Allen, James Millhollin, John Conwell, Nancy Rennick

Director: Douglas Heyes

The Mighty Casey

w Rod Serling
The manager of a baseball team on a losing streak hires a robot pitcher called Casey.
Cast: Robert Sorrells, Jack Warden, Don O'Kelly, Abraham Sofaer

Directors: Robert Parrish *and* Alvin Ganzer

A World of His Own

w Richard Matheson
A playwright describes characters into his tape recorder and they materialise in front of his eyes.
Cast: Keenan Wynn, Phyllis Kirk, Mary La Roche

Director: Ralph Nelson

Season Two
29 30-minute episodes

King Nine Will Not Return

w Rod Serling
A downed bomber pilot crash lands in the desert. When he regains consciousness he cannot find any of his crew members.

Cast: Bob Cummings, Gene Lyons, Seymour Green, Richard Lupino, Paul Lambert, Jenna McMahon

Director: Buzz Kulik

The Man in the Bottle

w Rod Serling
An impoverished pawnbroker is granted four wishes by a genie in a bottle and inadvertently finds himself transformed into Hitler in the last days of the war.
Cast: Luther Adler, Joseph Ruskin, Vivi Janiss, Lisa Golm, Olan Soule, Peter Coe, Albert Szabo

Director: Don Medford

Nervous Man in a Four Dollar Room

w Rod Serling
A small-time hood assigned to kill an old man finds himself confronted by his conscience in the shape of his own living reflection.
Cast: Joe Mantell, William D. Gordon

Director: Douglas Heyes

A Thing About Machines

w Rod Serling
A bad-tempered writer is convinced the machines in his home are conspiring to destroy him.
Cast: Richard Haydn, Barbara Stuart, Barney Phillips

Director: David Orrick McDearmon

The Howling Man

w Charles Beaumont
Taking refuge in a European monastery run by a 'Truth' order, a man hears someone howling and is told it is the devil who is being held prisoner. But he doesn't believe it . . .
Cast: H.M. Wynant, John Carradine, Robin Hughes, Ezelle Poule

Director: Douglas Heyes

The Eye of the Beholder

w Rod Serling
In a future state, a beautiful girl longs to
be like her peers – ugly, pig-like
humanoids. (This episode was also billed
under the title 'The Private World of
Darkness.)
Cast: Joanna Hayes, Jennifer Howard,
William D. Gordon, Maxine Stuart,
Donna Douglas

Director: Douglas Heyes

Nick of Time

w Richard Matheson
A superstitious newly-wed husband finds
a penny fortune-telling machine that
makes uncannily accurate predictions
about his life.
Cast: William Shatner, Patricia Breslin

Director: Richard L. Bare

The Lateness of the Hour

w Rod Serling
A young woman, bored with the precise,
faultless routine of her family's life, persuades her father to dismantle their robot
servants.
Cast: Inger Stevens, John Hoyt, Irene
Tedrow, Mary Gregory

Director: Jack Smight

The Trouble with Templeton

w E. Jack Neuman
A distinguished, ageing actor who reflects
on the happier days of his youth gets a
sobering glimpse of the past.
Cast: Brian Aherne, Pippa Scott,
Charles S. Carlson, Sydney Pollack

Director: Buzz Kulik

A Most Unusual Camera

w Rod Serling
A pair of petty thieves find that a camera
they have just stolen can predict the future
by the pictures it takes.

Cast: Jean Carson, Fred Clark, Adam
Williams

Director: John Rich

Night of the Meek

w Rod Serling
Henry Corwin, a down-at-heel department store Santa, dispenses Christmas
cheer to a mission house with the help of a
sack that will produce whatever one asks
for.
Cast: Art Carney *(Corwin),* John Fiedler,
Meg Wylie, Robert Lieb

Director: Jack Smight

Dust

w Rod Serling
An unscrupulous travelling salesman sells
some 'magic dust' he claims will save a
man due to hang for killing a little girl
during a drunken spree.
Cast: Thomas Gomez, Vladimir
Sokoloff, John Alonso, John Larch

Director: Douglas Heyes

Back There

w Rod Serling
A man tries to prevent the assassination of
Abraham Lincoln when he finds himself
thrust back in time.
Cast: Russell Johnson, Paul Hartman,
Bartlett Robinson, John Lasell

Director: David Orrick McDearmon

The Whole Truth

w Rod Serling
The disreputable patter of a used-car
dealer changes when he buys a haunted
car from an old man and finds he is
suddenly unable to lie to his customers.
Cast: Jack Carson, Jack Ging, Arte
Johnson, Nan Peterson, George
Chandler, Loring Smith

Director: James Sheldon

The Invaders

w Richard Matheson
A lone woman battles two miniature spacemen whose craft crashes into her isolated farmhouse, finally destroying the tiny invaders who come from . . . Earth.
Cast: Agnes Moorehead

Director: Douglas Heyes

A Penny for Your Thoughts

w George Clayton Johnson
Timid bank clerk Victor Pool discovers that a coin that lands on its edge as he pays for a paper leaves him with the power to read minds.
Cast: Dick York (Pool), Dan Tobin, Hayden Rorke, June Dayton, Cyril Delevanti

Director: James Sheldon

Twenty-Two

w Rod Sterling, based on an anecdote in 'Famous Ghost Stories'
A young woman complains of a recurring nightmare in which she always ends up in Room 22 – the hospital morgue. Discharged from hospital she goes to catch a plane to Miami and finds she's on – Flight 22.
Cast: Barbara Nichols, Jonathan Harris, Fredd Wayne

Director: Jack Smight

The Odyssey of Flight 33

w Rod Serling
A commercial airliner, en route to New York, breaks through the time barrier into the prehistoric past.
Cast: John Anderson, Paul Comi, Sandy Kenyon, Harp McGuire, Wayne Heffley, Nancy Rennick, Beverly Brown, Jay Overholt, Betty Garde

Director: Justus Addiss

Mr Dingle, the Strong

w Rod Serling
A timid little man is experimentally endowed with superhuman strength by a visiting Martian scientist.
Cast: Burgess Meredith, Don Rickles, James Westerfield, Edward Ryder, James Millhollin

Director: John Brahm

Static

w Charles Beaumont, based on a story by O. Cee Ritch
An old radio picks up signals from the past that unexpectedly rejuvenate a pair of elderly lovers.
Cast: Dean Jagger, Carmen Mathews, Robert Emhardt

Director: Buzz Kulik

The Prime Mover

w Charles Beaumont, based on a story by George Clayton Johnson
Two men try to make their fortune at Las Vegas from the power one of them has to move inanimate objects.
Cast: Dane Clark, Buddy Ebsen, Christine White, Nesdon Booth, Jane Burgess

Director: Richard L. Bare

Long Distance Call

w Charles Beaumont and William Idelson
A young boy keeps in touch with his dead grandmother via the toy telephone she once gave him.
Cast: Bill Mumy, Philip Abbott, Patricia Smith, Lili Darvas

Director: James Sheldon

A Hundred Yards Over the Rim

w Rod Serling
A 19th-century Western settler, desperate

for medicine for his sick son, takes an inexplicable journey into the future where he obtains life-saving penicillin.
Cast: Cliff Robertson, Miranda Jones, John Crawford, Evan Evans

Director: Buzz Kulik

The Rip Van Winkle Caper

w Rod Serling
Four thieves plot to hide out with their loot for 100 years in a state of suspended animation.
Cast: Oscar Beregi, Simon Oakland, John Mitchum, Lew Gallo

Director: Justus Addiss

The Silence

w Rod Serling
A garrulous man, bet half a million dollars that he can't keep silent for one year, goes to bizarre lengths to win the wager.
Cast: Franchot Tone, Liam Sullivan, Jonathan Harris

Director: Boris Segal

Shadow Play

w Charles Beaumont
A condemned man tries to convince the people around him that everything – and everyone – are merely part of a recurring nightmare that always ends in his execution.
Cast: Dennis Weaver, Harry Townes, Wright King

Director: John Brahm

The Mind and the Matter

w Rod Serling
A book about thought gives a clerk the power to accomplish anything just by willing it, leaving him free to create an ideal world.
Cast: Shelley Berman, Jack Grinnage, Jeane Wood, Chet Stratton

Director: Buzz Kulik

Will the Real Martian Please Stand Up

w Rod Serling
Seven people at a diner claim to be authentic Earthmen – but one of them is really a Martian.
Cast: Morgan Jones, John Archer, Bill Kendis, John Hoyt, Jack Elam, Jean Wiles, Barney Phillips

Director: Montgomery Pittman

The Obsolete Man

w Rod Serling
A librarian in a future society is declared obsolete and told he must die.
Cast: Burgess Meredith, Fritz Weaver

Director: Elliot Silverstein

Season One
37 30-minute episodes

Two

w Montgomery Pittman
A man and a woman, sole survivors of a nuclear holocaust, try to overcome their distrust and start the world anew.
Cast: Charles Bronson, Elizabeth Montgomery

Director: Montgomery Pittman

The Arrival

w Rod Serling
An airline official tests his theory that a newly arrived but totally empty plane is imaginary – with startling results.
Cast: Harold J. Stone, Robert Karnes, Jim Boles, Fredd Wayne, Bing Russell, Noah Keen, Robert Brubaker

Director: Boris Segal

The Shelter

w Rod Serling
A group of neighbours turn into a hostile mob when they try to invade one family's

bomb shelter, believing a nuclear attack is imminent.

Cast: Larry Gates, Peggy Stewart, Michael Burns, Jack Albertson, John McLiam, Jo Helton, Joseph Bernard, Moria Turner, Sandy Kenyon, Mary Gregory

Director: Lamont Johnson

The Passersby

w Rod Serling
A crippled Civil War soldier comes to realise that he and the people around him are not walking away from battle – they are dead.
Cast: James Gregory, Joanne Linville, Austin Green, Rex Holman, David Garcia, Warren Kemmerling

Director: Elliot Silverstein

A Game of Pool

w George Clayton Johnson
A pool master returns from the dead to play one last game with an eager young hustler for the highest stakes of all – the young man's life.
Cast: Jack Klugman, Jonathan Winters

Director: A.E. Houghton

The Mirror

w Rod Serling
A victorious revolutionary is shown a mirror in the presidential office which is reputed to show the watcher his own assassins.
Cast: Peter Falk, Richard Karlan, Tony Carbone, Val Ruffino, Arthur Batanides, Rodolfo Hoyos, Will Kuluva, Vladimir Sokoloff

Director: Don Medford

The Grave

w Montgomery Pittman
A hired gunman defies a Western outlaw's warning that if he ever came near his grave he'd reach up and snatch away his life.
Cast: Lee Marvin, Strother Martin, Lee Van Cleef, Stafford Repp, Richard Geary, James Best, Ellen Willrad, William Challee, Larry Johns

Director: Montgomery Pittman

It's a Good Life

w Rod Serling, *based on a short story by* Jerome Bixby
A six-year-old boy holds a town in terror with his powers to change or destroy anyone or anything at will.
Cast: Billy Mumy, Cloris Leachman, Alice Frost, Jeanne Bates, Casey Adams, John Larch, Tom Hatcher, Don Keefer, Lenore Kingston

Director: James Sheldon

Deaths-Head Revisited

w Rod Serling
A former Nazi is tried and sentenced to insanity by a phantom jury of his tortured victims, when he revisits Dachau concentration camp.
Cast: Oscar Beregi, Joseph Schildkraut, Ben Wright, Karen Verne, Chuck Fox, Robert Boone

Director: Don Medford

The Midnight Sun

w Rod Serling
The earth has fallen out of its orbit and is drawing closer to the Sun – inflicting ever increasing heat on its citizens.
Cast: Lois Nettleton, Betty Garde, Jason Wingreen, Ned Glass, June Ellis, John McLiam, William Keene, Robert J. Stevenson, Tom Reese

Director: Anton Leader

Still Valley

w Rod Sterling, *based on a short story by* Manly Wade Wellman
A troop of Confederate soldiers decline to

use a magical book that could guarantee their victory, because it would mean making a pact with the devil.
Cast: Gary Merrill, Jack Mann, Addison Myers, Ben Cooper, Vaughn Taylor, Mark Tapscott

Director: James Sheldon

The Jungle

w Charles Beaumont
A prospector, threatened with death by a native conjuror for violating African land, feels himself stalked in the deserted streets of Manhattan by some giant jungle beast.
Cast: John Dehner, Emily McLaughlin, Walter Brooke, Jay Adler, Hugh Sanders, Howard Wright, Donald Foster, Jay Overholts

Director: William Claxton

Once Upon a Time

w Richard Matheson
Nineteenth-century janitor Woodrow Mulligan tries on a time 'helmet' invented by his boss and is catapulted 72 years into the future. (Featured two of comedian Buster Keaton's most memorable routines – the lock step and putting on a pair of trousers while walking.)
Cast: Buster Keaton *(Mulligan),* Gil Lamb, James Flavin, Milton Parsons, Stanley Adams, Warren Parker, George E. Stone

Directors: Norman Z. McLeod, *and* Les Goodwins *(uncredited)*

Five Characters in Search of an Exit

w Rod Sterling, *based on a short story by* Marvin Petal
Five people – a ballet dancer, a major, a clown, a tramp and a bagpipe player – trapped in a deep enclosure, are revealed to be dolls due to be distributed to orphans at Christmas.
Cast: Bill Windom, Susan Harrison, Clark Allen, Murray Matheson, Kelton Garwood, Mona Houghton, Carol Hill

Director: Lamont Johnson

A Qualty of Mercy

w Rod Serling, *based on an idea by* Sam Rolfe
A fanatical soldier sees the futility of his militaristic thinking when he mysteriously experiences the situation through the eyes of his Japanese counterpart.
Cast: Dean Stockwell, Albert Salmi, Rayford Barnes, Leonard Nimoy, Michael Pataki, Ralph Votrian, Dale Ishimoto, Jerry Fujikawa

Director: Buzz Kulik

Nothing in the Dark

w George Clayton Johnson
An aged recluse barricades herself in an abandoned building to avoid meeting 'Mr Death'.
Cast: Gladys Cooper, Robert Redford, R.G. Armstrong

Director: Lamont Johnson

One More Pallbearer

w Rod Serling
A wealthy man devises an elaborate hoax to force three people to apologise for humiliating him earlier in his life.
Cast: Joseph Wiseman, Gage Clark, Trevor Bardette, Katherine Squire, Josip Elic, Ray Galvin, Robert Snyder

Director: Lamont Johnson

Dead Man's Shoes

w Charles Beaumont *and* O. Cee Ritch *(uncredited)*
A down-and-out steals the fancy shoes from the body of a murdered gangster and finds himself living in the dead man's footsteps.
Cast: Warren Stevens, Ben Wright, Harry Swoger, Joan Marshall, Eugene Borden, Richard Devon, Florence Marly, Ron Hagerthy, Joe Mell

Director: Montgomery Pittman

The Hunt

w Earl Hamner Jr
A hunter and his faithful dog are drowned while chasing a raccoon, and confront a gatekeeper who implies that he is St Peter and that Heaven lies inside. But when the dog declines to enter, the hunter wisely decides to stay with his trusty companion.
Cast: Arthur Hunnicutt, Titus Moede, Charles Seel, Dexter Dupont, Jeanette Nolan, Orville Sherman, Robert Foulk

Director: Harold Schuster

Showdown with Rance McGrew

w Rod Serling, based on an idea by
    Frederic Louis Fox
The ghost of Jesse James takes revenge on an insufferable cowboy star for his shabby film treatment of all the bad guys.
Cast: Larry Blyden, Troy Melton, Robert J. Stevenson, Arch Johnson (Jesse), Hal K. Dawson, Willam McLean, Jay Overholts, Robert Cornthwaite, Robert Kline

Director: Christian Nyby

Kick the Can

w George Clayton Johnson
The magic of a children's game enables a group of old people to recapture their youth.
Cast: Ernest Truex, Hank Patterson, Russell Collins, Earle Hodgins, Burt Mustin, Gregory McCabe, Marjorie Bennett, Lenore Shanewise, Anne O'Neal, John Marley, Barry Truex, Eve McVeagh, Marc Stevens

Director: Lamont Johnson

A Piano in the House

w Earl Hamner Jr
A strange piano allows the listener's hidden character to be suddenly revealed.
Cast: Barry Morse, Joan Hackett, Muriel Landers, Don Durant, Phil Coolidge, Cyril Delevanti

Director: David Greene

The Last Rites of Jeff Myrtlebank

w Montgomery Pittman
When a young man steps out of his coffin at his own funeral the townsfolk grow to suspect that the devil has assumed the man's body.
Cast: James Best, Ralph Moody, Ezelle Poule, Vickie Barnes, Sherry Jackson, Helen Wallace, Lance Fuller, Bill Fawcett, Edgar Buchanan, Mabel Forrest, Dub Taylor, Jon Lormer, Pat Hector

Director: Montgomery Pittman

To Serve Man

w Rod Serling, based on a short story by
    Damon Knight
Apparently benign alien emissaries show mankind how to end the misery of war, plague and famine. But the aliens' master manual for Earth turns out to be a cookbook.
Cast: Richard Kiel, Hardie Albright, Robert Tafur, Lloyd Bochner, Lomax Study, Theodore Marcuse, Susan Cummings, Nelson Olmstead

Director: Richard L. Bare

The Fugitive

w Charles Beaumont
A magical old man whose power to change his appearance delights the local children is really the revered king of another planet.
Cast: J. Pat O'Malley, Nancy Kulp, Susan Gordon, Russ Bender, Wesley Lau, Paul Tripp, Stephen Talbot, Johnny Eiman

Director: Richard L. Bare

Little Girl Lost

w Richard Matheson
A couple are awakened in the middle of the night by the cries of their six-year-old daughter who has fallen through a mysterious opening into another dimension.

Cast: **Sarah Marshall, Robert Sampson, Tracy Stratford, Charles Aidman**

Director: **Paul Stewart**

Person or Persons Unknown

w Charles Beaumont
A man awakens one morning to find that no one recognises him – not even his mother!
Cast: **Richard Long, Frank Silvera, Shirley Ballard, Julie Van Zandt, Betty Harford, Ed Glover, Michael Kelp, Joe Higgins, John Newton**

Director: **John Brahm**

The Little People

w Rod Serling
A space traveller terrorises the tiny inhabitants of a space station into accepting him as their God, but when another space ship arrives the tyrannical man discovers everything is relative . . .
Cast: **Joe Maross, Claude Akins, Michael Ford, Robert Eaton**

Director: **William Claxton**

Four O'Clock

w Rod Serling, *based on a short story by* Price Day
To combat all that he considers evil, a cranky man decides to make every evil person two feet tall at exactly 4 pm.
Cast: **Theodore Bikel, Linden Chiles, Moyna MacGill, Phyllis Love**

Director: **Lamont Johnson**

Hocus Pocus and Frisby

w Rod Serling, *based on a story by* Frederic Louis Fox
A celebrated yarn-spinner finds no one will believe his latest tale – that he was kidnapped by aliens.

Cast: **Andy Devine, Howard McNear, Clem Bevans, Milton Selzer, Dabbs Greer, Larry Breitman, Peter Brocco**

Director: **Lamont Johnson**

The Trade-Ins

w Rod Serling
Unable to afford a personality transplant for both himself and his wife, a pain-wracked old man has his mind placed in a new youthful body only to find he cannot face life without the companionship of his beloved wife.
Cast: **Joseph Schildkraut, Alma Platt, Noah Keen, Theodore Marcuse, Terrence de Marney, Billy Vincent, Mary McMahon, David Armstrong, Edson Stroll**

Director: **Elliot Silverstein**

The Gift

w Rod Serling
A crashed space traveller is hounded to death by mistrustful villagers who discover, too late, that the gift he bore was a formula to cure all types of cancer.
Cast: **Geoffrey Horne, Nico Minardos, Cliff Osmond, Edmund Vargas, Carmen D'Antonio, Paul Mazursky, Vladimir Sokoloff, Vito Scotti, Henry Corden**

Director: **Allen H. Miner**

The Dummy

w Rod Serling, *based on a story by* Lee Polk
A ventriloquist becomes convinced that his dummy has a will and a life of its own.
Cast: **Cliff Robertson, Frank Sutton, George Murdock, Bethelynn Grey, John Harmon, Sandra Warner, Rudy Dolan, Ralph Manza**

Director: **Abner Biberman**

Young Man's Fancy

w Richard Matheson
A man's intense longing for the happy

days of his boyhood succeeds in actually making the past reappear – to the chagrin of his new bride.
Cast: Alex Nicol, Phyllis Thaxter, Wallace Rooney, Rickey Kelman, Helen Brown

Director: John Brahm

I Sing the Body Electric

w Ray Bradbury
A widowed father buys his three young children an electronic grandmother to the delight of all but one of them – until she comes to realise that electric Grandmas have feelings, too.
Cast: Josephine Hutchinson, David White, June Vincent, Vaughn Taylor, Judy Morton, Dana Dillaway, Paul Nesbitt, Charles Herbert, Veronica Cartwright, Susan Crane

Director: James Sheldon *and* William Claxton

Cavender is Coming

w Rod Serling
A hapless apprentice angel is given one last chance to win his wings – by helping awkward, inept Agnes Grep. (Pilot for an un-made series – with laughter track.)
Cast: Carol Burnett *(Agnes),* Jesse White, Howard Smith, William O'Connell, Pitt Herbert, John Fiedler, G. Stanley Jones, Frank Behrens, Albert Carrier, Roy Sickner, Norma Shattuc, Rory O'Brien, Sandra Gould, Adrieene Marden, Jack Younger, Danny Kulick, Donna Douglas, Maurice Dallimore, Barbara Morrison

Director: Chris Nyby

The Changing of the Guard

w Rod Serling
A well-loved teacher feels his useful life is over when he is asked to retire.
Cast: Donald Pleasance, Liam Sullivan, Philippa Bevans, Kevin O'Neal, Jimmy Baird, Kevin Jones, Bob Biheller, Tom

Lowell, Russell Horton, Buddy Hart, Darryl Richard, James Browning, Pat Close, Dennis Kerlee

Director: Robert Ellis Miller

Season Four
18 one-hour episodes

Series now became known simply as *Twilight Zone.*

In His Image

w Charles Beaumont
A scientific genius creates an almost-perfect mechanical man, combining all the qualities he feels are missing in his own imperfect, human self.
Cast: George Grizzard, Gail Kobe, Katherine Squire, Wallace Rooney, George Petrie, James Seay, Jamie Forster, Sherry Granato

Director: Perry Lafferty

The Thirty-Fathom Grave

w Rod Serling
Sounds heard from a submarine sunk 20 years before cause the death of the man who believes himself responsible for the sinking.
Cast: Mike Kellin, Simon Oakland, David Sheiner, John Considine, Bill Bixby, Conlan Carter, Forrest Compton

Director: Perry Lafferty

Valley of the Shadow

w Charles Beaumont
A reporter comes upon a peaceful village which guards the secret of creating and obliterating matter. Once he learns the secret, it takes another miracle to release him from the responsibility of the knowledge.
Cast: David Opatoshu, Ed Nelson, Natalie Trundy, Jacques Aubuchon, Dabbs Greer, Suzanne Cupito, James Doohan

Director: Perry Lafferty

He's Alive

w Rod Serling

The ghost of Adolf Hitler inspires a young American hate-monger to achieve a short-lived success.

Cast: Dennis Hopper, Ludwig Donath, Paul Mazursky, Howard Cain, Barnaby Hale, Curt Conway, Jay Adler, Wolfe Barzell, Bernard Fein

Director: Stuart Rosenberg

Mute

w Richard Matheson

Experimenting with the powers of telepathy, a couple raise their daughter in a world free of verbal communication. But when they die she faces a world with which she cannot communicate.

Cast: Barbara Baxley, Frank Overton, Irene Dailey, Ann Jillian, Eva Soreny, Oscar Beregi, Claudia Bryar, Percy Helton

Director: Stuart Rosenberg

Death Ship

w Richard Matheson

A man's refusal to admit to his own death keeps him and his two companions alive in a world that has accepted their passing.

Cast: Jack Klugman, Ross Martin, Frederick Beir, Mary Webster, Ross Elliot, Sara Taft

Director: Don Medford

Jess-Belle

w Earl Hamner Jr

A girl strikes a deadly bargain with a witch to assure herself the attention of a young man.

Cast: Anne Francis, James Best, Laura Devon, Jeanette Nolan, Virginia Gregg, George Mitchell, Helen Kleeb, Jim Boles, Jon Lormer

Director: Buzz Kulik

Miniature

w Charles Beaumont

Charley Parkes, a shy bachelor, falls in love with a tiny, beautiful museum doll whom he believes is alive. (Parts of this episode have since been 'colourised'.)

Cast: Robert Duvall *(Parkes)*, Pert Kelton, Barbara Barrie, Len Weinrib, William Windom, John McLiam, Claire Griswold, Nina Roman, Richard Angarola, Barney Phillips, Joan Chambers, Chet Stratlon

Director: Walter E. Grauman

Printer's Devil

w Charles Beaumont

A newspaper editor who is facing bankruptcy hires the Devil as his chief reporter.

Cast: Robert Sterling, Patricia Crowley, Burgess Meredith, Ray Teal, Charles Thompson, Doris Kemper, Camille Franklin

Director: Ralph Senensky

No Time Like the Past

w Rod Serling

A time traveller attempts to alter history by vainly trying to warn the people of Hiroshima, assassinate Hitler, and persuade the captain of the *Lusitania* to change course.

Cast: Dana Andrews, Patricia Breslin, Malcolm Atterbury, Robert Cornthwaite, John Zaremba, Robert F. Simon, Lindsay Workman, Marjorie Bennett, Tudor Owen, James Yagi

Director: Justus Addis

The Parallel

w Rod Serling

An orbiting astronaut passes into a strange parallel world.

Cast: Steve Forrest, Jacqueline Scott, Frank Aletter, Philip Abbott, Shari Lee Bernath, Paul Comi, Morgan Jones, William Sargent

Director: Alan Crosland

I Dream of Genie

w John Furia Jr
A mild-mannered clerk finds Aladdin's lamp but decides that using his one wish for wealth, power or the girl of his dreams would be a waste of the lamp's power.
Cast: Howard Morris, Patricia Barry, Loring Smith, Mark Miller, Jack Albertson, Joyce Jameson, James Milhollin, Bob Hastings, Robert Ball

Director: Robert Gist

The New Exhibit

w Charles Beaumont (and Jerry Sohl – uncredited)
Discarded by a wax museum, the effigies of famous murderers kill people who would part them from their custodian, and when the custodian spurns them they murder him as well.
Cast: Martin Balsam, Will Kuluva, Maggie Mahoney, William Mims, Milton Parsons

Director: John Brahm

Of Late I Think of Cliffordville

w Rod Serling, based on a short story by Malcolm Jameson
A ruthless captain of industry strikes a deal with the Devil and goes back in time to the life he remembers as a young man.
Cast: Albert Salmi, John Anderson, Julie Newmar, Wright King, Guy Raymond, Christine Burke

Director: David Rich

The Incredible World of Horace Ford

w Reginald Rose
A toy manufacturer recalls his youth with such longing that he becomes a boy again.
Cast: Pat Hingle, Nan Martin, Ruth White, Phillip Pine, Vaughn Taylor, Mary Carver

Director: Abner Biberman

On Thursday We Leave for Home

w Rod Serling
The leader of an expedition to a remote asteroid cannot bring himself to face the dissipation of his authority that returning to Earth would bring.
Cast: James Whitmore, Tim O'Connor, James Broderick, Paul Langton, Jo Helton, Mercedes Shirley, Russ Bender

Director: Buzz Kulik

Passage on the Lady Anne

w Charles Beaumont
An unhappily married old couple find love when they sail the Atlantic aboard an old ship originally designed for honeymooners.
Cast: Gladys Cooper, Wilfrid Hyde-White, Cecil Kellaway, Lee Philips, Joyce Van Patten

Director: Lamont Johnson

The Bard

w Rod Serling
A hack TV writer conjures up William Shakespeare to act as his collaborator but his network bosses throw out the end script.
Cast: Jack Weston, John McGiver, Diro Merande, John Williams, Burt Reynolds, Henry Lascoe, William Lanteau, Howard McNear, Marge Redmond, Clegg Hoyt, Judy Strangis

Director: David Butler

Season Five
36 half-hour episodes

In Praise of Pip

w Rod Serling
Bookie Max Phillips learn that his son Pip has been critically wounded in Vietnam. Remorseful over the way he raised him, Max pleads with God to take his life in place of his son's.
Cast: Jack Klugman (Max) Billy Mumy (young Pip), Kreg Martin, Ross Elliott,

Stuart Nisbet, Russell Horton, Connie Gilchrist, Bob Diamond, John Launer, Gerald Gordon

Director: Joseph M. Newman

Steel

w Richard Matheson
A small-time promoter, desperate for his purse from a robot prize fight, takes the place of his robot when it gets damaged.
Cast: Lee Marvin, Joe Mantell, Merritt Bohn, Frank London, Tipp McClure, Chuck Hicks, Larry Barton

Director: Don Weis

Nightmare at 20,000 Feet

w Richard Matheson
A newly released mental patient is the only one able to see a gremlin ripping up the wing of his airliner.
Cast: William Shatner, Edward Kemmer, Christine White, Asa Maynor, Nick Cravat

Director: Richard Donner

A Kind of Stopwatch

w Rod Serling, based on a story by Michael D. Rosenthal
A talkative man acquires a stop watch with the power to halt all other action in the world.
Cast: Richard Erdman, Leon Belasco, Herbie Faye, Roy Roberts, Doris Singleton, Richard Wessel, Ken Drake, Ray Kellogg, Sam Balter

Director: John Rich

The Last Night of a Jockey

w Rod Serling
A down-and-out jockey yearns to be a giant of a man so that everyone would look up at him.
Cast: Mickey Rooney

Director: Joseph M. Newman

Living Doll

w Charles Beaumont and Jerry Sohl (uncredited)
A man is threatened with revenge by the expensive talking doll he is planning to dispose of.
Cast: Telly Savalas, Tracy Stratford, Mary LaRoche

Director: Richard C. Sarafian

The Old Man in the Cave

w Rod Serling, based on a short story by Henry Slesar
A small community has survived the aftermath of a nuclear holocaust by accepting the advice of The Old Man in the Cave.
Cast: James Coburn, John Anderson, Josie Lloyd, John Craven, Natalie Masters, John Marley, Frank Watkins, Don Wilbanks, Lenny Geer

Director: Alan Crosland Jr

Uncle Simon

w Rod Serling
A woman learns that she has inherited the estate of the uncle she left to die provided she looks after his latest invention – a robot that mysteriously takes on the nature of her dead uncle.
Cast: Sir Cedric Hardwicke, Constance Ford, John McLiam, Ian Wolfe

Director: Don Siegel

Night Call

w Richard Matheson
A bedridden spinster receives mysterious phone calls from her long-dead fiancé.
Cast: Gladys Cooper, Nora Marlowe, Martine Bartlett

Director: Jacques Tourneau

Probe 7 – Over and Out

w Rod Serling
The lone survivors of two devastated

planets meet on a new world, Earth, and introduce themselves – as *Adam* Cook and *Eve* Norda.
Cast: Richard Basehart, Antoinette Bower, Barton Heyman, Harold Gould

Director: Ted Post

The 7th Is Made Up of Phantoms

w Rod Serling
During manoeuvres near the site of Custer's Last Stand, three national guardsmen find themselves plunged into the battle of the Little Big Horn.
Cast: Ron Foster, Warren Oates, Randy Boone, Robert Bray, Wayne Mallory, Greg Morris, Jeffrey Morris, Jacque Shelton, Lew Brown

Director: Alan Crosland Jr

A Short Drink From a Certain Fountain

w Rod Serling, *based on an idea by* Lou Holtz
A wealthy man begs his doctor-brother to inject him with an experimental youth serum – but ends up regressing into an infant.
Cast: Patrick O'Neal, Ruta Lee, Walter Brooks

Director: Bernard Girard

Ninety Years Without Slumbering

w Richard DeRoy, *based on a story by* George Clayton Johnson
An old man believes that his life will end the moment his grandfather clock stops ticking.
Cast: Ed Wynn, Carolyn Kearney, James Callahan, William Sargent, Carol Byron, John Pickard, Dick Wilson, Chuck Hicks

Director: Roger Kay

Ring-a-Ding Girl

w Earl Hamner Jr
A movie star receives a gift from her home-town fan club that shows her images of the future.
Cast: Maggie McNamara, Mary Munday, David Macklin, George Mitchell, Bing Russell, Betty Lou Gerson, Hank Patterson, Bill Hickman, Vic Perrin

Director: Alan Crosland Jr

You Drive

w Earl Hamner Jr
A motorist's car won't let him forget his guilt over killing a young cyclist and fleeing from the scene.
Cast: Edward Andrews, Hellena Westcott, Kevin Hagen, Totty Ames, John Hanek

Director: John Brahm

The Long Morrow

w Rod Serling
A deep-space probe astronaut smashes the suspended animation device that will keep him young, so that he can age at the same rate as the woman he loves.
Cast: Robert Lansing, Mariette Hartley, George MacReady, Edward Binns, William Swan

Director: Robert Florey

The Self-Improvement of Salvadore Ross

w Jerry McNeeley, *from a short story by* Henry Slesar
A man finds he has the power to trade character traits, infirmities, even his life-span, with others.
Cast: Don Gordon, Gail Kobe, Vaughn Taylor, Douglas Dumbrille, Doug Lambert, J. Pat O'Malley, Ted Jacques, Kathleen O'Maley, Seymour Cassel

Director: Don Siegel

Number Twelve Looks Just Like You

w Charles Beaumont *and* John Tomerlin *(uncredited)*

A young woman resists pressure to be transformed into a state-controlled image of flawless beauty.
Cast: Suzy Parker, Collin Wilcox, Richard Long, Pam Austin

Director: Abner Biberman

Black Leather Jackets

w Earl Hamner Jr
An advance party of an alien invasion force arrive in a quiet residential neighbourhood disguised as leather-jacketed youths.
Cast: Lee Kinsolving, Shelly Fabares, Michael Forest, Wayne Heffley, Tom Gilleran, Denver Pyle, Irene Hervey, Michael Conrad

Director: Joseph Newman

From Agnes – With Love

w Bernard C. Shoenfeld
A computer programmer grows to realise that under the stainless steel exterior of the world's most advanced computer is the complex soul of a jealous woman who has fallen in love with him.
Cast: Wally Cox, Ralph Taeger, Sue Randall, Raymond Bailey, Don Keefer, Byron Kane, Nan Peterson

Director: Richard Donner

Spur of the Moment

w Richard Matheson
A young woman out riding fails to understand the significance of an encounter with her future, older self – until it is too late.
Cast: Diana Hyland, Marsha Hunt, Philip Ober, Roger Davis, Robert Hogan, Jack Raine

Director: Elliot Silverstein

An Occurrence at Owl Creek Bridge

w Robert Enrico, *from a short story by* Ambrose Bierce
A confederate spy is to hang in the civil war but appears to make a miraculous escape. (This was an award-winning French film recut for the series.)
Cast: Roger Jacquet, Anne Cornaly

Director: Robert Enrico

Queen of the Nile

w Charles Beaumont *and* Jerry Sohl
   (uncredited)
A magazine writer is determined to discover the secret of an ageless movie star's everlasting youth.
Cast: Ann Blyth, Lee Philips, James Tyler, Celia Lovsky, Ruth Phillips, Frank Ferguson

Director: John Brahm

What's in the Box

w Martin M. Goldsmith
A cab driver turns on the television and sees a portent of his wife's death after an argument. When he tries to tell his wife she won't listen and an argument starts . . .
Cast: Joan Blondell, William Demarest, Sterling Holloway, Herbert Lytton, Howard Wright, Ron Stokes, John L. Sullivan, Sandra Gould, Ted Christy, Douglas Bank, Tony Miller

Director: Richard L. Baer

The Masks

w Rod Serling
A wealthy old man compels his hateful family to wear masks they think are the opposite of their personalities. When they remove the masks a frightening change has taken place.
Cast: Robert Keith, Milton Selzer, Brooke Hayward, Virginia Gregg, Alan Sues, Bill Walker, Willis Bouchey

Director: Ida Lupino

I Am the Night – Color Me Black

w Rod Serling
The sun fails to rise on the morning that a

town's 'idealist' is due to be executed for killing one of his bigoted neighbours, and the community finds itself locked in the darkness of hate.
Cast: Michael Constantine, Paul Fix, George Lindsey, Terry Becker, Douglas Bank, Ward Wood, Eve McVeagh, Elizabeth Harrower, Ivan Dixon

Director: Abner Biberman

Sounds and Silences

w Rod Serling
A man who has lived his life joyously surrounded by loud noise suddenly finds that trivial sounds, such as dripping water, begin to drive him insane.
Cast: John McGiver, Penny Singleton, Michael Fox, Francis Defales, Renee Aubrey, William Benedict

Director: Richard Donner

Caesar and Me

w A.T. Strassfield
An impoverished ventriloquist accedes to his dummy's demands that he turn to crime to make some money.
Cast: Jackie Cooper, Susanne Cupito, Stafford Repp, Olan Soule, Sarah Selby, Don Gazzaniga, Sidney Marion, Ken Konopka

Director: Robert Butler

The Jeopardy Room

w Rod Serling
A KGB agent sent to kill a Russian defector plants a bomb in the man's hotel room and gives him three hours to find and disarm it and so win his freedom, or fail and die.
Cast: Martin Landau, John van Dreelen, Robert Kelljan

Director: Richard Donner

Stopover in a Quiet Town

w Earl Hamner, Jr
A young married couple awake to find

themselves in an unfamiliar artificial environment. As a giant hand starts reaching for them out of the sky, they hear the sound of a child's laughter.
Cast: Barry Nelson, Karen Norris, Nancy Malone, Denise Lyon

Director: Ron Winston

The Encounter

w Martin M. Goldsmith
A Japanese gardener finds that a samurai sword has vowed to avenge the murder of its master.
Cast: Neville Brand, George Takei

Director: Robert Butler

Mr Garrity and the Graves

w Rod Serling, *based on a story by* Mila Korologos
A con-man convinces the inhabitants of a Western town that he can raise the dead from the local cemetery.
Cast: John Dehner, Stanley Adams, J. Pat O'Malley, Norman Leavitt, Percy Helton, John Mitchum, Patrick O'Moore, Kate Murtagh, John Cliff

Director: Ted Post

The Brain Centre at Whipple's

w Rod Serling
A heartless industrialist sacks his entire factory staff and replaces them with machines. Then the machines start acting mischievously.
Cast: Richard Deacon, Paul Newlan, Shawn Michaels, Ted de Corsia, Burt Conroy, Jack Crowder

Director: Richard Donner

Come Wander With Me

w Anton Wilson
A bogus folk singer persuades a backwoods girl to sing an authentic ballad into

his tape recorder – and finds the song coming tragically true.
Cast: Gary Crosby, Bonnie Beecher, John Bolt, Hank Patterson

Director: Richard Donner

The Fear

w Rod Serling
A state trooper and an unstable woman both think they have found traces of a giant visitor from outer space.
Cast: Mark Richman, Hazel Court

Director: Ted Post

The Bewitchin' Pool

w Earl Hamner Jr
Two unloved children escape from their squabbling parents to a world which offers them a chance of happiness with a strange, kindly woman.
Cast: Mary Badham, Tim Stafford, Kim Hector, Tod Andrews, Dee Hartford, Georgia Simmons, Harold Gould

Director: Joseph Newman

UK Season A: 12 episodes
27 January–20 April 1963
(ITV, Border)

The Monsters Are Due on Maple Street
The Hitchhiker
Third from the Sun
Walking Distance
The Fever
What You Need
The Lonely
Escape Clause
A World of Difference
Elegy
Passage for Trumpet
The Purple Testament

UK Season B: 14 episodes
12 May–30 June 1964
(ITV, London)
(Double bills, each pair linked by a common theme)

Walking Distance
A Stop at Willoughby

I Shot An Arrow Into the Air
When the Sky Was Opened
Time Enough at Last
Eye of the Beholder
Third from the Sun
People Are Alike All Over
A Hundred Yards Over the Rim
The Trouble with Templeton
The Monsters Are Due on Maple Street
The Invaders
The Odyssey of Flight 33
The Arrival

UK Season C: 39 episodes
10 September 1983–20 January 1985
(BBC2)
This run consisted of the entire US first season, plus the first three of Season Two.

UK Season D: 50 episodes
5 January 1986–5 July 1987
(Channel 4)
Mix of double bills and single stories.

A Thing About Machines/
Mr Dingle, the Strong

The Odyssey of Flight 33/
The Howling Man

Nightmare at 20,000 Feet

A Young Man's Fancy/Living Doll

Night Call/Probe 71 – Over and Out

A Short Drink from a Certain Fountain
A Kind of Stopwatch
The 7th is Made Up of Phantoms
Black Leather Jackets
Hocus Pocus and Frisby
The Trade-Ins
Four O'Clock
The Little People
The Old Man in the Cave
The Long Morrow

Little Girl Lost/You Drive

Cavender is Coming/Kick the Can

Dead Man's Shoes/
Nothing in the Dark

Five Characters in Search of an Exit/
A Hundred Yards Over the Rim

The Fugitive/One More Pallbearer

Still Valley/Steel

The Arrival/Two

Number 12 Looks Just Like You
Will the Real Martian Please Stand Up
A Game of Pool

The Lateness of the Hour/The Mirror

It's a Good Life
The Eye of the Beholder
The Jungle
In Praise of Pip
The Gift
Night of the Meek
The Hunt

The Last Night of a Jockey/
The Rip Van Winkle Caper

The Silence

Ring-a-Ding Girl/Shadow Play

UK Season E: 25 episodes
28 July 1989–early 1990
(Channel 4)
Previously unscreened episodes were:
The Obsolete Man
A Quality of Mercy
I Sing the Body Electric
Spur of the Moment
Stopover in a Quiet Town
I Am the Night Color Me Black
The Jeopardy Room
Come Wander With Me
Queen of the Nile
What's in the Box
The Bewitchin' Pool

THE TWILIGHT ZONE (1985–86)

What's in a name? Everything, as far as this 1980s revival of a television icon is concerned.

It's not been a runaway commercial success and has never achieved the heights of critical acclaim reached by Rod Serling's original, but while it lacks his cohesive presence it's not at all bad. Some stories are excellent and most are a sight more entertaining than much of today's primetime TV.

Many of the industry's top names have brought their talents to bear – casts have included Bruce Willis, Danny Kaye, Elliot Gould, Tom Skerritt, Ralph Bellamy, Richard Mulligan, Martin Landau and H. Emmet Walsh, while Joe Dante, John Milius and William Friedkin are among the directors.

Besides many original scripts, the series culled short stories from leading sf writers as well as indulging in a few remakes of tales from the old Zone.

The first package was duly bought for Britain by ITV and has since circulated round the regions like a game of pass the parcel, with different episodes unwrapped and screened, each to his own, almost at random. The advent of 24-hour TV inevitably made more room in the companies' schedules and *The Twilight Zone* has been an uncomplaining lodger.

The revived *Twilight Zone* is still in production in America. For now, the first 80 segments first bought by ITV are listed here in the original episode packaging. Hopefully, sooner or later, they'll all get round to your area.

Creator: Rod Serling
Executive producer: Philip DeGuere
Supervising producer: James Crocker
Producer: Harvey Frand
Executive story consultant: Alan Brennert
Story editor: Rockne S. O'Bannon
Creative consultant: Harlan Ellison
Special effects coordinator: M. Kam Cooney

New main title theme: Grateful Dead and Merl Saunders

CBS Broadcast International Production
Series One (US): 24 60-minute colour episodes
Series Two: 19 30-minute colour episodes

UK premiere:
17 October 1987 (STV)

Season One
(one-hour episodes)

1a: Shatterday

w Alan Brennert, *based on a short story by* Harlan Ellison
Jay Novins absent-mindedly dials his home number from a bar and is jolted when the phone is picked up by . . . Jay Novins.
Cast: Bruce Willis

Director: Wes Craven

1b: A Little Peace and Quiet

w James Crocker
A harried wife and mother yearns for silence – a wish that comes horrifyingly true when she chances upon a way to 'freeze' time and motion.
Cast: Melinda Dillon

Director: Wes Craven

2a: Word Play

w Rockne S. O'Bannon
An overburdened salesman thinks he's losing his sanity when everyone's speech gradually becomes gibberish to him.
Cast: Robert Klein, Annie Potts

Director: Wes Craven

2b: Dreams for Sale

w Joe Gannon
A young woman goes on a picnic with her husband and twin daughters, where everything is so nearly perfect it seems too good to be true.
Cast: Meg Foster, David Hayward

Director: Tommy Lee Wallace

2c: Chameleon

w James Crocker
A space shuttle returns from a mission with something on board that wasn't there when it was launched.
Cast: John Ashton, Ben Piazza, Terrence O'Quinn

Director: Wes Craven

3a: Healer

w Alan Brennert
A young drifter becomes an overnight sensation as a hands-on healer after he steals an ancient Mayan stone that holds magic powers.
Cast: Eric Bogosian, Vincent Gardenia

Director: Sig Neufeld

3b: Children's Zoo

w Chris Hubbell, Gerrit Graham
A withdrawn little girl, caught between combative parents, receives an invitation to a most unusual zoo.
Cast: Steven Keats, Lorna Luft

Director: Robert Downey

3c: Kentucky Rye

w Richard Krzemien, Chip Duncan
A salesman with a drink problem who takes refuge in a bar after getting involved in a car crash is offered the deal of a lifetime.
Cast: Jeffrey Demunn

Director: John Hancock

4a: Little Boy Lost

w Lynn Barker
A professional photographer on the verge of a major career move finds she has been taking pictures of her own alternative future.
Cast: Season Hubley, Nicholas Surovy

Director: Tommy Lee Wallace

4b: Wish Bank

w Michael Cassut
A bargain hunter finds an Aladdin's lamp at a jumble sale, rubs it and is amazed to discover she will be granted three wishes. However, certain restrictions apply . . .
Cast: Dee Wallace

Director: Rick Friedberg

4c: Night Crawlers

w Philip DeGuere
A Vietnam veteran haunted by his memories of war is terrified of falling asleep in case his nightmares come true.
Cast: Scott Paulin

Director: William Friedkin

5a: If She Dies

w David Bennet Carren
A distraught father whose young daughter lies in a coma is drawn to a strange apparition in an abandoned orphanage.
Cast: Tony Lo Bianco

Director: John Hancock

5b: Ye Gods

w Anne Collins
An up-and-coming executive suffering the pangs of unrequited love discovers that Cupid and the other gods of Olympus are alive – but with hang-ups of their own.
Cast: David Dukes, Robert Morse

Director: Peter Medak

6a: Examination Day

w Philip DeGuere, *based on a short story by* Henry Slesar
Tale set in the future. A 12-year-old boy's birthday wish, to get a good mark in a government exam, makes his parents uneasy.
Cast: Christopher Allport, Elizabeth Normant, David Mendenhall

Director: Paul Lynch

6b: A Message From Charity

w Alan Brennert, *based on a short story by* William M. Lee
Peter, a boy living in present day Massachusetts, makes telepathic contact with Charity, a Puritan girl from the past, and each experiences the world through the other's eyes.
Cast: Robert Duncan McNeil, Kerry Noonan

Director: Paul Lynch

7a: Teacher's Aide

w Steven Barnes
An English teacher at a school terrorised

by a teenage gang falls under the spell of a gargoyle-like demon.
Cast: Adrienne Barbeau

Director: Bill Norton

7b: Paladin of the Lost Hour

w Harlan Ellison
An old man who holds the last hour of the world in a magical timepiece finds an unlikely keeper to assume the awesome responsibility.
Cast: Danny Kaye, Glynn Turman

Director: Gilbert Cates

8a: Act Break

w Haskell Barkin
A mediocre playwright, given a magic amulet by his dying partner, makes the one wish that will grant him dramatic immortality.
Cast: James Coco, Bob Dishy

Director: Ted Flicker

8b: The Burning Man

w J.D. Feigelson, *based on a short story by* Ray Bradbury
An aunt and her nephew, picnicking in the country on a scorching hot day, meet a crazed raggedy man who talks of 'genetic evil'.
Cast: Piper Laurie, Roberts Blossom

Director: J.D. Feigelson

8c: Dealer's CHoice

w Don Todd
The Devil sits in on a friendly poker game in New Jersey.
Cast: Garret Morris, Dan Hedaya, M. Emmet Walsh, Morgan Freeman

Director: Wes Craven

9a: Dead Woman's Shoes

w Lynn Barker, *based on an original story by* Charles Beaumont

Reworking of a 1961 'Zone story, *Dead Man's Shoes*, in which a derelict inherited a gangster's life along with his shoes. This time, a timid clerk slips on a pair of shoes once owned by a woman who was murdered, and becomes possessed by the victim's vengeful spirit.
Cast: Helen Mirren, Theresa Saldana, Jeffrey Tambor

Director: Peter Medak

9b: Wong's Lost and Found Emporium

w Alan Brennert, *based on a short story by* William F. Wu
A young man seeking answers to his bitter questions stumbles upon a warehouse in another dimension, where everything that's ever been lost is stored.
Cast: Brian Tochi, Anna Maria Poon

Director: Paul Lynch

10a: The Shadow Man

w Rockne S. O'Bannon
A timid 13-year-old boy, desperate to impress a beautiful classmate, finds a macabre ally in the Shadow Man, a ghoulish figure who emerges nightly from beneath his bed. But he gets just *too* cocky . . .
Cast: Jonathan Ward, Heather Haase, Jeff Calhoun

Director: Joe Dante

10b: The Uncle Devil Show

w Don Todd
A boy's parents have no idea what devilish tricks their young son will learn from the video of 'Tim Ferret and Friends' they've rented for him.
Cast: Murphy Dunne

Director: David Steinberg

10c: Opening Day

w Chris Hubbell, Gerrit Graham
Joe Farrell murders his lover's husband

and then finds that he has somehow replaced him in a new loop of time.
Cast: Jeffrey Jones, Martin Kove

Director: John Milius

11a: The Beacon

w Martin Pasko, Rebecca Parr
A doctor whose car breaks down on a deserted ocean road comes across the village of Bellwether which has an eerie lighthouse that only shines inland.
Cast: Martin Landau, Cheryl Anderson, Charles Martin Smith

Director: Gerd Oswald

11b: One Life, Furnished in Early Poverty

w Alan Brennert, *based on a short story by* Harlan Ellison
A writer who returns to his childhood home in search of the emblem of youth, is transported back in time to when he was a boy.
Cast: Peter Reigert, Jack Kehoe, Chris Hebert

Director: Don Dunway

12a: Her Pilgrim Soul

w Alan Brennert
A scientist experimenting with computer holography somehow captures the image of an infant which takes on a life of its own.
Cast: Kristofer Tabori, Gary Cole, Anne Twomey

Director: Wes Craven

12b: I of Newton

w Alan Brennert
A mathematician, obsessed with a complex equation, accidentally invokes a hellish curse and a very 'hip' demon materialises to claim his soul.
Cast: Sherman Hemsley, Ron Glass

Director: Ken Gilbert

13a: Night of the Meek

w Rockne S. O'Bannon
Remake of Rod Serling's original 1960 festive fantasy in which a down-at-heel department store Santa magically brings the true spirit of Christmas to his humble neighbourhood.
Cast: Richard Mulligan, William Atherton, Teddy Wilson, Bill Henderson

Director: Martha Coolidge

13b: But Can She Type

w Martin Pasko, Rebecca Parr
On Christmas Eve, the over-worked secretary of a tyrannical boss discovers the heaven-on-earth for all secretaries.
Cast: Pam Dawber, Charles Levin

Director: Shelley Levinson

13c: The Star

w Alan Brennert, *based on a short story by* Arthur C. Clarke
Space explorers from Earth discover the remains of an ancient civilisation on a burnt-out planet.
Cast: Fritz Weaver, Donald Moffat

Director: Gerd Oswald

14a: Still Life

w Gerrit Graham, Chris Hubbell
A photographer finds an antique camera used on an Amazon expedition 70 years earlier that still has exposed film on it – photos of fierce warriors who believed that to take their picture was to steal their souls.
Cast: John Carradine, Robert Carradine, Marilyn Jones

Director: Peter Medak

14b: The Little People

w J.D. Feigelson
The regulars at Kelly's Pub are sceptical

when Liam O'Shaughnessy comes in and swears he's seen the little people . . .
Cast: Hamilton Camp, Anthony Palmer, Michael Aldridge

Director: J.D. Feigelson

14c: The Misfortune Cookie

w Rockne S. O'Bannon, *based on a short story by* Charles E. Fritch
An arrogant food critic gets his just deserts at a Chinese restaurant he has panned without even dining there.
Cast: Elliot Gould

Director: Allan Arkush

15a: Monsters

w Robert Crais
A 10-year-old horror fan moves into a new neighbourhood where he meets a nice old man who informs him that he is a vampire.
Cast: Ralph Bellamy, Oliver Robins, Kathleen Lloyd, Bruce Solomon

Director: B.W.L. Norton

15b: A Small Talent for War

w Charlie Scholtz, Allan Brennert
An emissary of aliens who engineered Earth's evolution declares his race displeased with the planet's petty squabbles and gives world leaders 24 hours to get their act together or face total annihilation.
Cast: John Glover, Peter Michael Goetz, Stefan Gierasch, Fran Bennett

Director: Claudia Weill

15c: A Matter of Minutes

w Rockne S. O'Bannon, *based on a story by* Theodore Sturgeon
A couple awake to find themselves four hours ahead of 'real' time – in the minute 11.37 which is literally being built around them by a strange blue-clad workforce.
Cast: Adam Arkin, Karen Austin, Adolph Caesar

Director: Sheldon Larry

16a: The Elevator

w Ray Bradbury
Two brothers search an abandoned factory for their scientist father who's been experimenting on the formula for perfect food.
Cast: Stephen Geoffreys, Robert Prescott

Director: R.L. Thomas

16b: To See The Invisible Man

w Steven Barnes *based on a short story by* Robert Silverberg
In an alternate future, the state finds a man guilty of the crime of coldness and condemns him to a year of ostracism.
Cast: Cotter Smith, Karlene Crockett, Mary-Robin Redd, Peter Hobbs

Director: Noel Black

16c: Tooth and Consequences

w Haskell Barkin
A despondent dentist, near the end of his tether because all his patients hate to see him, is saved when the Tooth Fairy appears.
Cast: David Birney, Kenneth Mars, Oliver Clark, Theresa Ganzel

Director: Robert Downey

17a: Welcome to Winfield

w Les Enloe
Griffin St George, an agent of Death who's trying to get the hang of his new job, tracks his quarry to a dusty desert town that's not even on his map.
Cast: Gerrit Graham, Henry Gibson, Alan Fudge, Elish Cook

Director: Bruce Bilson

17b: Quarantine

w Alan Brennert, *based on a story by* Philip DeGuere *and* Steve Bochco
A space weapons engineer, cyrogenically

frozen at near-death in the 21st century, is revived 300 years later by a biologically perfect but technologically backward community who need his specialised skills to destroy a threat from space.
Cast: Scott Wilson, Tess Harper, Larry Riley, D.W. Brown, Jeanne Mori

Director: Martha Coolidge

18a: Gramma

w Harlan Ellison, *based on a story by* Stephen King
A young boy, left alone by his mother, is scared to death to go near his huge, grotesque grandmother in the shuttered room at the end of the hall.
Cast: Barret Oliver, Darlanne Fluegel, Frederick Long

Director: Bradford May

18b: Cold Reading

w Martin Pasko, Rebecca Parr
A flamboyant young radio prodigy, broadcasting in 1943, inadvertently invokes the powers of the air for authentic sound effects – bringing the *real* sights and sounds of Africa into his studio.
Cast: Dick Shawn, Janet Carroll, Joel Brooks, Lawrence Poindexter, Annette McCarthy, Ralph Manza

Director: Gus Trikonis

18c: Personal Demon

w Rockne S. O'Bannon
'Rockne O'Bannon', a hack screenwriter up against the biggest writer's block of his whole mediocre career, is confronted by his own personal demons.
Cast: Martin Balsam, Clive Revill, Joshua Shelley

Director: Peter Medak

19a: Three Irish Wishes

w Tommy Lee Wallace, *based on a story by* James Crocker

Shaun McGool, a Hawaiian-shirted leprechaun peeved at being caught by three boys while on his holidays, grants them their three entitled wishes – to the letter!
Cast: Cork Hubbert, Bradley Gregg, Joey Green, Danny Nucci

Director: Tommy Lee Wallace

19b: Dead Run

w Alan Brennert, *based on a short story by* Greg Bear
An unemployed truck driver gets a job driving in unfamiliar territory and learns to his horror that he's delivering a cargo of condemned souls to hell.
Cast: Steve Railsback, John Delancie, Barry Corbin, Ebbe Roe Smith

Director: Paul Tucker

20a: Button, Button

w Logan Swanson
A hard-up young couple are presented with a wooden box with a button on and told that if they push it, two things will happen: someone they don't know will die and they will immediately receive 200,000 dollars.
Cast: Mare Winningham, Brad David, Basil Hoffman

Director: Peter Medak

20b: Profile in Silver

w J. Neil Schulman
A historian from the future returns to 1963 to study President John F. Kennedy but unwittingly prevents his assassination, thereby initiating a disastrous chain of events.
Cast: Andrew Robinson, Lane Smith, Louis Gimbalvo, Barbara Baxley

Director: John Hancock

21a: Red Snow

w Michael Cassutt
A Russian KGB officer is sent to a

Siberian gulag to investigate the mysterious murders of party officials.
Cast: George Dzundza, Barry Miller, Vladimir Skomarovsky

Director: Jeannot Szwarc

21b: Need to Know

w Mary and Sydney Sheldon
In a small town, a government investigator finds insanity spreading from person to person. But the cause is not a virus – it's knowledge, a 'Chinese whisper' that overwhelms . . .
Cast: William L. Peterson, Robin Gammell, Frances McDormand, Harold Ayer, Eldon Quick

Director: Paul Lynch

22a: Take My Life . . . Please

w Gordon Mitchell
A callous stand-up comic, killed in a car crash, awakens on stage at the 'Club Limbo' where he's told he has to audition for his place in eternity.
Cast: Ray Buktenica, Tim Thomerson, Xander Berkeley, Jim Mackrell

Director: Gus Trikonis

22b: Devil's Alphabet

w Robert Hunter
In 1876, a group of cynical Cambridge men who call themselves the Devil's Alphabet Society sign a solemn oath in blood to meet annually on All Soul's Day – forever.
Cast: Ben Cross, Hywel Bennett, Robert Schenkkan, Osmund Bullock

Director: Ben Bolt

22c: The Library

w Anne Collins
A woman goes to work in a bizarre library containing a book on every living person, and innocently decides to make a minor change in one of them.

Cast: Frances Conroy, Lori Petty, Joe Santos

Director: John Hancock

23a: Shadow Play

w James Crocker, *based on a story and teleplay by* Charles Beaumont
Reworking of Beaumont's 1961 story. A man who waits on Death Row to be hanged is haunted by an obsession that everyone around him is a figment of his recurring nightmare.
Cast: Peter Coyote, Guy Boyd, Janet Eilber, Deborah May

Director: (not known)

23b: Grace Note

w Patrice Messina
A gifted young singer who dreams of performing grand opera but is held back by family responsibilities, is given a poignant glimpse into the future through her dying sister's last wish.
Cast: Julia Migenes Johnson, Sydney Penny, Rhoda Gemignani, Kay E. Kutter

Director: Peter Medak

24a: A Day in Beaumont

w David Gerrold
An earnest young scientist and his fiancée see a flying saucer land and bug-eyed aliens emerge carrying ray guns and large green pods. But oddly enough, they can find no one who will believe them.
Cast: Victor Garber, Stacy Nelkin, Jeff Morrow, John Agar, Kenneth Tobey

Director: Philip DeGeure

24b: The Last Defender of Camelot

w George R.R. Martin, *based on a story by* Roger Zelazny
A world-weary Lancelot, all but immortal and now living in London, is summoned

by his ancient nemesis, the enchantress Morgan Le Fey, to meet again with Merlin who has resurrected a grand scheme to restore Camelot.

Cast: Richard Kiley, Jenny Agutter, Norman Lloyd, John Cameron Mitchell

Director: Jeannot Szwarc

Series Two
(30-minute episodes)

1: The Once and Future King

w George R.R. Martin, Bryce Maritano
An Elvis Presley impersonator is transported back to 1954 where he meets his idol preparing for an historic audition. In a fight over the music the *real* Elvis is accidentally killed, so the impersonator assumes the mantle of the king.
Cast: Jeff Yagher, Lisa Jane Persky, Red West, Banks Harper

Director: Jim McBride

2a: Lost and Found

w George R.R. Martin, *based on a short story by* Phyllis Esenstein
A college student destined to become a famous anthropologist finds 'souvenir hunters' from the future have been taking items from her flat as mementos.
Cast: Akosua Busia, Cindy Harrell, Leslie Ackerman, Raye Birk

Director: Gus Trikonis

2b: The After Hours

w Rockne S. O'Bannon
Reworking of Rod Serling's 1960 tale. A young woman entering a shopping centre just as it closes finds herself trapped in a strange after-hours world of shop mannequins and learns that she, too, is a mannequin.
Cast: Terry Farrell, Ned Bellamy, Ann Wedgeworth, Chip Heller

Director: Bruce Malmouth

3: A Saucer of Loneliness

w David Gerrold, *based on a short story by* Theodore Sturgeon
A young woman refuses to disclose the 'personal' message given to her by a flying saucer. Driven to the brink of suicide, she finally meets a man who claims he knows what it was.
Cast: Shelley Duvall, Richard Libertini, Nan Martin, Edith Diaz, Andrew Massett

Director: John Hancock

4: The World Next Door

w Jeffrey Tambor
Saddled with a boring job and the antithesis of an understanding wife, a basement inventor discovers a 'doorway' into a parallel world where he and his creations are truly appreciated. (George Wendt – Norm in *Cheers* – co-starred with his real-life wife Bernadette Birkette).
Cast: George Wendt, Bernadette Birkette, Tom Finnegan, Jeffrey Tambor

Director: Paul Lynch

5: Voices in the Earth

w Alan Brennert
A mining ship in the distant future returns to find Earth a completely dead planet. As they prepare to destroy the planet for its internal minerals, the ship's historian becomes possessed by the ethereal souls of Earth's past inhabitants.
Cast: Martin Balsam, Jenny Agutter, Wortham Krimmer, Tim Russ

Director: Curtis Harrington

6: What Are Friends For

w J. Michael Straczynski
A man returns to his old holiday cabin with his eight-year-old son and discovers that his imaginary childhood friend is *real* and has been waiting for him all these years.

Cast: Tom Skerritt, Fred Savage, Luke Haas, Joy Claussen

Director: Gus Trikonis

7: The Storyteller

w Rockne S. O'Bannon
An elderly schoolteacher encounters a former pupil with an amazing gift. As a young man he kept his 131-year-old great great grandfather alive by reading stories to him.
Cast: Glynnis O'Connor, David Faustino, Parley Baer, Nike Doukas

Director: Paul Lynch

8: Aqua Vita

w Jeremy Betrand Finch, Paul Chitlik
A 40-year-old TV celebrity discovers a special brand of water which acts like a fountain of youth. But there is a hidden cost . . .
Cast: Mimi Kennedy, Joseph Hacker, Barbra Horan, Christopher McDonald

Director: Paul Tucker

9: Time and Teresa Golowitz

w Alan Brennert, based on a short story by Parke Godwin
A middle-aged man suffers a fatal heart attack, then finds he can relive any moment of his life he chooses.
Cast: Gene Barry, Grant Heslov, Paul Sand, Kriski Lynes, Wally Ward, Gina Gershon

Director: Shelley Levinson

10: Song of the Younger World

w Anthony and Nancy Lawrence
A pair of young lovers, forbidden to meet, seek happiness through a book of mystic teachings that allows them to leave their physical bodies and escape into the souls of wild wolves.
Cast: Pete Kowanko, Paul Benedict Jennifer Rubin

Director: Corey Allen

11: Nightsong

w Michael Reaves
When a lady disc jockey plays an obscure album made by a former lover, the musician magically appears in her life again, ten years after he suddenly 'disappeared'.
Cast: Lisa Eilbacher, Anthony Hamilton, Kenneth David Gilman

Director: Bradford May

12: The Convict's Piano

w Patricia Messina, based on a story by James Crocker
A prisoner wrongly convicted of murder plays a battered old piano in the prison chapel and finds himself transported back in time to 1920s New Orleans.
Cast: Joe Penny, Norman Fell, Tom O'Brien, John Hancock

Director: (not known)

13: The Card

w Michael Cassutt
A special credit card gives a wife unlimited spending power but when she forgets to settle the account she finds the penalties have unusually severe implications for her family.
Cast: Susan Blakeley, William Atherton, Ken Lerner

Director: Bradford May

14: The Road Less Travelled

w George R.R. Martin
A middle-aged family man confronts a bearded, wheelchair-bound 'intruder' and learns he is himself living, on a parallel plane. Each man gains a poignant insight into what might have been.
Cast: Cliff De Young, Margaret Klenck, Jaclyn-Rose Lester, Clare Nono

Director: Wes Craven

15: The Girl I Married

w J.M. DeMatteis
A married couple's mutual desire for the partner they knew years earlier is so strong that younger versions of themselves are conjured up – giving each the basis for a unique affair.
Cast: Linda Kelsey, James Whitmore Jr

Director: Philip DeGuere

16: Shelter Skelter

w Ron Cobb, Robin Love
A survivalist takes to his bunker when a nuclear bomb goes off and settles down for a 30-year wait, convinced that the rest of the world has been destroyed.
Cast: Joe Montegna, Joan Allen, Johnathan Gries

Director: Martha Coolidge

17: The Toys of Calisan

w George R.R. Martin, *based on a story by* Terry Matz
A 16-year-old retarded boy possesses the amazing gift of being able to conjure up anything after seeing its picture.
Cast: Richard Mulligan, Anne Haney, David Greenlee, Alexandra Borrie

Director: Tom Wright

18a: Joy Ride

w Cal Willingham
Two teenage brothers and their girlfriends 'hotwire' a classic old car, then find themselves reliving a 30-year-old murder.
Cast: Rob Knepper, Brooke McCarter, Heidi Kozak, Tamara Mark, Burr Middleton, Danny Spear

Director: Gil Bettman

18b: Private Channel

w Edward Redlich, *based on a story by* Edward Redlich *and* John Bellucci
A freak lightning strike on an airliner causes a teenager's 'Walkman' to malfunction, enabling him to tune in on the thoughts of other passengers, one of whom is planning to blow up the plane.
Cast: Scott Coffey, Andrew Robinson, Claudia Cron, Louise Fitch

Director: Peter Medak

19: The Junction

w Virginia Aldridge
Two coal miners – one from 1986 the other from 1912 – find themselves trapped in the same cave-in. When the 1912 man is rescued he writes a letter to be opened 74 years in the future.
Cast: William Allen Young, Chris Mulkey, John Dennis Johnston

Director: Bill Duke

TWIST IN THE TALE

Short-lived American anthology series that stuttered onto British screens in 1978. A cousin of *Tales of the Unexpected* (its US title), several of the stories had science fiction themes.

No Way Out starred Bill Bixby as a naval officer 'too busy' to pay much attention to his young son. He sails his boat through a time warp, emerging 25 years in the future when he discovers his grown-up son making the same mistake he did.

In *The Nomads*, a Vietnam veteran (David Birney) with a history of mental breakdown discovers that space-roving vampires are about to take over Earth. But no one will believe him.

The Mask of Adonis featured *Falcon Crest* star Robert Foxworth as a film producer offered eternal rejuvenation at an isolated clinic run by a sinister doctor.

And in *A Hand for Sonny Blue*, a baseball pitcher receives a new hand in a transplant, only to discover it came from a vicious young hoodlum, killed in a shoot-out, and is taking on a life of its own.

The series received a fragmented showing here, with episodes scattered round various ITV regions between 1978 and 1981.

REGULAR CAST
Narrator **William Conrad**

Producer: **John Wilder**

Quinn Martin Productions
Nine colour 55-minute episodes

The Final Chapter
The Mask of Adonis
Devil Pack
The Nomads
A Hand for Sonny Blue
Force of Evil (A 2-part story)
No Way Out
You Are Not Alone

UK premiere: 14 October 1978
(London)

(Author's note: This series is not to be confused with two 1988 dramas from Granada which went out under the same title, but which were really part of that company's contribution to an international package of *The Ray Bradbury Theater* – see separate entry.)

U.F.O.

With *U.F.O.* Gerry Anderson finally cut the strings that tied him to his Supermarionated puppets. He'd flirted with live action in *The Secret Service* and made the jump with his 1969 feature film *Doppelganger*, but *U.F.O.* was his first fully flesh and blood TV series.

It was a natural development, and one which offered the chance to dust off many of the props, vehicles and costumes lying around after *Doppelganger* (aka *Journey to the Far Side of the Sun*). All the same, production costs were high – around £100,000 for each of the 26 hour-long episodes.

U.F.O.'s format was similar to *Captain Scarlet and the Mysterons*, that of an alien force attacking an Earth defended by a powerful secret organisation. But this one was set in the 'near-future', 1980. The premise: for ten years a dying, sterile race has been raiding

Earth in search of human organs to keep itself alive. All that stops our planet from becoming one giant body bank is SHADO – Supreme Headquarters Alien Defence Organisation – operating from a secret base beneath the Harlington-Straker film studios (actually MGM in Borehamwood, where the series was made) which act as a cover for SHADO personnel led by ex-USAF colonel Ed Straker. SHADO also has a centre on the Moon – base for its interceptor craft and the first line of defence against marauding pyramid-shaped UFOs. Its high-tech resources include SID – Space Intruder Detector – a sophisticated computer satellite, submarine/aircraft called Skydivers and a range of tank-like SHADOmobiles to pursue UFOs that reach Earth.

The aliens themselves were rarely seen – and nothing was revealed of their possible origins. But they were shown to have a liquid environment inside their space helmets for interstellar travel – womb principle that Anderson told *TVTimes* he devised after hearing of genuine scientific experiments involving keeping a dog alive underwater for an hour by filling its lungs with a special combination of water and gases.

The series had one of the biggest semi-resident casts for any TV show, though not all the regulars appeared in every episode. In fact, only one had a 100 per cent record. That was Commander Straker, played by American actor Ed Bishop – the voice of Captain Blue in *Captain Scarlet and the Mysterons*. His right-hand men were Col. Alec Freeman and Col. Paul Foster, the former played by *Special Branch* star George Sewell who had also appeared with Ed Bishop in *Doppelganger*.

U.F.O. also boasted one of television's shapeliest regiments of women, dressed to kill in tight-fitting catsuits and mauve wigs. The glamorous commander of Moonbase, Lt. Gay Ellis, was played by Gabrielle Drake who later went on to head a very down-to-earth ITV outpost – the *Crossroads* motel.

Although many of Century 21's regular writers were used on *U.F.O.*, script editor Tony Barwick was responsible for 12 of the 26 scripts. There were notable contributions, too, from David Tomblin and Terence Feely.

This was a far more adult science fiction show than the Supermarionation adventures, often edgy and downbeat in its plots and characterisation. Straker, for example, was shown as having a broken marriage behind him. ITV, though, didn't know how to take it. First screened in September 1970, it didn't get a network launch and was buried by many regions. But the series has refused to die and still shows up in late-night schedules.

A planned second series, with the emphasis switched to Moonbase, turned into *Space 1999* – but that's another story.

Main Cast

Cmdr Edward Straker **Ed Bishop** Col. Alec Freeman **George Sewell**
Col. Paul Foster **Michael Billington** Lt. Gay Ellis **Gabrielle Drake**
Lt. Nina Barry **Dolores Mantez** Joan Harrington **Antonia Ellis**
Col. Virginia Lake **Wanda Ventham**

With:

Capt. Lew Waterman **Gary Myers** Miss Ealand **Norma Ronald**
Lt. Ford (SHADO Radio Operator) **Keith Alexander**
SHADO operative **Ayshea Brough** Skydiver navigator **Jeremy Wilkin**
Skydiver engineer **John Kelley** Skydiver operative **Georgina Moon**
Dr Jackson **Vladek Sheybal** General Henderson **Grant Taylor**
Lt. Mark Bradley **Harry Baird**

Format: **Gerry** and **Sylvia Anderson**
  with **Reg Hill**
Executive producer: **Gerry Anderson**
Producer: **Reg Hill**
Script editor: **Tony Barwick**
Special effects: **Derek Meddings**
Music: **Barry Gray**

*A Century 21 Pictures Ltd Production for
ITC Worldwide Distribution*
26 colour 60-minute episodes
16 September 1970–15 March 1973
(ATV, Midland)

Identified

w **Gerry** and **Sylvia Anderson, Tony Barwick**
Cmdr Straker discovers the grim secret behind the long-standing UFO attacks on Earth in which people have been mutilated or abducted, when an alien craft is forced down and its pilot captured. (Ed Bishop was 'rejuvenated' ten years for early flashback scenes, while two actors were used for the role of the alien who ages dramatically in a matter of moments.)
Minister **Basil Dignam**
Seagull X-Ray co-pilot **Shane Rimmer**
Capt. Peter Karlin **Peter Gordeno** (plus Eps 2, 4–5, 15, 22)
Ken Matthews **Michael Mundell**
Kurt Mahler **Paul Gillard**
Phil Wade **Gary Files**
Dr Harris **Matthew Robertson**
Dr Shroeder **Maxwell Shaw**
Alien **Gito Santana/Stanley Bray**

Director: **Gerry Anderson**

Exposed

w **Tony Barwick**
Civilian test pilot Paul Foster sees and photographs a UFO, and his quest to uncover its secret leads him to the heart of SHADO – and a new career.
Kofax **Robin Bailey**
Janna **Jean Marsh**
Co-pilot **Matt Zimmerman**
Dr Frazer **Basil Moss**
Nurse **Sue Gerrard**
Tsi **Paula Li Schiu**
Louis **Arthur Cox**

Director: **David Lane**

The Cat with Ten Lives

w **David Tomblin**
An innocent-looking Siamese cat turns out to be an alien being sent to take over the mind of SHADO pilot Jim Regan. (This was Alexis Kanner's first TV role since *The Prisoner*, and a reunion for him and David Tomblin.)
Jim Regan **Alexis Kanner**
Morgan **Windsor Davies**
Jean Regan **Geraldine Moffatt**
Muriel **Eleanor Summerfield**
Miss Holland **Lois Maxwell**
Albert **Colin Gordon**

Director: **David Tomblin**

Conflict

w Ruric Powell

An alien satellite uses space debris as a cover for its attacks – but Straker has a hard time convincing General Henderson to clear away the junk – until SHADO HQ itself is threatened.

Pilot Gerard Norman
Navigator Alan Tucker
Maddox Drewe Henley
Crewman David Courtland
Steiner Michael Kilgarriff

Director: Ken Turner

A Question of Priorities

w Tony Barwick

Straker faces an agonising dilemma when a chance to rescue an alien defector who could hold the key to saving the world means risking the life of his critically injured son.

John Rutland Barnaby Shaw
Mary Rutland Suzanne Neve
Rutland Philip Madoc
Dr Segal Peter Halliday
Mrs O'Connor Mary Merrall
Dr Green Russell Napier
Alien Richard Aylen

Director: David Lane

E.S.P.

w Alan Fennell

Straker and Freeman are threatened by an alien agent whose ESP powers are so pronounced he can predict their every thought and movement.

Croxley John Stratton
Stella Croxley Deborah Stanford
Dr Ward Douglas Wilmer
Dr Shroeder Maxwell Shaw
Gateman Donald Tandy
Security man Stanley McGeogh

Director: Ken Turner

Sub-smash

w Alan Fennell

Straker and Nina Barry become trapped on the ocean bed in Skydiver after a search for an alien craft. As hopes of rescue fade, a tender bond develops between them.

Lt. Chin Anthony Chinn
Lt. Lewis Paul Maxwell
Pilot Burnell Tucker
SHADO divers John Golightly, Alan Haywood

Director: David Lane

Kill Straker!

w Donald James

A close encounter with a UFO turns loyal SHADO officers Foster and Craig into ferocious adversaries and Straker faces a grim challenge to his command – and his life.

Craig David Sumner
Moonbase guard Steve Cory
Nurse Louise Pajo

Director: Alan Perry

Destruction

w Dennis Spooner

A beautiful Admiralty secretary is the innocent dupe in an alien plot to steal and release nerve gas which would destroy all life on Earth.

Sarah Bosanquet Stephanie Beacham
Naval captain Philip Madoc
Admiral Sheringham Edwin Richfield
Skydiver captain David Warbeck
Skydiver engineer Barry Stokes
Astronaut Steven Berkoff

Director: Ken Turner

The Square Triangle

w Alan Pattillo

Lovers Liz Newton and Cass Fowler are horrified when an alien pilot becomes the unexpected victim of their plot to murder her husband.

Liz Newton Adrienne Corri
Cass Fowler Patrick Mower
Jack Newton Allan Cuthbertson
Alien Anthony Chinn
Gamekeeper Godfrey James
SHADO Mobile navigator Hugo Panczak

Director: David Lane

Close Up

w Tony Barwick
A powerful new telescope could help SHADO track the origins of the UFOs. But one scientist, Dr Kelly, resorts to unusual methods to convince Straker that inner space is just as important as outer space!
Dr Kelly Neil Hallett
Dr Young James Beckett
Launch controller Frank Mann
Interceptor pilot Mark Hawkins

Director: Alan Perry

The Psychobombs

w Tony Barwick
Three average people – Linda, a secretary; Mason, a motorway construction boss; and Clark, a bank clerk – become super-humans when they are taken over by the aliens who plan to use them in a powerful plan to wreck SHADO.
Linda Deborah Grant
Clark David Collings
Mason Mike Pratt
Capt. Lauritzen Tom Adams
The Executive Alex Davion
Skydiver navigator Christopher Timothy

Director: Jeremy Summers

Survival

w Tony Barwick
Joining the search for a UFO that has attacked Moonbase, Col. Foster comes face to face with its alien pilot after their craft 'collide'. In the fight to survive on the Moon's inhospitable surface a surprising bond of friendship is forged.
Grant Robert Swann
Alien Gito Santana
Tina Duval Suzan Farmer
Rescue pilot Ray Armstrong

Director: Alan Perry

Mindbender

w Tony Barwick
A deadly Moon-rock causes two members of an interceptor crew to go berserk and attack their colleagues in the belief that they are seeing their enemies.
Conroy Ali Mancini
Dale Craig Hunter
Beaver James Charles Tingwell
Howard Byrne Stuart Damon
Radio operator Anouska Hempel

Director: Ken Turner

Flight Path

w Ian Scott Stewart
Threats to his wife force Moonbase officer Paul Roper to turn traitor, revealing vital information that will bring in a major UFO attack. But once the truth is uncovered, Roper gets the chance to even the score.
Paul Roper George Cole
Carol Roper Sonia Fox
Dawson Keith Grenville
Dr Shroeder Maxwell Shaw

Director: Ken Turner

The Man Who Came Back

w Terence Feely
Spaceship pilot Craig Collins is found alive and well two months after he disappeared and was presumed dead. But he's a changed man – now programmed by the aliens to kill Straker.
Craig Collins Derren Nesbitt
Miss Holland Lois Maxwell
Col. Grey Gary Raymond
Sir Esmond Roland Culver
Radio operator Anouska Hempel

Director: David Lane

The Dalotek Affair

w Ruric Powell
When all radio and video equipment on Moonbase breaks down, Col. Foster suspects that a lunar survey team may be responsible. But the breakdowns continue until the surveyors report seeing something strange at the bottom of a deep new crater.
Jane Carson Tracy Reed
Tanner Clinton Greyn
Mitchell David Weston

Blake Philip Latham
Reed John Breslin
Doctor Basil Moss

Director: Alan Perry

Timelash

w Terence Feely
Straker runs amok and when a dead body is found he is suspected of being a killer. But under the influence of a powerful truth drug he pieces together the startling mystery of an alien-controlled man with the power to cheat time.
Turner Patrick Allen
Casting agent Ron Pember
Actor Jean Vladon
Actress Kirsten Lindholm

Director: Cyril Frankel

Ordeal

w Tony Barwick
Abducted by an alien! That's the apparent fate of Col. Foster when he passes out in a sauna the morning after a very indulgent night before. What a nightmare!
Sylvia Graham Quinn O'Hara
Joe Franklin David Healy
Astronaut Mark Hawkins
Dr Harris Basil Moss
Perry Peter Burton

Director: Ken Turner

Court Martial

w Tony Barwick
Soon after interviewing a young starlet and her agent in his 'cover' capacity as a movie executive, Foster is accused of espionage and convicted at a court martial. With the death sentence hanging over his colleague's head, Straker decides to dig deeper.
Webb Jack Hedley
Carl Mason Neil McCallum
Diane Pippa Steel
Agent Noel Davis
Miss Scott Louis Pajo
Miss Grant Georgina Cookson

Director: Ron Appleton

Reflections in the Water

w David Tomblin
Investigating strange reports of a 'flying fish', Straker and Foster find themselves in a bewildering underwater replica of SHADO control, manned by doubles of all the staff – including themselves!
Skipper Conrad Phillips
Lt. Anderson James Cosmo
Film producer Richard Caldicott
Skydiver Capt David Warbeck
Skydiver operative Anouska Hempel
Skydiver navigator Barry Stokes

Director: David Tomblin

The Computer Affair

w Tony Barwick
The death of an astronaut in a UFO attack has strange implications for Gay Ellis of Moonbase Control and interceptor pilot Mark Bradley when a computer assessment shows they are in love.
Ken Matthews Michael Mundell
Dr Shroeder Maxwell Shaw
Dr Murray Peter Burton
Moonbase operative Nigel Lambert

Director: David Lane

Confetti Check A-O.K.

w Tony Barwick
Flashback episode in which Straker recalls the origins of SHADO and the call of duty that doomed his marriage – right from the start of his honeymoon!
Mary Suzanne Neve
Lt. Grey Julian Grant
CIA man Shane Rimmer
Mary's father Michael Nightingale
Hotel clerk Geoffrey Hinsliff
Porter Frank Tregear

Director: David Lane

The Sound of Silence

w David Lane *and* Bob Bell
A top showjumper mysteriously disappears after a UFO is reported to have landed near his family's farm.

Russ Michael Jayston
Anne Susan Jameson
Culley Nigel Gregory
Alien Gito Santana
Stone Richard Vernon
Doctor Basil Moss

Director: David Lane

The Responsibility Seat

w Tony Barwick
Col. Freeman finds it can be tough at the top when he takes over from Cmdr Straker who himself learns that a pretty girl can be as lethal as a UFO when he becomes entangled with reporter Jo Fraser.
Jo Fraser Jane Merrow
Film director Ralph Ball
Stuntman Royston Rowe
Astronaut Mark Hawkins
Russian base commander Patrick Jordan

Director: Alan Perry

The Long Sleep

w David Tomblin
The file on a long-standing UFO case is reopened when a girl regains consciousness after a ten-year coma. Straker pieces together a traumatic mystery that leads to a race against time to prevent a deadly alien bomb from being detonated. (A controversial episode with sepia-tinted black and white flashbacks, a drugs trip and an implied rape attempt, *The Long Sleep* was originally kept back by cautious ITV companies.)
Catherine: Tessa Wyatt
Tim Christian Roberts
Van driver John Garrie
Bomb disposal expert Christopher Robbie
Radio operator Anouska Hempel

Director: Jeremy Summers

UNDERMIND

'These people have been brainwashed to wage a silent war. They're part of a pattern – a pattern of evil. We've got to find the other pieces before they undermine the whole country.'

Highly unusual 1960s thriller about alien subversion – with not a rocket, flying saucer or extra-terrestrial in sight.

Its premise: an alien force, identified neither by name nor by location, seeks to establish a foothold in Britain by undermining society and morale. It has sent high frequency signals from space that are picked up by people who become brainwashed into subversive acts, to create a climate of unrest.

The series' villains are ordinary people from all walks of life – teachers, businessmen, politicians, clergymen, doctors and policemen – who have undergone a dramatic personality change. All have one thing in common – an acute susceptibility to high frequency signals, akin to dogs and dog whistles.

Undermind begins with personnel officer Drew Heriot returning from Australia to find his policeman brother Frank behaving strangely. In the course of the 11 more-or-less self-contained episodes, Drew and his sister-in-law Anne Heriot foil a string of brainwashed people plotting to undermine the nation in different ways, some violent, some subtle.

The series was devised by Robert Banks Stewart, better known later as the creator of TV 'tecs *Shoestring* and *Bergerac*.

REGULAR CAST

Drew Heriot Jeremy Wilkin   *Anne Heriot* Rosemary Nicols
Prof. Val Randolph (Eps 2–5) Denis Quilley

Devised and evolved by: Robert Banks Stewart
Producer: Michael Chapman

An ABC Television Production
11 60-minute episodes, black and white
8 May–17 July 1965
(ITV – Midlands)

Onset of Fear

w Robert Banks Stewart
Drew Heriot returns from Australia to find his policeman brother Frank has provoked a scandal involving a top politician. Appalled by this uncharacteristic behaviour, Drew and his brother's estranged wife Anne search for a cause behind Frank's strange actions. With the help of a psychologist, they discover that Frank has become 'emotionless' and uncover a web of similar cases – the victims all being susceptible to high frequency signals. Frank, meanwhile, kills Polson and tries to have Drew and Anne eliminated. But it is *he* who ends up being shot. As he dies, he tells Drew: 'There are more of us . . .'
Frank Heriot Jeremy Kemp
Hugh Bishop Tony Steedman
Dr Polson Paul Maxwell
Macridos David Swift
Paget Hugh Latimer
Inspector Frank Mills

Director: Bill Bain

Flowers of Havoc

w Robert Banks Stewart *(from a story by Jon Manchip White)*
Drew Heriot's search for clues about why his brother was brainwashed, takes him and Anne to a south coast resort where they find that the local vicar is the sur-

prising ringleader behind an invasion by hundreds of rioting teenagers.
Prof. Val Randolph Denis Quilley *(intro)*
Wilma Strickland Pauline Jameson
Charles Ogilvie Glynn Edwards
Rev. Austen Anderson Michael Gough
Dave Finn Gil Sutherland
Verger Edwin Finn

Director: Peter Potter

The New Dimension

w David Whitaker
Drew finds himself the victim of an elaborate plot to frame him for the murder of a call-girl, involved with an MP and a welfare worker. Anne goes undercover to get at the truth.
Smith Garfield Morgan
Fenway Patrick Allen
Beymer Derek Francis
Ellerway John Collin
Marion Gordon Judy Parfitt
Dorothy Vivienne Martin

Director: Bill Bain

Death in England

w Hugh Leonard
Drew and Anne uncover a plot to kill an old IRA revolutionary in London, and so spark off violence around Britain.
General Riordon Paul Curran
Sir Geoffrey Savage Robert James

Kennefick **David Kelly**
Pat Neary **Patrick Bedford**
Capt. Morrell **Mark Burns**
Rumbold **Terence Lodge**

Director: **Peter Potter**

Too Many Enemies

w **Robert Banks Stewart**
The trail of a mystery 'emotionless' man called Gill leads Drew and Anne to Prof. Randolph's radio telescope at Kimberley Vale and the shocking revelation that he, too, is one of the 'Undermind' and is out to brainwash them as well.
Gill **Aubrey Richards**
Dr Hepworth **Tenniel Evans**
Dr Burath **Lesley Nunnerley**
Alice Gill **Margaret Whiting**
Tubby Chalmers **Dave King**

Director: **Peter Dews**

Intent to Destroy

w **John Kruse**
A strange astrologer is the link between the poisoning of a thousand acres of Kent orchard, unsettling stock market tips, and a bomb plot to kill a famous TV celebrity on a live television show.
Stanley Shaw **Ewan Hooper**
Victor Liberton **Peter Barkworth**
Ursula Smythe **Jan Holden**
Mr Banbridge **John Garvin**
Mrs Banbridge **Margaret Gordon**
Effie **Lally Bowers**
Himself **Eamonn Andrews**

Director: **Bill Bain**

Song of Death

w **Bill Strutton**
Drew and Anne discover that a large number of doctors in London have committed suicide – each shortly after having a birthday on which they received a birthday greetings record. Clues lead them to a recording studio and they uncover a plot to hypnotise the doctors by 'doping' the records.

Dr John Rossleigh **Jeremy Burnham**
Donald Ames **William Wild**
Sam Freed **Ralph Nossek**
Dr Hugh Christian **David Bauer**
Dr Spring **John Wentworth**
Jesse Spring **Joan Heath**

Director: **Laurence Bourne**

Puppets of Evil

w **Max Sterling**
When children start behaving badly – influenced by a fictional child character – Drew and Anne suspect that the author, Kate Orkney, has been brainwashed. Unravelling a complex web of involvement, they find the true culprit behind the unsettling stories is a school headmaster, Edmonds.
Cyrus Benton **Norman Tyrell**
Homer Benton **Derek Nimmo**
Kate Orkney **Katherine Blake**
Morgan Fay **Stanley Meadows**
Edmonds **Philip Latham**
Nancy Long **Delena Kidd**

Director: **Patrick Dromgoole**

Test for the Future

w **David Whittaker**
With Anne held hostage by hired thugs, Drew is forced into cooperating with a brainwashed accountant's scheme to send government exam papers to potential failures, thus creating future havoc when inferior men achieve important posts.
Kennedy **Barrie Ingham**
Davies **Maurie Taylor**
Jeffreys **Godfrey Quigley**
Lodge **Dudley Jones**
Col. Matherson **Charles Carson**

Director: **Laurence Bourne**

Waves of Sound

w **Robert Holmes**
Investigating a pirate radio station, Drew and Anne find the trail leads to a cold cure clinic in Tunbridge Wells where the physician, Dr Whittaker, plans to spread a new flu virus that causes a middle ear

infection, making victims receptive to a new brainwashing signal from space. Drew is able to substitute ordinary cold pills and obtains a list of brainwashed people.

Dr Whittaker Ruth Dunning
Sir Geoffrey Tillinger John Barron
Ensign James George Moon
Ian Jenner John Barcroft
Billy Jarvis George Betton
Caper David Phethean

Director: Raymond Menmuir

End Signal

w Robert Holmes

Using Drew's list, security forces round up brainwashed people, and communications chief Tillinger prepares to jam the expected signal from space. Drew and Anne relax – until someone tries to kill them and they realise it's not yet over. As jamming is about to start, Tillinger reveals himself as the main Undermind and tries to stop the jamming. But in a struggle he is killed. Thus Britain is saved!

Thallon George Baker
Reynolds Richard Owens
Veronica Beryl Baxter
Killick Barry Warren
Raison Michael Lees
Prof. Emmett Alex McCrindle

Director: Peter Potter

THE UNFORESEEN

A prototype *Tales of the Unexpected*, this early fantasy anthology series from Granada Television appeared in 1960 (initially twice-weekly) as a late-night series of short plays covering the inexplicable, the supernatural, the occult and science fiction.

All these 'Tales of' *The Unforeseen* featured an element of intrigue to hook the viewer and a surprise ending to pull him up with a start. The series ran for 18 weeks in the Granada region, but was never picked up by the network.

Executive producer: Peter Francis

A Granada Television Production
24 30-minute episodes, black and white
28 June–8 November 1960

The Voice

w Hillary Waugh

A young woman, terrorised by a phone caller, agrees to act as a police decoy.
With: Susan Douglas, George Robertson

Director: Robert Christie

The Tintype

w Peter Francis, Vincent McConnor

A strange early form of photograph seems to confirm a young Victorian woman's belief that her former lover has returned from the dead.
With: Aileen Seaton, Patrick Macnee Sean Mulcahy

Director: John Ashby

When Greek Meets Greek

w Graham Greene

A crooked professor running a phoney

correspondence course meets his match in a new student.
With: Barry Morse, Paddy Croft, Adrian Waller

Director: Eric Till

The Freedom Fighters

w Edith Pargeter
The commander of an occupying force must take strong measures to stamp out a youthful Resistance movement.
With: Claude Rae, Barry Lavender

Director: Peter Francis

The Late Departed

(writer not known)
An unhappily married wife disappears. Has her errant husband murdered her?
With: Joseph Shaw, Norma Renault

Director: Eric Till

The New Member

(writer not known)
A hungover visitor to a country club is alarmed by the odd activities of the other members.
With: Peter Mews

Director: Melwyn Breen

The Mask

w Vincent McConnor
An executed murderer's sinister influence lives on in the form of his death mask.
With: Barry Morse, Henry Comor

Director: Charles Jarrott

The Monsters

w Bob Foshko
Two young scientists pilot their rocket into space – in defiance of their own government.
With: John Vernon, John Sullivan

Director: Leo Orenstein

Master Used-to-Be

w Hal Hackaday
An eight-year-old boy moves into an old house and starts talking about people and events from 200 years ago.
With: Hayward Morse

Director: Basil Coleman

Time Exposure

w Ralph Rose
A news photographer buys an old camera that takes pictures of non-existent scenes.
With: Dave Broadfoot, Pegi Loder

Director: Robert Christie

Rendezvous

w Gil Braun
An American airman is on a busy railway station – but no one seems able to see him or answer him.
With: Jill Foster, Frank Perry, Walter Massey

Director: Eric Till

Torgut

w Ralph Rose, Charles Smith
A scientist disappears, leaving just two clues – an unusual rock-like object and the strange word 'torgut'.
With: Frank Perry, Trudi Wiggins, Uriel Luft

Director: Robert Christie

The Three Marked Pennies

w Jack Paritz
Three marked coins hold a prize for their holder on a given date – two will bestow fabulous prizes, the third sudden death. Which is which?
With: Ed McNamara, Kay Livingston, George Luscombe, Alex McKee

Director: Melwyn Breen

Desire

w James Stephens, Cecil Bennett
A young man saves the life of a blind man who, in return, invites him to express a wish.
With: Barry Morse, Frances Hyland, Ted Borrows

Director: Peter Francis

Checkmate

w Michael Dyne
The owner of an amazing robot chess player invites all-comers to play against his machine, for very high stakes . . .
With: John Colicos, Marcia Morris, Chris Wiggins

Director: Norman Campbell

The Proposal

w Morris Hersham, Norah Perez
A man tries to stop his sister's marriage to a middle-aged suitor.
With: Anna Reiser, George Sperdakos, Alexander Dixon, Peg Dixon

Director: Ted Pope

The Brooch

w F. Britten Austin, adapted by Joseph de Courcey
An antique brooch has a sinister history – one that leads to murder.
With: Gillie Fenwick, Kathleen Kidd, Hedley Mattingley

Director: David Gardner

The Haunted

w Gil Paust
A young couple shipwrecked on an island beach seek refuge in a ruined house said to be haunted.
With: Frank Matthias, Rosemary Palin

Director: Leo Orenstein

The Metronome

w August Derleth
A woman is kept awake by a constant ticking sound. Has her small stepson returned from the dead to drive her crazy?
With: Norma Renault, Frank Perry

Director: Rex Hagan

Shelter for the Night

w Robert Arthur
A honeymoon couple lose their way at night and seek shelter at a derelict house where they accidentally uncover the owner's terrible secret.
With: William Bell, Sharan Acker, Larry Mann

Director: David Gardner

The Doomdorf Mystery

w M.D. Post, adapted by Lester Powell
Everything points to a supernatural death when a brutal farmer is found shot in a room no human being could have entered.
With: Charles Palmer, Ron Hartman

Director: Peter Francis

Man Running

w Timothy Warriner
A gangster gets his revenge on a man who double-crossed him – in a strange way.
With: Don Francis, Larry Mann, Laddy Denis

Director: Peter Francis

'V'

'V' was the last great science fiction 'event' to hit British television in the 1980s. The ten-hour American blockbuster cost around £25 million to make and was watched here by more than 10 million viewers – one of the biggest audiences ever for a science fiction show.

A thriller about aliens conquering the Earth and encountering a stubborn Resistance, 'V' was a clearly stated allegory about the evils of totalitarianism, and it pulled out all the stops to make sure its message got home. These aliens were intergalactic Nazis down to their jackboots, semi-swastikas and insidious propaganda. They rounded up Earth's scientists and herded them off to concentration camps, started a brown-shirted Visitor Youth corps and took over the media. Just in case you still hadn't twigged, up popped an elderly Jew to compare it to the rise of Nazi Germany.

Subtlety wasn't 'V's strongpoint, but then when you aim for the mainstream you go for the jugular. That meant easy-to-identify heroes and villains, lots of action and lavish special effects. 'V's make-up and hardware were well up to scratch, but it was something soft and furry that gave the series its most vivid and memorable image. Underneath their reassuring human exteriors the alien 'Visitors' were really a race of hideous reptiles with a taste for live meat, and one scene called for Diana, the alien leader, to 'eat' a live rat. To achieve the startling effect, actress Jane Badler dangled the rat in front of her mouth, but it was actually 'swallowed' by a mechanical head. The camera cut back to the real actress who was fitted with a false throat with built-in air sacs that inflated and deflated to give the illusion of the rodent sliding down her throat. Yuk!

If that wasn't enough, 'V' tossed in sex between a lounging lizard called Brian and an Earth girl, Robin, producing two babies – one a lizard creature which dies, the other a 'human' girl with forked tongue, Elizabeth, who eventually provides the key to defeating the aliens.

Heroes of the Resistance were TV cameraman Mike Donovan – capable of dodging umpteen laser blasts at a single bound – scientists Julie Parris and Robert Maxwell, and gruff mercenary Ham Tyler. They were aided by a handful of alien sympathisers, notably Fifth Columnist Martin and the soft-hearted Willie.

ITV scheduled 'V' in the summer of '84, as its alternative to the BBC's wall-to-wall Olympics. So, instead of hordes of Americans running and jumping in Los Angeles, you could watch . . . hordes of Americans running and jumping in Los Angeles. As a contest, 'V' made the Olympics look like a school sports. Two out of three viewers agreed and ITV won the ratings war – at least for the five nights 'V' was on.

Given the mini-series' phenomenal success, a sequel was inevitable. But *'V': The Series* never made the same impact. Most of the main characters returned, but the political overtones were largely discarded in favour of formula action-adventures, with the metamorphosis of the alien/human 'starchild' Elizabeth the only real sign of progress.

London, TSW and Channel viewers saw the sequel first, in June 1985. Other regions followed at irregular intervals.

'V' (THE MINI-SERIES)

MAIN CAST

Diana Jane Badler   *Mike Donovan* Marc Singer   *Julie* Faye Grant
Robert Maxwell Michael Durrell   *Brian* Peter Nelson
Robin Blair Tefkin   *Daniel* David Packer   *Elias* Michael Wright
Eleanor Dupres (Donovan's mother) Neva Patterson
Abraham Bernstein Leonardo Cimino   *Steven* Andrew Prine
Supreme Commander John Richard Herd
Willie Robert Englund   *Martin* Frank Ashmore
Kristine Walsh Jenny Sullivan
Ham Michael Ironside

Created by: Kenneth Johnson
Writer/Director/Executive producer:
  Kenneth Johnson
Producer: Chuck Bowman
Make-up: Leo Lotito

A Kenneth Johnson Production in association with Warner Bros Television
Five colour 110 minute episodes
30 July–3 August 1984

V/The Final Battle

Earth, present day: Out of the blue, gigantic UFOs hover above 31 cities around the world. Their humanoid occupants announce that they have come in peace, offering friendship and advanced technology in return for a few minerals. Earth agrees and the 'benevolent invasion' begins with the Visitors manipulating the hearts and minds of people in a propaganda campaign reminiscent of Nazi Germany. Then thousands of scientists start to disappear and communities split into collaborators and resisters. Suspicious TV cameraman Mike Donovan sneaks aboard the Mother Ship and discovers that the Visitors are really revolting lizards who devour live mice and rats for lunch. He learns, too, that their mission is to drain all of Earth's water and cart off as many people as they can – for food! Back on Earth he teams up with fugitive scientist Julie Parris and the Resistance movement grows, adopting the letter 'V' as its symbol of victory. Aided by a Fifth Column of sympathisers, they fight back, finally defeating the invaders by manufacturing a 'red dust' poison from the cells of 'starchild' Elizabeth, and sprinkling it into Earth's atmosphere from thousands of balloons around the world.

Kathleen Maxwell Penelope Windust
Stanley Bernstein George Morfogen
Ben Taylor Richard Lawson
Arthur Dupres Hansford Rowe
Tony Wah Chong Evan Kim
Josh Brooks Tommy Peterson
Lynn Bonnie Bartlett
Caleb Taylor Jason Bernard
Ruby Camila Ashlend
Sancho Rafael Campos
Brad William Russ
Sean Eric Johnston

'V': THE SERIES

REGULAR CAST

Diana Jane Badler   Donovan Marc Singer   Julie Faye Grant
Lydia June Chadwick   Willie Robert Englund
Elizabeth Jenny Beck (Eps 1–2)/Jennifer Cooke (from Ep. 2)
Ham Michael Ironside (Eps 1–12)   Nathan Bates Lane Smith (Eps 1–12)
Robin Blair Tefkin (Eps 1–12)   Elias Michael Wright (Eps 1–11)
Kyle Jeff Yagher (from Ep. 3)   Chaing Aki Aleong (Eps 5–12)
Charles Duncan Regehr (Eps 10–14)   Lt. James Judson Scott (from Ep. 11)
Philip Frank Ashmore (from Ep. 14)

Created by: Kenneth Johnson
Executive producers: Daniel H. Blatt, Robert Singer
Producers: Steven E. de Souza, Dean O'Brien, Garner Simmons, David Latt, Skip Ward, Don Boyle, Ralph R. Riskin
Make-up: Leo Lotito

A Daniel H. Blatt and Robert Singer Production in association with Warner Bros Television
19 colour 60-minute episodes
3 June–23 September 1985
(Includes two double-length episodes; 1/2, 18/19)
(Thames Television)

Liberation Day

w Paul Monash

One year after 'The Final Battle', the world celebrates the anniversary of Liberation Day. The evil Diana is due to stand trial for crimes against the human race, but is kidnapped by corrupt magnate Nathan Bates who wants to gain her knowledge. However, Diana escapes and rejoins the Visitors' armada on the dark side of the Moon. Meanwhile, 'star-child' Elizabeth begins a startling metamorphosis.
Robert Maxwell Michael Durrell
Martin Frank Ashmore
Steve Roller Burt Marshall

Director: Paul Krasny

Dreadnaught

w Steven E. de Souza

Reunited with her troops, Diana vows to take Earth by force and, under the guise of agreeing to make Los Angeles an 'open city', activates her Triax super-weapon to reduce the city to rubble. Donovan organises the Resistance to take over the Mother Ship; Elizabeth emerges from her metamorphosis as a fully-grown teenager;

Robert sacrifices himself to halt the deadly Triax.
Robert Maxwell Michael Durrell
Air Force General Linden Chiles
Roller Burt Marshall

Director: Paul Krasny

Breakout

w David Braff

Donovan and Ham are captured and imprisoned in a Visitor work camp guarded by a terrifying sand monster called a crivit. Bates mounts a desperate search for Elizabeth to exchange for his son Kyle who is in Diana's custody. At the camp, Donovan and Ham organise a mass escape.
Annie Pamela Ludwig
Billy Christian Jacobs
Vanik Herman Pope
Roller Burt Marshall

Director: Ray Austin

The Deception

w Garner Simmons

While the Resistance works to help Elizabeth escape to safety in New York,

Diana launches another scheme to capture the star-child by first seizing Donovan and drugging him into disclosing her whereabouts.

Sean Donovan **Nick Katt**
Alien captain **Sandy Lang**

Director: **Victor Lobl**

The Sanction

w **Brian Taggert**
Desperate to free his son Sean from the Visitors' influence, Donovan clashes with a powerful alien killer, Klaus. Meanwhile the relationship intensifies between Kyle and Elizabeth who is finally reunited with her mother Robin.

Klaus **Thomas Callaway**
Sean **Nick Katt**

Director: **Bruce Seth-Green**

Visitors' Choice

w **David Braff**
Nathan Bates resolves to crush the Resistance, starting with a showdown with his son Kyle. Donovan, Julie and Ham stage a daring sabotage at a convention of Visitor commanders where Diana plans to show off an 'encapsulator' – the ultimate device in processing humans for food.

Barry Boddicker **Jonathan Caliri**
Dean Boddicker **Chad McQueen**
Gen. Maxwell Larson **Robert Ellenstein**
Mary Kruger **Sybil Danning**

Director: **Gilbert Shilton**

The Overlord

w **David Abramowitz**
The Resistance runs into a double-cross when they go to help a mining community rid itself of alien-backed thugs. Back at Science Frontiers, Bates' oriental henchman Chaing finds evidence that could expose Julie's true allegiance.

Glenna **Sheryl Lee Raph**
Garrison **Michael Champion**
Daniel **Robert Thaler**

Director: **Bruce Seth Green**

The Dissident

w **Paul F. Edwards**
Diana tests a powerful new force field which she intends using to seal off Los Angeles. Donovan and Ham must kidnap the alien genius responsible for the invention, and find a way to destroy it.

Jacob **John McLiam**
Galen **Anthony DeLongis**

Director: **Walter Grauman**

Reflections in Terror

w **Chris Manheim**
Using a blood sample from Elizabeth, Diana creates a deadly clone which seeks out and ultimately *saves* the star-child. Bates sets a trap to test Julie's loyalty, once and for all.

Chris **Mickey Jones**
Elizabeth clone (aged 8) **Jenny Beck**
Dennis **James Daughton**
Laird **Anthony James**
Rev. Turney **William Wellman, Jnr**

Director: **Kevin Hooks**

The Conversion

w **Brian Taggert**
Ham and Kyle are captured by the Visitors. Aboard the Mother Ship, Charles, the Leader's special envoy, arrives to assume command of the alien forces, with Lydia as his second in command. Charles brainwashes Ham, programming him to kill Donovan, but his plan is thwarted by Elizabeth's uncanny powers.

Chris **Mickey Jones**
Lin **Catherine Nguyen**

Director: **Gilbert Shilton**

The Hero

w **Carleton Eastlake**
Aliens posing as rebels stage a terrorist raid on Science Frontiers hoping to turn public opinion against the Resistance. Chaing and Charles round up rebel sympathisers and announce that they will

kill one hostage a day until the leaders surrender. Robin falls for an apparently heroic comrade; Elias dies in a rescue bid.

John Langley Bruce Davison
George Caniff Robert Hooks
Carol Caniff Judyann Elder

Director: Kevin Hooks

The Betrayal

w Mark Rosner

When Willie is critically injured, Donovan and Ham kidnap a Visitor doctor who is sympathetic to the rebels' cause and reveals that Charles is smuggling arms into the city. Kyle has a poignant reconciliation with his father before Nathan is killed by his old henchman, Chaing. Robin is seduced by Langley and learns to her horror that he is a Visitor.

Langley Bruce Davison
Howie Richard Minchenberg

Director: Gilbert Shilton

The Rescue

w Garner Simmons

The scattered rebels struggle for survival in the war-torn city. Julie delivers a friend's baby in the midst of a battle. Charles forces Diana to marry him – but their wedding night ends in murder.

Alan Davis Terence Knox
Jo Ann Davis Darleen Carr
John Davis Ian Fried

Director: Kevin Hooks

The Champion

w Paul F. Edwards

Arriving to investigate Charles's death, Visitor General Philip allows Lydia and Diana to fight a laser duel. Donovan helps a beautiful widow organise the Resistance in her apathetic town.

Sheriff Roland Hugh Gillin
Kathy Deborah Wakeham
Jesse Sherri Sconer

Director: Cliff Bole

The Wildcats

w David Braff

Needing medicine to treat a deadly diphtheria epidemic, Julie and Kyle recruit a youth gang, one of whom may be a Visitor spy, to help steal the serum. Lydia and Diana conspire to frame a scapegoat for Charles' murder.

Tony Jeffrey Jay Cohen
Ellen Rhonda Aldrich
Andy Adam Silbar
Marta Gela Jacobson

Director: John Florea

The Littlest Dragon

w David Abramowitz

Philip, convinced that Donovan killed his brother, Martin, hunts down the rebel leader. But in the heat of their personal battle Philip learns that it was Diana who killed him, and he and Donovan forge a friendship and new understanding.

Robert Brett Cullen
Glenda Wendy Fulton
Angela Leslie Bevis

Director: Cliff Bole

War of Illusions

w John Simmons

When the Visitors install a high-tech computer, Battlesphere, to launch a final assault on Earth, the Resistance pin their hopes of thwarting the plans on a teenaged computer hacker.

Dr David Atkins Conrad Janis
Henry Atkins Josh Richman
Oswald Peter Eibling

Director: Earl Bellamy

Secret Underground

w David Braff *and* Colley Cibber

Alerted by Philip, Donovan and Julie sneak aboard the Mother Ship to look for a hidden list naming all the rebel leaders. Diana schemes to have Lydia's brother slain during a ritual celebration. Julie discovers a former lover seemingly helping the Visitors to develop a virus that would prove deadly to humans.

Dr Steven Maitland John Calvin
Oswald Peter Eibling
Nigel Ken Olandt
Judith Debbie Gates
Jonathan Derek Barton

Director: Cliff Bole

The Return

w David Abramowitz *and* Donald R. Boyle

The Leader stuns the Visitors by ordering a truce and travelling to Earth to negotiate peace, but Diana plots to disrupt the peace and it takes the combined powers of Elizabeth and the Leader to prevent an appalling holocaust.

Thelma Marilyn Jones

Director: John Florea

THE VOODOO FACTOR

'As my serial is fictional and involves scientists, it is, I suppose, a science fiction thriller. But at that point any resemblance to the conventional thing-from-outer-space story abruptly ends. This one not only could happen, possibly it will . . .'

For this contribution to ITV's *Saturday Serial* slot, in 1959, writer Lewis Greifer eschewed recourse to what he called the 'bug-eyed monsters from space' cliché to set his six-part tale within Earth-bound realms of suspense – the conflict between a scientific, rational attitude and superstition, voodoo, magic and myth.

Its hero, Dr David Whittaker, is detached and ruthlessly scientific – qualities which ill-equip him for a struggle against a legendary Polynesian goddess who died 2000 years earlier, and now seems to be reaching out across the centuries to make her power felt.

As *The Voodoo Factor* opens, Whittaker is called to treat a patient showing symptoms of a strange disease – identical to one he encountered two years before in the Timor Islands where 200 natives died in an epidemic of what they called Spider Fever, believing it the punishment of a malevolent deity, the Spider Goddess. Whittaker had put the deaths down to contaminated malaria serum. But that answer no longer fits.

Searching for his 'rational explanation', Whittaker and his more open-minded wife Marion find themselves caught up in an escalating crisis involving a world-threatening epidemic, an A-bomb test in the Pacific, a floating laboratory aboard a luxury liner and confrontation with the Spider Goddess incarnate (Anna May Wong).

Such blood-curdling thrills were familiar territory for the serial's producer Quentin Lawrence (see *Strange World of Planet X, The*

Trollenberg Terror). Lawrence, a former electrical engineer and stage designer, who joined ATV as a director in 1955, also worked on *H.G. Wells*'s *Invisible Man*.

CAST

Dr David Whittaker **Maurice Kaufmann**   *Marion Whittaker* **Maxine Audley**
The Malayan **Eric Young**   *Dr Tony Wilson* **Philip Bond**   *Alice Simms* **Jill Hyem**
Robin Horsman **Richard Bennett**   *Prof. Axhem/Simon Cave* **Tony Church**
Capt. Ross **Charles Carson**   *Malayan girl* **Anna May Wong**
Bob Busby **John Dearth**   *Riordan* **Dallas Cavell**
Smith **David Brierley**   *Jim Herring* **Richard Burrell**
Albert Williams **Frank Hawkins**   *Insp. Wilkins* **Reginald Marsh**
Renee **Jill Ireland**   *Dr Newman* **Trevor Reid**

Writer: **Lewis Greifer**
Designer: **Tom Lingwood**
Camera: **Warwick Ashton**
Music: **Johnny Dankworth**
Producer: **Quentin Lawrence**

The Malayan
The Professor
The Spiders
The Elixir
The Missing Factor
Operation Lifeboat

An ATV Network Production
Six 30-minute episodes, black and white   12 December 1959– 16 January 1960

VOYAGE TO THE BOTTOM OF THE SEA

Submarine adventures were in vogue in 1964 – we gave America *Stingray* and they gave us *Voyage to the Bottom of the Sea* . . .

These were the voyages of the supersub *Seaview*, a TV spin-off from Irwin Allen's 1961 film epic of the same name, and the first of his lucrative quartet of television sci-fi sagas.

Seaview was a 600-foot-long atomic submarine capable of diving farther and faster than any craft in history and equipped with mini-sub, diving bell, a 'flying' sub and atomic torpedoes. As if to underline the view that there were no half measures about the *Seaview*, even its creator and skipper was an admiral – Admiral Harriman Nelson, sailor-scientist head of the Nelson Institute of Marine Research. The crew's mission, though ostensibly scientific research, was to combat threats to world peace from anyone who felt a bit restless – be they foreign power, alien invader or one of many multi-tentacled monsters lurking in the gloomy depths.

Nelson was played by Richard Basehart, and his principal sidekick among the crew was Capt. Lee Crane (played by David Hedison, star of the 1959 movie original of *The Fly*).

The sub itself was a hand-me-down from the film *Voyage*, as were the sets, costumes, props and reel upon reel of underwater footage (Allen admitted that this saving in production costs was crucial to the TV series' birth). Special effects were masterminded by 20th Century Fox's William Abbott who picked up a brace of Emmys for his work on the show. And with the services of Oscar-winning cinematographer Winton Hoch, the series achieved a distinctive visual style.

But eventually that look became one of *déjà vu*, with the increasingly ludicrous plots and pictures being recycled more times than the crew's drinking water. In America, critics grew to loathe it, but *Seaview* kept on coming, for 110 episodes in four years, a persistence and stamina mercifully unmatched by British series (with only *Doctor Who* clocking up more episodes).

Over here, Northern viewers were the first to embark on the voyage, in October 1964 (barely one month after its US premiere), and the series surfaced and resurfaced throughout the ITV regions over the next two decades or so, with every episode turning up in one area or another.

REGULAR CAST

Admiral Harriman Nelson **Richard Basehart**   *Capt. Lee Crane* **David Hedison**
Lt. Commander Chip Morton **Robert Dowdell**
Chief Sharkey **Terry Becker** *(from Season Two)*
Kowalski **Del Monroe**   *CPO Curley Jones* **Henry Kulky**
Patterson **Paul Trinka**   *Sparks* **Arch Whiting**   *Sonar* **Nigel McKeand**

Creator/Executive producer: **Irwin Allen**
Special effects: **William Abbott**
Make-up: **Ben Nye**

An Irwin Allen Production for 20th Century Fox Television
110 60-minute episodes
black and white (Season One)
colour (from Season Two)

UK premieres:
Season One:
10 October 1964–29 May 1965
(ABC Weekend Television)

Season Two (incomplete run):
8 January–10 April 1966
(ABC Weekend Television)

(Author's note: After an initial Season Two run of 13 episodes, subsequent UK runs were made up of episodes from more than one American season. For ease of reference, all episodes are grouped in their original American seasons.)

Season One
(32 episodes)

Eleven Days to Zero

w **Irwin Allen**
The *Seaview* is sent to avert world-wide tidal waves by detonating a polar nuclear device – but finds its mission threatened by enemy agents.

Malone **Mark Slade**
Chairman **Hal Torey**
O'Brien **Gordon Gilbert**
Army General **Barney Biro**
Dr Fred Wilson **Eddie Albert**
Dr Gamma **Theodore Marcuse**
Dr Selby **John Zaremba**
Capt. Phillips **Bill Hudson**

Director: **Irwin Allen**

The City Beneath the Sea

w Richard Landau

While investigating the disappearance of two research vessels in the Aegean, Crane and a girl diver, Melina, are kidnapped and taken to a hostile underwater city.

Melina Linda Cristal
Zeraff Hurd Hatfield
Round Face John Anderson

Director: John Brahm

The Fear Makers

w Anthony Wilson

Enemy agents pump 'fear gas' into two atomic subs to slow down undersea research work.

Dr Kenner Edgar Dergen
Dr Davis Lloyd Bochner
Malone Mark Slade

Director: Leonard Horn

The Mist of Silence

w John McGreevey

Seaview is ordered to rescue a Latin American president who is the unwilling front man for a military junta and its new gas weapon.

Detta Rita Gam
Galdez Alejandro Rey
Gen. D'Alvarez Mike Kellin
Capt. Serra Henry Del Gado
President Fuente Edward Colmans
Malone Doug Lambert
Chairman Booth Colman

Director: Leonard Horn

The Sky Is Falling

w Don Brinkley

Rays from a mysterious space-craft knock out all *Seaview*'s power systems.

Rear Adm. Tobin Charles McGraw
Spaceman Joseph di Reda
Air Force General Frank Ferguson

Director: Leonard Horn

Turn Back the Clock

w Sheldon Stark

Investigating the story of a man who turns up tanned and healthy after being lost for nine months in Antarctica, Nelson, Crane and the man's fiancée Carol are led to a strange prehistoric world. (This episode used footage from Allen's film *Lost World*, and also featured Yvonne 'Batgirl' Craig.)

Jason Kemp Nick Adams
Carol Yvonne Craig
Dr Denning Les Tremayne
Native girl Vitina Marcus
Zeigler Robert Cornthwaite
Crewman Mark Slade

Director: Alan Crosland

Hot Line

w Berne Giler

One of two Russian scientists being taken by *Seaview* to disarm a defective Soviet atomic satellite is an impostor.

Gronski Everett Sloan
Gregory Malinoff Michael Ansara

Director: John Brahm

The Price of Doom

w Harlan Ellison

The *Seaview* is infiltrated by mysteriously expanding plankton.

Julie Lyle Jill Ireland
Dr Karl Reisner David Opatoshu
Phillip Wesley John Milford
Pennell Steve Ihnat
Mrs Pennell Pat Priest
General Dan Seymour
Crewcut man Ivan Triesault

Director: James Goldstone

Submarine Sunk Here

w William Tunberg

The *Seaview* blunders into a minefield, where an explosion cripples the sub and sends it to the bottom of the sea.

Evans Carl Reindel
Harker Eddie Ryder
Blake Robert Doyle

Director: Leonard Horn

The Magnus Beam

w Alan Caillou
Aided by a beautiful female spy and an offbeat team of Resistance men, Crane and Harriman attempt to destroy a fantastic new weapon that could start World War Three.
Juana Monique Lemaire
Gen. Gamal Malachi Throne
Abdul Azziz Jacques Aubuchon
Amadi Mario Alcalde

Director: Leonard Horn

The Village of Guilt

w Berne Giler
Seaview investigates the activities of a beautiful girl, a mad scientist and his terrifying creation – a sea monster that has a whole village frozen into silence.
Mattson Richard Carlson
Sigrid Anna-Lisa
Dalgren Steve Geray
Hassler Frank Richards
Anderson G. Stanley Jones

Director: Irwin Allen

No Way Out

w Robert Hamner
Smuggling a defecting Red agent to the US involves *Seaview* in a web of spies and counterspies.
Koslow Than Wyenn
Anna Ravec Danielle de Metz
Col. Lascoe Oscar Beregi
Victor Vail Jan Merlin
Wilson Don Wilbanks
Parker Richard Webb

Director: Felix Feist

The Blizzard Makers

w William Welch
A top scientist has been turned into a killer – programmed to eliminate Nelson before he discovers the truth behind a blizzard in Florida.
Dr Melton Milton Selzer
Cregar Werner Klemperer

Director: Joseph Leytes

The Ghost of Moby Dick

w Robert Hamner
A marine biologist becomes a modern-day Ahab when he enlists *Seaview*'s aid in pursuing a 200-ton whale that crippled him. (Also features *Lost in Space* 'mum' June Lockhart.)
Dr Walter Bryce Edward Binns
Ellen Bryce June Lockhart
Jimmy Bryce Bob Beekman

Director: Sobey Martin

Hail to the Chief

w Don Brinkley
Enemy agents plot to prevent the recovery of the US president aboard *Seaview* following an accident. (This episode features James Doohan – Scottie in *Star Trek*.)
Laura Rettig Viveca Lindfors
Dr Taylor Tom Palmer
Tobin James Doohan
Monique Nancy Kovack
Oberhansly Lorence Kerr

Director: Gerd Oswald

The Last Battle

w Robert Hamner
Nelson is kidnapped by a group of diehard Nazis who plan to use *Seaview* to destroy the world and build a Fourth Reich.
Schroder John Van Dreelen
Reinhardt Dayton Lummis
Miklos Joe de Santis
Brewster Ben Wright
Tomas Rudy Solari
Deiner Eric Feldary
Stewardess Sandra Williams

Director: Felix Feist

Doomsday

w William Read Woodfield
The nation goes on war alert following a sudden mass missile launching by a foreign power.
Corbett Donald Harron
Corporal Sy Prescott

Gen. Ashton Paul Genge
President Ford Rainey
Doctor Richard Bull

Director: James Goldstone

Mutiny

w William Read Woodfield
While investigating the loss of an experimental sub, Nelson shows signs of a mental breakdown.
Admiral Starke Harold J. Stone
Doctor Richard Bull
Captain Jay Lanin

Director: James Goldstone

Long Live the King

w Raphael Hayes
Racing to get young Prince Ang back to assume his throne before the Reds take over, the *Seaview* encounters an enigmatic stranger, Old John, floating on a rowing boat in mid-ocean.
Old John Carroll O'Connor
Prince Ang Michael Petit
Col. Meger Michael Pate
Countess Sara Shane
Georges Jan Arvan

Director: Laslo Benedek

The Invaders

w William Read Woodfield
A man-like creature preserved by suspended animation for 20 million years is found on the ocean floor and taken aboard *Seaview*.
Zar Robert Duvall
Foster Michael McDonald

Director: Sobey Martin

The Indestructible Man

w Richard Landau
Scientists aboard *Seaview* discover that a robot recovered from a space capsule has been converted into a destructive monster.
Dr Brand Michael Constantine

Director: Felix Feist

The Buccanneer

w William Welch *and* Albert Gail
A mad art collector takes over *Seaview* in a plot to steal the Mona Lisa from a French ship.
Logan Barry Atwater
Igor George Keymas
French captain Emile Genest

Director: Laslo Benedek

The Human Computer

w Robert Hamner
The *Seaview* sails on an automated mission with Capt. Crane supposedly the only human on board . . .
Man Harry Millard
Reston Simon Scott
Admirals Herbert Lytton, Walter Sande
Foreign general Ted De Corsia

Director: James Goldstone

The Saboteur

w William Read Woodfield
Crane is brainwashed by enemy agents into sabotaging the *Seaview*'s latest mission.
Forester Warren Stevens
Dr Ullman Bert Freed

Director: Felix Feist

Cradle of the Deep

w Robert Hamner
A microscopic particle of matter, taken aboard *Seaview* from the ocean floor, grows into an enormous protoplasm that threatens all aboard.
Dr Janus John Anders
Dr Benton Howard Wendell
O'Brien Derrick Lew
Helmsman Robert Pane

Director: Sobey Martin

The Amphibians

w Rik Vollaerts
Scientists in an undersea lab convert

themselves into amphibious creatures.
Doc Richard Bull
Dr Jenkins Skip Homeier
Dr Winslow Curt Vonway
Andie Zale Parry

Director: Felix Feist

The Exile

w William Read Woodfield
Nelson is stranded on a life-raft with
Brynov, ex-premier of a hostile foreign
power.
Brynov Edward Asner
Josip David Sheiner
Konstantin Harry Davis
Semenev James Frawley
Mikhil Jason Wingreen

Director: James Goldstone

The Creature

w Rik Vollaerts
Capt. Wayne Adams, sole survivor of a
missile disaster, joins *Seaview* to search
the ocean floor for the mysterious force
which foiled the missile launch.
Adams Leslie Nielson
Crewman Pat Culliton
Radar man William Stevens

Director: Sobey Martin

Secret of the Loch

w Charles Bennett
The *Seaview* follows a natural underwater
conduit leading to Loch Ness where a
scientist claims to have seen a monster kill
several men.
Prof. MacDougal Torin Thatcher
Insp. Lester Hedley Mattingly
Angus George Mitchell
Andrews John McLiam

Director: Sobey Martin

The Enemies

w William Read Woodfield
Nelson and Crane are captured by foreign
scientists who use them in an experiment

aimed at turning friends into bitter
enemies.
Gen. Tau Henry Silva
Dr Shinera Malachi Throne

Director: Felix Feist

The Condemned

w William Read Woodfield
Nelson and Crane are ordered to turn the
Seaview over to a publicity-seeking
scientist who plans to break the 'crush
barrier'.
Admiral Falk J.D. Cannon
Archer Arthur Franz
Hoff Alvy Moore

Director: Leonard Horn

The Traitor

w William Welch *and* Al Gail
Enemy agents in France capture Nelson's
young sister hoping to force him to reveal
the location of underwater missile silos.
Major Gen. Fenton George Sanders
Hamid Michael Pate
Girl Susan Flannery

Director: Sobey Martin

Season Two
(26 episodes)

Jonah and the Whale

w Simon Wincelberg
Trying to salvage information about an
underwater laboratory, Nelson and
Russian scientist Katya Markhova are
swallowed by a whale.
Katya Markhova Gia Scala
Helmsman Robert Pane
Crewman Pat Culliton

Director: Sobey Martin

And Five of Us Are Left

w Robert Vincent Wright
Admiral Nelson heads an expedition to
find the survivors of a sunken submarine
trapped for 28 years in an undersea cave.

Wilson James Anderson
Werden Robert Doyle
Hill Ed McCready
Ryan Phillip Pine
Brenda Francoise Ruggieri
Nakamura Teru Shimada
Johnson Kent Taylor

Director: Harry Harris

The Cyborg

w William Read Woodfield *and* Allan
    Balter
A deranged scientist creates a robot
duplicate of Nelson and orders it to target
Seaview's nuclear warheads at Washing-
ton, Peking and Moscow in a plot to rule
the world.
Tabor Ulrich Victor Buono
Gundi Brooke Bundy
Tish Sweetly Nancy Hsueh
Cyborg voices Fred Crane
Technician Tom Curtis
Sailor Stanley Schneider
Reporter Nicholas Colasanto

Director: Leo Penn

Escape From Venice

w Charles Bennett
Nelson engineers a daring rescue of Capt.
Crane from the clutches of enemy agents
in Venice.
Count Staglione Renzo Cesana
Lola Hale Danica D'Handt
Bellini Vincent Gardenia
Julietta Delphi Lawrence

Director: Alex March

Time Bomb

w William Read Woodfield *and* Allan
    Balter
An oriental secret agent's bid to turn
Nelson into a human time bomb almost
starts a war between Russia and America.
Katie Susan Flannery
Litchka Ina Balin
Adm. Johnson John Zaremba
Li Tung Richard Loo

Director: Sobey Martin

The Left-Handed Man

w William Welch
Nelson faces death several times as he
strives to foil a subversive plot to infiltrate
the Defence Department.
George Penfield Regis Toomey
Noah Grafton Cyril Delavanti
Left-handed man Charles Dierkop
Tippy Penfield Barbara Bouchet
Angie Judy Lang
Cabrillo Michael Barrier

Director: Jerry Hopper

The X Factor

w William Welch
Nelson and the *Seaview* crew battle enemy
agents in a toy factory to save a kidnapped
US scientist who has been coated in wax
and transformed into a life-size manne-
quin.
Henderson Jan Merlin
Liscomb George Tyne
Alexander Corby John McGiver
Capt. Shire Bill Hudson
Technician Anthony Brand

Director: Leonard Horn

Leviathan

w William Welch
Leaking radiation from a strange underwater fissure in the Earth's crust turns an
old scientist colleague of Nelson's into a
giant monster bent on destroying *Seaview*.
Cara Karen Steele
Dr Sterling Liam Sullivan

Director: Harry Harris

The Peacemaker

w William Read Woodfield *and* Allan
    Balter
A fanatical scientist, Everett Lang,
threatens to destroy the world with his
new super-bomb.
Lang John Cassavetes
Su Yin Iene Tsu
Policeman Lloyd Kino
Connors Whit Bissell

Premier Dale Ishimoto
Hansen Walter W. King

Director: Sobey Martin

The Silent Saboteurs

w Sidney Marshall, Max Elrich
Crane takes the flying sub on a daring
mission to destroy a secret computer being
used to intercept manned Venus space
flights.
Moana Pilar Seurat
Li Cheng George Takei
Halden Bert Freed
Lago Alex D'Arcy
Stevens Phil Posner
Astronauts Robert Chadwick, Ted
Jordon

Director: Sobey Martin

The Deadliest Game

w Rik Vollaerts
Nelson foils a plot by a US general to kill
the President and trigger a nuclear war.
Gen. Hobson Lloyd Bochner
President Robert F. Simon
Lydia Parrish Audrey Dalton
Gen. Reed Michaels Robert Cornthwaite

Director: Sobey Martin

The Monsters From Outer Space

w William Read Woodfield *and* Allan
Balter
A Saturn space probe re-enters Earth's
atmosphere with a strange tentacled
monster attached to it.
Seaview doctor Wayne Heffley
Space Centre technician Lee Delano
Flight director Preston Hanson
Naval commander Hal Torey

Director: James Clark

The Machines Strike Back

w John *and* Ward Hawkins
Unmanned submarines inexplicably turn
their devastating missiles towards
America.

Adm. Halder Roger Carmel
Capt. Verna Trober Francoise Ruggieri
Adm. Johnson John Gallaudet
Senator Kimberly Bert Remsen

Director: Jerry Juran

The Death Ship

w William Read Woodfield *and* Allan
Balter
Nelson averts an enemy plot to blow up a
seven-nation peace conference.
Stroller Lew Gallo
Tracy Elizabeth Perry
Ava June Vincent
Klaus Ivan Triesault
Chandler David Sheiner

Director: Abe Biberman

Killers of the Deep

w William Read Woodfield *and* Allan
Balter
Aboard a US destroyer, Nelson wages a
harrowing battle with an enemy sub trying
to steal undersea defence missiles.
Fraser Patrick Wayne
Capt. Tomas Ruiz Michael Ansara
Manolo James Frawley
Capt. Lawrence John Newton
Sonar men Dallas Mitchell, Gus Trikonis

Director: Harry Harris

Terror on Dinosaur Island

w William Welch
Nelson and Chief Sharkey parachute from
the flying sub onto a volcanic island
inhabited by prehistoric monsters (further
footage culled from Allen's film *The Lost
World*).
Benson Paul Carr

Director: Leonard Horn

Deadly Creature Below

w William Read Woodfield *and* Allan
Balter
Two escaped convicts try to hijack the

flying sub while a sea monster menaces the *Seaview*.
Dobbs Nehemiah Persoff
Hawkins Paul Comi
Seaview doctor Wayne Heffley

Director: Sobey Martin

The Phantom

w William Welch
The *Seaview* is nearly destroyed by a phantom sub and its ghostly captain who seeks to reincarnate himself through Crane.
Gerhardt Krueger Alfred Ryder

Director: Sutton Roley

The Sky's on Fire

w William Welch
While the Van Allen radiation belt burns, a fanatical UN official tries to sabotage Nelson's plan to explode the burning gases from the atmosphere.
Weber David J. Stewart
Carleton Robert H. Harris
McHenry Frank Martin

Director: Sobey Martin

Graveyard of Fear

w Robert Vincent Wright
The *Seaview* is menaced by a giant jelly-fish.
Dr Ames Robert Loggia
Karyl Marian Moses

Director: Jus Addis

The Shape of Doom

w William Welch
In a race to protect a ship carrying the President, Nelson and Crane battle a giant whale that has swallowed an atomic bomb.
Dr Alex Holden Kevin Hagen

Director: Nathan Juran

Dead Men's Doubloons

w Sidney Marshall
The flying sub is attacked by a ghostly underwater pirate ship.
Capt. Brent Albert Salmi
Sebastian Allen Jaffe
Adm. Howard Robert Brubaker

Director: Sutton Roley

The Monster's Web

w Al Gail, Peter Packer
The *Seaview* battles a giant spider while retrieving high-explosive fuel from a wrecked nuclear sub.
Capt. Gantt Mark Richman
Balter Barry Coe
Sonar man Sea Morgan

Director: Jus Addis

The Menfish

w William Read Woodfield *and* Allan Balter
The *Seaview* tangles with yet another monster – a half-man, half-fish creature created by a mad scientist.
Admiral Park Gary Merrill
Johnson Roy Jenson
Hansjurg Victor Lundin
Dr Borgman John Dehner

Director: Tom Gries

The Mechanical Man

w John *and* Ward Hawkins
A life-like robot uses the *Seaview* to seek control of the world.
Omir James Darren
Paul Arthur O'Connell
Jensen Seymour Cassel
Van Druten Cec Linder

Director: Sobey Martin

The Return of the Phantom

w William Welch
The Phantom returns from the dead in a

renewed attempt to capture Crane's body.
Gerhardt Krueger Alfred Ryder
Lani Vitina Marcus
Doctor Richard Bull

Director: Sutton Roley

Season Three
(26 episodes)

Monster from the Inferno

w Rik Vollaerts
A scientist-diver animates a brain-shaped
mass which tries to take over the *Seaview*.
Lindsay Arthur Hill
Doctor Richard Bull

Director: Harry Harris

Werewolf

w Donn Mullally
Nelson and the *Seaview* crewmen are
transformed into werewolves.
Hollis Charles Aidman
Witt Douglas Bank

Director: Jus Addiss

The Day the World Ended

w William Welch
The *Seaview* loses contact with the world
as a fanatical power-crazed senator
hypnotises the entire crew.
Senator Dennis Skip Homeier

Director: Jerry Hopper

Night of Terror

w Robert Bloomfield
Shipwrecked on a mysterious island,
Nelson, Sharkey and a geologist are
terrorised by a giant lizard and hallucina-
tions.
Sprague Henry Jones
Buccaneer Jerry Catron

Director: Jus Addiss

The Terrible Toys

w Robert Vincent Wright
Aliens aboard a UFO rig six wind-up toys
to destroy the *Seaview*.
Sam Burke Paul Fix
Old man Francis X. Bushman
Voice Jim Mills

Director: Jus Addiss

Day of Evil

w William Welch
An alien stranger tries to force Nelson to
destroy the Pacific fleet with a nuclear
missile.
Doctor Richard Bull

Director: Jerry Hopper

Deadly Waters

w Robert Vincent Wright
Kowalski's injured, unreasonable brother
Stan saves the *Seaview* crew from a deep-
sea death.
Kruger Lew Gallo
Stan Don Gordon
Commander Finch Harry Lauter

Director: G. Mayer

Thing from Inner Space

w William Welch
An adventurer leads the *Seaview* crew in
search of a monster that killed his camera
crew.
Bainbridge Wells Hugh Marlowe
Monster Dawson Palmer

Director: A. March

The Death Watch

w William Welch
Nelson and Crane are the subjects of an
experiment in which they are ordered to
kill each other. (No guest cast.)

Director: Leonard Horn

Deadly Invasion

w John *and* Ward Hawkins
Faceless aliens invade Earth and try to take over an underwater atomic base.
Sam Garrity Warren Stevens
Gen. Haine Michael Fox
Kelly Ashley Gilbert
Peters Brent Davis

Director: Jerry Juran

The Haunted Submarine

w William Welch
Nelson is plagued by a ghostly slave trader ancestor who has come to take him away.
Shaemus O'Hara Richard Basehart

Director: Harry Harris

The Plant Man

w Donn Mullally
The *Seaview* battles multiplying plant monsters and the twin scientists who created them.
John/Ben Wilson William Smithers

Director: Harry Harris

The Lost Bomb

w Oliver Crawford
An enemy sub vies with the *Seaview* for an activated super bomb that threatens to explode.
Dr Bradley John Lupton
Vadim Gerald Mohr
Zane George Keymas

Director: J. Mayer

The Brand of the Beast

w William Welch
Radiation exposure causes Nelson to suffer a recurrence of the Werewolf virus. (You can't keep a good plot down!)
Doctor Richard Bull

Director: Jus Addiss

The Creature

w John *and* Ward Hawkins
Nelson attempts to destroy a creature which threatens to grow large enough to demolish whole cities.
Dr King Lyle Bettger

Director: Jus Addiss

Death From the Past

w Sidney Marshall *and* Charles Bennett
The *Seaview* battles two Nazi officers left over from World War II who attempt to launch missiles at the Allied capitals.
Adm. Von Neuberg John Van Dreelen
Lt. Froelich Jan Merlin

Director: Jus Addiss

The Heat Monster

w Charles Bennett
The *Seaview* battles an invasion of alien heat monsters on the Arctic ice cap.
Sven Larsen Don Knight
Dr Bergstrom Alfred Ryder

Director: J. Mayer

The Fossil Men

w James Whiton
The *Seaview* battles hostile fossil men who want to take over the world.
Capt. Wren Brendan Dillon
Richards Jerry Catron

Director: Jus Addiss

The Mermaid

w William Welch
Crane captures a mermaid who eventually leads the sub to an undersea nuclear bomb about to explode.
The mermaid Diane Webber

Director: Jerry Hopper

The Mummy

w William Welch
A 3000-year-old mummy puts a spell on Crane and terrorises the *Seaview*.
Doctor Richard Bull

Director: Harry Harris

Shadowman

w Rik Vollaerts
The *Seaview* is taken over by a hostile energy mass from a distant galaxy. (No guest cast.)

Director: Jus Addiss

No Escape from Death

w William Welch
While trying to surface after a crippling collision, the *Seaview* is threatened by a gigantic Portuguese man-o-war.
(No guest cast.)

Director: Harry Harris

Doomsday Island

w Peter Germano
The sub encounters terrifying alien creatures who want to use *Seaview*'s power to take over the Earth.
Lars Jock Gaynor

Director: Jerry Hopper

The Wax Men

w William Welch
Hostile wax replicas of the crew take over *Seaview*.
Clown Michael Dunn

Director: H. Jones

Deadly Cloud

w Rik Vollaerts
The *Seaview* is sent to check out a mysteri-ous cloud which has caused widespread destruction around the world.
Jurgenson Robert Carson

Director: Jerry Hopper

Destroy Seaview!

w Donn Mullally
Nelson is brainwashed into trying to destroy the *Seaview* – and nearly succeeds.
Leader Jerry Catron
Dr Land Arthur Space

Director: Jus Addiss

Season Four
26 episodes

Man of Many Faces

w William Welch
A mad scientist imperils the Earth by drawing the Moon towards it.
Dr Mason Jock Gaynor
Page Bradd Arnold
Reporter Howard Culver

Director: Harry Harris

Time Lock

w William Welch
A man of the future tries to add Nelson to his collection of zombie-like military officers.
Alpha John Crawford

Director: J. Hoffer

The Deadly Dolls

w Charles Bennett
Nelson and Crane battle a puppet master, the tool of a machine-ruled civilisation.
Prof. Multiple Vincent Price
Puppeteer Ronald P. Martin

Director: Harry Harris

Fires of Death

w Arthur Weiss
The crew battle to stop an aged alchemist who's endangering the entire southern hemisphere to obtain an elixir of youth from an exploding volcano.
Dr Turner Victor Jory

Director: Bruce Fowler

Cave of the Dead

w William Welch
Nelson is the target of a seaman from the past, trying to transfer the curse of the Flying Dutchman onto him.
Doctor Richard Bull
Van Wyck Warren Stevens

Director: Harry Harris

Sealed Orders

w William Welch
Mass hallucinations grip the *Seaview* crew when a secret missile they are carrying begins to emit strange fumes.
(No guest cast.)

Director: Jerry Hopper

Journey with Fear

w Arthur Weiss
Nelson, Crane and Morton are captured by aliens and transported in a flash to their planet.
Maj. Wilson Eric Matthews
Centaur I Gene Dynarski
Centaur II Jim Goss

Director: Harry Harris

Terror

w Sidney Ellis
Alien plant creatures arrive to take over the Earth, possessing Nelson and some of the *Seaview* crew.
Dr Thompson Damian O'Flynn

Dunlap Pat Culliton
Crewmen Brent Davis, Thom Brann

Director: Jerry Hopper

Fatal Cargo

w William Welch
Nelson's decision to carry on with the animal experiments of a friend who has mysteriously died almost proves fatal to him, too.
Brock Woodrow Parfrey
Dr Blanchard Jon Lormer

Director: Jerry Hopper

Rescue

w William Welch
Nelson battles a saboteur and a mystery sub that threatens to destroy them.
CPO Beach Don Dubbins

Director: Jus Addiss

The Death Clock

w Sidney Marshall
The *Seaview* crew survive a fourth dimensional nightmare of death and destruction.
Mallory Chris Robinson

Director: Charles Rondeau

Secret of the Deep

w William Welch
A traitor nearly undermines *Seaview*'s mission to destroy a group of men threatening the world with sophisticated weapons.
John Hendrix Mark Richman

Director: Charles Rondeau

Blow Up

w William Welch
A whiff of gas gives Nelson temporary

paranoia and he tries to torpedo Navy subs.
Doctor Richard Bull

Director: Jus Addiss

Deadly Amphibians

w Arthur Weiss
An amphibian race try to take over the *Seaview* and use its nuclear power for their own ends.
Proto Don Matheson
Corpsman Joey Tata
Guard Pat Culliton

Director: Jerry Hopper

The Abominable Snowman

w Robert Hamner
In Antarctica, the *Seaview* is menaced by a strange creature created by weather experiments.
Corpsman Frank Babich
Guard Bruce Mars
Rayburn Dusty Cadis

Director: Robert Sparr

The Return of Blackbeard

w Al Gail
Blackbeard the pirate appears and tries to take over the *Seaview*.
Blackbeard Malachi Throne

Director: Jus Addiss

A Time to Die

w William Welch
The super-sub is menaced by an odd little man capable of moving people about through time.
Mr Pem Henry Jones

Director: Robert Sparr

The Edge of Doom

w William Welch
An enemy agent impersonates a crewman to sabotage a mission.
Helmsman Scott McFadden

Director: Jus Addiss

Nightmare

w Sidney Marshall
Crane finds the entire crew against him as he tries to stop Nelson from launching a missile attack on Washington . . . but it's all an alien trick!
Bentley Paul Mantee

Director: Charles Rondeau

The Lobster Man

w Al Gail
A lobster-like alien plots to destroy Earth. (Now that's what I call a plot!)
Alien Victor Lundin

Director: Jus Addiss

The Terrible Leprechaun

w Charles Bennett
The *Seaview* crew match wits with an unusual elfin enemy to prevent a nuclear explosion.
Leprechaun Mickey/Leprechaun Patrick Walter Burke
Somers Ralph Garrett
Corpsman Pat Culliton
Crewman John Bellah

Director: Jerry Hopper

Savage Jungle

w Arthur Weiss
A jungle growth planted by aliens threatens to overrun the Earth.
Alien Pat Culliton
Keeler Perry Lopez

Director: Robert Sparr

Man-Beast

w William Welch
Crane turns into a beast-like creature and
menaces all on board the *Seaview*.
Dr Kermit Braddock Lawrence
   Montaigne

Director: Jerry Hopper

Attack!

w William Welch
With the help of a peace-loving alien,
Nelson and Crane prevent an invasion of
Earth.
Robek Skip Homeier
Komal Kevin Hagen

Director: Jerry Hopper

Flaming Ice

w Arthur Browne Jr
The super-sub is sent to the polar ice-cap
to find the cause of destructive world-wide
floods.
Gelid Michael Pate
Frost men Frank Babich, George
   Robotham

Director: Robert Sparr

No Way Back

w William Welch
The mysterious Mr Pem returns to try to
use the *Seaview* to go back in time and
change the course of history.
Mr Pem Henry Jones
Benedict Arnold Barry Atwater
Maj. John Andre William Beckley

Director: Robert Sparr

THE WILD, WILD WEST

On the face of it, *The Wild, Wild West* sounds like just another
Western adventure series, set as it is in post-Civil War America.

The good guys are a debonair government undercover agent,
James T. West, and his aide, master of disguise and inventor
Artemus Gordon, who have been chosen by President Ulysses S.
Grant to spearhead the government's efforts to enforce law and
order on the frontier. They operate from a mobile base on a plush
private train with weapons and gadgets strategically hidden
throughout.

But the bad guys aren't your average rustler or gun-toting
outlaw. They're often criminal geniuses threatening the newly
united American nation with all manner of scientific devices from
robots to atomic bombs, wave-makers to time machines, cyborgs to
a volcano-creating device.

Thus, the elements of Western and tongue-in-cheek spy drama
combined to produce one of the purest and most outrageously
bizarre fantasies ever made for television.

The series' most charismatic 'super' villain, Miguelito Loveless,
is a dwarf with a fanatical hatred of everyone taller than himself! A
brilliant scientist, he invents robots, LSD and time travel devices.

He also devised the means to shrink people and to escape by passing into another dimension and hiding in oil paintings!

One episode even brought on the aliens – a trio of Venusians who land on Earth in their 'flying pie plate' in search of fuel. Another, *The Night of the Burning Diamond*, featured a thief who melted down diamonds to create an elixir with which he could travel faster than light.

In America, *The Wild, Wild West* was a big hit, running for four years and 104 episodes from 1965. Britain hasn't been so lucky: the series premiered in ITV's Northern region in May 1968 (a 13-week Sunday night run), billed as 'the first James Bond Western', and subsequently clocked up seasons in several ITV regions during the 1970s, notably London, Southern and Westward. But these were invariably mid-afternoon when no one was watching or late-night when they'd gone to bed.

REGULAR CAST

Major James T. West **Robert Conrad**   *Artemus Gordon* **Ross Martin**
Tennyson (a butler) **Charles Davis** *(Season One only)*
Dr Miguelito Loveless **Michael Dunn** *(semi-regular)*
Jeremy Pike **Charles Aidman***

Created by: **Michael Garrison**
Producers: **Michael Garrison, Fred Freiberger, Gene L. Coon, Collier Young, John Mantley, Bruce Lansbury**
Writers: Various, including **John Kneubuhl, Stephen Kandel, Oliver Crawford, Gene L. Coon, Paul Playdon, Edward J. Lasko**
Directors: **Various, including Irving Moore, Paul Wendkos, Richard Sarafian**

A Michael Garrison Production in association with CBS
104 60-minute episodes
black and white (Season One)
colour (from Season Two)
UK premiere run:
5 May–28 July 1968
(ABC Weekend Television)

A lot of ITV regions have seen *The Wild, Wild West*. But none of them have seen all 104 episodes which are listed here in their original US Seasons.

Season One
(28 black and white episodes)

The Night of the Inferno
The Night of the Deadly Bed
The Night the Wizard Shook the Earth
The Night of the Sudden Death
The Night of the Casual Killer
The Night of a Thousand Eyes
The Night of the Glowing Corpse

The Night of the Dancing Death
The Night of the Double-Edged Knife
The Night the Terror Stalked Town
The Night of the Red-Eyed Madman
The Night of the Human Trigger
The Night of the Torture Chamber
The Night of the Howling Light
The Night of the Fatal Trap
The Night of the Steel Assassin
The Night the Dragon Screamed

---

* stood in for several Season Four episodes while Ross Martin was recovering from a heart attack.

The Night of the Grand Emir
The Night of the Flaming Ghost
The Night of the Whirring Death
The Night of the Puppeteer
The Night of the Bars of Hell
The Night of the Two-Legged Buffalo
The Night of the Druid's Blood
The Night of the Freebooters
The Night of the Burning Diamond
The Night of the Murderous Spring
The Night of the Sudden Plague

Season Two
(28 colour episodes)

The Night of the Eccentrics
The Night of the Golden Cobra
The Night of the Raven
The Night of the Big Blast
The Night of the Returning Dead
The Night of the Flying Pie Plate
The Night of the Poisonous Posy
The Night of the Bottomless Pit
The Night of the Watery Death
The Night of the Green Terror
The Night of the Ready-Made Corpse
The Night of the Man-Eating House
The Night of the Skulls
The Night of the Infernal Machine
The Night of the Lord of Limbo
The Night of the Tottering Tontine
The Night of the Feathered Fury
The Night of the Gypsy Peril
The Night of the Tartar
The Night of the Vicious Valentine
The Night of the Brain
The Night of the Deadly Bubble
The Night of the Surreal McCoy
The Night of the Colonel's Ghost
The Night of the Deadly Blossom
The Night of the Cadre
The Night of the Wolf
The Night of the Bogus Bandits

Season Three
(24 colour episodes)

The Night of the Bubbling Death
The Night of the Firebrand
The Night of the Assassin
The Night Dr Loveless Died
The Night of the Jack o'Diamonds

The Night of the Samurai
The Night of the Hangman
The Night of Montezuma's Hordes
The Night of the Circus of Death
The Night of the Falcon
The Night of the Cut-Throat
The Night of the Legion of Death
The Night of the Turncoat
The Night of the Iron Fist
The Night of the Running Death
The Night of the Arrow
The Night of the Headless Woman
The Night of the Vipers
The Night of the Underground Terror
The Night of the Death Masks
The Night of the Undead
The Night of the Amnesiac
The Night of the Simian Terror
The Night of the Death-Maker

Season Four
(24 colour episodes)

The Night of the Big Blackmail
The Night of the Doomsday Formula
The Night of the Juggernaut
The Night of the Sedgewick Curse
The Night of the Gruesome Games
The Night of the Kraken
The Night of the Fugitive
The Night of the Egyptian Queen
The Night of the Fire and Brimstone
The Night of the Camera
The Night of the Avaricious Actuary
The Night of Miguelito's Revenge
The Night of the Pelican
The Night of the Spanish Curse
The Night of the Winged Terror
(A 2-part story)
The Night of Sabatini's Death
The Night of the Janus
The Night of the Pistoleros
The Night of the Diva
The Night of the Bleak Island
The Night of the Cossacks
The Night of the Tycoons
The Night of the Plague

There are also two TV movie revivals:
The Wild, Wild West Revisited (1979)
More Wild, Wild West (1980).

WONDER WOMAN

More properly billed as *The New Adventures of Wonder Woman*, this was America's second stab at liberating the comic-strip heroine from the printed page.

The first attempt (not shown in Britain) was set in the war years and ran for one season with the Amazon Princess, alias Diana Prince, leaving her idyllic home on Paradise Island to help World War Two Flying ace Major Steve Trevor battle the Nazis.

The New Adventures updated the scenario to the 1970s, with the ageless, leggy heroine now being recruited by Steve Trevor Jr's undercover organisation, the International Agency Defence Command (IADC), again to champion good and fight evil – this time in the shape of mad scientists, spies, would-be dictators, supercrooks and aliens.

Former Miss World and 1973 Miss USA Lynda Carter amply filled the star-spangled costume and bulletproof bracelets in a series that tried hard to avoid the camp elements of *Batman* but didn't always succeed.

Perversely, the BBC skipped the updated 'origins' episode, *The Return of Wonder Woman* (shown last!), and went straight into the action with the tale of a telekinetic Japanese seeking revenge on Wonder Woman for a 35-year-old grievance (*The Man Who Could Move the World*).

Other adversaries included: a rock musician hypnotising young women into stealing for him (*The Pied Piper*); Roddy McDowall as a crazy scientist who uses a laser weapon to create volcanic eruptions across the globe (*The Man Who Made Volcanoes*); the Skrill – alien mind-thieves out to take over the world's top brains (*The Mind Stealers from Outer Space*); an occult magician (*Diana's Disappearing Act*); Henry Gibson as an athlete-kidnapping megalomaniac (*Screaming Javelins*); Frank Gorshin as a mad toymaker using human androids to steal top-scret plans (*The Deadly Toys*); a group of Nazis plotting to clone Hitler (*Anschluss '77*); Wolfman Jack as a psychic vampire (*Disco Devil*); Joan Van Ark as a greedy 22nd-century scientist (*Time Bomb*); a billionaire's disembodied brain (*Gault's Brain*); and an alien criminal able to assume any shape (*The Boy Who Knew Her Secrets*).

REGULAR CAST

Wonder Woman/Diana Prince **Lynda Carter**   *Steve Trevor* **Lyle Waggoner**

Producer: **Bruce Lansbury**
Writers: Various, including **Stephen Kandel, Anne Collins, Alan Brennert, Bruce Shelley**

Director: Various, including **Alan Crosland, Michael Caffey, Seymour Robbie**

A Warner Brothers Television Production
45 colour 45-minute episodes (+ one × 80 mins)
1 July–26 August 1978
23 December 1978–4 May 1979
12 January–17 June 1980
(BBC1)

(Author's note: The BBC running order differed considerably at times from the US original but got there in the end. In America the series was shown in one 'strung out' season over two years.)

The Return of Wonder Woman (80 mins)*
Anschluss '77
The Man Who Could Move the World
The Bermuda Triangle Crisis
Knockout
The Pied Piper
The Queen and the Thief
I Do, I Do
The Man Who Made Volcanoes
The Mind Stealers from Outer Space *(A 2-part story)*
The Deadly Toys
Light-Fingered Lady
Screaming Javelin
Diana's Disappearing Act

Death in Disguise
Irac is Missing
Flight to Oblivion
Seance of Terror
The Man Who Wouldn't Tell
The Girl from Ilandia
The Murderous Missile
One of Our Teen Idols is Missing
Hot Wheels
The Deadly Sting
The Fine Art of Crime
Disco Devil
Formicida
Time Bomb
Skateboard Whiz
The Deadly Dolphin
Stolen Faces
Pot O'Gold
Gault's Brain
Going, Going, Gone
Spaced Out
The Starships Are Coming
Amazon Hot Wax
The Richest Man in the World
A Date With Doomsday
The Girl With the Gift for Disaster
The Boy Who Knew Her Secrets *(A 2-part story)†*
The Man Who Could Not Die
Phantom of the Roller Coaster *(A 2-part story)*

* Shown here as a 'special': 1 January 1981
† Shown here as one 90-minute episode: 17 June 1980

SINGLE DRAMAS/
ONE-OFF
PRODUCTIONS

A.D.A.M.

A psychological horror story, and a vindication of the neuroses of anyone who has ever lived in dread of household appliances taking on a life of their own.

Beautiful but disabled Jean Empson moves into her new home, built by her husband, to find it is a completely automated house in which everything is controlled by a computer called A.D.A.M. (Automated Domestic Appliance Monitor).

A.D.A.M. is programmed to talk and all goes well until it proceeds to take their relationship a step further, becoming emotionally involved with Jean. Put simply, it fancies her – a situation reminiscent of the film *Demon Seed*.

The play was produced by *Doctor Who* pioneer Verity Lambert and drew a strong performance from Georgina Hale as the crippled wife. In many scenes she was the only person on screen, acting with just a disembodied voice.

CAST

Roger Empson **Mark Jones**   *Jean Empson* **Georgina Hale**
Hanley **Richardson Morgan**   *Jean's mother* **Madge Ryan**
Kitty Perring **Cicely Paget-Bowman**
Brigadier Perring **Willoughby Gray**   *Vincent Metcalfe* **Tom Kempinski**
Voice of A.D.A.M. **Anthony Jackson**

Writer: **Donald Jonson**
Producer: **Verity Lambert**
Director: **Michael Lindsay-Hogg**
Designer: **John Emery**

London Weekend Television Production
60 minutes, colour
8 April 1973
(ITV)

ALTERNATIVE 3

Belated April Fool hoax that drew comparison with Orson Welles's famous *War of the Worlds* radio broadcast in the 1930s and drew protests from thousands of anxious viewers.

Alternative 3 purported to be a dramatic, shock-horror documentary revealing that America and Russia had founded a secret colony of scientists on Mars or the dark side of the Moon because, it was claimed, the Greenhouse effect – climatic disasters caused by the Sun's heat becoming trapped by thickening layers of pollution – had made dear old Earth a lost cause.

The 'three' alternatives put forward by one expert were: cut population, cut consumption or cut and run. Anglia Television's

Science Report team supposedly found out during an 18-month investigation that some 400 scientists had gone to the Moon and Mars, and even propped up an 'alcoholic ex-astronaut', Bob Grodin, to announce that 'those late Apollos were just a smokescreen to cover up what's going on up there'.

Using familiar and plausible tricks of investigative documentary such as case histories of vanished scientists, footage of droughts and disasters, plausible scientific doom theories, smuggled video-tape, 8mm 'home movie' sequences and the clinching authority of former newscaster Tom Brinton as frontman, *Alternative 3* pre-sented a compelling case, challenging the powers-that-be to 'tell us the truth'. A cast-list and the date 1 April appeared in the end credits but the ball was well and truly rolling by then.

The hoax misfired – or worked, depending on your point of view – with thousands of alarmed viewers failing to see the joke and calling on Anglia TV to tell *them* the truth! Writer David Ambrose and director Christopher Miles weathered the storm with a wry smile saying they had felt viewers would be sophisticated enough to take it, and that, besides the programme did have a serious point to make. Ambrose was quoted at the time as saying he was 'constantly amazed at the gullibility of people'. Most critics, being in on the joke, loved it, and *Alternative 3* was broadcast in several other countries. American networks turned it down, however, fearing another *War of the Worlds*.

Writer: **David Ambrose**
Director: **Christopher Miles**

Anglia Television Production
60 minutes, colour
Monday 20 June 1977
(ITV)

APE & ESSENCE

Horrific, bawdy satire by Aldous Huxley about the humanistic and religious consequences of dropping the bomb. In his vision of a Britain 80 years after the bomb, its inhabitants are not only badly mutated but are worshipping the Devil – Huxley's tongue-in-cheek contention that a race wicked enough to explode a nuclear device must, perforce, be damned.

Alec McCowen played a shy botany professor who was part of a New Zealand Rediscovery Expedition to Great Britain in 2048 which comes across a pocket of survivors near London. Under the sway of the Arch-Vicar of Belial, they are sacrificing their deformed babies and indulging in orgies of communal sex.

The play drew some calls of protest to the BBC, but was widely praised by the critics.

CAST

Alfred Poole **Alec McCowen**   *Miss Hook* **Hazel Douglas**
Craigie **Sydney Bromley**   *Chief* **Derek Sydney**
Loola **Petra Marknam**   *Flossie* **Jenny Lee**
Satanic Science Practitioner **Ken Parry**
Young girl **Yvonne Antrobus**   *Polly* **Amanda Reiss**
Arch-Vicar **Robert Eddison**   *Patriarch* **John Falconer**
Priest **Jonathan Scott**   *Director of Food Production* **Martin Carroll**

Writer: **Aldous Huxley**
Dramatised by: **John Finch**
Director: **David Benedictus**
Designer: **Norman James**
Producer: **Peter Luke**

A BBC Production
75 minutes, black and white
18 May 1966

ARTEMIS 81

'Disturbing, beautiful and almost incomprehensible'

(*Daily Mail*)

Mystical thriller about a battle between good and evil that ranged over a North Sea ferry, a Danish cathedral, a ravaged old tower by the sea and an alien planet, and tipped its hat to Hitchcock along the way.

Artemis 81 crammed extraordinary imagery into a bewildering plot that evolved into a kind of nightmare with disjointed sequences making little rational sense.

It opened on an alien world where Helith, the Angel of Life (dressed all in white), is ranged against his evil brother Asrael (the man in black) for control of man's destiny. The metaphysical plot thickened via pieces of a stolen pagan relic hidden in cars on a North Sea ferry, the subsequent suicides of ferry passengers, and a haunted-looking old organist, Von Drachenfels, who is terrified that a curse upon him will cause the devastation of the Earth.

To Gideon Harlax, novelist of the paranormal, such events are grist to the writer's mill. But as he coldly exploits human tragedies, angry powers are gathering.

Artemis 81 starred Hywell Bennett, Dinah Stabb and Dan O'Herlihy, and featured Sting in his first major dramatic role. Indulgently long, it ran for more than three hours. Too long by half was the critics' verdict.

CAST

Gideon Harlax **Hywel Bennett**   *Gwen Meredith* **Dinah Stabb**
Von Drachenfels **Dan O'Herlihy**   *Jed Thaxter* **Ian Redford**
Laura Guise **Margaret Whiting**

ALIEN PLANET:
Magog **Sevilla Delofski**   *Asrael* **Roland Curram**   *Helith* **Sting**

DANISH FERRY:
Tristram Guise **Anthony Steel**   *Sonia* **Mary Ellen Ray**
Pastor **Cornelius Garrett**   *Pastor's wife* **Siv Borg**

OXFORD LIBRARY:
Gorgon scholar **Sylvia Coleridge**   *Exhibitioner* **Daniel Day Lewis**
Hitchcock blonde **Ingrid Pitt**

Writer: **David Rudkin**
Director: **Alastair Reid**
Producer: **David Rose**
Designer: **Gavin Davies**
Original music: **Dave Greenslade**

A BBC Production
185 minutes, colour
29 December 1981

BEFORE THE SUN GOES DOWN

'We are interrupting the programme for an
urgent announcement'

The main story of this 1958 ITV play by American author Lester
Fuller was *not* science fiction – but its opening was, and it sparked
widespread alarm and anger that had Fleet Street luridly recalling
Orson Welles's 1938 *War of the Worlds* radio broadcast.

Without any introduction or on-screen credit sequence, the play
began with a simulated newsflash that took hundreds of frightened
viewers totally by surprise. After his initial interruption, the
newsreader unveiled this jolly little scenario:

'A new and terrifying satellite has been launched into outer
space. Defying all previous scientific theory, it hangs stationary
over London. Is this an enemy space platform armed with H-
bombs and aimed at the heart of the city?'

Viewers were told to clear the streets, stay in their homes and
keep watching their TVs. Unfortunately, hordes – especially in
London! – did quite the opposite, running *into* the streets to try to
catch a glimpse of the satellite. Once realisation had dawned – and
smelling salts been administered to elderly relatives – police,

newspaper, ITV (and BBC!) switchboards lit up as the complaints rolled in.

In response, Sir Robert Fraser, director-general of the Independent Television Authority, admitted that the announcement had been a 'bad blunder' – though advance publicity in *TVTimes* had made the fictional nature of the beast quite clear – and a hurriedly convened inquiry pledged to tighten up on possible areas of misunderstanding.

As for the play, the appearance of the satellite and the subsequent evacuation of London were simply a device to clear the stage for a slight romance between two maladjusted people, Vek, an eccentric Irish drunk, and Anna, a lonely, unhappy foreign maid, who elected to stay in the city. Their courtship ended in a sentimental mock marriage.

The *Daily Telegraph* critic Patrick Gibbs wrote: 'The play itself did not merit the attention drawn to it', while *The Observer*'s Maurice Richardson called it 'a "bad blunder" followed by a poor play'.

CAST

Vek Eddie Byrne   *Anna* Margot van der Burgh
Newsreader Paul Martin   *Bully* Charles Farrell   *Spiv* Harry Landis
Revivalist Gerald C. Lawson   *Madame* Joyce Barbour
Prime Minister Moultrie Kelsall   *Scientist* Colin Keith Johnson
General Richard Caldicott   *Admiral* Ewen MacDuff
Civil servant Douglas Bradley-Smith   *Doctor* Anthony Nicholls

Writer: Lester Fuller
Music composed by: Ron Grainer
Played by: Ron Grainer *and* Geoff Lofts
Settings: John Clements
Director: Robert Tronson

An Associated-Rediffusion Network Production
60 minutes, black and white
20 February 1959

BELLWEATHER NINE

Farcical nudge in the ribs for rockets and space travel. Its central character was Professor Humphrey Bellweather who, aided by his scatty sister Amanda, dotty secretary Doris and brainless assistant Monty, moves into the satellite business and prepares to beat the government in the space race. Everyone thinks Bellweather has been successfully launched into space in his rocket number nine. In fact, though suffering the same delusion himself, he was firmly earthbound in Bellweather Eight.

The *Daily Telegraph* said of the play: 'It got off to a shaky start . . . never gathered the necessary acceleration . . . and fell to Earth having failed to get into orbit.'

The Times was more succinct, calling it 'banal, witless and pointless'.

CAST

Humphrey Bellweather **Charles Lloyd Pack**   *Amanda* **Joyce Carey**
Monty **Peter Myers**   *Doris* **José Read**   *Fingle* **Anthony Sharp**
Bastable **David Conville**   *Jones* **James Belchamber**
Mervyn Dashwood **Derek Aylward**

Writer: **A.P. Dearsley**
Settings: **Frank Gillman**
Director: **John Rhodes**

An Associated-Rediffusion Network Production
60 minutes, black and white
15 May 1959

THE BURNING GLASS

The accidental discovery of a destructive weapon vastly more powerful than the H-bomb formed the basis of this sci-fi drama by novelist and playwright Charles Morgan which considered the issue of who should assume responsibility for such awesome power.

During his meteorological research into weather control, British scientist Christopher Terriford comes across a device that can harness the Sun's power. It can roast lizards, split rocks and sizzle cacti, but, more to the point, it can concentrate the Sun's rays accurately on any chosen city or other target on Earth and burn it totally. Terriford's problem: what to do with his celestial flame-thrower, his Burning Glass. Should he turn it over to the politicians who might misuse it? Or should he say nothing? In true British tradition he decides on a compromise and gives his wife Mary enough information to enable her to act in the event of his death. He then informs the Prime Minister, Montague Winthrop, offering to use it on Britain's behalf only in a supreme emergency. He also has to cope with being kidnapped for a foreign power by Hardlip, a drinking companion of his talkative assistant Tony Lack.

Originally performed as a two-hour stage play in 1953, *The Burning Glass* was adapted twice for television – once as a 60-minute 'distilled essence' for a 1956 Television Playhouse presentation, and secondly in 1960, as a 90-minute version, for the ITV network's Play of the Week slot.

Terriford 1956-style was played by John Robinson, another 'scientist with a conscience' role for the star of *Quatermass II*.

THE BURNING GLASS

w Charles Morgan

1956 (Television Playhouse)
CAST

Christopher Terriford John Robinson *Mary Terriford* Ursula Howells
Tony Lack Alfred Burke *Lady Terriford* Zena Dare
Gerry Hardlip Robert Rietty *Lord Henry Strait* Cyril Raymond
Montague Winthrop Donald Wolfit

Adapted for television by Barry Thomas
Settings: John Clements
Director: Cyril Coke

An Associated-Rediffusion Network Production
60 minutes, black and white
26 April 1956

(Generally praised by critics as a 'polished drama', this version caused a mild stir when scores of viewers rang a Whitehall phone number given in the play as 'getting you through to the PM' and found they had got through to the *real* Cabinet Office.)

1960 (Play of the Week)
CAST:

Christopher Terriford Michael Atkinson *Mary Terriford* Daphne Slater
Tony Lack Anthony Newlands *Lady Terriford* Noel Hood
Tamas Domokos Hardlip Peter Reynolds *Lord Henry Strait* John Shaplin
Montague Winthrop Roger Livesey *Insp. Wigg* Frank Forsyth

Adapted for television by Elizabeth Lincoln
Designer: Fredric Pusey
Director: David Boisseau

An Associated-Rediffusion Network Production
90 minutes, black and white
4 October 1960

CAMPAIGN FOR ONE

The 1965 BBC play was a Freudian drama wrapped up in a spacesuit. British astronaut, Squadron-Leader Osborne, is nearing the end of his ten-day solo mission orbiting the Earth. Due to a malfunction, the only way he can get back down is to fly his craft in manually. But Osborne's nerves have reached breaking point and he's not sure he wants to come down at all. He orbits the Earth broadcasting military secrets and private jokes, before finally pouring out his troubles to the psychiatrist on the ground as it is revealed that Osborne is a man trying to opt out of society because he has failed sexually.

Campaign for One was screened in BBC 1's midweek drama slot, *The Wednesday Play*.

CAST

Squadron-Leader Osborne **Barry Foster**   *Col. Anderson* **Jerry Stovin**
Squadron-Leader Cooper **Jeremy Kemp**   *Maj. Max Baker* **Robert Arden**
Helen Osborne **Pearl Catlin**   *Dr Gelner* **David Bauer**
Dr Marshall **George Roubicek**   *Dr Cutts* **Jack Stewart**
Group Capt. Austin **David Garth**   *John Kelly* **Redmond Phillips**
Flight Lt. Turnbull **Peter Jesson**   *Don Somers* **Chuck Julian**
with: **Norman Chancer, Marcella Markham, Anthony Morton, Lionel Murton,
Lesley Allen, Thomasine Heiner,
John Downey, John Bloomfield**

Writers: **Marielaine Douglas, Anthony Church**
Director: **Moira Armstrong**
Producer: **James MacTaggart**
Designer: **John Hurst**
Story editor: **Roger Smith**

A BBC Production
75 minutes, black and white
3 March 1965
(BBC1: *The Wednesday Play*)

THE CAVES OF STEEL

BBC 2's first venture into science fiction was this adaptation of Isaac Asimov's story combining an imaginative vision of the future with the more traditional narrative of a police murder hunt.

The Caves of Steel is set 200 years in the future, in a New York that has become a city of 14 million people living in one vast domed hall, looking on the open countryside as dangerous territory. Beyond is Spacetown, where scientists from other worlds that have subjugated Earth study the human race in the hope of saving it from self-extinction.

But when one of their scientists is found murdered and a human is suspected, the Spacers issue an ultimatum: unless the killer is found within 48 hours, New York will be destroyed or 'occupied'. City deputy police commissioner Elijah Baley is assigned the task of solving the case with the aid of a robot detective from Spacetown, called R. Daniel Olivaw.

The play was first shown in June 1964 as part of the new channel's *Story Parade* series of plays adapted from modern novels. It gathered good reviews and was chosen as one of five to be repeated as a 'Best of' showcase two months later.

CAST

Elijah Baley **Peter Cushing**   *R. Daniel Olivaw* **John Carson**
Simpson **Stanley Walsh**   *R Sammy* **Ian Trigger**
Commissioner Enderby **Kenneth J. Warren**   *Controller* **Richard Beale**
Clousar **John Boyd-Brent**   *Shop manager* **Richard Beint**

Customer **Patsy Smart**   *Jessie Baley* **Ellen McIntosh**
Ben **Hennie Scott**   *Dr Fastolfe* **John Wentworth**   *Dr Gerrigel* **Naomi Chance**
with: **Nicholas Brent, Bill Cartwright** *and* **Michael Earl**

Adapted by: **Terry Nation**, *from a story by* **Isaac Asimov**
Director: **Peter Sasdy**
Producer: **Eric Tayler**
Script editor: **Irene Shubik**
Special effects: **Jack Kine, Bernard Wilkie**

Music/special sound: **The BBC Radiophonic Workshop**

A BBC Production
75 minutes, black and white
5 June 1964 (repeated 28 August 1964)
(BBC2: *Story Parade*)

COUNTDOWN AT WOOMERA

Ambitious 1961 production presented live from Associated–Rediffusion's Wembley studios with a cast of 40, huge sets and a 'blind 'em with science' script. Set in the year 1968, it launched the first man to the Moon (British, of course), tossed in telepathic communication between the astronaut (Neil McCallum) and his Earthbound girlfriend (Sylvia Kay), and stirred up a new form of germ warfare capable of destroying all life on Earth and the Moon, all against a background of high-level treachery and misguided patriotism. Other stars included Patrick Barr as the tough Aussie mission controller, Allan Cuthbertson as a bigoted security chief and John Welsh as an Empire-loving tycoon. It was author Henry Bentinck's first TV play – he'd previously worked as a producer of radio shows and TV commercials.

'It was a play of pure hokum . . . phase three of the great launching looked more like the 9.30 steam engine leaving Liverpool Street.'

(*Daily Telegraph*)

MAIN CAST

Robert McKerrell **Neil McCallum**   *Margaret Paisley* **Sylvia Kay**
Sir Robert Trelevan **John Welsh**   *Gen. O'Connor* **Patrick Barr**
Supt. Steel **Allan Cuthbertson**   *Dr Newton* **John Glyn-Jones**
Prof. Leighton **John Tate**   *PRO* **Michael Blakemore**
Prime Minister **John Miller**   *Home secretary* **Edward Harvey**
Checkers: **Terence Bayler, Leon Thau, Maurice Travers, John Read, Charles Stanley, Alister Smart, John Matthews, David Ryder**
Trackers: **Fred Abbott, Brian Dent, George Roubicek, Roger Clayton**
with: **Paul Williamson, Jeffrey Gardiner, Ernest Hare, Robert Hewitt, Howard Pays, Lesley Jackson, Alan Wilson, Trevor Maskell, Terence Woodfield, Mira Tomek, Annette Kerr, Lorne Cossette, Benny Nightingale, Ian Anderson, John Herrington, Bobby Naidoo, Max Miradin, Edmund Otero**

Writer: **Henry Bentinck**
Designer: **Fredric Pusey**
Director: **Cyril Coke**

An Associated–Rediffusion Network Production
90 minutes, made in black and white
13 June 1961

COURSE FOR COLLISION

Early 'mid-air' drama from Arthur Hailey, father of the *Airport* disaster movies. Set in the future, it concerns the almost impossible decision taken by an American president flying to a last-minute summit conference in Mongolia, to avert World War Three by ordering his pilot to ram a Chinese A-bomber. Produced twice for TV, first in 1957 as part of a series of Canadian Television Theatre Productions, with a cast of just six, and again in 1962 with an enlarged BBC passenger list.

1957: CAST

The President **Ed McNamara**

1962: CAST

The President **Alexander Knox**   *Gen. Stewart* **David Garth**
Darrel Freedman **Bill Nagy**   *Capt. Shaw* **Anthony Sagar**
Maj. Hale **Lloyd Lamble**   *Brig. General Patrick* **Alan Gifford**
Maj. Peter McMahon **Graydon Gould**
with **Derek Tansley, Douglas Phair, George Golden, David Calderisi, Robert O'Neil, Chuck Julian, Douglas Stewart, John Philips, Robert MacLeod, Constance Wake, Don Mason, Burnell Tucker, Gene Sandys, Glenn Beck, Hal Galili, Harry Towb, Terence Fallon, Alan Cousineau**

Designer: **Tim Harvey**
Producer: **Patrick Dromgoole**

BBC Television Production
60 minutes, black and white
11 June 1962

THE CREATURE

A TV play by the prolific Nigel Kneale which furthered his reputation for original drama, back in the 1950s. Written against a background of speculation about the existence of the Yeti, Kneale called it a fictional guess at the answers.

The Creature provided another strong role for Peter Cushing, just two months after his acclaimed performance as Winston Smith in the Kneale/Rudolph Cartier production of *Nineteen Eighty-Four*. Cushing played scientist Dr John Rollason, whose expedition to the Himalayas in search of the Yeti brings him into conflict with colleague Tom Friend.

The play was performed live on a Sunday night, with a second performance the following Thursday. It was later filmed by Hammer as *The Abominable Snowman* (1957), with Cushing again in the lead role.

CAST

Tom Friend **Stanley Baker***   *Pierre Brosset* **Eric Pohlmann**
Dr John Rollason **Peter Cushing**   *Andrew McPhee* **Simon Lack**
Nima Kusang **Wolfe Morris**
The Lama of Rong-ruk Monastery **Arnold Marlé**
with Monks, Devil Dancers and Musicians

Writer: **Nigel Kneale**
Designer: **Barry Learoyd**
Producer: **Rudolph Cartier**

A BBC Production
90 minutes, made in black and white
30 January 1955
2nd performance: 3 February 1955
(BBC)

* by arrangement with British Lion Film Corporation.

THE CRITICAL POINT

Science fiction combined with murder in Evelyn Frazer's 1957 BBC drama (remade in 1960) about the first human guinea-pig to undergo a deep freeze experiment of 'hibernation anasthesia'.

Brilliant young scientist Philip Gage has been closely involved with tests that have so far been carried out only on animals. When he strangles his wife, he suddenly has a good reason to volunteer to be the first frozen man. But though he is successfully frozen, the murder hunt closes about him and he is eventually mercy-killed by his boss, Dr Andrew Mortimer.

Writing about the 1957 version, *The Observer*'s TV critic Maurice Richardson singled out one performance for particular praise, describing the play as 'redeemed by elementary tension and some fine underplaying by Leo McKern'.

1957: CAST

Dr Andrew Mortimer **Leo McKern**   *Dr Philip Gage* **Eric Lander**
Mason **Neil Wilson**   *Dr Helen Schroder* **Margo Johns**
Sir Keith Vernon **Nigel Arkwright**   *Prof. Hubbard* **Roderick Jones**
Margot Gage **Nicolette Bernard**   *Miss Armitage* **Norah Blaney**

Policemen **Brian Trueman/George Bancroft**
Det. Sgt Green **Bernard Horsfall**   *Det. Insp. Snaith* **Tom Chatto**
Dr MacPherson **John Rae**

Writer: **Evelyn Frazer**
Designer: **Charles Lawrence**
Producer: **George R. Foa**

Film sequences by the BBC North
Regional Film Unit
A BBC Production (Manchester)
90 minutes, made in black and white
5 December 1957

1960 CAST:

Dr Andrew Mortimer **Mervyn Johns**   *Dr Philip Gage* **Owen Holder**
Mason **Neil Wilson**   *Dr Helen Schroder* **Kay Hawtrey**
Sir Keith Vernon **Cyril Luckham**   *Prof. Hubbard* **Laidman Brown**
Margot Gage **Lana Morris**   *Miss Armitage* **Rosamund Greenwood**
Policemen **David Rendall** *and* **Bryan Bada**
Det. Sgt Green **Clifford Earl**   *Det. Insp Snaith* **Edward Harvey**
Dr MacPherson **Jack Lambert**

Writer: **Evelyn Frazer**
Designer: **Susan Spence**
Producer: **George R. Foa**

A BBC Production
80 minutes, black and white
31 July 1960
(BBC, shown under the heading '*Summer Theatre*')

THE CRUNCH

Could a former British colony somewhere to the east of Suez hold the mother country to nuclear ransom? That was the question posed by Nigel Kneale in this suspense drama.

The nuclear device is in the cellar of the Makangese embassy in London and will be detonated at midnight unless HMG coughs up a cool quarter of a billion pounds in cash. The capital is evacuated as a flustered PM, Goddard, debates whether to send in the troops or call the bluff of the megalomaniac Makangese President, Mr Jimson. The crunch comes when the mad dictator decides to detonate anyway and it takes a touch of the supernatural from his mystical ambassador Mr Ken to ensure London is spared.

A large cast included Anthony Bushell as a military chief – a few ranks higher than the colonel he played in Kneale's *Quatermass and the Pit*.

The play was the first in a new ITV approach to drama, *Studio '64* in which a group of directors and writers were brought together and given *carte blanche* to create a series of plays for television. Kneale teamed up with Michael Elliott, a partnership that later also produced the controversial *Year of the Sex Olympics* (see separate entry). When it came to *The Crunch*, critics tended to praise Kneale's 'gripping plot', but were less happy with Elliott's 'showy and strident production' (*The Times*).

CAST

Goddard Harry Andrews *Mr Ken* Maxwell Shaw *Mr Jimson* Wolfe Morris
Lt. Gen Priest Anthony Bushell *Capt. Buckley* Peter Bowles
Lovell Carl Bernard *Dr Kessel* John Gabriel *RAMC Major* John Cazabon
with: *Signal sergeants* Keith Smith, Arthur White, David Rose
Milkman Cyril Renison *Bradshaw* Frank Crawshaw
O'Day Michael Corcorran *Mrs Ken* Hira Talfrey
Her daughters Julia West, Olivia Hussey
and: Julian Sherrier, John Barratt, George Betton, John Trenaman,
Tracy Connell, Dean Francis, Bill Maxam

Writer: Nigel Kneale
Director: Michael Elliott
Designer: Tom Lingwood
Executive producer: Stuart Burge

An ATV Network Production
60 minutes, black and white
19 January 1964

DANGER ZONE

Keeping up with the nuclear arms race has been a global preoccupation since Hiroshima, and the apparent impotence of the individual to affect the outcome a regular theme of television plays. In this 1963 offering from Anglia Television, the individual is able at least to trip up one competitor, even if he doesn't force a total withdrawal.

Two hours before an American nuclear test in the Pacific, airline chief Henry Brunewald shanghais eight world-famous celebrities on a routine flight to Sydney and deliberately flies them into the danger zone in an attempt to blackmail the authorities into cancelling the test. After nearly 90 minutes of 'will they, won't they?' suspense, the test is indeed cancelled.

'The plot was creaky, the characters were marionettes and the dialogue was painfully banal.' (*The Observer*)

CAST

Henry Brunewald Oscar Homolka *Capt. Guy* John Sutton
Capt. Raffan Alan White *Jenny Earl* Jeanne Moody
Heinrich Niemeier Richard Marner *Bob Fellowes* William Sylvester
Margo Robertson Jean Marsh *Manning Maine* Ernest Clark
John Kolper Marne Maitland *Vera Rinkel* Hira Talfrey
Burns Guy Kingsley Poynter *Lee Smith* Ann Hamilton
J.L. Pierce John Hazor *Wilma Pierce* Pat Nye

WITH
Cherien Panache, Grant Holden, Nicholas Stuart,
George Golden, Patrick Dunn, John McGregor

Writer: N.J. Crisp, *from the novel* A Cry
to Heaven *by* James MacGregor
Designer: Reece Pemberton
Director: George More O'Ferrall

Anglia Television Production (networked
by Associated–Rediffusion)
90 minutes, black and white
22 January 1963

DAYS TO COME

Wellsian love story about two young people at odds with their world – a nightmarishly efficient society of the future where productivity is all.

Based on a novella by H.G. Wells, the story is set in the year 2122. London is an insulated, air-conditioned city, sealed in a vast plastic bubble. It never rains, and the temperature is thermostatically controlled. The world is at peace and society run as a benign Meritocracy in which children are streamed into three IQ grades – Alpha, Beta and Gamma – though there is a fourth category, the Deviants, who cannot adjust to society.

Elizebeth Moris is a problem girl, an old-fashioned romantic in love with Jon Denton, a mild-mannered rocket launchpad official. But her father wants to marry her off to up-and-coming bureaucrat, Bindon, and sees 'psychojustment', a genteel form of brainwashing, as the only way to bring her round. But Jon objects violently and the star-crossed Beta-class lovers escape from the city to rediscover the fresh air, flowers and birds of the countryside as well as the cruelty of nature.

Screened as the BBC's *Play of the Month* in October 1966, *Days to Come* was praised as 'an ingenious production' by *The Daily Telegraph*.

CAST:

Jon **Dinsdale Landen**   Elizebeth **Judi Dench**
Moris **Bernard Archard**   Eliut **Michael Gough**
Bindon **John Quentin**   Filips **Alan Rowe**   Blunt **Michael Brennan**
Stewardess **Peggy Sinclair**   Driver **Norman Mitchell**
Nurse **Pamela Strong**   Tomsun **John Roden**   Controller **Emrys Leyshon**
Rent steward **Raymond Mason**   Deviant clerk **Peter Hutton**
Girl clerk **Mirabelle Thomas**   Registration officer **Richard Coe**
Brother **Peter Birrel**

Writer: Ken Taylor, *based on the story by*
H.G. Wells
Producer: Cedric Messina
Director: Alan Bridges
Designer: Stuart Walker

A BBC Production
95 minutes, black and white
25 October 1966
(BBC: Play of the Month)

THE DEVIL'S EGGSHELL

Science fiction melodrama, shown in BBC 1's *Play of the Month* series in 1966.

Mysterious egg-shaped objects are found at the scene of train crashes, famines and deaths. They purport to be alien in origin, but turn out to be the work of a conspiracy of scientists intent on shocking politicans into behaving themselves by presenting the world with a universal scapegoat. Doubtless a good idea at the time, the conspiracy misfires, the scientists are publicly guillotined in Trafalgar Square, and power politics and tyranny return with renewed vigour and momentum.

The Devil's Eggshell received lukewarm reviews, and was generally felt to be a good idea which went on too long.

CAST

Dr Quilliam **Keith Barron** *Prime Minister* **Leonard Rossiter**
Sir Leonard Bell **David Langton** *Maj. Gen. Atkins* **John Phillips**
Home Secretary **Peter Copley** *Lord Portmanteau* **Bernard Hepton**
Jean Bell **Marian Diamond** *Holborn* **Michael Culver**
Wu Hsien Ching **Burt Kwouk** *Maudie* **Stephanie Bidmead**
Interviewer **P.J. Kavanagh** *Bland* **Lawrence James**
with: **Raymond Witch, Basil Moss, Edmond Bennett,
Nicholas Pennell, Edward Ogden, Anthony Jacobs,
Godfrey James, Colin Rix, Norman Scace, Betty Goulding**

Writer: **David Weir**, *from an idea by* Dr **Alex Comfort**
Director: **Gareth Davies**
Designer: **Roy Oxley**
Producer: **Cedric Messina**

90 minutes, black and white
28 June 1966
(BBC1: Play of the Month)

DOOMSDAY FOR DYSON

J.B. Priestley's third play for television, *Doomsday for Dyson* was a satirical fantasy that wore its heart on its sleeve in uncompromising fashion.

A passionate campaigner for nuclear disarmament, Priestley poured all his arguments into an emotive, deliberately shocking dream scenario intended to jolt his audience out of complacency.

Its central character, Tom Dyson, is an ordinary man plunged, in a dream, into the chaotic horror of an atomic explosion and an aftermath in which he shoots his blinded daughter and scorched wife, then turns his gun on himself. The play 'follows' Dyson into the next world, becoming a trial and investigation as Dyson attempts to find out who is to blame for the holocaust. Military men, scientists and politicians are all wheeled on to say their piece, but Dyson is painted as the *real* criminal, guilty of apathy and complacency.

In the end, Dyson awakens from his dream and decides to go with his wife and daughters to a Priestley protest meeting – the implication being that if all the Dysons of the world did likewise, mankind might be saved.

The 45-minute play was followed by an inconclusive studio discussion, with Peter Thorneycroft and Manny Shinwell in the anti-disarmament corner and Rev. Donald Soper and Barbara Castle on the pro side.

Doomsday for Dyson polarised its audience. *The Observer*'s Maurice Richardson called it 'an hour of compulsive viewing . . . as sincere as a reflex', while The *Daily Telegraph* line was 'a somewhat disappointing 45 minutes in which the performers seemed like platform puppets'.

A large cast featured George Baker (whose subsequent TV credits include *I Claudius* and *The Ruth Rendell Mysteries*), Bill Fraser, Harry Fowler and William Mervyn (ITV's *Mr Rose*).

CAST

Tom Dyson Ian Hunter   *Mrs Dyson* Frances Rowe   *Ann Dyson* Ann Firbank
Sally Dyson Alanna Bryce   *Magistrate* Frederick Leister
Dr Kenton Terence Longdon   *Goltsev* George Baker
Gen. Kuprin Hugh Latimer   *Marshal Kletsk* Ian Wallace
Gen. Schalz John Phillips   *Jackston* Bonar Colleano
Air Vice-Marshal Howard Marion Crawford
Porson Harry Fowler   *Mirolubov* Michael Segal
Scientists James Dyrenforth, Robert Arden, Barry Shawzin,
Arnold Yarrow, Reginald Marsh, Alexander Archdale
Journalist Ronald Howard   *Great Aunt Lucy* Jean Cadell
Civil servants Bill Fraser, William Kendall
Politician William Mervyn

Writer: J.B. Priestley
Designer: Tom Spaulding
Director: Silvio Narizzano

A Granada Production
45 minutes (out of 60-minute slot), made
in black and white
10 March 1958

FACE LIFT

Television musical set in the year 2074, with *Professional* Martin Shaw as workless-class hero Zax, dispensing pleasure to the impoverished idle masses through his Theatre of Glamour and Magic. But Zax aspires to be more than a mere conjuror and when a beautiful elite technocrat goes slumming at the theatre, Zax tries to capture her soul. *Face Lift* was shown first on Channel Four in 1983, with a repeat on ITV in 1984.

CAST

Zax Martin Shaw   *Bruce* John Le Mesurier
Bob Clarke Peters   *F9893* Eleanor David   *Ina* Sue Jones-Davies
M4327 Steven Mann   *F3425* Shelagh Stephenson

Writer/Director: Tony Bicat
Music: Nick Bicat
Designer: Martin Davey
Producer: Nicholas Palmer
Choreography: Arlene Phillips

Central Production
90 minutes, colour
8 April 1983 (C4)
21 April 1984 (ITV, network)

THE FLIPSIDE OF DOMINICK HIDE

One of the more unpredictable science fiction successes of the early 1980s, *The Flipside of Dominick Hide* was a simple, engaging time-travel adventure about a prim young man of the future on the loose in present-day London.

Dominick arrived in his flying saucer – and wearing a saucer-shaped hat – from a future shown as formal, hygienic and largely unimaginative, where Beatles' music is played by holograms of medieval musicians with lutes.

His naive bewilderment at the rough and tumble of the 20th century provided scope for a kind of topsy turvy nostalgia about the rituals and artefacts of our time. The play was also unfashionably optimistic and positive about the human spirit and its upbeat ending helped generate a tremendous response from the public and normally cynical critics. *Radio Times* reported a bumper postbag and the play carried off two awards at the 1981 Banff Television Festival.

A series was suggested, but resisted by writers Alan Gibson and Jeremy Paul who felt it would be impossible to sustain the novelty and humour. However they did find room for a sequel two years later, which performed new time tricks and added a thriller element. Called *Another Flip for Dominick*, it assembled the same cast, though his reappearance as Dominick's outwardly stern boss Caleb proved to be Patrick Magee's last TV role before his death, three months after filming ended.

MAIN CAST

Dominick Hide **Peter Firth**   *Jane* **Caroline Langrishe**
Ava **Pippa Guard**   *Caleb Line* **Patrick Magee**
Great Aunt Mavis **Sylvia Coleridge**   *Helda* **Jean Trend**

Writers: **Alan Gibson** *and* **Jeremy Paul**
Director: **Alan Gibson**
Producer: **Chris Cherry**
Music: **Rick Jones** *and* **David Pierce**

BBC Productions
Two colour plays

The Flipside of Dominick Hide

Dominick Hide, a young pilot from the London of 2130, time-warps his flying saucer back into 1980 for some historical research. Bewildered by the chaos of the 20th century, he is welcomed as a lovable oddball and is befriended (and bedded) by Jane with whom he ends up fathering his own great-great-grandfather.

Alaric **Trevor Ray**
Jim **Timothy Davies**
Felix **Denis Lawson**
Midge **Bernadette Shortt**
Harry **Tony Melody**
Brian **Bill Gavin**
Carl **David Griffin**
Geoffrey **Karl Howman**

Designer: **Roger Murray-Leach**

95 minutes
9 December 1980
(BBC1: *Play for Today*)
rpt: 7 December 1982

Another Flip for Dominick

Dominick is asked by Caleb to flip back to 1982, ostensibly to search for a colleague, Bonnington, who has gone missing while studying crime and violence in London. Naturally Dominick looks up old flame Jane and meets his two-year-old great-great grandad. Jane is now living with a rock musician (conveniently off on tour) but though she helps Dominick find Bonnington, she remains faithful to her new life, leaving Dominick to fly back to the future where his own wife, Ava, is glad to have home again, albeit with pangs of jealousy.

Pyrus Bonnington **Ron Berglas**
Prof. Burrows **Michael Gough**
Mrs Burrows **Antonio Pemberton**
Magistrate **Gillian Raine**
Police Sgt. **Godfrey James**
Duncan **Steve Alder**
Home help **Peter Cann**
Pilar **Mary Jo Randle**
Soo **Ysanne Churchman**
PC **Geoffrey Leesley**

Designer: **Dick Coles**
85 minutes

(BBC1: *Play for Today*)
14 December 1982

THE FRIENDLY PERSUADERS

The basic premise behind this 1969 play was that a similar planet to ours exists in another galaxy, but where man's evolution began 50,000 years earlier. When a delegation from this advanced civilisation, the Taraxans, arrive on Earth (Britain), they paint a Utopian picture of life on Tarax where machines do all the work, freeing the people to devote themselves to the typically 1960s pastimes of leisure and love. It's an irresistible vision, except to Whitehall sceptic Steve Leach who suspects that a sinister purpose lies behind the seductive facade.

MAIN CAST

Steven Leach Edward Judd   *Sir Terence Norrington* Grant Taylor
Michael Donnell Joe Melia   *Adrian Collingwood* Julian Curry
Sue Long Libby Glenn   *Bernard Webb* Jonathan Newth
Madame Alex Stella Tanner   *John Frisby* Milton Johns
Chris Stanford Robert Grange   *Director* Anthony Newlands
with: Betty England, Richard Corbet, Paul Bacon,
Michael Ashley-Davies, Lolly Cockerell, Geoffrey Denton,
David Grey, Jane Stonehouse, Audrey Teasdale,
Edward Brooks, Keith Hazelmore, Max Latimer

Writer: Paul Wheeler
Designer: Michael Bailey
Director: John Sichel
Executive producer: Cecil Clarke

ATV Network Production
90 minutes, black and white
23 June 1969

FRIENDS IN SPACE

Science fiction comedy co-written by John Ratzenberger (bar-room bore Cliff in *Cheers*) who also starred as one of a bunch of UFO freaks summoned to the secret hideaway of Prof. Rex Thornton for a special meeting of the Friends in Space Society.

Thornton announces that he has something to show them that will silence the sceptics once and for all and in an upstairs room introduces an alien creature who waves back at them.

A reliable cast was assembled for this 1980 ITV Playhouse which the *Daily Mail* called 'an unusual and unpolished piece which lacks a hard centre but is often very funny indeed'.

CAST

Reg G.X. Thornton Robert Stephens   *Don Saddler* Neville Smith
Tom Phillips John Ratzenberger   *Susan* Eleanor Bron
Mr Babcock Terence Rigby   *Esther Babcock* Pat Heywood

Written by: Ray Hassett, John
   Ratzenberger
Producer: June Roberts
Director: Robert Chetwin
Designer: Stanley Mills

An ATV Network Production
60 minutes, colour
5 March 1980
(*Playhouse*)

THE GALACTIC GARDEN

Entertaining natural history sci-fi drama documentary (phew!) set among the wildlife of an English garden.

The project was a labour of love for its star and co-writer Andrew Sachs, who played Vektor, a timid three-quarter inch tall time and space traveller who arrives from the artificial planet Orbito in the future, seeking data on how Earth people used to live.

But instead of gathering historical titbits, Vektor and his colleague Plasmid, a confident career spacewoman, find themselves in danger at the hands and jaws of the garden's natural – and giant – inhabitants. In quick succession, Vektor is waylaid by an array of wildlife from goldfish, a tortoise, worms and spiders.

CAST

Vektor **Andrew Sachs** *Plasmid* **Sarah Neville**
Chimaera **Mona Bruce** *Father* **Christian Rodska**
Mother **Stella Monsell** *Danny* **Richard Spencer**

Writers: **Andrew Sachs** *and* **John Downer**
Producer/director: **John Downer**
Designer: **Stephen Brownsey**
Photography **Alan Heyward**
Radiophonic music: **Elizabeth Parker**

A BBC Bristol Production
colour, 60 minutes
2 January 1985
(BBC1)

THE GIRL WHO LOVED ROBOTS

Ingenious murder thriller set in the near future. Nightclub hostess Victory Du Cann is found murdered. The investigating detective, Insp. Antrobus, tracks down his man – an arrogant astronaut about to fly off to the Moon – but is prevented from arresting him by the space project boss.

One critic described it as a play with dialogue rich in advertising copywriters' style, including the line 'She liked the smell of outer space on her men'.

Shown in the BBC 1 series, *The Wednesday Play*.

CAST

Victory **Isobel Black** *Cage* **Norman Rodway** *Antrobus* **Dudley Foster**
Doctor **Michael Gough** *Sgt* **Maurice Podbrey** *Toms* **George Betton**

Marina owner Mary Barclay   *Cafritz* David Dodimead
Xenia Judith Smith   *Lederman* John Bryans   *Gogel* Geoffrey Hinsliff
Vonnegut Kevin Stoney   *Minister* Howard Charlton

Writer: Peter Everett
Director: Brian Parker
Designer: Douglas Smith
Producer: James MacTaggart

A BBC Production
75 minutes, black and white
20 October 1965
(BBC1: *The Wednesday Play*)

HANDS ACROSS THE SKY

TV's first 'space opera', *Hands Across the Sky* was a one-act comic opera combining romance, science and a touch of the Jekyll and Hydes in a tale of two scientists and a visitor from outer space. Working in their laboratory are Professor Neutron and his assistant Miss Fothergill. She is devoted to science. He is devoted to her. All is changed by the arrival of Squeg, a green-skinned alien with whom Miss F becomes wildly infatuated. The comic resolution of the unusual triangle involved magic potions from Dr Jekyll's recipe book.

The enterprise was generally well received though there was an element of Jekyll and Hyde about the critics . . .

'Witty, tuneful and written with delightful economy' (*The Times*)
'Vocal monotony a stumbling block to enjoyment' (*Daily Telegraph*)

CAST

Prof. Neutron Eric Shilling*   *Miss Fothergill* Julia Shelley
Squeg Stephen Manton   *A voice* James Maxwell

Composed by Anthony Hopkins
Libretto by Gordon Snell
Designer: Richard Wilmot
Special effects: Jack Kline *and* Bernard
  Wilkie

Producer: Charles Lefeaux

BBC Production
45 minutes, made in black and white
7 February 1960

* By permission of Sadlers Wells Opera Co.

HUMAN INTEREST STORY

Part of the 1980s revival of *Alfred Hitchcock Presents*, this 30-minute tale was a toe-dipping venture into sf for what was otherwise a safe collection of mystery stories and suspense thrillers.

An American football game is suddenly interrupted by the appearance on screen of a man who announces: 'My name is Garo. I come from the solar system you people refer to as Alpha Centauri. You must listen to what I'm about to say. Some of them are here already and others are close behind. They are going to colonise the Earth.'

Newspaper reporter Maggie Verona follows up the story and meets Garo who explains that he is inhabiting the human body of one, Brian Whitman, and that soon everyone on Earth will be similarly taken over. If Maggie will go with him, he can supply the proof.

The twist – there's *always* a twist – is that once she has the proof we see Maggie returning alone to her office where – shock! horror! – we learn that she, too, is an alien and having got hold of Garo's 'proof' has killed him. The colonisation can proceed as scheduled . . .

CAST:

Brian Garo **John Shea**   *Maggie Verona* **Barbara Williams**
Alan Levy **Richard Marcus**   *Denise Whitman* **Rhonda Dotson**
Everett **James Callahan**

Writer: **Karen Harris**   for *MCA TV*
Director: **Larry Gross**   30 minutes, colour
Producer: **Alan Barnette**   24 April 1986
Executive producer: **Christopher Crowe**   (Thames)

I CAN DESTROY THE SUN

In 1958, ABC Television signed up Sydney Newman from the Canadian Broadcasting Corporation to guide its live drama output. Newman promised an increased commitment to contemporary drama on contemporary issues. *I Can Destroy the Sun*, part of his first season of *Armchair Theatre* productions, was one of the first fruits of that policy.

Written by Jimmy Sangster, who went on to script some of Hammer's best horrors, its theme was the quickening pace of the nuclear rat race – and told of one man's desperate attempt to halt it.

The central character (whose identity remains a secret until the last moment) is a man exasperated by the futility of top-level talks to thrash out the H-bomb problem. He conceives a means of destroying the Sun and uses that threat to blackmail world leaders to come to terms over the Bomb. The pivotal idea, that it *is* possible to destroy the Sun, came from Ingram D'Abbes who based it on the priciple of using a radio telescope to direct powerful signals at its heart.

A strong cast included Maurice Denham as observatory head Dr Lunn, John Robinson (from *Quatermass II*) as Foreign Office official Lloyd Crichton, John Barron as his cynical colleague, Leslie Sands as a ponderous Scotland Yard copper, and Carmel McSharry as a tea lady.

It all prompted one critic to remark: 'the mixture was original, the outcome ingenious and not without serious implications.'

CAST

Henry Walpole **John Barron**   Mary Harkness **Jennifer Wright**
Lloyd Crichton **John Robinson**   Bella **Carmel McSharry**
Supt Travers **Leslie Sands**   James Cartwright **Robert James**
Helen Dawson **Paddy Webster**   Igor Petrov **Jan Conrad**
Boardman **Robert Ayres**   Dr Lunn **Maurice Denham**

Writer: **Jimmy Sangster,** *based on an idea by* **Ingram D'Abbes**
Designer: **Voytek**
Producer: **Sydney Newman**
Director: **Wilfred Eades**

An ABC Network Production
65 minutes, made in black and white
12 October 1958
(ITV)

THE INCREDIBLE ROBERT BALDICK: NEVER COME NIGHT

One of the BBC's *Drama Playhouse* 'class of '72', *Never Come Night* was the pilot episode for a prospective series which never got made.

Written by Daleks creator Terry Nation, *The Incredible Robert Baldick* was originally conceived in 1969 as a possible replacement for a waning *Doctor Who*. Baldick was to be a Victorian adventurer striving to extend the boundaries of man's knowledge, who travelled the country in his private train, complete with laboratory.

Never Come Night was a tale of exorcism, of a supernatural force from the past or the unknown – 'a fear so old it can kill . . . a fear so old it defies reason.'

Character actor Robert Hardy took the title role, and turned in a typically larger-than-life performance.

(The honours graduate of Baldick's *Drama Playhouse* group was Iain Cuthbertson's Procurator Fiscal in *Sutherland's Law*.)

CAST

Robert Baldick **Robert Hardy**   Charles Aldington **Reginald Marsh**
Rev. Peter Elmstead **James Cossins**   Daniel Pluckly **Ron Welling**
Thomas Wingham **Julian Holloway**   Caleb Selling **John Rhys-Davies**
Lenham **Dave Mobley**   Seth Marden **Barry Andrews**
Sturry **Paul Humpoletz**

Writer: **Terry Nation**
Director: **Cyril Coke**
Producer: **Anthony Coburn**
Designer: **John Burrowes**

A BBC Production
50 minutes, colour
2 October 1972
(BBC1: *Drama Playhouse*)

INTO INFINITY

This 1976 outer-space odyssey was produced for NBC in America by Gerry Anderson as a contribution to an educational series called *The Day After Tomorrow*.

It was a £120,000 lesson in space travel in fantasy form which starred Brian Blessed, Joanna Dunham and Martin Lev as a family who set off to explore deep space, with Nick Tate (*Space 1999*'s eagle-eyed Alan Carter) as their pilot.

Launched from Earth in their prototype spaceship *Altares*, they accelerate to a faster-than-light top speed for a journey to a remote solar system – a voyage that would seem like 30 years to the folks back on Earth, but during which, thanks to Einstein's Theory of Relativity, they will hardly age at all. 'Ah, Einstein, what a genius he was!' says the Mother, as the scientific theory is dutifully spelled out.

The special effects were elaborate and spectacular, with the ship travelling past exploding stars and eventually being sucked through a black hole and into a new universe.

That could have been the cue for a new adventure, and Anderson had hoped to turn it into a series, but *Into Infinity* remained a one-off, and a pretty dull one at that.

It does, however, have the curious distinction of being the only Gerry Anderson production to have been screened by the BBC, who had bought the film with a possible series in mind – *if* it had been a success.

CAST

Tom Bowen **Brian Blessed**   Anna Bowen **Joanna Dunham**
David Bowen **Martin Lev**   Capt. Harry Masters **Nick Tate**
Jane Masters **Katharine Levy**
Jim Forbes **Don Fellows**   TV announcer **Ed Bishop**

Writer: **Johnny Byrne**
Producer: **Gerry Anderson**
Director: **Charles Crichton**
Designer: **Reg Hill**
Special effects designer: **Brian Johnston**

*A Gerry Anderson Production for NBC in
association with Richard Price Television*
52 minutes, colour
11 December 1976
(BBC1)

K9 AND COMPANY

The first and only TV spin-off from *Doctor Who* was a special Christmas show for 1981, starring the Doctor's canine computer and one of the most popular previous companions, Sarah Jane Smith.

The Earthbound story, called *A Girl's Best Friend*, involved Sarah Jane and K9 Mark III (who had arrived in a crate as a gift from the unseen Doctor) trying to prevent a coven of witches in the Cotswolds from sacrificing her Aunt Lavinia's young ward Brendan to ensure a fruitful future harvest.

It called for a lot of frantic to-ing and fro-ing as Sarah Jane did the rounds of the local churches, desperately trying to find the coven's meeting place, and the production veered from the banal to the atmospheric, notably the climactic sacrifice scenes.

Elisabeth Sladen reprised her assistant's role as Sarah Jane and Bill Fraser played market gardener Cmdr Pollock, successfully unmasked as the coven's High Priest.

CAST

Sarah Jane Smith **Elisabeth Sladen**   *Voice of K9* **John Leeson**
George Tracey **Colin Jeavons**   *Cmdr Pollock* **Bill Fraser**
Sgt Wilson **Nigel Gregory**   *Peter Tracey* **Sean Chapman**
Aunt Lavinia **Mary Wimbush**   *Brendan Richards* **Ian Sears**
Juno Baker **Linda Polan**   *Howard Baker* **Neville Barber**
Henry Tobias **John Quarmby**   *Lilly Gregson* **Gillian Martell**
PC Carter **Stephen Oxley**

Writer: **Terence Dudley**
Producer: **John Nathan-Turner**
Director: **John Black**
Designer: **Nigel Jones**
Music: **Fiachra Trench, Ian Levine,
  Peter Howell**

A BBC Production
One colour 50-minute episode
28 December 1981
(BBC1)
rpt: 24 December 1982
(BBC2)

LOOP

One-hour play, specially written for ATV's *Drama 63* season by Giles Cooper, previously a regular adapter of ghost stories for Associated-Rediffusion's *Tales of Mystery* series.

The world is facing its end – not now but millions of years hence. Mankind can no longer go forward, so an attempt is made to evacuate to the past and a group of people in 'the present' (1963) find themselves living in a nightmare. A sudden sound pulsating from TV sets puts viewers in a state of suspended animation (a wry warning if ever there was one). Among those unaffected, for various reasons, are a young lodger Peter, his landlord's daughter Fenella, and a neighbour Matthew Dowd.

CAST

Matthew Dowd Geoffrey Bayldon   *Commander Vincent* Roland Culver
Fenella Lee Moira Redmond   *Peter Morton* Rodney Bewes
PC Rogers Richard Burrell   *Bert* Ray Mort   *Sandra* Carol Austin
Tom Lee Frank Henderson   *Mrs Lee* Edna Morris
TV compere David Davenport

Writer: Giles Cooper
Producer: Herbert Wise
Settings: Richard Lake
Music: Max Harris

ATV Network Production
60 minutes, black and white
20 October 1963

MAN IN A MOON

'The time is tomorrow. Twenty-seven satellites are circling the Earth. The 28th is about to be launched – but what is the secret that it holds . . .'

While the world waited for the first manned space flight, this 1957 play by Michael Pertwee for ABC's popular *Armchair Theatre* series anticipated the event with more emphasis on the ethics than on the mechanics. Set in a country called Mittel Europa, its cornerstone was that while it might be possible to send a man to the Moon, that man might not return. After discussion on the morality of sending a volunteer on such a voyage of no return, a convicted murderer is plucked from his life sentence to be despatched into orbit as the human guinea-pig.

Director Stephen Clarkson told *TVTimes* that *Man in a Moon* was intended to break new ground as 'realistic drama, or dramatic reportage . . . using television as a news medium, in a way we hope will intensify the suspense of the play.'

Donald Pleasence starred as a cold-blooded scientist whose single-mindedness prevails in setting up the flight – his performance won praise, though the play itself was not so well received. *The Daily Telegraph* called it 'a play notable more for topicality than dramatic content', complained that viewers were left as much up in the air as the spaceman, and concluded that 'the script had been too hastily prepared and even more hurriedly produced'.

THE PLAYERS:

Donald Pleasence, Hilton Edwards, Derek Oldham,
Basil Dignam, Charles Houston, Jessica Spencer,
Hilda Fenemore, James Raglan, Job Stewart,
Barbara Everest, Bob Danvers-Walker,
Damaris Hayman, Neil Wilson, Keith Anderson

Writer: **Michael Pertwee**
Designer: **Bertram Tyrer**
Producer: **Stuart Latham**
Director: **Stephen Clarkson**

An ABC Network Production
60 minutes, made in black and white
17 November 1957

THE MAN OUT THERE

An *Armchair Theatre* essay in suspense that propelled Patrick McGoohan into space as a Russian astronaut, then jammed his escape mechanism, cut off contact with his base and gave him just five sweaty hours to live, trussed up in a spacesuit, grimacing and panting through his visor opening.

By a freak of radio reception the spaceman makes contact with Marie, a trapper's wife in a remote, blizzard-swept region of Canada, who is facing her own life and death struggle, with a daughter dying of diphtheria. With his own survival chances receding as rapidly as the Earth in his porthole, he, a doctor, is able to take her step by step through a life-saving tracheotomy on the child. The woman, in turn, takes down the information he needs to transmit before he becomes irrevocably lost in space, leaving the audience with a quiet moral of common humanity. (But only just. Critics complained that the play's 'extremes of hysteria' took it perilously close to absurdity.)

The Man Out There was McGoohan's second TV role as a space-traveller. In 1958 he played a returning astronaut in James Thurber's satire *The Greatest Man in the World*. (And in some areas it was ITV viewers' second sight of McGoohan that evening – he'd starred earlier in his superb spy'n'scuffle series *Danger Man*.)

CAST

Nicholai Soloviov **Patrick McGoohan**   *Marie* **Katharine Blake**
The General **Clifford Evans**   *Colonel* **Jack Watson**

Deputy Commander Marne Maitland *Olga* Hermione Gregory
with: Brenda Kaye, Martin Sterndale, Reed de Rouen,
Heather Lyons, Michael Adrian, Ivan Craig, Michael Peake

Writer: Donal Giltinan
Designer: Assheton Gorton
Director: Charles Jarrott
Producer: Sydney Newman

An ABC Television Network Production
65 minutes, made in black and white
12 March 1961
(ITV)

THE METAL MARTYR

Short drama screened in BBC2's *Thirty Minute Theatre* series in 1967. It depicted a society in which the robots had rebelled against man and now ruled. Then, one day, Robot Two has a new thought – he thinks he is a man. His thought has far-reaching consequences for mankind who, through him, learn something of their rich heritage.

CAST

The Father Alex Scott *Two* Geoffrey Matthews
Master Technician John Gabriel *Ed* Barry Jackson
Argo Jon Rollason *Eva* Elizabeth Proud
Old man Will Leighton
with: Children Graham Harboard, Susan Swain, Kim Goodey, Jonathan Deans

Dramatised by: Derrick Sherwin, *from a
story by* Robert Moore Williams
Director: Brian Hulme
Producer: George Spenton-Foster
Designer: Raymond Cusick

A BBC Production
30 minutes, black and white
27 December 1967
(BBC2: *Thirty Minute Theatre*)

MURDER CLUB

Runyonesque *Armchair Theatre* offering from 1961, starring Richard Briers as a naive 22nd-century social climber pressurised by his boss into taking up hunting to improve his promotion chances. A straightforward enough proposition, except that in the year 2110 murder is legal and 'the Hunt' its most socially acceptable form with the human victims selected by computer.

Stanley Frelaine is eager to get on in the world, but if he is to gain membership of the exclusive Tens Club he must notch up ten kills. After opening his account, Stanley is dismayed to find his next notified victim is a woman (Barbara Murray) and reluctantly heads for Manchester (conveniently 'preserved' as a historic monument) to search her out.

The comedy thriller also starred Patrick Magee as Stanley's boss and was initially set on Venus where an audience follow Stanley's quest as a documentary on 'Sporting Customs of the Universe'.

CAST

Venusian compere **Steve Plytas**   *Dr Swan* **Charles Lloyd Pack**
Stanley Frelaine **Richard Briers**   *Mr Morger* **Patrick Magee**
Stanley's mother **Patience Collier**   *Frelaine's hunter* **John Maitland**
O'Donnevan **Harold Berens**   *Spotter Three* **Edwin Finn**
Spotter One **John Ringrose**   *Virginia Douglas* **Barbara Murray**
Policeman **Danny Daniels**   *Landlady* **Doris Rogers**   *Man* **Robert Mooney**

Writer: **Robert Sheckley,** *adapted from*
 his short story 'Seventh Victim'
Designer: **Voytek**
Producer: **Sydney Newman**
Director: **Alan Cooke**

An ABC Network Production
60 minutes, black and white
3 December 1961
(ITV)

MURDER ON THE MOON

Take a dead body, a Moonbase full of suspects and a pair of contrasting investigators, and you've got the makings – if not the trappings – of a traditional country-house murder mystery.

Murder on the Moon was ITV's 1989 flirtation with science-fiction. Commissioned by LWT, the two-hour, £2½ million production was made in Britain by an American company and starred Brigitte Nielsen and Julian Sands as an initially mismatched detective duo.

This son (and daughter) of *Star Cops* is set in 2015, ten years after the superpowers have been to the brink of nuclear war – and back. Jake Elezar, Israeli security chief of an American titanium mine operating in the Russian sector of the Moon, is found dead at the bottom of a disused shaft.

As it's Russian territory, the Soviets send one of their military cops, the frostily-efficient Stepan Kirilenko, to investigate. As it's their man, the Americans send one of their NASA agents, the impulsive but intuitive Maggie Bartok, first seen overflowing a tight red dress after stepping out of a spacesuit.

Naturally, the two don't hit it off at first. But at the investigation pans out into a murder hunt you just know the frost is going to thaw. And, sure enough, the furtive glances conclude in an erotic detente as the duo seductively – and symbolically – disarm each other in their sexual foreplay.

As for the murder itself, Bartok and Kirilenko quickly conclude that Elezar had been looking for someone and was killed because he finally found him.

The mystery man turns out to be former terrorist Juan Pedro Vogler, the man responsible for a Jerusalem bomb attack that had nearly proved the spark to ignite a nuclear war. However, 'he' is now a 'she', with Mr Vogler having escaped capture via a sex-change to become Ms Louise Mackey.

A brief struggle in a draining airlock ends with Bartok and Kirilenko getting their 'man'. And, of course, they also get each other.

Murder on the Moon never gripped, but was quietly and claustrophobically absorbing, the low-key suspense broken by just two scenes of explosive action, with Ms Nielsen implausibly proving she can survive and talk in a dramatically depressurised room while a companion and contents are being sucked out to oblivion.

Notable names in cameo roles were Michael J. Shannon as an abrasive worker, David Yip as a computer operator and Georgina Hale as a barmaid!

CAST:

Maggie Bartok **Brigitte Nielsen**   Stepan Kirilenko **Julian Sands**
Louise Mackey **Jane Lapotaire**   Dennis Huff **Gerald McRaney**
Voronov **Brian Cox**   Dr Isabelle Klein **Alphonsia Emmanuel**
Patsy Diehl **Celia Imrie**   Sorokin **Tomek Bork**
Change **David Yip**   Allison Quinney **Georgina Hale**
Ivanov **Michael J. Shannon**   Kevin Faber **Stephen Jenn**
Contarini **Stuart Milligan**   Dr Trifonov **Berwick Kaler**
Alvarado **Ricco Ross**   Miner **Michael Brogan**
Driver **James Hamill**   Russian Rep **Andrzej Borkowski**
NASA Captain **Aaron Swartz**

Writer: **Carla Jean Wagner**
Director: **Michael Lindsay-Hogg**
Producer: **Tamara Asseyev**
Executive producer: **Nick Elliott**
Director of photography: **David Watkin**
Designer: **Austin Spriggs**
Music: **Trevor Jones**

Tamara Asseyev Productions Inc and Viacom International Ltd for London Weekend Television
(Filmed at Bray Studios and the Central Electricity Generating Board, Acton)
Colour, 120 minutes
26 August 1989
(ITV)

THE NIGHT OF THE BIG HEAT

'The warning that it was unsuitable for adults of a nervous disposition was highly necessary – I was positively limp at the end and so were the hard-working, sweat-soaked cast'

(Lynn Lockwood, *Daily Telegraph*)

'A poor man's *Quatermass*, more than a bit crude – yet remarkably good sport'

(Maurice Richardson, *The Observer*)

This 1960 adaptation of a novel by John Lymington about an alien invasion earned the unusual tag of TV's sweatiest play.

The big heat was an intense localised heatwave, caused by a short-wave radio beam on which maggot-like invaders materialised – in this instance at a remote village on Salisbury Plain. There, the fantastic combined with the everyday at the local pub where much of the action involved the landlord, his wife, his girlfriend – and a mysterious scientist – all contriving to look increasingly hot and bothered. In the end, the invasion was thwarted because the heat set fire to everything and roasted the unwelcome visitors, though with typical horror-comic perversity, the cunning invaders then switched their target to the Sahara Desert.

The Night of the Big Heat was filmed in 1967, though America lumbered it with the title *Island of the Burning Damned*.

CAST:

Richard Lee Montague   *Patricia* Melissa Stribling
Frankie Sally Bazely   *Cpl. Pearce* Bernard Cribbins
Sir James Murray Bernard Archard   *Dr Harsen* Karel Stepanek
Sqdn Ldr Grieves Patrick Holt   *Mick* Tony Quinn
Robert Lawrence James   *Ben* Charles Rea   *Brenda* June Ellis
Group Capt. Griffiths Nicholas Selby   *Charlie* Meadows White
Lindsey Stone Richard Meikle   *Flt Lt Morgan* Leonard Grahame

Adapted for television by Giles Cooper, *from the novel by* John Lymington
Designer: Frederic Pusey
Director: Cyril Coke

An Associated–Rediffusion Network Production
90 minutes, made in black and white
14 June 1960
(ITV: *Play of the Week*)

NINETEEN EIGHTY-FOUR

Television's capacity to shock its audience has rarely been more chillingly demonstrated than by the first British production of

George Orwell's classic novel. The play, adapted by Nigel Kneale and produced by Rudolph Cartier, was performed live on Sunday 12 December 1954, watched by some nine million viewers. The controversy it aroused led to calls for the scheduled second performance to be banned.

The production kept faith with Orwell's nightmare vision of a world in which the nature of human thought has been debased and morality turned upside down, to serve the totalitarian regime of Big Brother who sits atop a population pyramid which spreads down through an Inner and Outer Party to the unwashed masses, the Proles. Winston Smith, a member of the Outer Party, works in the Ministry of Truth, rewriting history to accord with the Party Line. His unease at his work turns to dissention as he falls in love with a co-worker, Julia, but his individual aspirations make him a thought criminal in the omniscient eyes of the Party regime. And in the bleak world Orwell depicts there is no happy ending – the rebellious sparks are cruelly extinguished.

Introducing the play in *Radio Times*, Nigel Kneale wrote: 'Orwell guessed at a final evil to consolidate all others – the abolition of ideas through the destruction of words to express them.' His audience, however, found plenty of words to express their opinions, ranging from outright hostility to stunned admiration. The shock waves spread rapidly to parliament where colourful motions for and against the play flew across the Commons floor. One, tabled by five Tory MPs, sharply delored 'the tendency . . . notably on Sunday evenings, to pander to sexual and sadistic tastes'. A barbed amendment expressed gratitude that 'freedom of the individual still permits viewers to switch off and, due to the foresight of her Majesty's government, will soon permit a switch-over to more appropriate programmes'. (The joys of ITV were just months away.)

The play's producer, Rudolph Cartier, strongly defended the broadcast, telling the *Daily Express*: 'Our job was to shake and if we have succeeded in shaking half of the nation then we have done the job we set out to do. It was right and wise to put this terrible vision before the largest possible audience – as a warning against totalitarianism in all its forms.'

And despite the furore, the BBC stood firm in its resolve to screen the second performance which went out, again live, on Thursday 16 December, and attracted the biggest TV audience since the Coronation. Although the novel had been around for about five years, its impact on the British public had been marginal. Television changed all that.

Nineteen Eighty-Four was the second collaboration between Kneale and Cartier, coming some 17 months after the success of their first, *The Quatermass Experiment*. An ambitious enterprise, it utilised 28 sets and used film sequences interspersed between the main live scenes to enable set changes to be made smoothly, without disturbing the dramatic flow. Cartier drew powerful performances from his leading players, notably Peter Cushing as Winston Smith, Yvonne Mitchell as Julia and André Morell as the odious O'Brien. Missing from the credits, though, was the 'face' of Big Brother – Roy Oxley, a 48-year-old television designer from Twickenham.

A telerecording of the second performance was shown in BBC2's Festival 77 season in August 1977, and Nigel Kneale's script was remade for a 1965 Orwell season as *Theatre 625: The World of George Orwell*. Kneale brought the narrative more into line with the situation 11 years nearer the title year – an updating shared by director Christopher Morahan.

Despite some solid performances – particularly from Joseph O'Conor as O'Brien – this version caused barely a ripple. Eleven years is a long time in television.

1984 (1954)

CAST:

THE PARTY: Winston Smith **Peter Cushing**   *Julia* **Yvonne Mitchell**
O'Brien **André Morell**   *Syme* **Donald Pleasence**
Emmanuel Goldstein **Arnold Diamond**   *Parsons* **Campbell Gray**
Mrs Parsons **Hilda Fenemore**   *Parsons girl* **Pamela Grant**
Parsons boy **Keith Davis**   *Woman supervisor* **Janet Barrow**
THE PROLES: First youth **Norman Osborne**   *Second youth* **Tony Lyons**
Third youth **Malcolm Knight**   *First man* **John Baker**
Second man **Victor Platt**   *Barman* **Van Boolen**
Old man **Wilfred Brambell**   *Mr Charrington* **Leonard Sachs**
Waiter **Sydney Bromley**   *Canteen woman* **Janet Joyce**
with Party workers, State prisoners, Thought police

Adapted by **Nigel Kneale** *from the novel by* **George Orwell**
Designer **Barry Learoyd**
Producer **Rudolph Cartier**
Incidental music composed and conducted by **John Hotchkis**

A BBC Production
120 minutes, black and white
First performance: Sunday 12 December 1954 (20.30–22.30 approx)
Second performance: Thursday 16 December 1954 (21.30–23.30 approx)
Repeated as *1954: Nineteen Eighty-Four*: 3 August 1977

1984 (1965)

CAST:

Winston Smith **David Buck**   *O'Brien* **Joseph O'Conor**
Julia **Jane Merrow**   *Syme* **Cyril Shaps**

WITH:

Soldier **Tony Cyrus**   *Arab colonel* **Mohammed Shamsi**
Russian Marshal **Alexis Chesnakov**   *French general* **Hugo de Vernier**
American general **John Brandon**   *British general* **Tom Macauley**

Telescreen announcers Brian Badcoe, Raymond Mason
Goldstein Vernon Dobtcheff   *Prole in canteen* Marjorie Gresley
Parsons Norman Chappell   *Mrs Parsons* Sally Lahee
Parsons girl Sally Thomsett   *Parsons boy* Frank Summerscales
Pedlar Henry Kay   *Blind man* Eric Francis   *Old man* Sydney Arnold
Proles Anthony Blackshaw, Edwin Brown
Prole youths John Lyons, David Baxter, Patrick Ellis
Barman Fred Hugh   *Charrington* John Garrie   *Waiter* John Barrett
Jones John Mincer   *Aaronson* Eden Fox   *Rutherford* George Wilder
Foster Peter Bathurst   *Singing prole woman* Julie May
Orator John Moore   *Martin* Paul Phillips   *Man with bread* Raymond Graham
Thin man William Lyon Brown   *Men in white coats* Norman Scace,
David Grey, John Abineri, Michael Sheard

Television screenplay by: Nigel Kneale
Director: Christopher Morahan
Producer: Cedric Messina
Designer: Tony Abbott
Music: Wilfred Josephs

A BBC Production
120 minutes, black and white
28 November 1965
(BBC2 – *Theatre 625: The World of George Orwell*)

NUMBER THREE

A group of atomic scientists at a nuclear research station in the north of England who are working on a process to drastically cut the cost of electricity face a crisis of conscience when they discover their leader plans to use the research to create an explosive rivalling the H-bomb.

Soul-searching drama on a now-familiar theme – but this was made in 1953, for the BBC's Sunday night drama slot, and marked an early, pre-*Quatermass* contribution from Nigel Kneale.

CAST:

Robert Matthews Philip Guard   *Bill Hollies* Jack Watling
Maureen Dartington Ursula Howells   *Maurice Crampton* Terence Alexander
Prof. Brander Raymond Huntley   *Joan Whitwell* Eileen Moore
Doris Myrtle Reed   *Mr Wheatfield* Carl Bernard
Harry Wall Jack Howarth   *Simpson* Peter Cushing

Writer: Charles Irving
Adapted for television by: George F. Kerr
  and Nigel Kneale
Producer: Stephen Harrison

A BBC Production
80 minutes, black and white
1 February 1953

THE OFFSHORE ISLAND

A parable on the suicidal inhumanity and futility of nuclear politics, *The Offshore Island* was a controversial first play by writer

Marghanita Laski, arousing a mixed reception from its 1959 audience.

Set in an England eight years after the country has been turned into a radioactive graveyard by nuclear war, the play centred on young widow Rachel Verney and her two adolescent children James and Mary who survived the holocaust and are now farming contentedly enough in an isolated valley which has somehow escaped contamination. Having remained completely cut off from the outside world, their idyll is shattered when an American patrol unit drops out of the sky and informs them that the war is still going on and that their tiny plot of uncontaminated England is to be nuked – in close cooperation with the Russians who also march in 'as friends'. The final suggestion, that the 'islanders' should go to America, to a special camp for contaminated people, is met with little enthusiasm, the family preferring to die with their chosen lifestyle.

The Offshore Island itself was received with little enthusiasm in some quarters. Protest callers complained to the BBC about the play's anti-American sentiment and strong language, while *The Times* described it as 'a gimcrack construction . . . with no strong dramatic impulse'. However, Nancy Spain in the *Daily Express* called it 'a brilliant and most moving adult play . . . entertaining, angry and full of passionate argument'.

CAST:

James Verney **Tim Seely*** *Mary Verney* **Diane Clare**
Rachel Verney **Ann Todd** *Martin* **Robert Brown**
Capt. Charles **Phil Brown** *Sgt Bayford* **George Margo**
Smithson **Dan Jackson** *Hale* **John Bloomfield**
Bertini **Jerry Green** *Capt. Baltinsky* **George Pravda**
Russian soldier **Paul Bogdan**

Writer: **Marghanita Laski**
Designer: **Barry Learoyd**
Producer: **Dennis Vance**

A BBC Production
90 minutes, black and white
14 April 1959

* By arrangement with Ealing MGM Artists Ltd

ONE

Billed as 'a story of the foreseeable future', this 1956 play was one of ITV's earliest forays into the realms of visionary drama. Adapted by John Letts from a novel by David Karp, it depicted a society of the future based on uniformity, with all personal ambition having been eradicated by an apparently benevolent

State. Then, from the midst of the unquestioning millions, emerges one man with the will of an individual.

Donald Pleasence starred as Burden, a Cambridge don who has been secretly reporting on his colleagues to the omniscient Ministry of Internal Security. Suddenly he himself is suspected of desiring to be different and the State turns to brainwashing to quash such desires. A new identity is created, turning Burden into a meek civil servant. But the experiment fails as the original personality breaks through again. In the end Burden is led away to face execution.

Less than two years' earlier, the BBC's production of George Orwell's *Nineteen Eighty-Four* had sent shock waves crashing round the country. *One* caused hardly a shudder. Describing the 90-minute play as 'a long-winded bore', the *Daily Express* said that 'not even the shadow of the ghost of *Nineteen Eighty-Four* crossed this brain-washing play of the future'.

CAST:

Conger Jack May   *Miss Allom* Ruth Trouncer   *Wright* Kenneth Hyde
Burden Donald Pleasence   *Wilkin* Jonathan Meddings
Dr Middleton Raymond Francis   *Emma Burden* Mary Jones
Richard Ronald Howard   *Lark* Kenneth Griffith   *Dr Emerson* Philip Ray
Duty doctor Victor Brookes   *Commissioner* Ian Fleming
Gray Tom Bowan   *Nurses* Fanny Carby, Jennifer Wilson
Victor John Woodnutt   *William* Victor Brookes   *Bernard* Keith Smith
Cumbers Roy Malcolm   *Mrs Greevy* Joan Young

Writer: John Letts, *from the novel by* David Karp
Settings: George Haslam
Director: Peter Graham Scott
Special effects: Edward Shankster

An Associated–Rediffusion Network Production
90 minutes, black and white
16 April 1956

ORION

Space-age musical that was a cross between Moses and Noah's Ark. A boy tells how his father escaped from a doomed planet in an enormous spaceship on a mission to lead the Earth's survivors to a new world. Good story, good visuals.

CAST

Hoan Richard Barnes   *Mrs Hoan* Leueen Willoughby
David Richard Kates   *Carol* Julia Lewis
Bruce Jeremy Truelove   *Chris* Anthony O'Keefe

WITH
Eric Roberts, Philippa Boulter, Julian Littman,
Pepsi Maycock, Paul Burton, Marlene Mackay,
Diana Martin, David Morris, Simon Gipps-Kent

Story: Melvyn Bragg
Music/lyrics: Ken Howard, Alan Blaikley
Choreography: Nita Howard
Designer: Rochelle Selwyn
Director: Jeremy Swan

A BBC Production
55 minutes, colour
rpt: 2 September 1979 (BBC1)

OUTPOST

Anglo-US pilot for a possible new 13-part family science fiction series.

Made by HTV at Pinewood Studios, with the cash put up by Columbia Pictures Television, *Outpost* is set in the year 2089, on Icarus, an Earth colony thousands of light years from this world.

It's a tale in the Western frontier spirit, with pioneering settlers, native inhabitants and an American marshal appointed to keep law and order. The pilot follows the marshal's efforts to deal with illegal Russian immigrants and track down a dangerous criminal.

At the time of going to print, *Outpost* had not yet been screened on British television.

CAST
includes: Pamela Stephenson

Writer/producer: Jeff Melvoin
Director: Tommy Lee Wallace
Executive producers: Patrick
  Dromgoole, Johnny Goodman

An HTV Production in association with Columbia Pictures Television
60 minutes, colour

THE POISONED EARTH

Didactic drama airing the pros, cons and 'don't knows' of the nuclear disarmament debate of the early Sixties. Set in a boom town beside a weapon-testing range, its premise was the invention of a new atomic bomb which contaminates only one square mile of Earth, thus making conventional warfare possible again – but with nuclear weapons.

The morality of such a device – and of the tests which form the scenario for the play – are brought into focus when a protest group arrives announcing its intention to be blown up with the bomb. There follows much posturing and manoeuvring, argument and counter-argument by characters on both sides of the fence – and astride it.

The protestors clash with the locals – farmers, shopkeepers, and even the town prostitute, all of whom have never had it so good. Tight-lipped scientists mingle with cynical reporters while the bomb's inventor wrestles with his own conscience. Caught in the middle are the 'honest copper' and the intelligence man 'just trying to do their jobs'.

All the views were strongly held and forcefully expressed – it was for the audience to decide where their sympathies lay.

As for the critics . . .

'Once again television proved itself a popular medium for deeply serious subjects. But we hadn't seen a play.'

(Maurice Richardson, *The Observer*)

CAST

Rev. Claude Bell Michael Gough   *James Whittier* Frederick Bartman
Dr Brockmeyer Joseph Furst   *Sayers* James Maxwell
Insp. Matthews Stratford Johns   *Charlie* J.G. Devlin
Len Beckett Barry Keegan   *Jack* Frank Windsor   *Barratt* Jack May
with: Joby Blanshard, Anne Jameson, George Hall, John Dearth,
Toke Townley, Philip Locke, Patrick Kavanagh, Roy Spencer,
Robert Pointon, Eric Thompson, Phyllida Law, John Wentworth

Writer: Arden Winch
Designer: Richard Negri
Director: Casper Wrede

ATV Network Production
90 minutes, made in black and white
28 February 1961

QUEST BEYOND TIME

Part of an Anglo-Australian series called *Winners*, shown on Channel 4 in 1988, which was intended to use stories to raise issues relevant to 'today's children'.

Quest Beyond Time was the series' only science fiction offering and propelled a young hang glider through a time warp 1000 years into the future. The youth, Mike, is mistaken by the clan Murray as a post-holocaust saviour, and he and a young warrior, Katrin, set out to 'glide' to a nearby island where a cure may be found for the clan's sickness. On the way they encounter various adventures which highlight each other's strengths and weaknesses. The friendship leaves Mike with a decision whether or not to return to his own time.

CAST

Mike Daniel Cordeaux   *Katrin* Rebecca Rigg

WITH:

Roger Ward, Tim Elliot, Marco Colombani, Jeanie Drynan

Writer: Tom Morphett
Producers: Richard Mason, Julia
  Overton
Director: Stephen Wallace

An Australian Children's Television Foundation/ITC Entertainment Production
60 minutes, colour
6 May 1988
(Channel 4)

THE ROAD

Presented as part of the BBC's *First Night* season in 1963, *The Road* was an 18th-century ghost story with a sci-fi punchline which maintained Nigel Kneale's reputation as a writer of ingenious television drama.

In 1770, Sir Timothy Hassall, a rural squire and self-taught scientist or 'natural philosopher', constantly striving for greater knowledge, comes into conflict with visionary Gideon Cobb as together they investigate a wood reputedly haunted by the spectres of a long-slaughtered army. After various red herrings more suited to a serial than a one-off play, the haunting turns out to be a traumatic ripple from the future – an echo of the dropping of the bomb and the panic of people trying to escape.

CAST

Sir Timothy Hassall James Maxwell   *Lavinia (his wife)* Ann Bell
Gideon Cobb John Phillips   *Big Jeff* David King
Lukey Chase Victor Platt   *Sam Towler* Rodney Bewes
Landlord Reg Lever   *Countrymen* Richard Beale, Beaufoy Milton
Tetsy Meg Ritchie   *Jethro* Clifton Jones

Writer: Nigel Kneale
Director: Christopher Morahan
Producer: John Elliot
Designer: Tony Abbott
Script editor: Vincent Tilsley

A BBC Production
55 minutes, black and white
29 September 1963
(BBC: *First Night*)

SALVE REGINA

The final bomb has fallen. In the basement of a gutted department store a raddled hag exercises imperious authority over two buffoon-like men, believing herself the only girl in the world. But she has reckoned without astronaut Marina, who was in space when the holocaust occurred, and who now makes a landing . . .

A strong cast was assembled for this half-hour drama, one of the six prizewinning entries from *The Observer* Television Play Competition, but they were eclipsed by the 'cast' of *Apollo 11* – the play was shown on the eve of man's first landing on the Moon.

CAST

The Queen **Miriam Karlin**   *Marina Palek* **Glenda Jackson**
Arlecchino **Al Mancini**   *Punchinello* **Graham Crowden**

Writer: **Edward Bowman**
Designer: **Andrew Drummond**
Director: **David Saire**
Producer: **Geoffrey Hughes**

London Weekend Television Production
30 minutes, black and white
19 July 1969

THE SHIP THAT COULDN'T STOP

The 40,000 ton nuclear-powered ship *Crusader*, making its maiden voyage, develops a fault in its reactor controls and becomes a runaway liner heading for an explosive docking in the heart of New York . . .

It sounds like a job for International Rescue, but this was *Armchair Theatre*, not *Thunderbirds* and in the absence of Scott and Virgil, it was down to young nuclear scientist Michael Holland (Donald Churchill) to step into the breach. Could he fix things in time to save the ship and its passengers? Of course he could – just like the climax of every disaster movie from *Airport* to *The Big Bus*, disaster was averted in the nick of time. Predictable suspense, but good clean fun.

(Incidentally, not many people know this, but down the cast, as a lowly Helmsman, was a young, little-known actor called Michael Caine . . .)

CAST

Commodore Grant **Frank Pettingell** *Michael Holland* **Donald Churchill**
Roman **Scott Forbes** *Mrs Bollanger* **Madeleine Burgess**
Mr Bollanger **Michael Balfour** *Ann Shields* **Jemma Hyde**
Sir Ronald Caterham **Philip Stone** *Wainwright* **Norman Bowler**
Sullivan **John Colin** *Steward* **Richard Klee**
Anderson **Harry Webster** *Helmsman* **Michael Caine**
Chief engineer **Peter Sinclair** *Engineers* **Graham Corry,**
Ian Anderson, Tony Veale

Writer: **Christopher Hodder-Williams**   *An ABC Television Network Production*
Designer: **Assheton Gorton**   60 minutes, made in black and white
Director: **Alan Cooke**   2 July 1961
Producer: **Sydney Newman**

SIN WITH OUR PERMISSION

Strong overtones of *The Prisoner* made this 1981 drama a gripping and intelligent *ITV Playhouse* production.

It was set in a futuristic New Town where all inhabitants are under constant surveillance and a daily soap opera is used to provide solutions for the individual problems of the citizens, including a small matter of euthanasia!

Gregory Floy played a social scientist who, in true Number Six style, discovers that the city is also a prison from which there is no escape; comic actor Paul Eddington played the head of the development corporation's Information Department – a strong Number Two-type character; and Robin Bailey played the actor who portrayed the central character in the city's soap opera.

CAST

Harry Dudley **Paul Eddington** *James Walton* **Gregory Floy**
Dr Perry **Robin Bailey** *Angela Birley* **Kate Fahy**
Ted Cunningham **Robert Austin** *Jenny Tevitt* **Sally Baxter**
Mrs Tevitt **Barbara New** *Barman* **Alan Thompson**
Chris Peterson **John Flanagan** *Zarah* **Gil Brailey**
Policeman **Martyn Read** *Floor manager* **Tom Kelly**

Writer: **J.C. Wilsher**   *ATV Network Production*
Producer: **Colin Rogers**   60 minutes, colour
Director: **Paul Harrison**   26 May 1981
Designers: **Richard Lake, Quentin**
Chases

STARGAZY ON ZUMMERDOWN

Billed as a visionary fable of Britain in the 23rd century, this was an optimistic look at the future by a historian specialising in the 17th century.

England, or rather Albion, has reverted to a country of peaceable rural communities and small towns, in a happy balance of high technology, industry and nature, called the Commonwealth of New Harmony.

At the Stargazy, the annual midsummer meeting of the agricultural folk (Aggros) and industrial workers (Toonies), among the megaliths on top of Zummerdown, the two communities come together to settle the terms for the following year's exchange of products and knowhow, and engage in the ritual discharge of mutual aggression.

Under the amiable supervision of the Reformed Celtic Church, they enjoy themselves in dancing contests, onion tastings and a swearing contest of Chaucerian earthiness.

Stargazy was science fiction that drew heavily on history. Author John Fletcher called it 'The Anglo-Saxon constitution, plus industrialisation'.

CAST

Father John Cuchlain **Stephen Murray**
Israel Tonge (the Pedlar) **Roy Dotrice**   *Abbot's secretary* **John Gillbyrne**

AGGROS
Opinionated Alice **Peggy Mount**   *Ruth Baxter* **Toni Arthur**
Contrary Harry **John Hartley**   *Goodman Barton* **Peter Schofield**
William Gurney **Declan Mulholland**   *Henry Gutch* **Aubrey Richards**
Alfred Treagle **Malcolm Stent**

TOONIES
Alf Smith **John Ringham**   *Sidney* **Frederick Haynes, Roy Marsden**
Heckler Jones **Alec Wallis**   *Toonie Curser* **Ron Pember**
George Weller **Jack Haig**

Writer: **John Fletcher**
Director: **Michael Ferguson**
Producer: **David Rose**
Designer: **Gavin Davies**
Music: **David Fanshawe**

A BBC (Birmingham) Production
80 minutes, colour
15 March 1978
(BBC2: Play of the Week)

THE STONE TAPE

A 'ghostbusting' play from Nigel Kneale that combined the supernatural and high technology in arguably the most creepy drama ever seen on television.

Originally commissioned as a Christmas ghost story, *The Stone Tape* was first shown on BBC2 on Christmas Day 1972 and proved a palatable antidote to the seasonal stodge.

A research team from Ryan Electric Products arrives at a Victorian mansion, Taskerlands House, where they are due to start work on finding a new, improved recording medium. In an old storeroom, computer programmer Jill Greeley has a strong psychic experience, hearing footsteps and a piercing scream, and seeing a ghostly figure on a stone staircase.

She and the team's director, Peter Brock, make enquiries about the house's history and discover stories of exorcism and mysterious death. When Brock, too, hears the scream he announces his plans to analyse and exorcise the ghost, using their modern technology. His theory is that traumatic emotions leave an impression trapped in the stone walls of the room. The team's first effort to 'play the Stone Tape', using amplified noise and ultra-violet light, appears instead to wipe it clean.

But Jill continues to investigate and believes something else now haunts the storeroom, that only the top layer of the tape was erased. Drawn back, she confronts a strange, terrifying force and in trying to escape 'falls' to her death in a bewilderingly surreal sequence, becoming the latest layer on the Stone Tape.

Kneale's script and Peter Sasdy's atmospheric direction drew some powerful performances from the cast, notably Jane Asher as the tortured Jill, and the play featured particularly eerie music from the BBC's Radiophonic Workshop.

CAST

Jill Greeley **Jane Asher**   Collinson **Iain Cuthbertson**
Peter Brock **Michael Bryant**   Eddie **Michael Bates**
Hargrave **Tom Chadbon**   Maudsley **John Forgeham**
Dow **James Cosmo**   Stewart **Philip Trewinnard**
Sergeant **Neil Wilson**   Bar helper **Hilda Fenemore**
Bar lady **Peggy Marshall**   Alan **Michael Graham Cox**
Vicar **Christopher Banks**   Crawshaw **Reginald Marsh**

Writer: **Nigel Kneale**
Director: **Peter Sasdy**
Producer: **Innes Lloyd**
Designer: **Richard Henry**
Script editor: **Louis Marks**
Music/special sound: **Desmond Briscoe**
and the **BBC Radiophonic Workshop**

A BBC Production
90 minutes, colour
25 December 1972
(BBC2)

STRONGER THAN THE SUN

'I hope my play gave a true picture of the urgency
of the situation as it appears to many people'.

(Stephen Poliakoff, author)

Powerful nuclear-age thriller with the plutonium industry rather than the bomb the target for the author's anxieties, as he charts one woman's attempt to halt what she sees as a suicidal nuclear energy programme.

Kate, a research officer at a nuclear fuel reprocessing plant, is recruited by a sombrely concerned colleague, Alan, to ferret out details of a covered-up mishap, and sets out to highlight the dangers of plutonium by showing how easy it would be to steal some.

At horrifing risk to herself, she smuggles some plutonium out of the factory only to find no one is interested. An anti-pollution group is too intent on achieving power through respectability to have anything to do with her; and a notorious investigative journalist can't be bothered to hear her out. In a final suicidal protest, Kate kills herself by taking a bath in plutonium-contaminated water.

Every bit as strong as the thriller angle was the play's psychological drama. As her mission becomes an obsession, Kate is transformed from an attractive, ambitious worker into a fanatical campaigner, growing more and more disturbed as she crumbles into a kind of repressed hysteria which ends with her final act of self-destruction.

Stronger Than the Sun launched the BBC's 1977 *Play for Today* season and both it and Francesca Annis's performance as Kate won widespread praise. *Daily Mail* critic Shaun Usher called it 'an ambitious and serious theme cast in human, emotional terms'.

CAST

Kate Francesca Annis   *Alan* Tom Bell
Gregory Clive Merrison   *Edwards* John Proctor
Higby Gerald James   *Bruce* Albert Welling
Joan Bridget Ashburn   *Margaret* Anne Aris
Urban guerrilla Duncan Faber   *Yorkshire journalist* Fred Gaunt
Brian Mark Wing-Davey   *Kendal* Hugh Thomas
London journalist Tony Doyle

WITH

Mark Hindley, Nick Ross, Fred Crossley, Peter Lorenzelli,
Nick Edmett, Toby Salaman, Robert Hamilton,
David Hargreaves, Bert Gaunt, Robert Lefever,
Philip Donaghy, Robert Milton, Ken Sicklen,
Hilary Gasson, Nial Padden

Writer: Stephen Poliakoff
Director: Michael Apted
Producer: Margaret Matheson
Designer: Susan Spence
Music: Howard Blake

A BBC Production
95 minutes, colour
18 October 1977
(BBC1: *Play for Today*)

THE TEST

A study in tension, based on the novel *Breakdown* by Patrick Marsh. A scientist, preparing for the testing of a top-secret defence project involving forces of terrifying potential power, never before harnessed, comes under increasing strain. Aside from bureaucratic pressure to hurry through the test before all the equipment has been fully checked, a suspicion of sabotage is in the air, plus the haunting fear that something could go wrong. Oh yes, and his wife's fallen in love with one of his colleagues. Nicholas Selby (who went on to join the staff of the BBC's soapy magazine *Compact*) played the stressed physicist.

CAST

Dr John Armstrong Nicholas Selby   *Mary Armstrong* Sheila Ballantine
Ian Campbell Jack Stewart   *Biggs* William Kendall
Wilson Jack May   *Miss Sheppard* Jocelyne Page
Capt. Snell Gary Watson   *Parnell* Blake Butler
Stevens Victor Brooks   *Miriam Kiall* Gillian Raine
Supt Harding John Arnatt   *Minister* Lockwood West
with: Frederick Rawlings, Alexander Donald, Margaret St Barbe West,
Charles Gilbert, Julia Worth

Writers: William Bast, Donald Bull
Producer: Alan Bromly
Designer: Clifford Hatts

A BBC Production
75 minutes, black and white
5 November 1961

THREADS

Chilling drama-documentary that imagined the unthinkable – the aftermath of a nuclear attack on Britain.

Threads picked on one city, Sheffield, and showed the horrific story of a nuclear strike through the eyes of two ordinary Sheffield families – the Kemps and the Becketts – and their designated wartime controller, the city's peacetime Chief Executive, Clive Sutton.

It traced the events of the four weeks that led up to the nuclear exchange, as the East and West power blocs stumbled to war over a crisis of control in the Middle East. It showed in graphic detail the inferno of suffering inflicted on the city and its population, and followed the scenario through the first post-holocaust decade as the 'threads' of civilisation unravelled.

Writer Barry Hines and producer/director Mick Jackson drew on reams of scientific studies to make *Threads* vastly more factual than the American TV movie *The Day After* and brought the images of the banned BBC film *The War Game* bang up to date. The city of Sheffield also responded with more than 1000 volunteers to be 'victims'.

There was no light relief in *Threads*. Watching it was a chastening experience.

MAIN CAST

Ruth Beckett **Karen Meagher**   *Jimmy Kemp* **Reece Dinsdale**
Mrs Beckett **June Broughton**   *Mr Beckett* **Henry Moxon**
Granny Beckett **Sylvia Stoker**   *Mr Kemp* **David Brierley**
Mrs Kemp **Rita May**   *Michael Kemp* **Nicholas Lane**
Alison Kemp **Jane Hazlegrove**   *Bob* **Ashley Barker**
Jane **Victoria O'Keefe**   *Clive Sutton* **Harry Beety**
Marjorie Sutton **Ruth Holden**   *Chief Supt Hirst* **Michael O'Hagan**
Medical officer **Phil Rose**   *Information officer* **Steve Halliwell**
Transport officer **Peter Faulkner**   *Food officer* **Anthony Collin**
Accommodation officer **Brian Grellis**
Scientific adviser **Michael Ely**   *Manpower officer* **Sharon Bayliss**

Writer: **Barry Hines**
Producer/director: **Mick Jackson**
Executive producers: **Graham Massey, John Purdie**
Film editor: **Jim Latham**
Photography: **Andrew Dunn**
Narrator: **Paul Vaughan**
Designer: **Chris Robilliard**

A BBC Production
115 minutes, colour
23 September 1984
(BBC2)

TIME SLIP

This 1953 BBC short drama had a premise worthy of *The Twilight Zone*. A man (Jack Rodney) dies and is brought back to life by an adrenalin injection. Everything about him is normal except that his time-sense is out of synch by 4.7 secs. He can even answer questions 4.7 secs before they are put to him.

A hospital psychiatrist who takes an interest in the case hits on an unorthodox treatment – he smothers him with a pillow, then revives him again with a more carefully administered dose of adrenalin.

(No further cast details available)

Writer: **Charles Eric Maine**
Producer: **Andrew Osborn**

A BBC Production
30 minutes, black and white
25 November 1953

TIMESLIP

This *Timeslip* was a futuristic 1985 thriller about a computer which locks a couple inside an office block and tries to hunt them down as intruders. John Taylor, of rock group Duran Duran, appeared as a computer hacker, while American actor Jeff Harding and Australian actress Virginia Hey shared a torrid love scene that raised tabloid eyebrows. The half-hour story was filmed as a pilot for a futuristic *Tales of the Unexpected*-style series that never materialised.

CAST

The Hacker **John Taylor**   *Greg* **Jeff Harding**
Jenny **Virginia Hey**   *Candy* **Liza Ross**
Lee **Manning Redwood**   *Billy* **Blain Fairman**

Writer: **Jim Hawkins,** *from a story by*
Robert Holmes
Director: **Willi Patterson**
Producer: **Colin Callendar**

A Yorkshire Television Production in association with the Callendar Company
30 minutes, colour
28 December 1985

2000 MINUS 60

Suspense drama about a runaway rocket heading for London, screened by ITV in its *Television Playhouse* series in 1958.

The one-hour play beings at 11 pm on New Year's Eve 1999, just 60 minutes before midnight and the year 2000. The peoples of the world have been at peace for 40 years. Yet suddenly they are menaced by a threat of destruction more terrible than war. A runaway freighter rocket, containing 1000 tons of high explosive, is due to detonate over London on the stroke of midnight.

As the minutes tick by, General Trent and his staff at the UNICON control centre try every means they can to intercept the runaway missile. But one by one their efforts fail until zero hour approaches.

John Robinson, whose rocket flight had *saved* the world three years earlier when he played Professor Quatermass in *Quatermass II*, starred as Trent, and there was a brief role for his daughter Jane Sothern as a girl who refuses to be evacuated from London because she wants to go to a wedding.

CAST

Devlin Eric Lander   *Lucy* June Thorburn   *Sinclair* Campbell Singer
Sergeant Douglas Blackwell   *Stevens* Murray Hayne
Lieutenant John Downing   *Prof. James* Charles Lloyd Pack
Gen. Trent John Robinson   *Young woman* Jane Sothern
Young man Barry Steele   *Drawbridge* Walter Horsbrugh
Chief engineer Jack Stewart

Writer: James Workman
Settings: Henry Federer
Director: Peter Graham Scott

Granada Production
60 minutes, made in black and white
4 April 1958

UNDERGROUND

This 1958 live *Armchair Theatre* drama about a group of H-bomb survivors trapped in the London Underground is remembered not for its story or dialogue, but for the macabre event of one of the cast dying in the middle of the production.

Actor Gareth Jones played one of a small band of people trapped when a nuclear explosion in London seals off a section of the underground network. The action called for him and other cast members to crawl through rubble in a sequence supposed to be taking place over the course of three days. This meant they had to appear progressively more dishevelled, so while the camera focused on two people crawling, one would nip off to be dirtied up. When it was Gareth Jones's turn to be dirtied he complained of feeling unwell and then died, leaving the show to go on without him, while director William (Ted) Kotcheff rearranged the dialogue and action to get round his unexpected demise.

The play itself was described as 'very depressing, and offering no hope' by another of its stars, Patricia Jessel.

CAST

Art Donald Houston   *Bob* Ian Curry   *Cassie* Patricia Jessel
Stan Warren Mitchell   *Carl Norman* Gareth Jones
Mr Thornton Andrew Cruikshank   *Elliot* Edward Dentith
Simpson Peter Bowles   *Old man* Launce Maraschal

Writer: James Forsyth, *based on the*
  novel by Harold Rein
Producer: Sydney Newman
Director: William Kotcheff
Designer: George Haslam

An ABC Television Network Production
60 minutes, black and white
28 November 1958
(ITV: *Armchair Theatre*)

VIRUS X

Hour-long suspense drama. A girl who has been on holiday in Bristol develops flu on her return to London and in two days she is dead. A member of the Virus Research Institute goes down with flu and dies. Something, it seems, is turning an ordinary flu virus into something much more deadly. Tests are made to find an antidote, but only one man can provide the answer – embittered scientist Dr Bennett, and he has disappeared . . .

Writer Evelyn Frazer drew on her experience as a secretary to the director of a medical research institute at Mill Hill in London to spice the drama with scientific authenticity, and character actor George Coulouris played the scientist whose wartime experiments take on a greater relevance. Other noteworthy names in a very large cast included Richard Carpenter (creator of *Catweazle* and *Robin of Sherwood*), Jean Anderson (*Tenko*) and Kenneth Kendall as the inevitable reporter.

CAST

Dr Cornish Richard Longman   *Dr Roberts* Brenda Kaye
Prof. Glenister Gilbert Davis   *Miss Reid* Jean Anderson
Dr Bennett George Coulouris   *Dr Nicholson* Richard Leech
Dr Maynard Richard Bebb   *Dr Lowden* Richard Carpenter
Jane Callan Jennifer Daniel   *Dr Rapier* A.J. Brown
Sid Symes Meadows White   *George Carter* Leslie Dwyer
Dr Bemmelman Richard Marner   *Rt Hon. Wybrow* Robert Sansom
with: Anne Hudson, Michael Raghan, Rosemary Rogers,
Dixon Adams, Wally Patch, Michael Alexander,
Marion Jennings, Kenneth Kendall, Joan Ingram,
John Keyes, Wendy Hall, David Haddon, Bay White,
Richard Steele, Christopher Hodge

Writer: Evelyn Frazer
Designer: Barry Learoyd
Producer: Stephen Harrison
Music: Tristram Cary

A BBC Production
60 minutes, black and white
25 June 1962

A VOICE IN THE SKY

Single science fiction plays had become a rare event on ITV when this *Armchair Theatre* drama was screened in March 1965. Reality rather than fantasy was in vogue, and it had been 18 months since ITV's last sf excursion (*Loop*, October 1963).

Its premise: one astronaut has been lost in space – another returns claiming to have heard 'the voice of the Almighty' telling him the world is evil and must be destroyed. The scene shifts between America and Britain, from Cape Kennedy to the London Planetarium, as the astronaut's secret space organisation 'The Angels' prepares to unleash a nuclear holocaust.

Jack Hedley starred as Jerry Noble, a failed astronaut who fights to thwart the Angels, aided by Paul Maxwell as a UN space expert and Ann Bell as the astronaut's girl friend. In a climactic scene Hedley balanced precariously on a rooftop trying to re-erect an aerial while Ms Bell performed a diversionary striptease. Very Sixties.

CAST

Mike Brixton **Denis Goacher**   *Flecker* **Paul Danquah**
Wallace Vestrey **Paul Maxwell**   *Robin Erickson* **David Bauer**
Helen **Roberta Huby**   *Jerry Noble* **Jack Hedley**
Tessa Bright **Ann Bell**   *Ken Stokes* **Jolyon Booth**
Dr McFeelan **Morris Perry**   *Dr Pritchard* **Lloyd Lamble**
Le Maitre **James Darwin**   *Richek* **Jack Niles**
Col. Orsett **Richard Coleman**   *Peter Winthrop* **Michael Newell**
Assistant **Michael Finlayson**

Writer: **Christopher Hodder-Williams**
Designer: **Patrick Downing**
Director: **Guy Verney**
Producer: **Leonard White**

An ABC Television Production
60 minutes, black and white
21 March 1965

THE VOICES

Barely a month after BBC audiences had been stunned by the nightmarish vision of *Nineteen Eighty-Four*, 1954-style, they were faced with another futuristic power struggle in this television adaptation by George F. Kerr of the novel *Hero's Walk*, by Robert Crane.

The play's theme was the perils of cosmic ambition in the interplanetary era and told the story of three days of world crisis in the year 2021. A world government runs Earth, and its delegates have met at the Palace of Intercos to discuss the latest programme of space exploration. One huge artificial planet, Platform One, already orbits Earth; Mars has been colonised and is fertile. Now plans have been developed for a second such satellite round Mars, to enable man to venture still further. Behind these plans is InterCos President, Dr Werner, a man with despotic ambitions. He is backed by the Russian and Chinese delegates and opposed by America and Britain.

But another voice is struggling to be heard. Prof. Mark Harrison, a scientist dying from radiation poisoning caused by atomic experiments, has sounded repeated warnings about signals from outer space. The Voices he has heard are those of an avenging alien force bent upon punishing man for having over-reached himself. Now the world faces annihilation in an interplanetary war. Ultimately the power struggle is resolved and Werner replaced by an Irishman (Terence Alexander, nearly 30 years before he became Charlie Hungerford in *Bergerac*) who charms the voices back home.

For the TV audiences watching the two live performances of the play, the most disturbing image was of the hero, Prof. Harrison, whose hideously scarred and bloated face filled the screen like a gruesomely benign Big Brother. The play had a generally fair reception, though *The Times* called it 'a trying essay in science fiction'.

CAST

Dr Werner **Walter Rilla**   *Helga von Horstmann* **Ursula Danera**
Crandall, USA **Launce Maraschal**   *Vernon-Cavendish, UK and Eire* **Carl Bernard**
Sir Alton Berkeley, UK and Eire **Terence Alexander**
Balatov, USSR **Stanley Zevic**   *Hsuan, China* **Andy Ho**
Dhevu, India **Paul Bahadur**   *Libby Harrison* **Ursula Howells**
Prof. Mark Harrison **Willoughby Goddard**
Dr Wooley **Kevin Stoney**   *Dr Luden* **Barry Letts**
Waterson, Australia **Bettina Dickson**   *McAllister, Canada* **Ronan O'Casey**
Locke, New Zealand **Vincent Ball**   *Admiral Gould* **Peter Bathurst**
Gen. Kirkland **Harold Ayer**   *Hadfield* **Paul Hardwick**
with: **Joan Angell, Joyce Chancellor, Sheila Chong, John Dunbar,
Mary Gillingham, Harcourt Curacao, Patricia Horder,
Arthur Hosking, Guy Mills, Liat Sahani, Frank Singuineau,
Jill Rowland, Joy Stewart, Veronica Wells, Felicitas Cottier,
Marti de Lyle**

Adapted by **George F. Kerr**, *from the
novel 'Hero's Walk' by* **Robert Crane**
Producer: **Dennis Vance**

A BBC Production
90 minutes, black and whtie
16 January 1955
Second performance: 20 January 1955

WINE OF INDIA

Two years after presenting a disturbing look ahead in *The Year of the Sex Olympics*, Nigel Kneale took a different, more civilised route into the future.

Wine of India was set in 2050, in a world where illness and natural death have been abolished through perfected medical techniques, enabling people to be maintained at an optimum age indefinitely.

But there is a price. To prevent the world from bursting at the seams, society and the individual make a contract guaranteeing people a set lifespan, at the end of which they must go quietly.

The play took the form of a funeral for Julie and Will, a couple of about 90 who barely look a day over 35. The funeral is like a sort of *This Is Your Life*, at which all the couple's relatives and friends gather for a farewell celebration during which film of the subjects' earlier life is flashed on screen by the 'undertaker' of Mortality Control. He carefully stage-manages the proceedings to ensure the couple go through with their side of the deal – even arranging for a 'spectre at the feast' in the form of Bee, a genuine old lady who has refused to sign a contract and is growing old naturally, so convincing the couple that their guaranteed youth has been worth the price. In the end the couple pass through the curtains to their death and the guests disperse. All very civilised . . .

CAST

Julie **Annette Crosbie**   *Will* **Brian Blessed**   *Russ* **John Standing**
Nita **Rosemary Nicols**   *Bee* **Catherine Lacey**   *Sam* **Ian Ogilvy**

WITH . . .

Adam **Donald Burton**   *Pat* **David Munro**   *Nonie* **Judith Bellis**
Dod **Nicholas Young**   *Jonna* **Vicky Williams**   *Celebrity* **Glenn Williams**
Mac **Reg Whitehead**   *Lexy* **Alexandra Dane**
Dave **Neville Hughes**   *Martin* **Roger Perry**

Writer: **Nigel Kneale**
Director: **Gilchrist Calder**
Producer: **Graeme McDonald**
Designer: **J. Roger Lowe**

A BBC TV Production
50 minutes, colour
15 April 1970
(BBC1: *The Wednesday Play*)

THE YEAR OF THE SEX OLYMPICS

'A highly original play written with great force and making as many valid points about the dangers of the future as any science-fiction work I can remember – including *1984!*'

(Sean Day-Lewis, *Daily Telegraph*)

Nigel Kneale's provocative 1968 parable of the future depicted a society totally dominated by television.

In his air-conditioned, fully automated England of the future – Area 27 – the population has become split into the two percent 'high-drive' people who make the TV programmes, and the 98 per cent 'low-drive' masses who watch them.

The television network, Output, uses techniques of mass voyeurism to stifle the population explosion and quell the attendant tensions such as war, love, hate and loyalty. Even language has become virtually redundant for the passive low-drives who don't need to read, write or even speak. Television runs their lives, dulling even the most basic urges. There are gluttony programmes such as the Hungry-Angry Show to put them off food, and 'applied pornography' programmes to put them off sex, including Artsex and Sportsex.

But when these start to lose their impact, Co-ordinator Ugo Priest (motto: 'watch not do') finds a new way to involve the viewers – The Live Life Show.

Volunteer family Deanie Webb, Nat Mender and their child go to a small island where life is far from feather-bedded. The cameras are on them 24 hours a day and their 'show' is soon top of the ratings. But there's a murderer about, and the outcome is violence and death – something that's greeted with glee and delight by the watching millions.

The Year of the Sex Olympics was first screened in BBC 2's *Theatre 625* series, with a repeat in BBC1's *Wednesday Play* slot in 1970.

CAST

Co-ordinator Ugo Priest **Leonard Rossiter** *Deanie Webb* **Suzanne Neve**
Nat Mender **Tony Vogel** *Misch* **Vickery Turner**
Lasar Opie **Brian Cox** *Grels* **George Murcell**
Kin Hodder **Martin Potter** *Keten Webb* **Lesley Roach**
Betty **Hira Talfrey** *Nurse* **Patricia Maynard**

Writer: **Nigel Kneale**
Director: **Michael Elliott**
Producer: **Ronald Travers**
Designer: **Roger Andrews**

A BBC Production
105 minutes, colour
29 July 1968 (BBC2: *Theatre 625*)
rpt: 11 March 1970 (BBC1: *The Wednesday Play*)

Z FOR ZACHARIAH

Nuclear parable by Anthony Garner set in a remote Welsh valley which, due to a climatic quirk, has been left virtually untouched by a nuclear attack that has devastated the rest of Britain.

Teenager Ann Burden is alone after her parents left to seek a new life and never returned. Ann has learnt how to survive and has built a life for herself within the valley. Then scientist John Loomis, sole male survivor of the holocaust, arrives at the valley in his prototype plastic radiation capsule.

The play traces their developing relationship which ends in tragedy when Loomis contracts radiation sickness after bathing naked in a contaminated stream.

Star Anthony Andrews had to endure a four-hour make-up job to present a convincing portrait of a radiation-ravaged victim.

The idea of an enclave touched by the holocaust was not a new one. It had been explored in Marghanita Laski's 1959 BBC play *The Offshore Island* (see separate entry).

CAST
Loomis **Anthony Andrews**   *Ann Burden* **Pippa Hinchley**

Writer: **Anthony Garner**
Producer: **Neil Zeiger**
Director: **Anthony Garner**
Designer: **Philip Lindley**
Make-up: **Carolyn Tyrer**
Music: **Geoffrey Burgon**

A BBC Production
120 minutes, colour
28 February 1984
(BBC1: *Play for Today*)

ANIMATION

Astroboy

In 1964, *Astroboy* became the first Japanese cartoon series to make an impact in Britain. Essentially, it was the adventures of a robot boy who, with superstrength, a computer mind and rocket jets in his feet, battles a never-ending stream of futuristic villains in the year 2000. But there was a poignant, almost Peter Pan-like side to the story. Astroboy's origins stem from the death in a car crash of the young son of scientist Dr Boynton. The distraught Boynton creates a robot duplicate of his son but later rejects him when the 'boy' doesn't grow any older. Sold to a robot circus, Astroboy is rescued by another scientist, Dr Pachedyrmus Elefon. In between fighting mad scientists, monsters or super-crooks, Astroboy yearns to be like 'real' boys so Elefon builds him a robot family to keep him company.

Astroboy debuted on ITV in the Anglia region, with other areas picking up the series later.

Creator/producer: Fumiro Suzuki
UK: 26 30-minute episodes, black and white
17 June–16 December 1964
(Anglia Television)

The Astronut Show

Animated adventures of the little man from space and his Earth pal Oscar. A frequent mid-1970s visitor to BBC1.

A Terrytoons Production
UK premiere: 11 September 1973
(BBC1)

Battle of the Planets

Cartoon adventure series revolving around the activities of G-Force, a group of five fearless young people with superhero powers, who fight to protect Earth from alien invaders, notably Spectra and the persistently villainous Zoltar. Among the voice stars were Janet Waldo (Judy Jetson and Penelope Pitstop), and Keye '*Kung Fu*' Luke.

A Sandy Frank Production, in association with Gallerie International Film
UK: 56 colour 25-minute episodes (out of at least 85 episodes)
3 September–19 November 1979
21 November 1980–2 January 1981
3/10 April 1983
16 April–2 November 1984
(BBC1)

Bleep and Booster

Cartoon adventures of a robot spaceboy (Bleep) and a young Earth boy (Booster) whose home-made rocket was intercepted by Space Freighter 2000. *Blue Peter* viewers followed their exploits around the galaxy for several years from March 1964.

Not an 'animated' series, *Bleep and Booster*'s adventures were told by means of still drawings.

A BBC Production

Centurions

Animated adventure series set in the late 21st century, in which a team of high-tech armoured warriors, based in their space Skyvault, battle an evil renegade scientist, Doc Terror.

The *Centurions* first showed up as part of the 1980s Saturday morning kids' show, *Get Fresh*.

A Ruby-Spears Production.

C-P and Qwikstitch

Cartoon series about two robots marooned on the planet Junkus Minor for a very long time. Nine five-minute episodes screened on BBC1 in August/September 1985.

Defenders of the Earth

Updated animated adventures of Flash Gordon and a group of heroic warriors who have sworn allegiance to the protection of Earth and the destruction of that merciless old villain, Ming. Mandrake the Magician, Lothar and the Phantom are among the good guys.

*King Features Entertainment Ltd
Production*
35 colour 20-minute episodes
UK premiere:
12 September 1988–12 June 1989

Droids

One of two animated spin-offs from *Star Wars* to reach our television screens. Along with its companion series *Ewoks*, *Droids* was set 15 years before the events of the *Star Wars* trilogy, and followed the adventures of the lovable droids C3PO and R2D2 and their assorted friends and masters. It benefited from having Anthony Daniels reprise his vocal role of the tall thin one, and from utilising many of the sound effects from the feature films – including the bleeps of the short fat one.

CAST
C3PO Anthony Daniels
R2D2 Himself *(Noises by* John Burtt*)*

LucasFilms Production
13 colour 25-minute episodes
UK premiere:
11 January to 11 April 1988 (BBC1)

Ewoks

Second of the animated spin-offs from the *Star Wars* movie cycle, *Ewoks* gave a series of their own to the furry little heroes of *Return of the Jedi* and *Caravan of Courage*, who live in tree-houses connected by wooden bridges, on the green moon of Endor.

Hero of the tales is young Wicket, usually joined by his friends Princess Kneesa, the trickster Latara, the show-off Paploo, and the dreamy Teebo. Baddies are the Duloks, lanky swamp-dwelling creatures whose king, Gorneesh, is always plotting to enslave the Ewoks. Other enemies include the witch Morag and the Phlogs.

A Lucasfilms Production
12 colour 20-minute episodes
UK premiere:
5 October–21 December 1987 (BBC1)

Fangface

Cartoon series, from America, about a teenage boy who samples a new soft drink and discovers it has a surprising side-effect – it turns him into a wacky werewolf. As *Fangface*, he and his friends, Biff, Kim and Pugsy, enjoy a series of unusual escapades such as combating alien space creatures, taming a gigantic dinosaur, fighting evil professors, magicians and assorted felons and generally solving mysteries. *Fangface* first showed his face on ITV in 1980 and was still growling as recently as 1987.

A Filmways/Ruby and Spears Production
32 colour 25-minute episodes
(not all shown in UK)

The Fantastic Four

Animated adventures of the original Marvel Comics quartet of heroes – Mr Fantastic, the Human Torch, The Invisible Girl and the grouchy monster called The Thing. Made in the States in 1967, it first played over here on ITV in November 1968, but was never widely aired.

An updated series, *The New Adventures of the Fantastic Four*, appeared in 1983, with a new 'hero' instead of the Torch – Herbie the Robot, a pint-sized mine of information.

The Fantastic Four
19 colour 25-minute episodes

The New Adventures of the Fantastic Four
13 colour 25-minute episodes
Hanna–Barbera Productions

Fantastic Voyage

Cartoon series inspired by the successful 1966 science fiction film of the same name. It followed the adventure of a team of scientists who are miniaturised – along with their submarine *Voyager* – to the size of microbes, enabling them to reach the parts other heroes can't reach, whether countering a threat to the Earth's oxygen supply from space crystals or operating internally on a critically injured colleague.

A Filmation Production
17 colour 25-minute episodes
UK premiere: February 1976
(ITV)

Gigantor

'The world's mightiest robot' hailed from Japan but was not one of their greatest exports to the UK. Set in the year 2000, this animated series' mechanical hero had no voice or brain but was controlled by 12-year-old Jimmy Sparks, son of the robot's late inventor. With their pals, scientist Dr Bob Brilliant and son Buttons, secret agent Dick Strong and comic cop Insp. Blooper, Jimmy and Gigantor regularly saved their corner of the world from the grand designs of various master criminals such as Swami Rivers, Mr Lurk, Prof. Stringer, Mr Double-Trouble and . . . the Space Pussies.

(The series was not widely shown in the UK, except in Scotland where Grampian and Scottish showed 37 25-minute episodes in 1967/68, with Grampian getting in first. Episodes also found their way south of the border – to the Granada region in May–June 1968, and to the West and Wales.)

UK premiere run:
29 October 1967–29 July 1968
(Grampian)

Godzilla

Animated adventures with the 600-ton monster who, after having been asleep for 1000 years, rises from the depths of the Pacific to aid mankind and, in particular, the crew of the research ship *Calico*. Light relief was provided by Godzooky, Godzilla's comical, cowardly little nephew.

A Hanna–Barbera Production
26 colour 25-minute episodes
UK premiere: Late 1970s
(BBC1)

He-Man and the Masters of the Universe

'By the power of Grayskull!'

This animated blend of sword'n'scorcery, science fiction adventure, comedy and morality, was based upon the hugely successful range of Mattel toys, but soon acquired a momentum of its own, becoming one of the longest-running cartoon series of the 1980s.

A heroic crusader 'with strength greater than a thousand mortal men', He-Man is really Prince Adam, cavalier heir to the throne of Eternia. A trustee of the secrets of the legendary Castle Grayskull, He-Man has a miraculous sword – and a mission. With his loyal companions, notably Teela, Man at Arms and Orko, he wages a tireless struggle against the Masters of the Universe, a surly alliance of evil foes led by Skeletor. Affectionately dubbed 'the wickedest creature that ever strode the cosmos', Skeletor is a sinister demon from another dimension who is constantly trying to destroy He-Man, Eternia and Grayskull (in no particular order).

The series was produced by Filmation, the American animation house responsible for a string of sf and fantasy cartoon series, from *Superman*, *Batman* and *Journey to the Centre of the Earth* to the Emmy award-winning animated version of *Star Trek*.

A Filmation Production
65 25-minute episodes
UK premiere: 5 September 1983

The Impossibles

American animated series following the adventures of a pop trio who are really super-powered crime-fighters – Coilman, Liquidman and Multiman. Also starring Frankenstein Jr, a lovable 30 ft monster robot controlled by a boy and his scientist father.

A Hanna–Barbera Production
18 colour 25-minute episodes
(first shown in black and white)
22 August–19 December 1967
(BBC1)

The Incredible Hulk

Animated adventures of the not-so-jolly green giant, alias gamma-ray afflicted scientist David Bruce Banner, and his companions Betty Ross and Rick. While searching for that ever-elusive cure, The Hulk combats a parade of super-villains including Spy-Master, Dr Octopus, Puppet Master, Doctor Proto and the Supreme Hydra. A time-travelling story also had the Hulk falling in love with a cavegirl, another introduced She-Hulk – Banner's cousin – and another saw him reduced to just 3 in tall.

Marvel Production
13 colour 25-minute episodes
2 April–23 July 1984
(ITV)

Jayce and the Wheeled Warriors

Fantasy adventures with Jayce, a 19-year-old battling through the cosmos to find his father who has the other half of the 'key' to destroying the evil Monster Minds who are taking over the Universe.

A Dic-Mattel Production
13 colour 30-minute episodes
UK premiere: 15 July 1986
(Thames)
13-week run on Channel 4:
9 July–10 October 1989

The Jetsons

The future wasn't all rampant aliens, ecological disasters or nuclear holocausts. The future could also be funny . . .

The Jetsons were essentially a space-age version of *The Flintstones*. Attempting to repeat the phenomenal success of the modern, stone-age family, creators William Hanna and Joseph Barbera simply transposed the formula into the future, presenting mid-Sixties middle-America with a reassuringly familiar picture of everyday family life in the 21st century – but with all the mod cons they could ever wish for.

The Jetsons were George, a hapless, harried dad who worked as an automated index operator for Spacely Space Sprockets, wife Jane who kept house and went shopping a lot, teenage daughter Judy who was into parties and pop music, and nine-year-old son Elroy, an electronics whizz-kid in a beanie hat. There was also a lovable family mutt called Astro and Rosie the robot maid. But what everyone who ever watched *The Jetsons* remembered best were the gadgets, from the nuclear-powered airmobile (with a 'side-saucer' for the dog), and videophone, to seeing-eye vacuum cleaner, voice-operated washing-machine, solar-powered stamp-licker, the amazing push-button cook, the Foodarackacycle, and the Supersonic Dressomatic – a must for sleepy-heads.

Among the voice talents were 'Yogi Bear' Daws Butler, Don Messick (better-known now as Scooby Doo), Jean Van Der Pyl (Wilma Flintstone), Mel Blanc (Barney Rubble) and Penny Singleton (star of the Forties *Blondie* movie series).

First shown in America in 1962, *The Jetsons* debuted in Britain in July 1963, with a full series run in the Granada area.

VOICE CAST:
George Jetson George O'Hanlon
Jane Jetson Penny Singleton
Judy Jane Waldo
Elroy Daws Butler
Rosie Jean Van Der Pyl
Astro Don Messick
Cosmo G. Spacely Mel Blanc

Creators/directors: William Hanna,
   Joseph Barbera
Gadgets: Tony Benedict, Don

A Hanna–Barbera Production
24 30-minute episodes, black and white

Rosie the Robot
A Day with Jet Screamer
The Space Car
The Coming of Astro
Jetson's Night Out
The Good Little Scouts
The Flying Suit
Rosie's Boyfriend
Elroy's TV Show
Uniblab
Visit from Grandpa
Astro's Top Secret
Elroy's Pal

Test Pilot
Millionaire Astro
The Little Man
Las Venus
Jane's Driving Lesson
G.I. Jetson
Miss Solar System
TV or Not TV
Private Property
Dude Planet
Elroy's Mob

3 July–11 December 1963
(Granada)

Jonny Quest

Highly respected American cartoon series about the adventures of a 12-year-old boy who travelled around the world with his scientist father Dr Benton Quest, and companions Race Bannon, their bodyguard; Hadji, a little Indian boy; and Bandit the dog. They sought lost treasures, Indiana Jones-style, encountered various monsters and tangled with Dr Quest's arch-enemy Dr Zin.

A Hanna–Barbera Production
26 colour 25-minute episodes (shown here in black and white)
6 January–30 June 1965
(BBC1)

Journey to the Centre of the Earth

American animated series inspired by Jules Verne's classic novel. Professor John Lindenbrook, his pupil Alec McEwen, niece Cindy and guide Lars are exploring a cave when they are accidentally entombed. The professor finds carved on the wall the initials of Arne Sacknussem, the original leader of an expedition to find the lost city of Atlantis at the centre of the Earth. They decide to take up the search by following the signs and clues he left behind.

But they are unaware that the villainous Count Sacknussem, nephew of the explorer, and his henchman Torg are watching their every move. The professor's party encounter all kinds of dangers en route to the Earth's core, from weird monsters, primitive underground races, lost civilisations, natural hazards and, of course, the evil Count.

A Filmation Production
17 colour 25-minute episodes
(first shown in black and white)
25 September 1968–29 January 1969
(BBC1)

Marine Boy

Japanese cartoon series about a boy who roams the world's oceans on his dolphin, Splasher, helping to keep the seas free of villains and monsters. He shared his adventures with a mermaid, Neptina and had various scientific aids such as Oxygum which he chewed to help him stay under water without needing to come up for air.

Seven Arts Production
UK: 26 25-minute episodes,
black and white
5 February–30 April 1969
6 July–6 October 1970
(BBC1)

The New Adventures of Batman

Animated update of the old bat-series, given added spice by the voices of the original caped crusaders Adam West and Burt Ward, who, with the help of Batgirl, continue to wage a ceaseless battle against crime and evil.

A Filmation Production
16 colour 25-minute episodes
31 December 1977–15 April 1978
(BBC1)

The New Adventures of Flash Gordon

Animated remake of the 1930s sf epic, following the exploits of Flash, Dale Arden and Dr Zarkov as they strive to save Earth from the evil dictator of the comet-world Mongo, Ming the Merciless.

(Until this 1979 American cartoon series reached Britain in 1983, our television experience of the legendary hero had been confined to screenings of the original black and white movie serials, starring Buster Crabbe. These appeared as far back as 1957 in some ITV regions, but the BBC's network runs of the three serials – *Flash Gordon* (1934), in December 1976; *Flash Gordon's Trip to Mars* (1938), in June–September 1977; and *Flash Gordon Conquers the Universe* (1940), in December 1977–January 1978 – introduced the character to a new generation and stirred memories in an older one.)

The New Adventures . . .
UK: 23 colour 20-minute episodes
A Filmation Production
UK premiere: 17–28 October 1983 (Ten episodes)
21 December 1983–6 January 1983 (13 episodes)
(BBC1)

Return to the Planet of the Apes

This animated extension of the quintet of Apes films and the television series had more than just a simian pedigree. It was produced by Friz Freleng, Oscar-winning creator of Bugs Bunny, Porky Pig, Tweety Pie, Daffy Duck and Sylvester the Cat.

The series revolved around three astronauts, Bill Hudson, Jeff Carter and Judy Franklin, who prove the theory of time thrust by projecting their space capsule some 200 years into Earth's future. There they find not just an ape-dominated world, but also two other groups – humanoids who have been there for centuries, and underdwellers, a group driven underground to escape an atomic holocaust. The philosophic orang-utan politican Dr Zaius again strives to keep the peace, opposed by General Urko, leader of the Gorilla army. The chirpy chimps are Cornelius and Zira, scientists intent on studying the humans.

Return's director, Doug Wildey was also the creator of Hanna Barbera's acclaimed 1960s cartoon series *Jonny Quest*.

Return to the Planet of the Apes ran for 13 weeks on ITV, debuting in the London and Anglia regions.

Producers: David DePatie *and* Friz Freleng
Associate producer/director: Doug Wildey
Music: Dean Elliott

A DePatie-Freleng Production in association with 20th Century Fox Television
13, colour 20-minute episodes
3 January–22 May 1976
(London Weekend Television)

Robostory

Animated series from France about two diametrically opposed robot communities on the distant Green Planet. The Robors are a clan of affectionate, clever robots; the Rotors are mean and warlike.

UK: 24 colour 25-minute episodes
UK premiere:
14 July 1986
(Thames)
(Longer run on Grampian, April 1989)

Rocket Robin Hood

In this 1960s cartoon series, Sherwood Forest was an asteroid in outer space in the year AD 3000. Robin and his Merry Astronauts fought the forces of evil with laser beams and ray guns as well as the odd bow and arrow. The series ran for around 18 weeks in ITV's Granada region from September 1968, and again in June–December 1969 but was not widely shown elsewhere.

The Shadoks

French cartoon series about two rival species of interplanetary explorers whose main purpose was to invade Earth. The Shadoks, led by Professor Shadoko, were hopelessly dim, while the Gibis were highly intelligent. Neither were successful.

The series, with English narration by Kenneth Robinson, had a 16-week run in ITV's London region, at the rate of one ten-minute episode per weekday.

9 July–26 October 1973
(Thames)

She-Ra: Princess of Power

Just so the girls wouldn't feel left out, here was the companion series to *He-Man and the Masters of the Universe*, with the same blend of sword'n'sorcery and the same moral message of loyalty, courage and honour.

She-Ra is He-Man's twin sister Adora, snatched as an infant by the evil Horde and raised on the planet Etheria. An encounter with He-Man unlocks Adora's conditioned mind and enables her to share the secret of Grayskull and lead her people's fight against the forces of evil and villainy.

A Filmation Production
65 colour 25-minute episodes
UK premiere: 2 September 1985

The Space Explorers

Children's fantasy cartoon film in which a young boy heads off into space in search of his missing father. Screened in two 30-minute instalments: 27 January and 3 February 1960, BBC (no credits available).

The Space Ghost

Enjoyable hokum about an inter-planetary crime fighter who possesses a magic belt that makes him invisible. He travels with two teenage wards, Jan and Jayce, and their pet space monkey, Blip.

A Hanna–Barbera Production
20 colour 25-minute episodes
US premiere: 1966
(Ran as part of TV-AM's *Wide Awake Club* 1983–4)

Space Kidettes

Uninspired US cartoon series about a bunch of space-age youngsters and their dog who are constantly foiling the bungling efforts of the notorious space pirate Captain Skyhook to get his grasping hands on their treasure map.

A Hanna–Barbera Production
UK: 28 colour episodes (lengths vary)
(first seven shown in black and white)
7 October 1969–14 August 1970
(BBC1)

The Space Sentinels

Selected from an earlier age and given incredible superpowers by friendly visitors from a distant planet, three teenagers return to Earth in their spaceship headquarters with a mission: to guard the human race from evil. The super trio are Hercules, Mercury and Astraea and they're assisted by their Super Computer S1, and Mo, the maintenance robot.

A Filmation Production
13 colour 20-minute episodes
10–31 October 1978,
4 January–1 March 1979
(BBC1)

Spiderman

Television has had a few goes at adapting the adventures of Marvel's web-spinning superhero. The first animated series appeared in America in 1967 and enmeshed the ITV schedules over here from 1969, with Peter Parker, college freshman, donning his superguise whenever supervillains threatened.

In 1983, ITV screened a new arachnid cartoon, *Spiderwoman*, featuring Spiderwoman and Spiderman battling assorted aliens and villains.

And in the same year BBC1 began showing *Spiderman and his Amazing Friends*, a lighthearted series set in a small college town, and featuring Spidey, his cool roommate Bobby Drake, the Iceman, and beautiful Angelic Jones who's hot stuff as Fire-Start. Together they save Earth from outlandish villains such as the Goblin, Swarm and Dr Doom.

Spiderman

52 colour 25-minute episodes
A Marvel Production

Spiderwoman

16 colour 25-minute episodes
De-Patie/Freleng/Lee Production

Spiderman and his Amazing Friends

32 colour 25-minute episodes
Marvel Production

Star Trek – Animated

The further voyages of the Starship *Enterprise* – in cartoon form with animated versions of Kirk, Spock and Co seeking out more life and new civilisations, plus a few familiar ones for old times' sake.

Nearly all the original cast supplied the voices for their animated selves, and with storylines supplied by many of the live series' writers, this production helped to meet the insatiable demand for new *Star Trek* tales.

The BBC showed the 16 first series episodes in 1974, with the second smaller batch of just six stories following in 1976.

VOICES:
William Shatner,
Leonard Nimoy,
DeForest Kelley,
James Doohan,
George Takei,
Michelle Nicholls,
Majel Barrett

Producer: Norm Prescott
Director: Hal Sutherland
Writers: various, including David
    Gerrold, Marc Daniels, D.C. Fontana,
    Walter Koenig, Margaret Armen

A Filmation Production
22 colour 25-minute episodes
31 August–22 December 1974
6 January–10 February 1976

Season One:
Once Upon a Planet
Jihad
The Infinite Vulcan
The Magicks of Megas-Tu
More Tribbles, More Troubles
The Survivor
Beyond the Farthest Star
Yesteryear
One of Our Planets Is Missing
Mudd's Passion
Time Trap
The Terratin Incident
The Ambergris Element
Slaver Weapon
The Eye of the Beholder
The Lorelei Signal

Season Two:
The Pirates of Orion
Ben
Practical Joker
Albatross
How Sharper Than a Serpent's Tooth
The Counter Clock Incident

Superfriends

Half-hour cartoon series featuring Superman, Batman and many other superheroes. It first appeared in America in 1973, where it ran for 13 years, making it the second longest-running Saturday morning cartoon on television. Its success in Britain was more modest, flitting in and out of the ITV children's schedules from the mid-1970s, but without establishing a solid run.

Various colour 30-minute episodes
A Hanna Barbera Production

Superman

A cartoon series of *Superman* arrived in Britain in 1968, with the man of steel aided by Superboy and Krypto the superdog of steel. And where George Reeves had mostly battled crooks, the animated heroes tended to face more alien threats.

Thames, in London, were the first to screen the cartoons, from 12 August 1968–3 March 1969. Other ITV regions were quick to follow.

A Filmation Production
UK premiere: 12 August 1968
(Thames)

The Telebugs

British cartoon fantasy series about a computer 'family' created by the eccentric Professor Brainstrain, who programmes the Telebugs to help people in trouble and fight against evil.

They are recruited by Arch McStarch, the boss of McStarch TV, who aims to boost his ratings by casting the Telebugs as his news-reporting team.

Their sworn enemy is Bullibyte who plans to dominate the world through the awesome power of Angel Brain, his very feminine multi-billion byte computer. But he is repeatedly frustrated by the combined processing powers of Chip, Samantha and Bug.

Zudo, the fourth Telebug, became evil by mistake when the Professor's cat tossed a handful of random chips into his system at the assembly stage.

The Telebugs' other main enemy is the pink-crested punk Arcadia who steals the electronic characters out of arcade games and uses them for a crime wave.

The series was created by John M. Mills and Elphin Lloyd-Jones. Mills, a former BBC producer and announcer, has spent more than 25 years in broadcasting and documentary film-making, and the Telebugs were born out of his desire to give high-tech hardware a softer 'face'. Elphin Lloyd-Jones is one of the country's leading animation directors who has worked with Hanna Barbera and Halas & Batchelor.

VOICES:
Ron Moody,
Susie Westerby

Devised by: John M. Mills, Elphin Lloyd-Jones
Executive producer: Anna Home
Music: Andy Murray

TVS Production
86 colour 10-minute episodes

Season One (26 episodes):
6 January–10 February 1986
Season Two (40 episodes):
10 November 1986–16 January 1987
Season Three (20 episodes):
17 November–15 December 1987

Thundercats

'Sword of Omens, give me sight beyond sight!'

Thundercats is a sword'n'sorcery saga featuring a group of feline heroes – Lion-O, Tygra, Cheetarah, Panthro, Snarf, Wilykat and Wilykit – who have escaped from their doomed planet Thundera. Prince Lion-O possesses a mystical sword which gives him great powers, all pretty vital in the Thundercats' never-ending battle against the forces of evil, principally Mumm-Ra and his mutant cronies. (A big hit with six-year-olds . . .)

A Marvel Production
32 colour 20-minute episodes
UK premiere:
2 January– 11 June 1987
10 September–22 October 1987
(BBC1)

Transformers

The cartoon of the toy: a numbing clash twixt good and evil in the shapes of Optimus Prime's Autobots and Megatron's Decepticons – two forces of 'robots in disguise'. Aired on TV-AM from 1986.

A Sunbow Production

Ulysses 31

Cartoon space adventure updating the ancient Greek odyssey. Ulysses, a space-commander from Earth, with his son Telemachus, a small girl called Yumi and Nono, a red robot, are lost among the galaxies of space, facing unknown and terrible dangers, in their spaceship Odyssey, striving to return to Earth if the Gods will allow . . .

26 colour 25-minute episodes
UK premiere:
7 November 1985–8 May 1986

A CHRONOLOGY

A year-by-year guide to some of the debut landmarks of science fiction on British Television.

1951 Oct Stranger from Space (BBC)
1952 Oct Stranger from Space (BBC: 2nd series)
1953 July The Quatermass Experiment (BBC)
1954 Jan The Lost Planet (BBC)
Dec Play: Nineteen Eighty-Four (BBC)
1955 Jan Return to the Lost Planet (BBC)
Play: The Voices (BBC)
Play: The Creature (BBC)
Oct Quatermass II (BBC)
1956 Jan Space School (BBC)
Feb The Adventures of Superman (ITV)
Science Fiction Theatre (ITV)
Apr Play: One (ITV)
Play: The Burning Glass (ITV)
Sept The Strange World of Planet X (ITV)
Dec The Trollenberg Terror (ITV)
1957 Dec Play: The Critical Point (BBC)
1958 Feb Play: Before the Sun Goes Down (ITV)
Mar Play: Doomsday for Dyson (ITV)
Sept H.G. Wells' The Invisible Man (ITV)
Oct Play: I Can Destroy the Sun (ITV)
Dec Quatermass and the Pit (BBC)
1959 Apr Play: The Offshore Island (BBC)
Dec The Voodoo Factor (ITV)
1960 Apr Target Luna (ITV)
July Men Into Space (BBC)
Sept Pathfinders in Space (ITV)
Dec Pathfinders to Mars (ITV)
1961 Jan The Avengers (ITV)
Supercar (ITV)
Mar Pathfinders to Venus (ITV)
June Play: Countdown at Woomera (ITV)
Sept Plateau of Fear (ITV)
Oct A for Andromeda (BBC)
Nov One Step Beyond (ITV)

1962 June The Big Pull (BBC)
The Andromeda Break-through (BBC)
Out of This World (ITV)
Sept The Avengers (Cathy Gale years) (ITV)
Oct Fireball XL5 (ITV)
Nov The Monsters (BBC)
City Beneath the Sea (ITV)
1963 Jan Dimension of Fear (ITV)
The Twilight Zone (ITV, Border)
Feb Secret Beneath the Sea (ITV)
July The Jetsons (ITV)
Space Patrol (ITV)
Sept Play: The Road (BBC)
Nov My Favourite Martian (ITV)
Doctor Who (BBC)
1964 Apr The Outer Limits (some ITV)
June Play: Caves of Steel (BBC2)
Oct Stingray (ITV)
Voyage to the Bottom of the Sea (ITV)
Nov R3 (BBC)
1965 March Play: Campaign for One (BBC)
May Undermind (ITV)
June The Man from UNCLE (BBC)
Sept The Avengers (Emma Peel years) (ITV)
Oct Lost in Space (ITV)
Thunderbirds (ITV)
Out of the Unknown (BBC)
Object Z (ITV)
Nov Play: Nineteen Eighty-Four (BBC)
1966 Jan The Master (ITV)
May Batman (ITV)
June Adam Adamant Lives! (BBC)
Nov Doctor Who: the Second Doctor (BBC)
1967 Jan The Invaders (some ITV)
Sept Captain Scarlet and the Mysterons (ITV)
The Prisoner (ITV)
1968 July The Time Tunnel (BBC)
Play: The Year of the Sex Olympics (BBC)
Sept The Avengers (exit Emma, enter Tara) (ITV)
Joe 90 (ITV)
Oct The Champions

Nov   Journey to the Unknown
(ITV)
Dec   Land of the Giants (ITV)
1969 July Star Trek (BBC)
Sept Counterstrike (BBC)
The Secret Service (some ITV)
1970 Jan   Doctor Who: the Third Doctor
(BBC)
Feb   Doomwatch (BBC)
Apr   Play: Wine of India (BBC)
July Ace of Wands (ITV)
Sept U.F.O. (ITV)
Timeslip (ITV)
Oct   The Adventures of Don Quick
(ITV)
1971 Apr   Out of the Unknown (4th and
final season) (BBC)
July The Guardians (ITV)
1972 June Doomwatch (3rd and final
season) (BBC)
Oct   The Incredible Robert Baldick
(BBC)
Dec   Play: The Stone Tape (BBC)
1973 Apr   Night Gallery (some ITV)
The Tomorrow People (ITV)
Sept Moonbase 3 (BBC)
1974 Aug   Star Trek cartoon (BBC)
Sept The Six Million Dollar Man
(ITV)
Oct   Planet of the Apes (ITV)
Dec   Doctor Who: the Fourth-
Doctor (BBC)
1975 Jan   The Changes (BBC)
Apr   Survivors (BBC)
Sept Space 1999 (ITV)
The Invisible Man (BBC)
1976 April Sky (ITV)
July The Bionic Woman (ITV)
Oct   The New Avengers (ITV)
Star Maidens (some ITV)
Dec   Into Infinity (Gerry Anderson
one-off) (BBC)
1977 Jan   Children of the Stones (ITV)
March The Fantastic Journey (BBC)
June TV hoax: Alternative 3 (ITV)
Sept 1990 (BBC)
Man From Atlantis (ITV)
Oct   Play: Stronger Than the Sun
(BBC)
1978 Jan   Blake's 7 (BBC)
Logan's Run (ITV)
May   The Incredible Hulk (ITV)
July The New Adventures of
Wonder Woman (BBC)
1979 Mar   Mork and Mindy (ITV)
May   Project UFO (some ITV)
July Sapphire and Steel (ITV)
Oct   Quatermass (ITV)
1980 Mar   The Outer Limits (BBC2)
Aug   The Martian Chronicles (BBC)

Buck Rogers in the 25th
Century (ITV)
Sept Battlestar Galactica (ITV)
Dec   Play: The Flipside of Dominick
Hide (BBC)
1981 Jan   The Hitch-Hiker's Guide to
the Galaxy (BBC)
March Brave New World (BBC)
May   The Nightmare Man (BBC)
Into the Labyrinth (ITV)
Sept The Amazing Spiderman
(ITV)
Kinvig (ITV)
Day of the Triffids (BBC)
Blake's 7 (4th and final
season (BBC)
1982 Jan   Doctor Who: the Fifth Doctor
(BBC)
Apr   Play for Tomorrow (BBC)
Dec   Play: Another Flip for
Dominick (BBC)
K9 and Company (BBC)
1983 Jan   Captain Zep – Space Detective
(BBC)
Sept He-Man and the Masters of the
Universe (ITV)
The Twilight Zone (BBC2)
Oct   Terrahawks (ITV)
Kolchak: The Night Stalker
(ITV)
1984 Jan   Chocky (ITV)
Feb   Play: Z for Zachariah (BBC)
March Doctor Who: The Sixth Doctor
(BBC)
Galactica 1980 (ITV)
July 'V' (ITV)
Sept The Invisible Man (BBC)
The Invaders (BBC2)
The Tripods (BBC)
Play: Threads (BBC)
1985 Jan   Chocky's Children (ITV)
Apr   Max Headroom – the Movie
(C4)
June 'V' – the Series (ITV)
Aug   Children of the Dog Star (ITV)
Nov   Edge of Darkness (BBC)
1986 Jan   The Twilight Zone (C4)
Sept Chocky's Challenge (ITV)
1987 April ALF (ITV)
July Space (ITV)
Star Cops (BBC)
Sept Knights of God (ITV)
Doctor Who: the Seventh
Doctor (BBC)
1988 Feb   Red Dwarf (BBC)
Oct   First Born (BBC)
1989 Jan   Superboy (ITV)
Mar   Max Headroom – the series
(C4)
Aug   Murder on the Moon (ITV)